Praise for *The Tao of Liberation*

"*The Tao of Liberation* is a path-breaking book. It brings together the insights of cosmology, ecology, and spirituality in a fresh and powerful way. With their creative collaboration, Mark Hathaway and Leonardo Boff offer us a remarkable new synthesis which will surely become an enduring classic."

—**Brian Swimme, Director, Center for the Story of the Universe, California Institute of Integral Studies**

"I love this book. Its inspiration lives up to its ambition—leading the reader through some of the most complex issues of our age (from globalization and the current recession to climate change and loss of species) while illuminating a path forward through religion and spirituality. Having had the great privilege of serving on the Earth Charter Commission with Leonardo Boff, it was not a new idea that our values and our faith have immediate relevance to the current interlocking web of crises in which we find ourselves. Together he and Mark Hathaway have written a transcendent work of eco-liberation and planetary survival."

—**Elizabeth May, O.C., Leader, Green Party of Canada**

"There is no other book that has so carefully identified the new cosmology of Thomas Berry and Brian Swimme as a liberating context for a sustainable future. This is a masterful and important work."

—**Mary Evelyn Tucker, Forum on Religion and Ecology, Yale University**

"*The Tao of Liberation* is a monumental contribution toward tackling the global crisis, including analyses that plumb the roots of the crisis and proposals for a fundamental change of direction. The text draws on science, economics, ethics and spirituality, integrating them in a scenario that just might pull us back from the precipice."

—**David G. Hallman, Advisor to the World Council of Churches Climate Change Programme**

"A sweeping, comprehensive and poetic manifesto of social and ecological change, as viewed through the eyes of a prominent liberation theologian in partnership with a hands-on spiritual change activist. They weave a vision of not only cultural change, but also spiritual transformation through a renewed, and renewable, relationship with the entire network of creation."

—**Neil Douglas-Klotz, author, *Prayers of the Cosmos***

"Leonardo Boff and Mark Hathaway give birth to a great marriage between liberation theology and creation spirituality. I welcome it—it is very timely—and I welcome the dimensions of ecology, cosmology and feminist philosophy applied astutely to the crisis of western capitalism and culture we are all undergoing at this time as well as the deep ecumenism which is so beautifully and aptly invoked in the use of the great *Tao Te Ching* throughout the text."

—**Matthew Fox, author,** *The Coming of the Cosmic Christ*

"Global poverty and global ecological destruction represent two of the most important challenges facing the human community. In *The Tao of Liberation*, Mark Hathaway and Leonardo Boff creatively and movingly explore the interconnection of these twin challenges, deftly blending the wisdom of the world's spiritual traditions and the insights of social science to explore the structural and cultural features underlying our present unsustainable behavior. This is a must read for all of those who seek to understand the critical nexus between the option for the poor and the option for the Earth."

—**Stephen Bede Scharper, University of Toronto**

"Drawing on compelling inter-disciplinary resources, Boff and Hathaway present us with a holistic, comprehensive, and integrated path toward the transformation required if the human experience is to have a future in our Earthly Home. The crisis we face is spiritual, and the 'The Tao of Liberation' is an exciting challenge we ignore at our peril."

—**Rev. Bill Phipps, Co-founder, Faith and Common Good network**

"As we reach a crossroads in the history of humanity, readers will find in this book a wealth of ideas and deep insights about the fundamental shift in human consciousness and the radical transformations in our world that are now required. Among all these ideas, the most important and profound, perhaps, is the one at the very center of the authors' endeavor. Rather than seeing the transition to a sustainable society primarily in terms of limits and restrictions, Hathaway and Boff eloquently propose a new and compelling conception of sustainability as liberation."

—**Fritjof Capra, author,** *The Tao of Physics*

"*The Tao of Liberation* is a seamless and creative gospel for our time. Through a vital and integral synthesis of wisdom both ancient and new, Mark Hathaway and Leonardo Boff craft a prophetic and timely work to address new challenges before us. Their guide to an ecology of transformation is a source of inspiration, engagement and hope for all who search for a comprehensive vision, and a new era of healing for earth and its peoples."

—**Jim Conlon, author,** *From the Stars to the Street*

"*The Tao of Liberation* . . . is lucid and inspiring, making connections between cosmology and ethics, science and spirituality, whole systems theories and consciousness—and explains how these insights, when united, point the way for us to join together in the struggle to renew the Earth."

—**Heather Eaton, co-author,** *Ecofeminism and Globalization*

THE TAO OF LIBERATION

ECOLOGY AND JUSTICE SERIES

THE TAO OF LIBERATION

Exploring the Ecology of Transformation

**Mark Hathaway
and
Leonardo Boff**

ORBIS BOOKS

Maryknoll, New York 10545

Founded in 1970, Orbis Books endeavors to publish works that enlighten the mind, nourish the spirit, and challenge the conscience. The publishing arm of the Maryknoll Fathers and Brothers, Orbis seeks to explore the global dimensions of the Christian faith and mission, to invite dialogue with diverse cultures and religious traditions, and to serve the cause of reconciliation and peace. The books published reflect the opinions of their authors and are not meant to represent the official position of the Maryknoll Society. To obtain more information about Maryknoll and Orbis Books, please visit our website at www.maryknollsociety.org.

Acknowledgments
Excerpts from *Desert Wisdom: Sacred Middle Eastern Writings from the Goddess through the Sufis* ("The Opening," "O Breathing Life," and "As the Cosmos Opens and Closes"), translations and commentary by Neil Douglas-Klotz. Copyright © 1995 by Neil Douglas-Klotz. Reprinted by permission of HarperCollins Publishers.

Commentary and excerpts of texts from *Prayers of the Cosmos: Meditations on the Aramaic Words of Jesus* by Neil Douglas-Klotz. Copyright © 1990 by Neil Douglas-Klotz. Reprinted by permission of HarperCollins Publishers.

Manufactured in the United States of America.

Library of Congress Cataloging in Publication Data

Hathaway, Mark.
   The Tao of liberation : exploring the ecology of transformation / Mark Hathaway and Leonardo Boff.
      p. cm.
   Includes bibliographical references and index.
   ISBN 978-1-57075-841-6 (pbk. : alk. paper)
   1. Environmentalism. 2. Environmentalism—Philosophy. 3. Sustainable development. 4. Deep ecology. I. Boff, Leonardo. II. Title.
   GE195.H385 2009
   333.72—dc22

                                                                    2009012895

To my daughter, Jamila, and my wife, Maritza,
who have sustained me during this journey
with their love and encouragement,
To all my teachers
who have inspired me with their insights and wisdom,
And to the living cosmos
whose unfolding beauty enkindles me with awe.
—Mark Hathaway

To Mirian Vilela and Steven Rockefeller,
for their deep love for the living Earth
and for their essential contribution to the process
of writing the Earth Charter.
—Leonardo Boff

We stand at a critical moment in Earth's history, a time when humanity must choose its future. As the world becomes increasingly interdependent and fragile, the future at once holds great peril and great promise. . . . The choice is ours: form a global partnership to care for Earth and one another or risk the destruction of ourselves and the diversity of life.... We must decide to live with a sense of universal responsibility, identifying ourselves with the whole Earth community as well as our local communities. (The Earth Charter)

By what name will our children and our children's children call our time? Will they speak in anger and frustration of the time of the Great Unraveling . . . or will they look back in joyful celebration on the noble time of the Great Turning, when their forebears turned crisis into opportunity, embraced the higher-order potential of their human nature, learned to live in creative partnership with one another and the living Earth, and brought forth a new era of human possibility? (David Korten)

We are not lacking in the dynamic forces needed to create the future. We live immersed in a sea of energy beyond all comprehension. But this energy, in an ultimate sense, is ours not by domination but by invocation. (Thomas Berry)

Contents

PART 3
THE TAO OF LIBERATION

Foreword

As our new century unfolds, two developments will have major impacts on the future well-being of humanity. One of them is the rise of global capitalism; the other is the creation of sustainable communities based on the practice of ecological design.

Global capitalism is concerned with electronic networks of financial and information flows; ecodesign, with ecological networks of energy and material flows. The goal of the global economy, in its present form, is to maximize the wealth and power of its elites; the goal of ecodesign is to maximize the sustainability of the web of life. These two scenarios are currently on a collision course.

The new economy, which emerged from the information technology revolution of the past three decades, is structured largely around networks of financial flows. Sophisticated information and communication technologies enable financial capital to move rapidly around the globe in a relentless search for investment opportunities. The system relies on computer modeling to manage the enormous complexity brought about by rapid deregulation and a dizzying array of new financial instruments.

This economy is so complex and turbulent that it defies analysis in conventional economic terms. What we really have is an electronically operated global casino. The gamblers in this casino are not obscure speculators but major investment banks, pension funds, multinational corporations, and mutual funds organized precisely for the sake of financial manipulation. The so-called global market, strictly speaking, is not a market at all but a network of machines programmed according to a single value—making money—to the exclusion of all other values. This means that economic globalization has systematically excluded all ethical dimensions of doing business.

In the last few years, the social and ecological impacts of globalization have been discussed extensively by scholars and community leaders. Their analyses show that the new economy is producing a multitude of interconnected harmful consequences. It has enriched a global elite of financial speculators, entrepreneurs, and high-tech professionals. At the very top, there has been an unprecedented accumulation of wealth. But overall, the social and environmental consequences have been disastrous; and, as we have seen in the current financial crisis, it has also severely endangered the financial well-being of people around the world.

The new global capitalism has resulted in rising social inequality and social exclusion, a breakdown of democracy, more rapid and extensive deterioration of the natural environment, and increasing poverty and alienation. It has threatened and destroyed local communities around the world; and with the pursuit of an ill-conceived biotechnology it has invaded the sanctity of life by attempting to turn diversity into monoculture, ecology into engineering, and life itself into a commodity.

It has become increasingly clear that global capitalism in its present form is unsustainable—socially, ecologically, and even financially—and needs to be fundamentally redesigned. Its underlying principle, that making money should take precedence over human rights, democracy, environmental protection, or any other value, is a recipe for disaster. However, this principle can change; it is not a natural law. The same electronic networks of financial and informational flows *could* have other values built into them. The critical issue is not technology but politics. The great challenge of the twenty-first century will be to change the value system underlying the global economy, so as to make it compatible with the demands of human dignity and ecological sustainability.

Indeed, the process of reshaping globalization has already begun. At the turn of this century, an impressive global coalition of nongovernmental organizations (NGOs) formed for this very purpose. This coalition, or global justice movement as it is also called, has organized a series of very successful protests at various meetings of the World Trade Organization (WTO) and the G7 and G8, and it has also held several World Social Forum meetings, most of them in Brazil. At these meetings, the NGOs proposed a whole set of alternative trade policies, including concrete and radical proposals for restructuring the global financial institutions that would profoundly change the nature of globalization.

The global justice movement exemplifies a new kind of political movement that is typical of our information age. Because of their skillful use of the Internet, the NGOs in the coalition are able to network with each other, share information, and mobilize their members with unprecedented speed. As a result, the new global NGOs have emerged as effective political actors who are independent of traditional national or international institutions. They constitute a new kind of global civil society.

To place the political discourse within a systemic and ecological perspective, the global civil society relies on a network of scholars, research institutes, think tanks, and centers of learning that largely operate outside our leading academic institutions, business organizations, and government agencies. There are dozens of these institutions of research and learning in all parts of the world today. Their common characteristic is that they pursue their work within an explicit framework of shared core values.

Most of these research institutes are communities of both scholars and activists who are engaged in a wide variety of projects and campaigns. Among them, there are three clusters of issues that seem to be focal points for the largest and most active grassroots coalitions. One is the challenge of reshaping the governing rules and institutions of globalization; another is the opposition to genetically modified foods and the promotion of sustainable agriculture; and the third is ecological design—a concerted effort to redesign our physical structures, cities, technologies, and industries so as to make them ecologically sustainable.

Design, in the broadest sense, consists in shaping flows of energy and matter for human purposes. Ecological design is a process in which our human purposes are carefully meshed with the larger patterns and flows of the natural world. Ecological design principles reflect the principles of organization that nature has evolved to sustain the web of life—continual cycling of matter, use of solar energy, diversity, cooperation and partnerships, and so on. To practice design in such a context requires a fundamental shift in our attitude toward nature, a shift from finding out what we can *extract* from nature, to what we can *learn* from it.

In recent years, there has been a dramatic rise in ecologically oriented design practices and projects, all of which are now well documented. They include a worldwide renaissance in organic farming; the organization of different industries into ecological clusters, in which the waste of any one organization is a resource for another; the shift from a product-oriented economy to a "service-and-flow" economy, in which industrial raw materials and technical components cycle continually between manufacturers and users; buildings that are designed to produce more energy than they use, emit no waste, and monitor their own performance; hybrid-electric cars that achieve fuel efficiencies several times that of standard cars; and so on.

These ecodesign technologies and projects all incorporate the basic principles of ecology and therefore have some key characteristics in common. They tend to be small-scale projects with plenty of diversity, energy efficient, nonpolluting, community oriented, and labor intensive, creating plenty of jobs. The technologies now available provide compelling evidence that the transition to a sustainable future is no longer a technical or a conceptual problem. It is a problem of values and political will.

It seems that this political will has increased significantly in the last few years. One notable sign is Al Gore's film *An Inconvenient Truth*, which has played a major role in raising ecological awareness. In 2006, Gore personally trained twelve hundred volunteers in Tennessee to deliver his famous slide show and spread the message worldwide. By 2008, they had delivered nearly twenty thousand presentations to a combined audience of two million people. In the meantime, Gore's organization, the Climate Project, trained more than a thousand equally committed individuals in Australia, Canada, India, Spain, and the United Kingdom. They now have twenty-six hundred presenters and have reached a worldwide audience of over four million people.

Another important development is the publication of *Plan B: Mobilizing to Save Civilization*, by Lester Brown, founder of the Worldwatch Institute and one of the most authoritative environmental thinkers. The first part of Brown's book is a detailed documentation of the fundamental interconnectedness of our major problems. He demonstrates with impeccable clarity how the vicious cycle of demographic pressure and poverty leads to the depletion of resources—falling water tables, wells going dry, shrinking forests, collapsing fisheries, eroding soils, grasslands turning into desert, and so on—and how this resource depletion, exacerbated by climate change, produces failing states whose governments can no longer provide security for their citizens, some of whom, in sheer desperation, turn to terrorism.

While this first part is predictably depressing, the second part—a detailed roadmap to save civilization—is optimistic and exciting. It involves several simultaneous actions that are mutually supportive, mirroring the interdependence of the problems they address. Every single proposal can be realized with existing technologies and, in fact, all proposals are illustrated with examples that have been successful somewhere in the world. Brown's *Plan B* is perhaps the clearest documentation to date that we have the knowledge, the technologies, and the financial means to save civilization and build a sustainable future.

Finally, the political will and leadership for moving toward sustainability increased dramatically with the election of Barack Obama to the presidency of the United States. Obama's family background is very diverse, both racially and culturally. His father was Kenyan, his mother American, his stepfather Indonesian. Obama was born in Hawaii and was raised partly there and partly in Indonesia. The great diversity of his background has shaped his outlook on the world; he moves comfortably among people of different races and social backgrounds.

Having spent many years working as a community organizer and civil rights lawyer, Obama is an excellent listener, facilitator, and mediator. His election has reshaped the political culture of the United States; it is transforming America's image abroad and the self-image of Americans at home.

President Obama's political program amounts to a serious course correction for the United States. Its main components are the repeal of market fundamentalism, an end to American unilateralism, and the development of green economic policies as a response to the global environmental crisis. Obama is well aware of the fundamental interconnectedness of the world's major problems, and many of the world's leading scientists and activists are ready to help him turn this awareness into effective policies.

Yet some fundamental questions remain. Why has it taken us so long to recognize the serious threats to the survival of humanity? Why are we so painfully slow to change the perceptions, ideas, lifestyles, and institutions that perpetuate injustice and destroy our planet's capacity to sustain life? How can we accelerate the movement toward social justice and ecological sustainability?

These are the issues at the heart of this book. The authors—one from the global South and the other from the North—have both reflected deeply on questions of theology, justice, and ecology. Their answer to the above-mentioned questions is that the fundamental challenge is much more than disseminating knowledge and changing old habits. All the threats we face, in their view, are symptoms of a deeper cultural and spiritual sickness afflicting humanity. "There is a deep pathology inherent in the system that currently dominates and exploits our world," they assert. They identify poverty and inequality, depletion of the Earth, and the poisoning of life as the three principal symptoms of this pathology, and they note that "the same forces and ideologies that exploit and exclude the poor are also devastating the entire life-community of the Earth."

To overcome our deep pathology, the authors maintain, will require a fundamental shift in human consciousness. "In a very real way," they write, "we are called to reinvent ourselves as a species." They refer to this process of profound transformation as "liberation," using the term as it is used in the tradition of liberation theology—both in the personal sense of spiritual realization, or enlightenment, and in the collective sense of a people seeking to free itself from oppression. In my view, this dual use of "liberation" is what gives their book its unique character, as it enables them to integrate the social, political, economic, ecological, emotional, and spiritual dimensions of the present global crisis.

As Hathaway and Boff state in the Prologue, *The Tao of Liberation* is a search for the wisdom needed to effect profound liberatory transformations in our world. Realizing that such wisdom, ultimately, cannot be captured in words, they have chosen to describe it by using the ancient Chinese word *Tao* ("the Way")—meaning both an individual spiritual path and the way the universe works. According to Taoist tradition, spiritual realization is achieved when we act in harmony with nature. In the words of the Chinese classic Huai Nan Tzu, "Those who follow the natural order flow in the current of the *Tao*."

In this book, the search for the wisdom needed to shift from a society obsessed with unlimited growth and material consumption to a balanced and life-sustaining civilization involves two principal steps. The first step is an understanding of the very real obstacles that stand in the way of liberating transformation. The second step is the formulation of a "cosmology of liberation"—a vision of the future, as Thomas Berry (quoted in the book) puts it, "sufficiently entrancing that it will sustain us in the transformation of the human project that is now in process."

The multiple and interdependent obstacles explored by Hathaway and Boff are caused by our political and economic structures, reinforced by a mechanistic and deterministic worldview, and internalized by feelings of powerlessness, denial, and despair. The external "systemic" obstacles are discussed at length. They include the illusion of unlimited growth on a finite planet, excessive corporate power, a parasitic financial system, and a tendency to monopolize knowledge and impose, in Vandana Shiva's apt phrase, "monocultures of the mind." As the authors explain, these external obstacles are reinforced by oppressive systems of education, manipulative mass media, pervasive consumerism, and artificial environments—especially in urban areas—that isolate us from living nature.

To overcome internalized powerlessness, which may take the form of addiction and greed, denial, psychic numbing, or despair, we need to expand our sense of self, the authors suggest. We need to deepen our capacity for compassion, build community and solidarity, reawaken our sense of belonging to the Earth, and thereby rediscover our "ecological self." They suggest that we should "reflect on the things that truly delight us, that truly give us pleasure—spending time with friends, walking outdoors, listening to music, or enjoying a simple meal." Most of what truly delights us, they point out, costs little or no money.

However, to fully awaken and reconnect, we also need a new understanding of reality and a new sense of the place of humanity within the cosmos.

We need "a living and vital cosmology." The authors use the term "cosmology" in the sense of a shared worldview that gives meaning to our lives, and they contrast a now-emerging "cosmology of liberation" with the "cosmology of domination"—including "the surrogate cosmology of acquisition and consumption" that currently holds sway over modern industrial societies.

The authors assert that a new understanding of the cosmos is now emerging from modern science, which in many ways recalls earlier aboriginal cosmologies. But unlike most of them, the new scientific worldview envisions an evolving universe and is therefore an ideal conceptual framework for the liberatory transformation we need. To make that case, Hathaway and Boff draw from a large reservoir of contemporary thinkers—philosophers, theologians, psychologists, and natural scientists. In the vast array of ideas, models, and theories they discuss, not all are compatible with one another; quite a few are esoteric and definitely outside the scientific mainstream; and at times the authors draw conclusions that go well beyond current science. Nevertheless, they succeed admirably in demonstrating the emergence of a new and coherent scientific understanding of reality.

At the forefront of contemporary science, the universe is no longer seen as a machine composed of elementary building blocks. We have discovered that the material world, ultimately, is a network of inseparable patterns of relationships; that the planet as a whole is a living, self-regulating system. The view of the human body as a machine and of the mind as a separate entity is being replaced by one that sees not only the brain but also the immune system, the bodily tissues, and even each cell as a living, cognitive system. Evolution is no longer seen as a competitive struggle for existence but as a cooperative dance in which creativity and the constant emergence of novelty are the driving forces. And with the new emphasis on complexity, networks, and patterns of organization, a new "science of quality" is slowly emerging.

The authors also argue, correctly in my opinion, that the emerging scientific cosmology is fully compatible with the spiritual dimension of liberation. They remind the reader that, within their own Christian tradition, the original meaning of spirit—*ruha* in Aramaic, or *ruah* in Hebrew—was that of the breath of life. This was also the original meaning of *spiritus*, *anima*, *pneuma*, and other ancient words for "soul" or "spirit." Spiritual experience, then, is first and foremost an experience of aliveness. Its central awareness, according to numerous testimonies, is a profound sense of oneness with all, a sense of belonging to the universe as a whole.

This sense of oneness with the natural world is fully borne out by the new conception of life in contemporary science. As we understand how the roots of life reach deep into basic physics and chemistry, how the unfolding of complexity began long before the formation of the first living cells, and how life has evolved for billions of years by using again and again the same basic patterns and processes, we realize how tightly we are connected with the entire fabric of life.

The awareness of being connected with all of nature is particularly strong in ecology. Connectedness, relationship, and interdependence are fundamental concepts of ecology; and connectedness, relationship, and belonging are also the essence of spiritual experience. Thus, ecology seems to be the ideal bridge between science and spirituality. Indeed, Hathaway and Boff advocate an "ecological spirituality" concerned primarily with the future of planet Earth and of humanity as a whole.

They point out that there are unique ecological insights and approaches in each religion, and they encourage us to see this diversity of teachings as a strength rather than a threat. "Each of us must look again into our own spiritual tradition," the authors suggest, "and seek out the insights that move us to reverence for all life, to an ethic of sharing and care, to a vision of the sacred incarnate in the cosmos."

The Tao of Liberation also contains many concrete suggestions of goals, strategies, and policies for effective transformative action to move toward a just and ecologically sustainable society. Two frameworks discussed in detail are bioregionalism, based on the idea of regaining a profound connection with nature at the local level, and the Earth Charter, "a truly liberating dream for humanity," which names as its first principle the respect and care for the community of life.

As we reach a crossroads in the history of humanity, readers will find in this book a wealth of ideas and deep insights about the fundamental shift in human consciousness and the radical transformations in our world that are now required. Among all these ideas, the most important and profound, perhaps, is the one at the very center of the authors' endeavor. Rather than seeing the transition to a sustainable society primarily in terms of limits and restrictions, Hathaway and Boff eloquently propose a new and compelling conception of sustainability as liberation.

—Fritjof Capra
Berkeley, First International Mother Earth Day, April 22, 2009

About the *Tao Te Ching*

We have chosen to use the *Tao Te Ching* (or *Dao De Jing*),[1] an ancient Chinese text written approximately twenty-five hundred years ago, as a source of inspiration in this book. The text is traditionally attributed to Lao-tzu (or Laozi), a sage who is believed to have lived from approximately 551 to 479 B.C.E., but most scholars think it is actually a collection of traditional sayings from a variety of sources. The text was probably developed between the seventh and second century B.C.E.

According to Jonathan Star, we can understand the meaning of the *Tao Te Ching*'s title as follows:

> Tao is the Supreme Reality, the all-pervasive substratum; it is the whole universe and the way the universe operates. Te is the shape and power of Tao; it is the way Tao manifests; it is Tao particularized to a form or a virtue. Tao is the transcendent reality; Te is the immanent reality. *Ching* means a book or a classic work. Hence, the *Tao Te Ching* literally means, "The Classic Book of the Supreme Reality (Tao) and its Perfect Manifestation (Te)," "The Book of the Way and its Power," "The Classic of Tao and Its Virtue." (2001, 2)

After the Bible, the *Tao Te Ching* is the most widely published text in the world. Innumerable translations of it exist, some more scholarly and literal, others more poetic. Ancient Chinese is a conceptual language, so in truth each word of the text evokes a host of images that can be translated in a variety of ways. No one translation, then, captures the whole breadth or depth of the text. In some sense, any translation of such a text is a form of interpretation, and none provides us with a complete picture of what is being said.

Since we are not attempting anything like an academic treatise on the text, we have chosen to draw on a variety of translations, most of them more poetic than literal in nature, combining them to create a version that was well suited

---

1. The modern transliteration from Chinese is actually Dao De Jing, which also corresponds to its correct pronunciation, but we have chosen to use Tao Te Ching in this text because the title is better known in this form in popular discourse.

to the chapter being introduced, but which still faithfully reflected the original text. To do this, we have used the translations of Mitchell (1988), Muller (1997), and Feng and English (1989), while drawing on the excellent literal translation prepared by Jonathon Star with C.J. Ming (Star 2001) as an overall guide.

Prologue

There was something formless and perfect,
both chaotic and complete.
There before Heaven and Earth.
Silent, vast, empty, and solitary,
Pervading all, ever in motion,
Sustaining all, yet never exhausted.
It is the mother of the cosmos.
For lack of a better name,
I call it the Tao.

It flows through all things,
inside and outside,
and returns to the source of all . . .

Humans follow the Earth.
The Earth follows Heaven.
Heaven follows the Tao.
The Tao follows only itself.

(*Tao Te Ching* §25)

The Tao of Liberation is a search for wisdom, the wisdom needed to effect profound transformations in our world. We have chosen to describe this wisdom using the ancient Chinese word *Tao*, meaning a way or path leading to harmony, peace, and right relationship. The Tao can be understood as a principle of order that constitutes the common ground of the cosmos; it is both the way that the universe works and the flowing cosmic structure that cannot be described, only tasted.[1] The Tao is the wisdom that lies at the very heart of the universe, encapsulating the essence of its purpose and direction.

---

1. Definitions of Tao are drawn from Dreher 1990; Heider 1986; Feng and English 1989; and Star 2001.

xxiii

While we use the image of the Tao and the texts of the ancient *Tao Te Ching*, this is not a book about Taoism per se. Indeed, the idea we point to by using the word Tao transcends, in some sense, any given philosophy or religion. Similar ideas can be found in other traditions. For example, the Dharma in Buddhism signifies the "way things work" or "orderly process itself" (Macy 1991a, xi). Similarly, the Aramaic word used by Jesus which is normally translated as "the kingdom" or "reign"—*Malkuta*²—refers to "the ruling principles that guide our lives toward unity" and conjures "the image of a 'fruitful arm' poised to create, or a coiled spring that is ready to unwind with all the verdant potential of the Earth" (Douglas-Klotz 1990, 20). While both the Dharma and the Malkuta frame the concept differently, for the sake of this book we can think of them pointing in some way to the same reality as the Tao—a reality that ultimately evades a hard and fast description but can only be intuited on a deeper level.

The Chinese ideogram used for the Tao combines the concepts of wisdom and walking, conjuring the image of a process that puts wisdom into practice— or in other words, a kind of *praxis*. In *The Tao of Liberation,* we seek this kind of "walking wisdom" inherent in the very fabric of the cosmos.

In the quest for this wisdom, we draw upon insights from such diverse fields as economics, psychology, cosmology, ecology, and spirituality. Still, in some sense it is impossible to outline fully the shape of the Tao of liberation. The Tao is an art, not an exact science. In a very real sense, the Tao is a mystery: We can provide signposts pointing to the path, but we cannot draw a detailed map.

---

2. It is virtually impossible to know the precise words that Jesus used in Palestinian Aramaic. Throughout this book, we have chosen to use these words as they appear in the gospels of the Aramaic (Syriac) version of the Bible employed by all Aramaic Christians today—the Peshitta text. Many Aramaic Christian scholars argue that these versions of the gospels could be as old as those found in the Greek New Testament.

The transliterations and interpretations of the words from the Peshitta text are drawn from the work of Neil Douglas-Klotz (1990, 1995, 1999, and 2006), who notes that, when Jesus spoke, he normally spoke in Aramaic since this was the everyday language of his people. Therefore, using a fully formed source text in Aramaic (like the Peshitta version) will give the clearest insight into Jesus himself as well as the wider meaning behind his words and the nature of his spirituality. As he explains, "The Peshitta is the most Semitic—the most Jewish if you will—of all the early versions of the New Testament. At the very least, it offers us a view of Jesus' thought, language, culture, and spirituality through the eyes of a very early community of Eastern Jewish Christians. No Greek text can give us this view" (1999, p. 6).

In addition, Douglas-Klotz notes that the key words that Jesus must have used are identical in root (and so in meaning) in both Palestinian and Syriac Aramaic. For Douglas-Klotz's method, see *The Hidden Gospel* (1999, pp. 1-24).

We search for wisdom in the hope of finding insights that will enable humanity to move away from perceptions, ideas, habits, and systems that perpetuate injustice and destroy our planet's capacity to sustain life. We do so in the hope of finding new ways of living that will allow the needs of all people to be equitably met in harmony with the needs and well-being of the greater Earth community, and indeed the cosmos itself.

We use the word *liberation* to refer to this process of transformation. Traditionally, liberation has been used either in the personal sense of spiritual realization or in the collective sense of a people seeking to free itself from oppressive political, economic, and social structures. We would include both of these uses, but frame them in a wider, ecological—and even cosmological—context. For us, liberation is the process of moving toward a world where all human beings can live with dignity in harmony with the great community of beings who make up *Gaia*, the living Earth. Liberation, then, entails repairing the terrible damage that we have inflicted both upon each other and upon our planet. On a deeper level, liberation is about realizing the potential of human beings as creative, life-enhancing participants within the unfolding evolution of Gaia.

We can even frame liberation in a cosmic perspective as the process through which the universe seeks to realize its own potential as it drives toward greater differentiation, interiority (or self-organization), and communion. Within such a context, human individuals and societies become liberated to the extent that they:

- Become more diverse and complex, truly respecting and celebrating differences;
- Deepen the aspect of interiority and consciousness, fostering creative processes of self-organisation; and
- Strengthen their bonds of community and interdependence, including their communion with the greater community of life on Earth.

This book begins with the question: How does transformation occur?—Or, perhaps more precisely, Why is it so difficult to effect the changes so urgently needed to save Gaia, the living Earth community of whom we are a part? A fundamental contribution of this book may lie in the very framing of this question. Hopefully, our text can serve as a starting point for others seeking creative new approaches to liberating transformation.

Our writing represents the confluence of the streams of thought of two authors, one from the South and the other from the North.[3] Leonardo Boff is probably well known to many who are reading this. As a theologian, he has

---

3. Throughout this text, we will often use the term "North" (or the "global North") to refer to the overdeveloped, high-consumption societies found predominantly in the north, and "South" (or "global South") to refer to the impoverished societies found predominantly in the south—particularly the tropical and subtropical belts of our planet.

reflected deeply on questions of liberation and ecology and has published over a hundred works on these subjects. He has taught theology for many years in his home country, Brazil, as well as in many other parts of the Americas and Europe. He is also the 2001 recipient of the Right Livelihood Award.

Mark Hathaway has worked for the past twenty-five years as an adult educator involved in questions of justice and ecology. Eight of those years were spent working as a popular educator and pastoral agent in a poor neighborhood in Chiclayo, a city on the north coast of Peru. Over the years, he has studied mathematics, physics, theology, creation spirituality, and adult education and has worked in Catholic, ecumenical, and interfaith justice and ecological initiatives. He currently lives in Canada, his home country, where he works both as South America program coordinator for the United Church of Canada and as a freelance "ecologian" who researches and writes about the interconnections between ecology, economics, cosmology, and spirituality.

The original core of this project consists of a paper that Mark wrote while finishing a master's degree in adult education entitled "Transformative Education." During Leonardo's visit to Toronto in 1996, the two of us had a chance to meet. After reading "Transformative Education," Leonardo suggested that we collaborate to write a book that also incorporates perspectives from the Latin American context. This volume is the result of our joint efforts.

Two central points of reference for the text are the preferential option for the poor and the preferential option for the Earth. We see these options as fundamentally linked: the same forces and ideologies that exploit and exclude the poor are also devastating the entire life community of the Earth. In this book, we explore the relationships between the many factors that serve as obstacles to authentic transformation. At the same time, we endeavor to come to a better understanding of the ways in which change occurs naturally in our world. Together, these insights can serve as a guide for those who struggle for life-enhancing transformation.

We have drawn inspiration from a wide variety of perspectives and insights; these have come from many different people and spiritual traditions, and we feel a deep debt of gratitude to all who have shared their wisdom with us. It is our hope that these threads will be woven over the course of our writing into a tapestry that is both clear and vibrant. In many ways, this is a challenging task. We have opted for a breadth of vision rather than a narrower, more careful analysis of the individual parts. By doing so, we hope to introduce readers to dimensions that they can explore in more depth on their own.

The image we would use for the way the text is written is that of a spiral. At times, it will no doubt seem that the same themes are revisited, but from a different perspective. As we move deeper into the spiral, these different perspectives may allow you to apprehend the whole that is greater than the sum of the parts, the weaving that is revealed only when we stand back from a close-up analysis of individual strands. As this happens, we hope you will begin to feel the flow and texture of the Tao of liberation at a deep, intuitive level, where its mysterious wisdom may guide your actions as you struggle for the renewal of the world.

1.

Seeking Wisdom in a Time of Crisis

When the best seekers hear of the Tao,
they immediately endeavor to embody it.
When average seekers hear of the Tao,
They follow it at times while at others they forget it.
When foolish seekers hear of the Tao,
they laugh out loud.
If they didn't laugh,
it wouldn't be the Tao.

Thus it is said:
The way into the light seems dark,
the path leading forward seems to go backwards,
the straight way seems crooked,
the greatest power seems weak,
the truest purity seems sullied,
authentic abundance seems insufficient,
genuine steadfastness seems unstable.

The most vast space cannot be contained,
the greatest talent takes long to ripen,
the highest note is hard to hear,
the perfect form cannot be embodied.

The Tao is nowhere to be found.
Yet it nourishes all things and brings them to fulfilment.

(*Tao Te Ching* §41)

Today we may be standing at the most important crossroads in the history of humanity, and indeed of the Earth itself. The combined dynamics of deepening poverty and accelerating ecological degradation are creating a powerful vortex of despair and destruction from which it is becoming increasingly difficult to escape. If we fail to act with sufficient energy, urgency, and wisdom, we will soon find ourselves condemned to a future in which the potential for living with meaning, hope, and beauty has been immeasurably diminished.

Indeed, for the majority of humanity struggling on the margins of the global economy, life already seems poised on the brink of disaster. Each year, the gap between rich and poor grows wider and wider. In a world selling the illusions of a consumer paradise, most must struggle hard just to obtain the minimum requirements for survival. The dream of achieving a simple but dignified lifestyle remains perpetually elusive. In fact, for many, life actually grows more difficult with each passing year.

The other creatures who share this planet with humanity are experiencing an even deeper crisis. As humans appropriate an ever-greater proportion of the Earth's gifts, less and less is available for other forms of life. As we foul the air, water, and land with chemicals and wastes, the intricate systems that sustain the web of life are rapidly being undermined. Many species are disappearing forever. In fact, our planet is experiencing one of the greatest mass extinctions of all time.

There are, of course, signs of hope: countless individuals and organizations are working creatively and courageously for transformation. Some have forged movements that are now truly global in scale. Their efforts are making a very real difference in communities throughout the world. At the same time, new means of communication are creating opportunities for dialogue among people of different cultures and faiths, so the possibility of sharing wisdom and insights has probably never been greater. Many people are more aware of their basic rights and more active in defending them. Real advances have been made in areas such as healthcare and access to basic services. There is increasing awareness of ecological issues, and many communities are endeavoring to work in harmony with nature, not against it. All of these trends open new possibilities for the renewal of the world.

Yet in many ways these are sparks of light amid the darkness. There is still little evidence of effective, concerted action on a scale sufficient to actually halt deepening poverty and ecological disintegration, much less to initiate a process capable of healing the Earth community. Global institutions, particularly governments and corporations, continue to act in ways that do not take into account the urgent need to change fundamentally the way we live in the world. Instead, the ideas, motives, habits, and policies that have caused so much devastation and injustice continue to dominate our political and economic systems. As Mikhail Gorbachev noted in 2001:

> While there are an increasing number of bold initiatives led by government and corporate leaders to protect the environment, I do not see emerging leadership and the willingness to take risks at the scale we need to confront the current situation. While there are an increasing number of people and organizations dedicated to raising awareness and provoking change in the way

we treat nature, I do not yet see the clear vision and united front which will inspire humankind to respond in time to correct our course. (2001, 4)

Joanna Macy and Molly Brown (1998) speak of the central challenge of our time—the shift from an industrial growth society to a life-sustaining civilization—in terms of the "Great Turning." Unfortunately, we have no assurance that we will make this essential transformation in time to prevent the unraveling of the intricate web that sustains complex life. If we are unable to make such a change, though, it will not be for lack of technology, sufficient information, or even creative alternatives, but rather a lack of political will and the fact that the dangers facing us are so painful that many of us choose simply to push them out of mind because of fear.

It is our belief, though, that the current cycle of despair and destruction can be broken, that we still have the opportunity to act fruitfully and change course. There is still time for the Great Turning to catch hold and heal our planet. In this book, we seek a path toward such a transformation, a change calling us to a new way of being in the world—a way that embodies just and harmonious relationships both within human society and within the wider Earth community. We seek a wisdom—a Tao—leading us to integral liberation.

We believe that the power to make these changes is already present among us. It is present in seed-form in the human spirit. It is present in the evolutionary processes of Gaia, our living Earth. It fact, it is woven into the very fabric of the cosmos itself, in the Tao that flows through all and in all. If we can find a way to attune ourselves to the Tao and align ourselves with its energy, we will find the key to truly revolutionary transformations leading to authentic liberation. The Tao, however, is not something that we can appropriate or dominate; rather, we must allow it to work through us, opening ourselves to its transformative energy so that the Earth may be healed. In the words of Thomas Berry:

> We are not lacking in the dynamic forces needed to create the future. We live immersed in a sea of energy beyond all comprehension. But this energy, in an ultimate sense, is ours not by domination but by invocation. (1999, 175)

Before we begin this task, however, we must understand the very real obstacles that stand in the way of liberating transformation. Perhaps the first step toward wisdom is simply to acknowledge the need for change. Many of us still do not appreciate the true magnitude and gravity of the crises we face. In large part, this is because our very perception of reality has been shaped in such a way as to hide what would otherwise be readily evident. We tend to see the world from a very restricted perspective, with respect to both time and space. We seldom look further afield than our immediate past or future, than our own community or region.

Part of the problem, too, is that many of the problems we face grow worse only gradually, especially when measured against the relatively short span of a human life. We tend to get used to new realities very quickly—at least on a superficial level—and therefore do not realize the seriousness of the crises we face. An illuminating analogy is that of a frog subjected to rising temperatures: If you place a frog in boiling water, it will immediately try to escape. If, on the other hand, you place a frog in cool water and gradually raise its temperature, the frog will not notice the danger until it is too late and, as a result, it dies of the heat.

THE CRISIS OF THE EARTH: A COSMIC PERSPECTIVE

To gain an insight into the gravity of the crises we face, therefore, let us stand back from our normal view of reality for a few moments and adopt a more "cosmic" outlook. Imagine that the entire fifteen-billion-year history of the universe is condensed into a single century.[1] In other words, each "cosmic year" is the equivalent of 150 million Earth years.[2]

From this point of view, the Earth is born in the seventieth year of the cosmic century and life appears in its oceans surprisingly soon afterwards, in the year 73. For nearly two cosmic decades, life is largely limited to single-celled bacteria. Still, these organisms do much to transform the planet, radically changing its atmosphere, oceans, and geology so that they can sustain more complex forms of life.

In the year 93, a new phase of creativity begins with both the invention of sexual reproduction and the death of unique organisms. In this new stage, the evolutionary process accelerates rapidly. Two years later, in the year 95, the first multicellular organisms appear. The first nervous systems develop in the year 96, and the first vertebrates less than a year later. Mammals arrive in the middle of the year 98, two months after the debut of the dinosaurs and the first flowering plants.

Five months ago, an asteroid impacts the Earth destroying many species of life, including the dinosaurs. Yet, within a short time the planet recovers and indeed surpasses its former beauty. This era—the Cenozoic—exhibits an exuberance and variety of life never before seen.

It is into this stunningly beautiful age that human beings are born. Twelve days ago, our ancient ancestors begin to walk upright. Six days later, *Homo habilus* begins using tools and, a day ago, *Homo erectus* tames fire. Modern humans, *Homo sapiens*, are born about twelve hours ago.

For the majority of the afternoon and evening of this cosmic day, we live in harmony with nature, close to both its rhythms and dangers. Indeed, our presence has little impact on the wider biotic community until forty minutes ago, when we first domesticate plants and animals with the invention of agriculture. The size of our interventions continues to increase, albeit slowly, as some of us begin to build and inhabit cities twenty minutes ago.

---

1. The times indicated here for the cosmic century are based on the time line given in *The Universe Story* (Berry and Swimme 1992, 269-78). A more recent estimate of the age of the cosmos is 13.73 billion years.

2. Similarly, a cosmic month is 12.5 million years; a cosmic day is 411,000 years; a cosmic hour is about 17,000 years; a cosmic minute is about 285 years; and a cosmic second about 4.75 years.

Humanity begins to have a much greater impact on the world's ecosystems just two minutes ago as Europe begins to transform itself into a technological society and expands its power through colonial exploits. It is during this time, as well, that the gap between the rich and the poor quickly begins to widen.

In the last twelve seconds (since 1950), the rhythm of exploitation and ecological destruction has accelerated dramatically. In this brief flicker of time:[3]

- We have destroyed nearly half of the Earth's great forests, the lungs of our planet. Many of the most important and extensive forests—including the great boreal forests, temperate rainforests, and tropical rainforests—are still experiencing an accelerating rate of destruction. An area greater than the size of Bangladesh is logged each year.

- We have released immense amounts of carbon dioxide and other greenhouse gases into the atmosphere, initiating a dangerous cycle of global warming and climatic instability. Global temperatures have already risen an average of 0.5° C and may rise between 2° and 5° C over the next twenty cosmic seconds.[4]

- We have created a gigantic hole in the ozone layer, the protective skin of the planet that filters out harmful ultraviolet radiation. As a result, UV levels have reached record highs, threatening the health of many living organisms.

- We have seriously undermined the fertility of the soil and its capacity to sustain plant life: 65 percent of once-arable land has already been lost—roughly half of this in the past nine cosmic seconds—and a further 15 percent of the planet's land surface is turning into deserts. In the past five cosmic seconds, the Earth has lost a quantity of topsoil equivalent to that which covers all the cultivated lands in France and China combined. Two-thirds of all agricultural land has been moderately to severely degraded through erosion and salinization.

- We have released tens of thousands of new chemicals into the air, soil, and water of the planet, many of them long-lived toxins that slowly poison the processes of life. We have created deadly nuclear wastes that will remain perilously radioactive for many hundreds of thousands of years—a time much longer than the twelve cosmic hours in which modern humans have been alive.

- We have destroyed hundreds of thousands of plant and animal species. Indeed, about fifty thousand species now disappear each year, almost all as a result of human activity. It is estimated that the rate of extinctions is ten thousand times greater than before humans inhabited the planet

---

3. The statistics in this section come from a variety of sources: Sale 1985; Nickerson 1993; Brown et al. 1991; Brown et al. 1997; Ayres 1998; Graham 1998. The Intergovernmental Panel on Climate Change Third Assessment Report (2001), Worldwatch Institute (2000 and 2005), and the International Fund for Agricultural Development (2006).

4. To put this change into perspective, the Earth is now 5° to 7° C warmer that it was in the midst of the last ice age.

and that we may now be undergoing the greatest mass extinction in the Earth's history. Scientist project that 20 to 50 percent of all species will disappear over the next thirty years (seven cosmic seconds) if current trends continue.

- Human beings now use or waste 40 percent of all the energy available for land-based animals on Earth (what is referred to as the "Net Primary Production" or NPP of the planet) and—if we continue on the same path—will take a total of 80 percent within another eight cosmic seconds (thirty-five years), leaving only 20 percent for all other animals.

So much destruction in so little time! And for what? The "benefits" of the process have gone to a very small proportion of humanity: the richest 20 percent of the world's population now earns approximately two hundred times more than the poorest 20 percent.[5] At the beginning of 2009, the world's 793 billionaires had a collective net "worth" equal to $2.4 trillion (Pitts 2009)—greater than the combined annual income of the poorer half of humanity. (At the beginning of 2008, before the current economic crisis began, there were actually 1,195 billionaires worth a total of $4.4 trillion, or roughly double what the poorest 50 percent earn in a year!). In terms of income, the richest 1 percent of humanity received as much income as the poorest 57 percent.[6]

Our planet, fruit of over four billion years of evolution, is being devoured by a relatively small minority of humanity and even this privileged group cannot hope to sustain its exploitation for much longer. It is hardly surprising, then, that a group of sixteen hundred scientists, including over a hundred Nobel Prize laureates, issued a "Warning to Humanity" when they met in 1992:

No more than one or a few decades remain before the chance to avert the threats we now confront will be lost and the prospects for humanity immeasurably diminished. . . . A new ethic is required—a new attitude towards discharging our responsibility for caring for ourselves and for the earth. This ethic must motivate a great movement, convincing reluctant leaders and reluctant governments and reluctant peoples themselves to effect the needed changes. (Brown et al. 1994, 19)

As we write this, seventeen years have passed since this warning was first issued. Yet, while some world leaders may be taking the problems of poverty and ecological degradation more seriously, there is still no concerted movement to mobilize the energies of humanity to address seriously the crises we

---

5. In 1992, the UNDP (United Nations Development Programme) Development Report estimated that the gap between the richest 20 percent of nations and the poorest 20 percent was 60 to 1 based on national averages, but when actual individual incomes were considered, this gap was actually 150 to 1 (Anthanasiou 1996). In 2005, the UNDP Development Report puts the gap, based on national averages, at 82 to 1, making it probable that the real income gap may actually be on the order of 200 to 1.

6. Statistics from Milanovic 1999, 52: Income distribution has actually become more unequal since these statistics were first compiled.

face. Indeed, far more energy is being devoted to the so-called war on terrorism (which, to a large extent, amounts to a war to protect oil supplies and to continue "business as usual") than to the threats that are actually destroying life at an unprecedented rate.

THE SEARCH FOR WISDOM

For the first time in the evolution of humanity, all the major crises we face—the destruction of ecosystems, the grinding poverty of billions as a result of greed and systemic injustice, and the continued threats of militarism and war—are of our own making. Combined, these crises have the potential to destroy not only a particular culture or a particular region of the world but human civilization as a whole, and indeed the integrity of the entire web of life on our planet. Not only present but also future generations of the Earth community are threatened.

The dangers we face understandably engender fear. It is important that we recognize both the situation and the feelings it evokes in us. So, while stressing the urgency of the crisis, it is vital that we avoid making apocalyptic warnings that lead to the paralysis of despair. We must remember that the very fact that these crises are of our own making means that there is hope of addressing them in a meaningful way. Indeed, many insightful and creative people have worked hard to formulate practical alternatives that could allow humanity to live with dignity without endangering the health of the Earth's ecosystems.

It is our belief that we have most of the information and knowledge we need to overcome our current crises. Indeed, as Macy and Brown note:

> We can choose life. Dire predictions notwithstanding, we can still act to ensure a livable world. It is crucial that we know this: *we can meet our needs without destroying our life-support system*. We have the technical knowledge and the means of communication to do that. We have the savvy and resources to grow sufficient food, ensure clean air and water, and generate the energy we require through solar power, wind, and biomass. If we have the will, we have the means to control human population, to dismantle weapons and deflect wars, and give everyone a voice in democratic self-governance. (1998, 16)

Obviously, hard work, concerted action, and organization will all be needed to put these alternatives into practice. Most of all, though, we require the energy, vision, perceptivity, and wisdom to guide our transformative action—we require an authentic Tao leading to liberation. We need to understand the various dimensions of the global crisis and the dynamics that conspire to perpetuate them; we need to find ways to overcome the obstacles in our path; we need an even deeper understanding of reality itself, including the very nature of transformation; and we need to sharpen our intuition and develop new sensitivities to be able to act creatively and effectively.

In searching for this wisdom, we must first recognize that all the threats we face can, in some sense, be seen as symptoms of a deeper cultural and spiritual sickness afflicting humanity, particularly the 20 percent of humans consuming the greater part of the world's wealth. This forces us to look deeper into our cultures, our values, our political-economic systems, and our very selves. As the psychologist Roger Walsh notes, the crises we face could serve to "strip away our defences and help us to confront both the true condition of the world and our role in creating it" (1984, 77). They have the potential of leading us to truly profound changes in the way we live, think, and act—indeed, in the way we perceive reality itself.

Times of crisis can be creative times, times when new visions and new possibilities emerge. The Chinese ideogram for crisis, *wei-ji*, is composed of the characters for danger and opportunity (represented by an unstoppable spear and an impenetrable shield). This is not simply a contradiction or paradox; the very dangers we face stimulate us to look deeper, seek alternatives, and take advantage of opportunities. Our own word—*crisis*—derives from the Greek word *krinein*, meaning "to separate." It implies a choice between distinct alternatives. If we do not act to change the situation of deepening poverty and ecological destruction, we will be choosing to continue a descent toward the abyss of despair.

Danger + Opportunity

But another choice is also possible: we have the opportunity to choose a new way of living on our planet, a new way of living with each other and with the other creatures of our world. There are many sources of inspiration for a world transformed. Some of these are ancient, coming from the heritage of the world's diverse cultural and spiritual traditions. Others are emerging from fields such as deep ecology, feminism, ecofeminism, and the new cosmology arising from science. A new vision of reality, a new way of being in the world, is becoming a possibility. Indeed, as Macy and Brown note:

> The most remarkable feature of this historical moment on Earth is not that we are on the way to destroying our world—we've actually been on the way for quite a while. It is that we are beginning to wake up, as from a millennia-long sleep, to a whole new relationship to our world, to ourselves and each other. This new take on reality makes the Great Turning possible. (1998, 37)

EXPLORING THE OBSTACLES

If authentic transformation leading to a world based on a new vision seems difficult, it is in large part because a whole series of interdependent obstacles conspire to make change seem impossible. An important step, then, in searching for a Tao of liberation is to understand the very real factors that impede change. In order to see this more clearly, we will examine the obstacles we face from three different perspectives. One way to image this is to see it as a process of peeling away a series of layers. At times we will return to the same obstacle viewed from a different, often more subtle, level. In some sense, though, all the different layers or perspectives are complementary ways of viewing a single reality.

From one point of view, the obstacles we face are *systemic*. The world's political and economic structures are actively destroying the Earth and at the same time impeding effective action to address the problems at hand. Increasingly, power resides in a small number of transnational corporations that are less and less accountable to democratic structures. The economics of global capitalism are based on an ideology of growth and quantitative progress. An ever-greater proportion of profits are generated through speculation, while the truly productive activities of nature and the social economy are assigned little value. Fewer and fewer benefit from this system as an ever-greater portion of humanity is simply excluded. The life of nature and the life of the poor are converted into lifeless capital in the form of money—essentially an abstraction that of itself has no inherent value. Since this is not a sustainable system, even the minority of people who benefit from it at present cannot hope to do so in the long term. In summary, our world is ruled by a pathological system out of control that, left on its own, threatens to destroy the Earth itself.

In examining this pathological system, we will seek to understand its dynamics more clearly while revealing its fundamental insanity. In so doing, we will see how transnational capitalism is rooted in both patriarchy (the domination of women by men) and anthropocentrism (the domination of nature by humanity). Part of the challenge of creating an alternative system is to reconceptualize the very nature of power, not as control, but as a creative potentiality interwoven through the bonds of mutual influence.

From a second perspective, the structures of global exploitation and domination conspire to disempower our capacity for change at a *psycho-spiritual* level. Objective oppression produces a psychological echo in the form of internalized powerlessness. The gravity of the crises we face also tends to produce dynamics of denial and guilt, and—if we dare to recognize the reality—despair. Addictions may result as a defense mechanism to avoid facing painful realities. Our spirits our deadened and we cease to live as fully human beings. The media, our educational systems, consumerism, and (in many nations) military repression— along with a whole series of more subtle cultural dynamics—reinforce this domination of the spirit. Our very perception of reality is distorted by a system that seeks to seduce us and impede any meaningful movement for change.

In order to overcome the psycho-spiritual impediments to transformation, we will consider the importance of acknowledging our fears, building community, and nurturing creativity and solidarity. In addition, we will reflect on the need to overcome our alienation from nature and recover true psychic health so that we may access the inner power we need to work for a profound transformation of our world. Ultimately, our goal is to reawaken spirit and develop a profound sense of compassion—the ability to identify with the joys and sufferings of all of Earth's creatures. This implies living at a much deeper and richer level of being than is common in most modern societies.

DELVING DEEPER: COSMOLOGY AND LIBERATION

Looking into the spiritual malaise of disempowerment, we are led to examine a third, and perhaps more fundamental, perspective—our very perception of the nature of reality. This perspective, which we refer to as the *cosmological*, is perhaps the most difficult to challenge, but also potentially the richest in new alternatives. Our cosmology encompasses our understanding of the origin, evolution, and purpose of the universe and the place of human beings within it. The way we experience and understand the cosmos—our "cosmovision"—lies at the very core of our beliefs about the nature of transformation.

For the past three centuries or so, a cosmology that is mechanistic, deterministic, atomistic, and reductionalist has increasingly dominated humanity. More recently, consumerism has even further narrowed and trivialized our perception of reality. Together, these factors have conspired to severely limit our capacity to envision change and act creatively.

Over the past hundred years, however, a new understanding of the cosmos has begun to emerge from science. In many ways, it recalls an earlier cosmology—still common among most aboriginal peoples—that views the universe as a single organism that functions holistically. Unlike some traditional cosmologies, however, the new cosmology arising from science envisions an evolving universe. The cosmos is not a static, eternal entity but rather a process constantly unfolding and creating itself anew. As we will discover, this cosmovision challenges the very way we understand the dynamics of change. As we awaken to our interconnectedness with the cosmos, transformation is seen within a new framework that uproots our assumptions of both linear causality and blind chance. The importance of intuition, spirituality, and ancient wisdom traditions becomes more apparent. Instead of passive consumers or spectators in a blind game of chance, we come to see ourselves as active participants in the subtle mystery of unfolding cosmic purpose.

THE ECOLOGY OF TRANSFORMATION

As we consider the multiple layers of obstacles to change and as we explore the new cosmology emerging from science, we also begin to see the interrelation between the dimensions of an integral process of transformation—something we could think of in terms of an ecology. The word "ecology" normally refers to the relationship between organisms and their surroundings. Essentially, it is a study of interrelationship and interdependence. More literally, it refers to the "study of the home" (where *oikos*, "home," could also be understood as the Earth itself). It seems fitting, therefore, to speak of an "ecology of transformation" to describe the inter-related processes that must be brought into play to restore health to our common home, the Earth.

An effective ecology of transformation will require a new vision of reality, something to serve as a concrete goal and give us hope. With the demise of "real socialism" in the past fifteen years or so (which, despite its limitations, at least inspired hope that some alternative was possible), the need for a compelling vision of a transformed world has seldom been more urgent. By conceiving realistic ways to live with dignity in harmony with the Earth, we can begin to create an alternative, life-enhancing vortex of inspiration that draws us forward toward a better future.

One concrete vision for a world that could allow humans to live with dignity in harmony with other creatures is that of "bioregionalism." Bioregionalism envisions a society based on small, local communities linked together in a network of relationships based on equality, sharing, and ecological balance instead of exploitation. This model seeks to build communities that are self-supporting and self-regenerating. The scale of the communities would correspond to natural "bioregions" based on the ecology, natural history, and culture of a specific area and would reflect the values of self-reliance, harmony with nature, achieving community control, meeting individual needs, and building local culture (Nozick 1992).

At first, such a vision may seem unrealistic, even utopian; but over the course of this book it will become increasingly clear that this model is much more in accord with the needs of humanity and the unfolding process of cosmic evolution than the structures of domination and exploitation that currently rape our planet. Indeed, adopting a model along these lines may be our only real hope for a future life worth living.

Finally, we will review, deepen, and integrate our insights by describing some possible processes for opening to and embodying the Tao of liberation. In this way, the outlines of the ecology of transformation will also become clearer. It is our hope that this will in turn generate new reflections and processes that can enrich the practice of all those concerned for the health and well-being of the Earth community.

Ultimately, the purpose of this book is to inspire new hope and creativity in all those struggling to enhance the quality and vigor of the Earth's living communities, both human and nonhuman. Certainly, there is a sense of urgency in our task. The path ahead will not be easy. Duane Elgin speaks of the time ahead as one of "planetary compression," where the crises of ecological degradation and depletion, climatic change, and poverty will draw us into a whirlpool of necessity where "human civilization will either descend into chaos or ascend in a spiralling process of profound transformation" (1993, 120). We can either avoid deep transformation—and slide into a future of greater misery, poverty, and ecological degradation—or we can awake to the urgency and radicality of the changes required and seek out the Tao of Liberation.

If we choose the latter, an opportunity exists for a collective spiritual awakening of humanity and a new planetary civilization where beauty, dignity, diversity, and the integral respect for life lie at the core of all—an authentic Great Turning. It is our hope that the reflections in this book can contribute to the wisdom needed to work effectively for such a transformation.

PART 1

EXPLORING THE OBSTACLES

2.

Unmasking a Pathological System

> . . . In harmony with the Tao,
> the sky is clear and pure,
> the Earth is serene and whole,
> the spirit is renewed with power,
> streams are replenished,
> the myriad creatures of the world flourish, living joyfully,
> leaders are at peace and their countries are governed with justice.
>
> When humanity interferes with the Tao,
> the sky turns filthy,
> the Earth is depleted,
> the spirit becomes exhausted,
> streams run dry,
> the equilibrium crumbles,
> creatures become extinct . . .
>
> (*Tao Te Ching* §39)
>
> . . . When rulers live in splendor and speculators prosper
> while farmers lose their land and the granaries are emptied;
> When governments spend money on ostentation and on weapons;
> When the upper class is extravagant and irresponsible,
> indulging themselves and possessing more than they can use,
> while the poor have nowhere to turn.
> All this is robbery and chaos.
> It is not in keeping with the Tao.
>
> (*Tao Te Ching* §53)

A first step in seeking out a path toward a world where life, beauty, and dignity can truly flourish is to understand the current reality of our planet. As we have already seen, we live in a time when the Earth's ecosystems are rapidly being destroyed while a small minority of humanity monopolizes the planet's wealth. Meanwhile, we are undergoing deep and rapid changes in the way we organize human society. In many ways, we stand at a crossroads. Technologically, breakthroughs in communications, computers, and genetics amplify human powers as never before. Economically, the world is being subjugated at every level to the dictates of "the market" and the profit motive. Politically, transnational corporations are converting themselves into the dominant powers of the globe, backed up by the military might of the nations that serve their interests. Culturally, the mass media impose the values and desires of consumerism around the world.

For many, this kind of "globalization" is seen as inevitable. Indeed, the voices of the world's prevailing powers assure us this is so. We must adapt to, and perhaps subtly influence, these trends as best we can. There is no other alternative.

But what if the crises of poverty and ecological destruction we face are not simply accidental side effects or "growing pains" of our economic, political, and cultural systems? What if they cannot be cured with some minor tinkering? What if, at the heart of these crises, there is an intrinsic pathology at work? Would we not then be forced to reassess the path we are on and seek out alternatives? Would we not be challenged to think and act in new and creative ways to change what has seemed inevitable?

It is, in fact, our belief that there is a deep pathology inherent in the system that currently dominates and exploits our world. In this chapter, we will seek to unmask this pathology. In so doing, it is not our intention to disempower or overwhelm readers. On the contrary, the first step toward health is to recognize and understand our sickness. In some sense, we live a kind of collective delusion in which what is both illogical and destructive has come to be seen as both normal and inevitable. Of course, the reality of a fundamental disorder may be self-evident for those on whom this pathology inflicts the greatest suffering— the creatures whose habitats are destroyed and the vast majority of humanity living on the margins of the new global economy. On the other hand, for those who (at least in the short term) reap the system's benefits, the very existence of pathology may be less apparent. For all, though, a deeper analysis of the system reveals insights that can help all of us to challenge the dominant dis/order[1] and envision alternatives.

---

1. There are many possible ways to name the systemic pathology that currently dominates our planet. In this book, we will most commonly use the terminology of *dis/order* to indicate a system, or "order," that is fundamentally pathological—essentially, a system that resembles in many ways a disease similar to cancer.

Others, including David Korten as well as some ecumenical organizations, describe this dis/order in terms of *Empire*. Korten, for example, defines Empire as "the hierarchical ordering of human relationships based on the principle of domination. The mentality of Empire embraces material excess for the ruling classes, honors the dominator power of death and violence, denies the feminine principle, and suppresses realization of the potential of human maturity" (2006, 20). Similarly, the World Alliance of Reformed Churches (WARC) defines Empire as "the convergence of economic, political, cultural, geographic and military imperial interests, systems, and networks that seek to dominate political power and economic wealth. It typically forces and facilitates the flow of wealth and power from vulnerable persons, communities and countries to the more powerful. Empire today

Just what is the nature of our world's sickness? A first step is to look more closely at the symptoms of the disease that plagues our planet, a disease that has its origins in the way that human society is organized in our time. In particular we will consider both the problems of poverty and inequality and the ecological problems that result from "overshooting" the Earth's limits through depletion and contamination.

Poverty and Inequality

A first symptom of pathology is the widening inequality between rich and poor. Many would argue that, at least in monetary terms, humanity is now richer than at any other time in history. We live in a world full of wonders that our ancestors a century ago could scarcely have imagined—rapid travel and communications, sophisticated medicine, labor-saving devices, and sumptuous comforts. By some estimates, there is now a greater diversity of consumer products than there are species of living organisms. Overall, humans now produce nearly five times more per person than they did a century ago (Little 2000).

Yet this incredible growth of wealth has not led to the elimination—or even to a significant reduction—of human poverty. Indeed, during the past half century, the proportion of people living in poverty has remained relatively constant (Korten 1995). Some real progress has been made in terms of reducing infant mortality, lengthening life expectancy, increasing literacy, and improving access to basic healthcare. Despite this, nearly one-third of the world's population still lives on less than a dollar (U.S.) per day. Looking deeper, especially considering the erosion of traditional cultures, livelihoods, and the ecosystems that supported these, the real quality of life for many of the world's poor may actually have deteriorated.

Meanwhile, the gap between rich and poor has grown into a gaping chasm. In relative terms, Asia, Africa, and Latin America are all actually poorer than they were a century ago. Globally, the income disparity in incomes between rich and poor has doubled. To make matters worse, massive amounts of wealth continue to be transferred from the poorer nations to the richer ones: For every dollar the North gives in aid, three dollars returns in the form of debt servicing. The

---

crosses all boundaries, strips and reconstructs identities, subverts cultures, subordinates nations and states and either marginalizes or co-opts religious communities." One advantage of the Empire terminology is that it clearly links the current system to a societal model that began roughly five thousand years ago and that includes the use of military power. On the other hand, the modern form of Empire has unique characteristics that the word "Empire" might not always evoke in most who hear it—particularly its voracious destruction of the Earth's living systems.

Yet a third, complementary way to name the systemic pathology is as an *Industrial Growth Society*. This term originated with the Norwegian ecophilosopher Sigmund Kwaloy and underlines the system's dependence on ever-increasing consumption of resources as well as a mentality that sees Earth as both "supply house and sewer" (Macy and Brown 1998).

In the end, all three of these terms are valid, complementary, and helpful and are used at different times in this text, along with others such as "global corporate capitalism."

net transfer of wealth increases even more dramatically when one considers the unfair terms of trade that condemn poorer nations to low wages and low commodity prices.

In terms of wealth, the scale of inequality is even more shocking. The three richest people in the world have assets that exceed the combined gross domestic product of the forty-eight poorest nations. As we have already noted, billionaires possess a combined net wealth of over $2.4 trillion, greater than the combined annual income of the poorest half of humanity. In contrast, the total cost of providing basic education and healthcare, adequate nutrition, and safe water and sewage for all those who currently do not have these essentials was once estimated to be a mere $40 billion a year—less than 2 percent of the wealth of the world's richest individuals (UNDP Development Report, 1998). More recently, the additional expenditures needed to achieve the Millennium Development Goals—which include the above objectives as well as reducing HIV/AIDS and malaria and ensuring environmental sustainability was estimated by the World Bank to be $40 to $60 billion per year. In contrast, the Stockholm International Peace Research Institute estimates that the world spent roughly $25 billion every *week* on military expenditures in 2007.

The immediate observation that emerges when one reflects on this reality is that poverty in human society is due fundamentally not to a lack of wealth or resources, but rather to the poor distribution of the world's riches. In Gandhi's words, "The Earth satisfies the needs of all, but not the greed of those bent on insane consumption."

A second reflection that emerges is that, while poverty itself causes untold suffering, inequality compounds this. This is especially true in today's world, where even the poorest of peoples are exposed to radio, television, and commercial advertising. As the mass media proffer a vision of a consumer "paradise" enjoyed by the few, alienation and despair among the poor grow. The media's vision also undermines traditional sources of social support (culture, family, and traditions). Meanwhile, as ecological devastation deepens, the material and spiritual sustenance provided by traditional livelihoods and the beauty of the natural world are also disappearing.

Depleting the Earth

The second major symptom of pathology lies in the rapid depletion of the Earth's riches—riches that include clean water, fresh air, fertile soil, and a diverse multitude of organic communities. The same greed that causes human poverty also impoverishes the Earth itself. Human consumption usurps an ever-greater proportion of the Earth's natural wealth, a wealth whose value transcends money because it sustains life itself. In more technical terms, we are witnessing the exhaustion of the Earth's "sources": our world is entering a period of "drawdown" in which humanity devours the Earth's common wealth faster than it can be replenished.[2]

---

2. Many of the statistics contained in this section were originally gathered from Brown,

This process of "drawdown" threatens our capacity to sustain food production. Modern agriculture uses chemicals to stimulate plant growth and increase yields in the short term, but trace nutrients are lost without having time for replacement, leading to soil degradation and a decrease in the nutritional quality of food. Soil is treated as a simple "growing medium" rather than as a complex ecosystem in which each gram of soil can contain a billion bacteria, a million fungi, and tens of thousands of protozoa: "The soil produces life because it itself is alive" (Suzuki and McConnell 1997, 80). It takes five hundred years to build just one inch (2.5 cm) of topsoil, yet we now lose twenty-three billion tons of soil each year—which means that in the past twenty years we have lost a quantity of soil equivalent to that which covers the agricultural lands of France and India combined. Each year, we either use, co-opt, or destroy 40 percent of the one hundred billion new tons of soil produced by the Earth's ecosystems.

Meanwhile, extensive irrigation is leading to widespread salinization while mechanization and farming on marginal lands lead to further soil erosion. Combined with the effects of climate change, these factors lead to the loss of arable lands to deserts: between 1972 and 1991, more land was lost to deserts than the area planted in crops in China and Nigeria combined. It is estimated that 65 percent of once-arable land is now desert.

The most biologically rich ecosystems on land, the forests, are also being destroyed. Over the past twenty years, deforestation has claimed an area larger than the United States east of the Mississippi; indeed, more than half of all forests on the planet in 1950 have now been felled. While some reforestation is also occurring, such forests are often little more than tree farms supporting a far lower diversity and density of life than the old-growth forests they have replaced. Not surprisingly, hundreds of thousands of plant and animal species have disappeared forever, and others are becoming extinct at a rate thousands of times faster than any period since the disappearance of the dinosaurs.

The oceans, which constitute 99 percent of the living space on our planet and where 90 percent of all beings make their home, are also undergoing fundamental changes. At least one-third of all CO_2 and 80 percent of the heat being generated by climate change is absorbed by the oceans. In turn, this is changing the acidity, ice cover, volume, and saltiness of the sea and may eventually alter ocean currents, which have a major influence on global climate. One-quarter of all coral reefs—the most biodiverse marine ecosystems—have already been destroyed, and fully half of those remaining are now endangered. Meanwhile, the fundamental changes taking place in the oceans' chemistry may well imperil the plankton that serves as a key source of nutrients for other marine creatures and which also constitute the primary lungs of our planet, producing fully 50 percent of the Earth's oxygen (Mitchell 2009).

Groundwater accumulated over millions of years in giant aquifers has been rapidly depleted over the past century, and the draw on these sources is likely

---

Flavin, and Postel 1991 and Sale 1985, with updates based on the Worldwatch Institute's *Vital Signs 2006-2007* and Suzuki and McConnell's *The Sacred Balance: Rediscovering Our Place in Nature* (1997) as well as additional sources such as the FAO (Food and Agriculture Organization).

to increase another 25 percent over the next quarter century. Many people are already facing chronic water shortages, and these problems are likely to become much more severe in many areas of the globe over the upcoming decades. Petroleum and coal, created over a period of five hundred million years, may be gone by the middle of the next century (and the carbon that the Earth had so carefully buried to stabilize its atmosphere will be free once again). We are already very close to having reached peak oil production, and demand will soon easily outstrip supply. In addition, many key minerals such as iron, bauxite, zinc, phosphate, and chromate could be nearly totally depleted over the course of this century.

Indeed, every minute of every day (Ayres 1999b):

- We lose an area of tropical forests equivalent to the area of fifty football fields, mostly through burning.
- We convert half a square kilometer of land into desert.
- We burn a quantity of fossil fuel energy that the Earth needed ten thousand minutes to produce through the capture of sunlight.

Already, it is estimated that the richest 20 percent of humanity use more than 100 percent of the Earth's sustainable output while the remaining 80 percent use a further 30 percent (and these are quite conservative estimates). In other words, we are already overshooting the limits of the Earth. It is immediately apparent that a relatively small portion of humanity is responsible for this situation—the overconsumption of the few is impoverishing the entire community of Earth. Some ecologists estimate that as much as a third of the Earth's "natural capital" may have been lost in the twenty-five years between 1970 and 1995 (Sampat 1999)—and the rate of this depletion has continued to accelerate since that time. Clearly, such a plundering of our planet's wealth cannot continue without serious, life-threatening consequences for us all.

Poisoning Life

The third symptom of pathology may represent the greatest threat of all. As we produce an ever-growing mountain of wastes, we overwhelm the capacity of the planet's natural "sinks" to absorb, break down, and recycle contaminants. More seriously still, we are introducing chemical and nuclear poisons that persist over the long term and we are transforming the very chemistry of the atmosphere. These *problems of tolerance* are seriously undermining the health of all living creatures as well as the habitats that sustain them. Consider the following examples:

- Seventy thousand human-made chemicals have been released into the Earth's air, water, and soil—most in the last fifty years or so—and a thousand new chemicals are created every year. Annual production of synthetic organic chemicals has risen from seven million tons in 1950 to nearly a billion tons today (Karliner 1997). Eighty percent of these have never been tested for toxicity (Goldsmith 1998). Fifty people die of pesticide poisoning every minute (Ayres 1999b) and one million tons of hazardous wastes are produced every day (Meadows et al. 1992).

- Nuclear wastes, some of which remain dangerously radioactive for 250,000 years, continue to be produced with no safe means of disposal. There are over eighteen hundred tons of plutonium in the world. Yet this element is so toxic that as little as one-millionth of an ounce can be lethal to a human being. A mere eight kilograms is sufficient to produce an atomic bomb as powerful as that which destroyed Hiroshima.

- We have released immense amounts of carbon into the atmosphere— three times more than natural cycles normally absorb—initiating a dangerous cycle of global warming and climatic instability. There are good reasons to believe that this may be the most significant change in the Earth's climate since the beginning of the Eocene era some fifty-five million years ago (Lovelock 2006). At the same time, through our destruction of forests and marine ecosystems, we have seriously reduced the Earth's capacity to remove carbon dioxide from the air. CO_2 levels are now higher than at any time in the past 160,000 years, and global temperatures have already risen an average of 0.5° C. At current rates, CO_2 levels will double in another fifty years and global temperatures will rise another 2° to 5° C by the end of the century (IPCC [Intergovernmental Panel on Climate Change]). As a result, weather is becoming more chaotic and storm damage is increasing. The number of people affected annually by weather-related disasters rose from an average of 100 million in 1981-85 to 250 million in 2001-5 (Worldwatch 2007).

Problems of tolerance represent a special challenge because of their long-term, persistent effects. Even if we were to cease the production of toxic chemicals tomorrow, even if all nuclear facilities were immediately closed, even if we ceased to emit greenhouse gases like methane and CO_2, the harmful effects of these would persist for centuries, millennia, or—in the case of nuclear waste— hundreds of millions of years to come. Yet the production of many of these substances continues to increase, in some cases at an accelerating rate. James Lovelock (2006) even notes that some of the changes we have initiated may actually become irreversible. For example, if we do not reduce greenhouse gas emissions soon, we could reach a tipping point that would lead to a permanently warmer climate for our planet in the future.

At times, we may not immediately see the interconnections between the problems of tolerance, depletion, poverty, and inequality. In particular, the connection between the ecological and social dimensions of the crisis can be difficult to perceive. In part, this is because the mass media often portray issues as a kind of competition between human needs and ecological protection. For example, should we preserve an old-growth forest or cut it down to provide new jobs? Should we protect a pristine river or open a new mine to stimulate a depressed economy? Should we use chemicals and genetic engineering to increase food production? Should we build a new dam to provide energy for industrial development?

Almost always, though, when we step back and take a broader view, this idea that we can *either* address poverty *or* protect ecosystems (but *not* both) is revealed to be a falsehood perpetuated by those who wish to continue to exploit both the Earth *and* the poorest and most vulnerable of humanity. The same pathologies that impoverish people also impoverish the Earth. To see this more clearly, let us examine six key characteristics of our current global dis/order produced by industrial-growth capitalism:

1. addiction to limitless growth
2. distorted understanding of development
3. increasing subjugation to corporate rule
4. reliance on debt and speculation as key generators of profit
5. tendency to monopolize knowledge and impose a uniform global culture
6. reliance on power as domination, including military power and violence.

CANCEROUS GROWTH

In a sense, the common belief in growth is justified, because growth is an essential feature of life . . . What is wrong with the current notions of economic and technological growth, however, is the lack of qualification. It is commonly believed that all growth is good without recognizing that, in a finite environment, there is a dynamic balance between growth and decline. While some things grow, others have to diminish, so that their constituent elements can be released and recycled.

Most of today's economic thought is based on the notion of undifferentiated growth. The idea that growth can be obstructive, unhealthy, or pathological is not entertained. What we urgently need, therefore, is differentiation and qualification of the concept of growth. (Capra 1982, 213-14)

In today's world, growth has become synonymous with economic health. When growth is stagnant, or worst still, when the economy "shrinks," we are in a recession and unemployment and other social ills are sure to follow. Few of us, then, question the conventional wisdom affirming the need for an ever-expanding economy.

Yet economic growth as it is normally understood implies the use of more natural resources and the production of more dangerous by-products such as chemical and nuclear pollutants. Meanwhile, as we have already seen, many key inputs for a growing economy are being rapidly exhausted. While some "optimists" may postulate that synthetic substitutes will be found for these, there seems to be little hard evidence to substantiate their hopes.

The crux of the matter is this: The planet we live on is limited. There is only a certain amount of clean air, fresh water, and fertile soil. The amount of energy available is also finite (it is being renewed by the sun, but at a fixed rate). As all economies and all human beings require these limited essentials, it is apparent that there are *limits* to growth.

Why, then, do most economists continue to insist that unlimited, undifferentiated economic growth is both necessary and good? In part this belief is due to a confusion between growth and development. As economist Herman Daly points out, "*to grow* means to increase in size by the assimilation or accretion of materials" while "*to develop* means to expand or realize the potentialities of, to bring to a fuller, greater, or better state" (1996, 2). Our economy needs to develop in this *qualitative* sense, but not necessarily grow *quantitatively*. Indeed, "our planet develops over time without growing. Our economy, a subsystem of the finite and non-growing Earth, must eventually adapt to a similar pattern of development" (H. Daly 1996, 2).

In earlier times, when humans were a relatively small population on the Earth and our technologies were relatively simple, we were often able to act as though the Earth was an endless storehouse of raw materials. True, the Roman Empire, the inhabitants of Easter Island, the lowland jungle civilization of the Maya, and other cultures did inflict grave damage on local ecosystems, often causing the collapse of their own societies in the process. Yet the health of the overarching global ecosystem was never greatly threatened, and, over time, local ecosystems were able to heal.

Today, human population has expanded rapidly, and human consumption has expanded far more rapidly still. We have moved from what Daly calls "empty-world" economics to "full-world" economics:

> Economic growth [has] made the world full of us and our things, but relatively empty of what had been there before—that which now has been assimilated into us and our things, namely, the natural life-support systems that we have recently started calling "natural capital" out of a belated recognition of both their utility and their scarcity. Further expansion of the human niche now frequently increases environmental costs faster than it increases production benefits, thus ushering in a new era of anti-economic growth [—] growth that impoverishes rather than enriches because it costs more at the margin than it is worth. This anti-economic growth makes it harder, not easier, to cure poverty and protect the biosphere. (H. Daly 1996, 218)

An Unsustainable Path

We have already mentioned one way of understanding the move to "full-world" economics: that of Net Primary Production (NPP). Humans now consume over

40 percent of the energy produced through photosynthesis on land; 3 percent is utilized directly while the rest is simply wasted or destroyed (through urbanization, deforestation, crop wastes, etc.). The proportion of NPP used climbs even further when we take into account the destructive effects of pollution, global warming, and ozone depletion (Meadows et al. 1992). At current rates of growth, we will be appropriating 80 percent of the terrestrial NPP by the year 2030 (Korten 1995).

Another way of understanding limits to growth is through the idea of "ecological footprints," developed by William Rees and Mathias Wackernagel of British Columbia. An ecological footprint is based on a calculation of the amount of land needed to produce the food, wood, paper, and energy for the average inhabitant of a given geographic region or nation.

Leaving a very minimal 12 percent of the Earth's land surface for the preservation of nonhuman species (an amount that seems almost scandalously small), there are 1.7 hectares per person currently available for human sustenance (or 1.8 hectares if marine resources are also included). Yet the average per capita ecological footprint is already 2.3 hectares.[3] In other words, we are already consuming 30 percent more than what can be sustained in the long term—primarily by consuming nonrenewable resources. If we were to reserve a more reasonable 33 percent of land for other species, less than 1.3 hectares per person would be available, meaning that we consume 75 percent more than what is sustainable.

At first glance one could conclude that the world's population must be reduced by at least a third. Certainly sheer numbers play a role, but they do not tell the entire story. The average inhabitant of Bangladesh, for instance, has an ecological footprint of only 0.6 hectares. A Peruvian needs 1.3 hectares. The Earth's wealthiest nations, on the other hand, need anywhere from 5.4 hectares (Austria) to 12.2 hectares (USA). If all the inhabitants of the Earth used as much as the average inhabitant of the global North (approximately 7 hectares per person) we would require nearly three to four more planets like Earth to sustain us. Clearly, then, overconsumption in the North is a primary cause of ecological stress.

Yet another indication of the impossibility of continued, unbounded economic growth comes from a sophisticated computer simulation used by the authors of the updated edition of *The Limits to Growth* (Meadows et al. 2004). If we continue to follow the current economic model of growth in the traditional manner, without a major change in the policies currently in place, our material standard of living and human welfare will begin to fall dramatically shortly after the first decade of this century—probably around the year 2015 or so, but by 2025 at latest.

Depending on the different strategies and scenarios used, of course, the onset of rapid declines in human welfare can be delayed. Surprisingly, though, even a doubling of available nonrenewable resources has a relatively minor effect. The addition of improved technologies combined with increased resource avail-

---

3. And by some estimates, the weighted average is as high as 3.1 hectares. See, for example, http://www.nationmaster.com/graph/env_eco_foo-environment-ecological-footprint.

"Business as Usual" Projections

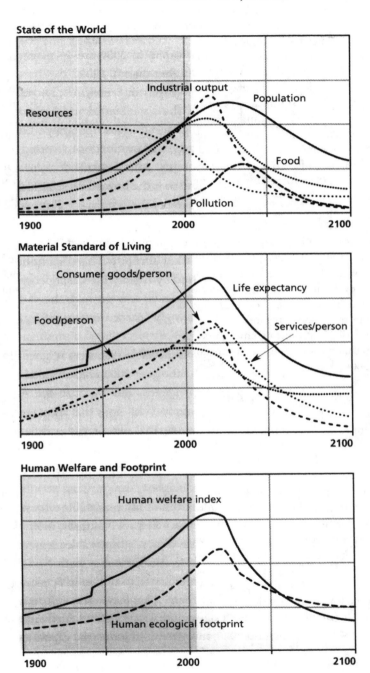

Source: Meadows et al. 2004, 169.

ability shows more promise, but it is only using the most wildly optimistic set of assumptions—a doubling of known resources, effective pollution control, significant gains in crop yields, land erosion protection, and much-improved resource efficiency technologies—that collapse can be avoided, albeit even in this case life expectancy dips around mid-century. In the longer term (beyond 2100), though, living standards ultimately become unsustainable as costs rise.

It should be noted, too, that if even one of this set of optimistic assumptions were changed significantly, it could be enough to provoke drastic declines in human welfare. (For example, removing the assumption that greatly improved resource efficiency technology will be developed and implemented results in a projection showing a collapse around 2075.) It may very well be, too, that this model actually underestimates the effects of climate change that we have already set in motion. (See, for example, the map on p. 1 of Meadows et al. 2004, showing the potential effects of climate change.) In the end, as Dennis Meadows notes:

> As long as you have exponential growth in population and industry, as long as those two embedded growth processes are churning away to produce larger and larger demands on the base, it doesn't make any difference what you assume about technology, about resources, about productivity. Eventually you reach the limits, overshoot, and collapse. . . . Even if you make heroic assumptions about technology or resources, it only postpones collapse by a decade or so. It's getting harder and harder to imagine a set of [such] assumptions that allow the model to produce a sustainable result. (Quoted in Gardner 2006, 38)

On the other hand, if population can be stabilized and per capita consumption significantly curbed (while also more effectively controlling pollution and protecting croplands), economic and ecological collapse can still be avoided. Unlike the previous scenario, this does not assume the—probably unrealistic—doubling of available nonrenewable resources.

But time is critical. Projections carried out by Meadows et al. show that beginning to implement the essential changes needed to institute this scenario twenty years earlier would have resulted in less pollution, more non-renewable resources for all, and a slightly higher overall index of human welfare. Conversely, the longer we wait to curb growth, the more disastrous the consequences and the more difficult the transition to sustainability. The authors observe:

> Growth, and especially exponential growth, is so insidious that it shortens the time for effective action. It loads stress on a system faster and faster, until coping mechanisms that have been able to deal with slower rates of change finally begin to fail. . . .

> Once population and the economy have overshot the physical limits of the Earth [something that the authors say has already effectively occurred], there are only two ways back: involuntary collapse caused by escalating shortages

Scenario with Optimal Technologies and a Doubling of Non-Renewable Resources

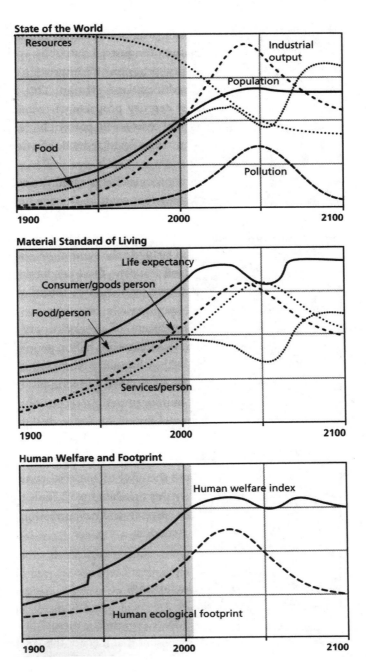

Source: Meadows et al. 2004, 219.

Stabilized Population and Consumption
with Improved Technologies

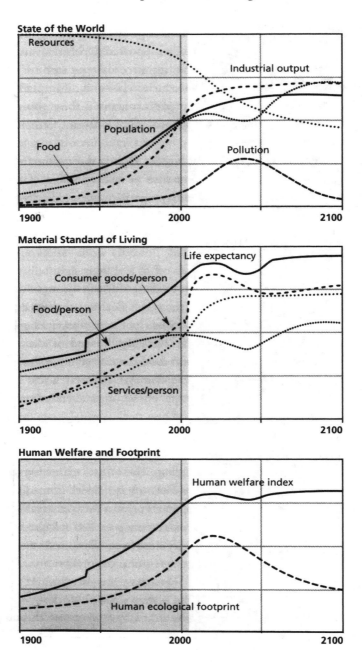

Source: Meadows et al. 2004, 245.

and crises, or controlled reduction of throughput by deliberate social choice. (Meadows et al. 1992, 180 and 189)

And more recently:

Putting off the reduction of throughputs and the transition to sustainability means, at best, diminishing the options of future generations, and, at worst, precipitating a collapse. (Meadows et al. 2004, 253)

The Attractiveness of Growth

Though we have already moved beyond any reasonable limit for a sustainable economy, we still seem far from voluntarily choosing to reduce consumption or "economic throughput." Indeed, most economists and politicians continue to insist that growth is an essential characteristic of a healthy economy. Why is it that growth remains so attractive?

Proponents claim that continued growth is necessary to reduce poverty. It is quite apparent that many people—probably the majority of humanity—do not have sufficient resources to live with dignity. Growth is seen as an "easy" way to address the problem: We need not redistribute the pie, only make it bigger.

Yet the existence of very real limits means that this path is simply not possible. Given the probability of population reaching more than nine to ten billion people in this century, the human economy would need to grow at least twenty times to provide for all people at the level of consumption currently enjoyed by the richest 20 percent. At a minimum, if we rely on growth alone to remedy poverty, the United Nations estimates that the human economy would have to grow five to ten times just to achieve a reasonable living standard for those who are now impoverished (McKibben 1998, 72). Since the human economy has already grown past sustainable levels, rapid ecological and economic collapse would ensue long before this could be accomplished. Why, then, do politicians and economists continue to advocate for growth as a means to address poverty? The Worldwatch Institute observes:

The vision that growth conjures up of an expanding pie of riches is a powerful and convenient political tool because it allows the tough issues of income inequality and skewed wealth distribution to be avoided. People assume that as long as there is growth, there is hope that the lives of the poor can be bettered without life-style changes by the rich. The reality, however, is that achieving an environmentally sustainable global economy is not possible without the fortunate [sic] limiting their consumption in order to leave room for the poor to increase theirs. (Brown et al. 1991, 119-20)

In any case, a century of unprecedented "growth" has not led to a real reduction in poverty, nor is it likely that it could do so in the future. Even if the economic growth rate of poor nations were doubled, only seven would close the gap with the rich nations in the next century—and only nine more in the next millennium! (Hawken 1993).

Indeed, development expert David Korten points out that the very policies that promote growth can actually make poverty worse, by shifting "income and assets to those who own property at the expense of those who depend on their labor for their livelihood" (1995, 42). Shifting to export crops, for example, may increase growth, but it also favors large agribusinesses at the expense of smaller farmers producing food. More logging increases economic growth, but also leads to the disruption of traditional livelihoods based on forest resources, while also increasing soil erosion and reducing rainfall.

Much of what is counted as growth is simply a shift from a nonmonetary to a monetary economy. Frequently this is accomplished by dispossessing the poor of their traditional economic base and forcing them to become laborers in a cash economy. Korten concludes:

> The continued quest for economic growth as the organizing principle of public policy is accelerating the breakdown of the ecosystem's regenerative capacities and the social fabric that sustains human community; at the same time, it is intensifying the competition for resources between rich and poor—a competition that the poor invariably lose. (1995, 11)

The only way of addressing the problems of poverty and inequality, therefore, is for those who have the most to drastically reduce consumption so that the world's limited wealth may be shared more equitably among all. Obviously some of this reduction might be achieved by making more efficient use of existing resources—converting to sustainable energy technologies and diverting resources from military expenditures. But a simultaneous reduction of overall consumption and an increase in resources for the poor would still require a significant change in lifestyle for the richest (and most powerful) 20 percent of humanity.

The challenge of reducing consumption in the North and redistributing wealth to the South may at first seem overwhelming, but it would benefit all. Some of these benefits would be ecological. As the Worldwatch Institute points out, the gaping gap between rich and poor is a major factor in ecological destruction. On the one hand, those living at the highest end of the income scale inflict the majority of ecological damage through high consumption and through the generation of large amounts of waste and pollution. On the other hand, those living in extreme poverty also contribute to the damage of ecosystems as they are pushed further and further to the margins. As a result, they may be forced to overgraze scarce lands, strip forests for firewood, or grow crops on fragile hillsides vulnerable to erosion. In contrast, the portion of human population with modest but sufficient means tends to have the least impact on the wider Earth community. Greater equity, then, would eliminate much of the damage associated with extremes of wealth and poverty (Brown et al. 1994).

Moreover, redistributing the world's wealth would free billions of people from the despair and misery of grinding poverty, allowing them to develop their human potential more fully and contribute meaningfully to a sustainable future. The benefits of redistribution for the North are not as immediately apparent, but it is certainly arguable that a move away from a consumer culture would ultimately benefit the overdeveloped world, leading to a renewal of community as people are liberated from a driven, competitive lifestyle. Indeed, a better distribution of income and wealth could result in better health for all people. As Korten observes:

> Clean water and proper sanitation are perhaps the most important contributors to get health and long life. Experience in places such as the state of Kerala in India proves that such necessities can be provided at quite modest income levels. By contrast, countries with high income levels are experiencing increases in rates of cancer, respiratory illnesses, stress and cardiovascular disorders, and birth defects, as well as falling sperm counts. A growing body of evidence links all these phenomena as to the by-products of economic growth—air and water pollution, chemical additives and pesticide residues in food, high noise levels, and increased exposure to electromagnetic radiation. (1995, 40-41)

A final benefit of greater equity is that it may well be the key to controlling overpopulation. Traditionally, population growth rates have only begun to decline once the basic needs of the population are satisfied and people feel secure enough to have fewer children (who represent a basic form of old-age security). It is worthy of note that, in the 1970s when incomes were rising in the South, population growth rates declined significantly. With the beginning of the debt crisis and the imposition of severe austerity measures in the 1980s, however, incomes fell sharply and population growth rates ceased declining, and in some cases increased. It is only in the 1990s that population growth rates again declined, but even then about one-third of this reduction could be attributed to deaths due to the AIDS pandemic.

Along with income security, the key to population stabilization lies in the empowerment of women, including their ability to make decisions regarding family size. Such empowerment, though, is arguably easier to facilitate in a society marked by lower levels of unemployment and social violence—but these conditions, too, are normally found only where at least a modicum of income equity and poverty reduction has been achieved. Ultimately, then, greater income security is essential in order to rapidly curb population growth.

A Flawed Indicator, a False Perspective

One of the key problems with growth economics is the way growth is gauged. Gross Domestic Product[4] (GDP), the principal measure of economic growth, is a seriously flawed indicator. Basically, GDP is the sum value of goods and services produced, including all economic activities in which money is involved. Thus, the cost of an expensive pollution cleanup, the production of a nuclear bomb, or

---

4. An older, slightly different indicator, is Gross National Product (GNP). It suffers from basically the same limitations as the GDP discussed here.

the price of labor to clear-cut an old growth forest is added to the GDP and inter-preted as an economic benefit. Ironically, other economic activities not entailing the use of money, such as subsistence agriculture (food production for family or community use), volunteer work, or raising children are not counted at all. Driv-ing a car a kilometer contributes far more to GDP than walking or cycling the same distance, even though the latter do not generate ecological costs.

In essence, GDP values many life-destroying activities positively while many life-enhancing ones are kept invisible. While calculations are made to account for the capital depreciation of buildings, factories, and machinery, no similar calcu-lation is made to account for the depletion of "natural capital"—the reduction in the carrying-capacity of the Earth. Artificial "wealth" is often "produced" by hiding the costs of the destruction of the real wealth of the planet, be it forests, water, air, or soil. For instance, cutting down a rainforest generates growth, but no one counts the cost of the lost wealth of creatures, air, soil, and water once sustained by the ecosystem. Korten goes so far as to say that GDP is little more than "a measure of the rate we are turning resources into garbage" (1995, 38).

In the film *Who's Counting*, feminist economist Marilyn Waring provides an interesting example of the kinds of distortions introduced by GDP. She points out that the economic activity generated by the oil spill of the *Exxon Valdez* off the coast of Alaska made it the most "growth"-producing voyage of all time. GDP counted the cost of the pollution cleanup, insurance payouts, and even the donations to "green" organizations as growth. Yet there was no debit side. The cost of dead birds, fish, and sea mammals, and the destruction of pristine beauty, simply didn't count.

From both an ethical and a practical point of view, using the GDP as a mea-sure of economic progress is therefore very questionable. The kind of undiffer-entiated economic growth measured by GDP is not necessarily good, and may often be harmful. As Herman Daly puts it: "There is something fundamentally wrong in treating the Earth as if it were a business liquidation" (quoted in Al Gore's *Earth in the Balance*, p. 91).

Yet that is what we do when we destroy the real capital of the planet—its capac-ity to sustain life—to accumulate artificial, abstract, and dead capital in the form of money (something that really has no inherent value). We are effectively borrow-ing from the future well-being of *all* life to produce short- term gain for a minority of humanity. This amounts to a very dangerous form of deficit financing.

As an alternative, many are now advocating the replacement of the GDP with a Genuine Progress Indicator (GPI). The GPI differentiates between life-producing activities and those that are life-destroying. The former are counted as productive, the latter as costs. All activities, including those that do not entail the exchange of money, are included. This allows a more accurate assessment of real economic progress—progress based on *qualitative* development rather than *quantitative* growth. Early applications of this indicator demonstrate that, over the twenty-five years before 1992, the GPI in the United States has actually fallen, even though the GDP had increased (Nozick 1992). Subsequent data seem to confirm that this trend is continuing with the 2002 GPI still slightly lower than the level reached in 1976.

Gross Production vs. Genuine Progress in the USA, 1950 to 2002

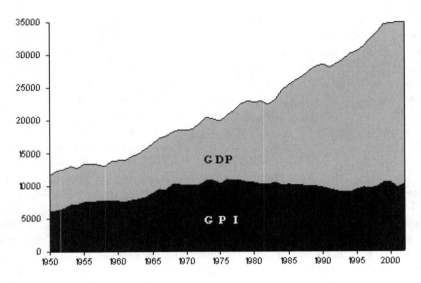

Source: http://www.redefiningprogress.org/

Moving beyond the traditional economics of quantitative, GDP-measured growth requires that we adopt a qualitative approach. Traditional ideas of profit, efficiency, and productivity must be questioned and redefined. Do we need growth? Certainly. We need growth in knowledge and wisdom, growth in access to basic necessities for all, growth in human dignity. We also need to foster beauty, preserve the diversity of life, and nurture the health of ecosystems. But we do not need growth in superfluous consumption. Nor do we need cancerous growth that destroys life simply to accumulate dead capital for a small fraction of humanity.

DISTORTED DEVELOPMENT

When anthropologist Helena Norberg-Hodge first arrived in the Ladakh region of Kashmir, India, in 1975, she encountered a people who had lived their entire lives isolated from the global economy. Yet the Ladakhis enjoyed a high quality of life. Local ecosystems were basically healthy, with pollution virtually unknown. True, some resources were hard to come by, but most people labored hard for only four months each year, leaving much of the remaining time for family, friends, and creative pursuits. As a result, Ladakhis produced a rich variety of artistic expressions. People lived in spacious homes suited to the region. Almost all basic needs, including clothing, shelter, and food, were produced and distributed without the use of money. When Norberg-Hodge asked a local inhabitant where the poor lived, the person she asked at first seemed perplexed, then replied that "We don't have any poor people here" (1999, 196).

Over the years, however, the local economy began to "develop." First, tourists came to the region, introducing the products and contrivances of the global economy. Soon, people felt the need for money to buy luxury goods. Little by little, people became oriented toward a monetary economy. As cash crops were introduced, the economy became dependent on oil, as modern transportation was required to ship production. The local ecosystem, too, began to degrade as chemically based agriculture began to take hold. As the traditional economy crumbled, Ladakhi culture was also eroded and people began to lose their sense of identity.

Perhaps our first reaction on hearing such a story is to look back nostalgically on a simpler time and culture. Most of us might consider what happened to the Ladakhis as sad, but in some ways inevitable. Others of us might ask whether another way of opening to the wider world might not have been possible, a way that did not require the deterioration of the local culture and ecosystem.

In any case, it seems reasonable to question whether the process of growth experienced by the Ladakhis was one of progress, or "development." As we saw earlier, development should imply qualitative improvements to the lives of people. Did the "benefits" of the global economy (television, access to consumer goods for those who can afford them, modern transportation) outweigh the costs in terms of poverty, ecological degradation, and cultural erosion? It seems unlikely. In any case, to call such a process "development" appears to be a gross distortion. Yet, since World War II, most of the world has been engaged in a massive "development" enterprise that shares many characteristics with the process experienced in the lives of the Ladakhis.

This is not to deny that, over the past sixty years, real progress has been made in terms of controlling diseases, raising life expectancies, and increasing access to education. Disturbingly, though, even these advances are now being eroded as poverty deepens in many countries in Africa as well as some in Latin America and Asia. Even some of the "miracle" economies of Asia, the darlings of the development ideologues, have experienced deep setbacks from time to time owing to financial crises.

Developing Poverty

Indeed, this process of development is often an exercise in "maldevelopment" based on the assumptions of growth-based economics that we have already explored. This is especially true of megaprojects like dams, irrigation schemes, free-trade zones, and many other industrial developments. All of these kinds of initiatives may indeed produce "growth" in the cash economy as measured by GDP (although they are just as likely to generate an onerous burden of debt), but they often also impoverish the majority of people and undermine the health of ecosystems. Consider the following examples:

- The Narmada irrigation project, now under way in India, will build 30 large, 135 medium, and 3000 small dams to harness the waters of the

Narmada and its tributaries. Overall, the project is expected to uproot more than a million people and destroy 350,000 hectares of forest, leading to the extinction of valuable plant species and the mass slaughter of wildlife. Many of those affected are *adivasi* (indigenous people) who will lose the lands they have inhabited for millennia.

- Throughout the world, the introduction of "green revolution" hybrid seeds has resulted in short-term gains in agricultural productivity, but at a high cost. The new crops need generous (and expensive) rations of chemical fertilizers and pesticides, harming the health of water, soil, and farm workers. Many of the crops require more water, demanding extensive irrigation (and leading to the construction of massive dam projects like the Narmada). Most of the new hybrids are cultivated as single crop monocultures, eliminating traditional crop mixes and making agriculture more vulnerable to drought, plagues, and infestations (Dankelman and Davidson 1988). More recently, the introduction of genetically engineered crops like herbicide-tolerant soybeans in South America has led to a further concentration of wealth for large landowners while facilitating the displacement of smaller producers and the destruction of complex ecosystems.

- The once-productive farming community of Singrauli, India, has become an ecological disaster zone since a dozen open-pit coal mines and a series of coal-fired generators were opened in the area. The contamination of the soil, air, and water has contributed to a virtual epidemic of tuberculosis, skin disorders, and other diseases. Seventy thousand people, many of whom once cultivated the land, now labor in the mines. Patricia Adams notes that the Indian press has compared Singrauli to "the lower circles of Dante's Inferno" (1991).

- In Lesotho, the South African government and the World Bank are implementing the Highlands Water Project, which will build five major dams, 200 kilometers of tunnels, and a hydroelectric plant. In the process, though, twenty-seven thousand local residents have been displaced from their farmlands as a result of flooding from the Mohale Dam. While they were promised help to relocate to urban areas, most have never received compensation for their losses (United Church of Canada 2007).

- The largest gold mine in South America, Yanacocha, has been developed near Cajamarca, in the highlands of Peru. While this has meant newfound wealth for a small portion of the population, most have been harmed by rising prices for land and essential products. Crime and prostitution are also on the increase. Cyanide has begun to leach into the local water table, poisoning many local water sources. Already, several streams show signs of contamination. Moreover, a mercury spill by a truck from the mine in 2002 contaminated a forty-kilometer stretch of road, leading to the poisoning of nearly a thousand local residents.

- The *maquila* free-trade zone on the United States-Mexican border was formed to spur the economic development of Mexico. Workers (mainly women) labor for low wages and are subject to a wide variety of human rights abuses. Meanwhile, the border zone is rife with toxic pollutants, and severe birth defects are common.

All of these kinds of "development projects" create growth as measured by GDP, but they have not led to a better quality of life for the majority of people. All of them are destructive of natural ecosystems and undermine the life-carrying capacity of the Earth. Yet most economists and "development experts" continue to insist that the way to progress lies through this kind of maldevelopment. Why?

Destroying Subsistence

One key problem is that Western-style development, by relying on distorted indicators like GDP, fails to value traditional subsistence economies—economies oriented toward production for immediate, local consumption. As with the Ladakhis several decades ago, people in subsistence economies may enjoy a quite high quality of life with time for family and cultural activities, but little money ever changes hands. Through the distorted lens of modern economics, this lack of cash transactions is interpreted as poverty, a "problem" that must be "cured."

Yet, as Indian ecofeminist Vandana Shiva notes, "Subsistence . . . does not necessarily imply a low physical quality of life" (Shiva 1989, 10). Local, unprocessed foods grown without chemical inputs are almost always healthier than Western diets; clothing and housing produced with natural materials are often better suited to local climates and are almost always more affordable. Shiva notes that the "culturally biased project" of removing perceived poverty "destroys wholesome and sustainable lifestyles and creates real material poverty, or misery, by the denial of survival needs themselves, through the diversion of resources to resource intensive commodity production" (1989, 10). "Commodities are grown, but nature has shrunk. The poverty crisis of the South arises from the growing scarcity of water, food, fodder, and fuel, associated with increasing maldevelopment and ecological destruction" (Shiva 1989, 5).

So the "cure" prescribed by development is to promote megaprojects, introduce cash crops for export, and increase the exploitation of natural resources. All these measures increase cash flow, but they also displace the poor from their livelihoods. Women are often the most severely affected by such a shift. "This poverty crisis touches women most severely, first because they are the poorest among the poor, and then because, with nature, they are the primary sustainers of society" (Shiva 1989, 5).

For example, subsistence farmers, often women, are frequently displaced by commercial agriculture, leaving families without an income. This often accelerates the process of urbanization as families displaced from the traditional economy move to cities to look for jobs, often in low-wage sectors like the *maquilas* of Mexico and Central America. At the same time, local ecosystems come under

attack as forests are felled, pesticides are introduced into agriculture, and factories and mines pollute the land, water, and air. David Korten concludes:

> After more than thirty years as a dedicated development worker, I've only
> recently come to see the extent to which the Western development enterprise
> has been about separating people from their traditional means of livelihood
> and breaking down the bonds of security provided by family and community
> to create dependence on the jobs and products that modern corporations
> produce. It is the extension of the process that began with the enclosure, or
> privatization, of common lands in England to concentrate the benefits of
> their production in the hands of the few rather than the many. . . . Locally
> controlled systems of agriculture, governance, health care, education, and
> mutual self-help [are replaced] with systems that [are] more amenable to cen-
> tral control. (1995, 251)

Adjusting to Maldevelopment

Over a decade ago, researchers from Yale University and two major botanical
gardens in the United States published a study on the value of the so-called minor
forest products harvested from a healthy rainforest. On average, the total value
of latex, edible fruits, and other goods gathered from the forest came to over
$6000 per hectare, more than double that which could be earned from grazing
cattle on cleared land or harvesting wood from quick-growing tree plantations.

Yet, despite this, tens of millions of hectares of rainforest are logged or simply burned each year. Often, governments like those of Indonesia and Brazil
offer direct or indirect incentives for this kind of activity. Why? In contrast to
traditional forest production, which is largely sold in local markets for local
needs, cattle, soybeans, and lumber can be sold in the global market, where
they generate "substantial amounts of foreign exchange." They are "highly visible export commodit(ies) controlled by the government and supported by large
federal expenditures" (quoted in Adams 1991, 36). This capacity to generate
foreign exchange on the world market is key because hard currencies are needed
to make payments on large external debts.

Indeed, there is tremendous pressure placed on indebted nations to make
debt payments. International financial institutions such as the International
Monetary Fund (IMF) and the World Bank impose harsh austerity measures—
called Structural Adjustment Programs (SAPs)—as a condition for guaranteeing
new loans. The objective of SAPs is to ensure the availability of foreign exchange
for debt payments. To this end, national governments must control inflation (by
reducing internal consumption), cut government expenditures, promote cash
crops and resource-extraction industries, weaken labor and ecological protections, and encourage foreign (mostly corporate) investment. Ironically, the problem of debt itself that SAPs are meant to address can largely be traced to the
kind of megaprojects associated with the practice of maldevelopment combined
with the effects of poor lending practices and high interest rates.

In practice, SAPs seldom reduce the burden of debt they are suppose to address—indeed they may well compound the problem. To control inflation, SAPs often provoke a recession by raising internal interest rates. As internal consumption, employment, and wages fall, tax revenues also diminish. Meanwhile, as more and more nations increase their production of the same export commodities, supply and international competition increase, effectively driving down prices, revenues, and wages. Debts continue to mount even faster. New loans are needed simply to pay interest on the old debt (often leading to further SAPs!) and often internal interest rates must be raised still higher to attract more money.

As a strategy to ensure debt repayment, then, Structural Adjustment Programs have been a dismal failure; yet Northern creditors have insisted on their implementation for further loans. Why? The real intent of SAPs seems to be to create a cheap pool of labor desperate for jobs, to generate cheap exports of raw materials for international markets, and to open new markets for transnational corporations. This process is usually referred to as the imposition of "neo-liberal economics"—a model of savage capitalism that sacrifices the well-being of the vast majority of humanity as well as the Earth to enrich a few. In many ways, SAPs can be seen as a kind of modern-day debtors prison, which holds entire peoples and ecosystems captive.

In an interview with the *New Internationalist* in 1999, shortly before his death, former president of Tanzania Julius Nyerere observed how SAPs had worked to impoverish millions and reverse the real gains made by authentic human development in his nation:

> I was in Washington last year. At the World Bank the first question they asked me was, "How did you fail?" I responded that we took over a country with 85 per cent of its adult population illiterate. The British ruled us for 43 years. When they left, there were 2 trained engineers and 12 doctors. This is the country we inherited.

> When I stepped down there was 91% literacy and nearly every child was in school. We trained thousands of engineers and doctors and teachers.

> In 1988 Tanzania's per-capita income was $280. Now, in 1998, it is $140. So I asked the World Bank people what went wrong. Because for the last ten years Tanzania has been signing on the dotted line and doing everything the IMF and the World Bank wanted. Enrollment in school has plummeted to 63 per cent and conditions in health and other social services have deteriorated. I asked them again: "What went wrong?" (Bunting 1999, http://www.newint .org/features/1999/01/01/anticolonialism/)

The failure of SAPs lies not only in the impoverishment of a great portion of humanity but also in the devastation of the Earth itself. Cash crops require the massive use of chemical fertilizers and pesticides; rainforests are logged for timber exports, destroying whole species, causing soil erosion, and leading to eventual desertification; delicate mangrove swamps are converted into shrimp farms; mines and smelters create a deadly brew of toxic chemicals.

Indeed, SAPs also neutralize the only market mechanism that might promote conservation of the Earth's natural wealth. In theory, as commodities become scarcer, prices should rise, forcing producers to become more efficient and to seek more ecologically sustainable alternatives. Likewise, as prices rise, consumption should drop, promoting conservation.

Unfortunately SAPs have severely distorted this form of market-based regulation. The neo-liberal model imposed through SAPs forces nations to compete in the production of exports to earn foreign exchange. As wood, minerals, oil, and agricultural products are exported at unsustainable rates, an artificial "oversupply" is temporarily created and prices are kept low. Thus market mechanisms, which might otherwise promote conservation or more sustainable alternatives, cannot work effectively. It seems likely that prices will only rise once many of the Earth's resources are virtually exhausted—leading effectively to the danger of economic collapse instead of a gradual transition to a more sustainable economy.

Rethinking Development

Both SAPs and the maldevelopment practices they promote are creating a huge and unpayable debt to the impoverished majority of humanity and to the entire community of creatures who share the Earth with us. If we are to redress this debt, we will need to rethink and challenge much that is currently named development. In particular, we must question everything that endangers traditional cultures and knowledge, everything that erodes participation and democracy, everything that undermines the health of ecosystems.

Even projects that appear to address basic human needs must at times be questioned. For example, building schools could have a negative impact if the education system encourages people to abandon traditional livelihoods in favor of consumerism and the cash economy. Hospitals and clinics can be used to impose Western-style medicine, marginalizing traditional healers and medicines. Roads may increase dependence on oil and encourage the production of cash crops for export.

That being said, not all that could go by the name of development is necessarily bad. Indeed, initiatives that genuinely improve health, nutrition, and education are urgently required. In addition, given the damage done by maldevelopment, much needs to be done to restore communities to health. The key is to carry out development in ways that empower people, affirm cultures, and safeguard local ecosystems.

Development, then, like growth, must be recast in qualitative rather than quantitative terms (especially when the quantities being measured—if money and GDP are used as measures—are themselves of questionable value). In this way, development must shift from valuing short-term expediency and profit for the few to long-term improvements in the quality of life for all people and all of Earth's creatures. We may even need to find new language that does not carry the negative burden now associated with the term "development." Some now speak of "sustainable development." In theory, this means development that does not endanger the well-being of future generations; however, in practice "development" always seems to take priority over sustainability. Another alternative is "sustainable community." This seems much better insofar as it describes the goal being sought (especially if we understand community as including other creatures), yet it may be too static. We might try "ecodevelopment," "sustainable community evolution," or even "participatory coevolution" as more appropirate terms.

To create truly sustainable communities, we must learn from the wisdom of healthy ecosystems where wastes are recycled by other organisms to produce life once again. An intriguing example of this is the Aigamo method for cultivating rice developed by Takio Furuno of Japan. Ducks are raised in the flooded paddies, providing a natural source of fertilizer to rice plants. In addition, the ducks eat most weeds (but not rice seedlings—which they find unappetizing), eliminating much backbreaking work. An aquatic fern is also used to provide nitrogen for the rice and additional food for the ducks. Over seventy-five thousand farmers in Asia now use this method. On average, crop yields rise 50 to 100 percent without the use of chemical inputs and the ducks provide farmers with an additional source of protein or earnings (Ho 1999).

Many other examples of this kind of creative, ecological thinking, can be found throughout the world. This kind of "ecodevelopment" shows that it is possible to improve the lives of human communities while preserving the health of the Earth. Indeed, in undertaking any kind of ecodevelopment, we should endeavor to live the wisdom of many native peoples in the Americas, who look at the consequences of their actions for the following seven generations to come. As Mike Nickerson points out: "More than seven thousand generations have cared and toiled to make our lives possible. They have given us language, clothing, music, tools, agriculture, sport, science, and a vast understanding of the world within and around us. Surely we are obliged to find ways to allow for at least another seven generations" (1993, 12).

CORPORATE RULE

We cannot hope to move away from unlimited, undifferentiated growth and maldevelopment unless we confront the key global powers driving both of these pathologies: transnational corporations (TNCs). The world's five hundred largest corporations employ only 0.05 percent of the world's population, but they control 25 percent of global economic output (as measured by GDP) and account for 70 percent of all international trade. Half of the world's top one hundred economies are not nations but corporations. The top three hundred corporations (excluding financial institutions) own nearly a quarter of the world's productive assets, while the fifty largest financial companies control 60 percent of all productive capital (Korten 1995, 222). Tom Athanasiou notes:

> TNCs are both the architects and the building blocks of the global economy.
> . . . [They] dictate the overall terms. . . . They are regional and global actors

in a world broken into nations and tribes. They play country against country, ecosystem against ecosystem, simply because it is good business to do so. Low wages and safety standards, environmental pillage, ever-expanding desires—all are symptoms of economic forces that, embodied in TNCs, are so powerful they threaten to overcome all constraint by the society they nominally serve. (1996, 196)

Transnational corporations have worked hard to shape the rules of the global economy to their advantage. In nations large and small they are able to exert considerable influence:

- by cultivating "friendly relationships" with political parties via political contributions
- through the promise (or threat) of moving investment and jobs
- by exerting pressure on global financial markets to effectively "vote" on a government's policies, through activities such as currency speculation

Given their control of the global economy, this political influence has become truly massive in the past twenty-five years. Not surprisingly, the policies embodied in Structural Adjustment Programs are extremely friendly to large corporations. Moreover, the new economic rules embodied in agreements and institutions governing trade and investment—such as the World Trade Organization (WTO), NAFTA, and the (at least temporarily failed) Multilateral Agreement on Investment—are largely a "bill of rights" for transnational corporations. Martin Khor, director of the Third World Network, observes that global trade agreements function as "world economic policemen to enforce new rules that maximize the unimpeded operations of transnational corporations" (Khor 1990, 6).

This new global framework is making it increasingly difficult for governments and citizens to protect both human and ecological well-being. For example, the Canadian government was forced to lift its ban on the inter-provincial trade of the fuel additive MMT—proven to be a powerful neurotoxin—because of NAFTA rules that effectively prohibit such restrictions. Ironically, MMT is not approved for use in the United States, the country where Ethyl Corporation manufactures the chemical. Another example is found in changes proposed to the WTO that would eliminate tariffs on all forest products and allow investors unrestricted access to another nation's woodlands, with no obligation to observe domestic labor and environmental laws.

Corporations and Ecological Destruction

In addition to promoting a global economic framework that makes effective ecological and labor protection nearly impossible, transnational corporations play a direct role in many of the most ecologically destructive activities. TNCs produce over half of all fossil fuels and are directly responsible for over half of all greenhouse emissions. Moreover, TNCs produce almost all ozone-destroying chemicals. They also control 80 percent of the land devoted to export-oriented agriculture. A mere twenty TNCs account for over 90 percent of all pesticide sales (Athanasiou 1996). Further, TNCs such as General Electric, Mitsubishi, and Siemens have a major stake in nuclear power generation.

More recently, TNCs have taken increasing control of the world's seed supply—and even of genetic material itself—through the patenting of life forms and even individual genes. The cultivation of genetically modified (or engineered) organisms (GMOs) produced and controlled by corporations like Monsanto and Aventis has expanded rapidly since 1995 to over a hundred million hectares today (roughly the size of Bolivia, or of France and Germany combined). Already, 60 percent of the world's soybeans and 25 percent of its corn contains genes spliced from other species.

The danger of these "transgenic" crops is twofold. First, since the seed is owned by the corporation that produces it, these crops take away control of the seed supply from farmers (a process that began to a lesser extent with the introduction of hybrid varieties during the past century). In order to use these seeds, farmers are forced to sign "technology use agreements" that forbid the saving of seeds from year to year. Corporations have even sought to introduce genetic controls in the seeds themselves that would effectively render them sterile; however, so far, this "terminator" technology has not been approved.

More disturbing, perhaps, is that transgenic crops are the result of artificially introducing genes from one species into another through the use of recombinant DNA. This essentially random insertion of foreign genes may have unintended effects on a plant's genome—and indeed, only a tiny proportion of genetic engineering experiments are successful. Yet genes replicate and spread, and any unintended effects—including subsequent mutations due to a less stable genome—could quickly spread through key crop species through cross-pollination.

Given the potential risks involved, why not ban GMOs? Large chemical and agricultural corporations argue that transgenic crops are necessary to increase food production, and even to reduce the use of chemicals in agriculture. Neither argument, however, seems to carry much weight. As we have seen, the key cause of hunger and poverty is the poor distribution of wealth and the impoverishment of ecosystems. Transgenic crops, by ensuring corporate control of the seed supply and introducing genetic contamination into ecosystems, will simply compound these problems. Even if food production were significantly increased, it would unlikely have any effect on poverty. Indeed, increased yields often suppress prices, actually impoverishing small farmers.

Furthermore, none of the commercial GMO crops created to date increase crop yields or food nutrition. Almost all modifications have focused on herbicide tolerance (allowing farmers to kill weeds without damaging the food crop) or insect resistance. Herbicide-tolerant crops actually increase the use of chemicals that are harmful to ecosystems. They also make it easier for corporations and large landowners to expand their cultivated areas. Indeed, in Argentina and Paraguay large landowners have sprayed herbicides indiscriminately on neighboring fields to kill the crops of smaller landholders and force them off their lands.

The best way to ensure food security lies in using a wide variety of open-pollinated plant varieties; this guarantees genetic diversity and thus a combination of traits that can adapt to varied weather and soil conditions. Open-pollinated seeds, however, cannot be patented and controlled by corporations in the way GMOs can. As Lovins and Lovins (2000) note, "The new botany aims to align the development of plants not with their evolutionary success but with their economic success: survival not of the fittest but of the fattest, those best able to profit from wide sales of monopolized products."

Given the massive investment of TNCs in ecologically destructive technologies, they have become a powerful force resisting more ecologically sound approaches. Far more money has been invested in the past forty years in nuclear energy than in solar- or wind-based technologies, primarily because it is easier for large corporations to profit from this centrally controlled technology (and the military spin-offs it generates). At the same time, oil companies have mounted massive publicity campaigns to try to throw doubt on the scientific evidence for global warming, despite the scientific consensus that human activity is having a discernible (and, most would argue, by far the predominant) effect on global warming.

Of course there are corporations that actually promote ecological well-being. Large insurance companies, concerned about storm damage caused by global warming, have begun to lobby for a reduction in greenhouse gas emissions. There are many companies—mostly smaller ones—that are developing more ecologically friendly technologies such as solar panels, wind generators, and hydrogen fuel cells. Overall, however, the largest and most powerful TNCs still resist alternative technologies unless they can find ways to control and dominate them for their own profit.

It is clear, then, that large TNCs still bear the bulk of the responsibility for the ecological devastation we are currently experiencing. This is unlikely to change until the way corporations are structured and regulated is radically altered. Paul Hawken (1993) notes that, at present, businesses are "better off" from the point of view of their bottom line if they simply ignore the fact that they are effectively stealing from the future to profit today. If a corporation tries to become truly ethical, just, and ecological, it incurs expenses others do not. In the long term, many corporations are undermining their own profitability, but stock prices rarely take into account long-term perspectives.

Corporate "Super-persons"

Many analysts observe that much of the problem with our current corporate model can be traced to the time when U.S. courts (and later those of other nations) granted corporations the right to be considered legal persons. By extension, a whole series of rights were granted, including the right to free speech and political participation. Yet, as Kalle Lasn points out, corporations are not really persons at all:

A corporation has no heart, no soul, no morals. It cannot feel pain. You cannot argue with it. That's because a corporation is not a living thing, but a process—an efficient way of generating revenue. . . . In order to continue "living" it needs to meet only one condition: its income must equal its expenditures over the long term. As long as it does that, it can exist indefinitely.

When a corporation hurts people or damages the environment it will feel no sorrow or remorse because it is intrinsically unable to do so. . . .

We demonize corporations for their unwavering pursuit of growth, power and wealth. Yet, they are simply carrying out genetic orders. That's exactly what corporations were designed—by us—to do. (1999, 221)

Simlarly, Joel Bakan argues that corporate super-persons have been created as pathological beings. We cannot expect them to behave ethically as long as they are structured to think and act like psychopaths:

By design, the corporate form generally protects the human beings who own and run corporations from legal liability, leaving the corporation, a "person" with a psychopathic contempt for legal constraints, the main target of criminal prosecution. . . . As a psychopathic creature, the corporation can neither recognize nor act upon moral reasons to refrain from harming others. Nothing in its legal makeup limits what it can do to others in pursuit of selfish ends, and it is compelled to cause harm when the benefits outweigh the costs. Only pragmatic concern for its own interests and the laws of the land constrain the corporation's predatory instincts, and often that is not enough to stop it from destroying lives, damaging communities, and endangering the planet as a whole. (2004, 79 and 60)

David Korten notes that corporate "super-persons" are now out of control—even those who "run" corporations have increasingly become expendable. Corporations now exist as "an entity apart" with no real bond to people or place. Indeed, he argues, the interests of people and all the Earth community increasingly diverge from the interests of corporations. Despite this, corporations continue to assume more and more control over our lives. "It is almost as though we were being invaded by alien beings, intent on colonizing our planet, reducing us to serfs, and excluding as many of us as possible" (1995, 74).

John Ralston Saul (1995) observes that this trend bears a close resemblance to the goals of corporatist movements like the fascism of the 1920s and '30s, which sought to: (1) shift power from peoples and governments to economic interest groups; (2) "push entrepreneurial initiative in areas normally reserved to public bodies" (we call this "privatization"); and (3) eliminate the boundaries between private and public interest. Reading his account, one is left with the impression that, despite the struggle of World War II, corporatism has now triumphed in a new, more subtle and powerful way. A less democratic and less ecological model of global governance is hardly imaginable.

At times, the overwhelming pathological power of corporations seems invincible, but already chinks are appearing in the corporate armor. People in parts of

Europe and Brazil—and even some counties in the United States—have successfully created GMO-free zones, for example. Progressive governments, particularly in South America, have begun to seriously critique the neo-liberal agenda promoted by TNCs. Global protests against the IMF, World Bank, and World Trade Organization—all key international instruments of corporate rule—have been growing in strength. In large part because of these movements and the election of governments critical of its agenda, "progress" in WTO negotiations has been nearly impossible in recent years.

Korten argues that today's global corporate capitalism bears a strong resemblance to the centrally controlled economies of the former Soviet bloc. "The West is now heading down a[n] extremist ideological path [similar to that of the former Eastern bloc]; the difference is that we are being driven to dependence on detached and unaccountable corporations rather than a detached and unaccountable state" (1995, 88-89). Both systems concentrate economic power in centralized institutions that resist accountability and popular participation; both rely on large structures that are inherently inefficient and unresponsive to human rights and authentic needs; and both create a distorted economy that treats other living creatures and ecosystems as resources that can be consumed without consequences. As we all know, the Soviet system—once seen as unassailable—collapsed in a matter of years. Global corporate capitalism may well be a more sophisticated system of control and exploitation, but there are good reasons to believe that it, too, could succumb to a similar fate if it does not radically change course. As Korten observes, "An economic system can remain viable only so long as society has mechanisms to counter abuses of either state or market power and the erosion of the natural, social, and moral capital that such abuses commonly exacerbate" (1995, 89).

PARASITIC FINANCE

The problems of growth, maldevelopment, and corporate rule are compounded by a parasitic financial system that increasingly shifts economics from the production and distribution of goods and services to an exercise in profiting from the manipulation of money. For instance, in 1993, two of the world's largest corporations—General Electric and General Motors—actually generated more profits through their internal financial subsidiaries than they did through the manufacture of real electronic or automotive products (Dillon 1997).

Overall, the world's "financial economy" has rapidly outgrown the economy dealing in real goods and services. Financial transactions are now "worth" (as money measures things!) over seventy times more than global trade in tangible commodities. The monetary value of the shares traded on the world's major stock exchanges rose from $0.8 trillion in 1977 to $22.6 trillion in 2003. As Korten observes, "This represents an enormous increase in the buying power of the ruling class relative to the rest of the society. It creates an illusion that economic policies are increasing the real wealth of society, when in fact they are depleting it" (2006, 68).

In total, daily transactions in stocks, currencies, commodity futures, and bonds reached about $4 trillion in 1997 (Dillon), while today the Bank of International Settlements calculates that foreign currency transactions alone reach that amount (up from about $1.5 trillion in 1997). As Dillon notes, "Most of these transactions [95 percent] are speculative; they are not in and of themselves necessary to finance the production of goods and services" (1997, 2). The introduction of new technologies has facilitated an increased pace and volume of financial transactions. Almost all these now employ the use of "cybermoney"—electronic transfers involving computers and near-instantaneous communications around the globe. Dillon notes, "Nothing tangible changes hands. Nevertheless, speculators grow wealthy doing nothing more tangible than rearranging zeroes and ones on computer chips as they buy and sell cybermoney" (1997, 3).

Many years ago, the economist John Maynard Keynes warned: "Speculation may do no harm as bubbles on a steady stream of enterprise. But the position is serious when enterprise becomes the bubble on a whirlpool of speculation." Yet this seems to be an accurate description of our current global economy. The volatility that this situation engenders can wreak havoc both quickly and unexpectedly. In 1995, a trader in Singapore bankrupted the 233-year-old Barings Bank of Britain after losing $1.3 billion on a transaction involving $29 billion in Japanese derivatives. More disturbing still were the financial crises in Mexico in 1994 and in Asia in 1998, provoked when investors suddenly pulled their money out of these regions causing their "bubble economies" to collapse. In both cases, the huge and volatile influx of speculative capital created the conditions that led to these crises. In both cases, foreign investors were largely protected from losses (after having made spectacular speculative profits earlier) by internationally financed bailout packages. The cost of these packages, however, was borne by the people and ecosystems of the affected nations—particularly through an increased burden of debt and the imposition of further Structural Adjustment Programs.

Finally, but on still a larger scale, the recent sub-prime mortgage crisis which began in the United States has caused financial markets to plunge around the world. Once again, speculation—particularly the trading of sub-prime mortgages sold as paper investments—led to a massive collapse of a bubble economy, but this time on a global rather than regional level. As economist Herman Daly notes:

> The turmoil affecting the world economy unleashed by the US sub-prime debt crisis isn't really a crisis of "liquidity" as it is often called. A liquidity crisis would imply that the economy was in trouble because businesses could no longer obtain credit and loans to finance their investments. In fact, the crisis is the result of the overgrowth of financial assets relative to growth of real wealth—basically the opposite of too little liquidity.
>
> The problem that we're seeing in the US has arisen because the amount of real wealth is not a sufficient lien to guarantee the staggering outstanding debt which has exploded as a result of banks' ability to create money, loans

given out on shaky assets and the US government's deficit, which has been stoked by financing the war and recent tax cuts. . . . To keep up the illusion that growth is making us richer, we deferred costs by issuing financial assets almost without limit, conveniently forgetting that these so-called assets are, for society as a whole, debts to be paid back out of future growth of real wealth. That future growth is very doubtful, given the deferred real costs, while the debt continues to compound to absurd levels. (2008)

Once again, governments have been forced to shore up the financial system through massive loans and even buyouts of financial institutions, leaving taxpayers on the hook for trillions of dollars. Meanwhile, the bursting of the bubble is resulting in very real costs, as unemployment rises, people lose their homes, and global trade rapidly contracts.

Financial speculation, then, while on one level divorced from reality, does generate real costs for people and the wider Earth community. Financial speculators wield immense economic power. As is evident from the crises in Mexico and Asia, they can quickly move their funds wherever they please, leaving economies to collapse in the wake of their decisions. Even the policies of the wealthiest of nations are subject to such pressure. In the early 1990s, for example, the threat of financial reprisals was cited by the Canadian government as a reason for drastically cutting government spending. International financiers effectively exercise a kind of veto power over the policies of all the world's nations, pushing them to adopt laws and regulations that increase corporate profitability through open investment policies (that further increase volatility), "free trade," low taxes, and weakened protections for labor and ecosystems.

Investors also wield power over individual corporations. To cut costs, raise profitability, and increase stock prices, companies eliminate jobs or move them to wherever wages are lower. Similarly, liquidating "natural assets" by depleting the Earth's wealth at unsustainable rates raises short-term profits and stock prices. Corporations that try to be responsible, who seek long-term sustainability over short-term profit, are subject to intense financial pressures to act otherwise. Those who fail to do so may also become vulnerable to "corporate raiders."

Ned Daly cites the example of the Pacific Lumber Company, which cuts timber in the ancient redwood forests of the California coast. During the 1980s, the company was considered a model in terms of its labor and ecological practices, including generous benefits for workers and innovative methods of sustainable logging. These same practices, though, caused it to generate only modest profits, leading to a low stock value. This in turn made it a prime target for a hostile takeover by corporate raider Charles Hurwitz. On assuming control, Hurwitz immediately doubled the company's rate of cutting timber and drained the company's pension fund of over half its assets. This allowed him to pay off the junk bonds he used to finance his takeover bid and turn a tidy profit. His gain, however, was achieved at the price of accelerating the destruction of one of the world's most unique and majestic forests (N. Daly 1994).

In some ways, the global financial system can be seen as a parasite sucking life from the real economy. This is not to deny that investment is necessary—productive investments that create jobs at living wages while living sustainably within the limits of ecosystems are often required for authentic innovation and progress. Most of the world's investors, though, now seem to be engaged in a kind of "extractive investment" that does not create wealth but simply "extract[s] and concentrate[s] existing wealth. . . . In the worse case, an extractive investment actually decreases the overall wealth [and health] of the society, even though it may yield a handsome return to an individual" or group of investors (Korten 1995, 195). The actions of Charles Hurwitz seem to be a perfect example of this kind of parasitic investment.

Illusory Wealth

At the heart of extractive investment and parasitic finance lies a mistaken understanding of money. Even Adam Smith opposed the idea of making money from money; money was meant to be an instrument, not an end in itself. John Ralston Saul notes, "The explosion of money markets unrelated to financing real activity are pure inflation. And for that matter, they are a very esoteric, pure form of ideology" (1995, 153-54).

Economist Herman Daly (1996) refers to this as the "fallacy of misplaced concreteness." We confuse money (or the zeroes and ones zipping through cyberspace that has largely replaced physical currency) with the real wealth it is meant to represent. Whatever is assumed to be true for the abstract symbol of wealth is assumed to hold true for real wealth.

Real wealth, however, is subject to spoilage. Grain cannot accumulate forever in barns and silos; clothing eventually wears out or is eaten by moths; and housing gradually decays. At best, natural wealth (like forests or crops growing in a field) can grow at rates fixed by the inputs of sun, clean water, air, and healthy soil. Real wealth, however, never grows at exponential rates for any significant rate of time and may indeed even decay with age.

Money, on the other hand, does not spoil. By equating the symbol (money) with the reality (wealth), wealth becomes an abstract quantity free of the laws of physics and biology. It can accumulate forever without rotting. Through the magic of debt and more sophisticated financial manipulations, money can even grow—often at exponential rates. Due to the fallacy of misplaced concreteness, most economists (and many politicians, investors, and common folk caught up in the money illusion) therefore assume that real wealth is also growing exponentially.

In fact, the money accumulating is not real wealth at all—it is simply a kind of lien against future production that, by social agreement, can be redeemed for real wealth at a later time.[5] To meet the growing liens against the future being

---

5. An intriguing example of how these liens can accumulate to truly ludicrous proportions via exponential growth is found in an article written by the Venezuelan researcher Luis Britto García

generated by this kind of capital accumulation, the economy must constantly grow or the value of money must be reduced via inflation to match the real wealth that exists. (Alternatively, as in the case of the sub-prime mortgage crisis, the bubble can simply burst, causing a chain reaction that includes the collapse of companies and the evaporation of the value of virtual assets.)

Here we begin to understand more clearly how the financial economy's quest for profit concentrates wealth in the hands of investors while impoverishing the poor and the wider Earth community. On the one hand, to meet the ever-mounting lien against future production, the world is forced to continue its obsession with unlimited growth—depleting the natural wealth of the planet in the process. At the same time, inflationary pressures particularly impoverish the poor who do not earn investment income at exponential rates.

A more direct example may be helpful. Between 1980 and 1997, the poorer nations of the world transferred $2.9 trillion in debt payments to banks, Northern governments, and international financial institutions such as the World Bank and the IMF. Yet, over the same period of time, their total debt still grew from $568 billion to over $2 trillion. Debt, then, transfers massive resources from the poor to the rich via the "magic" of compound interest. This ever-growing lien against the future production of poorer nations can never be met. Yet the world's parasitic financial system continues to suck the poor and the Earth itself dry, insisting that whatever wealth can be extracted be used to enrich the financial economy.

Money Colonizing Life

Most of us see economics as the science (or art) of producing, distributing, and consuming wealth. More crudely, many of us think of economics as the art of making money. In Greek, however, the word "economics" is *oikonomia*, the art of caring and managing the household—the community, a society, or the Earth. In fact, economics shares a common root with "ecology," the study of the home.

Aristotle made a clear distinction between economics and "chrematistics"—speculative activities that produced nothing of value, but which generated profits nonetheless. Chrematistics is defined as "the branch of political economy relating to the manipulation of property and wealth so as to maximize short-term monetary exchange value to the owner" (H. Daly and Cobb 1989, 138).

Aristotle uses the example of the philosopher Thales of Miletus to illustrate the difference between economics and chrematistics. For years, Thales had been ridiculed by his community for his simple lifestyle. "If philosophy is so impor-

---

(1990) in the form of a fictional letter from a Guatemalan indigenous leader named Guaicaipuro Cuauhtémoc to the leaders of Europe. The letter points out that, if Europe were to try to repay the "friendly loan" of 185,000 kilos of gold and sixteen million kilos of silver provided by the Americas to them over three hundred years ago at "market rates" of interest, Europe would owe "as a first payment against the debt, a mass of 185,000 kilos of gold and 16 million kilos of silver, both raised to the power of 300. This equals a figure that would need over 300 digits to put it down on paper and whose weight fully exceeds that of the planet Earth."

While the power of three hundred seems to be an exaggeration, it is true that at 13.5 percent interest, the amount of gold and silver needed to repay the loan after three hundred years would, in fact, exceed the weight of the Earth itself.

tant," they asked, "why have you been unable to accumulate wealth?" Thales then decided to prove a point. Through his knowledge of astronomy, he was able to predict a bumper crop of olives. So, while winter still lay over the land, he leased all the local olive presses at a discounted rate. When the bumper harvest arrived, he then used his monopoly to generate a generous profit for himself—but at a cost to the greater community.

In many ways, what Thales practiced is similar to that which takes place in today's global financial markets. He saw it, however, for what it was—an exercise in chrematistics rather than economics. After all, he had created nothing of value: he invented no new uses for olive oil, he built no new olive presses, he planted no olive trees. He simply enriched himself at the expense of others.

Much of our practice of "economics" is really little more than a sophisticated form of chrematistics. Indeed, the activities that generate the highest returns often have little or no real value (they neither sustain nor enhance life, and may even destroy it) while activities that are truly productive—caring for children, raising food, protecting nature—yield little in the way of money. We therefore see the investment banker as someone who is "worth" more than the peasant woman struggling to nurture the soil and her family. Vandana Shiva notes:

> The ultimate reductionalism is achieved when nature is linked with a view of economic activity in which money is the only gauge of value and wealth. Life disappears as an organising principle of economic affairs. But the problem with money is that it has an asymmetric relationship to life and living processes. Exploitation, manipulation, and destruction of the life of nature can be a source of money and profits but neither can ever become a source of nature's life and its life-supporting capacity. It is this asymmetry that accounts for a deepening of the ecological crisis as a decrease in nature's life-producing potential, along with an increase in capital accumulation and the expansion of "development" as a process of replacing the currency of life and sustenance with the currency of cash and profits. (1989, 25)

David Korten speaks of our time as one in which money has colonized life. It's an apt expression. Similarly, over fifty years ago the great economic historian Karl Polanyi warned that "the notion of gain" could overcome the social (and we would add, ecological) framework, so that human society (and the wider Earth community) become merely an "accessory of the economic system." He warned that if the laws of commerce (or, more accurately, chrematistics) took precedence over the laws of nature and the laws of God, the "self-regulating market" could not exist "for any length of time without annihilating the human and natural substance of society" (quoted in Athanasiou 1996, 197).

MONOCULTURE OF THE MIND

The pathological system dominating the globe does indeed seem to be converting human and other biotic communities into "mere accessories of the economic system." In so doing, it imposes a globalizing culture (or caricature of culture) that destroys local cultures and local knowledge, impoverishing all of humanity and potentially endangering our own survival as a species. Vandana Shiva points out that this "global culture" being foisted upon the world by corporate capitalism pretends to be in some sense universal, but in fact it is primarily the product of a particular culture (originating in North America and Europe). "It is merely the globalised version of a very local and parochial tradition" (Shiva 1993, 9).

This so-called global culture, so powerfully spread through advertising, the mass media, and westernized education, tends to negate the very existence of local knowledge and traditional wisdoms, effectively declaring them illegitimate, or even nonexistent. At best, the globalizing culture incorporates a few symbolic elements such as music, clothing styles, or art from non-Western cultures, but the essence and values of these cultures are largely ignored. At the same time, the globalizing culture "makes alternatives disappear by erasing and destroying the reality that they attempt to represent. The fragmented linearity of the dominant knowledge slips through the cracks of fragmentation. It is eclipsed along with the world to which it relates. Dominant scientific knowledge thus breeds a monoculture of the mind by making space for local alternatives disappear" (Shiva 1993, 12).

Fragmenting and Monopolizing Knowledge

One way in which knowledge is fragmented and destroyed, ironically, is through the multiplication of information—much of which is of only marginal value. Advertising is a particular case in point. The average North American child now watches thirty thousand advertisements before reaching the first grade, and teenagers spend more time soaking up commercials than they do in school (Swimme 1996). Such prolonged and persistent brainwashing beginning at an early age cannot help but narrow our perspectives and indoctrinate us into seeing the current global dis/order as normative. It is incredible to note, for example, that the average inhabitant of the United States can recognize over a thousand corporate logos but fewer than ten animal and plant species native to her or his area (Orr 1999). The dominant monoculture fills us with empty "information," but often distracts us from gaining real knowledge.

At the same time, the medium of television itself tends to split knowledge into bits of isolated information. Television news, composed mainly of brief "sound bites," teaches us to deal with complex issues by dividing them into fragments dissociated from any kind of integrating framework or analysis. Television programs, varying in length from thirty to sixty minutes, also tend to deal with simple questions (when they deal with questions at all!) that can be "resolved" quickly—thus largely avoiding more complex issues. Yet these mind-numbing entertainments often draw people away from traditional cultural pursuits like storytelling, conversation, music, art, and dance.

This whole process recalls the words of T. S. Eliot, who wrote in "Choruses from 'The Rock'":

> Where is the wisdom we have lost in knowledge?
> Where is the knowledge we have lost in information?

We might even add a third line for our own age:

> Where is the information we have lost in distraction?

As the globalizing culture extends its tentacles, it also attempts to monopolize whatever traditional knowledge might prove profitable. This can be most clearly seen in the drive of transnational corporations to patent life itself. The World Trade Organization opened the doors to this drive when it began permitting patent protection on seeds and genetic materials. Vandana Shiva notes that two U.S. corporations have used these provisions to apply for patents on basmati rice and neem—a natural pesticide and fungicide—both of which were developed by peasant communities in India centuries ago.[6] This type of "biopiracy" is becoming commonplace. There have even been attempts to patent genes from aboriginal peoples. That this kind of lunacy can actually seem logical to the global dis/order that currently dominates the planet is a clear demonstration of an inherent pathology.

Destroying Diversity

As the global "monoculture of the mind" spreads, it also obliterates other cultures, languages, and systems of knowledge like a cancerous growth. Just as local plant and animal species are lost and replaced by a few, economically expedient varieties, so too are entire cultural systems disappearing. Many of these took thousands of years to evolve and are uniquely adapted to a particular ecosystem—especially in the case of aboriginal cultures. Each culture lost represents a lessening of diversity, a lessening of the true riches of the Earth. As the destruction of plant species in the rainforests may represent the loss of a cure for cancer or the loss of a valuable new foodstuff, so too the destruction of the pieces in the global cultural mosaic represents the loss of potential solutions to our current crises. Moreover, such a loss entails a diminishment of the beauty and mystery of life itself, something that can never be adequately measured or quantified.

A particular example of this trend lies in the reduction of the languages being spoken in the world. Language is in many ways a central aspect of culture, for it embodies unique ways of thinking; the loss of each language, then, represents the loss of a unique perspective, a unique way of conceiving the world. Approximately ten thousand years ago, linguists estimate there were twelve thousand languages spoken by the five to ten million people living in the world. Today, only seven thousand of these remain, despite a current population that has ballooned to over six billion. At the same time, the rate of language loss has accel-

---

6. Fortunately, after a legal battle, the patent on neem has now been rejected and the patent claim on basmati rice restricted. In large part, though, this was because these highly publicized examples garnered significant attention; unfortunately, most such patent applications never come to public attention.

erated rapidly, particularly over the past century. We are now losing roughly one language every day. At current rates of loss, there will only be twenty-five hundred languages remaining a hundred years from now. Other experts are still less optimistic, believing that 90 percent of the remaining human languages will disappear by 2100 (Worldwatch 2007).

In his study of the rise and fall of the world's civilizations, cultural historian Arnold Toynbee noted that civilizations in decline tend toward ever greater uniformity and standardization. In contrast, thriving civilizations are marked by a growth in diversity and differentiation. Like healthy ecosystems, a healthy civilization allows for a diversity of cultures and ways of knowing. Uniformity is a sign of stagnation and decay (Korten 1995).

The ever-greater homogeneity of the globalizing culture parallels the imposition of an increasingly uniform global economy. In *The Ecology of Commerce*, Paul Hawken (1993) likens our current global economy to a pioneer community of weeds. In recently cleared areas, plants compete to cover the soil as quickly as possible. Much energy is wasted and diversity is low. The plants present in such biotic communities are generally not very useful to other species, including humans. In contrast, the ecosystems with the highest evolutionary potential are those with the greatest diversity (like old-growth forests and coral reefs). In a similar way, our global economy's obsession with untrammeled growth and expansion neglects other, more important characteristics such as complexity, cooperation, conservation, and diversity. It is an immature system.

The same analogy is also useful in thinking of the growth of a global monoculture. Ultimately, the loss in cultural diversity and local knowledge represents a threat to the human community similar to the threat that the loss of ecosystem diversity represents to the planet as a whole. We are replacing a diverse "ecosystem" of cultures with a weedlike monoculture, which grows rapidly but is of little real use. To make things worse, it is as though the weed culture that is spreading contains a death-dealing gene—like the genetically modified variety of cotton that produces the Bt pesticide—making it in many ways antithetical to life itself.

POWER AS DOMINATION

At the heart of the global pathology dominating the Earth is a conception of power as domination. In order to impose itself throughout the globe, capitalism (and its predecessor, mercantilism) has used force, initially in the form of colonialism. Between the years 1500 and 1800, European powers conquered or subjugated the greater part of the world to their domination. By the beginning of the nineteenth century, however, local peoples began to revolt against this domination, starting particularly in Latin America. While these (mainly) middle-class independence movements seldom led to significant changes for the poorest sectors of their societies, these struggles did force the hegemonic powers to rethink their strategy. By the end of the 1960s, traditional colonialism based on direct political domination had been almost totally replaced by an economic neocolonialism. In recent years, transnational corporations (together with the nations serving their political needs) have extended their controlling power, first through SAPs, and more recently through "liberalized" trade and investment agreements that destroy local control and the sovereignty of citizens while guaranteeing the "rights" of exploitative economic powers—particularly large corporations.

These economic weapons are compelling tools of domination, but they are also backed by the threat of arms. Military expenditures still consume a gigantic proportion of the world's resources. According to the Stockholm International Peace Institute, the world's governments spent over $1.3 trillion (or 2.5 percent of global GDP) to support military forces in 2007. Perhaps even more important, many of the world's brightest and most talented minds are still engaged in military research—what could happen if this same resource were applied to the world's most pressing problems? War, too, continues to destroy lives and communities, especially in internal conflicts often related to poverty, resource shortages, and the interests of large corporations. The threat of nuclear weapons also remains very real: About twelve thousand nuclear warheads still exist in the world—enough to destroy the Earth many times over.

For many of the world's peoples, then, war and military repression remain a real and present threat. In recent years, this has become more and more evident in the conflicts, repressive tactics, and human rights violations related to the so-called war on terror. Increasingly, labeling a person or group as a "terrorist" provides a license for indefinite imprisonment, torture, and even killing.

In a more general way, militaristic metaphors and ways of thinking continue to dominate the entire global pathology. We think in terms of "conquering disease" rather than promoting wellness; we speak of the "survival of the fittest"— or even "destroy or be destroyed"—rather than cooperation for mutual survival. We see domination—be it of rich over poor, men over women, one nation over another, or of humans over nature—to be somehow natural or inevitable.

Perhaps it is not surprising, then, that humans are now trying to manipulate and dominate the very processes of life itself through genetic engineering. Other technologies may further multiply the power to dominate—in particular robotics and nanotechnology (the latter of which could eventually result in self-replicating machines only slightly larger than molecules that in many ways mimic micro-organisms). Bill Joy (2000) warns that all these technologies hold the potential for harm on an unprecedented scale. Unlike nuclear warheads, these new technologies do not require difficult-to-obtain raw materials. They also all are potentially self-replicating. Finally, all of them are being developed by large corporations with little oversight from national governments—and are thus far removed from mechanisms of public accountability.

The danger of these new technologies is very real. Genes from transgenic crops have already crossed over to other plants, and even other species. Microscopic "nanites" could also reproduce themselves—opening the possibility, for example, that micro-machines could be created that would actually cover and consume the Earth, reducing it to dust, or systematically annihilate bacteria essential to sustaining life on the planet. As artificial intelligence advances, robots could also replicate themselves, possibly displacing humans in the future.

At first, hearing such predictions sounds like pure science fiction, but there are good reasons to believe that these technologies will become a reality within the lifetime of many of us—indeed the genetic genie is already "out of the bottle." Joy observes:

> The new Pandora's boxes of genetics, nanotechnology, and robotics are almost open, yet we seem hardly to have noticed. . . . We are being propelled into this new century with no plan, no control, no brakes. Have we already gone too far down the path to alter course? I don't believe so, but we aren't trying yet, and the last chance to assert control—the fail-safe point—is rapidly approaching. We have our first pet robots, as well as commercially available genetic engineering techniques, and our nanoscale techniques are advancing rapidly. While the development of these technologies proceeds through a number of steps, . . . the breakthrough to wild self-replication in robotics, genetic engineering, or nanotechnology could come suddenly, reprising the surprise we felt when we learned of the cloning of a mammal. (Joy 2000)

Human powers seem to be increasing far more quickly than human wisdom. Still, Joy believes that there are reasons to hope. He notes that humanity has been able to renounce the use of chemical and biological weapons, realizing that they were simply too terrible and too destructive to ever employ them. Can we renounce the knowledge and power that these new technologies imply—or at the very least, impose stringent safeguards on them based on the precautionary principle? Ultimately, perhaps, this depends on whether humanity—and particularly those with the most influence in the pathological system ruling our planet—are willing to turn away from the quest for ever-greater power, control, and domination.

FROM PATHOLOGY TO HEALTH

Is it, indeed, possible to turn away from the road of pathology and to choose instead a path leading to health and life? At first the sheer size and apparent power of the global dis/order seem overwhelming. Moreover, the sheer insanity manifest in its fundamental irrationality tends to push us toward denial (how could this really be happening?) or despair (how can it ever be stopped?).

Paradoxically, though, this irrationality may itself be a sign of hope. The dominant global economic, political, and ideological systems constantly try to convince us that the kind of "globalization" based on "free markets," financial speculation, deregulation, corporate power, and unlimited growth are in some sense inevitable. There is no other way—we may make minor course adjustments, but a fundamental change in direction is impossible. Yet a system as pathological and irrational as the current global dis/order is clearly not inevitable. It is an artificial and illogical artifice at odds with billions of years of cosmic and Earthly evolution.

Underlying Assumptions and Beliefs

If [humans] as individuals surrender to the call of their elementary instincts, avoiding pain and seeking satisfaction only for their own selves, the result for them all taken together must be a state of insecurity, of fear, and of promiscuous misery. (Einstein 1995, 16)

To see this more clearly, let us take a moment to review some of the underlying assumptions and beliefs inherent in the current pathology afflicting our world and compare them to what we might call "ecological common sense," or a way of thinking that embodies the wisdom of the Tao.

First, the current system is obsessed with quantitative, undifferentiated, unlimited "growth" as perceived through the distorted lens of GDP. Increasing "throughput" (the rate at which resources are used) is seen as a sign of health, even as natural wealth is depleted and poverty deepens through the process of maldevelopment. At the same time, a monoculture mentality attempts to impose a single culture and single economic model on the entire planet, resulting in immature "weed" societies that are high in energy use and low in diversity.

In contrast, healthy ecosystems display much more stable characteristics; they are what Herman Daly calls "steady state economies." This does not mean that change is not possible, or even desirable—all ecosystems evolve over time— but change is primarily qualitative, the growth of diversity that in fact leads to even greater system stability over time. Further, there is a wealth of diverse ecosystems—each one uniquely adapted to a specific climatic and geographic zone. The Tao lies in diversity, differentiation, and stability, not in the cancerous-growth monoculture.

Second, the current global dis/order gives primacy to the "notion of gain" or profits at all cost. In particular, the system centers on a fixation for short-term gain over long-term sustainability, a prioritization of profits for a few at the expense of the many. Often, those activities that generate the greatest "profit" are those that undermine the quality of life, while those which actually sustain and enhance life are considered "uneconomic." "Gain" is defined in purely financial terms: money is understood as "the only gauge of value and wealth," even if the quality and diversity of life are undermined as lifeless "capital" accumulates.

From the point of view of ecosystems, money is simply an abstraction created to facilitate exchanges. It has no inherent value. (What is the value of money if no healthy food, no clean air, and no pure water remain to be purchased?) Only the health and diversity of the web of life have real value. Activities that undermine this—including the destruction of life to accumulate capital—are evils, not goods. All activity is ultimately gauged by its long-term, enduring value. Short-term gain at the cost of long-term well-being is not gain at all—it is a loss. The Tao values life and looks to the good of the seventh generation and beyond.

Third, the hegemonic systemic dis/order concentrates power and wealth in the hands of corporate "super-persons"—artificial entities that evade accountability to the wider communities in which they operate. Power is understood and exercised fundamentally as domination. Competition is seen as the driving force of change and progress (even though large corporations simultaneously try to thwart competition by monopolizing markets and power).

From an ecosystem point of view, wealth best serves the community when it is most widely shared. Power is decentralized—in a healthy ecosystem no one species dominates. Dynamics of competition exist, but cooperation and interdependence are more fundamental. From an ecosystem point of view, a species that begins to expand beyond its natural bounds has become pathological—like cancerous cells in a body. Species who expand their niche beyond reasonable limits will inevitably exhaust their food supply, causing a collapse in population. The Tao looks to balance and interdependence, allowing all species and all people to coexist in harmony.

From an ecological point of view, then, there is nothing logical or natural about the current dis/order that dominates our planet. It is at variance with the Tao. Similarly, from the point of view of human ethics or values, the current system seems irrational. David Korten (1995) summarizes a few of the underlying assumptions about human behavior implicit in the current dominant ideology:

1. Humans are fundamentally motivated by greed and self-interest—expressed particularly as the desire for monetary gain.

2. Human progress and well-being are best gauged by increases in consumption—that is, we realize our humanity in the quest for acquisition.

3. Competitive behavior (and presumably, the desire to dominate) is more advantageous to society than cooperation.

4. The actions that yield the greatest financial gain are those that are most beneficial to society—and the greater community of life—as a whole. The pursuit of greed and acquisition will ultimately lead to an optimal world. (Korten 1995, 70-71)

Stated so clearly and blatantly, only a very few people would actually agree with such assumptions. Certainly, they are at odds with nearly every religion and philosophy traditionally practiced by humanity. The *Tao Te Ching*, for example, notes:

> Those who realise that they have enough,
> are truly wealthy. (§33)

Even Adam Smith, supposedly the guiding light of capitalism and "free market" economics, would have objected strongly to such a caricature of values: Smith believed sympathy (or compassion) to be the essential characteristic of humanity, not competition or greed. He defined virtue as consisting of three elements: propriety, prudence (judicious pursuit of self-interest), and benevolence (encouraging the happiness of others) (Saul 1995, 159).

Adopting a New Perspective

How can we move away from this distorted framework that subverts our values with anti-values? And how can we move practically from our current system based on chrematistics, monoculture, and domination to an authentic *oikonomia*, a way of caring for the household of the Earth, our home? How can we create a world where humanity lives within the ecological boundaries of the planet while also overcoming the staggering inequalities between rich and poor?

In posing these questions, it is helpful to remember that, despite its immense economic, political, and cultural power, the dominant global dis/order has not completely triumphed by any measure. The world still supports a wide diversity of cultures. In addition, around the globe, there are many pockets of resistance to the homogenizing trends that continue to exist and struggle. This is particularly true among those most marginalized and oppressed by the dominant system such as women, indigenous peoples, and those living in subsistence economies. But it is also true even near the "centers" of dominant power. Everywhere there are communities seeking alternatives to the globalizing economy and culture. Everywhere there are movements forming to resist the imposition of the hegemonic system and to create a new order based on equity, justice, empowerment, and ecological health. Everywhere there are people and organizations imagining innovative policies and creative technologies. There is nothing inevitable about the current dis/order: We can still choose another path leading to the Great Turning, and indeed many people are already deciding to do so.

Korten sees our choice of being between what he calls "Empire"—the global system of domination currently in place (or what Macy and Brown call the "Industrial Growth Society")—and Earth community—an order based on the principles of sustainable community that care for our home, an authentic *oikonomia*. The contrast in assumptions and values between the two alternatives can be illustrated as follows:

Empire (Industrial Growth Society)	*Earth Community (Oikonomia)*
Life is hostile and competitive	Life is supportive and cooperative
Humans are flawed and dangerous	Humans have many possibilities
Order by dominator hierarchy	Order through partnership
Compete or die	Cooperate and live
Love power	Love life
Defend the rights of self	Defend the rights of all/mutual responsibilities
Masculine dominant	Gender balanced

Adapted from Korten 2006, 32

To imagine an alternative framework or vision for an authentic *oikonomia*, it is helpful to visualize our economy in a new way using a cakelike diagram (adapted from Henderson 1996; see next page). Unlike the current economic pathology, which values the financial "hyper-economy" above all and which simply ignores both the nonhuman and subsistence economies, this model recognizes that the nonhuman economy is primary. Next, human activity that seeks the sustenance of life, such as childcare and subsistence agriculture—at present largely carried out by women without the exchange of money—is seen as the foundation of further human economic activity. Then comes the contribution of the public sector and social economy, including many activities carried out by popular and nongovernmental organizations. Finally comes the private sector (including cooperatives, small businesses, then larger corporations) and the financial sector (which is really just the "icing on the cake," meant to serve the other layers, but not very substantial in itself).

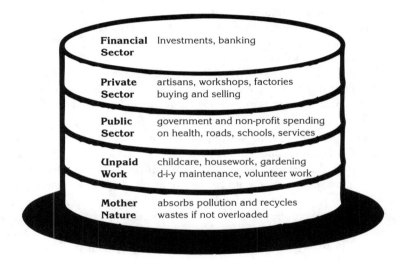

Adapted from *New Internationalist,* Issue 157, March 1986

The fundamental idea of this model is to turn current economics on its head. Instead of a financial and corporate economy sucking life from the layers below, finance and business exist to serve the wider community. The human community, in turn, recognizes its dependence on the wider Earth community and values the ecosystem as the foundation of all life and all human activity. In general, economic value is measured by the way an activity contributes to healthy relationships and to the sustenance of life, not the amount of monetary profit it generates.

At a practical level, there are many policies that could move us toward this kind of renewed practice of *oikonomia*. To a large extent, the current pathology perpetuates itself by rewarding activities that are harmful and simultaneously hiding the true cost of destruction. It is not hard to imagine policies that would do the opposite, for example:

- Reform our economic indicators, along the lines of the Genuine Progress Indicator mentioned earlier, so that the consumption of natural capital is seen as a cost, rather than income. At the same time, use the alternative indicator to recognize the value of nonmonetary human activities and the contribution of ecosystems to the sustenance of life.

- Tax labor and income less while taxing resource "throughput" more. Generally, workers bear the brunt of the current tax burden. "Green" taxes would constitute a much more fruitful alternative. On the one hand, energy, industrial water consumption, pollution, pesticides, and wasteful packaging should be taxed to encourage conservation and reduce harmful production. On the other hand, alternative energy sources, public transportation, organic agriculture, and conservation technologies should be subsidized to encourage their use. Similarly, a small tax on financial transactions (often called a "Tobin Tax" after the economist who first proposed the idea) would greatly reduce speculative activities while generating funds for poverty reduction, debt cancellation, and ecological restoration.

- Cancel the debts of the world's poorest nations and find ways to systematically reduce and eliminate the debts of so-called "middle-income" countries. As we have seen, debt and the Structural Adjustment Programs that accompany it serve as key mechanisms driving maldevelopment. Most of the debts in question have already been repaid many times over (and many were unjust or illegitimate to begin with). Just redirecting money from military spending or instituting a financial transaction tax would probably be more than sufficient to lift the burden of debt from the shoulders of the poor.

- Undertake a series of measures to curb corporate power: prohibit corporate donations to political parties; end the legal fiction that corporations are "persons" entitled to rights such as free speech and political participation; make shareholders legally liable for the damages caused by corporations to encourage ethical investing; and create provisions to revoke corporate charters of companies that repeatedly violate pollution laws, harm employees, or commit criminal offenses.

There is no lack of good ideas for policies and technologies that could enable us to create a sustainable and more equitable future. Nor is there a lack of economic resources. As Paul Hawken notes:

The U.S. and the former U.S.S.R. spent over $10 trillion on the Cold War, enough money to replace the infrastructure of the world, every school, every hospital, every roadway, building and farm. In other words, we bought and sold the entire world in order to defeat a political movement. To now assert that we don't have the resources to build a restorative economy is ironic, since the threats we face today are actually *happening*, whereas the threats of the post-war nuclear stand-off were about the *possibility* of destruction. (1993, 58)

What, then, is truly needed for the Great Turning to take place? How can we move forward toward an integral liberation for humanity and the Earth itself? In gaining an understanding that the current state of affairs is by no means inevitable, and is fundamentally irrational and pathological, we have taken the first step. The next will be to understand more clearly the origin of some of the beliefs, attitudes, perspectives, and practices that undergird the current system.

3.

Beyond Domination

The Tao of Heaven is like a bow:
It brings down the high and raises up the low.
It takes from those who have too much,
and gives to those who have too little.

The way of most humans is otherwise:
They use their power to take from that which is depleted,
and from those who have little,
so that they can give to those who have much.

The wise who follow the Tao can keep giving,
because they bear fruit without effort.
They act without expectation,
succeed without taking credit,
and do not need to prove their worthiness
to anyone else.

(*Tao Te Ching* §77)

Those who lead others in harmony with the Tao
do not use force to subdue others,
or attempt to dominate the world through force of arms.
For every force there is a counterforce.
Violence, even when well intentioned,
always rebounds upon oneself. . . .

(*Tao Te Ching* §30)

How could a system as irrational and destructive as the current pathological
dis/order have come into being? Ecopsychologist Theodore Roszak notes that
our current ecological and social crises must be seen as "more than a random

catalogue of mistakes, miscalculations, and false starts that can easily be made good with a bit more expertise in the right places." As we have seen, the values, beliefs, and assumptions at the very core of the systems of domination are themselves distorted—they breed a violence that attacks life. Therefore, "nothing less than an altered sensibility is needed, a radically new standard of sanity that . . . uproots the fundamental assumptions of industrial life" and corporate globalization (Roszak 1992, 232).

In this section, we will explore the perspectives of deep ecology and ecofeminism as tools for challenging the fundamental assumptions that undergird what we might call the "ideology of domination." Then we will apply these perspectives to look at the historical genesis of this ideology and examine how it has taken shape in the current form of global capitalism. Finally, we will draw on the insights gained to analyze and re-vision the very concept of power itself.

DEEP ECOLOGY

Deep ecology, like other ecological philosophies, concerns itself with the current destruction of the Earth's biosphere and the possibilities for the restoration of the planet's life systems. However, it goes well beyond some "shallow" forms of ecological thought that attempt to motivate people to save "the environment" because it is somehow useful to humanity. From the perspective of deep ecology, other species and ecosystems have an intrinsic value that does not derive from their usefulness or aesthetic value for human beings. Indeed, deep ecology argues that many versions of environmentalism are *anthropocentric* (human-centered) insofar as they continue to view the world as though humans were the measure of all value, the pinnacle of a hierarchy of creation. In the words of psychologist Warwick Fox, "Even many who deal most directly with environmental issues continue to perpetuate, however unwittingly, the arrogant assumption that we humans are central to the cosmic drama; that, essentially, the world is made for us" (1990, 10-11).

In fact, deep ecology questions the very idea of an "environment" separate from humanity. Humanity is seen as part of the natural world, a part of the greater "web of life." This is true on both a physical and more spiritual or psychic level. When we poison the air, water, and soil, we poison our very selves. When we diminish the beauty and diversity of the planetary community, we also diminish our humanity. As Wendell Berry notes, "The world that environs us, that is around us, is also within us. We are made of it; we eat, drink, and breathe it; it is bone of our bone and flesh of our flesh" (quoted in Hawken 1993, 215).

Deep ecology attempts to go beyond the symptomatic approach of some versions of environmentalism to seek out the deep roots of the ecological crisis: "Deep ecology recognizes that nothing short of a total revolution in consciousness will be of lasting use in preserving the life-support systems of our planet" (Seed et al. 1988).

Revolutionizing Consciousness

And just what is the nature of this "revolution in consciousness"? Arne Naess (1912-2009), who originally proposed the idea of deep ecology in 1973, maintains that its two key elements are *self-realization* and *biocentric equality*.[1]

Self-realization affirms that humans are deeply connected to the entire ecosphere. Humans do not stand apart from or above the greater web of life. All organisms—including humans—are seen as "knots in a biospherical net or field of intrinsic relations" (Arne Naess quoted in Roszack 1992, 232). Self-realization, then, comes from a profound empathy and compassion that connects us to all living creatures. In the words of Naess, "With maturity, human beings will experience joy when other life forms experience joy, and sorrow when other life forms experience sorrow" (quoted in Kheel 1990, 135). At the same time, because of this deep interconnection, we are enriched by the diversity and multiplicity of Earth's species and ecosystems:

> The self-realization we experience when we identify with the universe is heightened by an increase in the number of ways in which individuals, societies, and even species and life forms realize themselves. The greater the diversity, then, the greater the self-realization. . . . Most people in deep ecology have had the feeling—usually, but not always, in nature—that they are connected with something greater than their ego, greater than their name, their family, their special attributes as an individual. . . . Without that identification, one is not easily drawn to become involved in deep ecology. (Devall and Sessions 1985, 76)

Biocentric equality flows from a similar worldview. Each living thing, and each ecosystem, has an intrinsic right to existence that does not depend on its usefulness to humanity. Of course, one organism may need to kill another to survive, but no organism (including human beings) has the right to destroy another without reason, and no organism has the right to obliterate an entire species. Humans may therefore kill to satisfy basic needs—they may take from the Earth what is required to sustain their health and dignity—but they do not

---

1. In more detail, Naess (1989, 29) outlines the following basic principles of deep ecology: (1) The flourishing of human and nonhuman life on Earth has intrinsic value. The value of nonhuman life forms is independent of the usefulness these may have for narrow human purposes. (2) Richness and diversity of life forms are values in themselves and contribute to the flourishing of human and nonhuman life on Earth. (3) Humans have no right to reduce this richness and diversity except to satisfy vital needs. (4) Present human interference with the nonhuman world is excessive, and the situation is rapidly worsening. (5) The flourishing of human life and cultures is compatible with a substantial decrease of the human population. The flourishing of nonhuman life requires such a decrease. [This principle seems to be based on somewhat simplistic assumptions; it would be better to frame this in terms of decreases in overall human consumption, which might also require some overall reduction in human population over time.] (6) A significant change of life conditions for the better requires change in policies. These affect basic economic, technological, and ideological structures. (7) The ideological change is mainly that of appreciating life quality (dwelling in situations of intrinsic value) rather than adhering to a high standard of living. There will be a profound awareness of the difference between big and great. (8) Those who subscribe to the foregoing points have an obligation directly or indirectly to participate in the attempt to implement the necessary changes.

have the right to destroy biodiversity in order to accumulate capital and riches, nor to produce unnecessary luxuries. Ultimately, too, this implies that humans must put aside the quest to dominate—both other species and other humans:

> Ecological consciousness and deep ecology are in sharp contrast with the dominant worldview of technocratic-industrial societies which regards humans as isolated and fundamentally separate from the rest of Nature, as superior to, and in charge of, the rest of creation. But the view of humans as separate and superior to the rest of Nature is only part of larger cultural patterns. For thousands of years, Western culture has become increasingly obsessed with the idea of dominance: with dominance of humans over non-human Nature, masculine over the feminine, wealthy and powerful over the poor, with the dominance of the West over non-Western cultures. Deep ecological consciousness allows us to see through these erroneous and dangerous illusions. (Devall and Sessions 1985, 65-66)

Critiquing Anthropocentrism

From the point of view of deep ecology, the fundamental attitude at the root of the ecological crisis is that of *anthropocentrism*. Anthropocentrism can be defined as the belief that humans alone have intrinsic value. Everything else in the world is of relative value, important only insofar as it serves human interests.

Anthropocentrism separates us from the rest of the Earth community. We see ourselves as over and above other creatures. We reduce the rest of the sphere of life—the biosphere—to an environment separate from ourselves.

Anthropocentrism lies at the heart of our current anti-ecological understanding and practice of economics. Our very language—"raw materials," "natural resources," even "concern for the environment"—betrays us, underscoring the perception that the nonhuman world is at the service and disposal of humanity.

Most of us have never seriously questioned this understanding. It seems natural to view humanity as somehow above or apart from the rest of the Earth community. We believe we have the right to use the Earth, even if this harms or actually eliminates other species.

Some claim, of course, that we can be anthropocentric and still protect other life forms. Indeed, it is obvious that, to preserve the human species, we will have to protect at least some part of nature. But the question immediately arises: How much of nature needs to be preserved, and which species can we afford to lose? Ultimately this leads to a "slippery slope" that threatens to destroy humanity along with many other members of the Earth community.

Further, what might be sufficient for a limited human survival may not be sufficient for the sustenance of love, beauty, and the nurture of the spirit. The ecological cultural historian (or "geologian") Thomas Berry (1914-2009) points out that humans could have evolved only on a planet as beautiful as our own. The beauty of the Earth seems essential if we are to preserve what we most value in humanity.

In one way, some of the above arguments may in themselves seem anthropocentric. Yet, at another level, arguing that humans need other species in the broadest and most inclusive sense is also a recognition of our interconnection with all of life. Ultimately, though, as Warwick Fox explains (1990), anthropocentrism is both irrational and limiting because:

1. It is not consistent with scientific reality. Neither our planet nor humanity can be viewed as the center of the universe. Earth's biosphere constitutes a dynamic whole in which humans are interdependent with all other species. Nor can we consider ourselves the crown of creation; evolution is a branching reality, not a pyramidal hierarchy.

2. Anthropocentric attitudes have been disastrous in practice; they have led us to destroy species and ecosystems at the fastest rate since the time of the cosmic disaster that caused the disappearance of the dinosaurs.

3. It is not a logically consistent position, since no sharp division exists between us and other species—neither in an evolutionary nor in a physical sense. Our own bodies are actually symbiotic communities: nearly half of our weight is made up of other organisms such as the yeasts and enteric bacteria in our gut that help us metabolize our food and manufacture essential vitamins.

4. It is morally objectionable because it is not in accord with a truly open attitude to experience. Essentially, it is a selfish attitude that traps us in a delusion, blinding us to truth.

Anthropocentrism may feel "natural" to us, but it denies the ecological insight that we are fundamentally related to, and dependent upon, the entire web of life. We cannot exist without the Earth; we are part of a greater whole. There is no "environment" outside of us. We are constantly exchanging matter with our surroundings, drawing in oxygen, water, and nutrients that were once a part of other creatures. All life on Earth shares that same basic genetic coding mechanism. All other living beings are "our relations."

We are called, then, to move from an anthropocentric to a "biocentric" or "ecocentric" perspective. Anthropocentrism is essentially an *egocentric* mindset. But we are called to expand our empathy to all living creatures, and even to the soil, air, and water that are also part of us.

An Anthropoharmonic Alternative

Stephen Scharper (1997) proposes that the alternative to the anthropocentric mind-set would be one that is "anthropoharmonic." Instead of "conquering nature," humans need to develop and progress in harmony with the wider ecosphere. This does not mean that we need to deny that humanity is in some ways unique on Earth—indeed, we should celebrate our uniqueness while recognizing our interdependence with all other creatures. Nor does it mean that humans can never kill other forms of life—for indeed, there is no way to survive without consuming other organisms.

To live an anthropoharmonic ethic, however, does mean developing a profound respect and love for all life; it does mean ceasing to dominate, manipulate, devour, and pollute the Earth as though it were our private property; and it does mean consuming no more than what is necessary for a dignified, healthy life (and thus ceasing the quest for unlimited accumulation).

Arne Naess affirms that, ultimately, deep ecology calls us to redefine what it means to be human. This is not an exercise in denying our identity—our unique part in the unfolding evolution of the Earth—but rather of reframing it in the wider context of the "ecological Self." Such a shift must go beyond a mere intellectual acceptance—it must permeate every facet of our being and action. In particular, it calls humanity to put aside the quest for acquisition, consumption, and domination, affirming that this path can never lead to the authentic realization of humanity. Instead, we must seek out security, love, and community in harmony with the wider ecosphere. This kind of conversion to a new ethic is a very profound challenge—yet also one that could lead humanity to a more fulfilling way of living.

ECOFEMINISM

Ecofeminism in many ways deepens the critique that deep ecology makes of environmentalism. At the same time, it provides a broader analysis that also incorporates concerns for interhuman injustice. One way of understanding ecofeminism is as an integration of perspectives from both feminism and deep ecology—although arguably the synthesis that emerges is more radical (in the sense of getting to the roots of things) and more inclusive than a simple sum of its constituent parts.

Feminism itself is a diverse and pluriform movement that eludes a single definition. In our discussion here, however, we can understand feminism as a profound critique of patriarchy—where patriarchy is understood as the system through which men dominate women. Radical forms of feminism, however, make a causal link between domination and exploitation based on gender and all other forms of oppression, including those based on class, race, ethnicity, and sexual orientation. Thus, patriarchy is understood in very broad terms. Radical feminism, then, is not a simple search for equality between men and women within the dominant dis/order (which in any case, is not a real possibility); rather, it is a critique of all systems that perpetuate oppression and exploitation.

Indeed, Vandana Shiva (1989) affirms that feminism is ultimately a transgendered philosophy and movement. It recognizes that masculinity and femininity are socially and ideologically constructed and that the feminine principle of creativity is embodied in women, men, and nature. The recovery of this principle as a challenge to patriarchy is based on an inclusiveness that calls women to be productive and active while it calls men to redirect their activities to life-enhancing possibilities. While women have taken leadership in the feminist movement—as seems only right insofar as liberation normally begins from the side of the oppressed—men must also assume an active stance in favor of feminism and its challenge to the patriarchal system.

Feminism is arguably one of the most important and original movements of all times. Fritjof Capra (1982) notes that, until recently, patriarchy seemed so pervasive and so ingrained that it was seldom, if ever, seriously questioned. Yet it profoundly shaped all human relations and our relationship with the wider world. Now, though, the feminist movement has become one of the strongest cultural currents of our time; it has now crossed virtually every border and class barrier to become truly global in its reach.

Linking Patriarchy and Anthropocentrism

In synthesizing the insights of feminism and deep ecology, ecofeminism posits a dynamic link between patriarchy and anthropocentrism. From an ecofeminist perspective, it is not mere coincidence that western patriarchal thought has identified women with nature: this social construction has served to exploit and dominate them simultaneously since they are both cast as inferiors to men. Vandana Shiva notes, "The metaphors and concepts of minds deprived of the feminine principle have been based on seeing nature and women as worthless and passive, and finally dispensable" (1989, 223). Both women and nature are seen as passive, while men are considered rational, strong, and unemotional. In patriarchal society, the socially constructed masculine role is valued as superior, while nature and women are viewed basically as objects to be exploited. Because of this, ecofeminists affirm that it is far more accurate to speak of *androcentrism* (man-centeredness) than anthropocentrism. Charlene Spretnak observes:

> Modern, technocratic society [is] fuelled by the patriarchal obsessions of dominance and control. They . . . [sustain a] managerial ethos, which holds efficiency of production and short-term gains above all else—above ethics or moral standards, above the health of community life, and above the integrity of all biological processes, especially those constituting the elemental power of the female. The experts guiding our society seek deliverance from their fears of nature, with which they have no real communion or deep connection. . . .
>
> Ecofeminists say that this system is leading us to ecocide and species suicide because it is based on ignorance, fear, delusion, and greed. We say that people, male or female, enmeshed in the *values* of that system are incapable of making rational decisions. (1990, 9, 8)

For ecofeminism, then, the key to achieving liberation for both women and the wider Earth community lies in dismantling the very foundations of patriarchy and androcentrism, ending all forms of domination, particularly male control over women and the nonhuman world. To do so, it seeks to affirm the intrinsic value of all of nature while also "revaluing women's culture and practices" (T. Berman 1993, 16).

Broadening the Analysis

At the same time, ecofeminism affirms that the same logic used to oppress women and nature is also employed with slight adaptations to justify oppression on the basis of race, class, and sexual orientation. Just as women and nature are seen as weak, passive, and inferior, "non-whites" are depicted as closer to the animal world and less "civilized" than "whites." Working-class people are similarly seen as closer to "base" animal instincts and depicted as rapidly breeding "proletarians." Gay men are condemned for taking on "effeminate" characteristics, while gay women are condemned for usurping masculine roles. In all cases, the same logic of the dominating, patriarchal mind is at work.

In many ways, then, ecofeminism broadens the perspective of deep ecology by making a link between all systems of domination and control. At the same time, ecofeminism seeks to overcome a degree of abstraction found in some deep ecologists' idea of a generalized identification with nature. Ecofeminists are especially strong in affirming that an emotional bond to real places and real people is necessary to inspire action in favor of justice and ecological harmony. We must be rooted in real experience—not simply identify ourselves with an abstraction—if we open ourselves to the awe, wonder, and empathy that can sustain us: "The danger of an abstract identification with the 'whole' is that it fails to recognize or respect the existence of independent, living beings. . . . Our deep, holistic awareness of the interconnectedness of all life must be a *lived* awareness that we experience in relation to *particular* beings *as well as* the larger whole" (Kheel 1990, 136-37).

THE ORIGINS OF PATRIARCHY AND ANTHROPOCENTRISM

An ecofeminist perspective can provide insights that help explain how greed, exploitation, and domination have come to exercise such a powerful influence on the economic, political, and cultural systems that currently govern most human societies. In particular, they help us to understand how the beliefs, assumptions, and "values" of the current global dis/order are generated by the dynamics of both patriarchy and anthropocentrism (or androcentrism).

To gain such an understanding, it is helpful to look at the historical origins and evolution of both patriarchy and anthropocentrism. This in turn reveals the processes through which these social constructs emerged and gives clues to how just, equitable, and sustainable alternatives might be created to replace them.

Many ancient and modern aboriginal cultures have displayed a high degree of gender equity along with harmonious relationships to nature. Often, these cultures display a division of labor along gender lines, but this does not necessarily indicate an exploitative relationship between the sexes. Indeed, in ancient times, before the invention of large-scale agriculture and animal domestication, most human cultures were probably fairly egalitarian, and many were basically matricentric—that is, they worshiped feminine gods as their principal deities and accorded high prestige to women in their societies. Most tribes of hunter-gatherers, the societies of Neolithic Europe and Anatolia, and early Andean cultures seem to fit this matricentric pattern.[2]

Beginnings of patriarchy

By the year 5000 B.C.E., though, it seems evident that patriarchy was making inroads into Europe and the Middle East. In central Asia, it may have emerged even earlier, while in many other areas of the globe, it began much later, sometimes through the action of invasions and colonialism. (There are, however, cultures such as the Balinese and the !Kung-San of the Kalahari desert in southern Africa who have largely retained an equitable pattern of male–female relationships up to our current time.)

Maria Mies (1986) postulates that patriarchy gained its first toehold among pastoralists. As men began to observe and understand the reproductive processes of animals, they became conscious of their own generative role. Eventually, this led to a change in their relation to nature and to a new sexual division of labor. In nomadic societies in often-arid regions, women's traditional role as food gatherers became secondary. Because of this, women were relegated to a subordinate role as caregivers of children. A new mode of production based on coercion, control, and manipulation began to evolve.

Meanwhile, in agricultural societies patriarchy may have arisen with the invention of the plough. Rosemary Radford Ruether notes, "The plough was the tool of male dominance over animals and land. Together with the sword, these tools become the means for male conquest of other men and finally of their own women" (1992, 164).

Ken Wilber (1996) points out that the use of the plough requires a great deal of physical strength. Pregnant women who attempt to use a plough often miscarry, so it becomes biologically advantageous for women to refrain from this kind of work. Thus, the introduction of the plough tends to begin a shift of agricultural activities from women to men, with the result that men begin to assume the task of food production while women are increasingly isolated into the sphere of the household. Further, the plough helped generate food surpluses that freed a proportion of men to pursue tasks beyond those needed for daily sustenance, while women remained largely tied to reproduction and the maintenance of the household.

Over time, this resulted in the virtual removal of women from the public

---

2. At the same time, it should be noted that the search for an idyllic golden age of egalitarian male–female relationships, as has been evidenced in some recent literature, must be kept within bounds. Works such as *The Chalice and the Blade* (Eisler 1987) have recently romanticized the Neolithic cultures of Old Europe and Anatolia, as well as the pre-classical culture of Minoan Crete, as societies living with harmonious gender relations. Described as matrifocal or matricentric (rather than matriarchal, which would imply female domination) and goddess-worshiping, these cultures provide a powerful myth revealing the nonessentiality of patriarchal and anthropocentric domination; however, it is difficult to prove that truly harmonious relationships did in fact prevail in these societies—hence, there is a need for a degree of caution.

realm. Indeed, Wilber points out that, in horticultural societies (where agriculture is based on the hoe or digging stick), women produce about 80 percent of the food, there are egalitarian relationships between men and women (although there is a differentiation of roles), and many principal deities are feminine. In contrast, over 90 percent of agrarian societies (those using the plough) are male dominated—and primary deities tend to be masculine.

Predatory Production

Even in Neolithic times, improvements in agriculture began to allow villages to produce surpluses and accumulate wealth over time. Mies observes that this in turn made war economically expedient for the first time in history—it was often far easier forcibly to usurp the production of others than to produce for oneself. Thus, "predatory production" (in essence, nonproductive production!) was born in the form of conquest and pillage. Walls were built around villages, and the "arts" of warfare were developed. Men began to gain a monopoly over arms (probably due to their larger size and their freedom from the childbearing role), leading to a new concentration of power and prestige in the hands of men, and thus to the growth of patriarchy. Mies notes that "permanent relations of exploitation and dominance between the sexes" and the "asymmetric division of labour between women and men" were both ultimately "created and maintained" by direct violence and coercion based on this male monopoly over arms (1986, 65).

With the growth of agrarian societies, this process accelerated. As larger amounts of wealth accumulated, more and more men were freed from food production. On the one hand, this made possible the invention of writing, astronomy, metallurgy, and mathematics, but, on the other, it also freed up manpower for the creation of groups specialized in warfare. Professional armies, and even entire warrior classes, emerged for the first time.

Over time, the growth of populations in city-states also created competition for increasingly scarce natural wealth—fertile land, water for irrigation, precious metals, and so on. This in turn escalated inter-city conflicts and ethnic tensions. In addition, with warfare, the practice of capturing slaves came into being. Through this complex process, societies became increasingly divided along the lines of class, gender, and race.

Mies concludes that the "predatory mode of appropriation" eventually became the "paradigm of all historical exploitative relations between human beings" and, we might well add, between humans and the greater Earth community. In this process, certain groups of human beings (and the Earth itself) came to be seen as mere "natural resources" to be used to enrich others. The exploitation generated by this "predatory production" involved more than "the one-sided appropriation of the surplus produced over and above the necessary requirements of a community"; it extended beyond this to "the robbery, pillage, and looting of the *necessary requirements* of *other* communities. This concept of exploitation, therefore, always implies a relationship created and held up in the last resort by coercion or violence" (1986, 66).

Deepening Anthropocentrism

The same processes that progressively deepened the power of patriarchy also contributed to a deepening anthropocentrism. In most hunter-gatherer societies, the relationship between humans and the nonhuman world is close and direct. At times, certainly, a degree of fear of nature can be witnessed, but by and large a rigid separation between humans and the greater community of life simply does not exist. The very mode of production is one that relies not on control over nature but rather on harmony with it.

As societies develop horticulture, an element of control is introduced, but the change is still relatively minor. People continue to live close to the Earth, and the level of human intervention is still fairly minor. In pastoralist societies, perhaps, the domestication of animals leads to a greater sense of control and domination. This increases still further in agrarian societies as they employ the labor of animals to plough, and even more so as large-scale irrigation projects come into being.

As cities and city-states develop in agrarian societies, the shift toward anthropocentrism becomes even more marked. Even in Neolithic villages—especially once walls and fortifications were built—a psychological separation from the nonhuman community must have begun. With the genesis of cities, however, this same process accelerates rapidly. A city is largely a human creation—an artificial habitat where nature is controlled and human constructions become more and more central.

Duane Elgin (1993) also notes that city-state cultures were much more hierarchical than small villages. Society becomes progressively divided into classes and castes—with a clear division of labor among rulers, priests, warriors, artisans, and merchants. At the same time, city-states contribute to the growth of "predatory" modes of acquisition—there is more and more wealth to defend, and more and more sophisticated methods of warfare. Meanwhile, there is a shift in social psychology as wealth is systematically counted and accumulated and as a new worldview arises based on the "mathematical orderliness of the heavens." Along with this, deities shift from the Earth to the heavens, symbolizing perhaps a step of humanity away from direct relationship with the natural world.

At some point in this process, the idea of private property seems to have arisen. With the growth of city-states and the division of societies into classes, large tracts of land are often set aside as a source of wealth for the more powerful sectors of society (royalty, priests, etc.). Frequently, these properties are cultivated with the help of slave labor. The common lands of villages are reduced as a result, impoverishing the peasant classes. Through this process, land comes to be seen as a personal possession rather than a common wealth to be shared. (Albeit this shift was not total in early times—indeed, common lands have persisted in many cultures into modern times.) This change signals a significant shift in consciousness: land is now perceived as a resource, as private property, controlled by human persons—more often than not, by men. Previously, as is still evidenced in many aboriginal cultures today, land was something that could not be possessed, only shared. Land did not belong to humans; rather, humans belonged to the land—and, by extension, to the Earth itself.

The rise of city-state cultures was also often accompanied by ecologically destructive practices. In *A Forest Journey: The Story of Wood and Civilization*, John Perlin (2005) links deforestation in the ancient cultures of Mesopotamia, Crete, Greece, and Rome to the downfall of their civilizations. Similarly, many attribute the abandonment of the jungle cities of the Mayans to the ecological consequences of deforestation. Often deforestation was the result of an excessive demand for wood for construction (including ship building) or to fuel kilns and metalworks. At other times, it resulted from clearing lands for agriculture. In both cases, though, it was also associated with a change in worldview that licensed the domination and exploitation of both human and natural "resources" in order to accumulate wealth.

Some Implications for the Present

What can we learn from this story? Certainly, the evolution of patriarchy and anthropocentrism is complex, but it is clear that in some way all forms of domination, oppression, and exploitation share common origins. At the same time, it is helpful to move beyond the historical account and try to discern the psychological processes at work.

For instance, Rosemary Radford Ruether (1992) suggests that the early matricentric cultures may have contained the seeds of their own destruction. Unlike the female role that is linked by its very nature to the reproduction and sustenance of life, the male role has to be socially constructed.

In the hunter-gatherer societies that existed around the end of the ice age, male hunters still played an important role in food production owing to the presence of large mammals to hunt. The socially constructed role of man-as-hunter still carried a great deal of importance, allowing men to feel secure in their contribution to society. As the ice age ended, however, hunting became progressively less important and the role of women—as the primary gatherers—grew.

By Neolithic times, women were often both the primary producers of food *and* the primary parent. In such societies—for instance, those of Old Europe and Anatolia—men may have failed to develop a sufficiently affirmative and important role, thus giving rise to male resentment over the inherent prestige of women. As Mary Gomes and Allen Kanner (1995) point out, domination can be a way of denying dependence. In such a situation, men began to define their masculinity in terms hostile to women and the foundations of patriarchy were laid. Until this underlying resentment is addressed, then, it is unlikely that the patriarchal system in its current form can be effectively eliminated.

Ruether suggests that one concrete implication of this analysis is the need to structure new forms of parity among the genders—moving from dependence to interdependence. In particular, a new male role integrally involved in parenting and the domestic work that sustains life is an urgent priority in today's society. In general, gender roles will need to become more fluid and flexible, allowing both genders to participate meaningfully in life-producing rather than life-destroying activities. She gives the example of traditional Balinese society as a possible model of how a stable, nonexploitative relationship between the genders can be achieved.

Further, the analysis of Gomes and Kanner regarding domination as a mechanism for denying dependence has applications for our relationship to the greater Earth community. Humans attempt to dominate the Earth itself, and all living creatures, in our quest to deny our dependence on the greater web of life: "We in urban-industrial civilization have centered our identity as a species around the renunciation of this truth. Human dependence on the hospitality of the Earth is total, and this is extremely threatening to the separative self" (Gomes and Kanner 1995, 114). This process seems to have begun long ago with the advent of agrarian and city-state cultures, even if the degree of alienation has grown greatly with the development of industrial societies.

GLOBAL CAPITALISM: AN ANDROCENTRIC SYSTEM

From an ecofeminist perspective, modern capitalism represents the most sophisticated and exploitative of all patriarchal, anthropocentric systems. Global corporate capitalism—like the other systems of imperial domination that preceded it—has as its very foundation an "extractive, non-reciprocal, exploitative object-relation to nature, first established between men and women and men and nature" (Mies 1986, 71). As we saw in our examination of the pathology of limitless growth and maldevelopment, the contribution of the nonhuman economy (and very often, of women—particularly in the form of unpaid work) is rendered almost totally invisible by the current economic system. Indeed, the destruction of the Earth's natural wealth to create an artificial and illusory capital accumulation lies at the very heart of the industrial growth societies created by corporate capitalism. At the same time, as our analysis of corporate control and financial speculation demonstrates: "Those who control the production process and the products are not themselves producers, but appropriators." What may be less obvious, but which becomes apparent through a feminist analysis, is that "their so-called productivity pre-supposes the existence and the subjection of other—and in the last analysis, female—producers" (Mies 1986, 71). The "predatory means of production," then, lies at the very heart of capitalism.

The Foundations of Capitalism

From an ecofeminist perspective, the origins of capitalism are integrally related to several historical processes: the expansion of colonialism and slavery, the persecution of women during the great witch-hunts in Europe, and the rise of modern science and technology leading to the industrial revolution. Together, these processes served to remold nature from the image of Mother Earth into that of a lifeless machine serving "man's" need for a source of raw materials and a place for disposing wastes. At the same time, new and more sophisticated forms of patriarchy arose that effectively served to subjugate women to new levels of exploitation.

Many historians argue that the "primitive accumulation" of capital that formed the foundations for capitalism was possible only because of the violent usurpation of wealth from Europe's colonies in the Americas—especially gold, silver, and agricultural products from the colonies of Spain and Portugal. As we have already mentioned, the fictional letter from Guaicaipuro Cuauhtémoc to European leaders jokingly refers to the 185,000 kilos of gold and 16 million kilos of silver shipped between 1503 and 1660 from San Lucar de Barrameda as "the first of several friendly loans granted by America for Europe's development" (Britto García 1990). Of course, the reality is that this wealth was bought with the sweat, blood, and lives of hundreds of thousands of indigenous laborers working in mines throughout Latin America. To supplement this labor, millions of Africans were violently uprooted from their homes and freedom then shipped as slaves to the Americas. Many more were enslaved to work on agricultural plantations, providing valuable exports to Europe. While Spain and Portugal did not use this wealth to finance their own industrial development, these riches did create a pool of wealth and demand for luxury products that provided the seed for industrial expansion in northwestern Europe.

Over almost the same period—particularly between the mid-1400s and the mid-1700s—the great persecution of "witches," sometimes called "the burning times," was unleashed in Europe. It is estimated that 80 to 90 percent of those killed were women and that up to two million people may have died—by in large through genuinely horrific means. Many of the women killed were those who practiced traditional forms of healing and midwifery, and almost all those affected were poor. While the persecution of witches began as part of the Catholic Inquisition (which also extended to Latin America), the practice soon became widespread in Protestant Europe (and later, in New England).

On one level, the burning times can be seen as a manifestation of a fear of both the power of women and the power of nature—especially since those women practicing traditional healing crafts (which required a knowledge of herbs, and thus of the wild places where these could be gathered) were at special risk. Indeed, in English, the word "witch" comes from *wita*, meaning "the wise one." "Witches," then, were often those who possessed some form of nature-based wisdom.

In addition, Mies (1986) points out that the witch-hunts constituted an attack on women's sexuality and women's control over their fertility (hence the persecution of midwives). More generally, the witch-hunts tended to push women out of the public sphere: as a result of this persecution, women lost their jobs as artisans and their property was confiscated. On a psychological level, one can easily imagine the collective trauma that must have been generated by such a massive and horrific persecution. Women, no doubt, discovered that their best defense was to keep as low a profile as possible and to show themselves to be docile, obedient wives and daughters closely tied to the environs of the household.

It is interesting to observe that the witch-hunts and the first wave of European colonialism roughly coincide in time. Mies believes this is not coincidental:

The counterpart of the slave raids in Africa was the witch hunt in Europe.
. . . Just as the process of "naturalization" of the colonies was based on large-scale use of direct violence and coercion, so the process of domestication of

European (and later North American) women was not a peaceful and idyllic affair. Women did not voluntarily hand over control over their productivity, their sexuality and their generative capacities to their husbands, and the BIG MEN (Church, State). (1986, 69)

The third historical process that began over the same period was that of the scientific revolution. While this will be explored in greater detail later in this book, it suffices to note for now that this process profoundly affected the way Europeans saw the world—particularly the intellectual and political elites. Instead of seeing the Earth as *terra mater*, land, forests, and all living things were transformed into a lifeless machine and an inexhaustible source of "raw materials" for human use. This change, as Vandana Shiva points out, "removed all ethical and cognitive constraints against its violation and exploitation" (1989, xvii). By extension, women (and also aboriginal peoples)—who were identified as being closer to nature and thus as less rational and less valuable—were converted into little more than instruments at the "service of man."

From an ecofeminist perspective, modern science is a demonstrably patriarchal project insofar as it facilitates new forms of subjugation and exploitation. In the end, it spawns maldevelopment (which began with colonialism and continues with modern forms of economic domination) because it is based on forms of perception that are reductionist (trying to understand the whole by breaking it into smaller parts), dualistic (something must be this *or* that, but not both), and linear (direct cause-effect relationships). Shiva observes that these dominant modes of perception:

Are unable to cope with equality in diversity, with forms and activities that are significant and valid, even though different. The reductionist mind superimposes the roles and forms of power of western male-oriented concepts on women, all non-western peoples, and even on nature, rendering all three "deficient," and in need of "development." Diversity, and unity and harmony in diversity, become epistemologically unattainable in the context of maldevelopment, which then becomes synonymous with women's underdevelopment (increasing sexist domination), and nature's depletion (deepening the ecological crisis). (1989, 5)

Ultimately, Shiva argues, this mode of thinking and the industrial revolution it inspired converted economics

from the prudent management of resources for sustenance and basic needs satisfaction into a process of commodity production for profit maximisation. Industrialism created a limitless appetite for resource exploitation, and modern science provided the ethical and cognitive license to make such exploitation possible, acceptable—and desirable. The new relationship of man's domination and mastery over nature was thus also associated with new patterns of domination and mastery over women, and their exclusion from participation *as partners* in both science and development. (1989, xvii)

Capitalism and Exploitation

Capitalism, then, arose in a context in which androcentrism was reaching new heights in the consciousness of the intellectuals and ruling elites of Europe. "Man," defined as a rational, autonomous entity ("I think, therefore I am"), was seen as an apex of a hierarchy at whose base was "savage," untamed nature, with women, indigenous peoples, people of color, and peasants inhabiting the middle reaches of the pyramid. Patriarchy, understood here as a unified system of domination and exploitation, served a foundation upon which capitalism would be built.

Indeed, Maria Mies argues that capitalism cannot exist without patriarchy. Capitalist accumulation is based upon the appropriation of wealth produced by nature, women, and the poor of the world (especially non-European peoples). In other words, at its heart lies the "predatory" (or parasitical) mode of production that is justified and sustained by patriarchy. Capitalism depends on the unpaid work of women, the pillage of resources from the planet, and the poorly compensated labor of exploited classes and races. This process of endless accumulation of lifeless capital sucks life from the Earth and all its creatures. Meanwhile, those who control and profit from production are not themselves producers, but usurpers. This is particularly clear in the case of the modern "financial economy."

Like all forms of predatory production, capitalism depends on violence. Sometimes this violence is direct, involving the actual use or threat of arms. During the entire colonial period and up to the present, "gunboat diplomacy" has been used to maintain the current global dis/order (as could still be witnessed in the two wars and sanctions against Iraq that have killed millions of innocent people to guarantee the West's supply of oil). Today, what is even more common is the use of repressive mechanisms within nations. For example, governments imposing the dictates of Structural Adjustment Programs unleash armies and police against their own peoples to suppress legitimate protests.

The most pervasive form of violence in capitalism, however, is the structural violence exercised by economic coercion. On the one hand, debt and SAPs are excellent examples of such coercion exercised over entire peoples and nations. On a more general level, capitalism uses the unequal division of labor as a structure for appropriating wealth. Wage laborers are paid less than the value they create, thus allowing for capital accumulation. The exploitation of both women and ecosystems is greater still because their contribution to the economy is simply not recognized (it is kept invisible, for instance, by indicators such as GDP).

This failure to value the most basic of life-sustaining activities is not simply an oversight—it is based on the sexual division of labor that values "human" (largely male) work over "natural" activities (including subsistence production, household work, and the bounty of the greater Earth community). Non-waged work, carried out largely by women, is considered less valuable even though it is absolutely necessary for the sustenance and production of life.[3] Likewise, the

---

3. This is particularly true today in the face of Structural Adjustment Programs. Women often

services that a biotic community such as a forest renders to all in terms of producing oxygen, purifying and storing water, and building healthy soil count for nothing. Yet "this *production of life* is the perennial precondition of all other historical forms of productive labour, including that under conditions of capitalist accumulation" (Mies 1986, 47). Indeed, this unvalued work is the primary source of all true wealth, and its exploitation is the very foundation of the parasitical, predatory mode of production at the heart of modern capitalism. In contrast to Marxism, which basically sees the exploitation of wage labor as the key source of capital accumulation, an ecofeminist analysis goes further by affirming that capitalism depends on *both* the exploitation of wage-earners *and* the *super*exploitation of women and the wider Earth community. Mies concludes:

> Women's oppression today is part and parcel of capitalist (or socialist) patriarchal *production relations*, of the paradigm of ever-increasing growth, of ever-increasing forces of production, of unlimited exploitation of nature, of unlimited production of commodities, ever-expanding markets and never-ending accumulation of dead capital. . . .
>
> [Therefore,] women in their struggle to regain their humanity have nothing to gain from the continuation of [the paradigm of never-ending capital accumulation and "growth"]. . . . Today, it is more than evident that the accumulation process itself destroys the core of the human essence everywhere, because it is based on the destruction of women's autarchy over [or ability to govern] their lives and bodies. As women have nothing to gain in their humanity from the continuation of the growth model, they are able to develop a perspective of a society which is not based on exploitation of nature, women and other peoples. (1986, 23, 2)

It is simply not possible, then, for women to abolish exploitation and oppression in the context of the current economic paradigm. Likewise, it is impossible to protect the integrity of the greater Earth community. From an ecofeminist point of view, an integral struggle is required that will change the relationship between men and women, between humans and nature, and between North and South.

Beyond Capitalism: Ecofeminist Alternatives

What kind of alternative might ecofeminism envision to replace the current system of global, corporate capitalism? In place of predatory production based on exploitation, ecofeminism envisions a new economics that is fundamentally aimed at the *production and sustenance of life*. In place of exploitation, economic relationships would be reciprocal and nonhierarchical, both among peo-

---

take on new unpaid work to respond to the economic crises that SAPs generate. For example, the communal kitchens (*comedores populares*) of Latin America have provided a basic survival mechanism allowing the population to eat during a time of rising prices and high unemployment. Effectively, the unpaid work of women subsidizes an entire economy of survival. One could say, then, that debt payments are indirectly being made by the unpaid labor of women.

ple and between people and nature. Therefore, colonizing, dualistic divisions such as men/women, humanity/nature as well as those based on class and race are rejected. Similarly, the idea of infinite growth and progress is recognized as a dangerous illusion that begets inequality and destruction. The Earth is accepted as finite, and humanity strives to live harmoniously with it (Mies 1986).

Central to this new vision is a renewed understanding of work. The aim of human endeavor is no longer growth in terms of an expansion of quantity for the purpose of accumulation, but rather the enhancement of life processes and human happiness. This implies that labor is no longer seen simply as a burden to be borne, but as a unity composed of enjoyment and necessary struggle.

In such a vision, work that involves a direct, sensual contact with nature gains a special value. Machines and technology can still have their place, but their purpose is no longer to isolate us from organic matter, living organisms, or the material world. Work must first and foremost be purposeful, something useful and necessary for the production or sustenance of life. This implies, too, a new conception of time where we no longer divide our hours between work and play, but rather intersperse them both freely.

The processes of production and consumption must again be unified, and local communities on a regional level must develop economies that are essentially self-sufficient, where what is produced by the community is also consumed by it. Such a new form of work cannot, however, come into being until the existing division of labor along the lines of gender is eliminated. Mies maintains that the transformation of the sexual division of labor that currently exists must, indeed, be at the very center of the whole process of creating a new economy:

> Any search for ecological, economic and political autarky [self-sufficiency] must start with the respect for the autonomy of women's bodies, their productive capacity to create new life, their productive capacity to maintain life through work, their sexuality. A change in the existing sexual division of labour would imply first and foremost that the *violence* that characterises capitalist-patriarchal man-woman relations world-wide will be abolished not by women, but *by men*. (1986, 222)

Rosemary Radford Ruether (1992) speaks not only of the need for a revision in the sexual division of labor, but of gender roles in general. Women need to strengthen the aspect of autonomy and individuality in their lives, but this should be done not through the practice of domination (self-assertion at the expense of others) but rather by unifying ways of being simultaneously a person for others and for oneself in the context of a life-sustaining community.

Ruether agrees with Mies that the primary transformation, however, must come in the lifestyle of men. Men need to "overcome the illusion of autonomous individualism, with its extension into egocentric power over others, beginning with the women to whom they relate" (Ruether 1992, 266). The best way of doing so, she suggests, is for men to enter fully into life-sustaining relationships with women while assuming their share of such tasks as childcare, washing, cooking, making clothing, and cleaning:

Only when men are fully integrated into the culture of daily sustenance of life can men and women together begin to reshape the larger systems of economic, social, and political life. They can begin to envision new cultural consciousness and organizational structures that would connect these larger systems to their roots in the earth and to sustaining the earth from day to day and from generation to generation. (Ruether 1992, 266)

The transformation of work and gender roles must also be accompanied by a profound change in the way we perceive reality itself. Vandana Shiva points out that the male-constructed version of "rationality" that predominates in modern Western culture is in fact "a bundle of irrationalities, threatening the very survival of humankind." She maintains that we must recover the feminine principle "as respect for life in nature and society. Ultimately, this will allow all peoples—North and South—to move toward a new way of thinking and being in the world" (1989, 223).

When the feminine principle is undermined in women and nature, it is distorted into a principle of passivity. In men, this same process results in "a shift in the concept of activity from creation to destruction, and the concept of power from empowerment to domination." When the feminine principle dies in men, women, and nature simultaneously, "violence and aggression become the masculine model of activity, and women and nature are turned into passive objects of violence" (Shiva 1989, 53).

In order to reverse this process, the Jungian theorist Gareth Hill calls for the recuperation of the "dynamic feminine" in human society. In this context, "feminine" does not refer to women as a sex, but rather as a set of values or attributes that have systematically been denied by patriarchy. The dynamic feminine goes beyond the static images of nurturing and mothering—although it certainly does include qualities like compassion and the desire to sustain life. At the same time, though, there is a playful, vital quality to the dynamic feminine. It is simultaneously active and responsive, yielding and persistent. It recalls the chapter of the *Tao Te Ching* that speaks of the power of water:

> Nothing in the world
> is as soft and yielding as water.
> Yet for dissolving the hard and inflexible,
> nothing can surpass it.
>
> The soft overcomes the hard;
> the gentle overcomes the rigid.
> Everyone knows this is true,
> but few can put it into practice.
> (§78, Mitchell)

The dynamic feminine is also creative, with an element of chaos and surprise erupting from predictability. It contrasts strongly with the paradigm of domination and control (Gomes and Kanner 1995). In the end, then, the integration of the dynamic feminine into our practice of economics, politics, and culture calls us to conceive and exercise power in an entirely new way—not as domination, exploitation, and control but as something positive and creative.

RECONSTRUCTING POWER

As long as power continues to be exercised in a dominating, exploitative manner, patriarchy will continue to wreak havoc, undermining the ecological and social systems that sustain life. We need a whole new way of understanding and exercising power so that the feminine principle can be renewed and regenerated in our time.

The word *power* elicits many different thoughts and images. In some circles, it has come to have a purely negative connotation; power is seen simply as the imposition of one individual's or group's will on that of another. In contrast, the root meaning of the word power is in the Latin *posse*, which means "to be able," something reflected also, for instance, in the Spanish word *poder*. In essence, then, power is that which enables. Rather than destructive, the image inherent in its root is power as something productive or even creative.

In patriarchal societies, however, power has traditionally been viewed as something possessed by one group or individual at the expense of another. This is basically a distorted conception. Michel Foucault argues that power is not static, nor is it something that can be possessed. Rather, it is something that flows through a cluster of web-like relationships. Power is more like threads connecting beings: "Individuals are the vehicles of power, not its point of application" (1980, 98).

As noted earlier, Shiva links the exercise of assertive male power with the social construction of nature and the feminine as passive. Since power is relational, the former depends on the latter. The challenge is to recast power from being a relationship of active over passive, oppressor over oppressed, and exploiter over exploited, to a new relationship based on mutuality and creativity. To see how this can be done, however, we need a more practical analysis of power.

Analyzing Power

In her work *Truth or Dare* (1987), the ecofeminist writer, activist, and psychologist Starhawk delineates three basic types or modalities through which power expresses itself: *power-over*, *power-from-within*, and *power-with*.

Power-over is perhaps best described as power that restricts or controls. This is the way power is normally conceived and exercised in today's patriarchal society, and it is rooted in the predominant mechanistic paradigm that will be explored further in chapter 6. Power-over tends to organize itself hierarchically and works through systems of authority and domination. This is the kind of power that allows patriarchal capitalism to appropriate production through exploitation.

We are so accustomed to power-over and its implicit threats in our lives that it largely operates on a subconscious level, almost as though a jail keeper lived inside our heads. Generally, we only become conscious of power-over in its most extreme manifestations, such as open violence. Yet, while power backed by the gun, power backed by force, is the clearest example of power-over, more normally it operates through subtle mechanisms of coercion, manipulation, and control motivated at some level by fear.

It is noteworthy that power-over *is* in one sense "enabling": "Power-over enables one individual or group to make decisions that affect others, and to enforce control" (Starhawk 1987, 9). Yet power-over is essentially negative: it is power used to repress or crush the power of others.

A second type of power, which for Starhawk is the opposite of power-over, is what is called *power-from-within*. Power-from-within is the power that sustains all life: the power of creativity, of healing, and of love. It is experienced in a special way wherever people act in concert to oppose the control of power-over. Evidently, then, power-from-within is at the heart of what is often described by the term *empowerment*, and hence of many liberatory models of education and political action.

Interestingly, the Tao may be the purest and most essential form of this power—the intrinsic power manifest at the heart of the cosmos itself.[4] Power-from-within also relates to the Chinese idea of *Te* (the second word in the *Tao Te Ching*): *Te* is represented by an ideogram that combines the image of going straight with that of the heart (Dreher 1990, xiv, 12). Thus, it implies living authentically, from the heart (vital center), in a way combining intuition and compassion. From another perspective, *Te* is a personal power that enables one to see clearly and act decisively at the right place and time. *Te* is also the power inherent in seeds, the power to spring forth into life. We could therefore understand *Te* as the power of the life energy in each being, a power that connects to and channels the cosmic power of the Tao.

The third modality through which power is expressed is called *power-with*, or the power of influence or power-as-process. Its source lies in the willingness of others to listen to our ideas. It is power-with that enables us to act in concert and to form truly participatory organizations. While power-over utilizes the authority of position to impose its will through obedience, power-with is based on a personal respect earned in practice: "Power-with is more subtle, more fluid, and fragile than authority. It is dependent on personal responsibility, on our own creativity and daring, and on the willingness of others to respond" (Starhawk 1987, 11). Joanna Macy, a Buddhist ecological and peace activist, sees this kind of power as a type of synergy based on openness to others. "The exercise of power as process demands that we unmask and reject all exercises of force that obstruct our and others' participation in life" (quoted in Winter 1996, 258).

---

4. The word that Jesus used for power in Aramaic, *hayye*, also connotes this kind of power, best translated in this case as "life-force" or "the primal energy that pervades the cosmos" (Douglas-Klotz 1999, 65).

Power as process calls us to nurture our capacity for empathy. Activities such as facilitating popular education and organizing grassroots movements, at their best, employ this kind of power.

In practice, all three types of power coexist and interrelate in any concrete reality. For example, power-from-within and power-over often meld together (even though, conceptually, they are opposites). Domination ultimately relies on a certain degree of creativity, warped as it may be. Often, too, one person imposes his or her own ideas and creativity on another, converting power-from-within into power-over. Similarly, power-with can also convert itself into power-over. Starhawk notes that, in dominant culture, the two are easily confused. Influence can easily be converted into authority, especially because we have all been so indoctrinated into power as domination.

The reality that power-with is often mixed with and thus confused with power-over was analyzed in depth by the philosopher Hannah Arendt. Speaking of violence, the most extreme form of power-over, and of the power to act in concert (which corresponds to Starhawk's power-with), she notes:

> Power [power-with] and violence [power-over], though they are distinct phenomena, usually appear together. Wherever they are combined, power, we have found, is the primary and predominant factor. The situation, however, is entirely different when we deal with them in their pure states. . . . Violence can always destroy power; out of the barrel of a gun grows the most effective command, resulting in the most instant and perfect obedience. What never can grow out of it is power. . . .
>
> Politically speaking, it is insufficient to say that power and violence are not the same. Power and violence are opposites; when the one rules absolutely, the other is absent. Violence appears where power is in jeopardy, but left to its own course it ends in power's disappearance. Violence can destroy power; it is utterly incapable of creating it. (Arendt 1970, 52-53, 56)

Similarly, Starhawk says that "systems of domination destroy power-with, for it can only truly exist among those who are equal and who recognize that they are equal" (1987, 12). Unlike power-over, power-with can always be revoked by the group itself; it does not infringe upon the freedom of the other.

The relationship between power-with and power-from-within is perhaps clearer. In a group where each person's opinions are valued (i.e., where we have power-with), it is more likely that we will express and develop our power-from-within. Likewise, as our creative and life-giving potential grows, we are likely to gain the respect of others.

One way to visualize how the three types of power interact is to use the image of a netlike organization suggested earlier by Michel Foucault. Power-from-within could be represented as the nodes from which power originates; power-with as the lines that link together individuals and groups through influence; and power-over as barriers blocking the relationships of power-with while stifling the exercise of power-from-within.

Visualizing the Exercise of Power

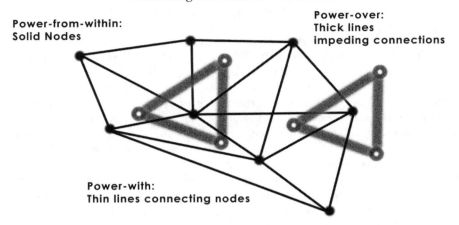

Power-from-within:
Solid Nodes

Power-over:
Thick lines
impeding connections

Power-with:
Thin lines connecting nodes

Transforming Relationships of Power

Moving from reconceptualizing power to actually reconstructing it is a difficult step, yet it is a step that we must attempt to take. Patriarchy's predatory mode of production depends on the exercise of power-over, the power of domination. If this power cannot be countered, if new forms cannot be cultivated that are life-enhancing rather than death-dealing, the possibilities for transforming the world along the lines envisioned by ecofeminists will remain minimal.

It is helpful at this juncture to recall that power is neither static nor fixed in quantity. The traditional politics of transformation spoke of "taking power." Yet another possibility exists: Creating new sources of power, beginning on the margins. At some point, of course, a confrontation with those who wield power-over may become inevitable, but first the resources of power-from-within and power-with must be nurtured at the grassroots. Indeed, the global movement of civil society embodied in both people's organizations and many nongovernmental organizations demonstrates that such power is already being created and nurtured.

One way, then, to foster both power-with and power-from-within is to create participatory organizations where an atmosphere of openness enables members to feel free to be and express themselves. At times, the use of guided imagery, playful techniques, and creative forms of expression can facilitate this. Those seeking to facilitate transformative processes must also ensure a certain degree of safety within the group that enables those who are most inhibited or most vulnerable to express themselves honestly without fear. To this end, a set of basic "ground rules" can be helpful in some situations.

A second strategy for cultivating liberating power is to foster awareness. Joanna Macy observes: "'Power-with' involves attentive openness to the surrounding physical or mental environment and an alertness to our own and others' responses. It is the capacity to act in ways that increase the sum total of one's conscious participation in life" (1995, 257). Starhawk notes, "Awareness is the beginning of all resistance. We can only resist domination by becoming and remaining conscious: conscious of the self, conscious of the way reality is constructed around us, conscious of each seemingly insignificant choice we make, conscious that we are, in fact, making choices" (1987, 79).

Developing power-with can happen only within the context of a group. By its nature, this type of power is the most intrinsically relational. Participants in liberatory initiatives can best develop their power-with when the group allows for genuine participation and the sharing of leadership functions. Starhawk observes, "To empower others, a group must not only be structured in ways that serve liberation, it must be conscious of how power in a group moves and flows" (1987, 268).

The liberating forms of power embodied in power-from-within and power-with are most fruitfully cultivated while engaging in interactions that produce value. Macy speaks particularly of "synergistic exchanges" generating "something that was not there before and that enhances the capacities and well-being of all who are involved" (1995, 257). Indeed, the word *synergy* may best encapsulate what we mean by power-with.

Ultimately, though, the restructuring of power in society as a whole will require strategies that go beyond these beginnings. Patriarchy has developed over thousands of years, and global corporate capitalism, the most recent manifestation of this imperial mentality, retains a firm grip on most of the world. To construct new forms of power and to confront the old, we will need deep resources from within and a new understanding of both the nature of reality and of transformation itself.

Our first task is to shake off the spell under which patriarchy, anthropocentrism, and the current system of domination hold us; we must overcome the paralysis that keeps us imprisoned in oppression, despair, denial, and addiction. The path toward this goal will be explored as we enter the next leg of our spiraling journey.

4.

Overcoming Paralysis

Renewing the Psyche

> . . . The sage desires freedom from desire,
> And does not treasure precious things.
> The sage learns to let go of learning.
> The sage simply guides others
> back to what they have lost,
> and assists all beings to find their true nature,
> while never daring to use force.
>
> (*Tao Te Ching* §64)
>
> . . . See the world as your body,
> Love the world as your own self,
> and you can be entrusted to care for all things.
>
> (*Tao Te Ching* §13)

Understanding the pathologies undermining human societies and the web of life itself is a first step toward liberation. As we unmask these disorders, delving into how anthropocentrism and patriarchy have colored our perceptions and shaped our actions, we are able to begin to shake off the belief that our current state of affairs is somehow inevitable or unchangeable. Yet the pathologies that affect our world have also rooted themselves deeply in our own psyches. Not surprisingly, then, at a deeper level we may still feel powerless to effect meaningful changes to the way we live with one another and with the greater Earth community.

Indeed, while the systems of exploitation and the organization of dominating power are major impediments to liberating transformation, our own feeling of powerlessness may be an even greater obstacle. What lies at the root of our paralysis? Why do we feel unable to act—or even to hope that another way might be possible? What is it that numbs and deadens our spirits?

Powerlessness could be defined as that which prevents us from realizing the fullness of both our power-from-within (the creative potential that serves as the basic foundation for our renewed vision) and our power-with (our ability to act in concert with others). If we are to revision and reconnect to power, then, we must first come to terms with the reality of powerlessness: In what forms does it manifest itself? How does it affect us? What are its roots? And how might we overcome it?

Psychologist and rabbi Michael Lerner has reflected deeply on the phenomenon of powerlessness. During the 1960s and 1970s, he was involved as an activist in the United States protesting the Vietnam War. At that time, he began to note that people involved in that struggle often acted in ways that undermined their own goals; they took powerlessness to be axiomatic, and this led them to plan and undertake actions that eventually confirmed their belief. More than the structural powerlessness created by the dominating systems, it was this "surplus"—or internalized—powerlessness that proved in the end to be most fatal to their movement.

Lerner does not deny the reality of the more "external" or objective sources of powerlessness—the way political, economic, and social structures prevent human beings from actualizing their capacities and effecting change. These exist, but they are greatly compounded by the reality of internalized (surplus) powerlessness: "Human beings contribute to this powerlessness to the extent that their own emotional, intellectual and spiritual makeup prevents them from actualizing possibilities that do exist" within the reality of systemically induced powerlessness (Lerner 1986, 23).

These dynamics of internalized powerlessness play a key role in impeding authentic transformation today at a global level. Despite the fact that we are faced with the most lethal threats in human history, we often either fail to act or we act in ways that ultimately endanger our own well-being. The dynamics of internalized powerlessness have become so powerful and so pervasive that they now extend to every sector of human society. Indeed, even the ruling elites often act in ways that, while profitable in the short term, actually undermine their own futures and those of their children.

Lerner observes, "Powerlessness corrupts us in a very direct way. It changes, transforms, and distorts us" (1986, 2). Our belief that major transformations are impossible becomes a self-fulfilling prophecy. Of course, the existing power structures are very real impediments to change. Yet one of the key ways that current structures actually block change is by exploiting and reinforcing our own feelings of powerlessness:

> The world could be changed. But one of the major reasons it stays the way it is is because of our deep belief and conviction that nothing can or will change. This is really a new development in history. In past historical periods, the main reason things stayed the way they were had little to do with people's beliefs and convictions and feelings about themselves. . . . The primary

change in the modern epoch is that the ruling classes rule by consent—they have managed to get the active participation of the people they rule in the process of policing the established order. We become our own jail-keepers. (Lerner 1986, 3-4)

If we can successfully confront our internalized powerlessness, if we can break out of the jails that have been constructed in our own psyches, the prospects for changing the current political, cultural, and economic systems are greatly improved. As Lerner points out, even though the existing structures of domination may wield overwhelming power, they do not wield *absolute* power. They can, in fact, be overthrown.

Indeed, much of the dominating power of the existing system of patriarchy embodied in global corporate capitalism comes precisely from the way it exploits internalized powerlessness. There is, then, a very close relationship between the objective powerlessness produced by the systems of domination and the psychological reality of internalized powerlessness. In the upcoming sections of this chapter, we will begin by first gaining a clearer understanding of the different forms of internalized powerlessness and how they relate to each other. We will then look at how the systems of domination reinforce and utilize these to perpetuate and strengthen themselves. Then, using the insights of ecopsychology, we will delve deeper to see the relationship between our sense of powerlessness and our very real alienation from the wider Earth community. Finally, based on all of these, we will explore some concrete ways for overcoming paralysis and moving toward authentic empowerment and liberation.

THE DYNAMICS OF POWERLESSNESS

The psychologist Roger Walsh (1984) has noted that classical Buddhism offers an analysis of both individual and social pathology that is useful in understanding the dynamics of internalized powerlessness. It classifies all pathology as falling into one of three "poisons": aversion, addiction, or delusion.

Aversion can manifest itself in a number of ways—as compulsive avoidance, anger, fear, defensiveness, or aggression. Aversion in the form of fear is particularly evident in two key forms of internalized powerlessness: *denial* and *internalized oppression*. Denial is most prevalent among those who are benefiting in some way from the current structures of power—who fear that acknowledging the reality of our crisis may mean giving up their feeling of security and comfort. In contrast, internalized oppression is especially apparent in those who suffer the most direct effects of structural powerlessness and who attempt to shield themselves from the most brutal forms of violence.

When we refer to *addiction*, we refer to something much wider than dependencies on substances like alcohol or drugs; in Buddhist psychology, addiction also includes all forms of greed and attachments. Addiction relates to aversion insofar as it is yet another way to hide or escape from our fears. It can also be seen as an attempt to fill the emptiness of lives lived in delusion with something—*anything*—that will ease the pain of hopelessness. At the same time, addiction combines with aversion to cloud our perceptions still further, leading us deeper into delusion.

Perhaps the purest form of internalized powerlessness is the delusion of *despair*. We begin to see the world as hopeless, change as an impossibility. We become so enchained by despair that we come to see this view of the world as "realistic"—any suggestion of an alternative is utopian and impractical. Consigned to this dreary fate, we may seek a false escape in addictions, or we may express our frustration and anger through irrational, aggressive forms of behavior.

In naming these different forms of internalized powerlessness, we must acknowledge that in fact they all tend to combine and reinforce each other—they are seldom found in an isolated form. Their complex interactions form a twisted web imprisoning our psyches. To begin to unravel this web, though, it is helpful to examine each strand more carefully so that a more complete picture of their interactions begins to become apparent.

Internalized Oppression

William Reich proposed that the fundamental question for psychology today must be: "What are the psychological forces that keep people from rebelling against a social order that is oppressive and prevents them from being all that they could be?" (Lerner 1986, v). This question seems particularly appropriate for the overwhelming majority of people who benefit very little—if at all—from the current political, economic, and social systems. Why do they not rebel?

For most of humanity, very real dangers are constant companions in life; the lack of basic necessities, susceptibility to potentially lethal diseases, and the threat of violence (be it domestic, social, or political) create a situation where security remains perpetually elusive. Fear is a natural result of this state of affairs, and this fear disempowers people, immobilizing them and inhibiting transformative action. It should be recognized that the fear that characterizes internalized oppression is the result of structural powerlessness and oppression; yet it is also distinct from it. In a sense, it is the psychological fingerprint left by a long history of subjugation and violence.

As an example of this, we could consider the peoples of Latin America.[1] For centuries, now, they have developed what might be termed a *culture of survival*, especially indigenous peoples. This culture of survival has normally avoided direct confrontation with the structures of oppression and exploitation, preferring instead to (at least superficially) submit and at the same time preserve what it can while resisting domination in subtle ways. This strategy has probably been necessary at times—and in some ways it could even be termed successful—but it has been purchased at the high price of internalizing oppression.

---

1. We choose this example because it is the one closest to our experience. Much of what is said here, though, would in many ways be more generally applicable to many other cultures that have experienced conquest or colonization.

The existence of this culture of survival does not imply pure passivity to oppression; nor does it deny the history of struggle of the peoples of Latin America, a history that often has erupted in courageous rebellions. Yet most of those rebellions have been unsuccessful, and a heavy price has been paid each time. Each unsuccessful struggle in some ways reinforced the power of the dominators and pushed resistance "underground," especially in the psychological sense. At the same time, despair accumulated as the hope for real change diminished.

During the past century, this history of oppression began to change with the success of many labor struggles, rural and indigenous movements, popular organizations, and even revolutions—albeit some of these successes proved to be short-lived. More recently still, we have witnessed the election of many progressive governments supported by popular movements in the region, some that desire to fundamentally reorient their societies (while others, less radical in nature, are at least carrying out meaningful reforms aimed at improving the lives of the poor). Despite these successes, however, old patterns of thinking and acting are slow to die: the fingerprint of past failures persists in the form of internalized oppression.

Paulo Freire (Torres 1986) speaks of this reality: The oppressed in some ways have adapted to their situation so that, while desiring a better life for themselves and their children, they may actually also fear freedom itself. In particular, they fear to struggle for liberation insofar as this represents a very real threat to their lives: the history of violent repression has been etched deeply into their psyches. Therefore, it is only natural that people begin to selectively "tune out" that which may in some way hold the key to liberation. As Freire writes:

> The naïve consciousness [of the oppressed person] is not so naïve; it is also a reflexive consciousness. It is the *consciousness of the possible* or, more exactly, *the maximum clarity of consciousness that can be represented* without the danger of the threat of discovering something that would be highly destabilising for the oppressed person. (Quoted in Torres 1986, 99)

This "naïve consciousness" to which Freire refers is essentially a type of delusion created by the psyche in response to the fear of repression, suffering, and violence. While in the past it may have served some purpose (and while, even now, it is very comprehensible), it inhibits effective transformative action and thus ultimately works to the disadvantage of the oppressed.

It should be noted as well that the dynamics of internalized oppression play an especially important role in the subjugation of women in society. Power dynamics within families, schools, and society in general begin the process of internalizing oppression in women from a very early age. The constant threat of violence and sexual abuse both in the home and outside it also contributes greatly to the insecurity that gives rise to internalized oppression. Similarly, dynamics of internalized powerlessness have reinforced racism as well as oppression based on sexual orientation.

Those working among the most marginalized and subjugated sectors of society need to take internalized oppression into account when attempting a trans-formative praxis (i.e., transformative action combining theory—or vision—and practice). At times, popular educators and activists have restricted themselves to activities of "conscientization"; these, however, are often in themselves ineffec-tive because internalized oppression represses both learning and further action:

> To "understand" what is happening does not mean we can change it. We are deeply invested in the "safety" of the ways we have learned to be, the "safety" of the known, the familiar. . . . It is quite terrifying to upset this, especially since those ways of being are not individual to us, but socially prescribed, mandated. Our fear of change, our sense of impending threat, is justified. (Rockhill 1992, 26)

This idea is echoed in Charlotte Bunch's observation: "Consciousness-raising helped us to verbalize our oppression, [but it] often has not led us to control over our lives and change in the conditions causing our oppression" (1987, 88). Overcoming internalized oppression, then, requires more than mere informa-tion: it requires a liberatory praxis that addresses its root causes and underlying dynamics.

Denial

Like internalized oppression, aversion in the form of fear lies at the heart of denial. For those suffering the death-dealing threats of the dominant system most directly, denial may be more difficult—it is hard, albeit not impossible, to maintain that all is well while having to struggle daily for survival or while enduring violence (although denial could still come into play in the case of eco-logical threats if these are not being too directly experienced).

Denial is no doubt deeper and more pervasive among those who reap certain benefits from the existing system. In such cases, denial only needs to block out certain aspects of reality and repress selected information. If the most pressing threats to one's survival are somewhat separated from immediate experience by time or distance, the mechanism of denial is facilitated.

Such is the case with many of the threats to global survival we presently face. For those living a relatively comfortable existence, the problem of poverty and the unjust distribution of world resources can be kept out of mind by shun-ning contact with the poor. Thought of ecological damage can be avoided if its effects are not too visible. The danger of nuclear war may still be a real threat, but there are few visible reminders of it in our daily existence.

Keeping problems "out of sight, out of mind," then, no doubt facilitates denial.[2] Certainly, this is something that is facilitated also by the way the mass media select and disseminate (or block) information. Essentially, though, denial

---

2. An interesting example of keeping things out of sight lies in the clear-cutting of forests in British Columbia, Canada, where forestry companies and government maintain "scenic corridors" around major highways to disguise the extent of the devastation being wrought. It is only when one travels on back roads or flies over the province that the true scope of destruction is evident.

depends on our internal filters to keep out painful information. Indeed, denial is such an effective defense mechanism that we are often completely unaware that we are employing it. When information is presented that could shake the false security we have constructed for ourselves, we tend to react in a number of ways (Macy 1995, 242-43):

- *Disbelief.* We simply try to ignore the problem, something facilitated both by the fact that many of the crises are hard to see (the depletion of the ozone layer or water resources) or they occur fairly gradually (for example, the rise in global temperatures).

- *Dispute.* Once it becomes impossible to ignore the problem, we may try to dispute the facts or argue that the severity is not so great. Alternatively, we may subscribe to "techno-optimism," maintaining that human ingenuity (or economic growth!) will magically solve the problem, even if no solution is apparent at present.

- *Double life.* Once it becomes impossible to ignore or debate, we retreat into a double life, somehow tucking the true knowledge of our reality into a dark corner of our minds while pretending to live as though everything were normal. In the words of Macy, "we tend to live our lives as if nothing has changed, while knowing that everything has changed" (1995, 243).

In truth, though, we are living a reality that is anything but normal. The threats we face are qualitatively different from at any other point in human history. As Macy points out, "Until the late twentieth century, every generation throughout history lived with the tacit certainty that there would be generations to follow" (1995, 241). Whatever hardships, whatever threats to personal survival, there was an unquestioning assumption that future generations would live to walk on the Earth—at least until the Creator might decide otherwise. That certainty no longer exists. Its loss is "the pivotal psychological reality of our time." This pain evokes a fear so great that it is more properly called terror, or even dread. Yet most of us never speak of this reality. It is too painful. We retreat instead into denial: "The very danger signals that should rivet our attention, summon up the blood, and bond us in collective action, tend to have the opposite effect. They make us want to pull down the blinds and busy ourselves with other things" (Macy and Brown 1998, 26).

The fear that this dread engenders in us is so deep that it results in a kind of "psychic numbing" that attempts to shield us from fully experiencing our pain. As Laura Sewall observes, "full awareness hurts. . . . In a culture with the luxury to do so, we turn down the volume" (1995, 202). In practicing this denial, though, we also block out much beauty and joy in the process. At the same time, we allow ourselves to continue the very kinds of behavior and attitudes that sustain the systems destroying our Earth community. Our denial, then, while caused by the crises we face, also perpetuates them.

The conspiracy of silence concerning our deepest feelings about the future of our species, the degree of numbing, isolation, burnout and cognitive confusion that result from it—all converge to produce a sense of futility. Each act of denial, conscious or unconscious, is an abdication of our powers to respond. (Macy 1983, 16)

The fear of pain at the heart of our denial is further compounded by the fact that Western societies consider pain itself to be dysfunctional. Moreover, we fear causing distress to others or sowing panic; we fear feeling guilty about our own share of responsibility for the problems we face; and we fear appearing stupid or powerless (since we are not supposed to admit a problem until we have a solution). All of these fears are understandable, yet the cost of repressing them is both very high and very real. Eventually, the energy we need for clear thinking and creative action drains away or dissipates, and we are left with even less power in our lives. Roger Walsh observes:

Denial, repression, and other defences are always purchased at the cost of awareness, authenticity, and effectiveness. When we deny our reality we also deny our full potential and humanity. When we distort our image of the world we also distort our image of ourselves. Therefore we remain unaware of the power and potential that lie within us and are us; the power and potential that are the major resources we have to offer to the world. (Walsh 1984, 76)

Out of touch with our power-from-within, denial blocks the potential for the organized power-with needed to confront the systems of power-over in our world. As we will see later in more detail, the psychic numbing of denial also blocks out the beauty and compassion that could truly motivate us and sustain us in the struggle for transformation. Denial can also lead to destructive behaviors like vandalism, violence, or suicide; to psychological projections that encourage us to demonize others (leading to racism, sexism, religious intolerance, etc.); and to diminished intellectual and creative productivity. Yet another possible effect is to escape into addictions to compensate for the life lost through the repressing mechanisms of denial. In all cases, though, denial essentially means living a lie—negating the truth of our situation. Inevitably, then, it leads to a state of delusion, a state whose most prevalent form today is despair.

Addiction

When we hear the word "addiction," our most immediate association is probably with substance abuse—for example, addictions to alcohol, tobacco, and other drugs. No one can deny the prevalence of these addictions, nor the immense damage they do to human society. Yet addiction in the sense we discuss it here encompasses far more than this. From the standpoint of Buddhist psychology (Walsh 1984), addiction includes any compulsive need to possess or experience something. Normally, it is characterized by the belief that "I must have _____ to be happy." One can be addicted to capital accumulation, possessions, shopping, power, work, entertainments, food, or sex.

The dependence and compulsion that characterize addiction result in a drastic narrowing of vision. Addictions focus on immediate experience, on the instant gratification of desires. Directly or indirectly, they tend to numb us and narrow our awareness. In the process, as Ed Ayres points out, addiction destroys our power to envision and to empathize with others. Yet "to be human is to be able to envision, as well as to see literally, and to empathize, as well to feel one's own needs" (1999a, 189). Addiction, then, is fundamentally dehumanizing.

In the modern world, some of the most prevalent (and interrelated) forms of addiction are the addictions to economic growth and consumption, as well as the related addictions to television and other forms of technology. Unlike some other addictions, these are actively promoted and condoned by corporate capitalism. As we have already seen, undifferentiated, quantitative "growth" and capital accumulation are seen as our principal economic objectives, even though these have not resulted in greater well-being and in fact have resulted in untold destruction. At a more popular level, consumption is promoted as the key to happiness, and a constant stream of advertisements in the mass media actively feeds this addiction. David Korten observes:

> Rather than teaching us that the path to fulfillment is to experience living to the fullest through our relationships with family, community, nature, and the living cosmos, the corporate-dominated media continuously repeat a false promise—whatever our longings, the market is the path to instant gratification. Our purpose is to consume—we are born to shop. Entranced by the siren song of the market, we consistently undervalue the life energy that we put into obtaining money and overvalue the expected life energy gains from spending it. (1995, 266)

So, while a large majority of the world's people are taunted by the visions of a consumer paradise they can never hope to attain, a small portion of humanity with the luxury to do so seeks to acquire ever-greater quantities of possessions. Yet the need for consumption is never satisfied. In fact, those in consumer societies are no happier today than they were in the 1950s, even though purchasing power has more than doubled (Winter 1996). In the United States, the percentage of people describing themselves as "very happy" has actually fallen from 35 percent in 1957 to 30 percent today (Gardner 2001).

Indeed, one of the characteristics of all addictions is that the compulsive needs that underlie them can never be satisfied. Ultimately, this is because the human need for joy, beauty, love, and meaning cannot be filled by any substance, possession, or immediate pleasure.

Despite this emptiness, the suffering underlying addiction is often masked. Some level of denial almost always accompanies addiction, whatever form it takes. The alcoholic who still drinks will try to maintain normal appearances, and will deny that any problem exists. Similarly, societies addicted to unlimited growth and ever-increasing consumption deny that there is any problem, as though limits to finite resources could simply be dismissed by a blind and irrational faith in yet-to-be-imagined solutions. Ultimately, then, addiction causes us to live a lie—to live in delusion.

Despair

Addiction, denial, and internalized oppression all tend to paralyze us, removing us from the struggle to create more equitable and life-sustaining communities. Our attempts to shield ourselves from fear and pain, however, actually lead us into an even deeper kind of suffering. In cutting ourselves off from participation in efforts to make a difference, "our lives begin to look so hopeless and bleak that many [of us] end up in a cycle of self-blame and self-destruction that is as bad and often worse than any price [we] would have to pay" if we had actually been involved in the struggle for transformation (Walsh 1984, 18). Despair, often manifested in subtle or not-so-subtle forms of depression, proves worse than the suffering involved in embracing the painful truth of our reality and seeking to change it.

Indeed, to lose hope, to fall into despair, is perhaps the purest form of internalized powerlessness. At its root lies a fundamental renunciation of our power-from-within, our power to create and contribute meaningfully to the world. It can lead to an even deeper state of denial or to addiction as we seek to avoid or escape the inevitable suffering that despair carries with it.

Despair is essentially a state of delusion because it causes us to perceive reality through a veil of falsehood that cuts us off from the joy of life. Despair is closely related to the psychic numbing that begins with denial. As we spend more and more energy repressing our fears and pain, as we try to isolate ourselves from the suffering of the world around us, we fall deeper and deeper into a black hole that sucks away the joy of life. This same isolation cuts us off from both the human and the wider Earth community, depriving us of a source of love, hope, energy, and the experience of power-with. Joanna Macy observes that in all of this:

> A marked loss of feeling results, as if a nerve had been cut. As Barry Childers has said, "We immunize ourselves against the demands of the situation by narrowing our awareness." This anaesthetization affects other aspects of our life as well—loves and losses are less intense, the sky is less vivid—for if we are not going to let ourselves feel pain, we will not feel much else either. "The mind pays for its deadening to the state of the world," observes Robert Murphy, "by giving up its capacity for joy and flexibility." (Macy 1995, 249)

Despair can also afflict those actively involved in the struggle for transformation. Indeed, when we honestly face the situation of the world, it can overwhelm us and throw us into despair. This can be compounded if our activities have led us to work compulsively for change—to the point that we grow overextended and fatigued. Indeed, *compulsive* action may be little more than yet another form of addiction.

Certainly, the severity of the crises we face does not inspire optimism. The problems are complex and time is truly limited. In many ways, it is even helpful to express our fears—admitting that we feel it may already be too late to effect the changes needed to move toward a just and ecologically harmonious future. Yet there is a fine line between hope and despair. Expressing our fears must serve as a first step in moving beyond the paralysis they engender. Ultimately, we need a realistic hope that admits the dangers, difficulties, and fears of the present but is able to move beyond these based on an inspiration that runs as deep as the life of the Earth itself.

SYSTEMIC REINFORCEMENTS

While internalized powerlessness serves to perpetuate the systems exploiting both the human and the wider Earth community, it is also in some measure the fruit of these same systems. As noted earlier, modern capitalism dominates us to a large extent with our own consent; but this consent—to coin the terminology of Noam Chomsky—has generally been "manufactured" in a very purposeful way.

Strangely, it would seem that those who direct the dominant system have become entangled in the same web that they themselves have woven. In particular, denial and addiction would appear to be just as prevalent (and perhaps even more so) among the rich and powerful as among other sectors of society. When considering systemic reinforcements, then, it is useful to keep in mind that many of these (especially those related to education and the mass media) serve to control and circumscribe the action of the powerful themselves. This certainly does not mean that no one is responsible for the current system of domination. It does, though, emphasize just how all-encompassing the system has become. In some ways, it would appear to have taken on a life of its own.

In the following subsections, we will explore some of the systemic reinforcements used to manufacture consent. To begin, we will look at how both the real threat of violence and our educational systems play a role in creating and sustaining internalized powerlessness. Most of this section, though, will focus on the role of the mass media in facilitating denial, feeding addiction, and maintaining us in a state of delusion.

Repression, Militarism, and Violence

In many parts of the globe, force exercised by the military and police is one of the principal means of sustaining structural powerlessness. This repressive force is one of the most direct and brutal instruments of the dominant system of power. As such, it is almost exclusively reserved for use against the poor and the oppressed.

At the same time, though, repression plays on the dynamics of internalized oppression. To do so, repression need not actually be exercised—the mere threat of it is often sufficient. Each time a protest is violently repressed, an activist is arrested, or a prisoner is tortured, the effects of the use of force reverberate far beyond those who receive its blows directly. By reinforcing internalized oppression, force is multiplied far beyond the bounds of its direct execution.

Repression also depends on internalized oppression to organize itself. The police and military forces of most nations are made up of people who themselves are poor and oppressed. It is only possible to control the majority if sufficient numbers of the oppressed are themselves co-opted into becoming a repressive force. Of course, this arrangement can quickly become unstable. In cases such as the "people's revolution" in the Philippines that removed the Marcos regime from power in 1986 as well as the more recent overthrow of Slobodan Milosevic in Serbia, the police and army changed sides at a critical juncture and stood aside—or even joined the people—allowing popular protest to bring down a dictatorial regime.

Around the world, to differing extents, the use of repressive force is being met by increasing pressures to protect human rights. While it is unlikely that brute force will disappear totally as a tool of domination, it is a fundamentally clumsy mechanism that is best reserved as a last resort. Increasingly, the dominant system is opting for more sophisticated means of playing on internalized powerlessness.

More persistent and harder to eradicate, perhaps, is the threat of domestic violence and sexual assault that is used to reinforce the internalized oppression of women in all parts of the world and in all social classes. Once again, the actual use of force is not always necessary: a woman does not have to have been sexually assaulted to fear for her safety and to restrict her activities to avoid potential dangers. Moreover, verbal abuse can take a toll that can be just as devastating as physical abuse—yet it may be harder to counter because it is more difficult to prove. The mass media, too, reinforce internalized oppression through its portrayal of violent acts being committed against women. (Despite all these threats, though, women's movements have made real progress in making violence against women increasingly unacceptable in many societies around the globe.)

Finally, we cannot forget the pervasive threat of nuclear war—a threat that still exercises a powerful effect on the collective psyche of the planet, despite the end of the cold war. As Joanna Macy (1983) has so convincingly demonstrated, it is a source of deep despair that works subtly but forcefully to keep us enchained in internalized powerlessness. Until nuclear disarmament occurs on a global scale, it will continue to distort our lives in countless ways—gnawing away at our spirits with the fear that a cataclysm could suddenly strike with little forewarning.

Education

Education, especially through its formal institutions, plays an important role in socializing us into the values and perspectives of corporate capitalism and the ideology of empire. It also tends to reinforce the dynamics of internalized powerlessness, albeit at times in subtle ways.

Particularly in the global South, educational methods still depend on the dynamics of internalized oppression. Education relies strongly on the authority of the teacher as the one who imparts knowledge. Learning is often reduced to the memorization of facts and formulas, and students themselves are basically treated as passive recipients of knowledge. Latin American popular educators often refer to this model as *educación bancaria* (banking education) because it conjures up the image of "depositing" knowledge into the heads of the students. Power-from-within is at best neglected and at worse actively repressed. Creativity and questioning are considered subversive, or at the very least annoying.

Such a methodology trains learners to view power as both authoritarian and static. Students are taught to be obedient, passive, and unquestioning. This in turn strengthens internalized oppression. The contents of the educational process may further reinforce this tendency. For instance, the teaching of history may extol the virtues of the oppressors (and highlight the failures of the oppressed), while literature and religious instruction may idealize the patriarchal vision of gender relations.

Those who have experienced more progressive educational systems may view such authoritarian education as a thing of the past—although it is still very prevalent in much of the world. Even more enlightened models of education that give some value to questioning, creativity, and cooperation, however, suffer from limitations.

Almost all educational systems play into the dynamics of denial by transmitting a distorted view of reality that either neglects the true crises affecting the globe or treats them in a superficial manner. Subjects are presented as distinct disciplines, making it more difficult to see the interconnection between different problems. We are taught to think for the short term, reflecting little on the long-term consequences of actions or plans. While children are often especially sensitive to the threat of nuclear war and ecological destruction, this sensitivity is only seldom developed constructively. Here, adult fears play a key role, especially the fear of causing distress and the fear of acknowledging pain. Indeed, since most educators are themselves suffering some degree of denial, they may unconsciously transmit this to students.

While educational systems may make an effort to discourage addictions to harmful substances, they still tend to feed the societal obsession with endless consumption by encouraging students to strive for a well-paying career that will allow for a high level of material comforts. Even in poorer societies and among marginalized peoples, where the realization of this aspiration is a virtual impossibility, the myth of "getting ahead through education" is used to reinforce the power of the formal education system and ensure that it is given high prestige in society.

The idea that transformative action is futile—a message of despair—is also transmitted subtly in a variety of ways. Children who dream of changing the world often receive a smile or a condescending comment rather than real encouragement. History is frequently presented in a deterministic fashion designed to quash utopian hopes for a better future. We are taught to be "practical" and "realistic" and to accept our inherent powerlessness.

Of course, there are many trends in education that run counter to those mentioned here. There are numerous educators who strive to awaken the imagination and creativity of students, who seek to give an accurate view of world problems, and who endeavor to support the emotional maturity of students and their capacity to deal with pain constructively. In many places and for many people, however, the net effect of the educational system is to make them more vulnerable to the dynamics of internalized powerlessness.

Perhaps of even greater importance, very few educational systems—or individual educators—seek to impart a vision of reality that truly values our relationship to the greater Earth community. Seldom are traditional forms of knowledge and the history of indigenous peoples valued. Students spend their time learning in sterile classrooms with little or no contact with the natural world—unless one counts keeping the occasional classroom pet or the dissection of some "specimen" during science class. The vision inspiring education is that of equipping students to compete in the global economy, to become consumers, and perhaps to be good citizens with a degree of respect for others. Unlike the systems of learning found in aboriginal societies, modern education does not initiate students into a relationship with the wider Earth community and with the cosmos that embraces it. Learners are taught how to function as autonomous individuals in a competitive society—not how to function as participants in the greater community of life.

Mass Media

The mass communications media, particularly television, may well be the most important means through which internalized powerlessness is reinforced in modern societies, both South and North. The power and coverage of the mass media have reached nearly incredible proportions: 97 percent of households in the United States, 90 percent in China, and over 80 percent in Brazil have at least one television set. While in some of the world's poorest nations, the percentage is significantly lower, other forms of mass media (especially radio) have near-universal penetration.

The rise of the mass media represents a relatively new phenomenon in the world. Until the beginning of the past century, almost all of humanity received information and knowledge from people they knew and trusted: parents, elders, teachers, physicians, and religious leaders. Today, the mass media have effectively supplanted many of these sources. In the United States, for example, the average five-year-old child spends fifteen hours a week watching television and is subjected at the same time to thousands of commercial advertisements (Swimme 1997). As these children grow older, many will actually spend more time in front of a television than they will in school. As adults, they will watch nearly five hours of television every day—which means that this activity will absorb more time than any other except work or sleep (Korten 1995). When one factors in the time spent with other forms of media—newspapers, radio, the Internet, and even billboard advertising—the influence of the mass media can be seen to be little less than overwhelming.

Perhaps just as disturbing is the degree of concentration in the control of the mass media. Today, fifty large corporations dominate the global media industry, and a mere nine of these wield the greatest influence[3] (Herman and McChesney 1997). Similarly, a mere fifty public relation firms produce the bulk of the world's advertising, and only ten of these account for 70 percent of global advertising revenue (Karliner 1997). Ed Ayres concludes that "our acquisition of information is increasingly filtered through large organizations—whether they be the corporate owners of newspapers or radio stations, their advertisers, or the industry lobbyists who help set the rules . . . by which the media draw their profits" (1999a, 165).

It is not surprising, then, that Paul Hawken asserts that "our minds are being addressed"—or should we say molded?—by "media serving corporate sponsors" (1993, 132). In the following sections, we will examine more closely the second part of his assertion: that they are attempting to "rearrange reality so that viewers forget the world around them." Just how is reality being rearranged? For what purposes? And how does this reinforce our own sense of powerlessness?

Blocking Perception, Perpetuating Denial

One of the main ways that the media disempower us is by facilitating denial. They do this in part by simply blocking our perception—never allowing us to get a clear picture of just what is happening in our world, or why.

At first, this may seem strange. Never has so much information been so readily available to such a large portion of humanity. Ed Ayres likens this, however, to being able to see only the tiny dots or pixels that make up a huge picture. We are overwhelmed with these tiny fragments of information, but seldom are we allowed to step back to see the larger picture. This is particularly a problem with a medium such as television that packages itself into brief "sound bites" produced to catch our attention and produce an immediate impact—but not to build a coherent understanding of just what is happening and why.[4]

Beyond fragmentation—which at first might seem accidental—the media go further by actually obscuring information and sowing doubt. For example, in the debate over climate change, the first line of defense of those with a vested interest in the status quo (like the petroleum industry) is simply to deny that climate change is occurring, or that it is being caused by "natural" phenomena like solar cycles. To facilitate their arguments, well-financed organizations like the Global Climate Coalition are created. Despite the clear bias of these groups, the media inevitably insist on giving them "equal time" in the name of supposed fairness—a strategy that we might call "false objectivity."

Eventually, as the scientific consensus pointing to human-induced climate

---

3. By 2006, just eight giant media firms dominated the U.S. market, three of them "new media" companies: Yahoo, Microsoft, and Google. The five other key media corporations were Disney (ABC), AOL-Time Warner (CNN), Viacom (CBS), General Electric (NBC), and News Corporation (FOX). Most of these are key global players as well.

4. This same fragmentation of knowledge occurs in other areas beyond the media as well—for example, the cult of specialization found everywhere from science to government that makes it difficult to draw information together and see the larger patterns at work.

change became overwhelming, the media changed tactics. Forced to give at least some attention to the reports issued by the International Panel on Climate Change (IPCC), which reached agreement among thousands of the world's leading climate experts, they still continued to publish and air the views of the occasional maverick scientist who might have a contrary opinion (especially at key times when these can have their maximum effect). These views are normally refuted quite easily, but the damage is still done—sufficient doubt is sown to facilitate disbelief and denial in the vast majority of the population.

At the same time, the media downplay the importance of the information available—or its full scope. It is argued that climate change may not happen so fast, that it may not be so severe, that we still have time to delay acting, that humans will be able to adapt, or even that there might be some benefits from climate change. The recommendation of the IPCC that humans should curb greenhouse gas emissions by 80 percent within the next forty years is seldom, if ever, reported. Instead, much of the debate has been restricted to whether or not we should reduce emissions by a mere 5 to 10 percent from the 1990 levels—and whether there is any urgency to make even these limited reductions. Indeed, emissions from the world's largest producer of greenhouse gases, the United States, have actually risen by 16 percent since 1990 while Canada's have risen a whopping 50 percent.[5]

Indeed, the media can be very effective at restricting the terms of a debate on almost any important issue. Noam Chomsky notes that democracies realize that they cannot stifle debate—but that there is no need to do so. If a debate can be kept within a safe range of views, there is no danger of really challenging those who hold power:

> Debate cannot be stifled, and indeed, in a properly functioning system of propaganda, it should not be, because it has a system-reinforcing character if constrained within proper bounds. What is essential is to set the bounds firmly. Controversy may rage as long as it adheres to the presuppositions that define the consensus of the elites, and it should furthermore be encouraged within these bounds, thus helping to establish these doctrines as the very condition of thinkable thought while reinforcing the belief that freedom reigns.
>
> In short, what is essential is the power to set the agenda. (Chomsky 1989, 48)

Together, by fragmenting and obscuring information, by sowing doubt, and by constraining debate, the media are able effectively to block a coherent vision of the crises facing humanity and the wider Earth community. A small number

---

5. The plan being debated by the U.S. Congress in June 2009, for example, will only reduce U.S. greenhouse emissions by 4 percent by 2020 in comparison to 1990 levels—much less than the target originally set by the Kyoto Protocol of a 7 percent reduction by 2012. The plan would reduce greenhouse emissions much more significantly in the longer term (to 83 percent of current levels by 2050), but the pace of reductions—initially, at least—seems to be painfully slow. Indeed, may experts argue that we should be aiming to reduce emissions by 80 percent over current levels *by 2020* to avoid the worst effects of climate change.

of people, no doubt, are able to break through these veils of distortion and deception, but they can largely be marginalized from the dominant discourse because they are viewed as a mere fringe beyond the bounds of rational debate. For most, though, these tactics are sufficient to maintain and reinforce denial.

Inculcating Inadequacy, Sapping the Imagination

The mass media also disempower us through a combination of more subtle yet still potent means. Michael Lerner (1986), for example, observes than television deepens internalized powerlessness by its very format: most programs run between thirty minutes and an hour, during which time a problem is presented in some form and then resolved. This simplification of life may unconsciously build a sense of inadequacy over time, making us doubt the strength of our own power-from-within.

Similarly, the mass media of all types portray people who are both beautiful (the media's idea of "beautiful," at least) and materially "successful." By doing so, they create the impression that it is "normal" to be wealthy and beautiful, thus denying the reality of the vast majority of people who have few possessions and a different ideal of beauty. This in turn creates a sense of inadequacy and even self-blame ("there must be something wrong with *me* if I am not like that . . .") that results in a kind of internalized oppression.

Today's mass media are also largely responsible for the homogenization of cultures that Vandana Shiva refers to as the "monoculture of the mind." By portraying one culture as normative, all others are in turn devalued. This, too, reinforces internalized oppression.

As well, the media disempower by isolating and alienating us from community. In times past, most entertainment occurred in group settings. The chance to listen to music, hear stories, dance, or watch a drama occurred in community, and often there was time for talking to neighbors and friends or to participate in some real, immediate fashion. Modern media are, in contrast, largely passive and individual in nature.[6] Television, in particular, tends to isolate us from others, even if viewed in a group setting. It draws us in and absorbs us. This in turn alienates us from the community around us, thus undermining the possibility of acting in concert with others, of creating and sustaining power-with. At the same time, it draws us away from relationship with the greater Earth community, alienating us further from nature.

Finally, television, movies, and related media (one could include here many video games) work to restrict our imagination or to warp it, thus circumscribing our creativity and vision. The visual nature of these media draws us in, effectively projecting images into our minds. The relaxed state in which we view them leads to a near hypnotic effect where values and ideas are accepted uncriti-

---

6. One could argue, no doubt, that the Internet may be different from other media in this respect—at least in terms of allowing us to link with other people and to interact. Yet, even here, corporations are also inundating the Net with advertisements, material encouraging the sexual exploitation of women, and often-violent games. The more positive use of the Internet is largely the result of individuals and people's organizations that are in some way able to subvert this new media for transformative action.

cally in a process of passive absorption. Unlike reading or listening to a story, we need not create our own images nor exercise our imagination. At the same time, we open ourselves to a subtle warping of the soul. The average child in the United States, for instance, views approximately forty thousand murders on television by the age of eighteen (Ayres 1999a) and may also take part in fictitious—though realistic—killings through video games. How can this not affect the way children will see the world, the kind of visions of the future they will have? Yet imagination—and the creativity that goes with it—provides the key foundation for our ability to develop power-from-within.

Reinforcing Addiction

Not only do the mass media reinforce denial and sap our imaginations, but they also actively feed and intensify modern capitalism's driving addiction— greed—by using advertisements and images to encourage consumption. We are bombarded with hundreds, even thousands, of messages every day that tell us with varying degrees of subtlety that our intrinsic worth depends on our capacity to acquire. As meaningless and empty as the pursuit of happiness through consumption may be, its message affects us all by reducing us to the position of mere receptacles for the latest products of the corporate economy.

The age of consumer capitalism began in earnest shortly after World War II in the United States. At that time, retailing analyst Victor Lebow made one of the clearest statements on the need to inculcate the addiction of consumption:

> Our enormously productive economy . . . demands that we make consumption our way of life, that we convert the buying and use of goods into rituals, that we seek our spiritual satisfaction, our ego satisfaction, in consumption. . . . We need things consumed, burned up, worn out, replaced, and discarded at an ever increasing rate. (Quoted in Durning 1995, 69)

In order to make consumption a way of life, modern capitalism has undertaken what psychologists Allen Kanner and Mary Gomes refer to as the "largest single psychological project ever undertaken by the human race" (1995, 80). The amount of money spent on this project of mass indoctrination is simply staggering, reaching nearly half a trillion dollars in 2008: more than $80 each year for every man, woman, and child on the planet and over six times the annual investment required to ensure adequate nutrition, healthcare, water, and education for all of humanity. The sheer volume of psychological expertise and research that these resources can purchase is little less than overwhelming.

Not surprisingly, then, the most frequent and persistent messages we receive are sales pitches. And just how do most of these work? By subtly instilling a sense of inadequacy or unhappiness in each of us. Often they accomplish this by creating an image of an "ideal consumer" that we will wish to emulate. We are told that if we want to be beautiful, successful, or happy, we must buy a certain product. In essence, then, advertising continually tries to create false needs in us by telling us that we must have "just one more thing" to be truly happy—that is, it works by encouraging addictive behavior.

Strangely enough, people actually remember few ads clearly. In some sense, the chief aim of advertising is to sell consumerism itself—to create a consumerist, addictive culture. The net effect is to construct in each of us what Kanner and Gomes call "the consumer self", a false self that "arises from the merciless distortion of authentic human needs and desires" (1995, 83). Our very identities are warped and twisted by the consumerist enterprise. At the heart of advertising is a falsehood that claims that our success or happiness depends on what we possess. Beyond the level of basic needs, however, this assertion is evidently false. It is repeated so frequently, though, that we begin to believe it. We seek to satisfy authentic human needs for love, beauty, friendship, and meaning with a hollow substitute. (Not surprisingly, wealthy societies are often less happy today than they were forty years ago!) We live in a state of delusion.

This affliction, however, is not limited to the wealthy. The same messages are fed to billions of people who must struggle daily simply to satisfy their basic needs. For them, the siren song of consumerism is a continual taunt. They can never hope to achieve the conspicuous levels of consumption displayed in advertisements. The message they receive, then, is that they can never hope to be truly happy, successful, or beautiful. At best, they can seek a momentary share in pleasure by buying a soft drink, cigarette, or a package of potato chips that they can probably ill afford. In the end, the consumerist message reinforces a sense of internalized oppression in the poor, or even despair.

In both North and South, consumerism deepens a sense of alienation and the breakdown in community. As more and more energy is directed toward consumer pursuits (or to the surrogate consumer world created by television and other media), less and less is available for authentic relationship, the contemplation of nature, community, and the creation of power-with. This leads to a deeper sense of alienation and emptiness, something that in turn feeds the frenzied addiction of consumerism.

Sustaining delusion

Consumer ideology has become so pervasive and so powerful that it now constitutes the virtual cosmology of modern capitalist societies. By cosmology we mean a vision of the nature of reality and the purpose of life—something we will explore in more depth in the upcoming chapters of this book.

Brian Swimme (1996 and 1997) is particularly adept at making this point. He speaks of reflecting on how, in traditional societies, children sat around the fire at night to hear the elders' stories of how the universe came into being, how humans emerged, and the place of humanity in the wider Earth community. Where, he pondered, is this happening today? What is the source of our functional cosmology? Then one day he realized:

> We take our children, we put them in the dark, we turn on the TV set, and it's not the shows, *it's the advertisements.* . . . The advertisement is the modern cosmological story. . . . The advertisement in a very concentrated form tells you everything that matters: It tells you the nature of the universe, it tells you the nature of the human, it gives you role models. The nature of the universe?

Storehouse of materials. Nature of the human? Get a job and buy commodities. The ideal human? Someone hanging out by the pool drinking a Pepsi and laughing. (Swimme 1997)

In the same lecture, Swimme goes on to lament that thousands of the world's most gifted psychologists work long hours trying to find ways to plant this message right into the soul of every child.[7] Indeed, most other sources of cultural transmission pale in comparison. As we have noted previously, children will be saturated with an average of thirty thousand advertisements before they ever go to school. By the time they are teenagers, they will have spent more time listening to ads than they will spend in high school classrooms.

From a very early age, then, we are indoctrinated into a trivialized cosmology that leaves us feeling forever hollow and empty. We are taught to substitute our authentic need for meaning, love, creativity, and communion with material possessions. Our existence is reduced more and more to working, earning money, and buying as much as we are able to. There is less and less space for what could make us feel truly fulfilled. Moreover, we are increasingly cut off from the deep sources of our own inherent power-from-within. Our imaginations and creativity are stunted and it becomes hard to imagine another way of being in the world. At the same time, our isolation and alienation from each other and from the other beings who share this planet with us reduces our capacity to act in concert to effect real change. The systems of domination weave a web of delusion that cuts us off from our power. As Roger Walsh concludes:

Our usual state of mind, say Eastern psychologists, is neither clear, optimal, nor wholly rational. Rather, our addictions, aversions, and faulty beliefs color and distort our experience in important yet subtle, unrecognized ways. Because they are unrecognized, these distortions constitute a form of delusion (*maya* is what Easterners call it), a form that is rarely appreciated because it is culturally shared.

Though such a claim may sound strange at first, it is actually consistent with the thinking of many eminent Western psychologists. "We are all hypnotized from infancy. We do not perceive ourselves and the world about us as they are but as we have been persuaded to see them," said Willis Harman of Stanford University. (Walsh 1984, 33)

DELVING DEEPER: PERSPECTIVES FROM ECOPSYCHOLOGY

Is there any hope of escape from the webs of internalized oppression, denial, addiction, and despair that entrap and paralyze most of humanity? At first,

---

7. Carol Herman, senior vice president, Grey Advertising, made this clear when she stated: "It isn't enough to just advertise on television. . . . You've got to reach kids throughout their day—in school, as they're shopping in the mall . . . or at the movies. You've got to become part of the fabric of their lives." Quoted in "Selling America's Kids: Commercial Pressures on Kids of the 90's" by the Consumers Union (http://www.consunion.org/other/sellingkids/summary.htm).

the bonds that hold us may seem unbreakable. Yet the hollow cosmology of consumerism that attempts to lull us into complacency never really manages to quench our deep yearnings for communion, creativity, and beauty. In our heart, we know that something is wrong, that we are somehow incomplete. Herein may lie a key to our liberation.

One sign that the lifestyle of consumerism fails to satisfy is the growing epidemic of depression in affluent societies. The World Health Organization now ranks depression as the second most common disease in the wealthy nations of the North—even more prevalent than cancer. Furthermore, there is strong evidence to suggest that depression becomes more common as societies move from the satisfaction of basic needs to conspicuous consumption. For example, adults in the United States born in the decade after World War II are three to ten times more likely to suffer depression than those born before World War I. The British psychologist Oliver James goes so far as to assert that "the closer a nation approximates the American model—a highly advanced and technologically developed form of capitalism—the greater the rate of mental illness in its citizens" (Gardner 2001, 14).

Given our preceding analysis, this should hardly come as a surprise; attempting to satisfy the need for communion and beauty with addictive consumption can never lead to real happiness. In contrast, Gary Gardner (2001) points to studies of the Old Order Amish people in the state of Pennsylvania (U.S.) who still live a life close to the land with strong community bonds. Their simple lifestyle eschews television, electricity, cars, and many other modern conveniences. At the same time, though, their strong local economies enable them to cover their basic necessities for food, clothing, and shelter quite ably. While their lifestyle is in some respects austere, the rate of mental illness among the Amish is very low—indeed, one-fifth the rate found among those living with modern comforts in the nearby city of Baltimore.

What can we learn from this? Certainly we need not conclude that all modern technology and material well-being are in and of themselves to blame. No doubt impoverished people living in conditions of violence and urban squalor also suffer high rates of mental illness. The key difference between the Amish and their neighbors in Baltimore is that the Amish still live in a close-knit community—a community that has not been undermined by a consumerist ideology and lifestyle. Looking deeper still, we can also observe that this sense of community is not limited to the people alone. The Amish cultivate the soil in a traditional way that allows them to live very close to the land. They have lived for generations in the same place: they live in community with the land itself and care for it as their primary source of sustenance.

In contrast, modern, urbanized societies both North and South are increasingly alienated from community—both with their human and nonhuman neighbors. Over 45 percent of the world's population now lives in cities, and this proportion continues to grow. In the nations of Latin America, Europe, and North America, the percentage often climbs to over 70 percent. At the same time, population is less and less rooted in a specific place. In the United States, this rootlessness has reached an extreme—20 percent of the population changes residence every year (Sale 2001). Together with the influence of consumer culture (which in itself is one of the driving forces of urbanization and mobility), these trends make it more and more difficult for us to experience a sense of community. We have become increasingly disconnected from our neighbors, the land, and the creatures who share it with us.

In order to analyze this sense of disconnection and alienation more deeply, it is helpful to turn to the emerging study of ecopsychology. Unlike most other branches of psychology—which seldom look further than relationships within immediate families—ecopsychology asserts that we must look at a much wider web of relationships, including our relationship to the Earth itself. At its heart is the belief that, at the deepest level of our psyches, we are still fundamentally and inextricably "bonded to the Earth that mothered us into existence." In looking at how we ruthlessly exploit our planet, ecopsychology maintains that this abuse is in some ways a projection "of unconscious needs and desires" similar to a dream or hallucination. It claims, though, that the way we subjugate our living planet reveals much more about our "collective state of soul" than do our dreams, which we do not easily mistake for reality. "Far more consequential are the dreams we . . . set about making 'real'—in steel and concrete, in flesh and blood, out of the resources torn from the substance of the planet" (Roszak 1995, 5).

Ecopsychosis: Living a State of Disconnection

In examining the dysfunctional lifestyle of people in modern societies, ecopsychology observes that we are living a kind of collective psychosis. If we understand psychosis as attempting to live a lie, the root of our current collective psychosis (or delusion) lies in our sense of disconnection from others, the perception that we somehow exist as isolated ego-selves. To the extent that we live disconnected from other beings—human and nonhuman—we accept the lie that we have no real ethical obligation to other people, no need to care for other living beings, and no real bond to the Earth that sustains us.

Many authors have tried to name and describe the nature of this psychosis; each reveals new facets of this collective disorder of our souls. Thomas Berry, a cultural and religious historian turned "geologian" (or "Earth scholar"), observes that "we have become autistic in relation to the natural world. We have closed it out as an acceptable world" (quoted in Scharper 1997, 116). Like those suffering from autism, we cannot seem to truly feel, hear, or perceive the presence of others. We have become cut off from the possibility of relationship or communion, including communion with the wider Earth community. As Ralph Metzner writes, "We have become blind to the psychic presence of the living planet and deaf to its voices and stories, sources that nourished our ancestors in preindustrial societies" (Metzner 1995, 59).

How did this kind of virtual autism develop? Largely through the process of psychic numbing that we previously explored in relation to denial. As Sarah Conn notes:

> Many of us have learned to walk, breathe, look, and listen less, to numb our senses to both the pain and the beauty of the natural world, living our so-

called personal lives, suffering in what we feel are "merely personal" ways, keeping our grief even from ourselves. Feeling empty, we then project our feelings onto others, or engage in compulsive, unsatisfactory activities that neither nourish us nor contribute to the healing of the larger context. Perhaps the currently high incidence of depression is in part a signal of our bleeding at the roots, being cut off from the natural world, no longer as able to cry at its pain or to thrill at its beauty. (1995, 171)

Psychic numbing and the autism it spawns, then, are also closely related to compulsive, addictive behaviors. Indeed, Metzner observes that "our inability to stop our suicidal and ecocidal behaviour fits the clinical definition of addiction or compulsion" insofar as we cannot cease this behavior even though we know that it is harmful to ourselves and to others (1995, 60). Similarly David Korten reflects:

No sane person seeks a world divided between billions of excluded people living in absolute deprivation and a tiny elite guarding their wealth and luxury behind fortress walls. No one rejoices at the prospect of life in a world of collapsing social and ecological systems. Yet, we continue to place human civilization and even the survival of our species [and that of many others on this planet] at risk mainly to allow a million or so people to accumulate money beyond any conceivable need. We continue to go boldly where no one wants to go. (1995, 261)

Why do we do so? In large part, it is because our very perception of what is normal and sane has been warped to an extreme degree. In contrast, for most of human history we lived in small tribal or communal groups in direct contact with the ecosystems that sustained us. From such a perspective, today's technological, urban civilization is not at all normal; in fact, as Edward Goldsmith points out, it is "highly atypical of humanity's total experience on this planet—necessarily short-lived, totally aberrant." To consider our current reality as normal is akin to mistaking cancerous tissue for "a healthy organism" (1998, xiii). Similarly, Theodore Roszak considers urban industrialism to be "at the outer limit of a particularly exaggerated oscillation" (1992, 307). Humans evolved in a context rich in tradition, community, and direct, sensual contact with the natural world. Not surprisingly, then, we are actually ill adapted for the isolating reality of our modern technological existence.

Psychology, as much as any other science, has emerged from a distorted framework colored by this aberrant state. By and large, psychology has analyzed humans as relatively isolated individuals with a strong emphasis on the immediate relationship to family, perhaps at times extended to friends and co-workers. The wider world is seen as something cold, objective, and even inhospitable. Yet, at one time (and to this day in many indigenous societies), psychology existed in a wider context:

Once upon a time, all psychologies were "ecopsychologies." Those who sought to heal the soul took it for granted that human nature is densely embedded in the world we share with animal, vegetable, mineral, and all the unseen powers of the cosmos. Just as all medicine was in times past understood to be "holistic"—a healing of body, mind, and soul—and did not need to be identified as such, so all psychotherapy was once spontaneously understood to be cosmically connected. It is peculiarly the psychiatry of modern Western society that has split the "inner" life from the "outer" world—as if what was inside of us was not also inside the universe, something real, consequential, and inseparable from our study of the natural world. (Roszak 1992, 14)

Most Western psychological perspectives, then, remain limited in helping us to analyze and understand the collective psychosis that disconnects and isolates us from the wider community of beings. Indeed, modern psychotherapy is almost always focused on the individual and takes place within the isolating confines of an office or consulting room. Insofar as it tends to dissociate the individual from the wider communal and ecological context, it is actually rooted in the same distorted view of reality that we are here attempting to understand. In contrast, an ecopsychological perspective can help us frame our collective psychosis in a wider context that allows us to gain new insights into both how it began and how it might be healed.

The Genesis of Ecopsychosis

How did the psychosis we are currently suffering come into being? How did we come to this state which, from the wider view of human history, is "highly atypical" and even "totally aberrant"? It is as though we have all forgotten something that was once common knowledge: we have lost touch with our need for shared community, an intimate bond with the land, a vital relationship to the wider biotic community, a feeling of respect and reverence for the Earth that sustains us, and a sense of awe for the cosmos that embraces all. Virtually every traditional culture—all of our ancestors—knew and lived these things. How has this knowledge, this way of life, been lost?

Ralph Metzner (1995) believes that we may be suffering a form of collective, traumatic amnesia. Just as a victim of some unspeakable act of violence may suppress memories, a collective trauma (or series of traumas) may have caused us to progressively forget what was once our shared wisdom. Interestingly, Chellis Glendinning notes that trauma is also at the root of all addictive behavior; addictions occur "because some untenable violation has happened *to* us." She proposes that:

The trauma endured by technological people . . . is the systemic and systematic removal of our lives from the natural world: from the tendrils of earthy textures, from the rhythms of sun and moon, from the spirits of bears and trees, from the life force itself. This is also a systemic and systematic removal of our lives from the kinds of social and cultural experiences our ancestors assumed when they lived in rhythm with the natural world. (1995, 51-52)

While it is unclear whom Glendinning considers to be "technological people," it seems evident that this same process has been experienced in different ways by most modern peoples of both the North and South. Some of the traumas that have occurred over generations include:

- The ancient trauma associated with the shift from hunter-gatherer to agricultural and city-state cultures. Often these shifts were not peaceful, but were the result of a violent imposition through war and conquest.

- The traumas that European peoples experienced as a result of the black death (mid 1300s), the beginning of "the little Ice Age" (1400s), and the witch-hunts. Together, these led to an increasingly hostile attitude toward both women and the natural world—something that was imposed on others as Europeans began invading and colonizing other lands.

- The traumas of those forcibly removed or displaced from their lands through slavery or conquest in Africa, Australia, Asia, and the Americas. The extent and depth of these traumas is hard to overestimate—especially since they were often accompanied by massive death and suffering wrought by violence, ill treatment, and disease.

- The traumas associated with the mass migration of Europeans to the Americas, Australia, and other parts of the world. This migration often involved a degree of coercion. Many of the migrants were fleeing some kind of persecution. Many more were poor peasants attempting to escape famine and poverty—often lured to a "new world" by false promises. In the extreme, there were those who were transported against their will, such as the impoverished prisoners of Britain and Ireland sent to Australia.

- The trauma of industrialization that directly or indirectly forced (and continues to force) people off the land into crowded and often-violent cities. This trauma continues today, particularly in the global South, as people migrate from rural areas to cities in the hope of escaping poverty and finding work, education, and healthcare.

All of these traumas have undermined the ancient connections that once bonded us to land and kin. Some aboriginal cultures still preserve, at least to some degree, these connections. For most of us, however, they have been seriously eroded over time. Deep within, we carry the scars of these traumas in our souls. They affect all of us—the oppressed and the oppressors, the exploited and the exploiters, the impoverished and the affluent—albeit our ways of dealing with or expressing these traumas may be different. Indeed, Chellis Glendinning concludes:

Technological society's dislocation from the only home we have ever known is a traumatic event that has occurred over generations, and that occurs again in each of our childhoods and our daily lives. In the face of such a breach, symptoms of traumatic stress are no longer the rare event caused by a freak accident or battering weather, but the stuff of every man and woman's daily life. (1995, 53)

Glendinning goes on to note that the classic response to trauma is the process of dissociation through which "we split our consciousness, repress whole arenas of experience, and shut down our full perception of the world" (1995, 53). One manifestation of this split consciousness is the humanly constructed dichotomies we have created such as mind/body, male/female, matter/spirit, human/nature, wild/tame. Similarly, Robert Greenway (1995) affirms that industrialized cultures have inflated the process of "distinction making" to the point where it dominates our entire consciousness. Dualism has become our cultural mode. Indeed, we experience consciousness as separation, even though in fact we can never really be separate from the biosphere that sustains us.

The artificial environments that we have constructed for ourselves, most notably in urban areas, compound this dislocation by further isolating us from the nonhuman world. Theodore Roszak reflects that cities began as the megalomaniac imperial fantasies of kings and pharaohs. They were "born of delusions of grandeur, built by disciplined violence, and dedicated to the ruthless regimentation of [humanity] and nature" (1992, 219). In many ways, modern cities continue in this tradition. In particular, the modern industrial city could be understood as a kind of collective "body armor" for our culture, a "pathological effort to distance us from close contact with the natural continuum from which we evolve" (1992, 220).[8] James Lovelock reflects on this reality:

How can we revere the living world if we can no longer hear the bird song through the noise of traffic, or smell the sweetness of fresh air? How can we wonder about God and the Universe if we never see the stars because of the city lights? If you think this is an exaggeration, think back to when you last lay in a meadow in the sunshine and smelt the fragrant thyme and heard and saw the larks soaring and singing. Think back to the last night you looked up into the deep blue black of a sky clear enough to see the Milky Way, the congregation of stars, our Galaxy. (1988, 197)

Lovelock notes that many of us living in cities see the greater world only through the window of the television screen. We are trapped in a world where we are reduced to spectators, not players, a world constructed and filtered by human dominance. He concludes, therefore, that "city life reinforces and strengthens the heresy of humanism, that narcissistic devotion to human interests alone" (1988, 198).

Our ecopsychosis is also transmitted and reinforced by the way we raise our children. Indeed, the creation of the separative self begins at a very early age,

---

8. Of course, many people—perhaps the majority of those living in cities—do not do so completely voluntarily. Many have been forced by economic circumstances, or the hope of a better education, to migrate to cities. Still, the isolating effect is the same. Indeed, those living in poor slums may be particularly affected, since they are seldom able to escape the confines of the city, and their neighborhoods often suffer a more degraded environment.

often from the moment of birth. Modern medical practice—at least until very recently (and to this day in many places)—separates newborns from their mothers almost immediately after birth and places them in the sterile surroundings of a nursery, surrounded by other distressed babies. In many cases, a bottle soon replaces the bond of breastfeeding. Young babies are left to sleep alone at night and parents are discouraged from holding their children too frequently. As Roszak concludes:

> What is the effect of all this but to break the bond between mother and child as early as possible, as if to force the child toward autonomy? . . . In contrast to traditional societies that often prolong the babe-in-arms phase of life well into the first year [and often continue to breastfeed for much longer], our habit in the modern West is to begin forcing the child toward relationless self-reliance from the first breath of life. Babies, fresh from the womb, the most intimate of all relationships, suddenly find themselves expected to become individuals, like it or not. (1999, 59)

Feminist psychology notes that this same process is especially accentuated in the case of males, who are expected to form their gender identity based on separation and differentiation from their mothers. Males are expected to root out "the woman within." This requires a tremendous act of will beginning at a very early age—something that permanently warps and stunts male identity. Marti Kheel observes, "The self-identity of the boy child is thus founded upon the negation and objectification of an other" (quoted in Roszak 1999, 88). Males are left emotionally isolated, trapped by the hard-shelled boundaries of their egos. To defend these boundaries and assert autonomy, dependence must be denied, often through competition, domination, exploitation, or violence. Indeed, we may see this as the fundamental psychological root of patriarchy.

As a result of the creation of the separative self from infancy, ecological philosopher Paul Shepard observes that people in modern industrialized societies (particularly males) are developmentally crippled from an early age. In fact, we "may now be the possessors of the world's flimsiest identity structure—by Palaeolithic standards, childish adults." As a consequence of this collective pathology, we display a tendency to "strike back at the natural world that we dimly perceive as having failed us" (quoted in Metzner 1995, 58). Similarly, our need to engage in endless competition against one another can be seen as a manifestation of this same pathology.

Not surprisingly, then, there is a link between our alienation from the wider Earth community and our quest for domination. The experience of separation and autonomy that has come to characterize modern consciousness is "the essential context for domination," and "domination is the root of exploitation" (Greenway 1995, 131). Why is this so? Psychologists have observed that domination is often an attempt to deny the reality of dependence. Just as men with a patriarchal mind-set may try to deny their dependence on women by subjugating them, so too do technological societies attempt to deny their dependence on the Earth through domination. As Mary Gomes and Allen Kanner point out, "human dependence on the hospitality of the Earth is total, and this is extremely threatening to the separative self. By dominating the biosphere and attempting to control natural processes, we can maintain the illusion of being radically autonomous." They also note that this kind of denial of dependence often results in a parasitic relationship, as we have seen in analyzing capitalism's quest for unlimited growth. "The unacknowledged dependence makes us act as parasites on the planet, killing off our own host" (Gomes and Kanner 1995, 115).

Widening Our Sense of Self: Awakening the Ecological Psyche

How, then, can we begin to overcome our collective psychosis? How can we heal our souls and move beyond the attitudes of domination and exploitation that cause us to harm each other and the greater community of life on Earth?

Ecopsychology teaches us that the first step is to begin to move beyond our limited sense of "self." Modern Western thought—of which mainstream psychology is a part—has generally restricted the "self" to that which lies within the bounds of our skin; all that lies beyond is the "external world." From a very early age, we are taught to repress what might be called "cosmic empathy" or any kind of "oceanic consciousness." Through a process of progressive psychic numbing, we isolate ourselves more and more from the wider community of life so that we may function as "normal individuals" in the modern world. Interestingly, Freud himself[9] observed that "our present ego-feeling is only a shrunken residue of a much more inclusive, indeed, all-embracing, feeling which corresponded to a more intimate bond between the ego and the world about it" (quoted in Roszak 1995, 12). Theodore Roszak sees this affirmation as a distant precursor to the perspective of ecopsychology. Indeed, ecopsychology could "be defined as the refusal to settle for that 'shrunken residue'" (1995, 12). Instead, it seeks to widen our concept of self, to expand it beyond the rigid confines of the boundary of the skin.

At first, the idea of a wider sense of self may seem strange to those of us whose minds have been formed by modern technological civilization. Yet traditional wisdom has often posited that the greater part of the soul actually lies outside of the body—that the body is *in* the soul, not the other way around. On a purely physical level, the idea of a clear boundary between self and external world is also in many respects an illusion. Our bodies are constantly exchanging materials with the "external world"—indeed, 98 percent of the atoms in our bodies are replaced every year. As well, over half of our dry body weight is made up of nonhuman cells—mainly enteric bacteria, yeasts, and other symbiotic microorganisms that are essential to our survival (Korten 1999). On a mental level, too, we are constantly exchanging ideas and information—our thoughts are the result of interchanges with others.

---

9. Who in other moments referred to nature as something "eternally remote" that "destroys us—coldly, cruelly, relentlessly" (quoted in Roszak 1995, 11).

Each "individual," then, is an open, dynamic system that can survive only through interaction with other people, other organisms, the wider ecosphere, and indeed the cosmos itself.

This does not deny, of course, that we each need a sense of our own uniqueness, of our identity; but this identity need not be formed in defensive opposition to others. The French philosopher Jacques Maritain once wrote, "We awaken to ourselves at the same moment as we awaken to things" (quoted in Barrows 1995, 110). Instead of seeing the separative self as normative, we could seek instead to value and nurture what some feminist psychologists call *the relational self*: "Rather than equating healthy development with increasing autonomy, relational theory suggests that as we mature, we move toward greater complexity in relationships" (Gomes and Kanner 1995, 117). Similarly, ecophilosopher Arne Naess maintains that the process of psychological maturation involves a broadening of one's identification with others, to allow the self to encompass wider and wider circles of being until it comes to include the greater Earth community itself (Barrows 1995).

This widening of our selves is also a deepening. Ecopsychologists believe that at the core of the psyche is what could be called the "ecological unconscious." In some mysterious way, this form of collective unconscious includes a living record of the entire process of cosmic evolution. At the same time, it is characterized by a deep sense of our abiding connection with the Earth. This inner wisdom in the depths of our souls has guided our evolution and permitted our survival. Roszak calls it the "compacted ecological intelligence of our species, the source from which culture unfolds as the self-conscious reflection of nature's own steadily emerging mindlikeness" (1992, 304). The repression of this "ecological unconscious is the deepest root of collusive madness in industrial society." In contrast, "open access to the ecological unconscious is the path to sanity" (Roszak 1992, 320). To the extent that we reawaken to our connection to the Earth and all its living beings, then, we also awaken to our own selves.

Regenerating the ecological unconscious involves a process through which we recover the "innately animistic quality of experience" of the child so that the "ecological ego" is rebirthed into being. As this occurs, "the ecological ego matures toward a sense of ethical responsibility with the planet," which it "seeks to weave . . . into the fabric of social relations and political decisions" (Roszak 1992, 320-21).

Broadening and deepening this expanded sense of self require that we extend our capacity for empathy and compassion. Warwick Fox refers to this as the process of developing "cosmologically-based identification," "having a lived sense of an overall scheme of things such that one comes to feel a sense of commonality with all other entities (whether [one] happen[s] to encounter them personally or not)" (W. Fox 1990, 257). Albert Einstein seems to refer to this same process when he noted:

[Human beings are] part of a whole, called by us the "Universe," a part limited in time and space. [We] experience [ourselves], [our] thoughts and feelings, as something separated from the rest—a kind of optical delusion of

[our] consciousness. This delusion is a kind of prison for us, restricting us to our personal desires and to affection for a few persons nearest us. Our task must be to free ourselves from this prison by widening our circles of compassion to embrace all living creatures and the whole of nature in its beauty. (quoted in Chang 2006, 525)

At first, this may seem to be a daunting task; compassion and interconnection, while valued by all the world's great spiritual traditions, receive little affirmation in the culture of competitive capitalism. Indeed, many believe that modern industrial growth societies are characterized by a kind of "Thanatos"[10]—a deadening of the soul caused by our resistance to the "invasion of boundaries of the individual" for "fear of personal disintegration" (Sliker 1992, 123). The thought of loosening our boundaries or expanding our sense of self may even evoke a sense of terror. Yet the great opening that compassion entails also opens us to the energy of Eros, the passionate embrace of life, and to the beauty and wonder of the cosmos itself. Further, when we acknowledge our dependence on others, including our dependence on the greater Earth community and the cosmos that envelops it, "we allow gratitude and reciprocity to come forth freely and spontaneously" (Gomes and Kanner 1995, 115). We liberate a new energy, a fire that can inspire and sustain us in the struggle to heal our world.

Beauty, Wonder, and Compassion

Certainly this is an inspiring vision, but how can we move toward it? First, we must remember that the knowledge of our deep connection to the Earth and its evolutionary processes is already present in us through the ecological unconscious. It need not be created *ex nihilo*; rather, it needs to be reawakened through a process that brings its deep memory to consciousness once again. Ultimately, this reawakening must be nurtured by love, beauty, and wonder—forces that open us to all that is best within us.

Here ecopsychology makes an observation that is of key importance to those of us working for integral liberation and the healing of the planet. If we assume that people are greedy and brutish by nature, or if we assume that people are stupid and self-destructive, our tone and discourse are likely to be contemptuous, overbearing, and authoritarian. We begin to use the tools of power-over, which in turn disempowers those we supposedly wish to motivate to action.

Of all these authoritarian tools, guilt and shame may well be the most dangerous. Certainly many of us, in our heart of hearts, feel guilty about the state of the world and our own responsibility for creating it. This is natural, and within bounds may even be healthy. Yet encouraging guilt, attempting to shock and shame people into action, will inevitably prove to be counterproductive: "Shame always [has] been among the most unpredictable motivations in politics; it too easily slides into resentment. Call someone's entire way of life into question, and what you are apt to produce is defensive rigidity" (Roszak 1995,

---

10. A Greek word meaning "death"; also the Greek god of death.

15-16). Shame closes us in on ourselves; it paralyzes us. Feeding guilt increases our sense of disharmony, leading to greater isolation, alienation, and denial.

Playing on guilt may also have other dangerous side effects. Roszak believes that "authoritarian politics roots itself in the guilty conscience" which begins by "convincing people they cannot trust one another, that they cannot trust themselves" (1992, 230). Similarly, Roger Walsh observes:

> Guilt always seeks someone to blame and it is not particularly fussy about who it is. If ourselves, we condemn and denigrate ourselves, thereby exacerbating the unworthiness and inadequacy that started the whole mess. If others, we look for people to scapegoat. These people may even include the victims themselves. (Walsh 1984, 76-77)

In contrast, ecopsychology suggests that we begin with the belief that people are fundamentally sensitive and compassionate. In our depths, we all carry a great love for our world and all the creatures that inhabit it. We are all capable of being moved by its beauty; we are all able to feel a sense of awe and reverence. By using these as the starting point, we can begin to open people to the power that lies deep within and around them, the mysterious Tao flowing through all and in all.

Indeed, if we can truly encourage ourselves to "widen the circle of our compassion" and expand our sense of self, we will need no external motivation to spur us to action. As Arne Naess observes, "Care flows naturally if the 'self' is widened and deepened. . . . Just as we need no morals to make us breathe . . . [so] if your 'self' in the wide sense embraces another being, you need no moral exhortation to show care" (quoted in W. Fox 1990, 147).

When our action is rooted in the expansive, ecological self, then the kind of moral "ought" associated with guilt or shame becomes superfluous. Love and beauty, rather than obligation, become the foundation of action—an insight long taught by the world's great spiritual traditions. The prayer of the Beauty Way of the Navajo people indigenous to the southwest United States exemplifies this sense of ethics: "My thoughts will all be beautiful, my words will all be beautiful, my actions will all be beautiful, as I walk my life the Beauty Way." As we extend our sense of self, encompassing the beauty around us and harmonizing ourselves with it, we become a part of this unfolding beauty ourselves.

At the same time, experiencing a widened self—including the ecological unconscious—should lead to a sense of fulfillment that enables us to disentangle ourselves from the webs of inadequacy, denial, addiction, and despair that ensnare us. This may be especially true with regard to the addiction of consumerism. As the ecological self grows, the emptiness of the consumer self is replaced by a growing sense of fulfillment and integration. The endless craving for more and more ceases as the void in our being is finally satiated. The ritual of perpetual shopping can then be replaced by more satisfying pursuits such as building community, engaging in artistic endeavors, and contemplating the beauty of nature. As we make this shift, new energies are freed for addressing injustice and healing the planet.

FROM PARALYSIS TO RECONNECTION

We have created a world situation that appears to demand unprecedented psychological and social maturation for our survival. . . . Because it demands greater development and maturation of us, our global crisis may therefore function as an evolutionary catalyst. Necessity may be not only the mother of invention but also of evolution.

This gives us a very, very different view of our situation. For from this perspective our current crisis can be seen not as an unmitigated disaster but as an evolutionary challenge, not just as a pull to regression and extinction but as a push to new evolutionary heights. . . . This perspective gives us both a vision of the future and a motive for working toward it.
(Walsh 1984, 81-82)

The crisis our world experiences certainly does seem to require a new level of collective psychological maturity, a new mode of *being* human in this world. Ecopsychology provides us with insights into what that new way of being human might entail: it provides us with a vision of living in touch with the power of beauty, awe, reverence, and compassion and of re-creating bonds of community with each other, other creatures, and the wider cosmos. How, concretely, might we move toward this vision?

As we have seen, there is no simple answer to this question. There are very real obstacles blocking the path to transformation. We have now come to understand more clearly how the dynamics of internalized oppression, denial, addiction, and despair entrap us and how the systems of domination reinforce these to maintain our state of collective paralysis. In seeking to move toward a new vision, a new way of being in the world, we must ask how we might free ourselves from these snares. At the same time, we need to look at how we might open ourselves to new sources of power and liberate energy for transformative action. In the final section of this chapter, we will explore processes for liberating ourselves from the forces that entrap us and reconnecting ourselves to the creative power of the Tao.

A first process involves the development of our awareness. To be aware means to open ourselves to reality, a reality that includes beauty and joy—but also fear and pain. To begin, we might start with those aspects of reality that facilitate opening most easily—experiences of beauty, awe, and reverence. As the barriers within us begin to dissolve, we can then bring into awareness the reality of disharmony—that beauty has been sullied, that needless suffering abounds, that things are not as they should nor could be.

Acknowledging and processing our emotional responses—particularly our response to the reality of pain—is another key process for reconnecting to authentic power. As Joanna Macy points out, feeling pain for our situation is both natural and healthy—it is only morbid or dysfunctional if we deny or repress it. Repression requires tremendous energy; it saps us of our vitality and dulls our minds and spirits. When we unblock and express our pain, we also unblock the energy of power-from-within. At the same time, sharing and expressing pain can actually weave a connection to others—and indeed a connection to the greater web of life—and help generate power-with (Macy 1995).

In delving deeper into our shared pain, we are also opened to the deep interconnection that bonds us to other people, other living beings, the Earth, and the entire cosmos. We can then begin to find ways of nurturing compassion and building community and solidarity. In so doing, we start to seek a deeper understanding of our situation and new sources of wisdom to guide our action. As we deepen our compassion and build community, we can also learn how to focus our attention and energy more effectively. At the same time, we can seek out a new vision and sense of purpose to inspire us and motivate us in our efforts to heal the Earth community.

As we explore these processes in more depth in the upcoming subsections, we will come to see that they are actually complementary parts of one greater, all-encompassing process of reconnecting to power. Certainly, these processes should not be seen in a linear fashion: it is not a matter of undertaking one, then another in sequential steps. Instead, we need to engage in all of them in a spiraling dynamic of continual deepening. Still, it is helpful to name the processes and explore each of them individually. In so doing, we will begin to see more clearly how we can overcome our paralysis and connect with the Tao of liberation.

Awakening through Beauty

> *Talking of beauty . . . is no mere exercise in aestheticism or babbling about the ineffable. It is a vitally compelling task, directly relevant to our possibilities for survival—or at least for decent and human survival. For this reason we can agree with Plato, who says in the* Republic *that "the aim of all education is to teach us to love beauty."* (Ferrucci 1982, 187-88)

How can we begin to overcome the psychic numbing induced by internalized oppression, denial, addiction, and despair? The psychologist James Hillman (1996) has suggested that we should begin by reawakening the soul through beauty and delight. As we start to recover our aesthetic sense, we also recover our sensuality and begin to dissolve the boundaries that separate us from other beings. As Laura Sewall notes, we then "begin to care for that which we see, and ideally, we find ourselves loving the material world, our Earth. Because love alters behaviour, honouring sensory and sensual experience may be fundamental to the preservation of the Earth" (1995, 203). Ultimately, reawakening the senses and reconnecting with beauty begin to change the way we perceive reality. We move beyond the numbing confines of the ego toward an open, mindful experience of the world.

At the heart of this process is the development of new levels of awareness. Silence and solitude may assist this process: We need to take time simply to pause, to attend to our breathing, to become aware of our bodies and the sensations we experience. In so doing, we develop greater mindfulness. For those involved in often-frenetic activity, it is important to take time simply to *be*, without any fixed agenda.

At the same time, as the Buddhist teacher Thích Nhât Hanh (1997) reminds us, simple acts—washing dishes, cleaning house, drinking a cup of tea, or walking—can also become opportunities for meditation if we focus on what we are doing rather than the thoughts in our minds. This is by no means an easy process, yet little by little we begin to learn to focus our awareness beyond the prison of the ego, essentially to widen our sense of self. Initially, our increased awareness may be limited to our own bodies and our own sensations, but slowly we can also move to expand our awareness to encompass wider and wider circles of the world around us.

On a practical level, a very interesting exercise is to reflect on the things that truly delight us, that truly give us pleasure. Often we find that most of these things require little or no money—for example, spending time with friends, walking outdoors, listening to music, or enjoying a simple meal. On the one hand, this reminds us just how dubious the path of consumerism is as a way to authentic happiness. Most of what truly delights us can be accommodated in a fairly simple lifestyle—indeed, if that lifestyle also includes more time, it might well allow for more opportunities to experience authentic enjoyment.

More importantly, however, the activities that truly delight us, the things that truly make us happy, serve as natural "gateways to reverence." It is particularly easy to pay attention to something we love. Each time we engage in something we enjoy, then, we can make a conscious effort to practice awareness. This in turn helps us to be more attentive in all aspects of our lives. At the same time, we can endeavor to spend more time engaging in these activities—something that brings us joy and renews our spirits (and may also steer us toward a more sustainable lifestyle).

The experience of nature is also particularly important as a way of expanding our awareness and developing mindfulness. Spending time walking in a forest, or by a river, or on the seashore, has a unique power to restore the spirit. As we open ourselves to the sound of birds, of wind in the trees, and of the movement of water, our sense of self can expand beyond the confines of the ego. As we contemplate the beauty of a flower, the sparkling dance of sun on water, the soft sensation of grass on bare feet, we open ourselves to a greater sense of community with all beings.

For some, however, recovering contact with the natural world may be a challenge in itself. This is particularly true for those who live in impoverished neighborhoods in large cities. Yet, even in these cases, possibilities exist. Some communities, for example, have started community gardens on vacant lands. These projects have generated many wonderful benefits: they create a space where communities gather to work together and connect; they produce healthy food that supplements and enriches people's diets; and they provide people with an opportunity to engage with soil, seeds, and plants in a direct, sensual way that heals the soul. Other projects with similar benefits include efforts to restore local watersheds and plant neighborhood trees.

As we reconnect with beauty, particularly the beauty of the land that we inhabit, we also begin to overcome our alienation from place, our sense of rootlessness. In this regard, we may even undertake conscious attempts to promote "land literacy"—learning to identify native species, studying local geography, and coming to understand the interrelation of these in the local ecosystem. These processes help us to recover our sense of being truly "native" to a place, whether we were originally born there or not. Instead of perceiving that we "own" the land, we come to see ourselves as part of it—indeed that in some sense *we* belong to the land. Ultimately, the aim of all these things is to develop *querencia*—a Spanish word that Kirkpatrick Sale defines as "a deep sense of inner well-being that comes from knowing a particular place on the Earth; its daily and seasonal patterns, its fruits and scents, its soils and birdsongs. A place where, whenever you return to it, your soul releases an inner sigh of recognition and realization" (Sale 2001, 41).

As we deepen our awareness, expand our perception, and reconnect to place, we also begin to acquire a profound sense of reverence and love for the Earth and all its creatures. In the terminology of ecopsychology, we develop the ecological self. We begin to care for all life spontaneously—not as a moral "ought" but as a result of love. Sewall observes:

> When fuelled by beauty and sensuality, our relationship with the visible world may move our hearts. As the visible world becomes meaningful and vital, we feel it in our bodies. The sensory world thus becomes directly embodied in us; the relationship is visceral, and subjective experience becomes sensuality. We fall in love. Participation in this way is essential if we are to care for the Earth; we need to view her through "love eyes." (1995, 209)

Despair and Empowerment Work

Just as beauty and delight can move us toward a greater sense of interconnection, so too can processing the emotions associated with our current state of crisis—particularly pain and fear. As we have noted earlier, fear underlies much of our internalized oppression, denial, despair, and addictions. Pain also plays an important role, for much of our fear is fear of pain: the pain we suffer now and the pain we may suffer in the future, our personal pain and our pain for those we love. Powerlessness results when we try to escape from our fear through aversion, addiction, or delusion. Pain, however, is such a strong emotion that it can actually bring us back to reality and force us to acknowledge our fears. This in turn creates new opportunities for growth. Walsh writes:

> Perhaps today's unprecedented threats may call us to more thoughtful living and greater contribution. If we choose to let them, they might strip away our defences and help us to confront both the true condition of the world and our role in creating it. They might call us to examine our lives and values with new urgency and depth, and to open ourselves fully, perhaps for the first time, to fundamental questions of existence. (1984, 77)

By acknowledging and experiencing our emotions, we actually generate solidarity and community, unblock repressed energy, and gain a new sense of clarity and purpose. Ultimately, working through our pain and fear reawakens our spirits and provides us with new resources in the struggle for transformation.

To do this, Joanna Macy suggests that we need to engage in a kind of "despair and empowerment work" (or "the work that reconnects"), which is in some ways similar to the grief work done by those dealing with personal loss:

> Just as grief-work is a process by which bereaved persons unblock their numbed energies by acknowledging and grieving the loss of a love one, so do we all need to unblock our feelings about our threatened planet and the possible demise of our species. Until we do, our power for creative response will be crippled. (Macy 1983, 18)

Macy identifies several stages in this despair and empowerment work. The first step is simply acknowledging our pain and our fear. As noted previously, pain is morbid only if it is denied. The power of fear to paralyze us, too, is greatly multiplied if it remains unspoken. We need to validate our fear and our pain, recognizing that it is both healthy and natural to experience these emotions. Indeed, Macy notes that "we perceive, for the first time in our history, the possibility of our death as a species. Facing our despair and anguish for our world is, in effect, a kind of initiatory rite, necessary to our growing up—to the fulfillment of the promise within us" (Macy 1983, 19).

Once we acknowledge our pain and fear, we must find the courage to truly experience these emotions. Giving information by itself is insufficient. Most of us already know, on some level, that we live in danger, that our future is threatened. We have difficulty acknowledging it, though, because we fear feeling helpless or hopeless. To move beyond paralysis, we need to drop our defenses and stay present to the flow of pain, allowing ourselves to express it. This involves a process of "positive disintegration" through which we learn to let go of our defenses and outmoded forms of being. Art, movement, or ritual can play a role in creatively facilitating this process of lament.

As we open ourselves to the flow of emotions, we can begin to move through them until we reach their true source. Ultimately, our pain—and even our despair—is rooted in compassion, our ability to suffer-with:

> Where, then, does despair fit in? And why is our pain for the world so important? Because these responses manifest our interconnectedness. Our feelings of social and planetary distress serve as a doorway to systemic social consciousness. To use [a] metaphor, they are like a "shadow limb." Just as an amputee continues to feel itches and twinges in the severed limb, so do we feel pain in those extensions of ourselves—our larger body—of which we have yet to become fully conscious. (Macy 1983, 35-36)

Our fear, too, is also often rooted in love; we fear seeing what we care about suffer or die. Once repressed feelings are unblocked, energy is released. "As each of us breaks the old taboos and conditioned responses, we begin to sense this promise within us; we feel new possibilities stir. We are like organisms awakening from sleep, stretching an arm, bending a leg, making sounds" (Macy 1983, 19). In many ways, this process is a kind of catharsis, yet it also goes beyond it:

> To present despair and empowerment work as just one of catharsis would suggest that, after owning and sharing our responses to mass suffering and the prospects of mass annihilation, we could walk away purged of pain for our world. But that is neither possible nor adequate to our needs, since each day's news brings fresh cause for grief. By recognizing our capacity to suffer with our world, we dawn to wider dimensions of being. In those dimensions there is pain still, but a lot more. There is wonder, even joy, as we come home to our mutual belonging—and there is a new kind of power. (Macy 1983, 23)

The final stage in this process, then, is recovering the power of interconnectedness. Ultimately, by unblocking our pain and acknowledging our fears, we open ourselves once again to the greater web of life of which we are a part. We are freed to move beyond the confining shell of the ego illusion and to reconnect with the power of the Tao that flows through all things.

In many ways, we can see despair and empowerment work as yet another way of coming to greater awareness without becoming "overwhelmed by the dread, grief, anger and sense of powerlessness" that pain and fear engender in us (Macy 1983, xiii). Indeed, a high degree of complementarity exists between the process of despair work and the process of awakening through beauty. On the one hand, reconnecting to beauty can strengthen us and give us courage to face our pain. On the other, our pain itself is rooted in love and compassion for the web of life around us. Combined, these processes can no doubt be more effective and powerful than they would be in isolation from one another.

Nurturing Compassion

Along with greater awareness, both despair work and awakening through beauty aim to nurture and deepen our capacity for compassion. Compassion entails a widening of the self beyond the ego, allowing care to flow out of a natural extension of our very being. To the extent that we are truly compassionate, we identify with others and indeed with the entire web of life. Compassion, then, enables us to experience interconnection.

Often compassion is seen narrowly as identification with the suffering of others, but in fact it extends as well to sharing joy, delight, and ecstasy. Beauty draws us out of ourselves and allows us to develop our sensitivity and awareness. We are inspired to awe, wonder, and reverence, all essential aspects of the ecological consciousness of interconnection.

We do not normally associate compassion and awareness with power—probably because most of us still think of power in terms of domination (or power-over) and may even view compassion as a weakness. In contrast, the synergy of power-with depends on both awareness and interconnection. It "involves attentive openness to the surrounding physical and mental environment and alertness to our own and others' responses. It is the capacity to act in ways that increase the sum total of one's conscious participation in life" (Macy 1995, 257). As we deepen our compassion and our awareness, then, we also reconnect to and reclaim our power to act in concert with others. Not surprisingly, Michael Lerner concludes that the fundamental task of a mass psychology of empowerment should be to generate compassion (1986).

Nurturing compassion is a process, indeed a life's journey. As we reawaken to our senses through beauty and delight, as we begin to experience our fear and pain, we develop compassion for ourselves and for others. Attending to the experience of our own bodies may also open our intuitive faculties, increase our sensitivity, extend our boundaries beyond ego, and put us in touch with new sources of power. In addition, creative activities can help us connect to our power-from-within, giving us the inner strength to leave isolating defenses behind and extend ourselves beyond the limitations of the ego.

As compassion is nurtured, we begin to reach new levels of consciousness effectively neutralizing the limiting effects of internalized powerlessness. We begin to gain a new intuition concerning the nature of reality itself—an intuition of the fundamental connection of all things and all beings.

Building Community and Solidarity

If we are truly going to nurture compassion and awareness, though, we cannot do so in isolation from others. Compassion is real only if interconnection becomes a living reality through community and solidarity. We can never hope to transform our way of being human in the world without the support and challenge of others committed to the same struggle. Further, the power-with needed to change attitudes and structures can only be exercised in concert with others.

At the same time, we must remember that many of the dominant system's mechanisms for reinforcing powerlessness serve to isolate us from one another and inhibit the development of power-with, as was already noted when in the discussion of the effects of mass media. Meanwhile, addictions such as consumerism attempt to placate our need for human relationships and community with false substitutes. Building community and solidarity, then, can lessen our internalized powerlessness both by alleviating our need for addictive behaviors and by freeing us from the prison of disempowering isolation.

Lerner (1986) notes, however, that entering with others into community must not be a simple return to the structures of the past, such as the dysfunctional families that have wounded so many. To be truly liberating, a community cannot be based on oppressive relationships or inequalities of power and respect. A new kind of community is called for, one that is founded on mutuality and a common commitment to growth and transformative action.

As Marcia Nozick observes, such communities are an indispensable component to the rediscovery of personal power. If it is indeed true that self-knowledge is essential to the development of power-from-within, it is equally true that this knowledge "seldom emerges in isolation, but is usually sparked by an interactive process of *identifying with other people in a common struggle*. Others of like mind and like situation serve as a kind of *mirror* to reflect back images of who we are and what we might become." Community, then, is essential for "the realization of one's own potential to act and affect change in one's life" (1992, 101-2).

To be truly liberating and empowering, community must also help us nurture and practice compassion. Lerner notes that we must first learn to be compassionate with our own selves, understanding that as we struggle to change we "will continue to make mistakes. The goals of our compassion must be to encompass that knowledge, to fight against discouragement, and to accept the limitations of our transcendence without abandoning the efforts to overcome them." At the same time, we must learn to forgive those around us—realizing that they, too, will make mistakes. This calls us to "know and understand the details of each other's life experiences, and possess a detailed understanding of how the social, economic, and political world shaped those experiences" (Lerner 1986, 283).

Community and solidarity, then, are challenging in and of themselves. Yet they are also essential if we are to grow and change, if we are to truly heal the pathology that afflicts and disempowers us. Roszak points out that, "the way out of our collusive madness cannot . . . be by way of individual therapy. We have neither the time nor the medical resources to place our hope in this approach" (1992, 311). Community must be the context in which we seek to heal and challenge each other toward new ways of being.

Cultivating Will

Once we begin to recover and reconnect to power, how can it be focused and made effective? The psychological insights of Roberto Assagioli, the founder of psychosynthesis, can be particularly helpful in looking at this question. Of particular interest to us is his concept of *will*.

The role of the will is often misunderstood and undervalued because it is confused with the Victorian idea of willpower: Will should not be confused with stern self-constraint or futile striving through brute force. In Assagioli's view, the real function of the will is to direct, not impose. Will may at times involve a degree of effort, but it is an effort analogous to that involved in steering a vehicle rather than that of pushing it up a steep hill (Ferrucci 1982).

The development of will enables us to act freely in accord with our own deepest nature rather than under external compulsion (Sliker 1992), thus allowing us to reconnect to our power-from-within. At the heart of many of the techniques that Assagioli describes for cultivating the will is the development of concentration. Piero Ferrucci, one of Assagioli's most prominent students, quotes the philosopher Hermann Keyserling to illustrate why concentration is so important:

The ability to concentrate is a real propelling power of the totality of our psychic mechanism. Nothing elevates our capacity of action more than its development. Any success, no matter in which area, can be explained by the intelligent use of this capacity. No obstacle can permanently withstand the exceptional power of maximum concentration. (Quoted in Ferrucci 1982, 30)

Learning to concentrate, learning to focus our attention, is thus a first step in cultivating the will and recovering our power to act. It is also important to remember that concentration is essentially a highly focused form of attention or awareness. As we have seen, this same capacity for attention lies at the heart of compassion; it enables us to extend our identification by encompassing wider and wider circles of beings. The development of will, then, can also help us to deepen our sense of interconnection with others, and thus our ability to exercise power in concert with others.

Recovering Vision and Purpose

In describing the process of exercising the will, Roberto Assagioli (1965) describes five stages. First, we need a clear goal or motivation toward which we wish to move—a vision that inspires and illuminates us. Only then can we move on to the other stages: deliberation (or discernment), affirmation, planning, and directing the execution of the plan.

Central to the entire process of exercising the will—and, similarly, to exercising power itself—is the existence of a clear vision and purpose. If we know not the direction in which we wish to move, we will remain paralyzed. As Meredith Young-Sowers explains:

> When we have no visions, our bodies and the body of the planet are unsure whether we accept the present state of depression, grief, disease, and annihilation. When we have no visions, the inner energies of our bodies and emotions settle in quietly and begin to resist movement and change. . . . Fear comes from having no plan, no internal story, to allow us to hope. No vision, in other words. (1993, 245-46)

David Korten reinforces this point. To him, it is clear that many of us already have a fairly good idea of the changes we need to make to survive as a species and to ensure the integrity of the biosphere. Yet simply "avoiding extinction is not a sufficient reason to draw us to the difficult changes we must make." In order to "make a choice for life, we must be drawn by a compelling vision of new possibilities grounded in a sense of meaning" (1995, 326).

To some extent, we have already begun to glimpse what such a vision might be. Certainly, it will include an economic system that supports a simple, dignified lifestyle and also respects and cares for the great economy—the Earth and its entire web of life. In addition, it will involve new ways of relating to one another and to all the other beings who share this planet with us—ways that move away from both patriarchy and anthropocentrism and toward a new way of exercising creative power in harmony with the Tao itself. It is also clear that this new vision entails moving beyond the paralysis of internalized oppression, denial, despair, and addiction. It will require that we overcome our ecopsychosis and expand our very sense of self through a new consciousness of interconnection and compassion.

Ultimately, though, the sources of this new vision must also include a new understanding of reality and a new sense of the place of humanity within the cosmos: it will require a living and vital cosmology. As Jim Conlon writes:

> Creativity happens in the psyche when our consciousness moves from being human-centered to creation-centered. This act of creativity is like a resurrection of the psyche. It makes mysticism possible and rescues us from an anthropocentric world view. Otto Rank, a colleague of Freud, writes, "When religion lost the cosmos, [humanity] became neurotic and invented psychology. . . ."
>
> Dr. Stanislav Grof, the prophetic psychiatrist and the author of *The Holotropic Mind*, sees psyche as co-extensive with the universe. The context for healing becomes the cosmos and not the person. We understand that we are in the cosmos and cosmos is in us. The psyche is not an object to be probed and analyzed; rather, it is a source of wonder, sacredness, and celebration. (1994, 31)

In the following chapters, we will explore new insights about cosmology emerging from modern science. As we do so, we will begin to glimpse new and surprising insights into the nature of the universe we live in and the nature of transformation itself. In addition, a deeper sense of purpose will emerge, together with the outlines of a compelling vision that can inspire us toward authentic transformation.

PART 2

COSMOLOGY AND LIBERATION

5.

Rediscovering Cosmology

The Tao gives birth to all things,
the power of Te sustains them.
Each takes on a physical form,
that is shaped by its surroundings.
Each honors the Tao,
and reveres Te,
not because of any compulsion,
but rather because it is their very nature to do so.

The Tao gives life to all beings,
the power of Te nourishes them,
cultivates them, guides their evolution,
comforts and protects them.

To create without possessing,
To act without expectation,
To guide without controlling:
This is the mystery of the power of Te.

(Tao Te Ching §51)

For most of us, the word "cosmology" evokes the image of something abstract, unrelated to our daily lives and certainly far removed from the great transformative challenges facing humanity. We see cosmology as belonging to the realm of philosophers, astronomers, and physicists. While it may be a fascinating area of study, it seems at best marginally relevant to the resolution of the crises currently facing our planet.

Yet we all hold basic—though often unconscious—assumptions about the very nature of reality. These assumptions influence our ability to perceive the problems we face. They may also limit our imaginations, making it more difficult to conceive of a path toward authentic liberation. Nonetheless, we seldom question these assumptions, in part because we may not even be aware that we hold them.

Each of us, however, has learned to see the world in a particular way. Each of us has a worldview, a cosmovision. Where does this view come from? What are the basic beliefs that underlie it? How does this view relate to our current scientific understanding of the universe as well as philosophical and religious thinking? All of these are cosmological questions.

Cosmology can be understood as the exploration of the origin, evolution, destiny, and purpose of the universe. It is a study that is probably at least as old as humanity itself. Brian Swimme (1996) speaks of how our distant ancestors—perhaps three hundred thousand years ago—may have begun the cosmological endeavor by gathering together under the night sky to ponder the great mysteries of the world, to tell stories, and to celebrate rituals. No doubt, they asked the same deep questions that have been posed through countless millennia: How did the world come to be? What is our place in the universe? What is our relationship to the other beings who inhabit the Earth? And how are we to live harmoniously with each other and with the greater community of life of which we are a part?

Cosmology is related to the concepts of worldview and paradigm. A paradigm, in the sense originally employed by Thomas S. Kuhn, refers to the "constellation of concepts, values, perceptions, and practices, shared by a community, that forms a particular vision of reality that is the basis of the way the community organizes itself" (Capra and Steindl-Rast 1991, 34). While a paradigm must be shared by a society, a worldview can be held by a single individual. In contrast, cosmology places less emphasis on the extent to which views are held by society yet is more systematic than an individual's worldview. At its foundation lies some kind of scientific, religious, or philosophical framework—in particular, a story of the universe's origins. In many ways, cosmology is the myth underlying the way we live where "myth" is understood as a story giving meaning (which may or may not be literally true). As such, it profoundly colors our perception of reality, including our assumptions about the nature of change itself. Its implications for transformative praxis, then, are fundamental.

Thomas Kuhn notes that humans cannot live long without formulating a cosmology because it is cosmology that provides us with a shared worldview that permeates everything, giving meaning to our lives (Heyneman 1993). Historically, at the heart of every human culture, there is a cosmology that orients it and imbues it with a sense of purpose. Yet, as Louise Steinman points out, "In the West, there is no longer one Big Story which we all believe in, which tells us how the world was made, how everything got to be the way it is, how we should behave in order to maintain the balance in which we coexist with the rest of the cosmos" (quoted in Heyneman 1993, 1).

Indeed, the culture of modernity that originated in Europe may well be the first human culture to have lost a functional cosmology. This process began nearly four hundred years ago with the Enlightenment and the scientific revolution initiated by thinkers like Copernicus, Galileo, Descartes, and Newton. Martha Heyneman notes that the philosopher Immanuel Kant, reflecting on the scientific laws formulated by Newton, eventually came to the conclusion that it was impossible to know whether the universe was infinite or finite or whether it had an origin in time. In so doing, he effectively renounced cosmological inquiry as futile.

Despite Kant's conclusion, the scientific orthodoxy of the late nineteenth century eventually came to see the universe as infinite and eternal. Yet such a universe could not be considered a cosmos, because an infinite expanse has no form. Therefore, we cannot orient ourselves or feel at home in it. Perhaps even more importantly, the static, eternal nature of such a universe means that it is also bereft of story, myth, and ultimately, meaning.

Until fairly recently, there were few people beyond scientists who embraced wholeheartedly this understanding—which we could call a "pseudo-cosmology." Many, even in Europe and North America, found in religion an alternative cosmology that continued to imbue the world with meaning. As education in modern science became more and more widespread, however, many people unconsciously adopted a split between their scientific and religious beliefs. Cosmology was effectively relegated to the "religious sphere" of their lives. As secularism grew, the idea of a purposeless, infinite universe deepened its roots in more and more people—including many of those with the greatest power to shape the dominant political, economic, and ideological forces in our world.

TRADITIONAL COSMOLOGIES

To gain a better appreciation of what it means to have effectively lost a functional cosmology in the culture of modernity, it is helpful to consider how traditional cosmologies instilled meaning in the world. It should be remembered that, in many cultures, these cosmologies still exercise a powerful influence. Looking at the entire history of humanity, it is the culture associated with modern technology and capitalism that is the aberration from the norm.

Of course, there is a wide diversity of indigenous and traditional cultures around the world. In speaking of these peoples and their cosmologies, then, there is a danger of overgeneralizing. Yet there are broad patterns of commonalities that may be discerned, even if there are also some exceptions. So, while recognizing the limitations to this approach, it is still helpful to look at the most common threads in the cosmologies of aboriginal peoples in order to contrast them with the pseudo-cosmology that now lies at the root of modern industrial growth societies.

At the heart of most indigenous cultures lies a creation myth. Among the Iroquois/Six Nations, for example, the story of creation speaks of Sky Woman coming down from heaven and being aided by the animals of the sea, who gather mud on the back of Big Turtle to form the continent of North America. In a myth of the Australian Aborigines, the Sun Mother awakens the spirits of the creatures and gives them form. In the myth of the !Kung-San of southern Africa, creatures begin living peacefully together underground with the Käng, the Great Master and Lord of All Life, until the world above is created and the first woman is pulled through a hole beside the roots of a wondrous tree, to be followed by other creatures and more people.

Most of these myths speak not only of beginnings but also of the relationship among people and between people and the rest of creation. Often, cultural norms flow out of the creation myth in some way—for example, the Hopi tell how Spider Woman assigned specific responsibilities and roles to both women and men. Creation myths may also explain how discord and disharmony crept into the world, and hint at ways of restoring the original state of balance. In most aboriginal myths, humans are seen as part of a greater family that includes other animals and often extends even further to encompass insects, plants, and "geographical beings" such as rivers, seas, or mountains.

As these myths illustrate, for most indigenous cultures, nature is seen as a closely woven community of living beings. Each thing—be it an animal, a plant, a rock, a river, or a mountain—has a spirit. Everything in the cosmos is perceived to be *alive*. The world has an enchanted quality where humanity feels at home, a part of a greater community of life. True, not all the beings in this extended community may be friendly, at least not all of the time; yet they are all in some ways subjects with their own dignity and place, not mere objects to be used or exploited. In such cosmologies, humans are not detached observers, but rather direct participants in the cosmic story (M. Berman 1981). The Earth itself is experienced as a living being. Indeed, even in Europe through the Middle Ages, the world was considered to have a soul, the *anima mundi*.

In these animistic cosmologies, a strong value is placed on respecting all living things, not only animals and plants but also the rocks, the water, the soil, and the air. The Earth is often understood as a mother who nurtures, but who also deserves a deep respect (and who, if mistreated, can also wreak havoc). To dig deep into the soil to find gold or gems, in such a cosmovision, is tantamount to opening the entrails of the living being who sustains all life. To pollute a stream is to sully the lifeblood of Mother Earth. Indeed, as long as the Earth is seen as something alive and sensitive, a natural constraint exists on a wide range of harmful behaviors.

Of course, peoples living out of such traditional cosmologies still need to take life in order to sustain their own, but only within certain bounds. Hunters can kill other creatures to satisfy a real need for food, but they must do so with a sense of gratitude and respect, never taking more than they truly require to live, and using every part of the animal with care to waste nothing. For example, in the Navajo culture in the southwestern United States, hunters traditionally say a prayer when they need to kill a deer:

A Navajo does not say a prayer to the inner form of a deer explaining his need for the deer and asking for the deer's indulgence simply because it is a kind and gracious thing to do; he [sic] does it because it reminds him of the deer's right to life and the necessity for him not to be excessive or overindulgent in his use of the deer, for such excessive behavior could throw the whole world out of harmony and balance and that would be dangerous to his own survival. (G. Witherspoon quoted in Winter 1996, 51-52)

Indeed, in animistic cultures, the ideas of balance, respect, and reciprocity are often central. In societies based on subsistence modes of production, the concept of persons working to further their own personal economic gain at the expense of others is seen as a perversion. Often, elaborate rituals have been devised to redistribute wealth in the community (such as the potlatch among the coastal aboriginal nations of the Pacific Northwest of Canada and the United States). Cooperation and harmony are valued over competition and personal achievement. The idea of private property is rare—or at least very limited. Certainly, the idea of owning land is an alien concept. How can one own the Earth, or any creature that lives on it, when all of these are understood to be living beings who deserve respect?

None of this means that traditional cultures or animistic cosmologies are perfect. At times, the idea of hostile spirits can lead to fears that paralyze or limit possibilities. The strong demand for harmony can also lead to conformity and a loss of independence and individual freedom. At the same time, most traditional cosmologies do not include a strong evolutionary aspect. Time is conceived as cyclic in nature. This, in turn, may reinforce a conservative tendency that can at times become oppressive. For example, if a cosmology justifies the subjugation of women by men, or the privileges of one class of society, it may be very difficult to change the perceived "natural order," even if it is inherently unjust. That being said, it is only fair to note that there is a wide variation among traditional cultures and cosmologies, and that many have led to a fairly high degree of equality and participatory decision making.

Drawing on the work of Deborah Du Naan Winter (1996, 54) and enriching it with our own reflections, we can summarize seven key characteristics of traditional cosmologies:

1.   At the heart of cosmology lies a myth of creation (implying both a beginning and a purpose for the cosmos) that also addresses some of the questions regarding the place of humans in the world, our relationship to other creatures and each other, and how to reestablish harmony in the face of imbalance.

2.   Nature, including the Earth and the entire cosmos, is viewed as being a living, interconnected web of existence, not as something inert made up of discrete parts.

3.   Humans consider themselves to be a part of nature—the cosmos is our home—and therefore people endeavor to work in harmony with it. A strong ethic of respect pervades human interaction with other creatures. Nature is something to be honored—even reverenced—not subdued, exploited, or even "developed."

4.   Land is understood holistically not as a piece of "dirt" or a collection of "natural resources"[1]—but as a community of living beings. There-

---

1. David Suzuki and Peter Knudtson (1992), for example, note: "One group of British Columbia Natives has translated the word in their language that most closely corresponds to the Western concept of 'natural resources' with the luminous English phrase 'Grasping the Handle of All Life.'"

fore, land cannot be owned but is rather held in common. People do not *own* the land—they *belong* to it.

5. Human society values a sense of kinship, inclusion, cooperation, and reciprocity rather than competition and personal economic gain.

6. Time is viewed as basically circular or cyclic, rather than as linear. Time follows the flow of the seasons and the cycles of birth, death, and rebirth.

7. The purpose of life is conceived in terms of harmony, balance, and sustainability rather than in terms of progress, growth, or economic development.

Thomas Berry, in reflecting on aboriginal cultures, sums up the essence of animistic cosmology as follows:

> The universe, as manifestation of some primordial grandeur, was recognized as the ultimate referent in any human understanding of the wonderful yet fearsome world about us. Every being achieved its full identity by its alignment with the universe itself. With indigenous peoples of the North American continent every formal activity was first situated in relation to the six directions of the universe, the four cardinal directions combined with the heavens above and the Earth below. Only thus could any human activity be fully validated. . . .
>
> The universe was the world of meaning in these earlier times, the basic referent in social order, in economic survival, in the healing of illness. In that wide ambience the Muses dwelled, whence came the inspiration of poetry and art and music. The drum, heartbeat of the universe itself, established the rhythm of dance, whereby humans entered into the entrancing movement of the natural world. The numinous dimension of the universe impressed itself upon the mind through the vastness of the heavens and the power revealed in the thunder and lightning, as well as through the springtime renewal of life after the desolation of winter. Then too the general helplessness of the human before all the threats to survival revealed the intimate dependence of the human on the integral functioning of things. That the human had such intimate rapport with the surrounding universe was possible only because the universe itself had a prior intimate rapport with the human as the maternal source from whence humans come into being and are sustained in existence. (T. Berry 1999, 14)

THE LOSS OF COSMOLOGY IN THE WEST

For people living in modern industrialized societies, the outlook of traditional cosmologies may seem strange and far removed, separated from us by

---

For an aboriginal society—past or present—with the ethos and vocabulary of a viscerally felt bond with the natural world, efforts to economically develop sacred tribal landholdings might well be a far more excruciating and soul searching process than it has historically been for the West."

an abyss of time and psychic space. Indeed, many would argue that humanity has gradually been moving away from animistic cosmologies for the past five thousand years or so, since the first city-state cultures emerged. As we noted in discussing the origins of patriarchy and anthropocentrism, with the advent of such cultures the ideology of domination and exploitation also became more deeply rooted. Social stratification, gender-based oppression, slavery, and—in many cases—ecologically destructive practices, also grew. It would be simplistic to say that the changes in these societies were caused by changes in their cosmologies; rather, as social structures changed, so did belief systems and worldviews. Each transformed and reinforced the other. Still, without a cosmology that in some way licensed the destruction of lives in order to generate and accumulate riches, it is difficult to see how such exploitative practices could have gained ascendency.

After the fall of the Roman Empire, Europe became very much a culture of small rural communities influenced by both Christianity and older worldviews. In medieval cosmology, the world was thought to have a soul—the *anima mundi*—and the cosmos was envisioned as a series of spheres encompassed by the celestial realms. In other cultures and other parts of the world, of course, a wide diversity of cosmologies existed, but the idea of a bounded and ordered cosmos was held nearly universally until the dawn of the scientific age only four hundred years ago. Even then, the new ideas about the universe and the nature of reality filtered only slowly into popular consciousness; they became widespread only through the combined processes of migration, industrial revolution, urbanization, and modern education.

Today, however, inhabitants of industrialized societies have largely lost the sense of the Earth as alive. Spirit has effectively been exorcised from matter, which is now conceived as simply dead "stuff" to be consumed. The celestial realms that once enveloped the Earth have become an endless expanse of cold space with distant stars and galaxies. (Indeed, those living in the illuminated nights of large cities seldom even see the night sky any more and so are rarely touched by the mysterious majesty of the stars and planets.) Morris Berman refers to this as a process of progressive "disenchantment" characterized by a rigid separation between subject and object that denies us a sense of real participation in the unfolding cosmic story. Only rarely do we experience ecstatic union with the universe—perhaps only for brief moments spent in nature when the old sense of connection may magically break through, enlightening us with awe.

Our "normal" experience, though, is one of a world that has become a collection of objects, no longer a community of living beings. In objectifying the world, however, we have also become objects ourselves. As Morris Berman observes, "The world is not of my own making; the cosmos cares nothing for me, and I do not really feel a sense of belonging to it. What I feel, in fact, is a sickness in the soul" (1981, 16-17). Martha Heyneman, reflecting on this process of disenchantment, notes:

> From a kind of cathedral filled with life, light, and music, our world was transmogrified—like those dynamited buildings we see pausing for a moment

in midair before they break up in a billion fragments and fall to earth—into what Alfred North Whitehead so accurately described as ". . . a dull affair, soundless, scentless, colorless; merely the hurrying of material, endlessly, meaninglessly. (1993, 17-18)

Brian Swimme believes that the most fundamental cosmological question may, in fact, be: "Is the universe a friendly place?" For people living out of an animistic cosmology, the answer to this question may be somewhat mixed—and no doubt depends on the traditional culture to which we refer. By and large, though, animism would probably say that, if we are friendly to the cosmos, if we respect it and endeavor to maintain ourselves in harmony with it, the cosmos itself will be friendly to us, at least most of the time.

For those who have adopted the pseudo-cosmology of a boundless, eternal, and amorphous universe, the answer seems much more pessimistic. Mathematician and philosopher Bertrand Russell, for example, reflecting on what seemed to him to be a random and purposeless universe, concluded that "the soul's habitation" could be safely built only "on the foundation of unyielding despair." More recently, geneticist and Nobel laureate Jacques Monad observed that we are alone in the "universe's unfeeling immensity, out of which [we] emerged by chance. [Our] destiny is nowhere spelled out, nor is [our] duty." Similarly, Nobel Prize–winning physicist Steven Weinberg, who sees life as the outcome of a mere chain of accidents, concluded that we live in an "overwhelmingly hostile universe" that, to the extent it becomes comprehensible, also seems to become more pointless (quotations from Roszak 1999, 82-83).

Humans in industrialized cultures, then, are now in some sense homeless people adrift in space and time. We have lost an all-encompassing story that gives us a sense of place in the world. The universe has become a cold and hostile place where we must fight for survival and eke out a habitation amid the meaninglessness that surrounds us. This has profound implications for the human spirit. For, as Heyneman concludes:

Whatever it is for the physicist as physicist or the astronomer as astronomer, a cosmological image is, for all of us, the frame of order of the psyche, the all-containing skin of the imagination and vessel of our knowledge. It is the house of the mind in which all of us, members of a given culture, live. Within some imagined picture of the whole of things we orient ourselves at any moment, make assumptions about what is real, decide what is possible or impossible. The cosmological image is our inner world. Everything we know or imagine is contained, consciously or unconsciously, within it. If the vessel is shattered and the image has no shape, impressions have no meaning. We have no stomach for them—no place inside ourselves to keep them. We are immersed in them, they flow over our surfaces in a ceaseless stream, but we are unable to extract any nourishment from them to add to the structure and substance of an understanding of our own upon which we might base a coherent and deliberate life. (Heyneman 1993, 5-6)

COSMOLOGY AND TRANSFORMATION

As a result of losing a living cosmology that could genuinely sustain and nourish our spirits, we have grasped instead to fill the void within with the surrogate cosmology of acquisition and consumption. In the process, as noted previously, we have become increasingly autistic in our relationship to other beings and to each other. We can no longer hear the voice of the trees, the mountains, the rivers, and the sea; nor can we hear the cries of the poor and marginalized in human society. We have become filled with despair and have lost a vision that could inspire and motivate us to confront the mounting crises around us.

The pseudo-cosmology that emerged from science from the seventeenth to nineteenth centuries, together with the surrogate cosmology of consumerism, has left us crippled in a way that Brian Swimme (1985) compares to the effects of a lobotomy: We are unable to feel the wonder, awe, and reverence that the true nature of the cosmos naturally evokes. At the same time, our imaginations and creativity have been severely circumscribed. It is difficult for us to envision the possibility of a fundamentally different way of living in the world, and nearly impossible for us to see *how* the profound transformations needed could actually come about. In the words of Fritjof Capra, all the world's crises are simply "different facets of one single crisis, which is largely a crisis of perception. . . . There are solutions to the major problems of our time, some of them even simple. But they require a radical shift in our perceptions, our thinking, our values" (Capra 1996, 4).

To illustrate this idea, Ed Ayres (1999a, 5) recounts the story of James Cook's first encounter with Australia's aboriginal people. When the ship *Endeavour* came into Botany Bay on Australia's east coast, it was, in the words of the lay historian Robert Hughes, "an object so huge, complex, and unfamiliar as to defy the natives' understanding." Indeed, it would appear that the Aborigines simply *did not see* the ship that entered the harbor because they had no way of fitting such an object into their worldview. So they simply continued to fish as though the ship were invisible—and indeed, in some sense it *was* invisible for them. It was only when members of the *Endeavour*'s crew boarded their landing boats and headed toward shore that most of the Aborigines fled and hid in the trees while two warriors stood their ground. Only on seeing the smaller boats— something within the scope of their own experience– could they react.

Perhaps we find ourselves in a similar situation. Ayres uses the example to illustrate how we can ignore the overwhelming evidence of crisis all around us: "The 6 billion natives of Earth . . . are being confronted by something so completely outside our collective experience that we don't really see it, even when the evidence is overwhelming" (Ayres 1999a, 6). Yet it is probably equally true to observe that we are also unable to conceive of a path toward authentic sanity and sustainability because our imaginations have been constrained by a particular understanding of reality—by our cosmology.

But what if the nature of reality was radically different from what we had been taught to believe? What if we did not live in an endless, eternal universe governed by mathematical laws and blind chance, but rather in a creatively unfolding cosmos imbued with a sense of deep and abiding purpose? What if evolution was propelled not primarily by ruthless competition, but rather by cooperation and a drive toward complexity—and perhaps even toward mind and consciousness? What if there was no rigid division between matter, mind, and spirit, but rather a close intertwining and intermingling of each? What if the relationship between cause and effect was far more mysterious and creative than we had ever imagined? How might such a shift in our perceptions and beliefs create new possibilities that we have never before been able to conceive?

Lewis Mumford notes, "Every social transformation . . . has rested on a new metaphysical and ideological base; or rather, upon deeper stirrings and intuitions whose rationalised expression takes the form of a new picture of the cosmos and the nature of [humanity]" (quoted in Goldsmith 1998, 433). Today, perhaps as never before, we need a new vision of the cosmos to inspire and guide the profound transformations that are required for the survival of complex life on Earth.

In many respects, this new cosmovision must recapture some of the key elements that made up traditional cosmologies for more than 99 percent of human history. As we have seen, humanity has normally understood itself to be part of a living cosmos imbued with spirit, a world full of a kind of enchantment. As Morris Berman observes, "The complete reversal of this perception in a mere four hundred years or so has destroyed the continuity of human experience and the integrity of the human psyche. It has very nearly wrecked the planet as well. The only hope, or so it seems to me, lies in a reenchantment of the world" (1981, 23).

Yet it is difficult to imagine people simply returning to the vision of animism, at least in its traditional forms. We have been marked by the scientific revolution, and our consciousness has been forever changed—in ways that are arguably both good and bad. It is difficult, for example, to imagine peoples of modern industrialized societies assimilating, in any meaningful way, the traditional myths that have inspired indigenous cultures. We need a way forward, not back, even if that way forward in the end integrates many elements of a more traditional vision.

Heyneman uses the metaphor of a flood to describe the meaningless, purposeless universe upon which we have now been adrift—to varying degrees—for the past four hundred years. Yet, with more optimism, she notes that it may rather be "an ocean we have been crossing, as our ancestors crossed an ocean to get to a new and unknown land" (1993, 18). Over the past century, a new vision of the cosmos has been emerging from science itself—and that vision is in many ways as radically different from the pseudo-cosmology of the nineteenth century as that one was from the cosmology of animism.

Once again, the cosmos is being seen to have a shape and a beginning—and some scientists even discern something that can only be described as purposefulness, or at the very least, directionality. We can now glimpse back in time and space, across the expanse of fourteen billion light years or so,[2] to glimpse

---

2. The current best estimate for the age of the cosmos is 13.73 ± 0.12 billion years, or roughly 14 billion years.

the beginnings of the universe. It is only now, at this time, that we have developed the sensitivities—through the tools of modern science—to do this. Yet, as Swimme (1996, 1) observes, the record of the beginning has always been with us, showering down upon us in the photons of light that have been present since the universe first flared forth eons ago. In contrast to the pseudo-cosmology of eternal space and deterministic laws, the story of the cosmos we are now discerning is marked by evolution and emergence—a process of unique and often unrepeatable stages of development.

As our vision of the macrocosm has changed, so too has the microcosm undergone a radical shift. No longer are atoms or subatomic particles considered to be hard, lifeless "stuff," the "building blocks" of matter. The microcosm is a world of dynamic activity that defies description in any human language. Some physicists compare subatomic entities to thoughts or ideas that can only be described mathematically, but never clearly visualized. The microcosm displays a fundamental unity: each "particle" is in some sense linked to all the others, reaching back to the first moments of the cosmic adventure. Cause and effect are no longer understood in linear terms, but rather intermingle and inform each other. Nor is there a strict division between the observer and the observed—they interact and form but one system. Mind and matter themselves seem to be mysteriously interwoven in a way that makes it difficult to discern whether mind somehow emerges from matter or matter from mind—or do they somehow co-emerge together?

At the level of our own planet and the life that has been birthed forth from it, the new cosmology increasingly suggests complex dynamics of emergence and evolution. In some ways, it would seem that Earth functions in a way analogous to a single organism—Gaia—that has carefully regulated and maintained the ideal conditions for life. While competition between organisms plays a role, cooperation and symbiosis seem far more important, as does the drive toward complexity and diversity. Once again the Earth, including its rocks, its water, and its air, seems to be in some sense alive, and perhaps even imbued with something we could describe as "soul."

At first, the new cosmology emerging from science may seem to be disorienting. Certainly, there are mysteries here that cannot be unraveled with simple explanations. Much is expressible only in the language of paradox, and often it seems we are struggling in the dark to grasp ideas beyond our comprehension. Yet there is also a profound hope in the creativity that emerges in a cosmos ruled by neither mechanistic determinism nor by blind chance. Throughout, ideas like community, relationship, complementarity, and reciprocity seem to come into play.

Could the new cosmology emerging from science rekindle our imaginations and give us new hope? Certainly, it is an important source for a new vision, especially if it is integrated with insights coming out of other sources of wisdom. As Swimme notes:

> The opportunity of our time is to integrate science's understanding of the universe with more ancient intuitions concerning the meaning and destiny

of the human. The promise of this work is that through such an enterprise the human species as a whole will begin to embrace a common meaning and coherent program of action.

One way to identify the significance of what is taking place is to say that science now enters its wisdom phase. . . . We are challenged here with understanding the significance of the human enterprise within an evolving universe. Upon our success in meeting this challenge rests the vitality of so much of the Earth Community, including the quality of life all future children will enjoy. (1996, 3)

Over the next few chapters, we will explore the new cosmology emerging from science in more depth, and at times make linkages to older sources of wisdom that enrich and enliven what is being revealed. In so doing, we must recognize that the mere *study* of cosmology in and of itself is insufficient to the needs of the moment. Ultimately, a shift in our cosmovision must entail an authentic "revolution of the mind," an inner turning, a profound conversion. It must fundamentally reorient our way of being in the world, our way of relating to other creatures, and our understanding of change itself.

First, though, we will seek out more clearly the characteristics and roots of the pseudo-cosmology that currently wields such a powerful influence over people in industrial growth societies. By doing this, we hope to begin to break down the walls that imprison our minds and circumscribe our creativity. Only then can we truly begin to apprehend a new mode of seeing, a new understanding of reality.

6.

The Cosmology of Domination

Do you think you can impose your own order upon the cosmos?
Do you seek to mold the world in order to improve it?
It cannot be done!

The cosmos is the Tao's own sacred vessel.
It cannot be improved.
If you tamper with it, you'll ruin it.
If you try to manage it, you will destroy it . . .

(*Tao Te Ching* §29)

Our common sense does not come directly from our experience, nor is it arbitrary or accidental. Instead our view of the world is shaped by centuries of intellectual tradition, so thoroughly embedded in our educational and social institutions that it is often difficult to appreciate it or its effects. (Winter 1996, 32)

On first reflection, it is probably difficult, if not impossible, for any of us fully to describe the characteristics of our worldview. Basic assumptions, by their very nature, are hard to identify. We take our view of reality as something axiomatic, as a given. While our personal views are in many ways unique, we have absorbed a host of basic beliefs from the cultural milieu in which we are immersed. In some sense, cosmology may be taught, but its teaching normally takes place on a largely unconscious level. We usually adopt a cosmology through a process that more closely resembles osmosis than it does formal learning.

Yet, if it is true that the dominant modern cosmology circumscribes our imaginations and limits the possibility of bringing about the radical transformations that our current crises require, then we must begin by naming and describing this view of the world as clearly as possible. What are its chief characteristics? And how did they come to take shape?

There is probably no single term that fully captures the cosmovision that currently holds sway over modern industrialized societies. Some call it "scientific materialism"; others "mechanism," and still others "reductionalism." While all these have validity, and all partially describe what we are speaking of, none is by itself complete. For now, though, we will call it the "cosmology of domination"[1] because, as we will come to see over the course of this chapter, this view of the world has to a large degree provided a license to "subdue the Earth" and to exploit and pillage the planet. Drawing on the works of Theodore Roszak (1999) and David Toolan (2001), we can outline the key characteristics of this pseudo-cosmology as follows:

1. There is an objective reality that exists outside of one's own mind. Other people also have their own unique centers of consciousness.

2. Mind and matter, including mind and body, are separate entities.[2]

3. The universe is composed of matter, a dead, lifeless substance composed of tiny, normally indivisible, atoms and even smaller, changeless, elementary particles.

4. All true phenomena can be perceived by the senses, often assisted by instruments. Anything that cannot be perceived in such a way—save perhaps the mind itself—is considered illusory, or at best subjective. Spirit and soul are therefore dismissed, ignored, or marginalized to the personal or emotional realm. The real world is reduced to the world of the material, and this world can be measured and quantified. In Galileo's words, "the book of nature is written in the language of mathematics" (quoted in Roszak 1999, 9).

5. The mode of thought preferred is discursive and analytical in nature—that is, an approach that categorizes, divides into pieces, and then delineates. Reality is most accurately studied by rigorous, objective observation and the application of logic. The more detached the observer, the more accurate will be the observation.

6. Nature and the cosmos are understood in mechanistic terms. The universe itself resembles a giant clockwork machine exemplified by the movement of the planets and stars.

7. Since the nature of reality is mechanistic, we can gain a complete knowledge of the whole by breaking it into—or reducing it to—its component parts and studying them one by one. (This approach is often called "reductionalism.")

8. There is no purpose to nature or to the cosmos. There are, though, fixed, eternal laws that have governed and ordered all things for all of

---

1. In using this term, we do not mean to imply that this is the only cosmology in history that has in some sense licensed domination and exploitation. It may well be true, however, that the pseudo-cosmology we examine here may do so to a greater extent than any other in the past.

2. Albeit, in more recent versions, mind is sometimes viewed in purely material terms, as arising as an epiphenomenon in the brain, which itself is understood in mechanistic terms.

time. Given the same initial conditions, then, an experiment will always yield the same results.

9. Time moves forward like a straight line, with cause always preceding effect. Each effect has a definite cause or set of causes, and the flow of causality is strictly unidirectional.

10. The cosmos is essentially deterministic, based on mechanical causes. If one could ever have a complete knowledge of the current state of all matter, it would be possible to predict the future with certainty. True novelty is essentially impossible.[3]

11. The universe is eternal and immutable in nature,[4] as is evidenced by its changeless laws. In terms of its large-scale structure, the universe does not change over time. Evolution on Earth is understood to be an isolated anomaly, not the norm for the cosmos.

12. All life on Earth is involved in a never-ending competition for survival. Evolution is driven by dominance, the "survival of the fittest." Change, when it occurs at all (and always within the bounds fixed by determinism), is change driven by competition, or even violence.

If we were truly to examine each assumption listed above critically, we might well come to see that these ideas are not unassailable truths; yet most people in modern industrialized societies, to one extent or another, accept most of these as being just that. Certainly, until fairly recently, science has rested on all of these tenets with relatively few changes during the past centuries. Even modern scientists continue to accept many of them with little critical awareness.

Yet, as Roszak (1999) points out, logic alone does not dictate that we accept these assumptions. Buddhists, using their own very logical analysis of experience, come to radically different conclusions. (For example, they believe that our sense of the individual self, and most of what we normally take to be reality, is in some sense illusory—or at the very least, something that we in some way construct ourselves.) Indeed, as we begin to examine the new cosmology emerging from science over the past century, it will become increasingly clear that most of these assumptions can be challenged; that many are, at best, questionable; and that some, in light of our current understanding, seem to be utterly false. Yet many of these beliefs continue to be the dominant ideas that shape the view of reality of people in post-traditional societies, though other assumptions, such as those coming from religious beliefs, certainly play an important role for some.

Arguably, these assumptions also distort our ability to perceive reality clearly and to act creatively. Vandana Shiva characterizes the cosmology of domination as fundamentally reductionist—not just because it breaks wholes into smaller parts but because it reduces "the capacity of humans to know nature" through the

---

3. In more recent versions, blind, purposeless chance also plays a role, particularly at the atomic or molecular level.

4. Once thermodynamics began to point to the gradual death of the universe and it was discovered that the cosmos was expanding, the idea of "continuous creation" was proposed as a way to maintain the timeless nature of the universe.

exclusion of "other knowers and other ways of knowing" and because it reduces "the capacity of nature to creatively regenerate and renew itself by manipulating it as inert and fragmented matter" (1989, 22). She goes on to state:

> The mechanistic metaphors of reductionalism have socially reconstituted nature and society. In contrast to organic metaphors, in which concepts of order and power were based on interconnectedness and reciprocity, the metaphor of nature as machine was based on the assumption of separability and manipulability. . . . [The domination of both nature and women] is inherently violent, understood here as the violation of integrity. Reductionalist science is a source of violence against nature and women because it subjugates and dispossesses them of their full productivity, power, and potential. (1989, 22)

Thomas Berry observes that this mechanistic view of the cosmos has facilitated "the growth of technological invention and industrial plundering" and that its objective has been "to make human societies as independent as possible from the natural world and make the natural world as subservient as possible to human decisions" (1999, 103). It would not be surprising, then, to discover that the cosmology of domination gained ascendancy in large part because it served the needs of the ruling classes who wished to promote capitalism, colonialism, and economic expansion. It gained rapid acceptance when it did because it fit the economic and political requirements of those in power. Moreover, it gained widespread acceptance in societies because the ruling elites were able "to convince people that the focus on manipulation of the physical world would produce a better and happier life." Hence, "the triumph of science was ultimately political" (Lerner 1986, 207).

A mechanistic, reductionalist cosmology is not a proven scientific fact, much less something flowing out of a set of eternal laws of the universe. It has been socially constructed. If we come to see this more clearly, if we come to understand the historical and ideological forces that have contributed to its genesis, we can also begin to deconstruct it and to break its power to distort our perceptions. To do this, we will now explore some of the people, ideas, and economic forces that shaped the pseudo-cosmology that has come to dominate the thinking and perceptions of so many in modern societies.

FROM ORGANISM TO MACHINE:
THE DEATH OF THE LIVING COSMOS

For most of history, in almost all human cultures, the world was understood to be a living organism with a soul or spirit at its heart. Matter was seen as something dynamic—in at least some sense, alive. Indeed, the word "matter" derives from the Indo-European word *mater*, meaning "mother." Matter was the living substance drawn from the body of our mother, the Earth. There was no rigid distinction between human consciousness and the material realm, no pretension of pure objectivity.

In Europe, this form of consciousness persisted throughout the Middle Ages and beyond, right up to the dawn of the scientific age. Morris Berman illustrates this in speaking of the worldview of alchemy. For the alchemist, there was no clear distinction between mental and material phenomena. Everything, in some sense, was symbolic because every material process had a simultaneous psychic equivalent. Berman notes that "if the state of [the alchemist's] mind can at all be imagined," we would have to "say that the alchemist did not *confront* matter; he *permeated* it" (1981, 92). In a similar vein, Jamake Highwater speaks of the ability of aboriginal peoples to "know something by temporarily turning into it" (quoted in Heyneman 1993, 27). Berman goes so far as to maintain that people did not simply once *believe* that matter possessed mind; rather, in some sense *it really did*. The animistic vision of the world was fully efficacious for those who lived out of it:

> Our ancestors constructed reality in a way that typically produced verifiable results, and this is why Jung's theory of projection is off the mark. If another break in consciousness of the same magnitude as that represented by the Scientific Revolution were to occur, those on the other side of the watershed might conclude that our epistemology somehow "projected" mechanism onto nature. (M. Berman 1981, 93)

The animistic vision in Europe was found not only in alchemy but also in the scholastic philosophy of St. Thomas Aquinas (1225-1274) that dominated the Catholic Church for centuries. According to St. Thomas, all of nature is alive and a wide variety of living beings have souls—though he believed that only the human soul is immortal. His philosophy drew on the work of Aristotle, who believed that each thing in nature has an imminent soul that endows it with purpose and draws it toward its goal. The soul of an oak tree guides its development from seed, to sapling, to mature tree. Even a rock falls to the ground because its soul draws it toward its home, the Earth.

By the time of the Renaissance, however, a revival of the Pythagorean and Platonic traditions was under way in Europe. The Pythagoreans had a fascination with mathematics and numbers. Each number was considered to have its own, unique nature with mystical qualities. More importantly, mathematics was understood as the key to understanding the cosmos. Plato, who drew on this tradition, concluded that, while the world itself was full of change, the realm of ideas, forms, and knowledge was changeless and eternal.

This philosophical outlook inspired the early scientists of Europe. Nicholas of Cusa (1401-1464), for example, conceived of the world as rooted in an infinite harmony based on mathematical proportions that could be measured. Cusa believed that "number is the first model of things in the mind of the creator" and that "knowledge is always measurement" (quoted in Sheldrake 1988, 22). Similarly, Copernicus (1473-1543), the proponent of the heliocentric model of the cosmos (which he adopted from the Pythagoreans), believed that the whole of the universe was composed of number. So, what is true in mathematics must also be true in the world of objective reality, including astronomy.

At first, Copernicus's idea of a heliocentric cosmos had relatively little impact, in part because there was no empirical evidence to support it. Copernicus did not adopt his ideas based on scientific observation, but simply because it seemed to him to be more rational and because it led to a more "harmonious geometry of the heavens" (Sheldrake 1988, 22). Not surprisingly, mathematicians were attracted to his ideas, but still his model was based on conjecture, not scientific data. (Indeed, it should be noted that the orbits of the planets and the motion of the sun can be described mathematically from a geocentric point of view—it is only that the motion becomes much simpler to understand and described from a heliocentric vantage point.)

It was Johannes Kepler (1571-1630) who gave a firm foundation to Copernicus's ideas by providing a mathematical theory of planetary motion based on observational evidence of the five known planets. Kepler conceived his theory in terms of three "laws" of planetary motion. In doing this work, he was once again inspired by the philosophy of Plato. Indeed, he "found to his delight that orbits of the planets bore a rough resemblance to the hypothetical spheres which could be inscribed within and circumscribed around the five regular Platonic solids." For Kepler, "the mathematical harmony discovered in the observed facts was the *cause* of these facts, the reason why they are as they are. God created the world in accordance with the principle of perfect numbers" (Sheldrake 1988, 23).

Galileo (1564-1642), using his invention of the telescope to observe the stars and the planets, came to support the theories of Copernicus and Kepler. Like them, he was drawn to a mathematical view of the cosmos. He postulated that the universe's order was governed by immutable laws that nature never transgresses. He also believed that "that which cannot be measured and reduced to numbers is not real" (quoted in Goldsmith 1998, 61).

The new view of the cosmos espoused by Copernicus, Kepler, and Galileo deeply challenged the whole Aristotelian-Thomistic synthesis elucidated in scholastic philosophy (albeit Copernicus continued to accept many of Aristotle's ideas). The Earth was no longer the center of the cosmos, and, by implication, Earth was no longer the center of God's action and purpose. The whole vision of a world encircled by the celestial spheres above and hell below began to dissolve, although the process was a slow one and it took centuries for it to filter into popular culture. At the same time, an integral view of reality that had imbued the cultures of Europe with a sense of place in the universe for more than a millennium began to fragment and shatter. Speaking of this process, Martha Heyneman comments:

> The revolution of the sixteenth century, in robbing the universe as a whole of any imaginable form, erased the image of a ladder of spheres up which an individual soul might aspire to climb from earth to heaven; robbed God and the angels of their habitations; and cast them, so to speak, out-of-doors. They might, however, have gone on dwelling indefinitely somewhere out there in infinite space . . . had it not been for another process that was taking place at the same time. This process, which E. J. Dijksterhuis calls "the mechanization of the world picture," and Carolyn Merchant, "the death of nature,"

transformed the world into a machine that runs by itself, with no need of angels or souls to account for its motions, and God into a "retired engineer." (Heyneman 1993, 13-15)

As the idea of a universe governed by eternal laws took hold, the belief that each thing has a soul was also gradually displaced. Universal laws mitigated the need for an individual soul guiding each thing toward its goal. Somewhere between 1596 and 1623, for example, Kepler decided to make a change to his *Mysterium cosmographicum* by replacing the word "soul" (*anima*) with "force" (*vis*) when referring to the planets. In so doing, he seems to have shifted from the concept of nature as a divinely animated being to one more closely resembling a clock, or a machine. Yet Kepler was still a transitional figure, for he did retain a belief in a soul of the world "in which the Divine Countenance is imprinted" (Heyneman 1993, 15).

It was René Descartes (1596-1650) who seems to have proposed the first truly mechanistic cosmology. For Descartes, the transcendent mind of humans stands over matter. The soul is composed of a mental substance that is entirely distinct from the body and is eternal in nature. What differentiates humans from all else is their ability to reason: "I think, therefore I am." Emotions belong to the realm of the body and are simply a contaminant to the pure realm of rationality that is the mind.

The physical world can be understood through the application of mathematics and is governed by unchangeable laws that come directly from God. Indeed, part of the dignity of the mind is that it has "a Godlike capacity to comprehend the mathematical order of the world" (Sheldrake 1988, 25). Truth itself is conceived in terms of mathematical knowledge.

For Descartes, all of reality—outside the transcendent realm of mind (which for Descartes included God)—is basically mechanical in nature. Everything is simply dead matter. Even animals are "automata" that only *appear* to be lifelike—they are really just complex machines. Since they have no souls, they cannot really experience pain or happiness, and thus humans can use them as they will.

Amazingly, many Christians today take the Cartesian worldview largely for granted, assuming that humans alone can have any kind of a soul. Yet, when it was first introduced, this idea was at odds with the then-orthodox understanding of a living world filled with living creatures, all with souls created by God. As Rupert Sheldrake points out, "Descartes was proposing a far more extreme form of monotheism than the orthodox doctrine of the Church. He thought his was a more elevated conception of God" (Sheldrake 1988, 26). Yet, over the centuries, the church itself seems to have unconsciously adopted much of Cartesian thinking as the new orthodoxy.

It is also hard to imagine a worldview more ruthlessly anthropocentric than that put forward by Descartes. Humans—particularly human minds—belong to a reality completely distinct from other creatures and from the entire material realm. They have totally free reign to exercise power over the Earth and all it contains, even if it means destroying other organisms (who are only "automata," not really living) in the process. At the same time, the preference given to "rational"—or, more precisely, discursive—ways of knowing along with a devaluation of both the emotions and the body seems to reinforce patriarchy, particularly because women were traditionally identified more closely with the emotional sphere and with nature itself. Moreover, the claim of superiority of mind over body lent dignity to intellectual pursuits (including both mathematics and science)—which were usually carried out by men of relatively high social standing—over physical labor, which was usually carried out by people of the poorer classes and by women. Thus, the Cartesian worldview serves as a justification for the domination and exploitation of other living beings by humans and of women by men.

Sir Isaac Newton (1642-1727) drew on Descartes' philosophy and applied it to science by formulating mechanical laws of motion and gravitation that could be verified through experimentation and observation. Using these laws, Newton could mathematically predict the motions of the stars and planets. The success of Newton's theories opened the door to the widespread acceptance of a mechanical worldview with its foundations in mathematical order. As Deborah Du Naan Winter points out:

Newton's work still provides the basis of our modern worldview: matter is seen as inherently inert; it is made up of objects that move only because outside forces move them, like billiard balls whose direction and motion can be successfully predicted. Although Newton agreed with Descartes that only God could have created such an exquisitely ordered universe, Newton helped pave the way for our modern secular worldview by demonstrating how orderly and precisely predictable the movements of objects is. (1996, 35)

The Cartesian-Newtonian synthesis gradually gained dominance—first in the world of science, but eventually more generally in society. As it did, soul and spirit were effectively extirpated from the world. The cosmos, which had once been a kind of cathedral of light, became an orderly but dull clockwork. The Earth was transformed from a living mother into dead matter, a mere storehouse of raw materials awaiting human exploitation. Even the animals, our closest creaturely companions, became but dumb beasts incapable of true feeling or emotion. The world, no doubt, became a tamer and perhaps less fearsome place as it became more predictable and as science exercised its powers to control it; yet ironically it also became a more cold and forbidding habitation as humanity saw itself standing alone, divorced from the greater community of life, truly homeless for the first time.

REDUCING THE WHOLE TO PARTS: ATOMIC MATERIALISM

He who breaks a thing to find out what it is has left the path of wisdom.
(Gandalf speaking in *The Lord of the Rings*; Tolkien 1999, 339)

Supplanting an organic view of the cosmos with a mechanistic one had a profound effect on our understanding of reality. We moved from a living home filled with mystery to a clocklike machine waiting to be dissected and controlled. The world became understandable in a new way that facilitated human mastery over nature. As Diarmuid O'Murchu points out, this new worldview was "neat, efficient, and easy to comprehend" (1997, 24). To illustrate some of the key characteristics, he uses the operation of a television as an example.

First, cause and effect take place in a simple, straightforward, and linear way. If I push a button, the TV goes on. Something happens because something else causes it to happen. Similarly, there are no souls directing the growth of the oak tree, just straightforward biological processes directed by chemicals called genes.

Second, the universe is predictable and deterministic. If I push the button, the TV will always come on unless, of course, there is a malfunction or no electricity at the moment. Pushing the "on" button will not, for example, result in a channel change sometimes and cause the color of the picture to change at others. Things work in a predictable, predetermined fashion. In the same way, a scientific experiment should always yield consistent, repeatable results.

Finally, every whole is comprised of smaller parts. If something is wrong with the TV, it suffices to find the faulty part or parts and replace them and all will work once again. Using the same logic, we can understand how a TV functions by studying the function of each of its parts, then seeing how each relates to the others. So, too, with anything else in the cosmos: We break something complex into simpler components to understand it.

This last characteristic of the classical, materialist cosmology is normally called reductionalism, and it is a key element of the scientific approach to reality. Using reductionalist thinking, it makes senses to search for the smallest possible component of matter in order to gain an understanding of the most basic workings of the universe. This smallest, indivisible, and indestructible component was called the atom. Newton, and other scientists of his time, postulated the existence of atoms, not because of any experimental evidence proving their existence but because the idea was philosophically attractive to them. In a world where everything can be broken into smaller and simpler parts, atoms simply *must* exist, even if it is impossible to see them.

The idea of atoms, though, is far older than Newton and his contemporaries. The Greek philosopher Anaxagoras (500-428 B.C.E.), followed by Leucippus and Democritus (460-370 B.C.E.), first postulated that matter was composed of tiny atoms that had existed for all time. Atoms were physically indivisible, and thus eternal and indestructible. Reality was composed of these atoms and the space through which they moved randomly, at times colliding like billiard balls and at times joining together with others of the same kind to interlock and form substances. In creating this theory, they took as their starting point the philosophy of Parmenides of Elea (early fifth century B.C.E.), who conceived of reality in terms of permanence and changelessness—in contrast to Heraclitus (ca. 535-475 B.C.E.), who viewed it as a dynamic, continuing flow in constant process. For the atomists, change was simply the movement and recombination of real but invisible particles. At the foundation of all reality, though, were changeless, eternal atoms.

Theodore Roszak (1999, 37) asks an intriguing question: Why was atomism so attractive to these Greek philosophers? He believes it is mainly because it freed them from the need to believe in temperamental gods. "Impersonal, law-abiding atoms make one feel secure: Nobody on Olympus was out to get you." Therefore, it is likely that, "the atom entered history as a tiny, philosophical tranquilizer, an intellectual solution to our deepest emotional dread. . . . It was therapeutic, not scientific."

For the Greek materialists who posited the existence of atoms, then, there was no need for either spirit or the gods. Humans were material entities like any other. The atomists of the early scientific revolution, however, wedded atomism to the Platonic idea of eternal forms, which were translated into the concept of universal laws. God created atoms and then set the universe in motion to be governed by the laws "he" established. As Rupert Sheldrake notes, this "cosmic dualism of physical reality and mathematical laws" first formulated by Isaac Newton "has been implicit within the scientific world view ever since" (1988, 28).

Newton's atomism differed somewhat from the cosmology of Descartes, who saw all of space filled with vortices of subtle matter. For Newton, like Leucippus and Democritus, atoms moved in the void. This meant that the attractive force of gravitation needed to act mysteriously at a distance through space itself. For Newton, gravitation arose from the very being of God as an expression of the divine will. Over time, though, scientists came to attribute the attractive force of gravity to matter itself. Once this happened, "what was left was a world machine in absolute space and time, containing inanimate forces and matter, and entirely governed by eternal mathematical laws" (Sheldrake 1988, 29).

Over time, the atomic theory continued to develop. In the nineteenth century, the English chemist John Dalton (1766-1844) used the idea of atoms to provide a mathematical foundation to chemistry. Since atoms could be weighed and counted, they provided a basis for the calculation of chemical formulas. This, together with Dmitri Mendeleyev's periodic table, took Newton's atomic vision to a new level. The only difference in elements was one of quantity—how much their respective atoms weighed—as opposed to one of quality. As Theodore Roszak remarks:

> It was all marvellously simple. Atoms gave the visible world a purely physical foundation. They supposedly moved in response to the same mechanical laws that neatly predicted the movements of heavenly bodies. There was a difference, of course: Heavenly bodies could be seen; atoms could not. But atoms offered something more valuable than visibility. Finality. They were the bedrock of reality. Religiously inclined scientists might wish to believe that God had created the atoms and set them in motion, but atheists were just as free to assert that atoms were eternal and required no God to make or move them. In either case, there was nothing more to explain in nature beyond them or below them. (1999, 39)

Eventually, of course, it was discovered that atoms (or at least, the entities to which we had given that name) were not, in fact, the smallest components making up matter. Other, "elementary particles" were discovered; yet these, too, were found to be divisible. Today, physicists continue to hunt for smaller and smaller pieces of matter using larger and larger machines to do so. Each time they discover a new particle, though, their search seems to become yet more elusive. There appears to be no bedrock, after all, just a mysterious reality that defies any kind of description in terms of our normative experience. Atoms and subatomic particles do not even follow the mechanical laws described by Newton, but rather something far more strange and exotic. Atoms, if we can still say that they exist at all, are something totally different from what was conceived by Leucippus, Democritus, Newton, or Dalton.

SUBDUING NATURE: THE QUEST FOR CONTROL

Behind the original theory of atomism lay the desire for a predictable, deterministic world. Like the early Greek philosophers looking for tranquillity and security, scientists were attracted to an idea of atoms that would enable them to understand, predict, and ultimately control the forces of nature. As Diarmuid O'Murchu notes, "once we have discovered the original bit(s), then, we assume, we will know how the universe began, how it is intended to work, how various forces within it can be conquered and controlled, and how it will eventually end" (1997, 25).

If we envision the universe as a vast machine composed of simple "building blocks" working in a deterministic fashion, we can then gain a degree of control over nature to the extent that we attain knowledge of the universal laws governing all things. By conceiving of the cosmos as being composed of dead, inert matter—and by even positing that other living creatures can feel no pain—ethical restrictions against domination and exploitation are largely removed. To what extent, though, have the formulation and adoption of a mechanistic cosmology actually been *motivated* by the desire to control, subdue, and even exploit nature?

Francis Bacon (1561-1626) is often considered to be the "father" of the scientific method. For Bacon, the universe was essentially a problem waiting to be solved. In his writings, he noted that "knowledge is power" and that truth, in some cases, can be considered the equivalent of utility. Edward Goldsmith (1998) observes that Bacon's replacement of the traditional values of good and evil with those of "useful" and "useless" provided a virtual license for exploitation at a time when colonial expansion in the New World was offering nearly limitless opportunities for plunder, enslavement, and economic gain.

In *The Plan of the Instauratio Magna*, Bacon wrote that nature would yield up its secrets more readily when it was "under constraint and vexed; that is to say, when by art and the hand of man she is forced out of her natural state, and squeezed and moulded." Similarly, in *The Masculine Birth of Time*, Bacon writes, "I am come in very truth leading to you nature with all her children to bind her to your service and make her your slave." The patriarchal tone of these passages is readily apparent. Nature, conceived as a feminine "she," must be squeezed, molded, bound, and enslaved by "man."

Not surprisingly, several feminist authors see Bacon as misogynist. He is often accused of using metaphors of torture such as "putting nature on the rack," though it seems unlikely that this oft-quoted phrase was actually used by Bacon himself.[5] What is apparent, though, is that he conceived of science as a tool through which "man" could violently subjugate "feminine" nature. Rosemary Radford Ruether notes that Bacon used the Christian story of fall and redemption to reinforce this concept:

> Through the sin of Eve, "nature" fell out of "man's" control, but through scientific knowledge this fall will be reversed and "nature" restored to man's dominion, as representative of God's dominion over the earth. For Bacon, scientific knowledge is fundamentally a tool of power, the capacity to subjugate and rule over "nature." (Ruether 1992, 195)

The philosophy of René Descartes also helped to remove ethical constraints against ruthless exploitation. Ruether observes that Descartes' dualistic separation of mind from matter also permits a split between values and facts. Scientific truth is considered to be both "objective" and "value free." Ethics and values, in turn, are relegated to the private sphere of the soul. This split of ethics from science is convenient insofar as it allows scientists to investigate freely without needing to worry about the religious implications of their findings. At the same time, though, this relegation of ethics to the private realm frees many other "material" pursuits from ethical considerations. Certainly, destroying things not possessing mind—anything except human beings—is of no real ethical importance. Even when ethics might come into play—in the case of the human realm—those involved in material pursuits (women and the lower classes) might be considered of implicitly lesser value than those involved in intellectual endeavors.

In the case of Newtonian physics, the creation of a cosmological framework based on rigid order and universal laws seems to be related, in at least some measure, to Newton's own personal need for security. Newton was born several months after his father's death and, when his mother remarried, was sent away to be raised by his grandparents. In his youth, he was described as a sober, silent thinker with few friends. At university, his interests included not only mathematics and natural philosophy but also alchemy.

Many of Newton's key discoveries, including the invention of calculus, the development of his theory of gravitation, and his initial studies of the nature of light, took place between 1665 and 1667 when the University of Cambridge was closed owing to an outbreak of the plague. No doubt, the time of solitude helped to spur Newton's creative genius, but the context of plague and death that surrounded him might also have subtly directed the course of his thought.

---

5. It is noteworthy, however, that Bacon was accused of torturing a prisoner while serving as Lord Chancellor of England, so certainly metaphors of torture may have played a role in his thinking.

Certainly, the image of an orderly, clockwork universe might have been comforting at such a time.

Morris Berman believes that Newton's evolution in thinking was influenced by his own psychological needs, as well as by a Puritan morality based on "austerity, discipline, and above all, guilt and shame" (1981, 120). Newton's own life, particularly his early youth, was marked by a climate that was in many ways hostile. For Newton, then, the universe was not a "friendly place"—it was rather something that required control and discipline. "A chief source of Newton's desire to know was his anxiety before and his fear of the unknown. . . . Knowledge that could be mathematicised ended his quandaries. . . . [The fact] that the world obeyed mathematical law was his security" (F. E. Manuel quoted in M. Berman 1981, 121).

Berman concludes that Newton, though not psychotic, did border on a kind of madness. In addition, he notes that portraits painted over the course of Newton's life seem to testify to a process of increasing rigidity. In his youth, Newton seems to have a gentle, nearly ethereal quality that witnessed to his sensitivity. As he grows older—and as his views become increasingly more mechanistic and reductionalist—he seems to put on a kind of "character armor" that eventually erases the earlier appearance of a sensitive soul.

Newton's adoption of mechanism and atomism was also linked to the social context in which he lived. It seems clear that alchemy exercised a great deal of fascination for Newton, and this interest seems never to have totally disappeared for him. His alchemical ideas, though, were driven underground and were eventually expunged from his published works. Berman notes that Newton's retreat from his earlier views took place in the years leading up to the Glorious Revolution when both Leveller and Republican sentiments were growing. The idea present in his earlier works that nature was "transformative and infinitely fecund" raised disturbing political parallels that bordered on being dangerous. Eventually, by 1706, when his disciple Samuel Clarke was working on a translation of *Opticks* into Latin,

> Statements such as "we cannot say that all Nature is not alive" were withdrawn before publications went to press; and most importantly, Newton adopted the position that matter was inert, that it changed not dialectally (i.e. internally) but through rearrangement alone. Thus, in . . . *Opticks* . . . Newton gives as his purpose "that nature may be lasting"; in other words, that it may be stable, predictable, regular—like the social order ought to be. As a young man, Newton had been fascinated by the fecundity of nature. Now, its alleged rigidity was somehow important. (M. Berman 1981, 125-26)

If Newton's need for security and predictability unconsciously shaped his science, the motivations of his contemporary, Robert Boyle, were much more explicit. Boyle clearly saw that one of the chief advantages of the new materialist philosophy was its ability to endow humanity—or perhaps more precisely, "men"—with power and to remove ethical constraints, which he refers to as mere "scruples of conscience":

The veneration wherewith men are imbued for what they call nature, has been a discouraging impediment to the empire of man over the inferior creatures of God. For many have not only looked upon it as an impossible thing to compass, but as something impious to attempt, the removing of those boundaries which nature seems to have put and settled among her productions; and whilst they look upon her as such a venerable thing, some make a kind of scruple of conscience to endeavor so to emulate her works as to extol them. (Robert Boyle, quoted in Roszak 1999, 100)

For Boyle, it was insufficient to simply to *know* nature; one had to "make it serviceable" to some particular end. Clearly, then, for Boyle and others like him, science was to be used as a method of control and domination.

This quest for power through science—conceived as "power-over," or the dominating power of the "empire of man"—persists into our time. Despite the new worldview inherent in such areas as quantum physics and systems theory, scientists continue to bash elementary particles together in the hope of finding the holy grail of the ultimate "basement" of nature. In the field of biology, genes now serve a function similar to the atoms of classical physics. Genes deterministically and mechanistically encode for specific traits—perhaps even for specific behaviors. All is reducible to genes, so if we can map out the genome completely and understand the discrete function of each gene, we will magically discover all the secrets of life and be able to refashion organisms as we see fit. In psychology, the theory of behaviorism extends mechanism into the realm of the mind itself: the brain is just a machine, and behaviors can be understood in terms of stimulus/response reactions without messy references to consciousness, motivations, or ethics. By manipulating behaviors, we can mold and reprogram the psyche itself.

According to Roszak, the psychologist Abraham Maslow believed that the entire modern scientific enterprise "was unconsciously dominated by a method of inquiry that was grounded in fear and therefore governed by the need to control" (Roszak 1999, 12). For Maslow, if this need were pushed too far, it could result in a kind of "cognitive pathology" that actually "distorted more than it illuminated." It is interesting to note, for example, that classical physics simply ignored the problem of nonlinear, chaotic systems because they could not be understood in terms of predictability and mechanistic science.

Similarly, Aldous Huxley once reflected that the vision of nature in Europe arose from the vantage point of a well-tended garden rather than from the mysterious complexity of a tropical rainforest. He, too, saw fear as one of the key motivations behind Eurocentric science: "It is fear of the labyrinthine flux and complexity of phenomena that has driven men to philosophy, to science, to theology—fear of the complex reality driving them to invent simpler, more manageable, and therefore, consoling, fiction" (quoted in Roszak 1999, 43), such as the comforting fiction of a clockwork universe reducible to inert atoms.

At this juncture, it is important to note an obvious characteristic of the scientific enterprise up until the end of the nineteenth—and indeed for much of the twentieth—century: it was an almost exclusively male preserve. Science was, by definition, "macho" science. Roszak notes that women have traditionally been given responsibilities over the messy details of the daily routines of living—caring for children, working in the kitchen, and cleaning. This reality "leads them to expect little in the way of neatness, order, or clarity in life. Perhaps they cannot help but cultivate an astute awareness of loose ends, subtle nuances, and ragged relationships. They may even learn to accept disorder as an integral part of the real world" (1999, 43). Roszak goes on to note that the recent willingness of science to contemplate "Chaos Theory" in order to understand nonlinear phenomena may have become possible only with the advent of a stronger feminine presence in the scientific community.

Given the male bias of classical science, it should not be surprising that it has been so sharply marked by clearly patriarchal methods and attitudes. As Jane Goodall notes, this "macho science" excluded "feminine" qualities from its methods such as "sensitivity, gentleness, warmth, compassion, and intuition" (Roszak 1999, x). The withdrawal of these qualities from science also removes ethical constraints against the use of violent and exploitative techniques, as is seen in the excessive use of animal experimentation—often for rather dubious research.

While the patriarchal bias of science may be considered largely a result of the sexual division of labor common at the time, there was also a measure of conscious intentionality in its approach. For example, Henry Oldenburg, the first secretary of Britain's Royal Society, stated that the highest priority of the society should be to establish a "Masculine Philosophy." "The Woman in us," he said, is "an Eve as fatal as the Mother of our miseries" (Roszak 1999, 56).

Given the patriarchal bent of Western science, it is perhaps not surprising that the French philosopher Michel Serres concludes that classical physics is the "strategy of the kill" where all is "stable, unchanging, redundant" and where "there is nothing to be learned, to be discovered, to be invented. . . . There is death forever" (quoted in Toolan 2001, 54). Vandana Shiva (1989), as previously noted, also believes that patriarchal science was instrumental in granting a license to the process of industrialization by converting the Earth from *terra mater* into a lifeless machine and storehouse of raw materials, effectively removing all ethical constraint against exploitation, which, in turn, led to new patterns of domination over women and their exclusion as partners in both science and in social-economic development.

ETERNITY, DETERMINISM, AND THE LOSS OF PURPOSE

As the idea of a mechanistic, clockwork universe gained ascendancy, the scientific view of the cosmos also became more immutable and deterministic. While the inspiration of the new model may have been largely Platonic, its God was the unmoved mover of Aristotle who was impassible, omnipotent, and unchangeable. Initially, this God was needed to "wind up the clock" from time to time to keep everything in motion, but by the beginning of the nineteenth century the cosmos had become a kind of perpetual motion machine.

Indeed, the French physicist Pierre Laplace (1749-1827) believed that, if one could gain knowledge of all the forces acting in the universe as well as the precise position of each body at a given moment in time, it would theoretically be possible to create a single formula that would allow one to see all the past and predict all the future perfectly, with no uncertainty. There could be nothing new under the sun—all was fixed, all was determined. As Rupert Sheldrake states:

> The machinery was eternal, and it would always go on, as it always had done, in an entirely deterministic and predictable way: or at least in a way that would in principle be entirely predictable by a superhuman all-knowing intelligence, if such an intelligence existed. . . . God was no longer needed to wind things up or start things off. He became an unnecessary hypothesis. His universal laws remained, but no longer as ideas in his eternal mind. They had no ultimate reason for existing; they were purposeless. Everything, even physicists, became inanimate matter moving in accordance with these blind laws. (1988, 4)

At the heart of this deterministic vision is the idea of linear causality or "unitary transformations." If every event in the universe is the result of causes that have preceded it, then "the present is always built out of the shadows of the past, and within the present is everything that will take place in the future" (Peat 1991, 125). This unidirectional flow of causality is linear because inputs directly determine outputs.

Linearity, in turn, is related to reductionism: variables are reduced to those that can be controlled and separated and tested one at a time. While such a method has borne some important fruits, it is limited insofar as the complex interplay of variables cannot be adequately examined. The goal is to analyze, control, and predict results, all of which assume one-way causality (Macy 1991a). The desire for a linear universe was so great in classical science that nonlinear systems, as we have noted, were largely ignored until the twentieth century. Yet even planetary systems, the original inspiration for the clockwork universe, can display chaotic, nonlinear dynamics when three or more large bodies interact.

By the end of the nineteenth century, the Western scientific cosmovision became even more depressing. The world could no longer be considered a perpetual motion machine because the newly formulated laws of thermodynamics proved that such a machine was not possible: Everything tended toward a state of energy equilibrium; everything moved gradually to a more disordered state. Eventually, the entire universe itself would die of heat death, becoming nothing more than an amorphous soup of matter and energy.

Even in the twentieth century, the idea of a static, eternal universe was so deeply entrenched that it led Albert Einstein to "cook" the field equations in his theory of universal gravitation. When Einstein first developed these equations, they provided only non-static solutions, indicating that the cosmos must be expanding. Einstein, believing this to be an error, "fixed" his equations by adding a "cosmological constant" to provide for a static solution. Einstein himself later referred to this as the greatest blunder of his life. It does, however, illustrate the power of established ideas to distort science, even in the case of a thinker as original as Einstein.

Once it was confirmed that the universe was, in fact, expanding, the theory of continuous creation helped to provide a way to envision the cosmos in a kind of ongoing "steady state." Indeed, static models of the universe continued to dominate physics until the 1960s. In such a worldview, novelty and change have little place. There is no goal, no purpose for the universe. Life, and even mind, are considered to be mere cosmic accidents without any real meaning. Even today, scientists are exceedingly careful to remove any hint of purposefulness from their descriptions of reality. Any hint of "teleology"—or some kind of final purpose—is ruthlessly expunged from scientific theories. Even living organisms must be assumed to be without a goal or aim, save, perhaps, raw survival.

Obviously, these kinds of beliefs color the way we think about change itself. In a deterministic, purposeless universe, ideas like revolution and radical transformation have no place. What will be is determined by what was. Authentic creativity, any kind of genuine emergence of novelty, is essentially impossible. This despairing view can perhaps best be summarized by quoting more fully the words of Bertrand Russell previously cited:

> That man is the product of causes which had no prevision of the end they were achieving; that his origin, his growth, his hopes and fears, his loves and beliefs, are but the outcome of accidental collisions of atoms; that no fire, no heroism, no intensity of thought and feeling can preserve an individual life beyond the grave; that all the labors of the ages, all the devotion, all the inspiration, all the noonday brightness of human genius, are destined to extinction in the vast death of the solar system; and that the whole temple of Man's achievement must inevitably be buried beneath the debris of a universe in ruins—all these things, if not quite beyond dispute, are yet so nearly certain, that no philosophy which rejects them can hope to stand. Only within the scaffolding of these truths, only on the firm foundation of unyielding despair, can the soul's habitation henceforth be built. (Quoted in Sheldrake 1988, 6-7)

The purposelessness of the cosmos also both flows from and reinforces the idea of science as value free. Ethics becomes largely superfluous, or at best a mere social convention: "the universe 'out there' apart from human subjects is inherently valueless and purposeless. Value is the product of human minds alone, and therefore cannot be an objective aspect of the cosmos" (Haught 1993, 28-29). As Martha Heyneman notes, in such a vision, humans themselves must ultimately lose their own sense of purpose as well:

> If we imagine the universe as "it"—a universe of "dead matter and blind force"—something in us goes dead and blind. We can engage without remorse (until we understand that our own existence is threatened) in the wholesale destruction of nature. If we imagine, moreover, a purposeless universe, we suffer, in the letdown that follows the momentary elation of achieving a prox-

imate goal, from a baffled feeling of depression. If the universe has no mean-ing, can my life have any ultimate meaning? If the whole has no purpose, can the part? (1993, 50)

PRIVATE GAIN, PROGRESS, AND THE SURVIVAL OF THE FITTEST

The vacuum of meaning inherent in the mechanistic worldview, together with the quest of science to control nature, led to the formulation of what we might call the first "surrogate cosmology." Living in a dead and hostile universe, humanity would find its purpose in improving its own living conditions by accumulating wealth and working for social and economic "progress." In time, these goals were largely combined into the pursuit of economic "growth."

Morris Berman (1981) observes that, for most of human history, the cosmo-logical endeavor was driven by questions of "why" because we viewed the cos-mos as alive, with its own goals and purposes. During the scientific revolution, however, we shifted to questions of "how," and the universe was transformed into a collection of inert atoms moving mechanistically without purpose. We replaced an approach based on *quality* with one based on *quantity*. Even human purpose, if it existed at all, came to be defined in quantitative terms:

> Atomism, quantifiability, and the deliberate act of viewing nature as an abstraction from which one can distance oneself—all open the possibility that Bacon proclaimed as the true goal of science: control. The Cartesian or technological paradigm is . . . the equation of truth with utility, with purpo-sive manipulation of the environment. . . . Not holism, but domination of nature; not the ageless rhythm of ecology, but the conscious management of the world. (M. Berman 1981, 45-46)

Given mechanism's quantitative approach, it is not surprising that a way needed to be found to measure manipulation, control, and domination them-selves. Money provided a convenient tool for this purpose.

In exploring the links between capitalist economics and the cosmology of domination, it is important to note that the rise of the money economy was closely related to the birth of the scientific revolution. It was during the Renaissance that finance and capital accumulation became a driving dynamic in Europe. German sociologist Georg Simmel maintains that an economy built around money "created the ideal of exact numerical calculation," which in turn led to the "mathematically exact interpretation of the cosmos" as the "theoretical counterpart of a money economy" (quoted in M. Berman 1981, 55). The ability of money to reproduce itself, seemingly without end, also "substantiated the notion of an infinite universe" (M. Berman 1981, 55), which in turn eventually lent support to the idea of limitless economic growth and development.

The merchants who were gaining power in the new economy came to see financial calculation as a way of understanding all reality, including the cosmos itself. "Quantification" came to be regarded as "the key to personal success, because quantification alone was thought to enable mastery over nature by a rational understanding of its laws." Since both money and mathematics had no "tangible content," they could be "bent to any purpose" and "ultimately, they became the purpose" (M. Berman 1981, 55).

Berman notes as well that, over the same period, a quantitative understanding of time entered European consciousness. Clocks became common and time shifted from a cyclical to a linear conception. Coupled with the money economy, the idea that "time is money" was first coined in the sixteenth century. Berman concludes that "the rise of linear time and mechanical thinking" as well as "the equating of time with money and the clock with world order, were parts of the same transformation, and each part helped to reinforce the others" (M. Berman 1981, 57). The idea of linear time is also closely related to the concept of unitary transformations and, in turn, to the deterministic conception of reality.

In a similar vein, the rise of individualism that characterized the beginning of the modern era no doubt made the ideas of reductionalism and atomism more attractive to early scientists. It also reinforced the concept of humans as separate from nature and the role of the scientist as a detached observer. Yet, at the same time, these tenets of science themselves served to reinforce notions linked to individualism, including both private property and individual rights. The idea that matter was inert and lifeless and that nature awaited the transforming hand of "man" to improve it also found their way into the political and economic ideals of a Europe involved in colonial exploits.

John Locke (1632-1704), for example, used Bacon's "ethics" of utility in his concept of private landownership. For Locke, unused land was wasted land. Native peoples did not really own the lands they inhabited because they had never "improved" them. So the wilderness was simply "virgin land" awaiting exploitation. For Locke, the private ownership of land was a God-given right and responsibility: "God, by commanding to subdue, gave authority so far to appropriate" (quoted in Winter 1996, 40). He advocated the use of labor to "enclose" land "from the common"—effectively arguing against any collective form of landownership. In Locke's conception of democracy, only landowners should vote because only they, through their work to "subdue the earth," merited a voice in government.

Our current understanding of individuals locked in competition may have originated with an even earlier philosopher, Thomas Hobbes (1588-1679), whose thought both preceded, and in some ways, superseded Locke's, though initially his ideas were not as well received. Hobbes argued for a completely mechanistic cosmovision where everything, including human beings, minds, and ideas, is purely material in nature. Hobbes conceived of humans as engaged in a constant state of competition with one another for both power and material goods. Humans must also fight for survival against nature, which is viewed as both dangerous and chaotic. "Thus, Hobbes saw competitive self-interest as the basis of human nature; because people are inherently in competition against each other, they must enter into market contracts to create some semblance of social order" (Winter 1996, 42-43). All is based on competitive self-interest. For Hobbes, humans owe society nothing.

The individualism advocated by Hobbes was reinforced by Adam Smith (1723-1790), who believed that, if individuals were allowed to amass wealth without undue interference by the state, the net result would be social well-being. In essence, "by behaving in the most egotistic way possible we maximize not only our own material interests but also those of society at large—a cheerful philosophy which rationalized the individualism and egoism that marked the breakdown of society during the industrial revolution" (Goldsmith 1998, 81). Over time, happiness itself was defined in terms of something that could be measured—the value of one's property and material possessions. Maximizing the accumulation of wealth, therefore, would also maximize happiness.

Yet, while the accumulation of wealth was lauded, spending wealth on luxuries was also discouraged through the influence of Protestantism—particularly Calvinism. According to Deborah Du Nann Winter, "one of the few things that one could in good conscience do with savings was to 'plough them back into the firm'; in other words, invest. In this way Calvinism encouraged the perfect combination of hard work and ascetic self-denial that enable capitalism to flourish" (1996, 45). Calvinism also encouraged capital accumulation by considering material rewards as a sign of God's blessings. In contrast, poverty was seen as a punishment of those who lacked effort. "In Protestant modernism, work and wealth are good; leisure and poverty are sin" (Winter 1996, 44).

In this emerging surrogate cosmology, then, individualism and capital accumulation were valued over community responsibility. Nature was valuable only insofar as it had been "improved"—or we would later say, "developed." Instead of having responsibilities to society as a whole, we were each endowed with inalienable, individual rights and liberties. As historian Richard Tarnas observes:

> While the classical Greek worldview had emphasized the goal of human intellectual and spiritual activity as the essential unification (or reunification) of man [sic] with the cosmos and its divine intelligence, and while the Christian goal was to reunite man and the world with God, the modern goal was to create the greatest possible freedom for man—from nature; from oppressive political, social, or economic structures; from restrictive metaphysical or religious beliefs. (Quoted in Winter 1996, 44)

The ideas of freedom and the dignity of the individual embodied in the idea of human rights, of course, are not in themselves negative. Certainly, too, liberation from oppressive political, economic, social, and religious structures seems to be a laudable goal. Yet these goals became so highly individualized that the well-being of society, and certainly the well-being of other creatures and of ecosystems, was largely forgotten. Further, the goal of "freedom from" is a kind of purpose through negation. It may be clear what one wants to move away from, but what does one desire to move toward in its place? Does the accumulation of wealth and personal possessions suffice?

The values of individual competition and personal gain promoted by Adam Smith and his followers eventually found their way back into science in the form of Charles Darwin's (1809-1882) theory of evolution based on competition and the "survival of the fittest." Edward Goldsmith (1998) sees strong parallels between Smith's "invisible hand" and Darwin's "natural selection"—both have nearly magical properties to result in progress and the common good through the promotion of individual self-interest.

Darwin did, of course, need to find some reason why evolution should happen at all in a purposeless cosmos heading toward an eventual thermodynamic death. *Why* should simple organisms evolve toward greater complexity in such a universe? Darwin needed an explanation that did not seem to involve any kind of deeper purpose or design—what is referred to as "teleology"—since any hint of such teleology would, of course, have been "unscientific." The idea of random variations and "survival of the fittest" provided an answer that made sense within the scientific and economic paradigms of his time. Rupert Sheldrake notes:

> The Darwinian doctrine is that the evolution of living organisms in no sense involves a process of purposive striving, nor is it divinely designed or guided; rather, organisms vary by chance, their offspring tend to inherit their variations, and through the blind workings of natural selection, the various forms of life evolve with no design or purpose, either conscious or unconscious. Eyes and wings, mango trees and weaver birds, ant and termite colonies, the echo-location system of bats, and indeed all aspects of life have come into being by chance, through the mechanistic operation of inanimate forces and by the power of natural selection. (1988, 6)

Competition between individuals with no real purpose, then, results in progress for a species as a whole. Today, Darwin's idea of a competitive struggle driving evolution continues to exercise a powerful influence. Indeed Richard Dawkins, a militantly reductionist biologist, actually speaks of genes themselves as competing with one another. He even describes genes as being "selfish" and compares them to both "war-gamers" and to "gangsters" (Roszak 1999, 129). What seems incredible is that scientists seem to take such explanations seriously. As Theodore Roszak points out, it is somehow acceptable to impute selfish motives to genes—which are really just complex molecules. Yet, if one were to make any suggestion that living organisms may have intentions or be motivated by cooperation or altruism, it would immediately be labeled "unscientific"!

Darwin's evolutionary thinking inspired others, such as the English philosopher Herbert Spencer (1820-1903), to promote the related idea of social progress. In this view, societies and economies evolve from the simple to the complex, just as species do through evolution. Hunter-gatherer societies progress to agrarian ones, and agrarian societies progress to industrialized ones. People begin as mere "savages" but eventually progress to become "civilized." As one can imagine, this theory of progress served as a convenient justification for colonization. Through the expansion of empire, Europe brought civilization to more "backward" societies. For the United States of America, this idea of progress served to support its belief in its "manifest destiny" to expand westward and conquer both the "savages" and the "virgin territories" they inhabited. In a similar fashion, it is easy to see how this same ethic of "progress" could be used as a justification for racism by claiming to "civilize" backward or "inferior" races.

The idea of progress was very much linked to Locke's earlier conception of "improving" the land and private ownership. As Winter notes, "progress occurs when individuals apply technology"—and we might add, human labor—"to convert their land to income" (1996, 48). With time, the idea of converting land was extended to include all kinds of "raw materials" or "natural resources." Progress became equated with "economic growth" as measured by an increase in GDP. This whole concept is intimately related to our cosmology and to our conception of power. As Winter concludes:

> Progress, through land ownership or economic wealth, is a fundamental feature of our worldview. The perception that human life is perched in *linear time* marked by progress toward something better is mirrored by the Greek and Christian view that we are perched in a *linear power order* as well. In the traditional Western view of the cosmos, God reigns over men, who rule over women, children, plants, and inorganic matter, in that order. (1996, 48)

A COSMOLOGY OF EXPLOITATION AND DESPAIR

The cosmology of domination that developed in the West over the past four centuries or so is a cosmology that licenses oppression and exploitation, promotes individualism and competition, and gives rise to a kind of existential despair born out of a sense of purposelessness. This cosmology, however, is not inevitable, nor is it the only "rational" or "objective" cosmology that can be conceptualized given our current knowledge of human societies, the Earth, its living organisms, and the cosmos that envelops all. Rather, the cosmology of domination is a social construct that was created in a particular historical context to support a particular view of the world that seemed convenient to those who held power. As such, it can be deconstructed and replaced. Indeed, for those who desire radical change, the cosmology of domination *must* be replaced.

As we have seen, the cosmology of domination—particularly that which has developed over the past four hundred years[6]—has supplanted a more ancient cosmology that envisioned the Earth, and indeed the entire cosmos, as a living organism full of life and purpose. In its place, we were given a universe that resembles a giant machine made up of dead, inert matter. This universe works

---

6. While we have focused on the modern cosmology of domination, as we have noted, transitional cosmologies that were neither fully animistic nor fully mechanistic/reductionalist have also existed. The actual process of moving away from animism has arguably taken millennia, as can be seen in our references to the Greek versions of atomism. Still, the past four hundred years have marked the sharpest movement away from the ancient animistic cosmologies.

on the principles of blind force and universal laws. By understanding these forces and laws, humanity—normally conceived as "man"—can dominate and control nature, molding it for its purposes. The cosmos is no longer a community of subjects, but rather a collection of dead objects.

Theodore Roszak believes that the idea of a dead universe leads to "the rape of nature" and that rape, in this case, is emphatically *not* a mere metaphor. Rape is rooted in "a mentality that licenses domination" and "a lust for power that is anything but metaphorical. . . . Rape stems from a distinct state of mind that is the same whether the victim is a woman or a rainforest. Rape begins by denying the victim her dignity, autonomy, and feeling. Psychologists now call this 'objectifying' the victim'" (1999, 96-97).

Roszak observes that rape normally results from a "compulsive need to control, to control completely" and that this in turn comes from the rapist's sense of inadequacy in the presence of women. Out of fear come anger and the need to punish or dominate. Similarly, the need to subjugate and control nature flows out of fear that comes from a sense of inferiority or inadequacy. The problematic female must be molded by the will of man and brought under control. To accomplish this, she is turned into an object and "stamped with her master's image" (1999, 106). In all of this, a sense of "man's" entitlement—be it to a woman's body or to the fruits of nature—comes into play. In the case of nature, we need not ask pardon or give thanks for what we have taken or destroyed because the world is essentially dead. The death of nature means that we are entitled to take what we want without any moral compunction. We are free to rape the Earth.

As was noted in the discussion of ecopsychosis, the fear of nature that seems to have motivated the shift from a cosmovision where nature was understood as living and fecund to one where nature was converted into dead, inert matter may be linked in part to the black death caused by the bubonic plague that wiped out roughly a third of Europe's population between 1347 and 1350. In addition, the onset of the "Little Ice Age" in the 1400s no doubt reinforced the desire to control forces of nature that were seen as destructive. As we have also reflected, the context of the witch-hunts and the use of torture may have played some role in the "inquisitorial" attitude toward nature conceived in feminine terms. Nature needed to be "vexed" so that "she" would give up her secrets; then "she" would be molded to "man's" needs and purposes.

The cosmology of mechanism and dead matter removes most, if not all, ethical constraints against the exploitation of the natural world. At the same time, the rigid separation of mind from matter inherent in the Cartesian paradigm also leads to a devaluation of the entire organic realm—including the human body. In this way, physical labor and all those engaged in it are also devalued. As a result, the oppression of women, slaves, and all those belonging to the laboring classes is facilitated.

Meanwhile, the idea that matter is composed of tiny, discrete, indivisible atoms reinforces an individualistic view of reality where relationships and cooperation are of little real importance. In a universe with no purpose, there is no place for altruism or compassion. Both evolution and progress are driven by ruthless competition that allows only the fittest to survive. Humans, like all animals, are engaged in a never-ending fight for survival in a cold, hostile world. Those who are most fit gain wealth—and wealth is a sign of God's blessing—while those less suitably adapted live in poverty, which becomes an indication of laziness and inferiority.

In a clockwork universe, all can be predicted if only we can gain sufficient understanding of the eternal laws governing motion and matter. Nothing genuinely novel or new is possible. Evolution on Earth is, at best, a curious anomaly. What *will* be is determined by what *has* been. As Michael Lerner observes:

> If human beings really are like the complex laws of [classical] physics, then it is rather silly for us to be engaged in struggles to change things. Our struggles are themselves predictable, and just as they have always failed in the past, they will fail in the future as well. "Just name a successful revolution that has produced a real transformation," we are challenged. "You can't—and the reason is that social science has already established that these kinds of dramatic changes are impossible. So stop kidding yourself." (1986, 213)

Indeed, Lerner observes that the "social unconscious"—something based on the deep assumptions that make up our cosmology—is indeed at the root of what he calls "surplus powerlessness," that is, "the totality of our beliefs and understanding about how the world is and how it can't be changed" (1986, 12). Even Marxism, which he considers the "deepest and most telling critique of capitalist society," ultimately fails because of its foundations in mechanistic cosmology which legitimate the idea that human beings are just things that "can be subjected to scientific laws" (1986, 219).

Kirkpatrick Sale concludes that the reason why the new scientific conception of reality was so readily accepted in Europe was because it filled the political and economic requirements of those in power: "It provided both the intellectual substructure and a practical mechanism for the rise of the nation-state out of feudal localism, for their chosen system of mercantile and industrial capitalism, and for their enterprise of global colonialism and exploitation (1985, 18). For example, the new force of nationalism found the concept of immutable laws a convenient idea for establishing control. Meanwhile, capitalism could thrive—indeed be seen as natural and inevitable—in a materialistic universe driven by the forces of competition and individual initiative. The process of colonization was supported by the scientific quest to control and subjugate nature, while the theory of evolution eventually added an additional justification for "developing virgin lands" and bringing "civilization" to the "savages."

Not only did the cosmology of domination remove ethical constraints against exploitation; it actually justified exploitation and made it seem both "natural" and "scientific." Yet this is not merely a historical observation, for the same cosmology continues to support the endeavors of those who wish to continue to transform the living Earth into dead and lifeless capital. We continue to live with the legacy of the cosmology of domination, even though many of its "scientific" foundations have long since turned to sand.

MOVING BEYOND MECHANISM

Real social transformation requires that we change our basic categories of thought, that we alter the whole intellectual framework with which we couch our experience and our perceptions. We must, in effect, change our whole "mindset," learn a whole new language. (Zohar and Marshall 1994, 38)

While we need to recognize the shortcomings of the scientific enterprise and its accompanying view of the world—while we acknowledge its role in justifying patriarchy, colonization, consumerism, and ecological destruction—it is also helpful to recognize some of the positive contributions it has made. Few people living in modern societies would desire simply to return to the way of life of Europe in the Middle Ages, for example. Few of us would like to live in a rigidly defined social structure with few comforts and with many life-threatening dangers. Most of us value the ideas of democracy and human rights that have slowly gained ascendancy. Science has brought genuine benefits to human societies, even if its blessings have been mixed with curses (and even though its effects on the ecological health of our planet have been almost wholly detrimental). Is there a way to preserve some of the benefits associated with both science and the cosmology it helped birth while at the same time mitigating or eliminating its detrimental aspects?

Philosopher Ken Wilber (1996) identifies three primary characteristics that he sees as constituting the "dignity of modernity"—what he calls the "Big Three." First, the differentiation of the individual self or "I" from one's culture or society helped give rise to modern democratic institutions including elected governments and human rights. Second, the differentiation of mind from nature may actually have contributed to movements for liberation insofar as "biological might" or brute strength could no longer serve as a justification for domination. Finally, the differentiation of culture from nature was the foundation for empirical science, where truth was no longer subservient to the ideologies of a state or a religion. In Wilber's view, the "good news of modernity was that it learned to *differentiate* the Big Three"—that is, self from culture, mind from nature, and culture from nature; "the bad news was that it had not yet learned how to *integrate* them" (Wilber 1996, 126). Indeed, instead of simply differentiating, we actually came to dissociate them. He concludes:

The ecocrisis is in large measure the result of the continued dissociation of the Big Three. We cannot align nature and culture and consciousness; we cannot align nature and morals and mind. We are altogether fragmented in this modernity gone slightly mad. (1996, 276)

Similarly, Morris Berman laments our loss of participating consciousness, the ability to identify with something—become it, as it were—which he calls "mimesis." Until the Renaissance, "the ego coexisted with participation more than it sought to deny it, and this attitude is what made it a viable structure for so many centuries. In denying participation, however, the ego denies its own source, for . . . the ego has no separate energy resources of its own. The unconscious is the ground of being" (1981, 179).

Our current fixation on ego and analysis is an exaggerated oscillation that results in destructive tendencies because it does not integrate participating consciousness. Berman does not, however, argue that we should simply abandon the ability to analyze and differentiate. Indeed, he notes that societies characterized by a strong component of non-participating consciousness, such as ancient Greece and Renaissance Italy, have produced cultures of "marvellous luminosity." The whole of the Middle Ages never produced artists and thinkers of the stature of Michelangelo, Shakespeare, or Leonardo da Vinci. The way to genuine psychic health and fruitfulness, then, lies in the *integration* of the mimetic and analytic modes of consciousness:

> Cartesian dualism, and the science erected on its false premises, are by and large the cognitive expression of a profound biopsychic disturbance. Carried to their logical conclusion, they have finally come to represent the most unecological and self-destructive culture and personality type that the world has ever seen. The idea of mastery over nature, and of economic rationality, are but partial impulses in the human being which in modern times have become organizers of the whole of human life. Regaining our health, and developing a more accurate epistemology, is not a matter of trying to destroy our ego-consciousness, but rather, as Bly suggests, a process that must involve a merger of mother and father consciousness, or more precisely, of mimetic and cognitive knowing. It is for this reason that I regard contemporary attempts to create a holistic science as the great project, and the great drama, of the late twentieth century. (M. Berman 1981, 189)

Indeed, over the past century a new cosmology has begun to emerge in diverse sciences, beginning with physics but now extending to biology, ecology, and the social sciences. We may well be standing at the doorway to a whole new way of viewing reality, a "great new synthesis" which understands the cosmos as an evolving process, "a complex, but holistic dynamic phenomenon of an universal unfolding of order which becomes manifest in many ways, as matter and energy, information and complexity, consciousness and self-reflection" (Jantsch 1980, 307). In diverse respects, it would be hard to envision a more startling contrast to the mechanistic cosmology that has been ingrained in us, yet this view is already well substantiated in many of its facets.

If this new cosmology remains virtually unknown to the vast majority of people, including many with a high level of formal education, we should not be completely surprised. Just as the old mechanistic, deterministic cosmology was promoted by the ruling elites because of the support it gave to their goals, the new cosmology may be neglected (or even subtlety repressed) because of its potential to subvert the dominant system. Even in the scientific community itself, mechanism continues to predominate in nearly every field outside of quantum physics and systems theory—though in all fields there are pioneers who are adopting nonmechanistic approaches. In part, the reluctance of scientists themselves to embrace change is due to the self-perpetuating nature of paradigms—they filter what we can and cannot see. Einstein's error in concocting a "cosmological constant" to produce a static cosmos is a case in point, as was the tendency of science simply to ignore, until very recently, nonlinear systems.

Indeed, a more holistic cosmology could prove deeply threatening to the existing social dis/order. As Edward Goldsmith observes, as long as we view nature and humanity itself as complex machines, we can maintain that our needs are only material and technological—so economic growth and "development" can satisfy all our needs and we can persist in following the surrogate cosmology of consumerism. On the other hand, if reality is really about relationships and all of nature is alive, then we may conclude that our real needs—"biological, social, ecological, spiritual and cognitive—*are ever less satisfied* by progress or economic development" (1998, 144).

Despite resistance, though, a new cosmology *is* emerging from science. In many respects, this cosmology is particularly noteworthy because it is emerging *in spite of* the long-standing prejudices and distortions of the old scientific worldview. "As in an unfolding fractal image, the universe keeps opening out and out, displaying more to be studied. The more science studies the world, the more it finds. And at every level, it discovers subtle structure, rich relationships" (Roszak 1999, 132).

This new cosmology provides fertile soil for our imaginations, opening us to new perspectives and new possibilities. Integrated with insights from more ancient sources of wisdom, the emerging cosmology could furnish us with a whole new impetus for our struggle for integral liberation. Instead of an atomistic universe composed of discrete particles that can be understood by breaking the complex into smaller, simpler components, the cosmos is increasingly revealed to be both relational and interconnected, a whole far greater than the sum of its parts. Indeed, the nature of matter itself as static and dead dissolves on closer examination into a dynamic dance of energy and relationality. Once again, the Earth, and the entire cosmos, begins to resemble a living organism, one marked by surprising bursts of creativity and emergence, one imbued once again with a deep and abiding sense of purpose—not understood as a final destination or as a static blueprint—but rather a directionality that manifests the underlying wisdom of the Tao.

7.

Transcending Matter

The Holistic Microcosm

The Tao is like a whirling void,
always at work but never exhausted.
It is like the fathomless abyss,
which is the origin of all things,
the guiding principle that fashions each being.

It blunts the sharp edge,
and loosens the knots that bind.
It softens the bright light,
and clears the dust, leaving tranquillity.

It is hidden but always present.
We cannot say from whence it comes.
It existed before creation itself.

(*Tao Te Ching* §4)

Atoms consist of particles, and these particles are not made of any material stuff. . . . When we observe them we never see any substance; what we observe are dynamic patterns continually changing into one another—the continuous dance of energy. (Capra 1982, 91)

Toward the end of the nineteenth century, mechanistic, materialist science seemed to be nearing its culmination, particularly in the field of physics. Some professors even discouraged students from undertaking graduate studies in physics since they saw few opportunities for making a truly original contribution in that field. Indeed, Lord Kelvin, one of the most respected physicists of his day, saw only two "small clouds" on the horizon remaining to be resolved.

Otherwise, our understanding of the material realm seemed virtually complete. Little did he realize that these two "small clouds" would lead to discoveries that would melt away the certainties of mechanism to reveal a new, and far more mysterious, view of reality.

One of the "small clouds" that remained was the problem of predicting the distribution of radiant energy at different frequencies from so-called "black bodies"[1]—a problem that would soon lead to the new field of quantum physics. The second was the failure of the Michelson-Morley experiment to detect the "ether" through which it was believed that light and other forms of radiation must travel. This "small cloud" became the inspiration for Einstein's Special Theory of Relativity.

According to Newton's physics, the speed of light should vary depending on whether the observer is moving toward or away from the source of the light. Light, like any wave form, requires a medium through which it must travel and that medium—the conjectural ether—must itself move (or be at rest) with respect to the observer's "frame of reference." For example, if one is moving toward the light's source, it should appear to be moving faster than if one is moving away from it.

In 1881, using newly developed instruments, Albert Michelson tried to test this theory but found no difference in the speed of light regardless of how the observer was moving. In 1887, he repeated this experiment with Edward Morley using even more accurate instruments, but they still obtained the same result. Yet how could this be? It simply made no sense in a universe governed by Newton's laws.

In 1905, Albert Einstein (1879-1955), postulated that there was indeed no ether and that the speed of light in a vacuum is constant, regardless of how fast an observer is moving toward or away from the light's source. At the same time, Einstein assumed that all observers moving at a constant velocity should observe the same physical laws.

By combining these two postulates, Einstein demonstrated that either time intervals or lengths must change according to the velocity of the moving system relative to the observer's point of view, or "frame of reference"—albeit these effects become noticeable only in systems moving close to the speed of light (like subatomic particles). According to his Special Theory of Relativity, observations will change depending on the observer's frame of reference.

Strange paradoxes result from this new view of the universe. For example, a body accelerating away from an observer, then turning around and accelerating back to return in a similar fashion, would apparently age much more slowly than the observer watching. This effect has since been proven using extremely

---

1. Black bodies are objects that absorb all the electromagnetic radiation falling on them. No radiation passes through them and none is reflected, yet they theoretically radiate every possible wavelength of energy. Despite their name, black bodies are not literally black, as they radiate light as well, particularly at higher temperatures.

accurate atomic clocks, even though the phenomenon becomes significant only at velocities near the speed of light. Moreover, two bodies with equal length while at rest will appear to be of different sizes if one is moving at speeds near that of light with respect to the other. Furthermore, *which* body appears longer will depend on one's frame of reference (i.e., from which body's "point of view" you observe things). In demonstrating these kinds of effects, the theory of relativity began to undermine the idea of objective observation lying at the root of classical Western science.

Another implication of Einstein's theory is that matter and energy are essentially interchangeable, as is demonstrated by the famous equation $E = mc^2$ (energy equals mass multiplied by the speed of light squared). Because of this, relativity challenges the static, unchanging view of matter that had dominated classical physics. Matter is simply a special form of energy, and atoms themselves can no longer be considered eternal and indivisible.

Further, relativity conceives of time itself as part of a continuum together with space. Einstein described the cosmos in terms of a four-dimensional geometry where time is treated in a way analogous to spatial dimensions. In this way, new ways of perceiving the universe are suggested which alter the way motion and change can be understood.

With the development of the General Theory of Relativity in 1916, Einstein proposed that gravitation was not a force acting at a distance, but rather a warping of the space-time continuum. Time will run more slowly, therefore, when under the influence of a gravitational field. The General Theory of Relativity was able to account for apparent aberrations in Mercury's orbit that Newtonian physics did not predict. Arthur Eddington also provided experimental backing for the General Theory of Relativity when he observed a star whose path of light had been "bent" by the sun's gravitational field during a solar eclipse in 1919 (due to the warping of space-time).

According to relativistic theories, the mass and size of objects—and even the flow of time itself—are no longer absolutes: they depend on the frame of reference of the observer. With relativity, Newton's neat, orderly, "commonsense" view of reality began to dissolve. In addition, new dynamics of wholeness were revealed including the unity of space and time and the complementarity of mass and energy.

It is in the field of subatomic physics and quantum theory, however, that scientific discoveries have most seriously undermined the Newtonian-Cartesian synthesis. The world of the very small—the microcosm—seems to be a reality that challenges our imaginations on every level. We simply cannot visualize it or conceive of it in terms of our everyday experience. In many ways, it appears to be a reality made up of unfathomable *koans*—the paradoxical mind problems used in Zen Buddhism to lead meditators to a new state of consciousness transcending discursive thinking. Even scientists seem baffled by the behavior of the subatomic world, where the field of quantum mechanics is used to describe reality. For example, the Nobel prize–winning physicist Richard Feynman has been quoted as saying, "I think I can safely say that nobody understands quantum mechanics."

At its heart, quantum physics begins by asserting that energy is composed of tiny packets called quanta. As mentioned previously, until the end of the nineteenth century it was assumed that light and other forms of electromagnetic energy consisted of waves—presumably moving through some kind of subtle medium called the ether. Experiments on blackbody radiation (examining the way bodies that absorb radiation emit heat) and the photoelectric effect (where light shining on a metal causes an electric current to flow), however, led to a new conception. First, Max Planck (1858-1947) showed that blackbody radiation is emitted in discrete multiples of a minimal amount of energy—which he called a "quantum." Then, Einstein demonstrated that the photoelectric effect results when quanta of light (called "photons") hit the metal surface, imparting their energy to the electrons there, and thus generating electricity. These discoveries set the stage for the development of quantum theory during the first half of the twentieth century.

Nick Herbert identifies three key characteristics of quantum physics that clearly differentiate it from the classical worldview of Newtonian physics. Interestingly, these same characteristics were the features that disturbed Albert Einstein: "Einstein was impressed by the success of quantum theory but could not accept the notion that at its core the world is random, is not made of things, and is connected in a peculiar way that seems to defy common sense and his own theory of relativity" (Herbert 1993, 172).

The first characteristic of the subatomic world of quantum physics could be described as *thinglessness*. Atoms, electrons, and other subatomic particles do not have objective attributes of their own until they are observed. Up until the moment of observation, they exist in some sense only as patterns of probability: one could almost think of them as potential entities, not yet manifest in reality. The way one goes about observing them also affects what one will discover. One can measure a particle's position, but if so one cannot determine its momentum, or vice versa. Further, entities like subatomic particles and photons are in some ways waves and in some ways particles. To put it another way, matter has been refined "into immaterial fields and forces," where matter itself turns out to be "a defunct idea" or a "nonconcept." "As Karl Popper once put it, in the new quantum universe, 'matter has transcended itself'" (Roszak 1999, 106).

A closely related second characteristic of the quantum microcosm is that of *randomness* or *indeterminacy*. In a world made up of probability patterns, there is simply no way to know for certain which possibility will actualize. As Nick Herbert notes, another way to understand this is to say that "identical situations can give rise to different outcomes. In the Newtonian world, identical situations always led to identical outcomes, but in the quantum realm, two atoms physically identical in every possible way can exhibit different styles of behavior" (Herbert 1993, 176) The world of linear determinism effectively dissolves with this new reality, at least when working at the subatomic scale.

Finally, the quantum world is characterized by *inseparability, relationality,* and *entanglement.* Once two objects interact, they remain connected at some level (or "entangled") for all time. What is more, this connection is instantaneous across any amount of distance, something that seems at first glance to violate the prohibition imposed by relativity against faster-than-light communication. While the connection is indeed mysterious—and is actually useless from a communications point of view owing to its random element—it does exist. The cosmos is not simply a collection of discrete objects, but rather an intertwined web of subtle relationships. As Fritjof Capra observes:

> In modern physics, the image of the [Cartesian-Newtonian] universe has been transcended by a view of one indivisible, dynamic whole whose parts are essentially interrelated and can be understood as patterns of cosmic process. At the subatomic level the interrelations and interactions between the parts of the whole are more fundamental than the parts themselves. There is motion there but there are no actors; there are no dancers, there is only the dance. (1982, 92)

In the following sections, we will explore the characteristics of the quantum microcosm more fully, drawing out insights in the process. In so doing, let us approach this strange reality as we would a creative paradox or a *koan,* realizing that, while we may not be able to comprehend the world it reveals using analysis, it *is* suggestive and creative if we can adopt a more intuitive and holistic form of cognition.

THINGLESSNESS

Since the latter part of the nineteenth century, science has shown the Newtonian atom to be a figment of the theoretical imagination. It never existed; there were never good grounds for believing it existed. The nucleus of the atom has proven to be more and more porous, as each newly discovered part reveals a deeper internal structure. "Atoms, like galaxies," the historian of science Timothy Ferris tells us, "are cathedrals of cavernous space." And like cathedrals, they have an exquisitely complex architecture that grows more baroque as we search deeper into the atomic nucleus. Or perhaps it would be a better choice of metaphor to say that the atom has opened out to reveal an infinitesimal world system as subtly complex as any ecosystem in macroscopic nature. One might almost think of the atom as having an ecology, a coherent pattern of connected parts. (Roszak 1999, 51)

Matter appears to be nothing more than ephemeral energy that flows together with exquisite coherence to produce waveforms with a dynamic stability and the appearance of solidity. (Elgin 1993, 277)

Most of us have studied the traditional image of the atom. We were taught to imagine a tight ball composed of smaller spheres—protons and neutrons—surrounded by other orbiting spheres called electrons. Already this atom is different from that of Newton, who certainly never conceived of particles smaller than the atom itself. For Newton, atoms, by definition, were the smallest possible bits of matter, indivisible by their nature.

Toward the end of the nineteenth century, however, J. J. Thomson discovered the electron, a small, negatively charged particle much, much smaller than an atom. Thomson proposed what is now called the "plum pudding" model of the atom consisting of electrons stuck on to the outer surface of a positively charged core. In 1911, Ernest Rutherford found that the positive charge at the atom's center must be concentrated in a tiny nucleus, so he proposed an image of the atom with a dense core and electrons orbiting around it. In 1914, Neils Bohr showed that the electrons must orbit in distinct shells depending on their energy level. Subsequently, Arnold Sommerfeld and Wolfgang Pauli determined the shape of the orbits and the behavior of the electrons in them. It was not until 1919, however, that Rutherford discovered the proton, a particle with a mass 1,836 times that of the electron. James Chadwick discovered the neutron—with a mass slightly greater than the proton—in 1936.

All of these discoveries and models advanced our understanding of the atom, but they are all in some ways misleading—especially once we try to visualize them or draw them. To begin with, no diagram can begin to capture the sheer spaciousness of an atom. On average, over 99.99999999999 percent of an atom's volume is empty space. Viewed another way, if the nucleus were the diameter of a pea (about 4 mm), the diameter of the atom itself would be about 100 m (about the length of a football or soccer field). If we also take into account that the electrons are much, much smaller than the nucleus, we begin to capture a basic truth: most of an atom is simply empty space. Already there appears to be very little hard, solid "stuff" in it at all.

But what about the "particles" themselves? Even these entities, which we normally visualize as hard spheres, are essentially ethereal in nature. In 1924, Louis de Broglie derived the wave-particle duality equation (using Einstein's equivalence for mass and energy, $E = mc^2$), showing that particles can also be conceived as waves. As understood today, particles are really not "things" at all in the way we normally conceive of them. Rather, they are "wave packets" or even simply "events." Theodore Roszak even notes that, "in superstring theory, one of the more esoteric schools of physical thought, particles are said to be vibrations on tiny strings that fold in ten dimensions." Based on this image, we could conceptualize particles "as musical notes that are palpably 'there' the way a chord struck on a piano is 'there'" (Roszak 1999, 32-33). Indeed, the great physicist Werner Heisenberg actually conceived of the cosmos as being composed of something more closely resembling music than either matter or energy.

According to the Sufi scholar and mystic Neil Douglas-Klotz, traditional Middle Eastern cosmology mirrors an idea similar to that of the wave-particle duality in which vibration and concrete manifestation are seen as two aspects of one reality. For example, the Aramaic word for "heaven" (*shemaya*) evokes the image of "a sacred vibration (*shem*) that vibrates without limit through the entire manifest cosmos (*aya*)" while the word for earth (*ar'ah*) can refer "to all nature with an individual form—from a plant to a star." In Genesis, both of these archetypes are created in the beginning, but they are not dualistic but rather complementary in nature. "From the 'earth' point of view, we are an array of infinitely diverse and unique beings. From the 'heaven' point of view, we are connected with every being in the universe through one wave of light or sound" (Douglas-Klotz 1999, 100). We are complete only when we can unite both visions of reality. In some sense, "heaven" is the realm of possibilities, potentiality, and visions, while "earth" is the realm of the forms made manifest at a concrete place and time.

A similar view of reality can be found in quantum physics. Not only are particles not "things" in the normal sense of the word; in some sense they are neither here nor there until they are observed by someone. According to Heisenberg's Uncertainty Principle, it is impossible to know *both* the position and momentum of a particle at any given moment: The more precisely we know one attribute; the less precisely we know the other. On one level, this is due to the nature of scientific observation itself. To observe something, at least one quantum of energy must be used. For example, we use light—made up of photons—to see something or detect it with an instrument. The quanta of energy we use—even if it is a single quantum—will affect what we observe because the particles we are dealing with are so tiny that the quanta of energy will disturb them. So, if we determine the position of a particle accurately, we will in the process affect its momentum, or vice versa.

Yet the Heisenberg Uncertainty Principle has deeper implications beyond the limitations of our ability to measure at the subatomic level. The wave nature of particles is made up of probability waves. In some sense, until it is observed, a particle exists in potential but in no one place in particular: There is simply a probability of where it is likely to be found. The very act of observation, in some mysterious way, forces it to manifest in a particular (and unpredictable) place. As Nick Herbert notes:

> By deciding what attribute you want to measure and deploying the appropriate instrument, you invite that attribute, but not its partner attribute, to manifest itself in the actual world. In the unobserved world of pure possibility, incompatible attributes [like position and momentum] can exist without contradiction, but there is room in the world of actuality for only one partner. Which partner appears is not specified in the quantum description but is decided by the type of measurement the [observer] decides to make. (1993, 177)

If it is true that particles have a wave nature, it is equally true to say that energy, including light, has a particle nature. Therefore, entities such as electrons and photons alike exist simultaneously as both waves of energy and as particles. In both cases, the Uncertainty Principle applies:

One could never say for sure whether they were particles or waves of energy, whether they could be said to exist at definite times and places or whether they tended to exist as probability waves. Today they tend to be understood as nonlinear waves, known as solitons, whose very existence makes sense only in terms of the medium to which they belong, namely, the information-rich subquantum field, hence the definition offered by Laszlo (1993, 138): quanta are observable soliton-like flows within an otherwise unobservable subquantum medium. (O'Murchu 1997, 27)

Another implication of the Heisenberg Uncertainty Principle is that, in the subatomic microcosm of quantum physics, there can be no rigid distinction between the observer and the observed—they form a single system. In some sense, the very act of observing causes the probability wave function "to collapse," forcing a particular reality to become manifest either as a wave or a particle. The physicist Wolfgang Pauli (1900-1958) noted that every observation, then, involves both choice and sacrifice: in choosing to know one thing, we sacrifice knowledge about the other (Wilber 1985). At the same time, what we find depends on what we are seeking. This implies a radically different epistemology, or way of knowing, than that of classical physics. One of the key physicists involved in exploring the wave-particle duality of quantum phenomena, Erwin Schrödinger (1887-1961), wrote:

> The idea of subjectivity in all appearance is very old and familiar. What is new in that present setting is this: that not only would the impressions we get from our environment largely depend on the nature and the contingent state of our sensorium, but, inversely, the very environment that we wish to take in is modified by us, notably by the devices we set up in order to observe it. . . .
> The world is given to me only once, not one existing and one perceived. Subject and object are only one. The barrier between them cannot be said to have broken down as a result of recent experience in the physical sciences, for this barrier does not exist. (Wilber 1985, 81)

Neils Bohr (1885-1962), in reflecting on the Heisenberg Uncertainty Principle, maintained that it was wrong to assert that a subatomic entity like an electron could even have a path, position, or velocity. According to Bohr, "the very concept of a path is ambiguous at the quantum scale of things" (Peat 1990, 45). In this more radical perspective:

> The quantum world is *actual*—things really happen in it—but not *real*, in the sense of containing *res*, things, as we perceive and identify various aspects of reality. "According to the Copenhagen view," writes Thompson (1990, 99), "until the observation is made particles have ambiguous, 'ghostly' states and then the observation 'reduces' the particles to the determinate states we observe . . ." Zohar (1993, 21ff.) adopts a similar view, considering reality as a vast sea of potential for which the scientist (and, indeed, each one of us)

acts as a midwife—evoking, at any one time, one or more aspects of the vast underlying potential. (O'Murchu 1997, 30)

For most of us, the idea that a single entity exists as a probability wave until it manifests as a particle defies the imagination. A related phenomenon can serve to illustrate just how strange quantum reality really is: the famous double-slit experiment. In this experiment, light is first passed through a single, very narrow slit to fall on a piece of photographic film. A single band of light will then be marked on the film. If we have two slits in close proximity instead of one, however, the waves of light from the two slits overlap and reinforce one another in some places, and cancel each other in others, forming a multi-banded interference pattern. All of this is perfectly understandable from the standpoint of classical physics.

What, though, if we weaken the intensity of the light so that only one photon is emitted at a time? This can, in fact, be done and the light will be detected using sensitive photographic film. As expected, using a single slit, the pattern that emerges is one of tiny dots where each photon—an indivisible quantum of light—has hit the film: so far, so good. Now, we repeat the experiment emitting one photon at a time, but with two slits open. Since each photon is indivisible, we would expect it to go through only one slit or the other. Therefore, we would expect two bands of dots, one band behind each of the two slits. *This, however, does not happen.* Instead, an interference pattern is generated. Yet how can that be? If each photon was emitted individually, how could it interfere with another? There was no other photon present for it to interfere with!

The inevitable conclusion is that quantum theory has thrown common sense out the window and that physicists have been forced to acknowledge that single, indivisible photons *act* as if they can pass through two slits at once and be in two places at the same time. Either that, or some new and mysterious communication is taking place that seems to inform a photon in one part of the universe what is happening in other parts. (Peat 1990, 10)

The results of the experiment are identical if, instead of light, we use a "particle" like an electron. The double-slit experiment not only demonstrates how strange the world of wave-particle duality is; it may point to some kind of deep, underlying unity that informs the behavior of the parts.

As we have noted, the double-slit experiment also seems to imply that it may be possible for a particle or a quantum of energy to be in more than one place at a time. In some sense, this should not surprise us. If a particle is nowhere in particular until it is observed, it is in one way present—at least in potential—in many places simultaneously.[2]

---

2. To clarify, one possible way to understand what is happening is that each photon (or electron), when it reaches the two slits, is still simply a potential entity since it has not yet been observed. So, one potential aspect of the photon passes through each of the two slits and interferes with its other potential self *before* reaching the film where it is finally observed. It is only on reaching the film, however, that it is forced to become manifest, but by then the interference has already occurred in the potential realm, so what we observe is an interference pattern.

Indeed, concepts like path and position make little sense when dealing with quantum phenomena. For example, it is actually possible for a quantum entity to move from one place to another without ever occupying the intermediate space in between. This occurs, for example, when a radioactive element emits an elementary particle from its nucleus. At one moment, it is in the nucleus and the next it is moving away at high speed, yet it is never in the process of escaping. What is more, this jump is instantaneous. It is as if the particle disappears from the nucleus and simply reappears outside of it.

Neils Bohr maintained that we simply cannot build a picture or create models of the atomic world because each time we do so the concepts of classical physics and our perceptions of our everyday reality will creep in. As David Peat writes, "All talk about paths, orbits, and intrinsic properties represents hangovers of classical thinking and traditional ways of visualizing the universe. As soon as we try to imagine pictures of the atom, such ideas enter, and the result is paradox and confusion" (Peat 1990, 64). The best we can do is use the approach of complementarity, for there is no "single, unambiguous account for the quantum world" (Peat 1990, 65). We must use words in pairs like space and time, or particle and wave. An elementary particle has both a localized, individual form and a distributed, wavelike form; or, in the concepts of Middle Eastern cosmology, it is simultaneously a part of the realm of *shemaya* (heaven) and the realm of *ar'ah* (earth).

At the level of subatomic reality, then, there seem to be no things in the sense we normally conceive of them. Nobel prize–winning physicist Steven Weinberg concluded that "out of the fusion of relativity with quantum mechanics there has evolved a new view of the world, one in which matter has lost its central view" (quoted in Roszak 1999, 51). In this same vein, as we have noted earlier, Werner Heisenberg eventually came to see the universe as being composed of music rather than matter or energy. In speaking of subatomic particles, Heisenberg noted that "the smallest units of matter are, in fact, not physical objects in the ordinary sense of the word; they are forms; structures or—in Plato's sense—Ideas" (Wilber 1985, 52). In speaking with David Peat, Heisenberg observed that "'the building blocks of matter' was a confused misrepresentation of the nature of quantum reality. Rather, they were the surface manifestations of underlying quantum processes. What was more fundamental . . . were symmetries rather than particles" (Peat 1994, 283). Another physicist, David Bohm (1917-1992), described subatomic particles as "concentrations and knots in a fundamental, continuous field" (quoted in Roszak 1999, 52). They are entities that somehow give shape and solidity to matter, but they themselves are insubstantial. At its foundation, the cosmos is made up not of "things" or "stuff," but rather dynamic, relational structures arising from something yet deeper and more subtle.

RADICAL RELATIONALITY

For physicists after Einstein, even the distinction between existing or not existing became fluid. Wave-like patterns in interdependent relation showed probable "tendencies to exist" as events or particles. Instead of decomposing the world into ultimate entities or "building blocks," scientists arrived at a void-like web of relationships in which events arise in interconnection with each other. This relational web is coterminal with the entire cosmos, in which everything is connected with everything, not only across space, but across time as well. (Ruether 1992, 38)

The realm of the quantum microcosm is one where the world of things dissolves into a world of process and relationship. "An elementary particle," writes physicist Henry Stapp, "is not an independently existing . . . entity. It is, in essence, a set of relationships that reach outward to all things" (quoted in Capra 1982, 81). Similarly, Stapp goes on to describe the atom itself as "*a web of relationships* in which no part can stand alone; each part derives its meaning and existence only from its place within the whole" (quoted in Roszak 1999, 126).

Experimental evidence of the profoundly relational nature of the microcosm comes to us in part from the giant accelerators used to tear subatomic particles apart. As smaller and smaller particles are found, it seems that the strength of the relationships binding them together also becomes stronger. The subatomic particles called quarks,[3] for example, coexist in tightly knit families. Even using truly titanic forces, it is possible to separate them only for an instant—less than one quadrillionth of a second—before they return, once again, to their closely bonded group. Drawing on this example, Theodore Roszak observes that "the complexity of patterned wholes in the atomic and subatomic level is turning out to be more tenacious, more resistant to disruption than anything built from them. It is almost as if nature were trying to tell us that relatedness is what came first and can never be meaningfully reduced to something more fundamental" (1999, 125).

The web of relations at the foundation of the cosmos exists also through what are called "non-local" connections that are both instantaneous and independent of distance. This phenomenon, sometimes called quantum entanglement, occurs whenever two particles interact with each other. From that time onward, they remain mysteriously linked together: the state of each particle remains forever correlated with that of the other.

The implications of this kind of entanglement were first discussed in 1935 when Einstein, together with Boris Podolsky and Nathan Rosen, published a paper critiquing quantum mechanics as incomplete. In the paper, they used a "thought experiment" that demonstrated that quantum theory implies that measuring an attribute of one particle would necessarily affect any other particles that had become "entangled" with it through a previous interaction. Since such an effect would have to be both instantaneous and independent of the distance separating the two particles, Einstein and his colleagues concluded that something must be missing from quantum theory because such instantaneous,

---

3. Protons and neutrons are actually made up of quarks. Quarks come in a number of "flavors" including up and down quarks as well as charm, strange, top, and bottom quarks!

non-local communication between particles seemed to violate the prohibition against faster-than-light communication imposed by the Theory of Relativity.

In 1964, John Bell (1928-1990) turned the argument of Einstein and his colleagues on its head when he proposed what is now called "Bell's Theorem." Instead of assuming that non-local connections were impossible, he assumed that they did, in fact, exist. If one observes one particle and therefore "collapses its wave function," forcing it to manifest in a particular way, the wave function of another particle entangled with it must also collapse simultaneously. Subsequent experiments have confirmed this phenomenon. These instantaneous connections are, however, subtle and do not allow for meaningful communication because they occur beneath the surface appearance of things. We can prove that they exist, but we cannot see them directly.

Not only do connections between particles transcend space; they also transcend time. As Robert Nadeau and Menas Kafatos note, other experiments demonstrate that "the past is inexorably mixed with the present and even the phenomenon of time is tied to specific experimental choices" (1999, 50).

Bell's Theorem and the phenomenon of quantum entanglement point to a deep, underlying unity connecting the entire cosmos at the level of quantum reality. Indeed, given our current understanding of the beginnings of the cosmos where energy, space, and time unfurl together in the so-called Big Bang, it seems safe to assume that all quantum entities have, in fact, interacted with each other and become entangled:

> Physicist N. David Mermin has shown, that quantum entanglement grows exponentially with the number of particles involved in the original quantum state and that there is no theoretical limit on the number of these entangled particles. If this is the case, the universe on a very basic level could be a vast web of particles, which remain in contact with one another over any distance in "no time" in the absence of the transfer of energy or information. This suggests, however strange or bizarre it might seem, that all of physical reality is a single quantum system that responds together to further interactions. . . . Nonlocality, or non-separability . . . could translate into the much grander notion of nonlocality, or non-separability, as the factual condition in the entire universe. (Nadeau and Kafatos 1999, 81)

The idea of non-local connections, even if of a very subtle nature, was so shocking for Einstein and his colleagues that they simply could not accept them. Indeed, non-locality deeply challenges some of the most cherished assumptions of science since the time of Descartes and Newton. When the universe was understood as a giant machine, we envisioned a cosmos where things were pushing and pulling on one another. Things moved because something else acted upon them. Causality was not only linear; it was also local and mechanistic in nature.

Yet, in the case of quantum entanglement, nothing is there to push or pull on anything else. The whole relationship of cause and effect becomes much more mysterious and complex. Indeed, in some ways, the entire quantum realm seems to be governed by blind chance and probability—something that scientists like Einstein found hard to accept: "I cannot believe that God would play dice with the Universe" (quoted in Herbert 1993, 173). Yet the existence of non-local connections opens another possibility for understanding causality at the level of the quantum realm:

> In quantum theory individual events do not always have a well-defined cause. For example, the jump of an electron from one atomic orbit to another, or the disintegration of a subatomic particle, may occur spontaneously without any single event causing it. We can never predict when and how such a phenomenon is going to happen; we can only predict its probability. This does not mean that atomic events occur in completely arbitrary fashion; it means only that they are not brought about by local causes. The behavior of any part is determined by its non-local connections to the whole, and since we do not know those connections precisely, we have to replace the narrow classical notion of cause and effect by the wider concept of statistical causality. (Capra 1982, 85-86)

Perhaps instead of "statistical causality," it would be preferable to speak of "holistic causality." We live in a cosmos whose foundations are built on deep rooted—or radical—relationality. On some subtle level, everything influences everything else. Cause and effect are neither linear nor local, nor are they simply random; instead, they are both mysterious and creative. The image of the clockwork universe is shattered, and what emerges in its place is something far more holistic in nature, something that more closely resembles a giant organism than a machine.

THE PREGNANT VOID

The fabric of space-time is . . . involved in [the] dance of creation. So-called empty space is no longer viewed as a featureless vacuum, as it was in classical physics. Space is not the simple absence of form, waiting to be filled with matter; instead space is a dynamic presence that is filled with an incredibly complex architecture. (Elgin 1993, 279)

In classical physics, the counterpart of hard, solid matter was the emptiness of space. As we have seen, the hard matter of Newton and his followers has now dissolved into something far more subtle and ethereal. Atoms themselves consist of scintillating wave forms; they are more like dynamic vortices than anything substantial. Electrons vibrate nearly five hundred *trillion* times each second, as many oscillations as would be made by a ticking clock in sixteen million years. The physicist Max Born (1882-1970) has written, "The deeper we penetrate, the more restless becomes the universe; all is rushing about and vibrating in a wild dance" (quoted in Elgin 1993, 277).

Yet, not only does modern physics change our conception of matter; space and time have also become intertwined, forming a dynamic unity. At any moment, a particle and its antiparticle can spontaneously spring into existence from this apparent emptiness, and then in the next moment annihilate each other again. Whence do they come? They seem to arise from the void—yet it is not clear if that void is simply space-time as we perceive it, or a hidden reality from which space-time itself arises. In any case, this "pregnant void" seems to be a kind of vast sea of energy seething with possibilities. Some physicists even speculate that, at times, waves of energy in the void may come together and that this brief surge could birth a whole new universe.

Classical physics taught us to see matter as fundamental—space was just a kind of canvas in which matter existed and moved. Yet, in the new understanding of the cosmos, space may have gained primacy: "Space is not static emptiness but a continuous opening process that provides a context for matter to manifest. Because space-time is inseparable from motion, and motion is another way of describing energy, it follows that vast amounts of energy must be required to generate the openness of the enormous volume of space-time that exists in our cosmos" (Elgin 1993, 279).

According to quantum field theory, what we perceive as "empty space" actually contains a huge "zero point energy," which arises from the combination of all the quantum fields it encompasses. The "empty" vacuum, not matter, is fundamental: matter is simply a small perturbation on an immense sea of energy. By some estimates, there is as much energy in a single cubic centimeter of the void (or the space being manifest from the void) than would be generated if all the known matter in the universe were to disintegrate (Bohm and Peat 1987).

The very nature of the atom may provide some evidence for this vast ocean of energy. In classical physics, one would expect electrons to radiate energy and gradually spiral inward until they fell into the nucleus. This does not, however, occur. Indeed, this is one of the original problems that inspired quantum theory: electrons are restrained to particular orbits, or energy levels. Therefore, they do not constantly radiate energy unless they jump from one orbit to another. In that case, they will emit energy as discrete multiples of a single quantum.

This does not, however, exactly explain why the electrons at the lowest energy levels do not eventually fall into the nucleus. The standard answer seems to be simply, "because they don't." One theory providing an alternative—and perhaps more satisfying—answer comes from Harold Puthoff, a physicist at the University of Texas. Puthoff believes that atoms constantly draw on energy inherent in the vacuum to compensate for the energy that radiates from the electron. According to Duane Elgin (1993, 278), Puthoff affirms that "the dynamic stability of matter verifies the presence of an underlying sea of immensely powerful energy that is universally present."

Some physicists even suggest a new kind of continuous-creation cosmology. Since matter is best understood as a kind of ongoing process—"patterns that perpetuate themselves; whirlpools of water in an ever-flowing river," as mathematician Norbert Wiener (1894-1964) put it—material objects can be understood as "dynamically constructed resonance patterns that exist within the larger resonance pattern of the 'standing wave' that is our cosmos" (Elgin 1993,

277-78). In this view, the entire universe is continually flickering in and out of existence at each moment. We perceive matter as solid simply because the oscillations occur so rapidly. Reality is a kind of vibration arising from the pregnant void, waves on a vast ocean of energy.

Brian Swimme compares the void to the "super-essential darkness of God" that is "the ground of all being" (quoted in Scharper 1997, 121). Zohar and Marshall (1994) compare it to the Buddhist concept of *Sunyata*, an emptiness filled with pure potentiality. We might also compare it to the Tao itself:

> The Tao is like a whirling void,
> always at work but never exhausted.
> It is like the fathomless abyss,
> which is the origin of all things,
> the guiding principle that fashions each being.

(*Tao Te Ching* §4)

In reflecting on the immense energy present in the pregnant void, the words of Thomas Berry quoted at the beginning of this book come to mind: "We are not lacking in the dynamic forces needed to create the future. We live immersed in a sea of energy beyond all comprehension. But this energy, in an ultimate sense, is ours not by domination but by invocation" (1999, 175). Berry may not have been referring to the zero point energy of quantum field theory, but somehow the two images seem to coincide. Is it possible to *invoke* the vast energy present in the void to realize new possibilities? How might we do this? Obviously, this is not a question of willpower, for we cannot hope to dominate or control such vast energies. Are there ways, though, to invoke it, to midwife new possibilities from the pregnant void?

Perhaps traditional practices of meditation, designed to lead us into a state of receptive emptiness, could hold a key in this process. In any case, reflecting on the vast potential present all around us may give new hope to the possibility of moving toward a deep and radical liberation that would fundamentally change our relationship to the cosmos, to the Earth, and to all the communities of beings to which we belong.

THE IMMANENCE OF MIND

Today there is a wide measure of agreement which, on the physical side of science, approaches almost to unanimity that the stream of knowledge is heading towards a nonmechanical reality; the universe begins to look more like a great thought than like a great machine. Mind no longer appears as an accidental intruder into the realm of matter; we are beginning to suspect that we ought rather to hail it as the creator and governor of the realm of matter—not, of course, our individual minds, but the mind in which the atoms out of which our individual minds have grown exist as thoughts. (Sir James Jeans, quoted in Wilber 1985, 151)

The Cartesian worldview was constructed on a strict dualism that separated mind from matter. Quantum physics, however, seems largely to dissolve this distinction. The nature of matter has been transformed into what the physicist Arthur Eddington (1882-1944) described as "mind stuff" (Wilber 1985). The Heisenberg Uncertainty Principle demonstrates that what is observed depends on the choices of the observer. The act of observation not only disturbs what is being measured; it actually seems to invite it to manifest in a particular way—or perhaps more poetically, to invoke it into being. Until the moment of observation, Heisenberg maintained that quantum entities like atoms and elementary particles "form a world of potentialities or possibilities rather than one of things or facts" (quoted in Peat 1990, 63). Building on this idea, the mathematician John von Neumann (1903-1957) believed that the entire physical world remains in a state of pure possibility (i.e., as probability waves) until a conscious mind "decides to promote a portion of the world from its usual state of indefiniteness into a condition of actual existence" (Herbert 1993, 156). Nick Herbert describes von Neumann's view as follows:

> The general idea of von Neumann and his followers is that the material world by itself is hardly material, consisting of nothing but relentlessly unrealized vibratory possibilities. From outside this purely possible world, mind steps in to render some of these possibilities actual and to confer on the resultant phenomenal world those properties of solidity, single-valuedness, and dependability traditionally associated with matter. (1993, 250)

In von Neumann's view, consciousness essentially midwifes reality into existence. It is an intriguing idea. Certainly, it moves us into deep questions of philosophy: Can we say that something has been observed if there is no center of consciousness involved? For instance, an instrument emitting a quantum of energy to detect the position of an elementary particle, by itself, cannot truly "collapse the wave function" any more than a random photon of light colliding with the same particle can. A real observer recording the measurement must be involved—and this implies consciousness. So, if consciousness is considered a prerequisite for observation, von Neumann's assertion seems to be a logical consequence of the Heisenberg Uncertainty Principle. As Morris Berman (1981) observes, this kind of interpretation of quantum mechanics implies a new form of participating consciousness—something closer to the worldview of alchemy than that of classical science.

Some have described this view as *quantum animism*. This perspective—that our minds in some way manifest or specify a reality—coincides with that of many religions and philosophies of the East. But does not such an idea seem to be deeply anthropocentric? By privileging consciousness in such a way, are we not assigning humans a central role? Only if we believe that mind and consciousness are exclusive attributes of human beings. In reality, there is no reason to believe that animals, for example, do not have some form of consciousness. Indeed, it is nearly impossible to *prove* that anything does or does not possess consciousness. We only know that we ourselves possess it because we experience it directly. We assume that other people also possess it because they affirm that they do, but we have no direct proof. Could not consciousness be far more wide-spread than we have been taught to believe? Certainly, there may be different forms of consciousness in different kinds of beings, but might not even plants have some kind of consciousness? We simply cannot know for certain one way or another.

If, as James Jeans (1877-1946) maintained, the cosmos itself resembles a great thought, might not mind be immanent in the cosmos? As we will examine in more detail in chapter 10, it now seems very improbable that the universe took form through mere random chance and the blind shuffling of particles, energy, and nascent matter. Might it not be, then, as Jeans believed, that mind ought to be conceived as the author and creator of the entire realm of matter, and indeed the entire cosmos? At the very least, if we see consciousness, including self-reflective consciousness, as an emergent property of the whole process of cosmic evolution, then we must say that the universe itself is conscious in some sense. Certainly, human beings are at least one aspect of the cosmos that has become conscious; but if this consciousness has emerged in humans, it may well have emerged in many other places as well, including other organisms on Earth (even if in different forms that may vary in their capacity for self-reflection). As Theodore Roszak writes:

> As long as time is understood to have had a start, then in some sense that science cannot yet find the language to clarify, the mind I use to write these words, the mind you use to read them, have always been *there*, enfolded in the first radiation that bulged into nothingness to create space. The laws and patterns of development were there, the structure-making thrust of time was there to yield this end. Now when we look back across cosmic history to study the background radiation of deep space or the outrushing of the far-thest astronomical bodies, we draw upon a consciousness that was born out of that very process, and we take in what we see as an idea: the idea of the cosmos. (1992, 134)

David Spangler notes that cultures imbued with a mechanistic cosmology have come to see mind and consciousness as ephemeral, while in some mystical and animistic traditions the opposite was the case—physical reality, including matter, was considered to be a projection of consciousness; reality was invoked into being by the mind. The latter view seems to more closely echo that of quantum animism. Yet, if mind in some way constructs our perception of physical reality, it does not do so in a controlling or dominating fashion: "Mind is not 'over' matter (nor matter 'over' mind). Each shapes and affects the other in a universal dance that creates and dissolves forms and patterns" (Spangler 1996, 59). Similarly, the philosopher Peter Koestenbaum writes, "There is no specific border in which mind becomes matter. . . . The area of connection is more like a gradually thickening fog" (quoted in M. Berman 1981, 148). Mind and matter interpenetrate each other: each gives rise to the other; or perhaps both are simply complementary manifestations of something that exists on a still more subtle level.

Given this understanding of mind and matter, the physicist Wolfgang Pauli maintained that we should see the body and mind as "complementary aspects of the same reality." Morris Berman believes that quantum physics implies that the relationship between the body and mind may be thought of as a kind of field, "alternatively diaphanous and solid" (1981, 148).

Indeed, just as matter may in some way be constructed by the mind, mind may also emerge from matter—or, more precisely, from quantum processes in the brain. As Danah Zohar and I. N. Marshall note, there is simply no mechanistic process that can account for the highly unified sense of "I" that results from the interaction of some one hundred billion neurons in the brain; in contrast, an "emergent, holistic quantum structure possibly could" (1994, 73). They propose that our brains may generate what is known as a "Bose-Einstein condensate," or perhaps a similar phenomenon. Bose-Einstein condensates are found in lasers, where photons become correlated into the same optical state, and in superconductors, where groups of linked electrons called Cooper pairs occupy identical quantum possibilities. Herbert Frölich, a physicist from Great Britain, has theorized that living systems might also be able to host this same kind of process using the phenomenon of ferroelectricity. In turn, Marshall believes that this kind of ferroelectric system could exist in the brain (Herbert 1993).

Bose-Einstein condensates are characterized by both fluid, ever-changing order and a highly correlated state of unity. Such a process might account for the inner unity of experience characteristic of consciousness: the highly coherent emergent electric field generated by the brain may form a kind of background state of consciousness giving us our sense of a unified "I." This background state would be analogous to a body of water upon which our thoughts, emotions, memories, and images ripple like tiny wavelets on a pool's surface.

Another reason for believing that the brain might involve quantum processes such as those found in a Bose-Einstein condensate is that this could account for its truly awesome processing capabilities. One neurobiologist calculated that a standard serial or parallel computer would need more time to process just one perceptual event that has passed since the beginning of the cosmos. In contrast, if the brain used quantum processes it would be capable of testing all the different possible combinations of data simultaneously, enabling it quickly to produce a unified sense of experience (Zohar and Marshall 1994).

If the mind somehow functions at the level of quantum reality, might it be able to interact directly with other quantum phenomena? Might mind even be able to act directly on what we normally call physical reality? An extensive study conducted by Robert Jahn and Brenda Dunne found that mind seems to be able to affect the operation of a random number generator. The effect is extremely small, yet quite measurable. After seven years of work, the overall psychokinesis effect was so significant that there was only a one in a million chance that it could be due to purely random causes. As Nick Herbert concludes, "If experiments of this sort had been continually carried out since the Stone Age, no more than one result this far from average would have occurred by accident" (1993, 199).

Another carefully constructed experiment demonstrates that separate minds seem to be able to link in a way that defies any ordinary physical explanation.

William Braud and Donna Shafer separated pairs of people in different buildings. One subject could view the other via a TV monitor connected to a camera viewing the other person. Every thirty seconds, the person being viewed was asked whether the person in the other building was staring at him or her or not. By chance alone, they should have been able to guess correctly only half of the time, and this was the result that was actually achieved; however, a galvanic skin response monitor connected to the persons being viewed detected an abnormally high stress reading 59 percent of the times that the person was being stared at—significantly higher than the expected 50 percent. On a subconscious level, then, those being viewed sensed that they were being stared at, even though on a conscious level they seemed unable to do so. Herbert concludes: "This experiment seems to suggest that separate minds can link via connections that defy ordinary mechanical explanation. The connection in this case seems to have been made below the level of the conscious mind, registered by a subtle bodily response rather than by a fully conscious perception" (1993, 241). Perhaps this could be an indication of some kind of non-local connection operating at the quantum level.

A third experiment, involving the relationship between prayer and healing, seems to indicate that thought and intention may influence biological processes over a distance. A cardiologist, Randolph Byrd, divided nearly four hundred cardiac patients into two roughly equal groups. The names of half of these patients were given to prayer groups throughout the United States. Four to seven people prayed for each of these patients—but neither the patients nor their physicians knew that this was happening. At the end of the experiment, though, it was found that the group of patients who had received the attention of the prayer groups were five times less likely to need antibiotics and three times less likely to suffer from fluid in the lungs. None of the prayed-for patients required endotracheal intubation to assist in breathing, versus twelve persons who needed this in the other group. At the same time, the effect of prayer seemed completely independent of distance (Herbert 1993). Of course, this phenomenon could equally be attributed to divine intervention, but such an explanation also defies purely mechanistic causes. Either the minds of the individuals praying for the patients affected them, or the operation of some kind of larger Mind was at work.

If intention and thought somehow interact with physical reality, there are important implications for transformative action. Liberation must be both liberation from oppressive social structures *and* liberation from oppressive ways of thinking. Vision and intention may have a very real and direct effect on our work for the health and well-being of the planet. To some extent, vision and intention may have a direct role in bringing about change. That is not to say that political action and organization are not important or necessary; it is only to say that work on what we might refer to as the level of intention (or spirituality) should also accompany all work aimed at transforming structures of domination and oppression. No dichotomy or dualism should exist between them.

If mind and physical reality somehow interpenetrate each other, what does that say about the place of humans in the cosmos? To return to Brian Swimme's question: Is the universe a friendly place? James Jeans observed:

The new knowledge compels us to revise our hasty first impressions that we had stumbled into a universe which either did not concern itself with life or was actively hostile to life. The old dualism of mind and matter, which was mainly responsible for the supposed hostility, seems likely to disappear, not through matter becoming in any way more shadowy or insubstantial than heretofore, or through mind becoming resolved into a function of the working of matter, but through substantial matter resolving itself into a creation and manifestation of mind. (Wilber 1985, 151)

Obviously, the relationship between the mind and what we have normally conceived of as physical reality is a complex one. What is apparent, though, is that the old Cartesian dualism that split mind from matter is simply not tenable given what we know about quantum physics. At the very least, consciousness seems capable of somehow "collapsing the wave function," inducing quantum reality to manifest in a particular way. At the level of quantum phenomena, mind in some sense seems to midwife reality into being. At the same time, it may be possible that mind itself has a quantum dimension in its functioning. It also seems probable that mind and matter interact in other ways that we do not yet understand and that mind-to-mind connections may also exist. In any case, an integral approach to liberation must seriously endeavor to unite thought, vision, and intention with more traditional approaches to organization and action for transformation.

THE HOLOGRAPHIC COSMOS

In the heaven of Indra there is said to be a network of pearls, so arranged that if you look at one you see all the others reflected in it, and if you move in to any part of it, you set off the sound of bells that ring through every part of the network, through every part of reality. In the same way, each person, each object in the world, is not merely itself, but involves every other person and object and, in fact, on one level is every other person and object. (paraphrase of the Avatamska Sutra by Houston 1982, 188)

In the quantum realm, a particularized reality seems to become momentarily manifest out of a vast sea of possibilities. Mind and consciousness appear to play a direct role in this process of manifestation. But is there a deeper reality, "beyond the veil" so to speak, from which elementary particles and waves become manifest? Do mind, energy, matter, space, and time emerge from yet another plane that we cannot perceive directly, but only through inference?

James Jeans believed that the most important implication of quantum physics is that scientists, for the first time in many centuries, were forced to recognize that they were dealing with only the shadows of reality, not reality itself. Schrödinger agreed, writing: "Please note that the very recent advance of quantum and relativistic physics does not lie in the world of physics itself having acquired this shadowy character; it had ever since Democritus of Abdera and even before, but we were not aware of it; we thought we were dealing with the world itself" (quoted in Wilber 1985, 7). Yet, if this is true, that we are dealing in some sense with shadows, just what is casting the shadows that we perceive?

One of the most intriguing ideas that attempts to grapple with this question is the "holographic analogy" proposed by physicist David Bohm. A hologram is an interference pattern produced on a photographic plate by two lasers, one reflected off the object being recorded and another, the reference beam, aimed directly at the film. While the image produced on the plate itself is indecipherable to the eye, a three-dimensional image of the original object is reproduced when a laser is passed through the developed film. What is more, even a tiny fragment of the photographic plate can reproduce the entire image at a reduced size. Like the Pearls of Indra, described in the Buddhist sutra at the beginning of this section, each part of the hologram contains the essence of the whole.

The holographic analogy postulates the existence of an *explicate* and an *implicate* level of reality. The *implicate* order, like the image on the photographic plate, is an "enfolded" reality—in essence, the unifying ground from which all phenomena arise, the formless void from which our perceived reality becomes manifest (which we might understand as the Tao itself). In contrast, what we normally experience is the *explicate*, or unfolded, order of space and time.

The implicate order is both holistic and non-local in nature, while the explicate order corresponds to the world of appearances composed of individual objects. We could think of the implicate order as a river and the explicate order as the movements on its surface that are actually created and sustained by the river itself:

> The whirlpool or vortex in a river, for example, has a definite location in space and time. It is even possible to generate in the river special sorts of waves, called solitons, that behave in many respects like particles—even to the extent of colliding with one another. Yet these vortices and solitons have no independent existence apart from the river that supports them. The vortex exists through the act of being constantly created. (Peat 1990, 156)

The idea of the implicate order, then, is perhaps in many ways equivalent to that of the pregnant void that we have previously discussed. For David Bohm, the implicate order enfolds space, time, matter, and energy. The explicate order—the world of our normal perceptions—is actually only a small portion of reality. The forms we see are simply a temporary unfolding of the implicate order, which underlies and sustains all. Interestingly, in searching for a mathematics to describe the implicate realm, Bohm and his colleague Basil Hiley considered Grassman algebra, originally formulated to describe the nature of thought itself (Peat 1994).

Working with Bohm, the neurologist Karl H. Pribram has theorized that the mind itself seems to exist—at least in some of its dimensions—in the implicate order, but transforms this into the explicate using a process mathematically similar to Fourier transforms (Peat 1987). As the laser shining on a photographic plate of an interference pattern constructs a hologram, the focus of consciousness constructs a perception of reality. The mind itself is analogous to a hologram enfolded in a holographic universe. Unlike a hologram, however, reality and the mind are dynamic. For this reason, David Bohm prefers the term "holo-flux" (or "holomovement") to describe the idea (Weber 1982).

The theory of the mind functioning in a way analogous to a laser becomes even more intriguing if we combine it with the idea of the brain generating a kind of Bose-Einstein condensate, the same kind of phenomenon actually at work in a laser. As Zohar and Marshall (1994) note, a hologram is simply a kind of ripple or modulation of the laser's underlying uniform field. Similarly, thoughts and perceptions in the mind may constitute ripples on the Bose-Einstein condensate generated by the brain. A deep meditative state, in contrast, returns the mind to a state of pure, undisturbed consciousness similar to a mirror-still pond or a laser unperturbed by a hologram.

If the mind is in some way similar to a hologram, we would expect that it would also display the same holistic dynamic that allows each part to include the whole. The nature of memory seems to be a case in point. As Karl Pribram has noted, memories do not appear to be localized within the brain but rather to be distributed in some mysterious way. Damage to the brain does not result in the loss of selective memories—even if the damage has been widely distributed. David Peat (1990) wonders if non-local correlations might not be involved in this phenomenon—suggesting, perhaps, some kind of quantum process at work. Others have speculated that memory is not stored anywhere at all, but rather that the mind is somehow able to look back in time to past events and experiences. Alternatively, if the mind exists in the implicate order, perhaps it has ways of storing memory outside of the physical brain. Maybe the brain only serves as a way of accessing memories, but not of actually storing them.

There are intriguing parallels between the idea of the implicate order—or the pregnant void to which it seems largely to correspond—and spiritual beliefs of many peoples. The aboriginal peoples of Australia, for example, see the universe as having two aspects: one corresponds to "ordinary" reality (or the explicate order) and another one from which the physical world is derived, called the "Dreamtime." The Dreamtime, which we could understand as corresponding to the implicate order, sings material reality into existence including rocks, rivers, trees, animals, and human beings. All is continually sustained by the Dreamtime (Elgin 1993). Similarly, the Tibetan Buddhist tradition believes that all phenomena arise from the void and that all is impermanent. Lama Govinda writes that "this apparently solid and substantial world [is] . . . a whirling of continually arising and disintegrating forms" (quoted in Elgin 1993, 284). These beliefs also relate to the idea of continual creation discussed earlier. Indeed, the holographic analogy implies that the world of phenomena is continually being sustained, is continually being created, out of the implicate order.

Even if the intricacies of the holographic theory are difficult to comprehend and are in many respects still quite speculative, it is interesting to consider some of the theory's implications, many of which coincide with earlier observations about the nature of quantum reality. First, there seems to be no such thing as pure energy or pure matter. Every aspect of the universe exists as a kind of vibrational expression—something that coincides, of course, with the whole idea of wave-particle duality and the Uncertainty Principle. This idea resembles the cosmology of the Sufis, which sees all reality in terms of vibration:

> The life absolute from which has sprung all that is felt, seen, and perceived [corresponding to the explicate order], and into which all again merges in time, is a silent, motionless, and eternal life which among the Sufis is called *zat* [corresponding to the implicate order]. Every motion that springs forth from this silent life is a vibration and creator of vibrations. (Inayat Khan 1983, 5)

Second, every facet of the cosmos is a whole, comprehensive system, containing all the information about itself. Yet, at the same time, each facet is also a part of a larger whole, the implicate order that pervades all. Since all the vibratory events intermingle within the unifying "holoflux," each facet also contains information about the whole. This part of the holographic analogy coincides with the idea of non-local connections implicit in Bell's Theorem, but also in some sense amplifies and expands it. The image of the Pearls of Indra once again comes to mind: each part of reality in some sense reflects the whole.

Third, time in the holographic universe is not restricted to a linear flow, but rather may exist multi-dimensionally, flowing out in different directions simultaneously. The old, mechanistic cosmology was deterministic, seeing all events within the framework of cause and effect. While such explanations may at times be useful, they are hardly complete as the many occurrences of "synchronicity" (Jung's term for mysteriously meaningful coincidences) demonstrate. In the holographic model, the unity of the psychic and material realms comes into play: synchronicities occur at those moments when the mind functions in its true order and its creative potential is realized (Talbot 1991, 158). This does not imply that reality is an illusion, but rather that our psyche can interact directly with the explicate order.

A holographic cosmology similarly implies that everything is in some sense caused by everything else, that all events are somehow related. This does not imply predetermination, though, as each moment allows for new creativity. Indeed, the insights of another new scientific field of study, systems theory, actually demonstrates that even the smallest of actions in complex systems can lead to very significant effects. Peat concludes:

> In claiming that "everything causes everything else," the suggestion is that the various phenomena of the universe arise out of the flux of the whole, and are best described by a "law of the whole." While linear causality may work well enough for restricted, mechanical, and well-isolated systems, in general something more subtle and complex is needed to describe the full richness of nature. (1987, 52)

Thus, a holographic cosmology opens us up to the true mystery of transformation and frees us of cold determinisms. Individual choices and actions can have a real and lasting impact—indeed, in the right circumstances a very small action may amplify and become much more powerful than could ever have been imagined. Within this holistic framework, individuals are challenged to live their full potential and to deal creatively with reality. This insight correspondingly reinforces the creative potentiality of both power-from-within and power-with. Liberating change is possible. The key to effective action lies not in the power to dominate and control, but rather in holding the right intention and in discerning the right action at the right time and place.

Finally, a holographic cosmology includes consciousness and spirituality as integral parts of reality. Marilyn Ferguson observes:

> Implicit to the theory is the assumption that harmonious, coherent states of consciousness are more nearly attuned to the primary level of reality, a dimension of order and harmony. Such attunement would be hampered by anger, anxiety, and fear, and eased by love and empathy. There are implications for learning, environments, families, the arts, religion and philosophy, healing and self-healing. What fragments us? What makes us whole?
>
> Those descriptions of a sense of flow, of cooperating with the universe—in the creative process, in extraordinary athletic performances, and sometimes in everyday life—do they signify our union with the source?
>
> . . . The holographic model also helps explain the strange power of the *image*—why events are affected by what we imagine, what we visualize. An image held in a transcendental state may be made real. (1987, 23-24)

Fostering attitudes of love, joy, awe, and reverence will have a central place in transformative action, then, within this cosmological framework. The value of art, creative visualization, and meditation practices becomes readily apparent.

A holographic cosmology also values the role of intuition. Intuition is not seen as a "special" or altered state of consciousness, but rather as "direct access to the implicit, which operates [analogously to] scanning a holographic-type blur with a diffuse attention that does not impose preconceived notions on it" (Welwood 1982, 132). In other words, intuition is seen as the mind's direct apprehension of the implicate order. Intuition is not irrational; it simply is a form of rationality distinct from discursive thought. Those involved in the struggle for integral liberation and healing of the life systems of the Earth, then, should work to develop the intuitive faculty and value it. This does not mean that linear logic should be neglected, however. In fact, the holographic view of reality rejects the creation of dualisms and seeks to integrate all the mind's facets.

In sum, the holographic metaphor challenges us to see mind, matter, and spirit as an inseparable whole: "Matter is saturated with spirit, and spirit embeds itself within matter. These two are not separate in reality" (Weber 1982, 207). The mind is a kind of interface between spirit and matter: It is itself a part of the implicate order, the ground of being which corresponds to the spirit, but it interprets reality in terms of the explicate order. Authentic liberatory praxis, then, must seek to integrate mind, matter, and spirit into a working whole.

QUANTUM HOLISM

Each atom turns out to be nothing but the potentialities in the behavior pattern of others. What we find, therefore, are not elementary space-time realities, but rather a web of relationships in which no part can stand alone; every part derives its meaning and existence only from its place within the whole. (Henry Stapp, quoted in Nadeau and Kafatos 1999, 195)

Whether or not the holographic analogy turns out to be a helpful metaphor for microcosmic reality, it is clear that the insights of quantum physics eliminate any possibility of understanding the cosmos in purely mechanistic or materialistic terms. The clockwork universe of Newton and Descartes has dissolved into a much more complex and mysterious—but also holistic—worldview. Heisenberg once stated that the cosmos needs to be described as, "a complicated tissue of events, in which connections of different kinds alternate or overlay or combine and thereby determine the texture of the whole" (quoted in Nadeau and Kafatos 1999, 195). Atoms and elementary particles are no longer seen to be things— indeed they contain very little if anything resembling "hard stuff"—but rather events or processes, like vortices in a stream. If we can say that matter exists at all, it is no longer as a noun but rather as a verb. As David Peat writes:

> Physics tells us that a rock is composed of a vast number of atoms. And these same atoms, which at the quantum level of description are enfolded in ambiguity, conspire to engage in a great dance whose collective manifestation is a rock. The rock is pure dance. Its very rockness, its inertness, its whole inner voice, are the manifestation of this constant movement and flux. (1991, 80)

The quantum realm reveals a deeply relational nature. What is a quark, for example, in and of itself when it stubbornly refuses to be isolated and analyzed? A quark exists only in relation to other quarks. Indeed, how can we describe any kind of elementary particle in and of itself? Every particle is linked to every other particle via non-local connections, so once again we cannot consider any particle in isolation. In such a cosmos, where everything is in some sense caused by everything else, we can understand the parts only in relation to one another. Matter, energy, space, and time coexist in a dynamic web of relationship. Indeed, all these manifestations of reality may well spring from a deeper level of unity, the pregnant void, a vast sea of energy that both creates and sustains them moment by moment.

What is more, in terms of the quantum scale of things, the entities we are dealing with do not even seem to have a position, path, or momentum in and of themselves. Until an elementary particle is observed, it exists in a state of pure potentiality and possibility, as a kind of probability wave. Specific qualities become manifest only when the particle is observed. The observer can never be considered to be separate from what is observed. Consciousness seems to draw out a certain aspect so that it becomes manifest. There is a holistic nature in the quantum realm, then, that also encompasses mind and consciousness. Similarly, relativity has demonstrated that the frame of reference of the observer affects what is observed. Once again, the observer cannot be separated from what is observed.

The holism of the quantum realm is evidenced also by its quality of complementarity. A particle is also a wave; space and time coexist as part of a greater whole; and matter and energy are two aspects of a single reality. This mirrors the complementary idea of *yin* and *yang* in Taoism or of *jemal* and *jelal* of Sufism (roughly analogous to feminine and masculine, or receptive and assertive). A dynamic tension of apparent opposites creates a dynamic unity. Or, alternatively, they may themselves be a complementary manifestation of something deeper from which they both arise.

Quantum physics reveals an authentic holism in which the whole is greater than the sum of the parts and where the parts also manifest the whole. Nadeau and Kafatos describe this kind of holism as follows:

> In a genuine whole, the relationships between the constituent parts must be "internal or immanent" in the parts, as opposed to a more spurious whole in which parts appear to disclose wholeness due to relationships that are external to the parts. The collection of parts that would allegedly constitute the whole in classical physics is an example of a spurious whole. Parts constitute a genuine whole when the universal principle of order is inside the parts and thereby adjusts each to all so that they interlock and become mutually complementary. This not only describes the character of the whole revealed in both relativity theory and quantum mechanics. It is also consistent with the manner in which we have begun to understand the relation between parts and whole in modern biology. (1999, 195-96)

The cosmos revealed in the modern physics of quantum mechanics and the theory of relativity, then, is deeply holistic in nature. The world of dead matter and blind determinism of Newton's clockwork is gone. Gone, too, is the rigid separation of mind and matter. Mind and matter seem to intermingle in a mysterious and even playful manner. Consciousness, we could say, evokes a particular manifestation of quantum reality while consciousness itself may arise from quantum phenomena—or perhaps mind and physical reality co-arise from something at once deeper and more subtle.

The vision of the cosmos emerging is profoundly relational, and therefore by definition ecological. Everything, at least at some level, is connected to everything else. Even consciousness seems to be imminent in the cosmos. Humans, then, cannot see themselves as separated from the world around them. We are challenged to take this new but ancient understanding to heart and attempt to live this consciousness of interconnection in our daily lives.

At the same time, the cold, clear linear rationalism of classical physics has given way to something much more paradoxical in nature. We find it impossible to build a clear picture of the quantum realm in our minds. Even the vocabulary of physics has become whimsical, including such terms as taste, color, charm (all qualities of quarks), gluons, and wimps. Physicists themselves claim that if we understand what they are talking about, we've missed the whole point!

For some, the end of a predictable, deterministic, and comprehensible cosmos may seem to be a cause for despair; but if we see mystery and complexity as creative, we can indeed take the opposite view. Perhaps determinism is a comfort for those who wish to see things continue as they are at present; but if we want to fundamentally change the way that humans live on Earth, then the paradoxical, surprising nature of the cosmos as revealed in quantum physics should in fact be taken as a sign of hope.

8.

Complexity, Chaos, and Creativity

The Tao gives birth to the one.
The one gives birth to the two.
The two gives birth to the three.
The three gives birth to all the diversity of things.

All beings return to the *yin* and embrace the *yang*
and the interplay of these two vital forces
fills the cosmos.

Yet only at the still point,
between the breathing in and the breathing out,
can one capture these two in perfect harmony . . .

(*Tao Te Ching* §42)

Act without doing,
work without effort,
savor without tasting.
Magnify the small,
increase the few.
Return kindness when receiving malice.

Confront problems
before they become too difficult.
Address complex situations
in a series of small steps . . .

(*Tao Te Ching* §63)

. . . When acting, proper timing is everything. . .

(*Tao Te Ching* §8)

[Picture] a universe in which every atom, rock, and star drinks of the same boundless waters of creativity. Nature is a symphony in which new themes, harmonies, and structures are ever-unfolding. These structures and processes remain in constant communication with each other and engage in a dance of form. Life swims in an ocean of meaning, in an activity and coherence that blur the distinctions between animate and inanimate, between thought and matter. New values unfold from this map, for as participators in a living universe, we are called to a new way of acting and being. (Peat 1991, 204)

We stand at the beginning of a great new synthesis. The correspondence of static structures is not the subject, but the connectedness of self-organization dynamics—of mind—at many levels. It becomes possible to view evolution as a complex, but holistic dynamic phenomenon of a universal unfolding of order which becomes manifest in many ways, as matter and energy, information and complexity, consciousness and self-reflection. (Jantsch 1980, 307)

While the view of the microcosm emerging from quantum physics is both fascinating and suggestive in terms of the cosmovision it reveals, it may also seem rather far removed from our everyday experience. It is true, of course, that quantum phenomena play an integral role in our daily lives—for example, all that we see is generated by the interaction of photons and our retinas. Yet the subatomic realm probably is in many respects too mysterious and alien to directly impact our perception of reality. Even physicists who deal with it on a daily basis claim that they cannot truly understand its paradoxical nature. At best, perhaps, the quantum worldview slowly seeps into our consciousness, infusing us with an implicit awareness that our perception of "solid" reality arises from an intricate dance of effervescent patterns of energy subtly interacting with mind.

The relational, holistic dynamics manifest in the microcosm, however, are equally evident in the complex systems that make up the world accessible to our senses. We may not, however, always be aware of these dynamics because of the worldview that has imprinted itself upon us. We still tend to perceive reality in mechanistic terms—as material parts working together in a relatively straightforward manner where the connection between cause and effect is direct and comprehensible.

In actuality, though, classical physics is only able to deal with relatively simple, isolated, linear systems operating close to equilibrium. Yet such systems are almost always idealizations; they are approximations that correspond to the real world only in very special cases. For example, while Newton's laws of motion brilliantly describe the interaction of two planets, the interaction of three or more celestial bodies results in nonlinear equations that defy any simple mathematical solution, making it impossible to predict their trajectories precisely. Similarly, a pendulum oscillating in a fairly narrow range can be easily analyzed, but a pendulum driven into wilder oscillations develops chaotic behavior that cannot be predicted.

The limitations of classical physics are even more apparent when we attempt to apply it to open systems (such as living organisms) that exchange matter and energy with their surroundings. According to the laws of thermodynamics formulated in the nineteenth century, entropy should always increase—that is, systems should always move to a state of greater disorder. Yet living organisms actually create and maintain order—and actually evolve toward more complex forms. Indeed, even systems that are not living organisms—including physical systems like lasers—demonstrate dynamics of self-organization that cannot be understood using the mind-set of classical physics.

Scientists have long been aware at some level of these limitations, but until relatively recently, they simply chose to ignore them. Effectively, they excluded the vast majority of real-world systems from their investigations because they could not be understood in mechanistic, deterministic terms.

Over the past fifty years or so, however, a new perspective—most often called "systems theory"—has been emerging as a way of understanding complex systems. In many respects, systems theory is not a theory at all in the normal sense of the word but rather "a coherent set of principles applying to all irreducible wholes" (Macy 1991a, 3); or, in the words of Ludwig von Bertalanffy, one of the originators of systems thinking, it is a new "way of seeing" the world. Indeed, it has spawned a whole series of theories applying to a wide variety of fields. Because of this, a host of different names are associated with the systems perspective, including chaos theory, emergence, complexity, and self-organization.

While we may at times consider simpler systems, we are most interested in those that display dynamics of self-organization and evolution—what some refer to as "living systems." Living systems certainly include organisms, but also include ecosystems and at times the term is extended to include organizations and societies. The Earth itself can be understood as a living system—something that we will examine in more detail when we discuss the Gaia theory in chapter 10—and some would even consider the cosmos as a whole to be one. "Living systems are essentially dynamic (as distinct from static). They grow, change, and adapt. They possess a will-to-live, an amazing and intriguing capacity to regenerate, usually through the cycle of birth-death-rebirth" (O'Murchu 1997, 167).

Some extend the idea of living systems to phenomena that are not normally associated with life per se—particularly to other open systems that maintain their coherence by dissipating energy. Certainly, dynamics of self-organization are often displayed in such systems. By and large, however, we will focus primarily on those systems that are most clearly alive in the more traditional sense, including organisms, ecosystems, and human societies. Drawing on the work of Joanna Macy (1991a) and Diarmuid O'Murchu (1997), we can identify some of the key characteristics of these living systems:

1. In such systems, the whole is always greater than the mere sum of its parts. A system cannot be reduced to its component parts without altering its characteristic pattern. Unlike a simple closed system (like a

brick wall), the parts can be understood only in the context and function of the whole system. If an organism is dissected, it ceases to be a living being—its very identity changes. In a sense, the pattern, rather than individual parts, is the essence of a living system.[1]

2. Every living system is not just a whole, but a part of a larger whole; every living system is a subsystem of a larger system (except, perhaps, if we consider the cosmos itself to be a living system). Such systems, therefore, are analogous to a treelike reality where branches (system) divide into smaller branches (subsystems), which themselves divide in turn into still smaller branches and twigs.

3. Living systems are homeostatic, stabilizing themselves over time through processes of negative feedback where outputs are constantly adjusted to match inputs. Material, energy, and information are constantly exchanged with the surrounding environment, but the overall pattern and order of the system are maintained. In other words, living systems always exist at a state far from thermodynamic equilibrium—and indeed, such equilibrium comes about only when the system dies, effectively breaking down.

4. Living systems are self-organizing and self-regenerating. If inputs and outputs cannot be matched, the system searches for a new pattern through which to function. This means that living systems are capable of development and evolution where true novelty can emerge—that is, living systems display dynamics of creativity.

5. Self-organization is simultaneously a process of learning, or a "cognitive process." For example, an immune system that has fought off an infection will "remember" how to do so again. This learning process does not require a brain or even a nervous system; it is an inherent characteristic of all living systems.

As quickly becomes apparent in reviewing this list, systems theory shares many perspectives with quantum physics, even though it arrives at these by reflecting on the nature of a different type of phenomenon. For example, relationships and organizational dynamics are far more important than substance in a systems view. In addition, living systems display a creative dimension that results in what some would consider a mental process—or even a form of mind—even when no nervous system is involved. Certainly, the systems view is organic and holistic rather than mechanistic and reductionist. Perhaps even more important, it can radically reshape our understanding of the relationship between cause and effect

---

1. Another example may shed further light on this idea: The human body is an open system that is constantly exchanging material with its surrounding environment. On average, over a period of seven years, every single atom in the body is lost and replaced through a process of constant regeneration (and indeed, 98 percent of the body's atoms are exchanged every single year!). From a strictly materialist point of view, then, we are totally different persons at the end of each seven-year period; yet, from a systems perspective, we remain the same because the overall pattern of our existence has remained intact, even if it has changed in some respects through growth or aging.

as well as our power to transform complex structures. To understand how, we will now explore systems theory in greater depth.

EXPLORING SYSTEMS THEORY

Modern systems theory has emerged over the past century or so in a number of fields of study, one of which is biology. During the nineteenth and twentieth centuries, many biologists attempted to explain living organisms in strictly mechanistic terms—an attempt that some would argue continues to this day via some of the more reductionalist understandings of genetics. Still, mechanistic explanations have faced very real limitations, particularly in the area of cell development and differentiation.

In opposition to this view, some scientists in the nineteenth century proposed theories based on *vitalism*, which asserts that some nonphysical force or entity must be added to the laws of chemistry and physics to understand life. Vitalists also maintained that the functioning of a living organism must be understood as an integrated whole where the activity of each of the organism's parts is comprehensible only in the context of the wider systems in which it is embedded.

Over the past eighty years or so a third alternative for understanding living organisms has been developed called *organicism*. Like vitalism, organicism maintains that life must be understood holistically, but unlike vitalism it does not posit any kind of outside force or entity at work. Instead, organicism maintains that physical and chemical processes *plus* "organizing relations" are sufficient to understand the dynamics of life. "Since these organising relations are patterns of relationships immanent in the physical structure of the organism, organismic biologists assert that no separate, non-physical entity is required for the understanding of life" (Capra 1996, 25). The idea of organizing relations has now largely come to be understood in terms of the dynamics of self-organization.

Philosophically, organicism draws on the insights of thinkers such as Aristotle, Goethe, and Kant. Aristotle, for example, believed that each entity, including living organisms, had its own pattern of organization—a kind of immanent soul that he called *entelechy*—which unified form and substance. Modern organicism continues this tradition in a new way that endeavors to overcome the old Cartesian dualism between mind and matter, a dualism that is still present in different forms in both mechanism and vitalism. Unlike Aristotle, however, organicism and the systems theories it helped inspire are dynamic and evolutionary in nature: new forms and patterns emerge through the process of self-organization. Some extend the organismic viewpoint to include all reality, affirming that, indeed, such an extension is inherent in the organismic perspective. For example, Rupert Sheldrake states:

> From the organismic point of view, life is not something that has emerged from dead matter, and that needs to be explained in terms of the added vital factors of vitalism. *All* nature is alive. The organising principles of living organisms are different in degree but not different in kind from the organising

principles of molecules or of societies or of galaxies. "Biology is the study of the larger organisms, whereas physics is the study of the smaller organisms," as Whitehead put it. And in the light of the new cosmology, physics is also the study of the all-embracing cosmic organism, and of the galactic, stellar and planetary organisms which have come into being within it. (1988, 54-55)

A second key thread that contributed to the development of modern systems theory is more philosophical in nature. In the early twentieth century, Alexander Bogdanov—a scientist, philosopher, economist, physician, and Marxist revolutionary who lived in Russia from 1873 to 1928—made the first attempt to formulate a general theory about systems, which he named "tektology," meaning the "science of structures." Tektology attempted to delineate systematically the principles of organization inherent in both living and nonliving systems. By demonstrating how an organizational crisis may lead to a breakdown of an old structure and the emergence of a new one, Bogdanov anticipated the work of Ilya Prigogine more than half a century later. He also explicitly recognized for the first time that living systems are open entities operating in a state far from thermodynamic equilibrium. Finally, he formulated a concept of regulation similar to the mechanism of feedback that would become central to the future field of cybernetics.

While Bogdanov's work was in many ways prophetic, it was also largely neglected in the West while—because of his political differences with Lenin—it was marginalized in Russia itself for many years. It was left to Ludwig von Bertalanffy (1901-1972) to formulate the more widely known General Theory of Systems starting during the 1940s and culminating with the publication of his *General System Theory* in 1968.

Bertalanffy was interested in the problem of explaining the evolution of life in light of the laws of thermodynamics. The second law of thermodynamics maintains that any isolated, closed system will move from a state of order to one of increasing disorder. This introduced the idea of the "arrow of time" into science, since mechanical processes always dissipate energy in the form of heat, and that energy can never be completely recovered. Thus, the entire universe itself must move toward an eventual "heat death" from which there can be no escape. In contrast, the theory of evolution showed that living organisms were evolving into ever more complex and ordered states of being. How was such a thing possible?

Bertalanffy postulated that living organisms do not fit the classical description of a closed system described by the second law of thermodynamics; rather, they are open systems working in conditions far from equilibrium that maintain a "steady state" through a continual flow of energy and matter. He went on to identify metabolism as the process that maintains a steady state, which he described in terms of "flowing balance." In open systems, entropy (or disorder) may actually *decrease*, but at the cost of *increasing* entropy in the surrounding environment. Hence, while the second law of thermodynamics still applies, living organisms manage to move to an increasing state of order by taking in energy and food from outside while expelling waste and heat (and increasing entropy) to their surroundings.

The third major thread involved in the genesis of modern systems theory comes from the field of cybernetics, a discipline that began to develop during the 1940s. Cybernetics deals with input-output systems and serves as the foundation for modern computer technology. Cybernetics attempted to create models of living organisms as complex "information-processing machines." As Fritjof Capra notes, "this school of thought is still mechanistic systems theory," but "it's a very sophisticated mechanism" (Capra and Steindl-Rast 1991, 72).

John von Neumann, a mathematical genius (whom we previously discussed in terms of his reflections on quantum physics, consciousness, and the construction of our perception of reality), was one of the early pioneers in this field. Von Neumann is often considered the inventor of the computer—and indeed, a computer is a good metaphor for understanding his approach to cybernetic theory.

When scientists first began to construct models of binary networks based on this cybernetics theory in the 1950s, they were surprised to discover that random activity, over a relatively short period of time, began to resolve into discernible patterns. The nonlinear nature of the networks consisting of feedback loops resulted in a kind of order emerging out of apparent chaos. This spontaneous emergence of order eventually became known as the phenomenon of "self-organization."

Another early cybernetics thinker, Norbert Wiener, took a somewhat different approach, focusing on the dynamics of self-organizing systems like living organisms. While von Neumann attempted to model the action of the brain in terms of logic, Wiener was more concerned about understanding natural, living systems. In the words of Capra, "Whereas von Neumann looked for control, for a program, Wiener appreciated the richness of natural patterns and sought a comprehensive conceptual synthesis" (1996, 54). Wiener's thinking inspired the work of Gregory Bateson (1904-1980), who approached systems theory from the point of view of the humanities.

Initially, Wiener's school of systems theory based on self-organization was largely neglected in favor of the more mechanistic cybernetics school inspired by von Neumann. During the 1970s and '80s, however, a revival of the organic approach, enriched by the perspectives of thinkers like Ludwig von Bertalanffy, took place. Some of the key figures involved in this new, integrated approach were Ilya Prigogine (1917-2003), James Lovelock, Lynn Margulis, Humberto Maturana, and Francisco Varela (1946-2001).

The concept of self-organization emerging in this work is much more far-reaching than that which had become apparent in the early work on cybernetics. Instead of simply looking at order arising out of chaos in networks involving feedback loops, the new theories include the "creation of novel structures and modes of behavior in the process of development, learning, and evolution" (Capra 1996, 85). Further, the new theories focus on open systems working in conditions far from equilibrium where matter, energy, and information are constantly being exchanged. Finally, all of the theories focus on systems involving feedback loops to regulate the system's activity that in turn result in a complex interconnection and interaction of all the system's components.

According to Ludwig von Bertalanffy, two essential properties are shared by all living systems. The first is the property of "biological maintenance," through which organisms work to preserve themselves via the process of homeostasis, or stability through flux. This could be seen as the property of self-assertion or subjectivity, which Humberto Maturana and Francisco Varela have named "autopoiesis," literally "self-making."

The second property manifests in a kind of dialectical tension with the first. Von Bertalanffy identified this as the property of hierarchical organization, the idea that every system is a subsystem of a larger system and is in turn composed of still smaller subsystems. We could think of this as well as the property of communion, relationality, or even contextuality. In some sense, "Parts and wholes in an absolute sense do not exist at all" (Capra 1982, 43). The idea of relationality is actually embedded in the very meaning of the word "system," which comes from the Greek word *synhistanai*, meaning "to place together." "To understand things systematically literally means to put them into a context, to establish the nature of their relationships" (Capra 1996, 27).

Some refer to the existence of these two, apparently opposite, properties as the "Janus nature" of systems, named after the ancient Roman god with two faces. Another way to think of this is in the Taoist terms of *yin* and *yang*. The two tendencies—self-assertion (*yang*) and communion (*yin*)—must exist in healthy tension and balance for a living system to thrive.

As noted above, systems maintain their identity—their subjectivity—through the process of *homeostasis*, which can be understood as a kind of stillness in motion, or stability in the midst of flux and change. Unlike the old materialist view of classical physics, a system is defined not by substance but by a pattern of organization. The image of a whirlpool illustrates this point: the water flowing through the whirlpool is constantly changing, but the whirlpool itself—its pattern of organization—remains essentially the same. In the words of Norbert Wiener, "We are but whirlpools in a river of ever-flowing water. We are not stuff that abides, but patterns that perpetuate themselves" (1950, 96).

Closely related to the idea of homeostasis is the concept of *autopoiesis*, or "the characteristic of living systems to continuously renew themselves and to regulate this process in such a way that the integrity of their structure is maintained" (Jantsch 1980, 7). In a living system, each component of the weblike network works to sustain, transform, and replace the other components so that the system continually regenerates itself. In the human organism, for example, the pancreas replaces almost all of its cells within the span of a day and nearly all (98 percent) of the protein in the brain is cycled through within the space of a month. Yet, despite these changes, the overall patterns of organization remain stable (Capra 1996).

Living systems maintain their structure by taking in energy—for example, plants absorb sunlight and animals consume other organisms as food. This allows them to exist in a state far from equilibrium. Ilya Prigogine referred to open systems that maintain order by using energy as "dissipative structures." In terms of thermodynamics, a living system decreases its internal entropy (creates order) by increasing entropy in its surrounding environment (increasing disorder): "In the living world, order and disorder are always created simultaneously" (Capra 1996, 188).

A key process involved in the maintenance of structure is the use of negative feedback loops. For example, when a person becomes too hot, processes come into play that cause the sweat glands to excrete water, which, through evaporation, cools the body. Similarly, when blood sugar levels rise, the pancreas produces more insulin to enable the body to utilize the sugar and convert it into energy. Through these kinds of processes, living systems can maintain their overall pattern of organization, even as they constantly exchange energy, matter, and information with their surroundings.

While the process of autopoiesis enables living systems to maintain their identity in the midst of constant flux, that identity is always in turn conditioned by the relationship of the system both to its own subsystems and to the larger systems of which it, in turn, is a part. In other words, systems do not have intrinsic properties but rather characteristics that emerge from their relationships. We could refer to this as the contextual or relational nature of systems. A system cannot be dissected or reduced to its component parts without its integrity—its very identity—being destroyed: "Although we can discern individual parts in any system, the nature of the whole is always different from the mere sum of its parts" (Capra 1982, 267).

In systems, properties emerge in a way that at times can seem mysterious. This can even be seen at the level of atoms, where the same elementary particles conspire to create nearly a hundred different natural elements. The subsystems involved—which we call protons, neutrons, and electrons—are essentially the same (though they vary in number), but through different patterns of organization they produce elements with totally different properties. Similarly, hydrogen and oxygen unite to form water molecules, which have very different properties from those of their constitutive elements. Complex biological organisms—different species of mammals, for example—may have similar subsystems (organs), but the way these are patterned means that each species can, in fact, be very different from others.

It is also interesting to note that, in the case of living organisms, a high degree of symbiosis comes into play. Lynn Margulis has shown that eukaryotic cells (those with a nucleus) actually carry more than one set of DNA and were probably originally formed through a process she names "symbiogenesis" in which two or more distinct microbes came together to form a new, more complex cell (Capra 1996). On a larger scale, roughly 50 percent of a human's body weight is made up of "nonhuman" organisms such as the enteric bacteria and yeasts that enable us to metabolize our food and manufacture vitamins, and without which it would be impossible for us to survive. "Each cell and microorganism in our body is an individual, self-directing entity, yet by joining together they are able as well to function as a single being with abilities far beyond those of its parts" (Korten 1999, 13). Our identity, then, is not a matter of substance alone—not even in terms of our genetic makeup, for example—but rather the integral pattern of relationships that make up our living system.

One way to understand the relational nature of living systems is in terms of what Arthur Koestler has named "holons." Holons are subsystems that are simultaneously wholes and parts. Each holon has both a tendency to integrate and a tendency to assert itself. This model of organization, which can be referred to as "holarchy," resembles in some way the concept of hierarchy, and the two ideas are often confused. (Indeed, Ludwig von Bertalanffy cast the property of relationality in hierarchical terms.) Holarchy, however, is based not on rank or the power to dominate, but rather on ever-greater levels of inclusion and depth. The larger system both includes and transcends the smaller systems that make it up. The subsystems, in turn, are not dominated by the larger system, but rather are sustained by it and in turn serve it.

In a hierarchical view, systems were imaged as rigid, pyramidal structures. In contrast, the holarchical view of systems is like that of circles within wider circles, which in turn are encompassed by even more inclusive circles. Alternatively, holarchy can be visualized in terms of a branching tree dividing into smaller and smaller subsystems. The overall system (the trunk) depends of the health of the branches—and indeed, the health of the tree in turn depends on the health of the ecosystem in which it, in turn, is imbedded. While a certain stratification of order occurs, it is not based on the exercise of control from the top down—or power-over. Instead, nourishment, information, and energy flow in both directions, maintaining a dynamic interaction between systems and subsystems. In essence, power in systems demonstrates the relationality and interdependence of mutual influence—of power-with—rather than the power-over inherent in many human hierarchies.

This difference between the hierarchical and systems perspectives becomes even more apparent when we examine another characteristic of living systems: differentiation. Joanna Macy notes that, in the systems view,

> Order and differentiation go hand in hand. Subsystems are able to integrate *as* they differentiate (like nerve cells in the brain). This is in direct contrast to the mechanistic and patriarchal views which assumed that order requires uniformity, the better to be subordinated to a separate and superior will. Here, instead, order manifests within the system itself, where components diversify as they interrelate and respond to the environment. (1983, 26)

Therefore, in open systems, health and integrity are maintained and strengthened through differentiation, in direct contrast to the ideology of monoculture. A diverse ecosystem, for example, is inherently more stable than a simpler one. Dynamics of domination and homogenization, in contrast, weaken a system and make it more rigid and more susceptible to destruction.

Indeed, while the vision of reality encapsulated in systems theory is certainly holistic in nature, it can perhaps best be described as *ecological*. In Capra's words, "It looks not only at something as a whole but also at how this whole is embedded into larger wholes. . . . At the deepest level, ecological awareness is an awareness of the fundamental interconnectedness and interdependence of all phenomena and of this embeddedness in the cosmos" (Capra and Steindl-Rast 1991, 69-70).

David Suzuki and Amanda McConnell point out that this ecological awareness challenges us to transform the very way we perceive and understand the world around us: "Our language falls short of our apprehension because of the way we have been taught to identify the world. We belong to, are made of, that world that surrounds us, and we respond to it in ways beyond knowing" (1997, 199). They provide the example of trying to perceive a tree in a new way, in relationship to all that is around it. The very idea of boundaries begins to dissolve. In the words of Neil Evernden in *The Natural Alien*:

> A tree, we might say, is not so much a thing as a rhythm of exchange, or perhaps a centre of organizational forces. Transpiration induces the upward flow of water and dissolved materials, facilitating an inflow from the soil. If we were aware of this rather than the appearance of a tree-form, we might regard the tree as a centre of a force-field to which water is drawn. . . . The object to which we attach significance is the configuration of the forces necessary to being a tree . . . rigid attention to boundaries can obscure the act of being itself. (Quoted in Suzuki and McConnell 1997, 199)

THE EMERGENCE OF CREATIVITY AND MIND

This spontaneous emergence of order at critical points of instability is one of the most important concepts of the new understanding of life. It is technically known as self-organization and is often referred to simply as "emergence." It has been recognized as the dynamic origin of development, learning and evolution. In other words, creativity—the generation of new forms—is a key property of all living systems. And since emergence is an integral part of the dynamics of open systems, we reach the important conclusion that open systems develop and evolve. Life constantly reaches out into novelty. (Capra 2002, 14)

The emergence of novelty and creativity is perhaps the most intriguing and surprising insight to arise from the study of open systems operating far from equilibrium. The cosmos is not doomed endlessly to repeat itself, trapped in a rut circumscribed by universal laws. Instead, the universe evolves and changes. It continually births forth new forms. The cosmos no longer appears moribund, condemned to a slow and intractable heat death, but rather creative and fecund. Indeed, mind itself seems to be an emergent quality of the universe.

From a mathematical point of view, this creativity is bound up with the non-linear nature of systems operating far from equilibrium. In such systems, "what happens in one region depends sensitively on another region and, in turn, feeds back to it; . . . different parts behave cooperatively; . . . [and] the whole engages in a sort of dance" (Peat 1991, 202).

As we have seen, negative feedback loops help maintain stability by regulating a system and maintaining functions within a bounded range. Mathematically, the kind of stability-in-flux sustained by negative feedback loops can be understood using the concept of "attractors." An attractor can be visualized as a region in space (or a set of points) toward which a system "gravitates" or tends to move over time.

More precisely, if one plots the position and velocity of a system as a kind of graph during a time interval—like the motion of a pendulum—a picture emerges of its "phase space" in which a pattern becomes evident. We can think of this pattern as a "basin of attraction" that can be a single point (in the case of a simple system at rest), a curve, or a manifold. In nonlinear systems, there are often several such "basins," each with its own attractor.

Sometimes an attractor may take the form of a fractal—a complex geometric shape in which the parts resemble smaller versions of the greater whole. This kind of "strange attractor" is associated with what may be described mathematically as "chaotic" activity. Yet this chaos is not mere disorder, for the activity associated with it is neither random nor erratic. Rather, it is a highly complex but nondeterministic order. The behavior of a chaotic system cannot be predicted with any precision, but the behavior is effectively maintained within a certain boundary—or basin of attraction—characterized by its attractor.

Metaphorically, we can think of the attractor as "pulling" or shaping the system, but in fact there is no force involved. The attractor is inherent in the system, not something that directs it from outside—it is a characteristic of the system itself. In some sense, we may think of it as the pattern of the system—but this pattern can be very complex and, although it is ordered, it is not always predictable or deterministic.

Along with the dynamics that maintain stability, however, others—characterized by positive feedback loops—can also come into play, especially when a system comes under stress. Instead of dampening fluctuations, positive feedback actually amplifies them, often leading to rapid and surprising changes. For example, positive feedback loops are readily evident in the phenomenon of climate change. At the beginning of an ice age, the growing expanse of reflective ice and snow causes the Earth to reflect more radiation back into space, cooling the planet and leading to the formation of yet more ice. Conversely, when the planet begins to warm, forest fires can become more common and permafrost melts, both of which release more carbon dioxide into the atmosphere, accelerating the greenhouse effect and global warming.

Over successive iterations, positive feedback can rapidly multiply the effects of relatively small changes. This kind of "runaway feedback" was always considered destructive in cybernetics theory, but Prigogine discovered that this was not always the case in open, dissipative systems. True, when the flow of matter and energy reaches a critical point—in mathematical terms a "bifurcation point"—the system does become unstable. The attractors of the system at such a point then may in fact disappear altogether—and the system will break down. But another possibility also exists: the attractors may transform themselves, allowing the system to break through to a totally new order, often one that is more complex than the one that preceded it.

From the point of view of living systems, this means that stresses (such as new conditions in the surrounding environment, or in the wider system that encompasses the subsystem) can lead to breakdown in the form of death, but they can also lead to the evolution of a totally new form. This breakthrough to a new form is not deterministic—the system in some sense "chooses" between several possible paths of transformation. Which choice it will make, however, is not predictable, although it depends on both the system's history and on the external stresses driving the transformation.

The nonlinear nature of natural systems, illustrated both by their "chaotic" stability and by their "jumping" to new states at bifurcation points, means that they are extraordinarily sensitive to small changes. This "vulnerability," however, is not a weakness but rather a strength insofar as it enables rapid adaptation to new conditions. On the other hand, it also means that when dealing with complex systems, we can never predict the future.

One illustration of this lies in the so-called "butterfly effect," first encountered by the meteorologist Edward Lorenz (1917-2008) in the 1960s. In designing a simple mathematical model of weather patterns based on three interlinked, nonlinear equations, Lorenz was surprised to find that the solutions to his equations were extraordinarily sensitive to the initial starting point he specified. In effect, starting from two, only slightly different sets of initial conditions resulted in a totally different genesis of the system over time. Long-range prediction, even in this simple system, was impossible. If one applies this to the example of weather, it is theoretically possible for the action of a butterfly's wings to "cause" a storm halfway around the world the following month.

While complex systems spell the end of determinism, they also open the way to creative engagement. Since such systems are extraordinarily sensitive, even the action of a single individual can have an effect—albeit that effect can never be predicted. Still, this understanding can be tremendously empowering and hopeful. What is more, the argument that "something cannot happen because it has never happened before" becomes empty. As Capra notes, "Near equilibrium we find repetitive phenomena and universal laws. As we move away from equilibrium, we move from the universal to the unique, toward richness and variety" (1996, 182). The world is not condemned to repeat the past forever—true novelty, authentic transformation, is always a possibility, even if the process through which it comes about will always contain an element of mystery and surprise.

The ability of dissipative systems to spontaneously create new structures makes them appear, in some sense, to have a will of their own. Certainly, self-organizing systems seem to have an inherent creativity that we would normally associate with the phenomenon of mind. Gregory Bateson, for example, saw this as a "mental process" at work. Capra notes that, for Bateson, "mind is not a thing, it's a process. And this mental process is the process of self-organization, in other words, the very process of life. So at all levels the process of life is a mental process" (Capra and Steindl-Rast 1991, 103). Similarly, Humberto Maturana and Francisco Varela (Capra 2002) envision the process of life itself as being a process of knowing—or as "cognitive process." All the interactions of living systems with their surroundings are in some sense acts of cognition, so in one way mind, understood as mental process, is immanent in life, and indeed, in all living systems at all levels.

To understand this idea more clearly, consider the process of self-organization in living systems. An organism responds to its environment through structural transformations—and the organism simultaneously affects and modifies its environment. As we have seen, in the phenomenon of bifurcation, the choice of new structure is not predetermined but rather creative. As Capra notes:

> Living systems, then, respond autonomously to disturbances from the environment with structural changes, i.e. by rearranging their pattern of connectivity. According to Maturana and Varela, you can never direct a living system; you can only disturb it. More than that, the living system not only specifies its structural changes; it also specifies which disturbances from the environment trigger them. In other words, a living system maintains the freedom to decide what to notice and what will disturb it. This is the key to the Santiago Theory of Cognition. The structural changes in the system constitute acts of cognition. By specifying which perturbations from the environment trigger changes, the system specifies the extent of its cognitive domain; it "brings forth a world," as Maturana and Varela put it. (2002, 37)

Similarly, in Bateson's conception, mind involves processes such as memory, learning, and decision making. These processes, however, begin long before a brain or nervous system is ever present, as we have seen in our earlier example of an immune system that learns to respond to an infection, remembers how to do so, and then decides when a new response is necessary. All life, from its simplest of forms, is associated with these kinds of processes. For Maturana, cognition is not the representation of some kind of external reality, but rather a kind of "bringing forth of a world" through the act of specifying a particular reality—by making a choice. This "bringing forth of a world" (or midwifing a specific reality into being) is inherent in the process of self-organization itself; so all living systems can be considered cognitive systems with an active mental process.

The idea of "bringing forth a world," however, should not be understood to mean that the "material" world does not exist—although our discussion of quantum reality should make us well aware that what we perceive to be material is something that more closely resembles an intricate dance of energy or wave forms. Maturana and Varela's insight is similar in spirit. For example, the way a cow perceives a blade of grass will be very different from the way an earthworm perceives the same object. Even individuals of the same species will perceive things somewhat differently, albeit not nearly to the same extent. As Capra notes, when we see an object, then, we are not conjuring a reality from the void, "but the ways in which we delineate objects and identify patterns out of the multitude of sensory inputs we receive depends on our physical constitution. Maturana and Varela would say that the ways in which we can couple structurally to our environment, and thus the world we bring forth, depend on our own structure" (1996, 271). Similarly, Joanna Macy reflects from a Buddhist perspective:[2]

> We create our worlds, but we do not do so unilaterally, for consciousness is colored by that which it feeds, subject and object are interdependent. . . . Sensory experience shapes us and we in turn shape it. The conditioning is mutual. Never is the world presented as independent of the viewer, nor the viewer as independent of perception, for cognition is transitive. (1991a, 122)

Like the view of quantum physics, then, the systems view of mind implies the impossibility of a truly "objective" observer somehow independent of the reality they observe. From a systems perspective, the observer is always a part of the system they are observing, and their interaction with the system inevitably colors their perception. Knowledge is, in some sense, always an approximation. As Heisenberg stated, "What we observe is not nature itself, but nature exposed to our method of questioning"—and, we might add, nature seen from the perspective of our own unique place in the wider system of which we, too, are a part.

If mind—or at least mental process—is inherent in all living systems, how do systems thinkers understand consciousness? Certainly, a systems view would affirm the "dynamic and irreducible nature of psychic activity," which cannot be equated or reduced to "externally observed phenomena" (Macy 1991a, 110). But how, exactly, does consciousness arise?

Humberto Maturana holds that consciousness cannot be understood in terms of chemistry or physics, but only in terms of language and social context. Yet, while his rejection of a more mechanistic understanding of consciousness seems laudable and in keeping with the systems perspective, it also seems too limiting. How, for example, could such a theory explain the experience of consciousness of those individuals who think in terms of images, or other sensory impressions, rather than language? And how would it account for what many experience as the "higher states of consciousness" evidenced in mystical experiences, where words and language are totally transcended? Finally, through its emphasis on language, this conception of consciousness seems to be strongly anthropocentric: Cannot other creatures, particularly more complex vertebrates, experience some kind of consciousness, even if somewhat different from that experienced by humans?

In this context, Francisco Varela's understanding of consciousness seems more helpful. For Varela, all higher vertebrates probably experience some form of consciousness that involves a "unitary mental space," even if it may not yet be self-reflective in nature. While "mental states are transitory, continually aris-

---

2. Interestingly, Francisco Varela became a Tibetan Buddhist in the 1970s. Perhaps his own Buddhist outlook helped shape his theories around "bringing forth a world."

ing and subsiding," each sensation and each thought are composed of "a single, coherent mental state composed of sensory perceptions, memories, and emotions" (Capra 1996, 292). Varela believes that this coherent state arises from the unified, rhythmic oscillation of neural networks—both in the cerebral cortex and in other parts of the nervous system. This seems to be supported by experimental evidence demonstrating the synchronization of rapid oscillations in the neural network that both surge and abate rapidly. Yet this experience is not "identified in terms of specific neural structures. It is the manifestation of a particular cognitive process—a transient synchronization of diverse, rhythmically oscillating neural circuits" (Capra 1996, 293).

While Capra himself seems to reject any quantum explanations for consciousness, his description of Varela's theory seems very similar in some ways to that of neural networks generating some kind of Bose-Einstein condensate (such as those involved in lasers) as we discussed in the section on the "Immanence of Mind" (in chapter 7). This coincidence becomes even more significant when we consider that Bose-Einstein condensates are themselves self-organizing systems existing far from equilibrium. Whether or not a Bose-Einstein condensate is actually involved—or whether another similar, highly correlated phenomenon involving systems dynamics is at work—is impossible to confirm at this juncture. In any case, though, the two theories certainly seem to share important similarities.

COMPLEXITY AND TRANSFORMATION

A difficulty in understanding the interplay between living systems and both mind and consciousness often results from our view of causality—that is, the relationship between cause and effect. Mechanistic cosmology has taught us to see causality in linear terms: so either the world of material reality must somehow produce mind (as a purely materialist science would posit) or mind must somehow conjure reality (as some kinds of idealism might posit). But what if something far more creative and mysterious is in play? What if systems somehow condition the process of mind and the process of mind in turn conditions systems? What if causality is in some sense reciprocal?

The nature of causality is a key question for transformative praxis. Causality is all "about how things happen, how change occurs" (Macy 1991a, 1). While quantum theory began to undermine the determinism of linear causality inherent in classical physics, it was unable to formulate a truly satisfying alternative. Joanna Macy points out that the "blind and purposeless play of atoms" and subatomic particles, governed by the laws of chance, is almost as "bleak to the spirit" as the determinism of a clockwork universe (1991a, 70).

While the non-local connections evidenced in Bell's Theorem do point to the possibility of a more mysterious, holistic understanding of causality (where everything may in some sense cause everything else), this understanding still provides few concrete insights into *how* change really comes about. Systems theory, in contrast, offers a clearer understanding of the relationship between cause and effect with intriguing implication for liberatory praxis. In essence, it represents a kind of "middle way" between determinism and chance, where change, while mysterious, is not random, but rather creative.

Unlike linear systems, where input determines output, the nonlinear dynamics of living systems produce an extremely complex relationship between cause and effect. As we have noted, in such systems feedback loops and chaotic behavior lead to a high degree of sensitivity where what happens in one region affects all other regions in a nondeterministic fashion and where the entire system works cooperatively to create a kind of "whirlpool that abides." Because of these holistic dynamics, cause and effect interact mutually in such a way that the effect becomes a cause, and vice versa. The idea of feedback loops is helpful in imaging this kind of circular, interactive causality. Causality, then, is not linear and unidirectional, but reciprocal—or even circular. Outcomes are determined less by inputs than by the complex dynamics of the system itself.

In *Mutual Causality in Buddhism and General Systems Theory: The Dharma of Natural Systems*, Joanna Macy (1991a) gives an insightful analysis of the implications of systems theory for understanding causality, supplementing it with parallel ideas drawn from Buddhism. Insofar as causality is the basic foundation upon which our view of transformation and change is built, it is worthwhile to examine her analysis in more detail.

In Buddhism, the concept of Dharma refers not to a substance or essence but to the "way things work," or "orderly process itself" (p. xi)—an idea that closely resembles the Tao. As in systems theory, all phenomena are considered to be interdependent, and experience is therefore considered both workable and spacious. Central to all this is the doctrine of *paticca samuppada,* which means "dependent co-arising"—that is, mutual or reciprocal causality. This corresponds to the ecological, self-organizing view inherent in systems theory, which also sees reality as a process involving self-organizing patterns of mental and physical events. In systems theory, as in Buddhism, cause and effect arise "from interweaving circuits of contingency" (p. xii).

Mind and spirit are not isolated from the interactive causality implicit in systems theory and Buddhism. Here, the dynamics first glimpsed through the holographic analogy come into play. Matter and mind interact and affect each other in a reciprocal fashion. This idea becomes even clearer when supplemented with the insights of *paticca samuppada*:

> Integral to the concept of dependent co-arising is the belief that the preconceptions and predispositions of the mind itself shape the reality it sees. This runs counter to commonsensical notions of a world "out there" distinct from and independent of the perceiving self. A genuine understanding of mutual causality involves a transcendence of conventional dichotomies between self and world, a transformation of the way experience is processed, which amounts to an overhauling of one's most ingrained assumptions. *Paticca samuppada* is not a theory to which one assents, so much as a truth one is invited to experience, an insight one is encouraged to win, by virtue of disciplined introspection and radical attentiveness to the arising and passing away of mental and physical phenomena. (Macy 1991a, 19)

The new understanding of causality arising from systems theory, supplemented with insights from Buddhism, presents a world in which novelty becomes a real possibility. Open systems, in response to the wider reality in which they are immersed, can and do change in fundamental ways. Both the determinism of the clockwork universe and the purposeless play of chance of quantum theory's statistical mechanics are rejected. In its place, an understanding of causality emerges that admits both the possibility of authentic transformation and our ability to participate meaningfully in it.

As long as causality was restricted to either determinism or blind chance, our power to change the world seemed to be at best a wishful illusion. Indeed, our unconscious assumptions about causality may well lie at the heart of the despair many of us experience in the face of the global crisis:

> In a hierarchical view of reality, and in the linear, one-way causality to which it leads, both value and power are attributed to an absolute or entity or essence, unaffected by the play of phenomena. . . . Even when belief in an absolute erodes, habits of thought bred by the one-way view persist in the assumption that power works from the top down. This notion is particularly dangerous in a time of increasing planetary disruptions and scarcities. It tempts people to assume that personal freedom is inimical to collective survival, and that order is imposed from above. Indeed the political fanaticisms and religious fundamentalism of our time give voice to the belief that common will and coordinated action require subservience to a particular leader or deity. (Macy 1991a, xiii)

The reciprocal, interactive view of causality resulting from a systems perspective changes this. Our ability to affect reality no longer depends on the brute force of our input, but on the subtle webs of relationality inherent in the exercise of power-with. In the systems view, "order is not imposed from above, by mind exerting its will [i.e., willpower] on dumb material forces; it is intrinsic to the self-organizing nature of the phenomenal world itself" (Macy 1991a, xiii). Indeed, this intrinsic power for self-organization could be understood as the source of power-from-within. Because of this, the effectiveness of an action depends on its quality (timing, place, etc.) rather than its quantitative "force." In the words of the *Tao Te Ching*, "When acting, proper timing is everything" (§8).

Indeed, not only do our actions have the potential for impact—our very thoughts and intentions may influence reality. In some sense, as our perception of reality changes, this in turn has an effect on the systems we live in. Our power to change the world becomes real. It then remains for each of us to discover how to make it effective. As Macy notes, "When we recognize our participation in its co-arising patterns, we can claim our power to act. We can then, through our choices, give expression and efficacy to the coordination at play in all life-forms" (1991a, xiv).

In the Buddhist conception, the tendency to "cling to fixed forms and categories created by the mind instead of accepting the impermanent and transitory nature of all things" is the root of human suffering. Indeed, all fixed forms—be they concepts, categories, or things—are a kind of *maya*, or illusion: "Out of ignorance (*avidya*), we divide the perceived world into separate objects that we see as firm and permanent, but which are really transient and ever-changing. Trying to cling to our rigid categories instead of realizing the fluidity of life, we are bound to experience frustration after frustration" (Capra 1996, 294-95).

As Macy notes, this analysis of suffering is also a key to understanding the process of liberation—particularly liberation from our own internalized power-lessness in the form of denial, despair, addiction, and internalized oppression:

> Our suffering is caused by the interplay of these factors and particularly by the delusion, craving, and aversion that arise from our misapprehension of them. We fabricate our bondage by hypostatizing and clinging to what is by nature contingent and transient. The reifications we construct falsify experience, imprison us in egos of our own making, doom our lives to end-less rounds of acquisition and anxiety. Being so caused, our suffering is not endemic; it is not inevitable. (Macy 1991a, 18)

One of the key ways of overcoming our internal bondage, according to Bud-dhism, is through the practice of meditation—developing a state of pure, open awareness or mindfulness. This same practice is also a key to developing a deep intuition into the nature of dependent co-arising itself, and thus a way to engage creatively in transformation. The mind "is liberated, not through setting itself apart from phenomenality, but increasing its awareness of it. This rigorous attention brings insight into the dependent co-arising of phenomena" (Macy 1991a, 155).

In reflecting on causality, power, and the dynamics of complex systems, we can gain a number of insights into the nature of economic, social, and cultural transformation. First, it is important to note that no open system—no matter how large and complex—is immutable. Often, we can feel overwhelmed by the sheer complexity of the systems we wish to change. The possibility of a single individual, or even a single social movement, truly contributing to change in a meaningful manner may seem infinitesimally small.

Yet systems theory suggests that this is not at all the case. The more complex a system is, the more sensitive it becomes to change. If the system is healthy and is functioning well, this means that it will be able to adapt easily, responding with necessary changes in a positive manner. Alternatively, if the system is no longer able to adapt to the requirements of the moment—as would seem to be the case with our current economic and political system—dynamics of positive feedback may force it to come to a bifurcation point where the current structure may rapidly be replaced by a new one that is better adapted to the new situation. This is precisely what happens in the evolutionary process: External stresses lead to sudden jumps—often with surprising rapidity—through a phenomenon called "punctuated evolution" (which we will explore in greater depth in the following chapter).

In acting to transform social, economic, and cultural systems—including the common paradigms these may share—we should recall that a system is often most sensitive in those places where it is subjected to the greatest pressures. Just as new species often appear where an ecosystem is under stress—in regions considered to be on the margins—so too may it be in human societies; we should therefore seek out creativity on the periphery of our social, economic, and cultural systems, for it may be precisely in those regions where structures and paradigms are beginning to break through with creativity into new forms.

In working for authentic liberation, we should also view crises as opportunities for radical change. In the systems view, crises represent potential bifurcation points where a social structure, an economic system, or a cultural paradigm may be particularly vulnerable to change. As Ilya Prigogine and Isabelle Stengers observe:

> We know that societies are immensely complex systems involving a potentially enormous number of bifurcations exemplified by the variety of cultures that have evolved in the relatively short span of human history. We know that such systems are highly sensitive to fluctuations. This leads both to hope and threat: hope, because even small fluctuations may grow and change the overall structure. As a result, individual activity is not doomed to insignificance. On the other hand, this is also a threat, since in our universe the security of stable, permanent rules seems gone forever. We are living in a dangerous and uncertain world that inspires no blind confidence. (1984, 313)

While security may be elusive in a world such as this, hope for deep, profound transformation is not. Given the phenomenon of reciprocal causality and the amplifying effects of positive feedback, the thoughts, motives, and actions of each individual carry the potential to effect significant changes. In such an understanding, the role of individuals, organizations, and social movements can become critical. As Macy points out, from a systems perspective our social, economic, and political systems—and, by extension, our systems of values and our cosmovision—are not some kind of static, preordained order to which individuals must accommodate themselves. Rather, they are fluid patterns in which we ourselves participate and in which we have influence. The dynamics of dependent co-arising always come into play. As Margaret Mead once wrote, we should "never doubt that a small group of thoughtful, committed citizens can change the world. Indeed, it is the only thing that ever has" (quoted in Suzuki and McConnell 1997, 218).

Our ability to effect change will not, however, depend on the sheer force and size of a movement—although in some circumstances it may be necessary to create a certain amount of "critical mass" to be successful. More important, though, will be our ability to discern the right action with the right intention at the right time and place. While good analysis can play a role in this process, contemplation, intuition, and creativity may be even more important. To influence a situation, we need to apprehend the subtle undercurrents at work and make use of them, gently redirecting the flow of the system in a new direction. This kind of subtle, intuitive action may require the use of practices such as meditation, visualization, art, and other methods normally associated with spiritual paths.

One way to illustrate this kind of intuitive apprehension is through the story of the cook who butchers an ox in the Taoist text of *Chuang Tzu*:

Carving Up an Ox

A cook was butchering an ox for Duke Wen Hui.
The places his hand touched,
His shoulder leaned against,
His foot stepped on,
His knee pressed upon,
Came apart with a sound.

He moved the blade, making a noise
That never fell out of rhythm.
It harmonized with the Mulberry Woods Dance,
Like music from ancient times.

Duke Wen Hui exclaimed: "Ah! Excellent!
Your skill has advanced to this level?"

The cook puts down the knife and answered:
"What I follow is Tao,
Which is beyond all skills.

"When I started butchering,
What I saw was nothing but the whole ox.
After three years,
I no longer saw the whole ox.

"Nowadays, I meet it with my mind
Rather than see it with my eyes.
My sensory organs are inactive
While I direct the mind's movement.

"It goes according to natural laws,
Striking apart large gaps,
Moving toward large openings,
Following its natural structure.

"Even places where tendons attach to bones
Give no resistance,
Never mind the larger bones!

"A good cook goes through a knife in a year,
Because he cuts.
An average cook goes through a knife in a month,
Because he hacks.

"I have used this knife for nineteen years.
It has butchered thousands of oxen,
But the blade is still like it's newly sharpened.

"The joints have openings,
And the knife's blade has no thickness.
Apply this lack of thickness into the openings,
And the moving blade swishes through,
With room to spare!"

"That's why after nineteen years,
The blade is still like it's newly sharpened.

"Nevertheless, every time I come across joints,
I see its tricky parts,

I pay attention and use caution,
My vision concentrates,
My movement slows down.

"I move the knife very slightly,
Whump! It has already separated.
The ox doesn't even know it's dead,
and falls to the ground like mud.

"I stand holding the knife,
And look all around it.
The work gives me much satisfaction.
I clean the knife and put it away."

Duke Wen Hui said: "Excellent!
I listen to your words,
And learn a principle of life."

(Translated by Derek Lin of the Tao Study Group posted at http://www
.truetao.org/chuang/butcher.htm)

What if we could approach the art of liberatory praxis in the same way as the cook approaches the butchering of an ox? What if we could intuit the Tao in the same way and act accordingly? In the case of social and cultural transformation, the challenge is even greater, for we are dealing with a host of intricately related, self-organizing systems in a constant state of flux. Yet the same spirit is certainly called for—an intuitive apprehension of the whole through which we endeavor to discern the right approach for the context at hand.

It is interesting to note that the Aramaic version of the prayer of Jesus ("The Lord's Prayer" or "Our Father") can also enrich our insights into appropriate action in this regard. The word that Jesus used for "good" (*taba*) essentially means "ripe," while the word used for "evil" (*bisha*) means "unripe" or "rotten." So, drawing on the old roots of the Aramaic words, the phrase normally translated "Lead us not into temptation, but deliver us from evil" could perhaps more accurately be rendered as, "Let us not be deluded by superficiality or seduced by appearances, but free us from inappropriate (unfruitful) actions," or even "Let us not be captive to uncertainty, nor cling to fruitless pursuits."

As Neil Douglas-Klotz (1990; 1999) points out, the idea here is very much one of finding the right action for the moment at hand: "Those who are 'good' are at the right place and the right time with the right action. In this sense, they are prepared for any event—ready, with full presence in the moment." In contrast, evil implies that one has "fallen out of rhythm with Sacred Unity." It may be that the action may "not yet be ready for the purpose for which it is meant" (it is not yet ripe) or that the action "is no longer ripe: at one time and place it was appropriate, but it has now departed from the rhythm of the sacred 'I Am' and has become rotten, so to speak" (Douglas-Klotz 1999, 132).

To embody a truly liberatory praxis, then, means becoming acutely sensitive to the moment at hand and maintaining an attentive receptivity toward it. It means entering into the mystery of reciprocal causality, recognizing that discursive, analytical thought alone can never plumb the depths of the complexity involved. It also means utilizing the power of relationality and creativity as the energy to undertake the transformative journey. Finally, it means breaking through the delusions that imprison our minds, the threads of internalized powerlessness that ensnare and bind us.

Liberation itself is an art, a self-organizing process in which we are each called to discern and act through contemplation, creativity, and relational engagement. The final results of such a process are never predictable, but the value of each individual, each community, and each movement should never be underestimated. As Macy notes, "Within the context of [a] larger body—or living web—our own individual efforts can seem paltry. They are hard to measure as significant. Yet, because of the systemic, interactive nature of the web, each act reverberates in that web in ways we cannot possibly see. And each can be essential to the survival of the web" (1983, 36).

9.

Memory, Morphic Resonance, and Emergence

Look and it cannot be seen.
Listen and it cannot be heard.
Grasp and it cannot be touched.

Intermingling in oneness,
it eludes the senses.

From above it is not bright.
From below it is not dark.
Like an unbroken thread that cannot be described,
it returns to the void.

Formless form that includes all forms,
image without substance,
subtle, beyond all conception.

Approach that which is beyond beginnings,
follow that which has no end.
Hold fast to the timeless Tao,
and move to the rhythm of the present moment,
and you will apprehend the origin in the unbroken thread of the Tao.

(Tao Te Ching §14)

The regularities of Nature are more like habits than laws, . . . they're not fixed for all time from the beginning. They're habits which have grown within Nature. Nature has a kind of inherent memory rather than an eternal mathematical mind. Each kind of thing has a collective memory of previous things of that kind. . . . Memory depends on the process I call morphic resonance, the influence of like upon like through space and time. Similar patterns of activity or vibration pick up what's happened to similar patterns before. (Fox and Sheldrake 1996a, 163-64)

Systems theory serves as an excellent foundation to begin to understand the nature of transformation in complex systems. Yet the phenomenon of emergence at some level remains mysterious. Positive feedback loops and the mathematics of chaos do help us to describe some of the key phenomena involved, but they do not exactly explain *why* creativity seems to be inherent in the very fabric of the cosmos. Nor do they explain some of the more puzzling aspects of creative emergence—particularly, how new behaviors and new learnings seem to "take on a life of their own," rapidly spreading in ways that seem to defy our accustomed way of viewing learning and change.

One of the most intriguing examples of this kind of mysterious transmission of learning can be seen in the series of experiments carried out by William McDougall at Harvard in 1920 (Sheldrake 1988). Hoping to find evidence for the hereditary transmission of learning, McDougall trained a group of standard white laboratory rats to pass through a complex water maze with two exits: one illuminated (where the rats received an electric shock) and one darkened (which was safe). The exit with the light and electric shock was periodically changed. Over time, the rats learned that it was safe to leave by the darkened exit and that they should avoid the illuminated one.

The first generation of rats chose the illuminated exit an average of 165 times before they learned that they must consistently avoid it. The next generation of rats, in contrast, learned to avoid the illuminated exit after only the twentieth try—even though McDougall had chosen the least intelligent rats from the previous generation as the parents for the second one. He concluded that some kind of inherited memory was at work, leading to a vast improvement in learning in the second generation.

Then, a scientist in Edinburgh, Scotland, tried to replicate McDougall's experiment, starting with a totally new set of rats; however, his first generation of rats learned much more quickly than McDougall's, consistently avoiding the illuminated exit after a mere twenty-five errors. Similarly, another group of scientists in Melbourne, Australia, found that their first generation learned much more quickly than McDougall's. What is more, after working with fifty more generations of rats over a period of twenty years, the rate of learning continued to increase—even with control rats not descended from the previous generation. The learning of subsequent generations of rats—even those with no direct link to those who had preceded them—kept improving over time.

Certainly, this is an intriguing experiment—and one that could potentially have important implications for transformative praxis. As we will see over the course of this chapter, it does not seem to be simply an isolated incident but rather a particularly clear and scientifically rigorous example of a more widespread phenomenon. What is the nature of the process at work? Systems theory alone does not seem to provide an adequate explanation. The non-local quantum-level connections implied by Bell's Theorem may suggest some possibilities, but it is not immediately apparent how such connections might play a role in the transmission of learning. More promising still might be the idea of the implicate order—especially since it implies that mind and memory themselves may not be local phenomena, but rather that the brain somehow simply accesses memory, which itself exists in the implicate order—or if one prefers an alternative term— in the pregnant void.

As we have seen in our discussion of systems theory, mind—including the process of memory—need not be associated with a nervous system at all. The immune system, for example, remembers the configuration of a foreign substance (such as a virus or bacterium) for decades after it has first been identified. Indeed, as Diarmuid O'Murchu (1997) points out, we could think of the immune system as a kind of a field of memory. Similarly, he notes that the DNA of a cell could be thought of as a kind of storage system for the transfer of information:

> DNA never budges so much as a thousandth of a millimetre in its precise structure, because the genomes—the bits of information in DNA—remember where everything goes, all three billion of them. This fact makes us realise that memory must be more permanent than matter. Consequently, a cell may be described as a memory that has built some matter around itself, forming a specific pattern. The carrier of information, therefore (and dare we add, *meaning*), is the memory rather than the matter. (1997, 70)

In this understanding, the concepts of form and of memory are closely related. As we have seen, form takes primacy over matter in the systems perspective. Insofar as form requires constant regeneration through the whirlpool-like dynamic of stability-through-flux, we could say indeed that a system is a kind of manifestation of memory. Yet, at the same time, the nature of reciprocal causality (or dependent co-arising) would in turn imply that the system also continually creates (or re-creates)—or at least contributes to—memory.

In this chapter, we will explore the dynamics of memory in more detail. In so doing, we will see that memory, which itself could be considered one aspect of the broader concept of mind, seems to be inherent in all systems, not only those that we would normally consider to be "living." For example, protein molecules and chemical crystals could be thought of as having a kind of memory, as could societies and ecosystems. In exploring these ideas, we will draw heavily on the ideas of Rupert Sheldrake, a somewhat unconventional British biochemist. While Sheldrake's theories are not considered "mainstream" science, differing as they do from the accepted orthodoxies of our day, they do explain a host of intriguing phenomena that many scientists seem to have ignored, perhaps because of the challenge they represent to traditional scientific thinking. At the very least, Sheldrake's theories raise excellent questions and provide clues that may lead to a new understanding of memory and the evolution of new habits and behaviors. They also seem to point to a new way of viewing reality that could have important implications for transformative praxis.

The heart of Sheldrake's thesis is contained in his theory of "Formative Causation," which proposes that memory is inherent in nature and is contained or embodied in "morphic fields" (taken from the Greek *morphē*, meaning "form"), which are immaterial (and in some sense, both local and non-local), but still in some sense "physical," in character:

> Morphic fields, like the known fields of physics, are non-material regions of influence extending in space and continuing in time. They are localized within and around the systems they organize. When any particular organized system ceases to exist, as when an atom splits, a snowflake melts, an animal dies, its organizing field disappears from that place. But in another sense, morphic fields do not disappear: they are potential organizing patterns of influence and can appear again physically in other times and places wherever and whenever the physical conditions are appropriate. When they do so they contain within themselves a memory of their previous physical existences. (Sheldrake 1988, xvii-ix)

In many ways, morphic fields correspond to the idea of "organizing relations" (or the "dynamics of self-organization") in the philosophy of organicism;[1] indeed Rupert Sheldrake sees his theory as an extension or elaboration of the organicist perspective. For Sheldrake, the field is imminent in the system, much like Aristotle's idea of the soul (as opposed to the Platonic idea of eternal, transcendent forms). Despite this, many critics, including Fritjof Capra, consider Sheldrake's ideas to be a sophisticated form of vitalism—something that Sheldrake himself vigorously rejects.

In considering the accusation of vitalist tendencies in Sheldrake's theory, it should be recalled that vitalists insist that their "vital force" is somehow unique to living organisms, something distinct from morphic fields which are seen to be at work in all systems in the cosmos. As we have previously noted, Sheldrake believes that "from the organismic point of view, life is not something that has emerged from dead matter and that needs to be explained in terms of the added vital factors of vitalism. *All* nature is alive. The organizing principles of living organisms are different in degree but not different in kind from the organizing principles of molecules or of societies or of galaxies" (1988, 54-55).

Furthermore, Sheldrake's morphic fields are considered to be just as "physical" as other fields in physics (such as gravitational or electrical fields), even if their nature is also in some sense unique. Further, it should be noted that morphic fields and systems interact through reciprocal causality—that is, creativity in a system also interacts with its morphic field, effectively adding new knowledge and new experiences to the collective field of memory.

---

1. As discussed earlier (see p. 199 above), organicism maintains that physical and chemical process plus "organizing relations" are sufficient to understand the dynamics of life and, in contrast to vitalism, do not posit any kind of outside force or entity at work. The idea of organizing relations has now largely come to be understood in terms of the dynamics of self-organization.

According to the theory of formative causation, memory—"the process by which the past becomes present"—occurs through "morphic resonance," which involves the "the transmission of formative causal influences through both space and time" (Sheldrake 1988, ix).[2] Since the memories contained in the morphic fields accumulate over time, things become increasingly habitual. In the case of the "behavior" of such things as atoms, molecules, or elementary particles, these have recurred over such a huge expanse of time that they now appear to be changeless. Yet what we take to be "eternal laws" should actually be understood as very ingrained habits of nature.

Even though morphic resonance can make some habits appear to be nearly changeless, the spirit of the theory of morphic resonance is thoroughly evolutionary and dynamic in nature. Morphic fields can and do change over time, and when they do so, sudden bursts of creativity often come about.[3] Indeed, at the root of the theory of morphic resonance is the conviction that, in an evolving cosmos, there can be no fixed or eternal laws. Everything, including the organizing field of the cosmos itself, must evolve over time.

Over the course of this chapter, we will explore a number of areas where the theory of morphic resonance can contribute to our understanding of a new cosmology. In particular, we will examine how morphic fields can provide a unique perspective on the nature of memory—and also of mind itself—which enables us to uncover new insights into learning and the dynamics of self-organization and creativity. In addition, we will look at how the morphic perspective enables us to move beyond a mechanistic understanding of genes so that we can see the development and evolution of living organisms in a new light. We will also discuss how morphic fields help us to envision a truly evolutionary cosmology, one where eternal laws no longer reign like some kind of "unmoved mover" governing the cosmos. Finally, we will consider how morphic resonance can help us discover new insights into transformative praxis.

THE REVERBERATIONS OF MEMORY

What we learn and what we think can affect other people by morphic resonance. Our souls are bound up with those of others and bound up with the world around us. The idea of the mind being inside our heads, a small, portable entity isolated in the privacy of our skulls, is extraordinary. No culture in the past has had this idea, and it's amazing that the most educated and sophisticated culture that has ever existed (as we'd like to think

---

2. From here onward, we will mainly use the term "theory of morphic resonance" instead of "formative causation" because the latter term seems to conjure the image of fields "causing" a form to arise in a linear, unidirectional fashion. In contrast, the term "resonance" carries a strong connotation of reciprocity and is thus more consistent with a complex understanding of causality.

3. From our experience with systems theory, we might well postulate that the more complex a system, the more vulnerable its morphic field is to modification.

of ourselves) could have such an extraordinary view. (Fox and Sheldrake 1996a, 94)

Most of us think of our brains as both the seat of consciousness and the container of our memories. Certainly, the brain is a wonderful organ, one so complex that we are far from understanding all the mysterious dynamics at work in it. Yet the quest to find the seat of memory within the brain has so far been elusive.

Neuroscientists working out of a purely materialist paradigm have postulated that memory should be understandable in terms of some kind of physical or chemical modification of the nervous system—a material "trace"—presumably located in the brain. To find evidence of such a trace, scientists have used animal experiments in which they teach an experimental subject something and then attempt to remove portions of the subject's brain—in some cases up to 60 percent—to see just when the animal ceases to remember. The results of such experiments, however, are inconclusive at best: specific memories cannot be removed by eliminating a specific part of the brain. Memory seems to be somehow distributed throughout the brain—to be both everywhere in general and nowhere in particular (Sheldrake 1990).

Indeed, people afflicted by amnesia due to traumatic brain damage normally lose their memories in a holistic fashion rather than particular segments of memory. If memory is recovered, it often returns in a chronological order, the oldest memories being recovered first. This seems at odds, once again, with the idea of localized "memory traces" stored in the brain.

Rupert Sheldrake suggests that memory traces may not, in fact, exist at all. The brain may not store memories, but rather simply access memory in a manner analogous to the way a television tunes into a field of electromagnetic radiation (a radio signal). Damaging the brain can certainly affect its ability to tune in to the field of memory—resulting in either the inability to recall a past memory (receive) or to store a new one (transmit). Memory traces, however, cannot be found: "A search inside your TV set for traces of the programs you watched last week would be doomed to failure for the same reason: the set tunes into TV transmissions, but does not store them" (1990, 93).

Sheldrake believes that memory is stored in morphic fields and that memory works through the process of morphic resonance instead of any kind of material memory store:

Morphic resonance depends on similarity. It involves an effect of like on like. The more similar an organism is to an organism in the past, the more specific and effective the morphic resonance. In general any given organism is most like *itself* in the past, and hence subject to highly specific morphic resonance from its own past. (1990, 94)

This does not mean that physical or chemical disturbances in the nervous system cannot affect behavior—only that these disturbances are analogous to damage to a computer's hardware rather than to its programming (or software). In fact, the ability of the brain to recover from traumatic memory loss can be explained in terms of morphic fields:

> After damage to parts of the brain, these fields may be capable of organizing the nerve cells in other regions to carry out the same functions as before. The ability of learned habits to survive substantial brain damage may be due to the self-organizing properties of the fields—properties which are expressed in the realm of morphogenesis in regeneration and embryonic regulation. (Sheldrake 1988, 168)

The idea of memory being stored in morphic fields is closely related to psychologist Carl Jung's idea of the collective unconscious, a kind of collective field of memory shared by all humanity that manifests itself in common symbols or "archetypes" in myths and dreams. Jung believed that all people shared a common set of archetypes, but that at the same time particular cultures might also share a more specialized set of unconscious memories. Marie-Louise van Franz has further developed this idea; she envisions the collective unconscious in a holarchical fashion where the individual unconscious is nested in the unconscious of the family, which in turn is nested in that of the clan, the culture, and so on, in ever-widening circles. For this reason, the mythologies of each culture may have unique elements as well as those shared with neighboring cultures and those that are common to humanity itself (Sheldrake 1988, 252).[4]

We could envision the morphic fields of memory in this same way—as nested holarchies reaching out in ever more inclusive circles. These circles presumably would reach beyond humanity into the memories of other species as well, although our ability to "resonate" with those fields progressively weakens as similarities diminish.

The idea of memory stored in morphic fields may explain in part the "past life memories" that some people experience and which seem to become clearer through hypnosis. It may be that, due to similarities in personality or psychic structure, we tend to "resonate" in some way with the memories of certain individuals who have lived in the past, and are thus able to access and experience their memories more easily.

The concept of fields itself may initially seem somewhat mysterious. Is this just some kind of metaphysical abstraction, an idea rather than something with a more concrete manifestation? Even in asking such a question, we must be careful to examine our own materialist assumptions. As we have already seen, even "physical" realities like subatomic particles are more like subtle dances of energy, waves of probability swimming in the pregnant void. Indeed, one way

---

4. Similarly, morphic fields are related to the idea of the "ecological unconscious"—what Roszak (1992, 304) calls the "compacted ecological intelligence of our species"—which we discussed on p. 114.

of expressing the wavelike nature of matter is in terms of "quantum fields" (or "quantum matter fields"). As Sheldrake points out: "In these quantum matter fields, there is no duality of field and particle in the sense that the field is somehow external to the particle. Indeed, the essential physical reality has become a set of fields, and the fields specify the probabilities of finding quanta at particular points in space. The particles are manifestations of the underlying reality of the fields" (1988, 118). In the new physics, then, we can think of fields (organizing or formative entities) as being more essential than matter or substance. The concept of morphic fields should be considered in this light—indeed, morphic fields may well involve quantum phenomena.

One way to conceive of morphic fields is to consider them as fields of information, analogous in some ways to the idea of a program in conventional biological usage. At the same time, morphic fields are probabilistic in nature, just as quantum matter fields are. (Indeed, at the level of atoms and subatomic entities, Sheldrake suggests that what is described in quantum field theory may well be identical to the morphic field of the atom or subatomic particle.) In terms of biological phenomena, this probabilistic nature is demonstrated by the fact that no two organisms or biological systems are ever identical, even when they develop under similar conditions—or even when they are genetically indistinguishable. Always, there is an element of indeterminacy that comes into play. At the same time, though, the morphic field does create a kind of boundary for behaviors and forms. In this sense, morphic fields are analogous to the "attractors" of systems theory—albeit in systems theory the attractors are not considered to be in any way causative.

The phenomenon of morphic resonance also contributes to the probabilistic nature of morphic fields. A morphic field resonates with innumerable fields from the similar organisms or systems in the past, yet there is variation in all these past fields as well. These variations, once again, create a kind of composite boundary that delineates the range of forms or behaviors in a probabilistic fashion. Therefore, a morphic field can never be rigidly deterministic in nature: it is always a probability structure (although in some cases—such as the case of some physical phenomena—the range may be so small as to be essentially undetectable).

Morphic resonance, unlike most forms of physical resonance (such as nuclear-magnetic resonance or acoustic resonance), does not involve the transfer of energy between systems, but rather "a non-energetic transfer of information." On the other hand, morphic resonance resembles other resonance phenomena insofar as it "takes place on the basis of rhythmic patterns of activity," including the vibrations of atoms, the oscillations of cellular activities, the waves of electrical activity in the nervous system, and the innumerable cycles of living organisms.

According to the hypothesis of formative causation, morphic resonance occurs between such rhythmic structures of activity on the basis of similarity, and through this resonance past patterns of activity influence the fields of subsequent similar systems. Morphic resonance involves a kind of action at a distance in both space and time. The hypothesis assumes that this influence does not decline with distance in space or in time. (Sheldrake 1988, 109)

Morphic fields resemble Aristotle's entelechies insofar as they do not exist as transcendent ideals independent of actual organisms or systems. They are very different, for example, from the Platonic concept of ideal forms that shape reality in a unidirectional and deterministic fashion. In the case of morphic fields, information does not simply flow from the field to the form, but also from the form back to the field in an interactive or reciprocal fashion. Morphic fields are therefore dynamic and evolutionary in nature.

In considering how morphic fields convey information through space and time, Sheldrake maintains that we do not need to postulate some kind of "morphogenetic ether" or some phenomenon working in another dimension, but rather we should "think of the past as pressed up, as it were, against the present, and as potentially present everywhere" (1988, 112).

If this idea seems strange to us, we should take into account that the Newtonian idea of immutable laws is just as mysterious and perhaps even stranger—it is just that we have become used to thinking in such a manner and do not question our basic assumptions:

We are so used to the notion of immutable physical laws that we take them for granted; but if we pause to reflect on the nature of these laws, they are profoundly mysterious. They are not material things, nor are they energetic. They both transcend space and time and are, at least potentially, present in all places and at all times.

Although morphic resonance seems mysterious, the conventional theories seem no less so when we stand back and look at the remarkable assumptions they embody. The hypothesis of formative causation is not a bizarre metaphysical speculation that contrasts with a hard, empirical, down-to-earth theory of mechanism. The mechanistic theory depends on assumptions that are, if anything, *more* metaphysical than the idea of formative causation. (Sheldrake 1988, 112)

As we have noted, the idea of morphic fields can easily be related to systems theory if we consider these fields analogous to the idea of an attractor that constitutes a kind of boundary for forms and behaviors. Essentially, we might think of an attractor as a kind of mathematical description of a morphic field. At the same time, the idea of morphic fields and morphic resonance is also related to the theory of the implicate order and the holographic analogy. In some sense, the entire nested holarchy of morphic fields taken together could be thought to correspond to the implicate order. David Bohm, one of the originators of the holographic perspective, sees the relationship as follows:

The implicate order can be thought of as a ground beyond time, a totality, out of which each moment is projected into the explicate order. For every moment that is projected out into the explicate there would be another movement in which that moment would be injected or "introjected" back into the implicate order. If you have a large number of repetitions of this process, you'll start to build up a fairly constant component to this series of projection and injection. That is, a fixed disposition would become established. The point is that, via this process, past forms would tend to be repeated or replicated in the present, and that is very similar to what Sheldrake calls a morphogenetic [or morphic] field and morphic resonance. Moreover, such a field would not be located anywhere. When it projects back into the totality (the implicate order), since no space and time are relevant there, all things of a similar nature might get connected together or resonate in totality. When the explicate order enfolds into the implicate order, which does not have any space, all places and all times are, we might say, merged, so that what happens in one place will interpenetrate what happens in another place. (Quoted in Sheldrake 1988, 305-6)

The concept of memory stored in morphic fields becomes much clearer when we consider concrete examples that seem to demonstrate this phenomenon. While such examples are not definitive experimental proof of morphic resonance, they do suggest that something beyond memories physically stored in the brain are at work.

One such example is that of the acquisition of language. Noam Chomsky has postulated that the rapidity with which children learn language simply cannot be explained through a behaviorist model of learning. To Chomsky, it appears that language effectively grows in the mind and that the organizing linguistic structures are essentially innate. Because of this, Chomsky has proposed that there is a kind of universal grammar that he believes must be in some way genetically programmed.

An alternative explanation for this phenomenon, however, can be found in the theory of morphic resonance. Given the morphic fields of all human beings who have spoken different languages in the past, morphic resonance should facilitate the learning of these languages. As Sheldrake notes, "Morphic resonance gives young children a general tendency to learn language, but as they begin to speak a particular language, such as Swedish, they enter into morphic resonance with the people they hear speaking it; their learning of its particular grammar and vocabulary is facilitated by this resonance" (1988, 185).

Indeed, morphic resonance seems to provide a more satisfactory explanation for the ease of language acquisition than any kind of genetic programming. If genetic programming were in play, we might expect far less diversity and far more rigidity in linguistic structure than what we actually encounter. On the other hand, morphic resonance can account both for a degree of regularity in languages—common features such as words and sentences—while also allowing for a great diversity of linguistic systems.

Rupert Sheldrake designed a linguistic experiment that illustrates how morphic resonance comes into play in language acquisition. He asked a Japanese poet to supply him with three rhymes: one a traditional nursery rhyme recited by generations of children in Japan and two others that resembled it, one of which was meaningful in Japanese, and the other of which was not. These three rhymes were then taught to children in the United States and the United Kingdom who did not know any Japanese. Roughly two thirds of the children found the genuine nursery rhyme to be the easiest to learn, even though the three rhymes were of equivalent difficulty—a very significant result from a statistical point of view.

While not conclusive, this experiment does lend support to the idea that morphic resonance facilitates language acquisition: the repetition of a rhyme by generations of children would create a strong field of memory that could be accessed via the phenomenon of morphic resonance. Other experiments, involving the direct or indirect recognition of real and fabricated written words in languages unknown to the experimental subjects, give further support to the theory of morphic resonance (Sheldrake 1988, 190-93).

Morphic resonance may also account for the power of traditional rituals, chants, and mantras in the world's religious traditions. Religious rites repeated over and over—sometimes for thousands of years—would create a powerful collective morphic field of memory. Because of this, such rituals should accumulate a kind of spiritual power (associated with the spiritual states of those who have experienced these rituals in the past) that newer rituals cannot. Similarly, traditional mantras—prayer words repeated over and over again by millions of people over vast spans of time—should take on a deep power by tapping into the memory of meditative states of countless individuals over the centuries. Because of this, traditional mantras have a unique ability to facilitate meditation.

Morphic resonance might also account for the rapid spread of new habits in animal populations. One particularly interesting case that illustrates this process can be seen in blue tits, a bird species living in western Europe. During the 1920s through to the 1940s, the habit of blue tits of opening the caps of milk bottles spread throughout the UK, even though blue tits seldom travel more than twenty-five kilometers from their homes. The habit did not spread continuously in geographic order, but rather popped up independently in different locales. (Milk bottles were first introduced in the UK in 1880, so it took at least forty years for the first discovery by a blue tit to take place.) Sheldrake (1988) points out that detailed records show that the habit's spread accelerated as time went on, and that it was discovered independently by at least eighty-nine different blue tits over the decades in question. Moreover, the habit spread to the Netherlands, to Denmark, and to Sweden. In the case of the Netherlands, where milk bottles practically disappeared during World War II, the habit quickly reappeared following the end of the war, even though the German occupation of the Netherlands (and the suspension of milk deliveries) had lasted much longer than the average life span of a blue tit.

The hypothesis of morphic resonance could explain why the habit of opening milk bottles seemed to accelerate in its diffusion as time went on. As more and more birds adopted the habit of opening milk bottles, morphic resonance made it easier and easier for the new habit to be acquired, making new, independent discoveries more and more frequent.

The phenomenon of morphic fields may even extend beyond memory to encompass other aspects of what we normally conceive of as mind. Consider, for example, the complex collective behavior of termites that enables them to construct immense structures built of pellets of soil and saliva. Termite nests are extremely complex: for instance, the nests of the African fungus-growing termites can reach three meters in height and house two million inhabitants. The nests are ingeniously designed to radiate heat and maintain adequate ventilation. As E. O. Wilson observes:

> It is all but impossible to conceive how one colony member can oversee more than a minute fraction of the work or envision in its entirety the plan of such a finished product. Some of these nests require many worker lifetimes to complete, and each new addition must somehow be brought into a proper relationship with the previous parts. The existence of such nests leads inevitably to the conclusion that the workers interact in a very orderly and predictable manner. But how can the workers communicate so effectively over such long periods of time? Also, who has the blueprint of the nest? (Edward Osborne Wilson 1971, 228, quoted in Sheldrake 1988, 228-29)

Other naturalists have observed how termites on opposite sides of large breaches are able to coordinate their activities to perfectly match up the two halves of the structure, even though no physical communication was possible (for example, owing to the insertion of a large steel plate between the two halves).

While no satisfactory mechanistic explanation has been provided for these phenomena, the hypothesis of morphic fields and morphic resonance could provide a way of understanding what is happening. Sheldrake suggests that the structure of termite nests is organized via social morphic fields that reside in the colony of termites as a whole. In one sense, this is similar to a kind of collective mind shared by the entire colony of insects. A similar phenomenon may be at work in large schools of fish that are able to coordinate their movements with amazing rapidity—as little as a fiftieth of a second. Indeed, experiments on fish show that even those who have been blinded using special contact lenses are able to move as a coordinated unit. Once again, a social morphic field—a kind of collective mind—may be able to account for what is happening in ways that mechanistic explanations cannot.

BEYOND GENETIC DETERMINISM

The theory of morphic resonance—or of formative causation—provides an intriguing new way of conceiving of memory, and indeed of mind itself. As we have seen in our discussion of systems theory, however, our concept of mind must be broadened to include all kinds of life, not just organisms with nervous systems. Indeed, memory and mind are inherent in all living systems—and perhaps even more broadly, in all natural systems.

One specific area in which this broader conception of memory and mind comes into play is that of the process of inheritance in living organisms. Current scientific orthodoxy ascribes to genes the powerful role of guiding the development of an organism's form—its morphogenesis—as well as the mechanism for inheritance itself. While the theory of morphic resonance does not ignore the important role of genes, it ascribes to them a much more modest function. In this section, we will explore the limitations of current genetic theory and examine how morphic fields and morphic resonance might provide an alternative— and perhaps more satisfactory—explanation for the processes of inheritance and biological development.

At first, it might seem strange to challenge current genetic theory. Certainly, genetics has had important successes and provides a valuable theory that explains a range of biological processes. Indeed, many would argue that we are now living at the dawn of a "genetic era" characterized by powerful techniques such as genetic engineering, which might well reshape our planet in important respects.

Yet it can also be argued that genetics—or molecular biology—has become one of the most atomistic and reductionalist disciplines in modern science. Indeed, Theodore Roszak maintains that genes now serve a role in biology analogous to atoms in the physics of the late nineteenth century and are, in many respects, little more than a mental projection of biologists on reality. Some molecular biologists go so far, for example, as to project the trait of selfishness onto genes.[5]

This, perhaps, should not be totally surprising if we consider the origins of the modern genetic enterprise. In *Cloning the Buddha*, Richard Heinberg (1999) observes that two streams came together at the initiation of the discipline of molecular biology. One, funded by a number of wealthy families in the United States, was based on the eugenic philosophy that sought to prove that everything was genetically determined. One implication of this perspective is that social improvements do not come about through political or economic changes—nor through shifts in paradigms—but rather through an improvement in the "genetic stock" of humanity. If one is poor, commits a crime, or suffers from alcoholism or from a psychological disorder, genes, not social conditions, are to blame. Science, not social transformation, holds the key to solving problems. Obviously, such a philosophy can be comforting to the ruling elite (who, of course, must be members of the elite because of their genetic superiority!).

The second stream of influence comes, perhaps not surprisingly, from Newtonian physics. Two applied mathematicians, Max Mason (1877-1961) and Warren Weaver (1894-1978), worked with the Rockefeller Foundation to reconstruct biology along mechanistic, reductionalist lines. According to Philip Regal, a professor of ecology, evolution, and behavior at the University of Minnesota, Mason and Weaver

> . . . were even more strongly committed to the deterministic, reductionalistic ideology than the biologists were. The biologists were flirting with it, but Mason and Weaver were totally swept up in it. That has to do with the rea-

---

5. See, for example, Richard Dawkins, *The Selfish Gene* (Oxford: Oxford University Press, 1989).

son they left physics—which was because they were disgusted with quantum physics. The whole idea of uncertainty was totally against their grain. They had this old Newtonian idea of the billiard-ball universe: once we understand mechanics, then we can build upon that and everything will reduce to mechanics. (Quoted in Heinberg 1999, 36)

Regal goes on to note that biologists at first resisted the reductionalist methods introduced by Mason and Weaver (and also by the many chemists and physicists who entered the field of molecular biology in subsequent years). The mechanists, however, had an "inside track" on both private and government funding, which eventually pushed biology toward the mechanistic paradigm.

Given the origins of molecular biology, we should, perhaps, be suspicious of its apparent successes. Indeed, Mason and Weaver and those who thought like them assumed that, with time, quantum theory would be proven to be deeply flawed—something that has not happened to date. If we accept that physics is not, in fact, mechanistic in nature, it would be very strange to find that biology, whose physical and chemical processes involve quantum phenomena at some level, could be mechanistic and reductionalist. If anything, given the increased complexity (and nonlinearity) of the systems involved, one would expect biology to be the least mechanistic and deterministic scientific discipline of all.

Paul Weiss (1898-1989), one of the first biologists to propose the idea of morphogenetic fields (essentially morphic fields guiding the development of living organisms), asserted that it was ridiculous to attribute mindlike attributes to genes. He accused molecular biologists of

> . . . glossing over the difficulty of the problem of bestowing on the gene the faculty of spontaneity, the power of "dictating," "informing," "regulating," "controlling," etc. the ordering process in its unorganized milieu, so as to mould the latter into the co-ordinated teamwork that is to culminate in an accomplished organism. But they never explain just how this is done. (Quoted in Goldsmith 1998, 272)

In actual fact, the proven role of genes is much more modest: genes (specific sections of the DNA molecule) code for the structure of an organism's proteins, including its enzymes, serving in a sense as a kind of protein template via the intermediary action of the RNA molecule. Even this process is, in fact, not as straightforward and linear as was first assumed, as we will see in our subsequent discussions. In any case, though, this is quite a different role from "dictating, informing, regulating, and controlling" an organism.

Indeed, if genes alone determined the structure and behavior of the organism, then cells with an identical genetic makeup should, in fact, be identical. Yet this is not the case. The liver cells, the blood cells, and the bone cells in your body all share the same genes, but they have distinct structures and functions. All your organs have the same genetic makeup, but they are very different from each other. As Sheldrake points out, to assume that "given the right genes and hence the right proteins, and the right systems by which protein synthesis is controlled, the organism is somehow supposed to assemble itself automatically" is "rather like delivering the right materials to a building site at the right times, and expecting a house to grow spontaneously" (1990, 86).

The mechanistic theory of genes that forms the foundation of molecular biology—particularly genetic engineering—rests largely upon what is often referred to as the "central dogma" of genetics first proposed by Francis Crick (1916-2004), one of the scientists who discovered the DNA double helix structure. At its simplest, the central dogma asserts that a specific gene (essentially a portion of a DNA molecule), through the intermediary agency of an RNA molecule, codes for a specific protein, which ultimately manifests as a trait in the organism. Because of this, there should be a one-to-one correspondence between the number of genes an organism has and its number of proteins. The progression from genes to proteins is always linear in nature—that is, DNA determines the structure of the protein in a unidirectional manner.

$$DNA \rightarrow RNA \rightarrow Protein \rightarrow Trait$$

While most molecular biologists might agree that this version of the dogma is now somewhat simplistic, the basic idea that genes—specific portions of the DNA molecule—ultimately determine traits in a fairly linear, straightforward manner does, in fact, form the foundation of modern "genetic engineering," which attempts to add or delete specific traits to an organism by inserting genes using what is called "recombinant DNA" technology.

Indeed, while the "central dogma" is attractive in its simplicity, it is at best a "special case" scenario that does not apply universally. Based on the number of proteins in the human body, for example, geneticists expected there to be roughly one hundred thousand protein-coding genes in the human genome. In actual fact, the number of such genes now seems likely to be in the neighborhood of twenty to twenty-five thousand (roughly similar to the nineteen thousand found in roundworms). Obviously, then, there is not a one-to-one correspondence between genes and proteins.

It is also now understood that the way that genes code for proteins is often much, much more complex than was originally thought. One process that contributes to this complexity is that of "alternative splicing," which allows one gene to code for a multiplicity of proteins. For example, a single gene encoding for a protein found in the inner ear of chickens can give rise to 576 different proteins, while a single gene found in the fruit fly can code for over thirty-eight thousand variations of protein molecules (Commoner 2002). As Barry Commoner explains:

> Alternative splicing thus has a devastating impact on Crick's theory: it breaks open the hypothesized isolation of the molecular system that transfers genetic information from a single gene to a single protein. By rearranging the single gene's nucleotide sequence into a multiplicity of new messenger

RNA sequences, each of them different from the unspliced original, alternative splicing can be said to generate new genetic information. (2002, 42)

The process of alternative splicing contradicts the central dogma in yet another way insofar as it involves "spliceosome" proteins that influence the way that genetic information is conveyed: "This conclusion conflicts with Crick's second hypothesis—that proteins cannot transmit genetic information to nucleic acid (in this case, messenger RNA)—and shatters the elegant logic of Crick's interlocking duo of genetic hypotheses" (2002, 42) that genes code for proteins in a one-to-one correspondence and that information always moves from gene to protein in a unidirectional manner. According to Commoner, Crick himself had asserted that, "'the discovery of just one type of present-day cell' in which genetic information passed from protein to nucleic acid or from protein to protein 'would shake the whole intellectual basis of molecular biology'" (2002, 41).

Indeed, genes alone are not even responsible for the fidelity of their own replication: specialized proteins intervene to prevent most errors. So, while genes do play a key role in determining the shape of proteins, proteins also play a role in determining how genetic information is replicated and conveyed suggesting a kind of reciprocal (rather than linear) causality. Indeed, the successful replication of DNA depends holistically on the entire cellular environment (or "epigenetic network").

The assumption that a specific gene taken from one organism will work the same way in another is also false in many circumstances. For example, many genes associated with cancer in mice are not associated with cancer in humans (Capra 2002). In fact, the same gene can play completely different roles in different species. The functioning of the genes, then, seems to depend upon the wider genetic (and perhaps, cellular) context in which they are found. The role of isolated genes as the exclusive transmitters of inheritance, then, has been significantly exaggerated.

Indeed, we might go so far as to challenge the whole notion of "genes" altogether. The idea of a specific section of a DNA molecule coding for a specific protein—and even more so, determining one trait—simply does not hold true in many cases. Not only can one gene code for more than one protein (contributing to the rise of multiple traits), but at times a single trait seems to be determined by multiple genes, sometimes found on completely different chromosomes (Capra 2002). Could it be that the whole idea of separating out and delineating specific sections of DNA and calling them "genes" does not really make sense? Certainly, genetic material seems to function much more holistically than had at first been theorized.

The whole question of so-called junk DNA—which could more appropriately be called "mystery DNA"—should be considered in this light. In the case of humans, roughly 97 percent of our genetic material seems to play no role in coding for proteins. What is the role of this DNA? Some biologists see it as artifact of genetic material no longer in use, but why, then, do we retain it? And why are so many genetic sequences redundant? Could this DNA have some function that we simply do not yet understand? Certainly, given that the same gene can have different roles in different organisms, it might not be unreasonable to postulate that this wider "genetic context" plays some role in the organism.

What seems very clear is that the role of genes—or perhaps stated more broadly, the role of DNA—is far more complex than was originally supposed in molecular biology. The idea of a one-to-one correspondence between genes and proteins (much less between genes and traits) seems at best simplistic—a rather special case from which we cannot generalize. It now appears that only about 2 percent of all human diseases are associated with single genes, for example. The idea that we can excise a gene from one species and insert it randomly into another and that it will function normally there—the premise of genetic engineering based on recombinant DNA technology—seems to be false in most cases. Indeed, only about 1 percent of all such genetic experiments are successful (Capra 2002) and normally these involve rather simple traits. Even then, given that DNA depends on complex cellular processes to ensure its faithful replication, we cannot assume that foreign DNA will continue to replicate faithfully in future generations. If in fact genes function holistically in the wider context of their "mystery DNA," questions are raised also about how a foreign gene might subtly distort the wider genome of an organism, perhaps causing effects that are not immediately apparent.

If the idea of genes determining specific proteins in a linear, unidirectional manner is problematic, the idea of a "genetic program" determining an organism's traits, form, and development seems even more difficult to accept. As we have noted, cells in an organism share a common genome, yet they develop and function differently. Even identical twins, who share the same genome, are only 90 percent concordant when ten major physical characteristics are compared (Hillman 1996). Sydney Brenner, an adjunct professor of biology at the Salk Institute, for example, notes:

> At the beginning it was said that the answer to the understanding of development was going to come from a knowledge of the molecular mechanisms of gene control. I doubt whether anyone believes that any more. The molecular mechanisms look boringly simple, and they don't tell us what we want to know. We have to try to discover the principles of organization. (Quoted in Sheldrake 1988, 94)

One way of explaining these principles of organization is, in fact, through morphic fields. Indeed, the whole concept of morphic fields had its origin in the study of embryonic development—or morphogenesis—where the idea of a "morphogenetic" field was proposed by scientists like Hans Spemann (1869-1941), Alexander Gurwitsch (1874-1954), and Paul Weiss to explain how cells with the same genetic inheritance differentiate and develop differently. They proposed that the morphogenetic field both organized the organism's development and guided the process of regeneration after an injury.

In Sheldrake's theory of morphic fields, genes still have a role to play, but that role is limited to the coding of proteins and does not extend to programming the form and development of the entire organism. (Indeed, given the complexity of the protein-coding process and the relationships of reciprocal causality involved, morphic fields could play a role in protein formation, as well.) This role for genes—while still quite important—is much more modest than that proposed by most molecular biologists.

From the perspective of morphic fields, it seems easier to understand how humans can share between 96 percent and 99 percent of their genomes with chimpanzees. Such a similarity does not mean that our *forms* are almost identical (although we obviously bear a very close kinship), but rather that our *proteins* (i.e., our chemical makeup) are almost identical. Indeed, 29 percent of our genes code for the same proteins, and even our proteins that differ generally vary only very slightly from their counterparts in chimpanzees.

One possible additional role for genes that Sheldrake suggests is that they might in some way "tune in" to the morphic field in a way analogous to that of a radio or television tuner. This could also indicate a possible role for the mystery DNA that accounts for such a large proportion of the genomes of living organisms. In any case, from a morphic-resonance perspective genes alone do not determine form and development, but rather interact with the nested holarchy of morphic fields that contain the formative information. This interactive process could very well involve quantum phenomena. For example, David Peat notes:

> The DNA molecule itself would be constantly informed about its wider surroundings, and in turn, certain of its "hidden information" could, for example, be made active. It is even possible that the whole cell could act in an intelligent way and cause modifications within its own DNA. In other words, a mutation of the organism would be the cooperative response to some overall change in the global context in which the cell lives, rather than a purely random and purposeless event. Evolution would become a cooperative process, the outcome of a constant dialogue between other life forms and their entire environment. (1991, 108)

In the morphic-fields perspective, then, genes still have a role, but genes are no longer seen as mechanistic agents containing a program for the formation and development of the organism. Indeed, Sheldrake maintains that genes—just like brains—have been overrated. Certainly both brains and genes are important, but they serve the role of interfaces between the organism and morphic fields. The phenomenon of morphic resonance, manifest in the dynamics of self-organization and memory, is primary—not mechanistic, materialistic agents likes genes and brains.

FROM ETERNAL LAWS TO EVOLVING HABITS

As we have seen in our discussion of both the nature of mind and the limitations of genetic determinism, the perspective of morphic resonance challenges mechanistic explanations of memory, mind, inheritance, and biological development. Another key feature of morphic fields, as we have previously noted, is their dynamic, evolutionary nature. Morphic fields change over time. New information is added, collective memory grows, and new fields emerge.

Indeed, according to the theory of morphic resonance, the cosmos is innately evolutionary in nature. This perspective challenges the dualistic vision that we inherited from the nineteenth century that envisioned life on Earth as an evolutionary process but continued to see the rest of the universe as essentially static, governed by eternal laws. Since that time, physicists have gradually come to see that the structure of the cosmos itself evolves; yet the idea of eternal, mathematical laws persists, virtually unchallenged.

Yet, the belief in eternal laws is precisely that—a belief—and one that has never really been subject to serious scrutiny. Given its origin in the science of the Newtonian revolution, there are reasons to question whether this belief corresponds, in fact, to reality. In many ways, it seems to flow out of the theological concept of God as a kind of "unmoved mover" and eternal lawgiver. What if, indeed, eternal laws did not really exist? What if they are simply a philosophical projection imposed on the world so that we can make sense of it—and perhaps, control it?

If we accept modern cosmological theory, which maintains that the universe was birthed into being in a sudden unfurling of space and time in what is commonly called the Big Bang, then the void that preceded the genesis of the cosmos was bereft of matter, energy, space, and time. Perhaps indeed mind—in the form that many of us conceive of as God—existed in that "pregnant void" (or implicate order) filled with possibility. But need that mean that the laws of physics were laid out beforehand, never to change? Does that not seem to be at odds with the evolutionary nature that appears to be woven into the very fabric of the cosmos? As Sheldrake notes:

> This assumption that the laws of nature are eternal is the last great surviving legacy of the old cosmology. We are rarely even conscious of making it. But when we do bring this assumption into awareness, we can see that it is only one of several possibilities. Perhaps all the laws of nature came into being at the very moment of the Big Bang. Or perhaps they arose in stages, and then, having arisen, persisted changelessly thereafter. For example, the laws governing the crystallization of sugar may have come into being when sugar molecules first crystallized somewhere in the universe; they may have been universal and changeless ever since. Or perhaps the laws of nature have actually evolved along with nature itself, and perhaps they are still evolving. Or perhaps they are not laws at all, but more like habits. Maybe the very idea of "laws" is inappropriate. (1988, 11)

If we envision the cosmos as a kind of living system, as something that more closely resembles an organism than a machine, then the idea of a cosmos with memory and habits contained in evolving morphic fields should seem at least as plausible as eternal, unchanging laws. Certainly, of the possibilities that Sheldrake outlines, the idea of evolving laws or habits would seem to be the most consistent with an evolutionary outlook.

Indeed, the whole concept of physical laws—on closer examination—seems in many respects to be far more mysterious than that of morphic fields. We know that fields of many types do exist, and indeed in a quantum worldview fields seem to be more fundamental than either matter or energy. Laws, on the other hand, are much more ineffable. Why should we believe that laws of physics should exist at all?

In the context of the seventeenth century, of course, the metaphor of a law seems quite understandable. If God is envisioned as an eternal, unchanging law-giver, then eternal laws must govern the cosmos. On a more ideological level, the concept of eternal, unchanging laws is also convenient for those in power, or those who find comfort and security in a universe that must be molded to resemble a well-ordered English garden.

From the point of view of the twenty-first century and of modern physics, however, such a view is far less "natural" than we might at first think. Even in the realm of theology, the idea of God as an unchanging, eternal lawgiver is restricted to the more conservative elements of different religious traditions. The God of the mystics, the God who continually creates and renews, the God who is compassion, the God who hears the cries of the poor and who responds, the God who is libera-tor stands in contrast to the God who dictates rigid, eternal laws.

Returning to the realm of physics, there certainly do seem to be observable regularities in nature. The cosmos has recognizable form and order of which minds can make sense, at least to some degree. But as Sheldrake observes, "There is no basis for assuming that these regularities are eternal. The regu-larities within an evolving universe evolve: this is what evolution means" (1988, 13). Instead of laws, the cosmos may very well have habits—some of them very deeply ingrained, but all open to evolution over time.

The idea of evolving habits rather than eternal laws is not altogether new. One suspects that for traditional peoples who view the cosmos as a living organ-ism, such an idea would come naturally, even if it were not made explicit. At the beginning of the twentieth century, some philosophers like Charles Peirce (1839-1914) and Friedrich Nietzsche (1844-1900) began to propose the idea of evolving habits as a natural extension of evolutionary theory. For Peirce, the cosmos as a whole should be considered a living entity with mind and, as he noted, "the law of habit is the law of mind." Matter, too, is pervaded by mind, although in mat-ter mind has become "deadened by the development of habit to the point where the breaking up of these habits is very difficult" (quoted in Sheldrake 1988, 14). Nietzsche believed that the "laws" of nature had evolved and had even under-gone some form of natural selection.

Indeed, many philosophers toward the end of the nineteenth and the begin-ning of the twentieth century speculated on the evolution of cosmic habits or laws. According to Sheldrake (1988), these ideas gradually became less fashion-able as physicists, including Einstein[6], insisted that the universe itself was eternal

---

6. As we have noted earlier (see p. 156 above), Einstein actually "cooked" his fields equations,

in nature, governed by unchangeable laws. Yet, since that time, physicists themselves have changed their views—at least in terms of the evolution and development of the large-scale structure of the cosmos. No longer does it seem that life on Earth is an exception in an otherwise static universe. Instead, eternal laws now seem to be the exception. Yet, if the basic character of the cosmic process seems to be evolutionary, the idea of evolving habits of nature (even if we prefer to call them "evolving laws" to make the term more palatable to our ingrained mind-set) seems more logical and coherent with a cosmovision that has emerged over the past decades.

It is interesting to note that a world governed by eternal laws at some fundamental level of its existence is a world that is essentially conservative and static in nature. A cosmology based on eternal laws—at a subtle, perhaps even unconscious level—perpetuates certain assumptions about the limits of authentic transformation. We come to believe that what will be will always, at best, be a rearrangement of what has come before. True novelty seems impossible: fundamental changes to the world order simply cannot come about.

Obviously, an evolutionary worldview already challenges some of these conservative assumptions—but not totally, as long as eternal laws lie at the foundation of all. In contrast, the idea of habits is much more hopeful. True, habits can be difficult to change, especially if they have become ingrained, but the possibility of change always exists. What is more, a group of persons working together can always model different behaviors and create new habits. True novelty is always a possibility—what shall be is not predetermined by what has come before.

In the case of phenomena normally associated with physics, it is difficult to actually prove that ingrained habits are at work, rather than eternal laws, since ingrained habits, by their nature, appear to be nearly changeless—particularly over the tiny fragment of time that corresponds to the development of modern science. Despite this, there are some intriguing examples that lend support to the idea of a cosmos ordered by morphic fields containing habits rather than changeless laws.

There is some evidence, for example, that several of the fundamental constants in physics fluctuate over time—albeit only very slightly. For instance, the gravitational constant (normally designated by the letter G) is normally calculated to be $(6.674 \pm 0.003) \times 10^{-11}\,\mathrm{m^3\,kg^{-1}\,s^2}$. Yet, in 1986, researchers in Australia determined G to be 6.734 ± 0.002, and other measurements in the United States, Germany, New Zealand, and Russia have also demonstrated significant variations. The possibility exists, of course, that these can be traced to some limitation in the experimental apparatuses employed, yet most measurements of G use the same basic kind of apparatus (Sheldrake 1995).

inserting a "cosmological constant" to ensure a static solution—something that later in his life he saw as one of his greatest blunders. More recently, the cosmological constant has been revived, but with a small *positive* value—not to provide a static solution—but rather one corresponding to an expansion that is actually *accelerating* due to the presence of "dark energy."

Similarly, there are some indications that the speed of light (c) itself could fluctuate over time. In particular, it appears that the speed of light during the period 1928 to 1945 may have dropped by about 20km/s before returning to its current value (Sheldrake 1995). This result is particularly interesting because different scientists using different methods obtained similar results within that given time period. Once again, this cannot be taken as definitive proof that constants are, in fact, changing—but certainly this type of small variation would be consistent with an ingrained habit rather than an eternal law.

In the field of chemistry, the evidence for evolving habits in nature appears stronger—perhaps in part because new chemical compounds and structures continue to be developed, and thus not all the habits involved have had enough time to become ingrained. Sheldrake (1988) notes that newly synthesized compounds are often exceedingly difficult to crystallize, taking many weeks to form in a supersaturated solution. As time goes by, however, it becomes progressively easier to crystallize the compound anywhere in the world. It would seem that, once the habit of crystallization is established, it becomes easier to synthesize the crystal in question.

Moving closer to the field of biology, the phenomenon of protein folding also seems to be consistent with morphic fields and habitual activity. Once a protein is denatured (i.e., unfolded into a flexible chain of polypeptides, losing its original shape), it quickly enfolds itself into its previous configuration once again. Yet the way the polypeptide chains can unfold themselves is virtually limitless. For example, a protein consisting of a hundred or so amino acids has approximately 10^{100} (one followed by a hundred zeroes—or "googol") possible configurations. If the protein needed randomly to try each of these configurations until it found the correct one, it would take an interval of time much longer than the entire history of the cosmos to find its proper shape. Yet, in fact, the process takes a matter of seconds. It would seem that the protein somehow "remembers" the proper configuration amid all the countless possibilities. How this is accomplished is not at all clear. No one has yet found the information needed encoded in the protein itself. On the other hand, the theory of morphic resonance does provide a possible explanation for the retention of a collective memory of proteins, essentially a long-formed habit. As Sheldrake notes:

Fields . . . canalize the folding process towards a characteristic end-point. . . . Out of the many possible ways of folding and the many possible final forms, the fields stabilize particular folding pathways and final forms. . . . The morphic fields are themselves stabilized by morphic resonance from innumerable past structures of the same kinds. The long evolutionary process has indeed stabilized those structures that have been useful and therefore favored by natural selection; and the vast numbers of these past molecules have a powerful stabilizing effect on the fields by morphic resonance. (1988, 126)

To further support the hypothesis of morphic resonance, Sheldrake notes that many proteins have similar structures even though their amino acid components vary greatly—what one might expect if the information for protein enfolding was contained in a morphic field rather than in the amino acids themselves. For example, hemoglobin molecules, found in most animals and in some plants, share a common structure, but only three of a total of 140 to 150 amino acids are consistently found in the hemoglobin molecules of different species.

Morphic resonance could also account for the similarities found in ecosystems made up of very different species. For example, Tim Flannery observes that the savannah fauna of North America fifteen million years ago bear a striking resemblance to that found in Africa today:

> Some researchers have sought explanations in the idea of co-evolution. They say that each species on Earth is shaped by interactions with the other species in its environment and that on the savannah there are only limited choices available as the various species compete. Large browsers, they believe, have to be shaped like giraffes in order to reach food in the treetops, while grazers are best off being fast and migratory like horses, semi-aquatic like hippos or enormous and well-armored like white rhinos. Other researchers dispute this argument, explaining that any similarities may be due to coincidence. . . (2001, 113)

Even more striking an example can be found in the evolutionary history of Australia, where marsupials took on a wide variety of forms amazingly similar to those assumed by placental mammals elsewhere. For example, the marsupial flying phalanger looks very much like a placental flying squirrel, and the Tasmanian wolf is very much like a placental wolf. In a slightly different vein, the eye of an octopus is structurally quite similar to that of humans, although it evolved separately.

This kind of "convergent evolution" is easy to explain if one sees memory as being held in morphic fields, leading to forms that tend to repeat themselves—even in different contexts—once they have become established. It also explains why evolution may occur in "jumps" (a rapid explosion of new species followed by long periods of relative stability). Once new habits, forms, and traits become established, they quickly become more widespread, but the first emergence of a new trait may take much, much longer because its morphic field has not yet emerged.

CREATIVITY AND CHANGE

While the idea of habits in nature is more dynamic and evolutionary than that of eternal laws, it still implies a certain conservative element that might seem to limit the possibilities of transformative praxis. Physical phenomena do follow recognizable patterns, and organisms do behave and develop along established lines. This does not mean, however, that novelty does not emerge from time to time. The whole evolutionary nature of life on Earth—and the whole drama of cosmic evolution—makes clear that an innate creativity is at work.

From the perspective of morphic resonance, two orders of creativity are evident. The first—and the weaker of the two—is at work within the context of existing morphic fields. In this case, there is a degree of adaptability, flexibility, and even resourcefulness that contributes to the evolution of the morphic field, but the attractors (or pattern of behavior) characteristic of the field remains essentially the same. This phenomenon is evident in the example of the blue tits acquiring a new habit (opening milk bottles) that enables them better to adapt to their surroundings.

At the same time, a higher order of creativity also exists that is evidenced by the emergence of completely new fields with a whole new set of attractors. The synthesis of a totally new chemical compound is an example of this phenomenon. A "jump" in the evolutionary process, or the emergence of a new kind of social organization in human society, also evidences this higher order of creativity.

What is clear from the perspective of morphic resonance is that changes to form affect the morphic field and changes to the morphic field in turn affect form. Both field and form co-evolve over time in a reciprocal fashion. Sheldrake (1988) summarizes four key characteristics to this evolutionary process from a morphic perspective:

1. The appearance of new forms—or new patterns of organization (or even new paradigms)—is always associated with the emergence of a new morphic field.

2. Not all morphic fields that emerge will continue into the future: morphic fields are subject to a process of natural selection. Those that are not viable will disappear, while those that are successful will stabilize over time.

3. Inheritance in living organisms takes place primarily through the inheritance of morphic fields via morphic resonance, not through the selective modification of genes.

4. Morphic fields differentiate and specialize over time, some becoming more probable and stable than others.

As a concrete example of this evolutionary process at work, Sheldrake cites the phenomenon of punctuated evolution, where evolution appears to take a sudden jump and then stabilizes over time:

Many palaeontologists have deduced from the fossil record that when new evolutionary lines begin—when new basic body-plans appear—there is often an "intense radiation of types, an 'explosive phase' in the early part of their phylogeny, and that only a limited number of the branches continue to develop, and with decreasing speed" (Rensch 1959). One example is the adaptive radiation of the mammals after the sudden extinction of the dinosaurs over 60 million years ago. Most of the orders of mammals came into existence within about 12 million years: carnivores, whales, dolphins, rodents, marsupials, anteaters, horses, camels, elephants, bats, and many others.

Indeed most of the basic mammalian forms that appeared then still exist. (1988, 284-85)

From the perspective of morphic fields, the phenomenon of punctuated evolution is easily understood. Morphic fields are normally quite stable, but when a breakthrough to a truly novel form is made (i.e., when a bifurcation point is reached), the new morphic field that accompanies it opens the way for a whole new series of patterns or "variations on the theme" to come about through the phenomenon of morphic resonance. Over time, through the process of natural selection, some of the new morphic fields are eliminated, while others stabilize, becoming increasingly habitual over time.

This does not, of course, negate that a process of natural selections also occurs on a genetic level. Those organisms whose forms are best adapted to their habitats will be more successful, and their genes will, of course, propagate more quickly and become more common over time, while the genes of those who are less successful will correspondingly decrease. Genetic selection, then, will occur; but from the perspective of morphic resonance, the key process at work in evolution is the natural selection and stabilization of morphic fields and their corresponding forms or patterns of organization. Sheldrake notes that, while this way of understanding evolution concords well with Darwin in the sense that it recognizes the power of habit, it also differs insofar as it allows for both sudden and gradual changes over time. In contrast, Darwin's theory explains gradual changes quite well, but it cannot explain the sudden "jumps" that characterize the "explosive phase" of evolution.

The morphic perspective seems to gain further support when we consider that "punctuated evolution" takes place not only in organisms but also in other phenomena. As Sheldrake notes, "Comparable explosive phases may have occurred in the evolution of patterns of instinctive behavior, as well as in the evolution of human languages and social, political, and cultural forms. A similar process occurs in the evolution of religions, arts, and sciences as distinct sects, schools, and traditions arise within them" (1988, 320).

Why does this occur? At first, when a new theme or form comes about, there is a wide experimentation with variations—but there are also a limited number of truly novel variants that can be tried out. Over time, some of these prove themselves to be better than others. Many variations are discarded or die out as a few, more successful ones, gain dominance. These versions then become increasingly habitual over time.

Morphic fields, then, seem to exhibit a kind of *yin* and *yang* tension between habit and creativity. On the one hand, the patterns or attractors of the field are conservative in nature. Yet, even within habitual behavior, as we have seen in our discussion of systems theory, a certain amount of flexibility and adaptability is essential. This corresponds to the behavior of a system around an attractor. It is never predictable, but it is constrained by certain limits created by the attractor.

Yet, occasionally, a "jump" is made and a totally new attractor comes into being—a totally new field is born. What causes this to happen? Once again, drawing on our examination of systems theory, we can see that a stress can push a system beyond the limits of the old attractor, field, or paradigm. In some cases, this stress can result in the outright elimination of the old morphic field and its accompanying forms, but in other cases, a totally new field comes into being, organized around a new attractor or pattern.

From the perspective of the theory of morphic resonance, the creativity embodied by these kinds of jumps is seen as an inherent property of morphic fields. It is not, however, as though the new fields were somehow always present from eternity, in the sense of Platonic forms, waiting for a form to embody them. Rather, the fields are themselves dynamic and evolving. Nothing is predetermined in this view; authentic creativity is inherent in the very nature of the cosmos. That does not mean that there may not be an ultimate goal or purpose in the cosmic story, but the path to such a goal is certainly not predetermined. It is possible, too, that the goals themselves may evolve over time.

MORPHIC RESONANCE AND TRANSFORMATIVE PRAXIS

The morphic perspective has important implications for transformative praxis. On the one hand, the conservative nature of morphic fields underlines the difficulty of overcoming long-ingrained habits. Yet we see also that authentic creativity and qualitative "jumps" to new forms, paradigms, and practices is always a possibility, particularly in times when the old forms are under stress, no longer able to cope with reality in a time of crisis.

A cosmos where morphic fields are in play—like the cosmos of systems theory—is one where neither the rigid determinism of linear causality nor blind chance holds sway, but rather one where creative emergence is always a possibility. Form affects field, and field affects form in a reciprocal fashion. Causality, then, is understood to be both complex and creative. Not even the laws of physics themselves are truly static and unchangeable—all habits are open to modification. Authentic transformation is always a possibility; truly liberating change can come about.

As we have seen, morphic fields enable us to understand the phenomenon of punctuated evolution in a new way. If this phenomenon is governed by the emergence of new morphic fields, the same kind of "creative jumps" can (and do) occur in other arenas. Sheldrake himself has observed that the conservative nature of paradigms is a good example of the habitual nature of morphic fields, but that the creative, evolving nature of morphic fields also makes clear that a jump to new paradigms is always possible. Indeed, such a jump can be both sudden and radically creative in nature. Referring to scientific paradigms, Sheldrake observes:

> The appearance of new morphic fields, new paradigms, cannot be explained entirely in terms of what has gone before. New fields start off as insights, intuitive leaps, guesses, hypotheses, or conjectures. They are like mental mutations. New associations or patterns of connection come into being sud-

denly by a kind of "gestalt switch." Scientists often speak of "scales fall-ing from their eyes" or of a "lightning flash" that "illuminates" a previously obscure problem, enabling its components to be seen in a new way that for the first time enables it to be solved. (1988, 268)

On a more spiritual level, what Zen Buddhists describe as *satori* ("enlighten-ment") seems to correspond to this same kind of creative jump. After years of meditation and intense spiritual practice, a person can suddenly break through to a totally new way of perceiving reality and of living in the world. What is inter-esting about this example is that Zen practices are actually designed to incubate a kind of internal crisis—often using paradoxical questions called *koan*—that essentially force one to move beyond one's habitual way of perceiving the world. From the morphic perspective, it is as though one's personal morphic field sud-denly jumps to a new state.

Is such a creative jump possible at a social level? Could humanity—with surprising suddenness and radicality—shift to new habits, perhaps even on a planetary level? What might it take to provoke such a shift? There are no simple answers to these questions, but certainly the morphic perspective would imply that we could indeed make a radical shift more quickly than we might at first expect.

In this light, the phenomenon of morphic resonance seems particularly prom-ising. As we have seen, morphic resonance implies that new learnings and new habits can spread through a community much more quickly—and perhaps more mysteriously—than we might ever have imagined. Are there ways of amplifying this phenomenon? How could those working toward a more just and sustainable future use morphic resonance to effect change?

Once again, there are no easy answers, but the idea of creating "communities of vision" might be one way of doing this. To the extent that we try to live in new ways that model the future we wish to create, we begin to create new hab-its and ways of being that—through morphic resonance—make it progressively easier for others to do likewise. It would seem likely that, as more and more people put into practice a new habit or way of living, the morphic field for this behavior would also become increasingly stronger.

The phenomenon of morphic resonance, then, underlines the importance of what some have called "anticipatory fidelity"—being faithful to what we wish to come about. A key part of this process may well be the very envisioning and imagining of a different way of living; but the perspective of morphic fields would lead us to posit that the visioning must ultimately begin to change our habitual way of being—it must be put into practice—in order to truly affect others more widely.

The theory of morphic resonance may also help us to deepen our reflections on the nature of relational power. Is power-with strengthened not only by our relationships with others, but by our interaction with a collective morphic field? Do our relationships, insofar as they create a kind of community, develop a morphic field that, through resonance, amplifies its strength? If so, the strength of such relational power might well depend not only on the number of relationships involved but perhaps more importantly on the quality of the relationships that bind the community together.

A final series of questions worthy of further reflection concerns the Tao itself. What relationship does "the Way"—the Dharma, the Malkuta—have to morphic fields and morphic resonance? If morphic fields are envisioned as a holarchy of nested fields, what is the relationship of the Tao to this holarchy—what role does it play in shaping these fields? Perhaps we could envision the Tao as a kind of universal attractor that characterizes—or as even as an overarching morphic field that subtly draws—cosmic evolution in a general direction without predetermining the precise evolutionary paths taken—a "formless form that includes all forms," which is followed but "which has no end" (*Tao Te Ching* §14). If so, the Tao might also be seen as the embodiment of the creative principle at work—or better yet, at play—in the cosmos.

10.

The Cosmos as Revelation

In the beginning,
was the Mother of the cosmos.
By knowing the Mother,
one also knows her offspring.
By knowing her offspring,
one stays close to the Mother,
and becomes free from fear and sorrow . . .

(Tao Te Ching § 52)

The great Tao flows everywhere.
It reaches out in all directions,
pervading all things.

All beings depend on it,
and it does not reject any of them.

It fulfills its purpose,
yet it asks for no recognition.
It nourishes every being in the cosmos,
yet it does not attempt to chart their courses.

It is free of desire and seems insignificant,
yet it is the home to which all beings return.
Even so, it claims no lordship for itself,
It strives not for greatness,
yet accomplishes great things.

(Tao Te Ching § 34)

When we reverence Earth for its own sake, we create the possibility of prophetic cultural action. We have experienced what happened when cul-

ture fails to understand the reality of Earth's story: It becomes cut off from people and planet. This cultural death is where we are now, facing the ruin and devastation of the planet. This watershed moment of cultural collapse awakens us to the opportunity for understanding and new health.

There is a new story being told. This story is about a living universe. We have failed to understand that the universe is alive. The best way to get in touch with the immense notion of a living universe is through story. In this way we come to see that the universe story is, in fact, our story too. (Conlon 1994, 3)

This story, as told in its galactic expansion, its Earth formation, its life emergence, and its self-reflexive consciousness, fulfils in our times the role of the mythic accounts of the universe that existed in earlier times, when human awareness was dominated by a spatial mode of consciousness. We have moved from cosmos to cosmogenesis, from the mandala journey toward the center of an abiding world to the irreversible journey of the universe itself, as the primary sacred journey. This journey of the universe is the journey of each individual being in the universe. (T. Berry 1999, 163-64)

The integral nature of the universe is revealed in its actions. (T. Berry and Swimme 1992, 19)

One of the key revolutions in scientific understanding in the last fifty years or so has been the shift away from a static, eternal vision of the cosmos to one that is dynamic and evolving. Most scientists now agree that the universe burst into being roughly fourteen billion years ago and that it has been expanding and transforming itself since that time. We can conceive of the cosmos not so much as a thing but rather as a living entity in the process of becoming or as a process of unfolding evolution.

Indeed, the very idea of space-time as a single reality seems to reinforce this insight. A cosmos that has a beginning, a cosmos that changes over time, is a cosmos that is also a story. And the story of the universe being revealed to us by science is, perhaps, the most awe-inspiring, magnificent, and mysterious cosmic myth of all time—a myth not because it is in some way untrue, but rather because it is a story that enables us to understand our place in the universe. In this sense, the cosmos is not only our habitation, not only our story, but also an ongoing process of revelation that can guide and orient our lives. The cosmos is our teacher.

As David Peat has pointed out (see p. 196 above), humans are active participants in this story; we actively engage in this process of evolution and revelation. As participants in a living cosmos, we cannot understand our role to be that of simple spectators; nor can we content ourselves with exploiting the fruits of nature, as though we were some kind of parasite or, worse yet, a cancer. No, we are called to be much more than that. As integral participants of the cosmos, our consciousness, creativity, and insights are also a part of a greater cosmic process of self-reflection and discovery. We are called, then, to strive to understand the cosmos, to find our place in it, and to participate in its creative process.

By engaging in this enterprise of mythic proportions, we return in truth to the ancient cosmological endeavor that has been a part of all of human history—save, perhaps, for the anomalous Western scientific culture of the past five hundred years or so. In so doing, perhaps we begin to heal the split between ourselves and the rest of the cosmic community—the cultural autism that has imprisoned us in a world of our own making and blinded us to the reality of our current, destructive path. We can begin to hear, once again, the voices of nature, equally present in the blazing fury of a supernova and in the caressing touch of a springtime breeze.

To truly open ourselves to these voices, we need to make cosmology come alive; we need to experience the story in our hearts, in our blood, in our very bones. Reflecting on the story in our minds is insufficient—we need to *live* the story to truly understand that it is part of us and that we are part of it. Indeed, we have no authentic meaning outside of the cosmic story. As Jim Conlon observes, "We humans are that dimension of this story whereby the universe emerges into awareness of itself. . . . I cannot know my culture apart from the unfolding of the universe. Through telling the Earth's story, I have come to realize that I am deeply interconnected in a common evolutionary adventure" (1994, 17).

We are fortunate, indeed, to live precisely at the time when we have developed, as Brian Swimme observes, the sensitivity to perceive, for the first time, the very echoes of the cosmos's birth. Perhaps this is not purely coincidental, but is rather a kind of serendipitous synchronicity; perhaps we needed this revelation at this time of human history to help set us again on the path toward health and wholeness, a path that will enable us to work harmoniously with the Tao as it leads us toward the unfolding of its ultimate purpose.

Not only have we now been able to sense the reverberations of the primordial flaring forth; we have also come to discern more clearly the series of unrepeatable steps that form the outline of the cosmic story. This story has a definite beginning and may too have a definite end—although that is not yet clear. In its stages, we can also perceive a kind of plot, a pattern, an attractor, or allurement giving shape to the cosmos as it moves toward the future. As the cosmos unfolds, it seems to be moving toward greater complexity, diversity, and relationality. Some, indeed, perceive a kind of purposefulness at work, a "Way" that seems to orchestrate the cosmic story. As Theodore Roszak notes:

As nature around us unfolds to reveal level upon level of structured complexity, we are coming to see that we inhabit a densely connected ecological universe where nothing is "nothing but" a simple, disconnected, or isolated thing. Nor is anything accidental. Life and mind, once regarded as such anomalous exceptions to the law of entropy, are rooted by their physiochemical structures, all the way back to the initial conditions that followed the Big Bang. (Roszak 1992, 8)

Over the course of this chapter, we will reflect on the nature and meaning of the cosmic story as it is now being revealed, particularly the story of our home planet and the community of life that makes up the biosphere. In so doing, we will try to discern the direction, the sense of purpose, the Way, or the Tao that seems to be woven into the very fabric of the cosmos. This is not a set of eternal laws but something more subtle, more dynamic, and more creative. What is this wisdom that the cosmos reveals to us? What does it teach us about our role, as humans, within the context of the larger story? Most important of all, perhaps: How can we open ourselves to the mystery of the Tao so that we may truly become creative, harmonious participants in the unfolding of this cosmic story?

COSMOGENESIS

It's really simple. Here's the whole story in one line. . . . You take hydrogen gas, and you leave it alone, and it turns into rosebushes, giraffes, and humans. (Swimme 2001, 40)

The Big Bang is like the primal orgasm, the generative moment. Or it is like the breaking open of the cosmic egg. The cosmos is like a growing organism, forming new structures within itself as it develops. Part of the intuitive appeal of the story is that it tells us that everything is related. Everything has come from a common source: all galaxies, stars and planets; all atoms, molecules and crystals; all microbes, plants and animals; all people on this planet. We ourselves are related more or less closely to everyone else, to all living organisms, and ultimately to everything that is or that ever has been. (Sheldrake 1990, 101)

In the beginning, there was nothing—there was no *thing*; nor was there time, space, or energy. What was there? The pregnant void, the ground of being, the generative thought, that which is beyond thought and things and even being: the Tao. We cannot say exactly what "it" was, for all naming, all conceptualizations, cannot capture it. It is the mystery behind all mysteries that births all into being.

Scientists do not know what was before the birth of the cosmos. Indeed, the very word "before" may have no meaning here. When the cosmos was birthed into being, time was born with it. Stephen Hawking, using mathematical terms, speaks of the cosmos as having open boundaries, in some sense with no clear beginning or end.[1] If this is true, one can get closer and closer to the initial moment of birth, but one can never reach the actual instant when the cosmos sprang forth from the pregnant void. Yet there is still a beginning from which all-that-is issued forth, an initial moment which Martha Heyneman refers to

---

1. Using quantum theory, one can postulate that space-time may form a closed surface without boundary, implying that it has no beginning and no end: "All the complicated structures we see in the universe might be explained by the no boundary condition for the universe together with the uncertainty principle of quantum mechanics" (Hawking 1998, 140).

as "the point or zero doorway between the timeless and time, the spaceless and space" which is "also here and now, everywhere and always" (1993, 92).

Our imaginations and our comprehension are also challenged when we try to picture the early moments of the cosmic birth, what is commonly called the Big Bang. This rather unfortunate expression conjures the image of looking from afar at a massive explosion bursting out into space, perhaps something akin to a supernova, but on a far larger scale.

Yet such an image is misleading. There was no "outside" from which to view the event; there was no "empty" space; all that was was caught up in the primal firestorm. The physicist Stephen Weinberg describes it as "an explosion that occurred simultaneously everywhere" (quoted in Heyneman 1993, 92). Not only energy but also space and time themselves were born in that initial generative moment. The heat and fury of that instant defy our comprehension. Certainly, this birthing was in some sense exceedingly violent—at least from our perspective as living organisms who could not possibly survive in such conditions—but it was a violence more akin to the pain and labor of birth than to a destructive cataclysm. As Thomas Berry and Brian Swimme note:

> In that primordial reality the greatest of the Himalayan mountains would dissolve more suddenly than would a child's sand castle hit by a tsunami wave. The Earth's solidity becomes smoke in the beginning. In that beginning time, the briefest human reverie, an unnoticed flicker of a mind on a summer's day, would be an interval of time in which the primeval fireball thundered through a thousand universe annihilations and as many universe rebirths.
>
> At the base of the serene tropical rainforest sits this cosmic hurricane. At the base of the seaweed's column of time is the trillion-degree blast that begins everything. All that exists in the universe traces back to this exotic, ungraspable seed event, a microcosmic grain, a reality layered with the power to fling a hundred billion galaxies through vast chasms in a flight that [has] lasted fifteen billion years. The nature of the universe today and of every being in existence is integrally related to the nature of this primordial Flaring Forth. The universe is a single multiform development in which each event is woven together with all others in the fabric of the space-time continuum. (1992, 21)

The power and mystery of the primal firestorm inspire such awe that it seems to require spiritual imagery to capture it. Indeed, the world's great religious traditions often invoke the memory of the beginning moments in their most sacred phrases. For example, in Islam the first word of the *Sura Fateha* (the opening chapter, or *sura*, of the Qur'an)—and indeed of each and every *sura*—evokes the image of the cosmic birth: *Bismillâh*, normally translated as "In the name of Allah," elicits the image of the SM (name, light, sound, vibration) that goes forth from Allah, who can be understood as the One, the "Cosmic Unity" that is the "ultimate force behind being and nothingness" (Douglas-Klotz 1995, 15). Similarly, the first line of Jesus' prayer in Aramaic evokes the image of the *shem* (once again, name, light, sound, or vibration) emanating (or breathed forth) from the One, the unity, who gives birth to all (Douglas-Klotz 1990, 13). Both the Qur'an and the Prayer of Jesus (what we normally name "The Lord's Prayer or "Our Father"), then, on one level recall the first generative moment of the cosmos as well as the essential unity binding all things and all beings together.

Indeed, every time we remember the moment of beginning, we affirm the fundamental unity of the cosmos. We all sprang from the same source. All things and all beings have a common origin. Yet this unity is not only a memory but rather a living reality. As we will recall from our discussion of Bell's Theorem (see p. 179 above), the phenomenon of "quantum entanglement" means that all the elementary particles in the universe remain in some way bound together through mysterious, instantaneous connections. A fundamental unity ties all together. As Berry and Swimme observe, "The fireball manifests itself as a quintillion separate particles and their interactions, but the nature of these particles speaks of the universe as indivisible whole. No part of the present can be isolated from any other part of the present or the past or the future" (1992, 29).

After bursting forth from the primeval generative seed, after a mere hundredth of a second or so, the cosmos cooled rapidly to a mere hundred billion degrees and consisted of an amorphous mix of energy and matter (in the form of hydrogen nuclei—i.e., free protons). After three minutes, the first helium nuclei began to organize themselves. Within thirty minutes, most of the primeval matter—hydrogen and helium nuclei—had been birthed into being and, at the same time, the universe became transparent for the first time (i.e., light could travel freely through it). It took another seven hundred thousand years of further expansion and cooling, however, to create the conditions for stable atoms consisting of nuclei and electrons. By the end of the first billion years, the seeds of the galaxies had been sown.

Over the next four billion years, the great galactic clouds formed, to be followed by the primeval stars. These stars are the crucible for the formation of more complex forms of matter, but it is only with the first supernovas that elements such as carbon and oxygen—and all the elements heavier than helium—were dispersed for the first time. The second- and third-generation stars such as our own formed from the remnants of these supernova explosions. Indeed, it is only in these later-generation star systems that organic life as we know it could possibly form. Our entire solar system—and we ourselves—are made up of ancient stardust.

This cosmic story reveals an ongoing creativity and evolution. While the primeval fireball set the stage for what was to come afterwards, the universe continued to manifest new forms of creativity over time. Creation does not happen once-and-for-all time; rather, creativity is an ongoing process that manifests as a series of—often unrepeatable—stages or steps.

There was, for example, only one moment when the galaxies could form. If the opportunity had not borne fruit, our cosmos would have remained an amorphous soup of energy and primitive matter with no real form or structure. In such a cosmos, life and mind would never have emerged.

Similarly, the galaxies need never have given birth to the stars. There are actually two common kinds of galaxies. Spiral galaxies, like our own, are able to birth new stars. Yet many galaxies are of the other type: elliptical galaxies. These lack internal structure and new stars are not formed in them. If an elliptical galaxy collides with a spiral galaxy, the ability of the resulting galaxy to create new stars can be destroyed. The stars gradually burn out and die, and no new ones take their place.

Creativity, then, is not inevitable. Indeed, our cosmos's creativity rests upon a figurative knife's edge. There are two basic opposing forces that are held in a delicate balance that have permitted structure to evolve: the contractive force created by the action of gravity on matter; and the expansive force that bursts forth with the primal fireball. These form the fundamental *yin* and *yang* of cosmic physics.

If the gravitational force had been only slightly greater, the whole universe would have contracted rapidly back in on itself, to be crushed in a black hole. If the gravitational force had been only slightly weaker, the cosmos would have never been able to form galaxies or any kind of structure. A difference of a mere one part in 10^{59} (10 followed by 59 zeroes!) or less than a trillionth of a trillionth of a trillionth of a trillionth of one percent either way, and a cosmos with galaxies, stars, planets, and life would never have emerged.

Thomas Berry sees this delicate balance of attraction (or limitation) and expansion (or wild exuberance) as the "first expression and the primordial model of artistic discipline." He considers "the wild and disciplined" as "the two constituent forces of the universe, the expansive force and the containing force bound into a single universe and expressed in every being in the universe" (1999, 52). It is out of this *yang* and *yin* that all expressions of creativity in the cosmos are born.

Strangely, the amount of known matter in the universe does not account for the gravitational attraction that is at work. It is now hypothesized that most of the cosmos is invisible—or "dark"—in nature, consisting of particles and energy that rarely interact with visible things and are thus undetectable to scientific instruments. It is currently estimated that dark matter makes up 22 percent of the universe and dark energy a further 74 percent, meaning that a mere 4 percent of the cosmos can be directly perceived. Rupert Sheldrake observes that "it is as if physics has discovered the unconscious. Just as the conscious mind floats, as it were, on the surface of the sea of unconscious mental processes, so the known physical world floats on a cosmic ocean of dark matter" (1990, 74).

The delicate balance between expansion and contraction suggests that the nature of the cosmos is not the result of pure chance. Indeed, the fundamental forces of the cosmos and all the "laws" of physics seem to have been selected to allow for the possibility of a self-organizing, emergent cosmos. Did the cosmos, in its first flickering moments when universes were created and annihilated innumerable times, select one of the few—or perhaps the only—one that made authentic creativity possible? Or did the habits of the cosmos, its morphic fields, evolve in some way to allow for creativity? We will examine these questions in more detail later in this chapter, but for now it suffices to observe that the drive toward creativity and complexity seems to be woven into the very fabric of the cosmos from its beginnings.

Paul Davies (1988) points out that there is a difference between predestination and predisposition. The cosmos was not "predestined" to give birth to the galaxies, to the stars, to life, to mind. These were not inevitable results of the initial conditions of the primal flaring forth; rather, the possibility of self-organization—and even, perhaps, a direction or inclination—were somehow present. The cosmos was "predisposed" toward creativity and emergence, but as the example of the elliptical galaxies shows, self-organizing dynamics are not inevitable. True freedom exists. As the *Tao Te Ching* (§34) says, the Tao "fulfills its purpose. . . . It nourishes every being in the cosmos, yet it does not attempt to chart their courses."

Brian Swimme believes that the current moment in which we live is a critical juncture in the cosmic story, or at least the Earth story. We have a choice to make as humans—but our time for making that choice is in some ways limited. Once past, it will not come again. It is like the moment when the first galaxies were birthed into being:

> There was one moment when the galaxies could form, not before or after. That's like our moment right now, I think. See, this is the moment for the planet to awaken to itself through the human, so that the actual dynamics of evolution have an opportunity to awaken and to begin to function at that level. It couldn't happen before, you know. And the amazing thing is, it probably won't happen afterwards. If we don't make this transition, most likely the creativity of the planet will be in such a degraded state that we won't be able to make that move. The chilling thing is that, in the universe, the really creative places *can* lose their creativity. [For example,] elliptical galaxies are just sitting there, and the stars go out one by one, and that's it. So you can actually move off from the mainline sequence of creativity in the universe. (Swimme 2001, 41)

While creativity and emergence are not, then, inevitable—while there are real choices to be made—there is also immense hope revealed in the story of the cosmos. Despite all odds to the contrary, creativity has prevailed. We cannot know, of course, what opportunities were forever lost, but we do know that creative emergence continues and that the universe seems to continue to strive toward greater complexity and, ultimately perhaps, toward greater beauty and greater depth of mind.

In adopting this perspective, it seems best to understand the entire cosmos as being in some sense a living entity, an organism that grows and develops over time. Certainly, the dynamics of emergence that the modern universe story reveals make clear that the cosmos does not resemble a machine. Rather, it is a living entity with its own freedom and creative dynamism. This becomes even more apparent as we consider the story of our own planet, the living Earth of which we ourselves are a part.

THE UNFOLDING OF LIFE

Evolution takes place not in response to the demands for survival, but as creative play and cooperative necessity of an entire evolving universe. (Lemkow 1990, 136)

The driving force of evolution, according to the emerging new theory, is to be found not in the chance events of random mutations, but in life's inherent tendency to create novelty, in the spontaneous emergence of increasing complexity and order. (Capra 1996, 227-28)

Mutual aid is as much a law of animal life as mutual struggle, but . . . as a factor of evolution, it is most probably of greater importance, in as much as it favors the development of such habits and characters as ensure the maintenance and further development of the species, together with the greatest amount of welfare and enjoyment of life for the individual, with the least waste of energy. (Peter Kropotkin, quoted in Goldsmith 1998, 239)

We consider naïve the early Darwinian view of "nature red in tooth and claw." Now we see ourselves as the products of cellular cooperation—the cells built up from other cells. Partnerships between cells once foreign and even enemies to each other are at the very root of our being. (Lynn Margulis, quoted in Suzuki and Knudtson 1992, 23)

Life did not take over the globe by combat, but by networking. (Margulis and Dorion Sagan, quoted in Capra 1996, 231)

The dynamics of creativity and emergence inherent in the fabric of the cosmos are revealed, perhaps most clearly for us, in the story of life's evolution here on Earth. The story of our home planet exhibits a drive toward greater complexity, consciousness, and beauty that cannot be fully explained by the dominant evolutionary theory of neo-Darwinism based on random mutations, competition, and the survival of the fittest. Something more subtle seems to be at work, something that hints at a goal, or at least a direction, toward which life itself seems to be striving.

The origin of life on our planet in many ways remains shrouded in mystery. Most current theories propose that basic organic molecules such as amino acids somehow formed in the primordial sea and that lipids then gave rise to primitive cellular membranes. Later, RNA and proteins arose, and finally primitive cells themselves. To date, however, no one has been able to produce a living cell in a laboratory. It may well be that subsequent research will bear more fruit in this area, but there are very real difficulties in imagining what processes could have given rise to the complex organic molecules necessary for life, much less the creation of viable cells. Because of this, some scientists wonder if life—or at least its immediate precursors—might not have had an extraterrestrial origin, arriving here via the collision of a comet or some other body with Earth. Even that theory, however, in one sense simply moves the problem rather than solving it. In any case, "blind chance" alone does not seem to be sufficient to account for the emergence of the first living organisms.

What does seem to be clear is that primitive bacteria evolved very quickly on our planet: a mere half-billion years after the formation of Earth, the first prokaryotes (cells without a nucleus) were born. Cells developed the process of photosynthesis, allowing them to tap into the energy of the sun, within another hundred million years. In so doing, however, they produced free oxygen—something that actually killed primitive cells when it reached high enough concentrations. Indeed, photosynthesis fundamentally altered the chemistry of the Earth's atmosphere, oceans, and soil. In addition, by taking the greenhouse gas CO_2 out of the atmosphere, it allowed the planet to cool considerably, which resulted in the first ice ages approximately 2.3 billion years ago.

It took almost two billion years from the development of photosynthesis for cells to learn how to deal successfully with oxygen, that dangerous gas which we now consider to be essential for life. Around the same time, the first eukaryotes (cells with nuclei) emerged. It took another billion years or so for life to develop sexual reproduction. Around the same time, the first heterotrophs came into being—that is, organisms that consume other organisms to provide their source of energy. Three hundred million years later (that is, 700 million years ago), the first multicellular organisms appear. From this point on, the pace of evolution seems to accelerate rapidly (T. Berry and Swimme 1992).

What was the driving force behind this explosion of creativity and diversity? Why do organisms evolve into more complex forms? And what processes allow these changes to take place? Charles Darwin observed that there are natural variations in individual organisms of any given species. Some of these variations are more advantageous than others. For example, a certain color of skin pigmentation might allow a species of lizards to blend in with its surroundings more effectively—like green skin in place of brown among lizards living in a forest. This green pigmentation makes the lizard less vulnerable to predators, and its progeny who inherit it likewise have a greater likelihood to survive and reproduce. The "survival of the fittest" means that, over time, the green skin color becomes more frequent—at least in habitats such as forests and grasslands where it provides more effective camouflage. Eventually, the population of green lizards in these habitats may become a species distinct from the brown lizards, who, for example, might continue to be more successful in the desert, where their skin blends more effectively with their surroundings.

Darwin's theory of natural selection was eventually combined with Mendel's theory of genes, and this new synthesis came to be known as neo-Darwinism. In this perspective, all variations in species arise through spontaneous genetic mutations. While most of these are not beneficial, occasionally beneficial mutations do occur. In the case of our example above, the gene coding for brown skin pigmentation mutates and results in a gene for green pigmentation instead. The genes coding for the more successful traits get passed on more frequently, so that—via the process of natural selection—they become more common over time. In this view, the combination of chance (spontaneous mutation) and necessity (the survival of the fittest) drives all evolution. To use the words of Jacques Monod, "Chance alone is at the source of every innovation, of all creation in the biosphere" (quoted in Capra 1996, 224).

Neo-Darwinism is still the theory of evolution that is most commonly taught in schools. In many ways, it is brilliant in its simplicity, yet it also suffers from serious shortcomings. First, its view of simple genetic mutation seems to assume a one-to-one correspondence between genes and traits. Certainly, in some instances, such a correspondence does seem to exist, but as we have seen, this is not always the case. Often a whole host of genes—sometimes located on distinct chromosomes—are related to the expression of a single trait. In the neo-Darwinist vision, these would presumably need to mutate spontaneously simultaneously to result in a useful trait that could then become more common via natural selection. This hardly appears to be a sufficiently probable occurrence to serve as the key evolutionary process.

Similarly, one gene can affect multiple traits. If a spontaneous mutation occurs, one of these traits might be beneficial, but it is unlikely that all the resulting trait changes would be useful. Indeed, it is much more probable that most will be harmful, so it is extremely unlikely that the spontaneous mutation of such a gene will ever result in a net benefit for the organism. In the end, then, most genetic mutations in an organism would need to be highly coordinated within the genome to be beneficial. To compound the problem, we now know that chance errors in genetic replication are much rarer than was originally thought (Capra 1996). What is more, when such mutations do occur, cellular mechanisms exist to eliminate these errors.

Combining all these observations together, spontaneous mutation—in the sense of random, chance genetic changes—seems an exceedingly unlikely process to account for the emergence of useful new traits and adaptations. Indeed, in the case of bacteria, at least, mutations do not, in fact, seem to be random at all, but rather highly directive. Harvard biologist John Cairns and Rochester University's Barry Hall have both concluded that "certain mutations in bacteria occur more often when they are useful to the bacteria than when they are not" (Goldsmith 1998, 164). What is the process that directs which mutations occur? This is not yet clear, but something much more selective than random mutations—some would say much more purposeful—seems to be at work.

Second, neo-Darwinism does not really explain the evolution of complex, multicellular organisms. From the standpoint of "survival of the fittest," there can be no doubt that bacteria are the most successful organisms on the planet. Indeed, bacteria are able to freely exchange genetic material with each other, allowing them to adapt far more quickly than more complex organisms. The bacteriologist Sorin Sonea goes so far as to argue that bacteria should not be divided into separate species because, essentially, they all draw on a common pool of genes. Each "individual" bacterium typically changes up to 15 percent of its genetic material every day, leading Sonea to observe that "a bacterium is not a unicellular organism, it is an incomplete cell . . . belonging to different chimeras according to circumstances" (quoted in Capra 1996, 230). In some sense, then "all bacteria are part of a single microcosmic web of life" (Capra 1996, 230).

One can certainly argue, then, from a survival and adaptability point of view, that the bacterial web is the oldest, most adaptable, and most successful organism on Earth. It had no "need" to evolve into eukaryotes or to develop into organisms using sexual reproduction, much less into what we traditionally consider to be multicellular life forms. Certainly, then, competition and the struggle for survival alone cannot drive the evolutionary process toward great complexity.

A third objection to neo-Darwinism lies in its failure to explain the evolution of more complex adaptations. True, the theory can account for small changes, such as the skin color example we mentioned earlier. Similarly, the emergence of the trait allowing plants to resist the herbicide glyphosate (controlled by one gene) could be accounted for by the neo-Darwinian theory. What, though, could account for the evolution of far more complex structures, such as the eye or the ear? One might imagine that a photosensitive cell could emerge spontaneously (although its usefulness to the larger organism seems doubtful without a connection of some kind to the nervous system), but not all the supporting structures that work together to form a functional eye. Similarly, an ear cannot function without a whole series of structures working in concert: the auditory nerves, the middle ear bones, the eardrum, and even the outer ear. Yet these structures—until they are complete and working together in a coordinated fashion—confer no advantage to an organism. Why, then, would they evolve at all? Even Charles Darwin himself found this inconsistent with his theory:

> To suppose that the eye with all its inimitable contrivances for adjusting the focus to different distances, for admitting different amounts of light, and for the correction of spherical and chromatic aberration, could have formed by natural selection, seems, I freely confess, *absurd in the highest degree*. (Quoted in Goldsmith 1998, 197)

Fourth, if neo-Darwinism alone explained evolution, we would expect the fossil record to display gradual, ongoing changes to species over time. Yet, in fact, what we see is the phenomenon of "punctuated evolution" characterized by long periods of relative stability followed by comparatively brief periods of explosive creativity and evolutionary experimentation. Why is it that, in certain periods, so few changes take place while in others, the changes take place far more quickly than we might expect? As we have seen, both systems theory and the hypothesis of morphic fields provide valuable insights into understanding this phenomenon. In contrast, punctuated evolution seems to be nearly totally inconsistent with neo-Darwinist explanations.

Indeed, Edward Goldsmith (1998) observes that neo-Darwinism may place far too much emphasis on change and not enough on stability. What explains the constancy of species, sometimes over the period of hundreds of thousands, or even millions, of years? In the neo-Darwinist vision, gradual changes—minor fine-tuning of organisms—should be a continual, ongoing process. Yet this is seldom actually the case. In part, the processes of genetic stability we have mentioned account for this. Most mutations are repaired before they ever propagate, and those that are not repaired are almost always harmful and may even result in the death of the organism. The hypothesis of morphic fields may provide an additional insight: the field of an organism is habitual in nature and is only changed with great difficulty. It is only when a new stress arises—a crisis that threatens the viability of the old habitual form—that new forms emerge. In the systems perspective, a chaotic state eventually leads to the formation of totally new attractors, and with it, the appearance of new forms. Natural selection then might well enter into play, effectively testing the new forms that have emerged and helping determine which are best suited for long-term survival.

A final objection to neo-Darwinism lies in its underlying assumptions. As we have noted earlier, Darwin was very much influenced by the economic theories of his day as well as by Thomas Malthus' (1766-1834) "law" of population, which envisioned life in competition for scarce resources. As Theodore Roszak notes:

> All the harsh, competitive assumptions of Malthus and the Manchester School got mixed into the foundations of Darwinian biology. Far from reading the ethos of the jungles into civilized society, Darwin read the ethos of industrial capitalism into the jungle, concluding that all life had to be what it had become in the early milltowns: a vicious "struggle for existence." (1992, 153)

Not all biologists of Darwin's day or those who have come afterwards assume that competition is the primary force driving evolution. The zoologist Peter Kropotkin (1842-1921), for example, believed that complex dynamics of cooperation were much more fundamental. Even the action of predators can be understood from a cooperative perspective. By culling the weak and the sick, they strengthen their prey and help ensure that food resources are not exhausted. Indeed, the intricate relationships between species and the dynamics of complex ecosystems are now much clearer to most of us than they were in Darwin's time (with the important exception, of course, of indigenous peoples, who have commonly been keenly aware of such relationships).

For example, when wolves were reintroduced into Yellowstone Park in the United States, it was discovered that elk were less likely to graze on tree saplings along riverbanks, where they were an easy target for the newly returned predators. As a result, soil erosion along waterways was reduced, allowing for healthier fish stocks in streams and rivers. Strange as it might sound, wolves were found to play a key role in the prevention of soil erosion and the health of freshwater fish.

Indeed, emerging scientific research suggests that cooperation and symbiosis are key dynamics in evolutionary processes. As we have seen, bacteria routinely share their genetic material, essentially constituting a microcosmic web of life. That does not deny the fact that individual bacteria may on one level compete with each other for food and other necessities, but they still cooperate together—in some sense sharing knowledge and experience via their genetic exchanges. Indeed, they can share genetic information globally within the space of just a few years. It is this bacterial web that actually created the conditions essential for more complex forms of life on Earth:

> During the first two billion years of evolution, bacteria were the sole inhabitants of the Earth, and the emergence of more complex life forms is associated

with networking and symbiosis. During these two billion years, prokaryotes, or organisms composed of cells with no nucleus (namely bacteria), transformed the Earth's surface and atmosphere. It was the interaction of these simple organisms that resulted in the complex processes of fermentation, photosynthesis, oxygen breathing, and the removal of [CO_2] gas from the air. Such processes would not have evolved, however, if these organisms were atomized in the Darwinian sense, or if the force of interaction between parts existed only outside the parts. (Nadeau and Kafatos 1999, 110)

Lynn Margulis has now demonstrated that all eukaryotic cells are in themselves results of a symbiotic alliance of simpler organisms. This is particularly evident in the case of a cell's mitochondrion, the organelle that enables it to utilize energy through chemical reactions involving oxygen. The mitochondrion actually has its own DNA distinct from that of the cell's nucleus. It seems probable that eukaryotes are the result of an alliance between early oxygen-consuming bacteria (who formed the mitochondria) and other organisms, forming a more complex, symbiotic whole. Perhaps the mitochondrial bacteria initially invaded or "infected" the host cells, but then gave up their independence in exchange for protection and a steady supply of nutrients. Other cell organelles may have a similar origin.

Margulis goes so far as to refer to nucleated cells as "microbial collectives" or "bacterial confederacies" which "cooperated and centralized, and in doing so formed a new kind of cellular government" (quoted in Roszak 1999, 126). As Fritjof Capra observes, this "theory of symbiogenesis implies a radical shift of perception in evolutionary thought. Whereas the conventional theory sees the unfolding of life as a process in which species only diverge from one another, Lynn Margulis claims that the formation of new composite entities through the symbiosis of formerly independent organisms has been the more powerful and more important evolutionary force" (1996, 231).

Symbiosis exists not only within cells, but within multicellular organisms. As we have previously observed (see p. 203 above), roughly 50 percent of our own body weight is made up of other organisms—particularly bacteria—most of which are essential for our own survival. Every human being, and indeed every multicellular organism, is a kind of close-knit confederacy of diverse organisms. Similarly, we depend on an entire web of organisms—many of them microscopic—to maintain the basic conditions that make life possible at all. All organisms on Earth live in these kinds of symbiotic relationships. All living things not only adapt to their surroundings but also shape and transform their habitats. Living things, particularly microbial organisms, have fundamentally altered the chemical composition of the atmosphere, the geology, and the climate of our planet.

At another level, individual species, such as the wolves of Yellowstone National Park, play often surprising roles that maintain the health and viability of other species with whom they may at first appear to have only minimal interactions. Could it be, then, that all evolution is really a kind of coevolution? As the marine mammalogist Victor Scheffer observes, "Never since the Achaean Period has a living thing evolved alone. Whole communities have evolved as if they were one great organism. Thus all evolution is coevolution and the bio-sphere is now a confederation of dependencies" (quoted in Suzuki and Knudt-son 1992, 158).

In this perspective, we need to reinterpret the whole idea of "survival of the fittest" to mean the ability not to kill and destroy other species but rather to *fit in* well and contribute to the rest of the biotic community. This does not mean that competition plays no role whatsoever, but rather that its role is complemen-tary—and normally secondary—to the role of cooperation. Competition seems to play a stronger role in pioneer ecosystems where it helps to space out living organisms and favor the development of greater diversity over time. "As living things evolve, however, as ecosystems develop from their pioneer states toward climax states . . . competition give[s] way to cooperation and . . . homeostasis [is] correspondingly increased" (Goldsmith 1998, 253).

In considering the idea of coevolution, it may help us to reflect on the rela-tionship between a butterfly and a flower. Flowers have evolved to attract pollina-tors such as butterflies, while butterflies are dependent on the nectar of flowers as their source of food. One cannot really exist without the other. Which, then, came first? Did they not need to evolve together? And how do we view their relationship? Does the flower somehow trick the butterfly into pollinating it, or has the butterfly somehow tricked the flower into providing it with nectar? One could choose to look at things that way: We could assume that each organism is focused only upon its own survival, its own needs.

Yet might it not be otherwise? Might not the flower, in some way, care about the survival and well-being of the butterfly, and vice versa? Might not something akin to love be at work here? Most would view such a perspective as "unscien-tific"; yet are there really any grounds for supposing that egoism and selfishness are more "scientific" than love, compassion, and mutual care? If cooperation and symbiosis are really more fundamental than competition and the "struggle for survival," perhaps love—or at least some kind of attraction, allurement, or care—is actually more essential than—or at the very least, just as essential as—self-assertion or egoism.

The cooperative, creative view of evolution emerging from both systems theory and the theory of symbiogenesis differs fundamentally in many respects from the neo-Darwinian perspective. No longer is evolution seen as the result of the mere combination of chance (random mutations) and necessity (survival of the fittest). Indeed, a drive toward greater cooperation, complexity, diversity, and even mindfulness seems at work. Even the worldwide exchange of genetic information throughout the microcosmic bacterial web in some ways conjures the image of mind which shares genetic "memories" or "experiences."

How, we must ask again, did the myriad of related changes necessary for the evolution of complex structures such as an eye or an ear actually take place? Certainly, this seems to have required a series of highly coordinated genetic mutations to result in something that was truly functional. Yet, as we have seen, genes alone may very well not determine form. If morphic fields or something like them exists, might they not have played a role in coordinating the needed transformations? This could help explain how an eye, once evolved, might be more easily developed in another, completely unrelated species, as we have seen in our discussion of convergent evolution. But just how did the coordination necessary for the evolution of the very first eye—or any other such complex structure—initially take place?

While there are yet no clear answers to this question, it would appear that a series of changes that took place seemed to be aiming toward a certain goal, such as the development of an eye. A goal seems to imply something like purposefulness, or at least a direction. It is interesting to note that the original theory of evolution was proposed by both Alfred Russel Wallace (1823-1913) and Charles Darwin. While both agreed on the process of natural selection, Wallace diverged from Darwin as time went by since he did not believe that blind chance alone could explain the changes driving evolution, but rather that it was guided by some kind of creative intelligence, which he conceived of as organizing spirits in some ways analogous to the idea of morphic fields (Sheldrake 1988, 53).

That does not mean that we need to adopt some version of "intelligent design"—which seems to conjure the image of a blueprint laid out from the beginning of time. The insights of systems theory help us to envision something more creative than this. What it does seem to require, though, is some kind of mindful activity at work at the heart of the cosmos, something that draws evolution toward greater complexity and diversity—something that we could refer to as the Tao, the Dharma, or the Malkuta. However we might want to envision this, it seems to be woven into the very fabric of the universe. It is not, however, something static like a "law," but rather something that is dynamic, something that itself may evolve and unfold over time.

One way to conceive of this is to see the cosmos as moving toward an attractor, or better yet, a vision, which itself may still be evolving. This is similar to the idea of the Jesuit paleontologist Pierre Teilhard de Chardin (1881-1955), who proposed that evolution is not "directed in its details according to some preexisting plan, but that it is shaped overall to converge on a yet-to-be-achieved superior final stage, which he called the 'Omega point'" (Davies 1988, 110). We cannot say what, exactly, this Omega point will look like, but it does seem clear that moving toward it involves ever-increasing levels of complexity, interrelationship, diversity, and self-awareness.

GAIA: THE LIVING EARTH

The entire range of living matter on Earth, from whales to viruses, and from oaks to algae, could be regarded as constituting a single living entity capable of manipulating the Earth's atmosphere to suit its overall needs and endowed with faculties and powers far beyond those of its constituent parts. (James Lovelock, quoted in Goldsmith 1998, 115)

The Gaia Hypothesis states that the Earth's surface conditions are regulated by the activities of life. . . . This environmental maintenance is effected by the growth and metabolic activities of the sum of the organisms, i.e., the biota. The hypothesis implies that were life to be eliminated, the surface conditions on Earth would revert to those interpolated for a planet between Mars and Venus. Although the detailed mechanisms of Earth's surface control are poorly understood, they must involve interactions between approximately thirty million species of organisms. (Lynn Margulis, quoted in Joseph 1990, 86)

The cooperative dynamics evident in the evolution of Earth's biosphere have led James Lovelock and Lynn Margulis to hypothesize that the planet's climate, oceans, and atmospheric composition are actually regulated by living organisms working together in a coordinated fashion to maintain the conditions necessary for life. In the most widely accepted version of the theory, this coordination takes place through complex cybernetic feedback loops such as those we considered in our examination of systems theory. This life-sustaining system encompasses the Earth's entire biosphere (or ecosphere)[2]—that is, its living organisms plus the water, air, and soil with which life interacts. James Lovelock goes so far as to assert that this system actually functions as a single living entity. Margulis and Lovelock call this entity "Gaia," from the name of the Greek goddess of the Earth.

In many ways, the relationship of the biosphere to the planet as a whole can be compared to a tree. There is only a thin outer layer of living cells in a tree, 97 percent of which actually consists of dead wood. Similarly, the biosphere is like a thin covering stretched over the planet—thinner than a coat of paint would be if the planet were the size of a basketball. The biosphere consists of both biological organisms and the rocks, soil, air, oceans, rivers, and aquifers that these organisms inhabit. Thus, it reaches downward into the depths of the oceans and even several kilometers into the Earth's crust as well as upward nearly ten kilometers into the atmosphere.

> Just as the bark of a tree protects the tree's thin layer of living tissue from damage, life on Earth is surrounded by the protective layer of atmosphere, which shields us from ultraviolet light and other harmful influences and keeps the planet's temperature just right for life to flourish. Neither the atmosphere above us nor the rocks below us are alive, but both have been shaped and transformed considerably by living organisms, just like the bark and the wood of the tree. (Capra 1996, 214)

The biosphere works together as an integrated, living system that is greater than the mere sum of its constituent parts. As Lovelock notes, "Gaia, as a planet sized entity, has properties that are not necessarily discernible by just knowing individual species or populations of organisms living together" (Lovelock 1988, 19). From a systems perspective, self-regulation is seen as an emergent property of this integrated entity.

In this entity, bacteria play a key role. As Margulis notes, over the history of the planet, over 99 percent of all species have become extinct. In contrast, the bacterial web has survived throughout the billions of years of life on the

---

2. Indeed Lovelock, unlike Margulis, believes that this entity may encompass the Earth down to its very core, but most discussion normally focuses on the biosphere.

planet, playing a key role in the regulation of the conditions necessary for life: "The concept of a planetary autopoietic network is justified because all life is embedded in a self-organizing web of bacteria, involving elaborate networks of sensory and control systems that we are only beginning to recognize. Myriad bacteria, living in the soil, the rocks, and the oceans, as well as inside all plants, animals, and humans, continually regulate life on Earth" (Capra 1996, 216).

The evidence for the self-regulating activity of the ecosphere is very strong. If we consider Gaia as a living entity, the atmosphere is analogous to a semi-permeable cell membrane, allowing certain substances to enter (for example, sunlight) while keeping others (harmful radiation, most meteorites) out.

One could argue, of course, that many planets without life have atmospheres, which of course is true. Yet Earth's atmosphere is unique—at least in our solar system and what little of others we know—insofar as it exists in a state far from chemical equilibrium. Without the constant activity of life, its composition would be fundamentally different. Both Venus and Mars, for example, have atmospheres consisting mainly of CO_2 (96.5 percent and 95 percent respectively), while CO_2 makes up a mere 0.03 percent of Earth's atmosphere. Nitrogen makes up only about 3 percent of the Martian and Venusian atmospheres, but 79 percent of Earth's. Only traces of oxygen are present on Mars and Venus, but its concentration in Earth's atmosphere reaches 21 percent (Lovelock 1988).

James Lovelock points out that, without life, Earth's atmosphere would very closely resemble that of Mars or Venus. Indeed, free oxygen reacts so readily with other gases and chemicals that its presence on Earth can be maintained only because it is constantly being produced by photosynthesis. Similarly, free nitrogen results from the activity of bacteria. Meanwhile, biological organisms have found ways to remove CO_2 from the atmosphere, mainly by burying carbon (in the form of oil and coal, created by the heating and compression of ancient organisms) or by locking it into rock (in the form of the calcium carbonate that makes up limestone, which was formed from the shells of oceanic plankton deposited on the floor of the sea).

The removal of CO_2 from the atmosphere has been a key reason why the Earth has maintained a relatively constant surface temperature over the past four billion years, even though the sun has grown 30 to 50 percent warmer over that time. Initially, CO_2 formed a protective greenhouse blanket that enabled life to develop on the planet. If, however, this CO_2 had not been gradually removed by the action of living organisms, surface temperatures on Earth would now have reached 240° to 340° C, much more like the infernal climate of Venus than the average 13° C we currently enjoy.

Another important vehicle for regulating temperatures lies in the great tropical rainforests that—increasingly—are disappearing from our planet. Tropical forests, by evaporating vast quantities of water and forming reflective clouds, act as Earth's air conditioning system. Indeed, if we were to assign a monetary value to the cooling services they provide, it would cost roughly $450 trillion annually (Lovelock 1988).

In addition to temperature and CO_2 levels, it seems evident that Gaia also regulates the level of oxygen in the atmosphere. If the level of oxygen were to fall too low, the planet could not support many current forms of life, while if it rose just a few percentage points higher, spontaneous combustion would result, destroying much of the biosphere in a storm of fire and smoke. Yet, despite ongoing photosynthetic activity, the concentration never reaches dangerous levels.

It was the release of oxygen into the atmosphere that led to the formation of the ozone layer, which protects life by blocking out most harmful ultraviolet radiation. Before the formation of this protective shield, life was restricted to the oceans. Indirectly, then, the release of free oxygen via the photosynthetic process of organisms created the conditions necessary for life to spread to land.

In the seas, it would seem that life might also regulate the salinity of the water. The planet's oceans have maintained a nearly constant concentration of salt for the past 3.5 billion years. If the salt concentrations were to rise by a mere 3.5 percent, most sea organisms would no longer be able to survive. Yet salt is constantly being added to the oceans: as rocks weather and soil erodes, rains wash salt into rivers and thus into the oceans. At the rate of salt being added, it should take only eighty million years to double the amount of salt currently in the ocean. How is it, then, that the oceans' salinity remains nearly constant? While the processes are not entirely clear, it is suggested that microorganisms may play a role by separating out evaporative lagoons from the sea, effectively moving salt from the sea onto the land (Sheldrake 1990). In any case, it seems far more than coincidence that the ocean's salinity is maintained within the range that permits the flourishing of life.

It is also probable that the continued presence of water on the planet is the result of life processes. Water and CO_2 will react with the oxides in basalt rock to produce a variety of carbonates. In the process, free hydrogen is released into the atmosphere, which eventually escapes from Earth completely since it is too light to be held by the planet's gravitational pull. David Suzuki and Amanda McConnell point out that, during the first billion years or so of the planet's history, all of Earth's water could have been lost through this process. Fortunately, living organisms prevented this from happening:

> Instead, when plants evolved photosynthesis and produced oxygen as a by-product, some of the hydrogen of the water was held in the carbon ring of glucose, thus holding the hydrogen on the planet. In addition, the free hydrogen produced by the oxidation of iron in rock was exploited by bacteria as a source of energy. Oxygen, hydrogen and sulphur react chemically to produce water and hydrogen sulphide, which has recoverable energy within its structure. Thus, the forces of life may very well have prevented the desiccation of the planet by capturing the hydrogen that is necessary for water and thus preventing it from drifting into space. (1997, 58-59)

Not only have Earth's atmosphere and oceans been shaped and regulated by life, but also its rocks and soil. As we have already noted, limestone rock is itself the by-product of the shells of tiny sea organisms. Limestone is sufficiently heavy that it slowly sinks into Earth's mantle. There is some speculation that the pressure on the mantle that this process generates may play a part in Earth's continued geological activity, and perhaps even the formation of the continents. Others have posited that the presence of granite—a rock that seems to be unique to Earth, at least in our solar system, and a key constituent in continental formation—may also depend on life processes. Minik Rosing (quoted in McLeod 2006) believes that photosynthesis could have played a key role by making sufficient energy available for the geochemical processes needed to form granite.[3] One concrete way this could occur is through the action of microbial life forms that live near thermal vents which break down basalt into illite and smectite clays, both of which contribute to the formation of granite. Since granite is lighter than the basalt found in the Earth's mantle, it floats to the surface, helping to form a stable continental crust.

While the extent to which life processes have contributed to the formation of Earth's rocks and continents is still open to some question, it is clear that soil is very much the creation of life—and, indeed, could be said to be living. Every cubic centimeter of soil contains billions of microflora and micro fauna including bacteria (up to one billion/gm), fungi (up to one million/gm), algae (100 thousand/gm), protozoa (100 thousand/gm), nematodes (100/gm), and earthworms (up to 300 per cubic meter). As Suzuki and McConnell note:

> Almost all of the nitrogen that is essential for life must be made available through the action of nitrogen-fixing microorganisms, most of which are in the soil. The soil is a microcosm where all the relationships of the larger world play out; in this element, earth, the other three unite—air, water and energy together create the vitality of the soil. . . . Soil organisms comprise a major portion of the total diversity of life. In this dark, teeming world, minute predators stalk their prey, tiny herbivores graze on algae, thousands of aquatic microorganisms throng a single drop of soil water, and fungi, bacteria and viruses play out their part on this invisible stage. In their life and death these organisms create and maintain the texture and fertility of the soil; they are caretakers of the mysterious life-creating material on which they, and we, depend absolutely. (1997, 80-81)

Soil organisms actually make up a very large proportion of the total biomass on land, especially when we consider that they reach far below the surface of the Earth. Some core samples of solid rock taken from four kilometers deep have been found to be filled with microorganisms. As Suzuki and McConnell observe, the very rocks of the Earth are in one sense alive.

While there is strong evidence for many aspects of the Gaia theory, there is no scientific consensus around it. In part, the degree of consensus depends on what version of the theory one puts forth. What might be called *Weak Gaia*—that life

---

3. Currently, photosynthesis provides "three times as much energy to the Earth's overall geochemical energy cycle as geological activity driven by the Earth's interior" (McLeod 2006, 12).

has had an influence, indeed perhaps, a very marked influence, on many non-biotic aspects of Earth such as the atmosphere and oceans—is probably acceptable to most scientists.

A somewhat stronger position, which could be called *Moderate Gaia*, maintains that the biosphere actually modifies its environment and that organisms and habitat co-evolve together. This version, while somewhat more controversial, also seems to enjoy fairly widespread support.

On the other hand, the versions of the theory that could be called *Strong Gaia* are far more controversial insofar as they maintain that living organisms, working collectively, in some way actually regulate or control their environment in order to maintain—or perhaps even to optimize—the conditions necessary for life.

One objection to the strong versions of Gaia is that its hypothesis can never be proven via scientific experimentation. Indeed, it may well be true that in this sense Gaia is not a hypothesis in the traditional sense of the word—but this in itself does not negate that it may well be true. Certainly in many respects it seems to be the explanation that most clearly corresponds to the facts as we know them.

Another objection lies in the suspicion that science has for anything that might hint of purposeful activity among nonhuman organisms. To purport that organisms in some way work together to achieve a goal, then, is a serious challenge to scientific orthodoxy. To try to counter this objection, James Lovelock created a simple mathematical model called Daisy World involving a planet with two types of daisies—white (that reflect heat) and black (that absorb it)—that effectively regulate surface temperatures via natural selection. In brief, as the planet cools, the black daisies multiply relative to the white daisies because they absorb heat more effectively and this in turn warms the planet (since it reflects less solar radiation). If the planet gets too hot, the white daisies, who reflect heat, are favored, and their reflective action also cools the planet. This model is meant to demonstrate, in a very simplified form, how cybernetic feedback loops might account for the regulatory activity of Gaia.

It should be noted, as well, that there are some differences in the Gaia theories proposed by Lovelock and Margulis. Lovelock often speaks of Gaia as a living entity, or even as a living organism. Many scientists, including Margulis, reject this terminology. What is meant by an organism in this case? Must not an organism be able to reproduce itself?[4] Margulis maintains that the Earth is simply a highly complex system, a "series of interacting ecosystems that compose a single huge ecosystem at the Earth's surface. Period" (1998, 120). She does add, however, that "the surface of the planet behaves as a physiological system in certain limited ways," which in some sense could be "best regarded as alive" (1998, 123).

From our point of view, the evidence for a Gaia that truly regulates the conditions that allow life to thrive seems sufficiently strong that we would consider it

---

4. Albeit some, like Carl Sagan, believe that humans could eventually serve to reproduce Gaia via space travel. In this view, Gaia simply has not yet quite reached the stage of reproductive maturity.

to be a truly living entity in some ways comparable to an organism, or perhaps a superorganism of some kind. While scientific orthodoxy may still want to reduce the complex, highly coordinated activity of our living planet to a series of cybernetic feedback loops or, worse still, a series of fortuitous accidents, to us the activity of Earth does in fact appear to be purposeful in its nature in the sense that it strives to maintain the conditions necessary for life to exist on our planet.

One particularly intriguing example of this kind of activity can be found in the sulphur cycle. Sulphur is an essential element for living organisms, but on land sulphur (in the form of sulphate ions) is constantly being lost in the runoff of rivers. Indeed, sulphur would long since have been depleted from the Earth's continents and islands if it were not being replenished by the large quantities of dimethyl sulphide emitted by many marine organisms. As Lovelock notes, however, "Why should marine algae out in the open oceans care a fig for the health and well-being of trees, giraffes, and humans on the land surfaces?" (1988, 136). While he proposes a possible evolutionary process that might have caused algae to emit dimethyl sulphide, this does not seem to adequately account for this process in other marine organisms. Furthermore, Lovelock notes that the presence of land-based organisms, in turn, benefits marine life by increasing rock weathering and increasing the flow of essential nutrients to the sea.[5]

Could this not be evidence for something that does, in fact, resemble altruism, or at least a kind of cooperative coevolution requiring a larger vision of the whole? Could it not be that all living organisms work together in some mysterious fashion actually to optimize the conditions for life on the planet? From this point of view, the contribution of land-based organisms to sea-based ones and vice versa seems quite logical. At the very least, the perspective of systems theory would assert that a living system like that of the Earth functions in a way that is both mindful and intelligent. Capra (1996) maintains that this kind of mindfulness does not require an overall design or purpose, but it would seem to us that, while a design or destiny may not be required, there does seem to be a general kind of purposefulness in the sense of striving to maintain the conditions necessary for life, and indeed, moving toward ever greater complexity, diversity, and communion.

In many cultures, and even in Europe up to the Middle Ages, people often believed that the Earth (or indeed the entire cosmos as it was then understood) had a soul: the *anima mundi*. Rupert Sheldrake believes that this idea of a world soul corresponds to the morphic field of the Earth itself and that this field is related to a yet greater field on a cosmic scale. Might not such a field, in some way, help coordinate the activities of the parts for the good of the greater whole?

---

5. Yet another intriguing example provided by Lovelock in *The Revenge of Gaia* (2006, 18-19), is that of the urea cycle, which also seems to demonstrate a kind of enlightened altruism. The nitrogen that animals excrete as urea in their urine could, for example, be excreted more efficiently (with less water loss) if animals simply breathed nitrogen out instead. Yet then our urea would not provide an essential compound needed by plants. Of course, helping plants does, ultimately, benefit animals as well but, as Lovelock concludes, "How on Earth did we evolve to be so altruistic and have such enlightened self-interest?"

This does not require consciousness, albeit it might imply at least some kind of mindful activity. As we have seen, morphic fields are formative in nature, and they also evolve themselves over time. Sheldrake observes:

> The purposive organizing field of Gaia can be thought of as her morphic field. . . . We would expect the morphic field of Gaia to coordinate her various constituent processes, such as the circulation of molten rocks in the interior, the dynamics of the magnetosphere, the movements of the continental plates, the circulatory patterns of the oceans and the atmosphere and their chemical composition, the regulation of global temperature, and the evolution of ecosystems. These regulatory activities, like those of morphic fields in systems of all other levels of complexity, would involve an ordering of otherwise indeterminate, probabilistic processes. (Sheldrake 1990, 135)

From the standpoint of transformative praxis, one advantage of the Gaia theory is that it carries a strong mythic quality that could serve to help motivate humanity to work to heal our planet. The idea of Gaia—Mother Earth—has ancient resonances that may awaken in us a sacred, reverential attitude toward our home. Within the Gaia framework, we see ourselves very much as part of a greater community of life, a community that works together to maintain the conditions that allow life to flourish and evolve. This awakens in us both a sense of responsibility and a sense of connection to a greater whole of which we are a part. At the same time, though, as Deborah Du Nann Winter points out, there is a danger in the feminine imagery that Gaia evokes:

> The terms *Mother Earth* and *Gaia* (to the extent that people understand *Gaia*'s feminine identity in Greek mythology) will also carry with them our unconscious sexist attitudes about the status and abilities of women and men. If mothers and women are seen as endlessly generous, attending, and caring, we will be more likely to overestimate the regenerativity of the planet. Alternatively, seeing nature as a wanton, recalcitrant female as both Freud and the Enlightenment thinkers did, will encourage our attempts to control and constrain "Her." (1996, 253)

One wonders, however, if these objections are not overcome to the extent that we also overcome our old stereotypes about women and nature. Certainly, there is no need to think of Earth as either feminine or masculine, but many traditional peoples who have referred to Earth as mother have also been highly respectful of both women and the Earth itself. In any case, whether or not we think of Gaia as feminine, the personification of Gaia does serve to make the living entity it represents more real and even suggests a spiritual dimension. While this has had the advantage of helping to capture the imagination of a wide number of people, it has also, unfortunately, alienated some scientists who, perhaps, gave less serious consideration to the theory precisely because of its mythic imagery.

From the standpoint of transformative action, the Gaian perspective can also help us to reframe issues and problems in a wider context, helping us to see situations in new ways. In the case of our current climate crisis, we must view the rise of greenhouse gases through human activity in the light of Gaia's whole history. The Earth's organisms have been working for the past three to four billion years to remove CO_2 from the atmosphere so that Earth's temperature would not increase. Indeed, from a Gaia perspective, cooler can be seen as better since, during ice ages, large expanses of land appear as sea levels drop, actually allowing for a greater expanse of rainforests in the tropics and, with it, greater biodiversity. At the same time, as greenhouse gases have been systematically removed from the atmosphere, plants have been adapting to survive on lower and lower concentrations of CO_2.

Yet, in a brief blink of an eye—two centuries or so—humans have been digging up the carbon (oil and coal) so long buried and, by burning it, returning it to the atmosphere. In that space of time, we have begun a shift in the planet's climate. In the past fifty years, global temperatures have already risen 1° C, and they will likely rise 1° to 2° C more over the next fifty years and perhaps 3° to 4° C by the end of the next century. To put this in perspective, temperatures now are only an average of 5 C warmer than they were during the last ice age. Indeed, through positive feedback loops, the damage we have done may well be amplified further over time. From a Gaia perspective, it is clear that we are acting in a truly reckless manner, undoing the work of the biotic web performed over hundreds of millions of years in what, from a planetary perspective, is a mere instant of time. As Lovelock notes:

> If the present warm period is a planetary fever, we should expect that the Earth left to itself would be relaxing into its normal comfortable ice age. Such comfort may be unattainable because we have been busy removing its skin for farm land, taking away the trees that are the means for recovery. We also are adding a vast blanket of greenhouse gases to the already feverish patient. Gaia is more likely to shudder, then move over to a new stable state, fit for a different and more amenable biota. It could be much hotter, but whatever it is, no longer the comfortable world we know. These predictions are not fictional doom scenarios, but uncomfortably close to certainty. We have already changed the atmosphere to an extent unprecedented in recent geological history. We seem to be driving ourselves heedlessly down a slope into a sea that is rising to drown us. (1988, 227)

Personally, we are less pessimistic about the fate of humanity than Lovelock is, but his warning is not without merit. Certainly, we should not assume that Gaia will be able to maintain the ideal conditions for humans in the face of our current practices. Indeed, humanity may well destroy both itself and a host of other species if it does not awaken to the fact that it is but a part of a much greater whole, a whole with whom we must work cooperatively if we truly wish to flourish on this planet. If we can rise to this challenge and understand our own role within the broader evolution and purpose of Gaia, and indeed that of the entire cosmos, then too we can learn to live and act in ways that actually contribute to the collective well-being of our entire planet.

The Distribution of Life Now and on a Hotter and a Colder Earth
Source: Lovelock 2006, 63

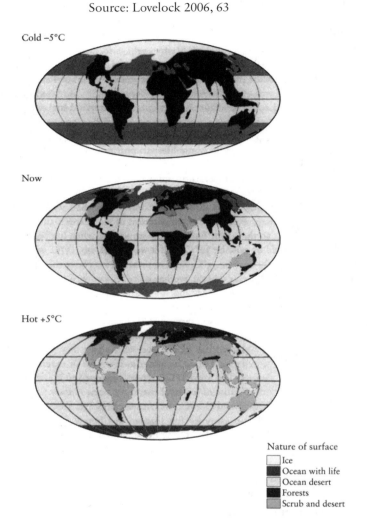

Nature of surface
☐ Ice
■ Ocean with life
☐ Ocean desert
■ Forests
▨ Scrub and desert

Compare [the current situation] with two imaginary sketches: the lower an Earth 5°C hotter than now, roughly that predicted by the IPCC for the end of this century, and the upper 5°C cooler than now, close to the temperature of the last ice age. To judge from the abundance of life, Gaia seems to like it cold, which is why perhaps for most of the past two million years, and maybe much longer, the Earth has been in an ice age. . . . It [is] important that we recognize that a hot Earth is a weakened Earth. On the hot planet, ocean life is restricted to the continental edges, and the desert regions of land are much extended. (Lovelock 2006, 62-64)

A SENSE OF PURPOSE

The sense of purpose is all-pervasive and deeply ingrained in the fabric of the universe. Even the curvature of space itself is delicately pointed— between the demise of collapse into a massive black hole, had the initial curvature been a fraction larger, or an explosion into a scattering of life-less particles, had it been a fraction smaller. (O'Murchu 1997, 99-100)

The idea that [the cosmos's] complexity is the result of random interaction is no longer viable. . . . There is a strong current within scientific discussion that is convinced that somehow or another the universe from the very beginning was pressing toward . . . complex communities. (Swimme 1997)

There is . . . at the level of the most fundamental physics, strong suggestive argument for a single evolutionary principle that selects for life and consciousness at every stage of the universe's unfolding. (Zohar and Marshall 1994, 176)

The evidence for the purposiveness of life processes at every level of organization within the hierarchy of the ecosphere is so great that its denial seems inconceivable. (Goldsmith 1998, 168)

Without direction toward a goal, we just can't account for the phenomena we observe. Unless we see that purposefulness is present even in the subatomic particles, we risk putting humans way up there above nature. We humans know purpose, we act purposefully. Does that set us apart from the rest of nature? I don't think so. (David Steindl-Rast in Capra and Steindl-Rast 1991, 199)

If humanity is to orient itself within the story of the cosmos, and particularly within the unfolding story of the Earth itself, the question of purpose is a key one. As we have noted, a living cosmology is one that helps us find meaning within our own lives. Yet, if the cosmos is in itself random and purposeless, what hope do we have of finding such a meaning? If we ourselves are mere accidents, part of a long string of accidents, can life have any true purpose? In the words of Bertrand Russell that we previously quoted, is it true that we are just the "product of causes which had no prevision of the end they were achieving; that [our] origin, [our] growth, [our] hopes and fears, [our] loves and beliefs, are but the outcome of accidental collisions of atoms" and that, "the soul's habitation" can be safely built only "on the foundation of unyielding despair" (quoted in Sheldrake 1988, 6-7)? If the cosmos were to reveal no meaning, our lives would ultimately be reduced to a struggle for survival, or perhaps the pursuit of momentary pleasure. Would it really matter, in the larger scheme of things, to strive for authentic liberation, searching for a way to live harmoniously within the greater biotic community of Earth?

Perhaps some of us could still find a noble purpose amid such a despairing view of the world around us, but it seems unlikely that such a purpose would have the power to engage humanity collectively. If there were truly no purpose inherent in the cosmos, it would indeed seem that much of this book would have been written in vain. Yet our examination of cosmology does, in fact, seem to reveal a kind of purpose woven into the cosmic fabric. Why did the universe, against all odds, form galaxies, stars, and planets? Why did life emerge? Why did bacteria, perfectly adapted to our planet, evolve into more complex organisms? All these things suggest a movement, a drive toward complexity, that cannot be explained by random chance alone.

By purpose, though, we do not mean predestination. The cosmology emerging from both subatomic physics and systems theory does not support the idea of a Laplacian universe where, if we were only to know the precise initial starting conditions of all, we could predict the entire course of history. No, by purpose, we mean something both more subtle and creative. It is not so much a destination as a direction, an orientation to cosmic evolution that implies a deeper meaning and, in some sense, a goal. Yet the goal itself may be evolving, and there may be an infinite variety of paths that still move in the same general direction. It is a Tao, a kind of walking, evolving wisdom that is woven into the fabric of the cosmos. It cannot be defined, but it can be perceived. Like the idea of the Malkuta, it is a creative principle, a "'fruitful arm' poised to create, or a coiled spring that is ready to unwind with all the verdant potential of the earth. It is what says 'I can' within us and is willing, despite all odds, to take a step in a new direction" (Douglas-Klotz 1990, 20). It is like the Dharma which somehow orients the "way things work," something that could even be described as "orderly process itself" (Macy 1991a, xi).

Rather than predetermination, the unfolding of the cosmos comes about by self-organizing dynamics that can never be predicted because of the interplay of reciprocal causality, or "dependent co-arising." Yet this creativity in itself implies a kind of direction, a movement toward greater complexity, diversity, relationality, and mindfulness. In such a cosmos, there is meaning and purpose, but there is not a defined blueprint. Some paths may be tried and found to be dead-ends. Others will prove to be successful, at least for a certain stage of the journey. The patterns unfold over time and move, at least broadly speaking, in a certain direction, but the future shape of the design can never itself be known. It is "neither random nor determined but creative" (T. Berry 1999, 169).

There is, indeed, a wide range of scientific evidence that supports the idea that the universe could not have evolved as it did by mere chance. As we have already noted, if the rate of expansion of the cosmos had been infinitesimally smaller, or if the force of gravity had been infinitesimally stronger, the cosmos could never have developed any kind of structure at all. Similarly, Brian Swimme (1997) notes that the precise shape of the four basic forces (gravity, electromagnetism, and the strong and weak nuclear forces) needed to be perfectly balanced to allow for the evolution of a structured cosmos. In fact, the probability of this balance occurring by mere chance has been estimated to be only 1 in 10^{229} (that is, one over one followed by 229 zeroes!). To put this in perspective, the total number of elementary particles in the universe is estimated to be only 10^{90} (1 followed by 90 zeroes). Odds like this are so small that the human mind cannot begin to grasp them. It would seem that the balance of forces had to have been selected by some process: How did they emerge just so?

> Perhaps their final form . . . depended to some extent on the experimentation and exploration of a former, freer era. Perhaps their structure was determined to some degree by what had preceded the moment of symmetry, when a pure or at least original activity had settled into a particular form. If so, these four interactions can be regarded as analogous to habits that the universe adopted for its primary actions . . .
> The universe established its fundamental physical interactions in a manner similar to the way it unfurled its space—with stunning elegance. Had it settled on a slightly different strong interaction, all the future stars would have exploded in a brief time, making an unfurling of life impossible. Had the universe established a slightly different gravitational interaction, none of the future galaxies would have taken shape. The integral nature of the universe is revealed in its actions. The universe as it expands itself and establishes its basic coherence reveals the elegance of activity necessary to hold open all the immensely complex possibilities of its future blossoming. (T. Berry and Swimme 1992, 19)

When considering the probability of life emerging by random activity, we are met with similar levels of improbability. For example:

- All life as we know it depends on carbon atoms. Yet, if the nuclear resonance of carbon was even infinitesimally different, virtually no carbon would ever have been formed in the heart of stars and life on Earth would never have begun (O'Murchu 1997).

- Calculations estimate that not enough time has passed since the beginning of the cosmos to form a single amino acid via the random collision of atoms, yet amino acids exist, not only on Earth but throughout our galaxy (T. Berry and Swimme 1992).

- In the case of an enzyme consisting of a short chain of twenty to thirty amino acids, the probability that these formed by mere chance is simply beyond comprehension: Fred Hoyle and Chandra Wickramasinghe estimated that the probability of this occurring by random processes is on the order of one in $10^{40,000}$—that is, one over one followed by forty thousand zeroes (Roszak 1992).

Probabilities like these have led scientists to formulate what is called the Anthropic Cosmological Principle. In its weak form, this principle states that "the observed values of all physical and cosmological quantities are not equally probable but they take on values restricted by the requirement that there exist sites where carbon-based life can evolve and by the requirements that the Universe be old enough for it to have already done so" (Barrow and Tipler 1986, 16). An alternative statement of the same idea, from the Merriam-Webster Dictionary, says simply that "conditions that are observed in the universe must allow the observer to exist."

In this version of the Anthropic Principle, one need not assume that any kind of purpose or direction actually exists. One could even assert that this is simply a statement of the obvious: given that life exists in the universe, the cosmos's physical "laws" (or habits) and conditions must be of a certain shape that allows for the existence of life. According to one view, there may even be an infinite number of universes, most of which never develop any kind of structure, much less any kind of life. We just happen to inhabit one of the infinitesimally small proportion of universes where life is possible.[6] This is the ultimate appeal to blind chance, analogous to the idea that, given an infinite number of monkeys typing randomly, at least one of them by chance will create the complete works of Shakespeare. As Theodore Roszak observes, "Such ideas have about them the character of a Zen Buddhist koan: they boggle the mind with contradiction. They seem to say, at one and the same time, we reside in a unique condition that is nothing special" (1992, 125).

Another version of the Anthropic Principle, referred to as the "strong" version, takes another tack. It declares that "the Universe must have those properties which allow life [or more generally, observers] to develop within it at some stage of history" (Barrow and Tipler 1986, 21). Once again, this statement has a kind of tautological flavor to it: if the universe has observers, it must have those properties that permit the existence of such observers. Yet this version is highly controversial insofar as it hints at some kind of purpose, or even a design, in the cosmos.

The real significance of the Anthropic Principle—in either of its versions— may be that scientists are discussing these questions at all. As Theodore Roszak notes, even in its most "flippant formulation, the Anthropic Principle echoes a certain subdued amazement at the very fact of intelligent being. It loiters to wonder at the fact that the universe has generated self-conscious life that survives within such a narrow zone of probabilities" (1992, 125). He goes on to note that "what is original in the Anthropic Principle is the fact that it places life and mind at the center of cosmology as matters to be accounted for and reckoned with" (1992, 126-27). One of the scientists who seems to adopt this view most wholeheartedly seems to be the mathematical physicist Paul Davies, who goes so far as to assert that "a hidden principle seems to be at work organizing the cosmos in a coherent way" (quoted in Roszak 1992, 126).

---

6. While one cannot refute the infinite universe theory, its appeal to random processes does seem to be at odds with the observed behavior of self-organizing systems. Certainly, for example, mere random processes do not seem to be able to account for the rapid re-enfoldment of a denatured protein that we previously discussed (see p. 239). Similarly, while random processes could account for the formation of an amino acid—or even different amino acids—in an infinite number of universes, it is hard to imagine that these would form in sufficient quantities ever to become widespread in places devoid of life. Of course, when dealing with infinity, anything is possible—but, in the end, such an argument appears to be more of a mathematical mind game than a reality.

Yet, for generations, scientists completely avoided anything that hinted of an underlying purpose in the cosmos. Even now, there is a strong resistance in most of the scientific community to anything that hints of "teleology"—that is, the idea of design, purpose, directive principle, or finality in nature. For example, when the Gaia hypothesis was criticized as being teleological—since it seemed to imply that the Gaia superorganism acted purposefully to maintain the conditions necessary for life—Lovelock responded to critics by creating the Daisy World model (with Andrew Watson) to demonstrate that a simple combination of cybernetic feedback loops and natural selection could explain the regulatory functions of Gaia (although in truth this rudimentary model seems far too simplistic to explain the apparently purposeful behavior of our planet).

Indeed, much of scientists' efforts to avoid teleology—particularly when referring to living organisms—seems actually to be an exercise in semantics. For example, Goldsmith (1998) notes that while it is not acceptable to say that "the function of the vertebrate heart is to pump blood" (something most of us would take to be obvious), it is acceptable to state that "the heart is a necessary condition for the circulation of blood in vertebrates." This so-called "teleonomy" is acceptable because it is essentially mechanistic in nature and avoids any hint of metaphysics: it allows one to ask "why," but only within very restricted limits.

A similar tack is to state that organisms simply *appear* to have purpose. Julian Huxley, for example, says that "at first sight the biological sector seems full of purpose. Organisms act *as if* in purposeful pursuit of a conscious aim. But the truth lies in those two words 'as if'" (quoted in Goldsmith 1998, 29). Similarly, Charles Darwin asserted that any hint of purpose was only an appearance, that organisms did not act purposefully but rather "seized opportunities."

Yet, as Goldsmith points out, "seizing opportunities" does in itself imply a purpose: "An adaptive individual does not seize any opportunity to bring about a random change, but the one that best suits its purposes, the one that it judges to be 'hypothetically best' for itself and for the hierarchy of natural systems of which it is a part" (1998, 29). Indeed, the "struggle for survival" is itself a purpose. Why should an animal, a plant, or a microorganism struggle to survive at all if it has no purpose? If its goal is to survive, and presumably to propagate, then a purpose is already presumed. The biologist Richard Dawkins, as we have previously noted, goes so far as to assert that genes are "selfish." Essentially, then, one can ascribe a purpose to a molecule (DNA) as long as it is based on self-interest, but as soon as one hints of any kind of purpose that might be more altruistic or cooperative in nature—even in complex organisms with well-developed nervous systems—suggesting purposefulness is no longer acceptable.

Similarly, natural selection itself implies purpose. What is being selected? As French zoologist P. P. Grassé notes, "There cannot be selection without purpose (intention)" and "by explaining the evolution of the fittest in terms of selection, they (the neo-Darwinists) are endowing all living things with an inherent goal" (quoted in Goldsmith 1998, 32). Ultimately, then, the rejection of teleology in science—particularly in biology—is essentially an illusion. Biology has not rejected teleology, only those teleological explanations not based on selfishness, competition, and survival; that is, it accepts purposes in synch with the mentality of capitalism, but rejects those that are not. Similarly, it favors mechanistic descriptions of purpose over those that are more organismic in nature.

The appeal to random processes as a motor of creativity in the cosmos as a whole is also rooted in ideological assumption related to capitalist economics. As Goldsmith notes:

> Randomness is seen as essential because it is impossible to justify the Promethean enterprise to which our industrial society is committed and which involved systematically transforming the biosphere so that it may best satisfy short-term commercial interest if it is seen as organized to achieve a grand overall project of its own. By seeing the ecosphere as random, on the other hand, it is possible to make out that what order there is in the world has been created by science, technology and industry, rather than by God or the evolutionary process. "The cardinal tendency of progress," as J. D. Bernal writes, "is the replacement of an indifferent chance environment by a *deliberately created one.*" (1998, 165)

Finally, it should be noted that the rejection of teleology is firmly rooted in anthropocentrism. Humans are assumed to have purpose, but we are assumed to be unique in this respect. Yet why should humans alone be so endowed? If other creatures display behavior that appears to be purposeful, is not the simplest explanation, based on our own experience, to conclude that the behavior *is* purposeful?

To be fair, perhaps in part there is some confusion in just what is meant by "purpose." For example, Fritjof Capra asserts that while "the systemic understanding of life recognizes the pervasive order, self-organization, and intelligence manifest throughout the living world" (and might we not say, the entire cosmos?), "the teleological assumption that purpose is inherent in natural phenomenon is a human projection, because purpose is a characteristic of reflective consciousness, which does not exist in nature at large" (2002, 120). Yet purpose, in the sense we are using it here, does *not* require self-reflective consciousness. One does not need to be conscious of a goal in order to have one—indeed, many people are motivated by goals that remain unconscious. No, purpose as we understand it is very similar to an organizing principle, a hidden wisdom that manifests itself in the unfolding of the cosmos.

In the end, the avoidance of teleology seems to be driven primarily by ideological assumptions, not by logic. There is, indeed, overwhelming evidence that the cosmos has been evolving in a certain direction, which in turn implies both a goal and a purpose. The probability that our cosmos would be able to evolve the complexity it has birthed by random activity alone is, for all intents and purposes, nil. As some scientists have termed it, the universe is "finely tuned" to allow for the evolution of complexity and, ultimately, life and consciousness themselves. At the level of our own planet, the evidence for the Gaia hypothesis, once again, points to a kind of collective planetary purpose in the sense of a movement toward ever greater complexity, diversity, cooperation, and mindfulness. As Edward Goldsmith notes, "It is only in terms of a teleological ecology that we understand the role of living things within the Gaian hierarchy, in particularly their fundamentally . . . whole-maintaining character . . . which above all makes possible the order, integrity and stability of the living world. . . . Ecology has to be teleological, for purposiveness is possibly the most essential behaviour of living things" (1998, 29).

Humanity itself was birthed by the living Earth, and we, too, are called to work for the greater purpose revealed in the holistic dynamics of the planet and, indeed, of the entire cosmos. As the theologian John Haught notes:

> The cosmos is not forced, but invited, to allow into itself continually more diverse forms of patterned novelty. It does not always accept this invitation in a straightforward fashion. It is allowed to wander and experiment with various forms of beauty. It deserves our care, then, not because it is precarious, but because it is an instance of divinely inspired beauty. (1993, 34)

The use of the idea of "invitation" is very insightful. There is no blueprint, perhaps even no clear, defined goal, but there is a dynamic of allurement (or attractor) that is drawing the cosmos in a certain direction. In this sense, certainly, the activity of the cosmos is mindful. Further, insofar as we are part of the cosmos—and are here only because a myriad of forces, entities, systems, and living things have created the possibility of our existence—we know that the *possibility* of developing self-consciousness itself was woven into the fabric of the universe from the very beginning. Once again, there was no predestination involved—things could have turned out differently (and indeed probably have turned out differently in other parts of the cosmos)—but the possibility of manifesting our particular kind of mind has existed since the moment that the cosmic seed first burst into being.

What is clear is that humanity must understand that we, and the planet we live on, are not merely a cosmic accident. In some sense, the universe has been striving for nearly fourteen billion years to give birth to us. That is not to say that we are at the apex of some kind of hierarchical ladder: each creature and each thing has its place in the cosmos. We are all, in some sense, both special and necessary. Certainly, from our own perspective, Gaia itself might be understood to be the most precious child of the cosmos. Gaia, taken as a whole, is far more complex—and might we not say, far more beautiful—than any one of the beings that are part of this planetary superorganism. As Roszak notes, despite "desperate efforts to assert the omnipotence of the accidental, in a sense that is both poetic and astronomically accurate, we can now say that the entire cosmos mothered the living Earth into existence" (1999, 124).

As for humanity itself, we are very much children of the cosmic process and the evolution of Gaia itself. Our own role and our own purpose must be understood within the context of the more all-encompassing purpose of Gaia, and indeed that of the cosmos itself. To the extent that we can align ourselves—as individuals and as a species—with this greater purpose, new possibilities may emerge that we can scarcely imagine. But to do so, we must first try to discern more clearly just what this purpose is: What is the wisdom that the cosmos reveals to us?

THE WISDOM OF THE COSMOS

The cosmogenic principle states that the evolution of the universe will be characterized by differentiation, autopoiesis, and communion *throughout time and space and at every level of reality. These three terms—differentiation, autopoiesis, and communion—refer to the governing themes and basal intentionality of all existence.* (T. Berry and Swimme 1992, 71)

The basic drive of evolution is to increase depth. . . . Consciousness unfolds more and more, realizes itself more and more, comes into manifestation more and more. . . . Because evolution goes beyond what went before, but because it must embrace what went before, then its very nature is to transcend and include, and in this it has an inherent directionality, a secret impulse, toward increasing depth, increasing intrinsic value, increasing consciousness. . . . We—and all beings—are drenched in this meaning, afloat in a current of care and profound value, ultimate significance, intrinsic awareness. (Wilber 1996, 40-42)

Ecology . . . is a faith in the wisdom of those forces that created the natural world and the cosmos of which it is part; it is a faith in the latter's ability to provide us with extraordinary benefits—those required to satisfy our most fundamental needs. It is a faith in our capacity to develop cultural patterns that can enable us to maintain its integrity and stability. (Goldsmith 1998, 96)

As we wrote in the prologue of this book, the *Tao of Liberation* is a search for wisdom, the wisdom needed to effect profound and liberatory changes in our world. We chose to describe this wisdom using the ancient Chinese word Tao, a way or path leading to harmony, peace, and right relationship. The Tao can be understood as a principle of order that constitutes the common ground of creation; it is the flowing structure of the universe that cannot be described, only tasted. The Tao is the wisdom that lies at the very heart of the cosmos, encapsulating the essence of its purpose and direction. Our exploration of cosmology has very much been an attempt to taste the Tao, to feel its contours, to intuit its ways. Ultimately, this wisdom cannot be encapsulated in words, but words may at least serve to point us in the right direction.

In order to contemplate this wisdom of the cosmos, it may be helpful briefly to review some of the insights that our exploration of cosmology has provided us:

1. From Machine to Organism

In the mechanistic, reductionalist cosmology we have termed the "cosmology of domination," the universe was understood as analogous to a great machine. By breaking down things into their component parts, it was possible to gain a fundamental understanding of reality that in turn enabled humanity (or "man") to have control—or "mastery"—over nature. Matter was seen to consist of tiny, indivisible entities called atoms. Matter, energy, space, and time were all understood to be distinct entities.

In the holistic, evolutionary cosmology that we call the "cosmology of liberation," the principal metaphor is that of an organism. The essence of reality lies not in substances but in systems and their relationships. A system is like a vortex which maintains its organizational identity even as the matter within it changes. All systems are embedded in larger systems, and all systems are made up of smaller ones—that is, systems always exist in relationship to something else, and their identity is always an identity-in-relationship determined in part by the entire "holarchy."

In this new view, atoms have dissolved into effervescent whirlpools of pure relationality. The deeper one plunges into the microcosm, the more deeply relational and interconnected it appears to be. All subatomic wave/particles are understood to be interconnected through both space and time. Matter, energy, space, and time coexist in a dynamic web of relationship. Indeed, all these manifestations of reality may well spring from a deeper level of unity, the pregnant void, a vast sea of potential energy that both creates and sustains them moment by moment.

In this cosmology of liberation, matter is no longer considered to be dead or inert; rather, all of reality is in some sense alive. All systems have the capacity to give birth to new forms through the process of creative emergence. Insofar as all systems are related to one another, the cosmos itself is also considered to be alive. In particular, our own planet demonstrates coherent dynamics that both maintain the conditions necessary for life and continue to birth forth new forms over time.

2. From the Deterministic and the Random to Creative Emergence

In its early manifestations, the cosmology of domination was essentially deterministic in nature. By knowing the precise starting conditions of every body in the cosmos and by understanding the eternal laws of physics, it was theoretically possible to predict all that would come in the future. Cause and effect were related in a clear, straightforward manner. Later, determinism was supplanted by random chance and the laws of probability, particularly on the atomic and molecular scale. In both views, however, the possibility of creative causality and the emergence of authentic novelty did not really exist.

In the cosmology of liberation, true creativity and novelty are a fundamental dynamic of the cosmos. In complex systems, nothing can be predicted with certainty. Cause and effect are related through nonlinear dynamics: each depends on the other, resulting in reciprocal causality or dependent co-arising. Yet things do not occur randomly. There is an order characterized by attractors (and possibly formed by morphic fields), but these attractors do not fully determine what is to be. Further, one attractor can be transcended and a new one can come into being, allowing for genuine creativity. Authentic transformation is always a possibility, and given the right conditions, radical change can happen in a very short period of time. In such a context, the power to transform is not determined by brute force, but rather by sensitive intuition of timing and place.

3. From Eternity to Evolution

In the cosmology of domination, the universe was understood to be essentially eternal and largely changeless in nature. Yet the laws of thermodynamics also implied that the cosmos would eventually die a slow but inexorable heat death. Evolutionary dynamics on Earth were seen as an exception, and these dynamics themselves were driven by random mutations, the drive for survival, and ruthless competition.

In the new cosmology, the universe is understood to be—not just a place, but a process—a story of cosmogenesis unfolding toward greater levels of complexity, diversity, self-organization, and communion. The cosmos has a definite beginning and may even have a definite end. The unfolding of the cosmos occurs in stages marked by a series of unrepeatable moments. There was time for the cosmos to be born, a time for hydrogen to organize itself, a time for the formation of the galaxies. The heavier elements necessary for life were not available until they were formed in the heart of stars and then dispersed through the galaxy by the explosive force of supernovas. On our own planet, there was a limited window of opportunity when life could evolve before the warming sun would make such an act impossible. Fortunately, life seized this opportunity and began to transform our planet, regulating conditions so that life could continue to develop and flourish.

Here on Earth, we can see that evolution cannot be explained solely—or even primarily—by random mutations and the survival of the fittest. Indeed, evolution is marked by dynamics of cooperation and symbiosis, and mutations seem to happen in a coordinated, purposeful fashion. Evolution moves toward ever greater levels of complexity and depth—one might well say, toward greater mindfulness.

In an evolving cosmos, the so-called "laws" of physics could themselves evolve over time. The fine balance of the four fundamental forces, for example, may actually be a carefully chosen habit. Indeed, the evolution of the cosmos could well be accompanied by the evolution of fields of memory—morphic fields—which are themselves related to one another in nested holarchies and which together may form a great cosmic field analogous in some ways to the *anima mundi* of old, but dynamic and evolutionary in nature.

4. From Objectivity to Participation

In the cosmology of domination, the observer was understood to be separated from what they observed. Indeed, the entire foundation of scientific objectivity rested on this assumed separation. Relationship implied emotional attachment and this was seen to undermine objective knowledge. Ideally, a scientist was most effective when most detached from their object of study.

In the new cosmology, we understand that the observer is always related to what is observed. Indeed, subatomic physics would suggest that the observer always affects what is observed through the very act of observation. We are all participants in a greater whole, so we can never separate ourselves from what we would endeavor to know. In this perspective, relationship and participation are understood as keys to authentic knowledge. We can only truly know that which we ourselves are part of. Knowledge, then, is in some sense bound up with love for what we desire to know.

5. From Purposelessness to Meaning

The dominant cosmology of the past few centuries vigorously rejected any sense of purpose outside the sphere of human affairs. The unfolding of the cosmos was understood to be based on the laws of random chance combined with eternal laws. At best, life itself was the result of fortuitous circumstances, but there was no purpose, no drive, and no direction evident in the unfolding of the cosmos. Even living organisms—apart from humans—were devoid of purpose. They may have *appeared* to be purposeful, but in many ways they were little better than machines, or *automata*, who simply created the illusion of purpose.

In the cosmology of liberation, the entire universe is understood to be imbued with a deep and abiding sense of purpose. This is not, however, a design or blueprint, but rather a kind of allurement drawing the evolution of the cosmos in a certain direction or toward a nondeterminative pattern like an "attractor," or a hidden wisdom (or "Tao") that subtly shapes the unfolding of reality. In one sense, this implies a goal, but that goal may also itself be evolving.

Humanity, as a creation of the cosmos, is bound up in its purpose. Our choices, perhaps, may at times impede the unfolding of the cosmic purpose—and we may even be capable of thwarting certain paths that could have furthered cosmic evolution. Ultimately, though, our own fulfillment lies in aligning ourselves with the Tao and finding our own unique contribution to the writing of the cosmic story.

How, though, are we to do this? In seeking such a path, it is helpful to identify some of the key dynamics that seem to manifest the Tao woven into the fabric of the cosmos. One useful framework for doing this is that of the so-called cosmogenic principle outlined by Thomas Berry and Brian Swimme in their lyric book *The Universe Story* (1992). According to this principle, three key characteristics mark the cosmic story of evolution: differentiation, autopoiesis, and communion.[7] Indeed, these three characteristics are so fundamental that the very existence of a structured cosmos depends on them: "Were there no differentiation, the universe would collapse into a homogeneous smudge; were there no subjectivity [or autopoiesis], the universe would collapse into inert, dead,

---

7. These same dynamics were first introduced from the perspective of systems theory; see pp. 202-3 above.

extension; were there no communion, the universe would collapse into isolated singularities of being" (T. Berry and Swimme 1992, 73).

Differentiation is used to speak of cosmic dynamics associated with the words "diversity, complexity, variation, disparity, multiform nature, heterogeneity, [and] articulation" (T. Berry and Swimme 1992, 72). The universe, over time, continually gives birth to new forms, new beings. As Berry and Swimme put it, the universe has "an outrageous bias for the novel, for the unfurling of surprise in prodigious dimensions throughout the vast range of existence" (1992, 74). Not only that, but the "creativity of each place and time differs from that of every other place and time" (1992, 74-75). In one way, we can think of differentiation as the cosmic drive toward *breadth*—an expansiveness not of quantity but of multiplicity.

The cosmos did not remain an undifferentiated soup of elementary particles, but instead chose to form structure. As we have noted, this was possible only because the great expansive surge of the cosmos's birth was finely balanced with the attractive dynamics of gravitation. Because of this delicate tension of *yin* and *yang*, the four basic forces came into being, hydrogen atoms formed, galaxies coalesced, and stars and planets were birthed forth. Eventually, life began on our own planet, and with it a new explosion of creativity and differentiation followed. In each of these stages, unique individuals sprang forth: no two galaxies, no two stars, no two living cells, are truly identical. Coming to know something is always, in part, a process of recognizing its uniqueness:

> The multiform relatedness demanded by a differentiated universe rests upon the fact that each individual thing in the universe is ineffable. Scientific knowledge refers ultimately to the way in which structures are similar, whether stars, or atoms, or cells, or societies. But in the universe, to be is to be different. To be is to be a unique manifestation of existence. The more thoroughly we investigate any one thing in the universe—the Milky Way galaxy, the fall of Rome, the species of a particular tree in the rainforest—the more we discover its uniqueness. Science simultaneously deepens our understanding of a thing's structure and its ineffable uniqueness. Ultimately each thing remains as baffling as before, no matter how profound our understanding. (T. Berry and Swimme 1992, 74)

On Earth, the diversity of life forms has grown increasingly rich over time. This differentiation, as we have seen, was not driven primarily by the need for survival—indeed, bacteria, the most primitive life forms, are in some ways also the most resilient and adaptable. What is it, then, that impels the cosmos to become more differentiated? Could it be that the universe strives to engender beauty? That it, in some sense, delights in creativity? It would seem, indeed, that its very nature is found in its quest to give birth to novelty.

The drive toward diversity and differentiation seems to be in stark contrast to the monoculture mentality that undergirds the imperial enterprise of modern industrial capitalism. The idea of growing a single kind of crop in a field or creating a giant tree plantation; the push to impose a single, monolithic culture on the globe (even if it draws, at least superficially, on many cultural expressions); or the drive to promote a single political or economic model for the world, all seem to run counter to the path of cosmic evolution. On a personal level, the quest to "fit in" as opposed to having the courage to express one's own unique gifts and way of being can also be seen as a refusal to act in accordance with the Tao. Indeed, as Bruce Bochte points out, the way of differentiation requires strength and courage insofar as "differentiation is a path that has intrinsic loneliness involved with it" (1990, 18).

Indeed, mortality and death are in some sense bound up with differentiation. Insofar as unique individuals exist, death also becomes a reality. Bacteria, as a kind of collective microcosmic web, are nearly immortal—they were born four billion years ago and will probably persist for billions of years to come.[8] The same is not true for other organisms, particularly those who reproduce sexually to create genetically unique—and unrepeatable—individuals. We could even understand death as a process that creates space for new individuals to arise, so that the creativity of our planet may be continually renewed. In this light, we must also learn to see that "mortality is a blessing to us—an awareness that our time is finite. We have [only] this moment to be who we are" (Bochte 1990, 18).

From a more cosmic perspective, we could say that differentiation and the creation of novelty are inseparable from dynamics of violence and loss. The universe continually makes space for novelty through the destruction of what has come before. Creation itself is often violent. The original cosmic seed burst forth with an unimaginable violence that we cannot begin to fathom, yet that violence proved to be the mother of creativity. Supernovas explode with a ferocity capable of destroying their surrounding planetary systems, yet without the heavy elements formed in such explosions, no life would have been possible on our own planet. Mass extinction events on Earth have often been followed by surges in evolutionary creativity. Indeed, over the course of Earth's history, 99 percent of species that once existed are now extinct. Without such a loss, however, the variety of forms that we see today could never have come into being. Like the dance of Shiva, creation follows destruction, and destruction follows creation. There can be no novelty without loss. As Bochte observes:

> The primeval fireball is lost forever. Our sun will perish in five billion years, forever. The dinosaurs were magnificent creatures. They had their day. Without the elimination of the dinosaurs, the mammals would never have developed [as they have]. So, too, the mammals will have to deal with the demands of the universe. We must embrace loss as an ultimate reality.
>
> Evil is the demand that loss is not real. Our society has organized itself for the denial of that reality. . . .
>
> The denial of loss is the refusal to enter into the sacrificial event of the

---

8. As each bacterium reproduces by mitosis, or simple cellular division, there is effectively a continuity between each modern bacterium and the first bacterium that was birthed into existence four billion years ago.

universe. If loss is embraced, every moment of our lives is understood as disappearing into the ongoing story of the universe. Our creativity is energizing the whole. (1990, 23)

While it can be difficult to embrace the reality of loss, with it comes the possibility of constant renewal and change, including authentic liberation. The cosmic drive toward differentiation, diversity, novelty, and complexity means that the creative impulse is woven into the very fabric of the universe. In other words, the Tao is always moving toward the birth of new forms. What will come will build on what has come before, but it is not determined by it. If humanity at this moment seems entrapped in oppressive and destructive habits, practices, and systems, this does not determine our future. We can move toward something new, although this will inevitably require that we let go of the old. In the case of those benefiting disproportionately from the current system, this will mean sacrificing some of what is held to be dear; but if we can embrace that loss, we open the way for truly liberating creativity.

The second major cosmic dynamic, *autopoiesis*, refers to cosmic dynamics associated with "subjectivity, self-manifestation, sentience, self-organization, dynamic centers of experience, presence, identity, inner principle of being, voice, [and] interiority" (T. Berry and Swimme 1992, 72). We could think of this as the cosmos's drive toward greater *depth*, including the drive toward increasing mindfulness, and even consciousness. Autopoiesis is closely related to differentiation. As entities become more distinct from each other, their own identities as unique individuals become clearer. At the same time, the maintenance of their own individual identities depends on the dynamics of self-organization. Indeed, the essence of each entity lies not in their substance—matter and energy may constantly be exchanged with the being's surroundings—but rather on the coherence of their inner organizational dynamics, on autopoiesis.

Berry and Swimme observe that autopoiesis "refers to the power each thing has to participate directly in the cosmos-creating endeavour." A star, for example, organizes the hydrogen and helium within it to generate energy. "That which organizes this vast entity of elements and action is precisely what we mean by the star's power of self-articulation" (1992, 75). Similarly, an atom also organizes the subatomic particles within it, and a cell—though in constant flux—maintains its coherent organizational structure. As we have seen, we can also think of the living Earth itself—or Gaia—as a self-organizing system with characteristics transcending its component parts. Over time, the depth of interiority manifest in the cosmos has grown:

Autopoiesis points to the interior dimension of things. Even the simplest atom cannot be understood by considering only its physical structure or the outer world of external relationships with other things. Things emerge with an inner capacity of self-manifestation. Even an atom possesses a quantum of radical spontaneity. In latter developments in the universe this minimal dimension of spontaneity grows until it becomes a dominant fact of behavior, as in the life of a gray whale. (T. Berry and Swimme 1992, 75-76)

We could also think of this growth in spontaneity as a growth in playfulness. Creativity and play go hand in hand. An artist must be willing to try new things, to dare experiments that might very well not be successful. Indeed, one could argue that an artist is at her or his best when that person has no thought of success or failure, but simply enters into the moment and rejoices in the act of creation. So too, the cosmos itself is at play, experimenting with new forms, many of which presumably come to naught. In our own planet's evolution, the phenomenon of punctuated evolution has a flavor of playful experimentation to it. There can be an explosive creation of new forms in a short period of time, but few of these are actually successful in the longer term.

In the realm of animal behavior, we can see the growth of what we might term the more whimsical aspect of play. Mammals and birds, for example, seem to display more playful behavior than reptiles, fish, or insects. Indeed, much of mammalian behavior seems to exude a kind of joyful freedom that is not directly related to survival in any apparent way—albeit it may increase social bonding. (Think, for example, of the playful frolicking of dolphins or seals.) In the case of humans, Brian Swimme (1985) points out that what differentiates us from our closest genetic relative—the chimpanzee (who shares 98 percent of our genetic heritage)—is a characteristic called *neoteny*, or delayed development. Stephen Jay Gould (1977) even argued that humans are essentially a neotenous species of chimpanzees insofar as our bone structure resembles that of juvenile chimps. Unlike chimps, who have difficulty learning new things once they reach maturity, humans retain the ability to learn throughout life. In essence, we remain in some respects like children, with all the playfulness and sense of wonder that this implies. Like the universe itself, we are made for creative play. Could we not understand this capacity for play as an expression of the growing interiority of the cosmos itself?

Another way to think of the increasing depth and subjectivity of the cosmos is as a growth toward increasing mindfulness. As we saw in our discussion of systems theory, this growth of mindfulness involves processes such as memory, learning, and decision making that allow self-organizing entities to "bring forth a world" through the act of specifying a particular reality. This process does not require consciousness, but certainly the development of self-reflective consciousness in the cosmos can be seen as a part of this evolutionary movement toward greater depth, greater interiority, and greater mindfulness.

Why, exactly, does the cosmos move in this direction? Ultimately, of course, that is a mystery, but perhaps—as we saw in our discussion of quantum physics—mind is in some way immanent in the cosmos, present from the beginning in the implicate order. Over time, the process of cosmic evolution increasingly manifests mind in the explicate order. Humanity is certainly one example of that manifestation, but we may not be unique in our consciousness. Indeed, on our own planet, other—perhaps in their own way just as complex—forms of consciousness may exist. Certainly, in a cosmos as vast as our own, many other conscious beings may exist.

The philosopher Ken Wilber sees the movement toward greater depth, interiority, and mind as the cosmos giving birth, in some sense, to the divine into the realm of manifestation, or the explicate order:

> We are part and parcel of this immense intelligence, this Spirit-in-action, this God-in-the-making. We don't have to think of God as some mythic figure outside of the display, running the show. Nor must we picture it as some merely immanent Goddess, lost in the forms of her own production. Evolution is both God and Goddess, transcendence and immanence. It is immanent in the process itself, wove into the fabric of the Kosmos; but it everywhere transcends its own productions, and brings forth anew in every moment. (1996, 42)

In this perspective, we can understand the mindful activity of humanity as a part of the deepening consciousness of the universe itself, and perhaps even as a manifestation of "God-in the-making." We cannot know all the ways in which the cosmos is evolving mind, but at the very least we know that it has become conscious through us. How, then, as a species, can we contribute to the mindful activity of the universe? Insofar as we deepen our own spirits, do we not deepen the spirit of the cosmos itself? Do we not, to paraphrase the words of the great Christian mystic Meister Eckhart, give birth to God in our own time? In some sense, then, our responsibility as a species is not just to our own heritage, nor even to that of our beautiful planet; rather, we are called to contribute to the deepening of the cosmos's own interiority and spirit.

The third great cosmic dynamic, *communion*, is associated with "interrelatedness, interdependence, kinship, mutuality, internal relatedness, reciprocity, complementarity, interconnectivity, and affiliation" (T. Berry and Swimme 1992, 72) as well as contextuality. We could also think of this aspect in terms of the growth in *relationality*, or even of intimacy, that in some sense binds the cosmos together. In the mystical tradition of the Sufis, this underlying dynamic of communion or attraction is called *Ishq*: it is a deep, divine love that acts as a kind of cosmic glue, binding all together.

This communion is manifest in part through the phenomenon of quantum entanglement which mysteriously connects every wave/particle in the universe with every other one reaching back to the first moment when all was one. Because of this, what affects one subatomic entity, in some sense, simultaneously affects them all. Atoms themselves, instead of substance, are best understood as a kind of nexus of pure relationality. At another level, gravity binds the entire universe together, making it possible for galaxies, stars, and planets to form. Our entire solar system—from the sun to the tiniest microorganism on Earth—is bound in communion to other stars that have existed in the past and that birthed forth all the elements heavier than helium. As Berry and Swimme observe:

> The universe evolves into beings that are differentiated from each other, and that organize themselves. But in addition to this, the universe advances into

community—into a differentiated web of relationships among sentient centers of creativity. . . .

In the very first instant when the primitive particles rushed forth, every one of them was connected to every other one in the entire universe. At no time in the future existence of the universe will they ever arrive at a point of disconnection. Alienation for a particle is a theoretical impossibility. For galaxies, too, relationships are the fact of existence. Each galaxy is directly connected to the hundred billion galaxies of the universe, and there will never come a time when a galaxy's destiny does not involve each of the galaxies of the universe.

Nothing is itself without everything else. (1992, 77)

On Earth, all organisms are related through their radical interdependence on each other; indeed, this communion is so strong that they form a single entity—Gaia—that transcends the mere sum of the parts and that acts holistically to maintain the conditions necessary for life to thrive, modifying the atmosphere, hydrosphere, and geology of the planet in the process. Similarly, the cooperative, symbiotic nature of the evolutionary process on our planet manifests the relational wisdom of the cosmos. This does not deny dynamics of competition and self-assertion—which we can understand as related to both differentiation and autopoiesis—but even competitive dynamics are embedded in the context of a greater whole that functions as a living community.

One particular aspect of the relational nature of the cosmos—and of life on Earth in particular—that stands out is generosity. The universe is full of lavish excess, but such excess also nurtures the relational bonds that sustain the cooperative dynamics of the whole. As Martha Heyneman writes:

From a thermodynamic point of view, living things are dissipative systems, productive of entropy. Enormous quantities of energy are spent in evolving and maintaining them. Just as in chemistry huge excesses of reagent are needed to drive a reaction away from the "attractor" of equilibrium, huge expenditures of energy, productive of entropy, are required for just "stayin' alive." It is like the lavish excesses of nature, wasting billions of acorns to produce one oak tree—but then, the waste of one is the food of another. One [being's] garbage is another['s] gourmet dinner. The decaying acorns fertilize other trees. The sun produces enormous quantities of energy, and a minute fraction of this "waste" suffices to sustain all life on Earth.

We living things are like tiny Dixie cups in the magnanimous Niagara of the sun. This huge excess seems to be required to keep us alive. We are expensive. We are bought with a price. (1993, 132)

While we may think of differentiation, autopoiesis, and communion as three distinct dynamics, in fact they are part of a single cosmogenic principle: the cosmos grows in breath, depth, and relationality as part of a single movement. At first, this may seem strange to us. The relationship between differentiation and subjectivity is clearer perhaps: as an entity differentiates itself from others, it is not surprising that its own self-identity would also deepen. But might not this make its communion with others less strong? Surprisingly, though, greater diversity and greater complexity actually strengthen the bonds of communion. This can perhaps be seen most clearly in the example of the maturation of ecosystems.

As Edward Goldsmith (1998) points out, simpler and less integrated systems—like a pioneer ecosystem—are able to adapt to a wider variety of environmental conditions, but have a relatively weak ability to actually regulate the conditions, leading to a certain kind of vulnerability. As ecosystems become more evolved, they become more complex and the species that make up the ecological community become more specialized.

For example, goats are generalists that can eat nearly anything, and they often inhabit relatively simple ecosystems. In contrast, the species of a rainforest tend to be far more specialized. A particular tree may have a preference for very particular conditions, while animals and insects may eat only certain plants, or even certain parts of certain plants, allowing them to make better use of their habitat. Similarly, predators may choose a very particular kind of prey. Because of this, the rainforest ecosystem can support a wider variety of life.

Yet the degree of specialization also makes the species who take part in it more interdependent. Therefore, increased differentiation actually requires increased integration or communion. As differentiation and communion grow, so too does the level of complexity of the system as a whole—that is, its self-organizing dynamics are deepened. At the same time, it gains a greater ability to actually create and sustain its own environmental conditions. For example a rainforest actually moderates its own temperature and facilitates the formation of clouds, which in turn provide it with rain.

The example of ecosystems is instructive for human societies. One could argue that, in the age of modernity, we have emphasized a particular kind of subjectivity—in the form of individualism. We have grown, in some respects, in knowledge—and certainly we have become more and more specialized. Yet it would be hard to argue that this has always led to greater *depth* of interiority in most respects. One could even venture to say that we have gained knowledge, but lost a degree of wisdom. Moreover, we increasingly seek our happiness—not in creative endeavors, in spiritual practices, or in cultivating the bonds of communion—but rather in the pursuit of material gain in the form of consumerism. In reality, then, we seem to have chosen to emphasize *exteriority* over *interiority*.

Meanwhile, our sense of community has been eroded. In many modern urban societies, we have retreated into nuclear families, and increasingly even these are breaking down. Few of us know our neighbors well. The bonds of relationship and community have been weakened, in some cases to an extreme. At the same time, as we have previously noted, we have often been subsumed into a superficial monoculture that threatens authentic diversity.

Certainly, not all is negative. In many places, there is a growing appreciation for diversity: racism, sexism, and religious intolerance are being challenged.

Indeed, there is a movement to go beyond mere tolerance, to actually celebrate diversity. In some places, too, people are experimenting with new forms of community that transcend the old compartmentalizations into family, tribe, village, or state.

Yet, as a whole, we have not created a society that truly endeavors to broaden diversity, to deepen interiority, and to strengthen relationality. This becomes particularly apparent when we consider the vast chasm that separates rich from poor, and perhaps even more so when we consider the psychic separation of human society from the larger community of life on our planet. Indeed, we seem to be systematically destroying the diversity of life and replacing complex ecosystems with much simpler and more fragmented ones. If we are truly to rise to the challenge of the crises that confront us, we must radically re-envision our place in the universe, and particularly in the Earth community, which genuinely draws on the wisdom of the cosmos, the Tao, as is illustrated in the dynamics of the cosmogenic principle.

REINVENTING THE HUMAN

[The solution to this crisis] would be to reinvent ourselves, at a species level, in a way that enables us to live with mutually enhancing relationships. Mutually enhancing relationships—not just with humans but with all beings—so that our activities enhance the world. At the present time, our interactions degrade everything. (Swimme 2001, 39)

When we began our exploration of cosmology, we noted that a fundamental question for humanity is whether the universe is a friendly place. What is certainly apparent is that we are, very much, creatures of the cosmos. Earth is our home and we are part of a larger planetary entity that maintains the conditions of life. We can even understand ourselves as one expression of the emergent mind of the cosmos itself. In one sense, then, we need to transcend the question totally, for the universe is not so much a place as a process, or a story, of which we ourselves are a part. Yet, in another sense, insofar as we are truly "at home" in the cosmos, insofar as Earth birthed us into existence, we could say that, yes, we are in an essentially friendly place. That does not deny the reality of suffering, the need for sacrifice, the times of grief, or the pain of loss. Yet most of us do cherish the gift of life. We also know that Earth—together with the sun, which bathes us in energy—provides us with sustenance, both material and spiritual, and that we are utterly dependent on its generosity for our own continued existence.

Unfortunately, we do not seem to be very friendly to the cosmos, and particularly to our home planet and the community of creatures with whom we share it. Indeed, many of our actions seem to run counter to the course of evolution on Earth. Instead of nurturing the complexity and diversity of ecosystems, we are replacing mature forests, savannahs, and marshlands with primitive, unsustainable monocultures. In the process, tens of thousands of species are driven to extinction each year. At a cultural level, thousands of human languages are also disappearing, and with them thousands of unique ways of conceptualizing and interacting with the world. As people are displaced from their traditional lands and move to cities, they are further alienated from the wider ecosphere, and cultural diversity erodes.

As evolution progresses, competition should give way to increased cooperation—something that ecologists call "mutualism." In contrast, we have been reducing complexity and accentuating the competitive element. At a cultural level, this is evident as "progress" leads to the breakdown of traditional communities and families. In its place, we have been creating societies that value competition over cooperation, destroying the deep relationality that gives life its meaning.

Similarly, as evolution advances, systems become increasingly self-sufficient as they learn to recycle materials and energy more effectively. Indigenous cultures, too, have traditionally been able to produce and sustain the essentials for life from local resources. In contrast, the society of modernity has created an unparalleled level of waste and inefficiency. Local communities are no longer self-sufficient, but rather depend on exports to generate income and to buy imports from afar, leading to vast expenditures of energy in transportation.

Not surprisingly, Edward Goldsmith has concluded that humanity in the age of modernity has actually been "reversing ecological succession," transforming a complex ecology into a much simpler, less efficient, and less sustainable one: "Today, with the globalization of progress, we are rapidly heading toward a global ecospheric disclimax in which modern [humanity] will have effectively reversed three thousand million years of evolution to create an impoverished and degraded world that is ever less capable of sustaining life" (1998, 424).

Thomas Berry refers to this process of ongoing degradation as "biocide" and "geocide"—which we might alternatively term "ecocide"—and considers this the greatest ethical challenge that humanity has ever faced:

> We find ourselves ethically destitute just when, for the first time, we are faced with ultimacy, the irreversible closing down of the Earth's functioning in its major life systems. Our ethical traditions know how to deal with suicide, homicide, and even genocide; but these traditions collapse entirely when confronted with biocide, the extinction of the vulnerable life systems of the Earth, and geocide, the devastation of the Earth itself. (1999, 104)

We do not, however, need to continue on this path. As we have seen, there is nothing "natural"—much less inevitable—about this course. Humanity is part of the cosmic process, so the cosmogenic principle must be part of our essential nature. Indeed, looking at the long history of indigenous cultures on our planet, we can see that diversity, interiority, and cooperation have all been marked characteristics of autochthonous peoples. Even in agricultural societies, these dynamics clearly played an important role. It is only in the age of modernity—as the project of empire building took on a global dimension—that ecological destruction has become truly widespread and systematic on a planetary scale;

it is only now that we have created societies that seem fixated on monoculture, consumerism, and competition.

Thomas Berry refers to our current, anti-ecological time as the "Technozoic" era. He proposes that our challenge is to leave this destructive paradigm behind and to inaugurate a new, "Ecozoic" era:

> We are now experiencing a moment of significance far beyond what any of us can imagine. What can be said is that the foundations of a new historical period, the Ecozoic Era, have been established in every realm of human affairs. The mythic vision has been set into place. The distorted dream of an industrial technological paradise is being replaced by the more viable dream of a mutually enhancing human presence within an ever-renewing organic-based Earth community. The dream drives the action. In the larger cultural context the dream becomes the myth that both guides and drives the action. (1999, 204)

At the same time, though, Berry warns that this "moment of grace" will not last forever. The transformation must take place quite soon, or the opportunity will be lost forever. Yet we are not without hope:

> In the immense story of the universe, that so many of these dangerous moments have been navigated successfully is some indication that the universe is for us rather than against us. We need only summon these forces to our support in order to succeed. It is difficult to believe that the purposes of the universe or of the planet Earth will ultimately be thwarted, although the human challenge to these purposes must never be underestimated. (Berry 1999, 204)

Indeed, we must clearly understand that as a species—despite our apparently vast powers—we cannot, acting alone, hope to heal the planet that we have ourselves have so grievously harmed. Our only hope is to allow the cosmos itself to act through us. We cannot control this process, but we can allow ourselves to become part of it. Indeed, the Earth is no doubt doing all it can to heal the harm done, but humans often impede this process. We cannot "master" the life-giving power of the Earth, but we can invoke it. We cannot direct the healing process, but we can actively cooperate and participate in it.

Essentially, this requires that we open ourselves to the Tao, that we receptively tune ourselves to its whispered wisdom, and that we allow it to work through us. Will this ensure the continued flourishing of complex life on Earth? We cannot say for sure. When Brian Swimme was asked whether we still have time to make the changes needed to overcome the crises we face, he remarked:

> Well, I think the universe is carrying this out. But we get to participate in it consciously. And in a real sense, it's very important that we participate. At the same time, it's important to remember that we're not doing it. I mean, the universe has been working on this for a long time, and right now, it's exploding within human consciousness. But we're not in charge of it. So I

haven't got the slightest idea if we have enough time. That's almost a second-ary question to me. It just seems so deeply right that we be thinking about this and working on this. But I think all of the spiritual traditions are going to be accelerated as they learn about this new cosmology and this moment that we face as a human species. There'll be an amplification taking place. So, it could go very quickly. Or it might take thousands of years. I don't know. (2001, 135)

We can understand the conscious participation of humanity in the movement toward greater diversity, interiority, and communion as the process of *liberation*. In other words, to the extent that we actively cooperate with the cosmogenic principle, we set ourselves on the path of liberation. At a personal level, the liberation that Buddhists call enlightenment—or *satori*—illustrates this process. *Satori* can be understood as a radical breakthrough that enables a person to apprehend reality directly, allowing one to perceive the very nature of *suchness*. In so doing, the enlightened one becomes keenly aware of communion with all other beings, and the cosmos itself. Indeed, Zen Buddhists speak in terms of nonduality, overcoming the subject/object distinction. That does not, however, negate the reality of diversity, but rather allows for a new kind of differentiation. An enlightened individual can be truly one's own, unique self, different from all others, but at the same time has no need to change others. Indeed, relationship to all other beings is characterized by a deep sense of respect and compassion. At the same time, enlightenment leads to a deepening of interiority. In fact, a deep sense of awareness or mindfulness is a key aspect of *satori*.

At a social level, we can also think of liberation in terms of the cosmogenic principle. Liberation means creating a society where diversity is truly valued, celebrated, and broadened—including gender, sexual, spiritual, cultural, and ecological diversity. This calls for a renunciation of the paradigm of monocul-ture in all of its manifestations.

Liberation also requires a deepening of subjectivity or interiority, valuing our participation in the "cosmos-creating endeavor"; we must no longer seek our fulfillment in the pursuit of material wealth or consumerism, but rather strive to enhance life-giving expressions of creativity, be they what have traditionally been considered artistic activities, or the creative participation in the restoration of complex ecosystems. Liberation also means valuing what we might call the "spiritual arts" including meditative practices, spiritual dance and movement, and the cultivation of mystical identification with the Earth and the cosmos itself, all of which aim directly to deepen interiority.

Further, liberation is the process of deepening communion and relationality at every level. As individuals, this means that we need to revalue and reclaim the "relational self" by moving toward more complex relationships and broadening our sense of identification with other beings, that is, widening the circles of our compassion. At the level of human society, this means overcoming injustices that divide people from each other and from the living community of Earth as a whole, working to overcome the vast inequality between rich and poor and the rebuilding of authentic community. Ultimately, it requires that we find ways peacefully to coexist with the other creatures who inhabit our planet, finding new ways of truly living in harmony with the greater community of life of which we, too, are a part.

We can also understand liberation as a process that will move us from the Technozoic to the Ecozoic era, bringing about the Great Turning. This process will require, above all, a fundamental shift in human consciousness. In a very real way, we are called to reinvent ourselves as a species; indeed, a key aspect of our liberatory process consists of this reinvention. While this is no small challenge, it is not one beyond our capabilities. Of all creatures, humans seem to be the least habitual in nature. We need to learn nearly everything and have very few, if any, instincts. As neotenous beings, we have the capacity to learn even after we have reached maturity.

Indeed, in our relatively brief history on this planet, we have reinvented ourselves time and time again. We were born in the forests and savannahs of Africa, but we were able to adapt to life in the ice age. We began as hunter-gatherers, moved on to become farmers, and then reinvented ourselves as industrial, city-dwelling people. There is no reason why we cannot reinvent ourselves yet again. Indeed, it should be easier to move toward a paradigm that is in harmony with evolutionary processes than it was to make the transition to our current, anti-ecological way of being. If we open ourselves to the wisdom of the cosmos itself, to the Tao, there can be little doubt that we can indeed fundamentally remake ourselves once again. But just how do we go about doing so? There can be no simple answer to such a question, but four key interrelated challenges seem apparent:

- We must learn to embrace limits, definitively renouncing the pseudo-cosmology of consumerism and the economics of growth.
- We must find our meaning and fulfillment in our active participation in the process of cosmic evolution, and particularly in what we can call the "Dream of the Earth."
- We must deepen our communion with our living planet, which is the material and psychic source of our sustenance.
- We must seek out a new kind of ethics based on care and the enhancement of life, creativity, and beauty.

Embracing Limits

As the power of humans has grown, so too have our appetites. As we have seen, unbounded, cancerous economic growth threatens the well-being of our planet, seriously eroding its capacity to sustain complex ecosystems. In the process, the diversity of life is undermined, leading to the greatest mass extinction since the disappearance of the dinosaurs sixty-five million years ago.

At the same time, if all of humanity were to consume the Earth's bounty at the same level as the peoples of North America and Europe, we would require approximately four more planets like Earth to sustain such consumption over the long term (at current population levels). If we are to achieve a just and sustainable lifestyle for all people, then those of us who consume the most will need to drastically reduce our level of consumption.

A key challenge for the reinvention of humanity as a species, therefore, will entail the need to embrace limits, effectively renouncing the addictive behavior of consumerism. Indeed, as Thomas Berry (1999) points out, the "law of limits" is a fundamental cosmological and ecological principle, recognized as an integral demand for humans in both the principle of the Dharma and that of the Tao. Yet much of modernity has represented a rejection of this fundamental imperative:

> Recently humanity has attempted to relate to . . . cosmic realities by destroying resistance, denying intrinsic cost, and magnifying the intensity of its desires. If we meet resistance, we work to eliminate it. If we are asked by the universe to make the payment necessary for development, our response is to avoid the bill. On the other hand, if we discover any new human desires, we invest tremendous effort in fanning these desires, no matter how superficial and costly they are for other members of Earth. Our refusal to accept any limitations for movement in space has resulted in our destructive transportation systems, imposed on the planet without regard for the rest of the Earth community. Our refusal to accept limitations on our desire for consumer items has resulted in the disruption of ecological communities throughout the planet. Our desire to have children without regard for the capacities of the biome has resulted in the explosion of human numbers and the consequent sufferings inflicted upon many billions of them. (T. Berry and Swimme 1992, 57)

The culture of modernity has come to see limitation as a negative, yet any kind of authentic balance requires a degree of restraint. The creative impulse of the cosmos springs forth from the creative tension of *yin* and *yang*, for example, the finely balanced forces of expansion and contraction which permitted the universe to develop structure, or the complex dynamics of reciprocity at the heart of a thriving ecosystem. As we have noted previously, "the universe thrives on the edge of a knife." Without balance, without limitation, creativity ceases and, ultimately, we are destroyed in the process.

Morris Berman (1981), drawing on the work of Gregory Bateson, suggests that we must renounce the "ethics of maxima" and replace them with an "ethics of optima." Optimizing is distinct from maximizing. For example, we need a certain amount of food to maintain our health, but too much leads to obesity and disease. Similarly, we need to balance the types of food we eat. The current lifestyle of many living in the global North has now far exceeded the bounds of optima, leading to the destruction of biodiversity, the exacerbation of inequalities between rich and poor, and the undermining of the life-sustaining systems of the planet itself.

In contrast, the ethics of optima draws on the insights of systems theory, noting that all living systems seek to optimize—not maximize—certain variables. The sustenance of life, as well as fulfillment and happiness, depends on striking a balance. Indeed, we could argue that the attempt to maximize in the material realm has caused us to neglect other aspects of living: Our obsession with *externality* has led to a loss of *interiority*. Embracing self-limitation in the material sphere challenges us to shift our idea of "progress" from the accumulation of wealth to the deepening of the spirit, the broadening of diversity, and the strengthening of bonds of relationality and reciprocity. This rebalancing, in turn, can actually lead to a greater sense of fulfillment and contentment. As Thomas Berry observes:

> As physical resources become less available, psychic energy must support the human project in a special manner. This situation brings us to a new reliance on powers within the universe and also to experience of the deeper self. The universe must be experienced as the Great Self. Each is fulfilled in the other: the Great Self is fulfilled in the individual self, the individual self is fulfilled in the Great Self. Alienation is overcome as soon as we experience this surge of energy from the source that has brought the universe through the centuries. New fields of energy become available to support the human venture. These new energies find expression and support in celebration. For in the end the universe can only be explained in terms of celebration. It is all an exuberant expression of existence itself. (1999, 170)

The Dream of the Earth

Our ability to embrace limits, then, depends in large part on our ability to deepen our interiority through conscious participation in the creativity of the cosmos itself. If we understand the movement of evolution as a process of increasing complexity and mindfulness, we can understand ourselves as one aspect of the emerging cosmic mind. In this light, when we act on behalf of the Earth, our perspective changes. For example, as John Seed points out, I will no longer see myself as "protecting the rainforest" but rather that "I am part of the rainforest protecting myself. I am that part of the rainforest recently emerged into thinking" (Seed et al. 1988, 36).

Ken Wilber refers to the emergence of this type of consciousness as the experience of the "Eco-Noetic Self" and notes that this does *not* mean that we simply recognize that we are "strands in the web" but rather that we try to perceive reality from the perspective of the web as a whole. "You are doing something no mere strand ever does—you are escaping your 'strandness,' *transcending* it, and becoming one with the entire display. To be aware of the whole system shows precisely that you are *not* merely a strand" (1996, 205).

It is only by adopting this wider perspective that we can truly find the wisdom to constrain the vast powers now available to us and to put them at the service of the greater whole. If we fail to broaden our sense of self to embrace the Earth, and perhaps the entire cosmos, we will always be in danger of using our powers for narrow, short-term goals that ultimately prove destructive to the greater whole, including future generations of humanity. On the other hand, if we can adopt this new perspective, if we can reconceive of progress in terms of deepening our conscious identification with the process of cosmic evolution, we can hope to channel our creativity in ways that will truly enable us to move into the Ecozoic era. We can reconceive of technology itself, ensuring that our creativity works *with*, not *against*, the natural world. Science and innovation will then have to be exercised in harmony with the needs of the Earth and be developed in an ecological context. Indeed, "our primary concern must be to restore the organic economy of the entire planet" by fostering its "entire range of life-systems" and establishing "our basic source of food and energy in the sun, which supplies the energy for the transformation of inanimate matter into living substance capable of nourishing the larger biosystems of Earth" (T. Berry 1999, 148-49).

One way of moving into this new mode of consciousness which serves as the foundation for harmonious creativity involves the remything of the cosmic story so that, at the deepest level of our beings, we feel its movement and understand its directionality. In so doing, we can gain a sense of the cosmic purpose in terms of an unfolding vision, or even of a dream. In fact, Thomas Berry speaks of our conscious involvement in the creativity and life-sustaining processes of the Earth in terms of participation in a "shared dream experience"—something that resonates with ancient wisdom of the aboriginal peoples of Australia:

> The creative process, whether in the human or the cosmological order, is too mysterious for easy explanation. . . . This process can be described in many ways, as a groping or as a feeling or imaginative process. The most appropriate way of describing this process seems to be that of dream realization. The universe seems to be the fulfilment of something so highly imaginative and so overwhelming that it must have been dreamed into existence.
>
> This awakening is our human participation in the dream of the Earth, the dream that is carried in its integrity not in any of Earth's cultural expressions but in the depths of our genetic coding. Therein the Earth functions at a depth beyond our capacity for active thought. We can only be sensitized to what is being revealed to us. We probably have not had such participation in the dream of the Earth since earlier shamanic times, but therein lies our hope for the future for ourselves and for the entire Earth community. (1999, 64-65)

Communion and Consciousness

The call to deepen our interiority is, at the same time then, a call to deepen our communion with the Earth and the entire cosmos. In some ways, this movement resembles a return to an earlier mode of consciousness, one still evident among many of the Earth's indigenous peoples. Yet it is also a return with a subtle but important difference. Joanna Macy (1991b), for example, notes that in traditional cultures, there existed a kind of "participation mystique" in which people felt no separation from the natural world around them. Then, in the next stage, humans moved into self-consciousness, where from the early agrarian cultures through to the Enlightenment and the age of modernity, we progressively distanced ourselves from nature. As noted earlier, this movement brought real gains in the sense of new forms of understanding, the ideal of human rights, as well as significant (and often life-saving) innovations, but it was also accompanied by a high cost in terms of the vast inequalities and the ecological destruction that it spawned.

We are now entering the third stage, when we are truly ready to begin to return to the sense of the whole. We do so, however, having developed self-reflective consciousness and a new vision of the cosmos that is the fruit of science. Unlike the second stage, however, we must now broaden our sense of self to include the embrace of the entire cosmos. If we began indeed as strands in the web—then painfully attempted to separate ourselves out—we now return to the web, relinquishing our sense of separateness but retaining our capacity of self-reflection, which enables us to see the web as a whole. In the words of Macy, "we are the world knowing itself. We can come home again—and participate in our world in a richer, more responsible and poignantly beautiful way than before, in our infancy. . . . [The world] can appear to us now both as self and as lover" (quoted in M. Fox 1994, 206).

Indeed, Thomas Berry warns that critical reflection is necessary if we are to avoid any romanticism as we move into an ecological mode of consciousness. He goes so far to say that "our intimacies with the natural world must not conceal the fact that we are engaged in a constant struggle with natural forces." Yet, he notes, even these struggles "strengthen the inner substance of the living world and provide the never-ending excitement of a grand adventure" (1999, 162). Ultimately, "the greatest human discoveries in the future will be the discovery of human intimacy with all those other modes of being that live with us on this planet, inspire our art and literature, reveal that numinous world whence all things come into being, and with which we exchange the very substance of life" (T. Berry 1999, 149).

A New Ethic

Within the context of deepening communion with the Earth, a new basis for ethics also emerges. From an ecological perspective, "a thing is right when it tends to preserve the integrity, stability and beauty of the biotic community. It is wrong when it tends to do otherwise" (Aldo Leopold, quoted in Goldsmith 1998, 97). Erich Jantsch, too, defines "ethical behaviour as behaviour which enhances evolution" (1980, 263). Similarly, the cosmogenic principle itself suggests a basis for ethics in its threefold call to broaden diversity, deepen interiority, and strengthen the bonds of relationality.

All of these foundations of ethics cause us to rethink—or at least to deepen—what we may have traditionally thought of as "good" or "evil." Yet, to some extent they hark back to older traditions. For example, as we have previously noted (p. 216), in the Aramaic language that Jesus spoke, the word normally translated as "evil"—*bisha*—presents the image of a fruit that is either unripe or rotten, indicating an action that is inappropriate for a certain time or place. In contrast, to be "blessed," "happy," or "aligned with the one" (the Aramaic word *tubwayhun*) is to bear ripe or appropriate fruit (Douglas-Klotz 1990). A good action is understood, then, as one that is appropriate for this time and place.

One way of thinking of this would be to say that, when our actions are truly an expression of the creativity of the cosmos, they are appropriate. Otherwise, they will not bear good fruit.

In addition, we should recall here the insight coming from the Navajo indigenous culture of the southwestern United States, where spirituality is conceived in terms of the Beauty Way (see p. 116). An ethics based on thinking beautiful thoughts, speaking beautiful words, and doing beautiful actions is one that truly aims at promoting harmony and right relationship. Moreover, such a way of being comes about not by force of will but by extending our sense of self, encompassing the beauty around us and harmonizing ourselves with it, so that we become a part of this unfolding beauty ourselves. In so doing, we become motivated by the desire to enhance the beauty of the Earth, to maintain harmony, and to create right relationships. We will then act naturally in accord with ecological ethics.

The philosopher Immanuel Kant observed that, when we are motivated by a morality of "duty," we will not delight in the good but will see it as a burden. In contrast, ethics based on the creation and sustenance of beauty make doing the right thing something attractive, even joyful. The morality of duty is based on guilt, which, as we have seen, tends to paralyze more than motivate. Its counterpoint, the ethics of beauty, is based on allurement and passion. As Jim Conlon observes, when we are "drawn forward, allured, enchanted by a passion, a desire and fascination for beauty . . . , something erupts and shifts. There is an experience of being carried forward and embraced by the energy of the universe" (1994, 25), or being caught up in the Tao itself, being empowered by the sense of "I can" characteristic of the Malkuta. It is this kind of ethics that can be a powerful motivator for liberation and the healing of our planet. Indeed, Brian Swimme (1997) observes that we must create "a culture that enables us to do virtuous acts with delight."

Not only ethics, but the entire challenge of reinventing the human, requires vision and passion. We will not make the changes we need to by cultivating guilt or by shaming people into action. True, we need to recognize the seriousness of the situation we face, but ultimately we will be able to remake humanity only if we are passionately drawn toward a new way of living in the world, if we sense a strong allurement to creating an Ecozoic era. Beauty, awe, and wonder along with a deep love for all living things must be central sources of energy in the struggle to come. Only if we understand our own role within the larger cosmic purpose can we make this transition. The challenge is immense, but also exciting and revitalizing. Moreover, if we can learn to trust in the cosmos, to intuit the Tao at the heart of all, we may well open the gates to an energy greater than we could ever have imagined.

THE EARTH CHARTER AS A COMMON FRAMEWORK

In reflecting on the reinvention of the human and the need for a new way of conceiving ethics, a key resource on which we can draw is the Earth Charter, a document that is arguably the fruit of the broadest consultations with civil society in human history. The Earth Charter represents an important contribution to a holistic and integrated vision of the socioecological problems currently facing humanity. In essence, the charter has selected many of the best and most solid intuitions of ecology and the new cosmology to create a fertile vision of reality based on a new spirituality and a new ethic. The charter does not understand ecology in a reductionalist way—that is, as the administration of scarce natural resources—but rather as a new paradigm of relationship with nature in which all beings are connected, forming an immense, complex system.

One key advantage of rooting our transformative vision in the Earth Charter is the fact that this is not just the thought of a single person, organization, or even community; rather, it draws on the wisdom and insights of nearly a hundred thousand people from a wide diversity of cultures around the globe. As such, it represents an exceptionally broad and inclusive "common ground" that enables us to reframe the relationship of humanity with the wider Earth community. Indeed, the very process of writing the charter reflects a new paradigm—a new way of collectively reflecting and creating as humans—that has allowed us to envision a shared framework that unites us both in our diversity and in our common heritage as part of a planetary community of life.

The Origins and History of the Earth Charter

In 1992, during the Earth Summit held in Rio de Janeiro, it was proposed that an Earth Charter be written that would be discussed worldwide by both nongovernmental organizations and national governments. The charter would function as a kind of "ethical glue" that would provide unity and coherence to all the projects proposed at that important meeting, but particularly to the summit's key plan of action: Agenda 21. There was no consensus on the charter proposal among governments, perhaps because the text was not yet sufficiently mature or perhaps because many participants at the summit still lacked the state of consciousness needed to truly welcome the Earth Charter. Instead, the summit adopted the Rio Declaration on the Environment and Development. The rejection of the Earth Charter proposal provoked great frustration in the most conscious sectors who were committed to an ecological future for the Earth and humanity.

Two international nongovernmental organizations—Green Cross International and the Earth Council—were asked to support the government of the Netherlands to assume the challenge of seeking out ways to formulate the Earth Charter. In 1995, they cosponsored a meeting in The Hague in the Netherlands where sixty representatives from widely diverse sectors, together with other interested parties, created the Earth Charter Commission with the purpose of organizing a global consultation process over the course of two years that would culminate in the drafting of the document.

At the same time, the key principles and instruments of international law were identified and compiled from the vast body of existing official documentation on ecological matters. The result was the report entitled "Principles of

Environmental Conservation and Sustainable Development: Summary and Survey" (Rockefeller 1996).

In 1997, the Earth Charter Commission was created, composed of twenty-three respected personalities representing every inhabited continent of the Earth. The commission's role was to accompany the consultation process and to put together the first draft of the charter text under the coordination of then-UN under-secretary general Maurice Strong and Green Cross International president Mikhail Gorbachev.

During 1998 and 1999, a broad-based global discussion of the Earth Charter took place including such diverse organizations as primary schools, grassroots faith communities, NGOs, think tanks, and ministries of education. In the end, more than a hundred thousand people from forty-six countries were involved in the process, which resulted in a wide variety of proposals for the charter.

Then, in April of 1999, Steven Rockefeller, a practicing Buddhist as well as a professor of religion and ethics, wrote the second draft of the charter, bringing together the principal resonances and convergences from around the world. From March 12 to 14, 2000, in Paris, UNESCO incorporated the final contributions and ratified the Earth Charter. In 2003, UNESCO officially adopted the Earth Charter as an effective instrument to be used in schools to nurture ecological consciousness.

The Earth Charter springs forth from a holistic, integral vision. It considers poverty, ecological degradation, social justice, ethnic conflicts, peace, democracy, ethics, and the spiritual crisis to be interdependent problems that demand inclusive, integrated solutions. The charter is an urgent cry in the face of the threats that weigh down the biosphere and the planetary human project. The charter also represents an affirmation of hope in favor of the Earth and humanity.

The authors of the Earth Charter—including Mikhail Gorbachev, Steven Rockefeller, and Leonardo Boff—state clearly:

> The Earth Charter is conceived as a declaration of fundamental ethical principles and as a practical guide of lasting significance, widely shared by all people. In a way similar to the UN Universal Declaration of Human Rights, the Earth Charter will be used as a universal code of conduct to guide peoples and nations toward a sustainable future. (*The Earth Charter*, San José, Costa Rica, 4)

A Holistic Vision

The charter creatively assimilates the four great streams of ecological discourse: environmental, social, deep, and integral ecology.

The Earth Charter enriches the *environmental vision* by inserting the environment into the context of the greater "community of life." The Earth itself is presented as "alive with a unique community of life," effectively embracing the vision of Gaia as a living superorganism.

Social ecology emerges in themes such as democracy, social and economic justice, nonviolence, and peace.

Deep ecology appears when the charter refers to the "sense of universal responsibility," "the spirit of human solidarity," and "reverence for the mystery of being, gratitude for the gift of life, and humility regarding the human place in nature."

Finally, *integral ecology* is expressed in the consciousness that human beings are "part of a vast evolving universe" and that the "Earth has provided the conditions essential to life's evolution."

Only this holistic vision permits us to see that our "environmental, economic, political, social, and spiritual challenges are interconnected, and together we can forge inclusive solutions." These solutions should be effectively inclusive and should encompass all the different spheres of human activity—personal, social, and planetary—because humanity has arrived at a critical juncture in its history, and because the very "foundations of global security are threatened."[9]

Humanity must therefore "choose its future" and either "form a global partnership to care for Earth and one another or risk the destruction of ourselves and the diversity of life." If we choose life, this change will be the fruit of a new ethic, derived from a new perspective—an ethic of life, care, precaution, solidarity, responsibility, and compassion.

If we were to summarize in one phrase the grand political-ethical-spiritual-cultural proposal of the Earth Charter, a truly liberating dream for humanity, it would be *a sustainable way of life*. This sustainable way of life presupposes a consciousness that human beings and the Earth have the same destiny and that their fates are inseparably intertwined. Either together we care for each other and thus guarantee a common future or together we run the risk of destruction.

A sustainable way of life is that which permits the Earth—with all its beauty and integrity and with all its abundant yet limited riches—both to meet the authentic needs of humanity (including current and future generations) and at the same time to allow the Earth to reproduce, regenerate, and evolve as it has been for the past 4.5 billion years. The way we live now globally is absolutely unsustainable. Continuing on this path might lead us to share the destiny of the dinosaurs.

Never in its history has humanity confronted such a serious challenge. To rise to it, we must urgently undergo deep transformations. If not, we will face tragedy. In this lies the importance of the Earth Charter—it serves to awaken us all to the dramatic life and death situation we face. At the same time, it inspires hope and confidence, because the situation is not yet fatal: "Together in hope" we can find liberating solutions, noted in the four principles and sixteen key paths toward transformation. As Mikhail Gorbachev stated so eloquently in his book *Perestroika*: "This time, there is no Noah's Ark that will save some while allowing the rest to perish. Either we save ourselves together or we perish together" (1987, 134). If we can make the proposals of the Earth Charter a reality, we will have a future and we will witness a new flowering of human civilization unified in its diversity by the common home it shares.

---

9. Unless otherwise noted, all citations in this section are taken from the preamble of the Earth Charter.

The Centrality of the Community of Life

With great wisdom—but perhaps surprisingly—the Earth Charter does not center its attention on sustainable development, a theme that normally dominates the official documents of governments and international organizations. Instead, it focuses on that which is most threatened—the entire community of life in all its splendid diversity. Together with this, it focuses on the attitudes that are most clearly connected to the preservation of this community: *respect* and *care*. For this reason, it names as its first principle the *Respect and Care for the Community of Life*.

Why does the document refer to the "community of life" instead of simply "life"? Because, according to the Earth sciences and modern biology, all living beings—beginning with the first bacteria that burst into being some four billion years ago, to the plants, animals, and, finally, human beings—possess the same basic genetic alphabet. All the Earth's living beings possess the same twenty amino acids and the same four phosphate base pairs. Because of this, we are all relatives—we are all brothers and sisters—with each other. In reality, no "environment" exists at all, but rather a true community of life in which all beings are interdependent and intertwined in a fabric of interrelationship that guarantees the biodiversity and subsistence of all, even the most weak.

Since life and the community of life cannot exist without the physical-chemical infrastructure on which it depends and feeds, these elements must also be inserted into our comprehension of life. In order for life to be birthed forth, the entire cosmos needed to labor from its first moments of chaotic creativity until now, always reaching toward deeper levels of order and complexity. Life itself arose when matter, in an advanced process of evolution, became more complex in an act of self-organization out of chaos. In this mysterious way, life burst forth as a "cosmic imperative," as the Nobel Prize–winning (1974) biologist Christian de Duve puts it. Life, then, is a chapter in the story of the universe in which matter possesses nothing truly material, since it is essentially highly condensed and stabilized energy woven together in a field involving colossal interactions.

Human beings are a subchapter of the chapter of life, a link in this vital current and a unique member of this community of life. In the past few centuries, however, humanity has chosen to exile itself from this community, attempting to place itself above and, many times, against it—demonstrating our capacity to become the "Satan" of the Earth when we were called to be good angels instead. As the Earth Charter states so well, human beings have the "right to own, manage, and use natural resources," but with this also "comes the duty to prevent environmental harm" (section 1.2).

Today, much of humanity feels the urgent need to return to the community of our sisters and brothers and to assume a dual function: on one hand, to feel itself once again immersed in the community of life together with its other members, and, on the other—what seems to stand out with reference to the community of life—to be able to creatively (but humbly and carefully) intervene to empower the evolutionary process and, responsibly, to be a guardian of other species. This is the ethical mission formulated in the Book of Genesis when it affirms that humans are to be the "gardeners of Eden" who care for, protect, and complete—with labor and creativity—the work of the Creator.

In the context of the community of life, we must no longer think of human beings individualistically (as the dominant global culture tends to do) but rather as a community and a society. Community better conforms to the nature of human beings, since this form was born out of the cultural experience of peoples as well as from our political reflection and the practice of democracy. In community, we express our willingness to participate and build together, our sense of the common good, and our sense of co-responsibility for all that concerns us together. It is with good reason, then, that under the first principle—Respect and Care for the Community of Life—that the imperative to "build democratic societies that are just, participatory, sustainable, and peaceful" is placed.

Respect the Community of Life

Let us now analyze the two fundamental attitudes that are important to cultivate with respect to the greater community of life: *respect* and *care*.

Respect presupposes, in the first place, recognizing the other in his or her uniqueness and "otherness" and, in the second place, perceiving his or her intrinsic value.

Human intervention in nature began roughly 2.3 million years ago when *homo habilus* first began using tools. With intervention, the risk of disrespect also arose, as did the risk of denying the "otherness" of other beings—or the risk of understanding the other not as a subject but rather as an object valued for its usefulness to humans.

This is the principal sin of anthropocentrism so common in almost all cultures around the globe with the exception of those indigenous cultures still living in deep communion with the community of life. Anthropocentrism tries to make us believe that all other beings have meaning and value only to the extent that humanity can organize and use them according to its pleasure.

Yet humans arrived on the evolutionary scene only after 99.98 percent of the Earth's history had already passed. So clearly, nature does not need humanity to order its vast complexity and biodiversity. Rather, humanity sees itself in its true place when it understands itself as living in communion with the wider community of life, as but one link in the great chain of life. While it is true that this link is unique insofar as it possesses consciousness that clearly enables it to act (if it so chooses) both ethically and responsibly, it is equally true that—as one of the last links in this chain—we are dependent on those who have come before us.

Respect implies that we recognize that other beings are older than we are and, for all the more reason, deserve to exist and coexist with us. Respecting them, we impose a limit on our will-to-power over others and our arrogance.

In reality, however, humans have historically almost never really limited their power; we have seldom truly lived with respect in creation. The well-known researcher of biodiversity Edward Wilson, carrying out a balance of the relationship of respect/nonrespect that humans have had with nature, concludes heavily:

The somber archaeology of vanished species has taught us the following lessons: the noble savage never existed; Eden occupied was a slaughterhouse; paradise found is paradise lost. Humanity has so far played the role of planetary killer, concerned only with its own short-term survival. We have cut much of the heart out of biodiversity. The conservation ethic, whether expressed as taboo, totemism, or science, has generally come too late and too little to save the most vulnerable of life forms. (2002, 102)

Today, we have arrived at an impasse that we can overcome only if we recover the attitude of respect as a limit to our capacity to destroy and as a condition for both the preservation of nature and our own survival.

Second, respect implies that we must recognize the intrinsic value of other living beings. Each living being is of value in and of itself, because it exists and, in the act of existing, expresses something of Being itself—of the original Source of energy and virtues from which all beings come and to which all beings return, the quantum vacuum, the pregnant void. In religious terms, each being expresses the Creator. For this reason, value belongs to the realm of excellence. Each being, especially living beings, is a bearer of this excellence "regardless of its worth to human beings" (1.1.a). Apprehending the value of each being, we feel arising within ourselves the feelings of reverence and veneration.

Buddha and Hinduism in the East and Saint Francis, Arthur Schopenhauer, and Albert Schweitzer in the West developed an ethics based on respect and reverence which affirms that all that exists deserves to exist and all that lives deserves to live. The guiding principle of this ethics of respect and veneration (Ehrfurcht and Verehrung) was formulated by Albert Schweitzer: "Good is all that conserves and promotes beings, especially the living, and among the living, the weakest; evil is all that undermines or diminishes beings or which causes them to disappear." He continues, stating that "ethics is the unlimited reverence and responsibility for all that exists or that lives."

Care for the Community of Life with Understanding, Compassion, and Love

Let us analyze now the second key attitude toward the community of life, care. This attitude has a long tradition in the West, as is evidenced by the famous fable-myth on care (fable #220) recounted by Caesar Augustus's famous slave (and later, freedman), the writer Gaius Julius Hyginus (64 B.C.E.-A.D. 17).[10] This myth received a very detailed commentary by the philosopher Martin Heidegger in Being and Time (§§39-44). From this myth comes the idea that care is not just one fundamental attitude or virtue among others; rather, care is the concrete essence of the human being. Care is the precondition that allows a conscious, rational, and free being to emerge. Only through the exercise of care can a being, through the act of living, mold its existence together with others as they move into the future.

---

10. A detailed analysis of this myth-fable can be found in Leonardo Boff's *Essential Care: An Ethics of Human Nature* (2008a, 33-41).

Thinking cosmologically, without the careful synergy of all the universe's energies, life and consciousness would never have emerged and we would not even be here reflecting on these matters.

Concretely, care is the essential guide to all conduct. All that we do with care is well done. That which we do without care can be destructive.

The degraded state of the Earth and the eroded quality of life on our planet are due, fundamentally, to a lack of care on the part of human beings. The psychoanalyst Rollo May stated it eloquently:

> Our situation is that in our heyday of rationalistic and technicalistic episodes, we have lost sight of and concern for the human being; and we must now humbly go back to the simple fact of care. . . . It is the mythos of care—and I often believe, this mythos alone—which enables us to stand against the cynicism and apathy which are the psychological illnesses of our day. (2007, 305, 306)

The same idea was fervently presented by the International Union for Conservation of Nature (IUCN), United Nations Environment Programme (UNEP), and by the World Wildlife Fund (WWF), which in 1991 together published a book with practical recommendations on ecology that carried a programmatic title *Caring for Earth: A Strategy of Sustainable Living*. The theme of care oriented all the recommended practices of preservation, regeneration, and treatment of nature, emphasizing the fact that the ethics of care is the most universal of all because it can be exercised and experienced at all levels, from the personal to the global.

Care is a loving and nonaggressive relationship with reality. Care is attentive to the vital processes and is concerned with all beings so that they can continue participating in the community of life in such a way that no one is excluded and left alone in their suffering. It is with care, as stated in the charter, that we can "ensure that communities at all levels guarantee human rights and fundamental freedoms and provide everyone an opportunity to realize his or her full potential" (1.3.a).

The charter also emphasizes that care must be exercised with *understanding* (1.2). Understanding is not an abstract process of acquiring the truth about things, but rather a form of communion with them—essentially, a kind of love. In truth, we can only really know that which we love.

The charter then states that we should care for the community of life with *compassion* (1.2). The idea of "compassion" is better understood if we take the Buddhist perspective that encompasses two dimensions. The first is to respect each living being and to entirely renounce the desire to possess that being (detachment). The second is to care for each being, to be together with that being in all circumstances—in happiness and in sadness—and, in particular, to not allow that being to suffer alone.

Finally, it is necessary to care for the community of life with *love* (1.2). Love is the most powerful energy that exists in human beings and in the universe. It is a force of indomitable attraction and union, which seeks a kind of fusion—

or perhaps more precisely, an experience of nonduality. If, objectively, we are sisters and brothers because of our shared genetic code, love in turn moves us to subjectively desire to be brothers and sisters and to consciously propose to live out this reality. To care with love is to feel united with the most distant star, with our brother bird, and with our sister ant, and to be interested in the destiny of each person on this planet. To care with love is to be able to declare with emotion: "You are infinitely important to me; you cannot suffer unjustly; you cannot disappear; you must live."

As we conclude our reflections on the Earth Charter, we can say that the ultimate effect of this ethics of respect and care will be peace *on* Earth and *with* Earth. After thousands of years of hostilities between human beings and nature, and the devastation we have wreaked on the gifts of our Great Mother, we must now, if we want to have a future, make a covenant of peace. We must allow the words of the covenant that God made with the survivors of the great flood to become our own: "Never more devastation and death; . . . on the contrary, I will make an eternal covenant between myself and all living beings and with all creatures that live on Earth" (Genesis 9:11, 16). The rainbow is the symbol of this covenant for life. We are all invited to be the rainbow's daughters and sons.

PART 3

THE TAO OF LIBERATION

11.

Spirituality for an Ecozoic Era

. . . Fully embrace life, abiding in the Mother,
and you will share in the glory of creation.
The Mother herself will be your guardian,
And all her creation your guide . . .

Return home to your own inner light,
Be aware of your own awareness.
On the darkest nights you will not stumble,
On the brightest days you will not blink.

This is called
"Cultivating the Eternal."

(*Tao Te Ching* §52)

Express yourself completely,
but use few words.
Follow the way of nature:
the wind does not blow all morning;
the rain does not pour all day;
when the storm passes, the sun shines again . . .

Open yourself to the Tao,
Become one with Te,
And you will become its embodiment.
Then trust your natural responses;
and you will receive all that you need with joy.

(*Tao Te Ching* §23)

In reflecting on the need to reinvent the way we live as humans in the world, it is clear that what is required is nothing less than a spiritual revolution. As Thomas Berry points out, the current threat of ecocide confronts us with deep ethical questions that our spiritual and religious traditions have never before needed to consider. This crisis, though, also invites us to break through to a new understanding of the world and our place in it. In so doing, it summons humanity as a whole to a great spiritual awakening. Indeed, our survival as humans, as well as myriads of other complex forms of life on our planet, may well depend on such an awakening.

In looking at the importance of renewing the psyche in chapter 4, we already began to consider questions of spirituality; in fact, the original meaning of the word "psyche" is actually "soul," something intimately connected to spirit. The call to widen our sense of self could easily be restated in terms of the need to transcend the ego, a key concept in many spiritual traditions, as is the importance of deepening our compassion.

Cosmology and spirituality also have a close relationship. Insofar as cosmology deals with questions related to the origin, evolution, destiny, and purpose of the universe, it very much speaks to our own sense of purpose and place in the larger scheme of things—which certainly can also include our relationship to the Source of all, or God.

One way of thinking of spirituality would be to understand it as the concrete way in which we embody, or live out, a cosmology in our daily lives. How can we participate in the evolution and unfolding purpose of the cosmos itself, and thus find our own meaning and fulfillment within it? And how can we open ourselves to the energies and wisdom of the great "Way"—the Tao, the Dharma, or Malkuta—at work in the cosmos? These are ultimately spiritual questions.

In the preceding chapter, we also spoke of the importance of deepening the aspect of interiority or subjectivity as a way of overcoming our obsession with the acquisition of material wealth. To embrace limits, we noted, we must shift our idea of "progress" from the accumulation of wealth to the deepening of the spirit, the broadening of diversity, and the strengthening of bonds of relationality and reciprocity.

So, to a large extent, we have already been reflecting on many aspects of spirituality throughout this book; we simply have not named them as such.

We have spoken less about religion—although we have drawn on insights from many different religious traditions. Yet religion and spirituality, while not identical, are certainly intimately intertwined.

Spirituality can exist outside of formal religious traditions. Indeed, the spirituality of each person is in some sense unique, and our own spirituality may draw on a variety of religious or philosophical traditions, as well as our own personal experience. That being said, most of humanity draws on religious traditions as a key source of spiritual insight. It is nearly impossible to consider spirituality without also considering the influence—both potentially positive and negative—of religion.

In terms of the ecology of transformation, then, it is important to consider the role of both spirituality and religion in the quest to move from our current path of destruction to another where humans actively participate in the preservation and enhancement of the integrity, beauty, and evolution of life on Earth.

UNDERSTANDING SPIRITUALITY

The word *spirituality* comes from *spirit*. To understand what spirit is we must develop a conception of the human being that is deeper and more fertile than the conventional one transmitted by the dominant culture, which affirms that humans are composed of both a body and soul, or of matter and spirit. Instead of understanding this in a holistic, integrated form, dominant culture still holds a dualistic, fragmented vision in which these aspects are juxtaposed. Because of this, some areas of study focus on the body and matter (natural sciences) while others are linked to spirit and soul (social sciences and the humanities). We have lost the vision of the sacred unity of the living human being as a dynamic, interconnected, and interwoven coexistence of matter, energy, and spirit.

Does Spirituality Concern the Whole or the Part?

Spirituality, in this fragmented view, means cultivating one side of the human being—the spirit—via meditation and by looking inward, in order to find one's deepest Self or God. These forms of discipline can often be taken to imply the need to distance oneself from the material or corporeal dimension.

Seen in this way, spirituality is viewed as a task—of course, an important one—but only one among many. Spirituality is viewed as a part and not as a whole.

Since we live in a society with fast-paced historical and social processes, the cultivation of spirituality—when understood in this way—obliges us to find a space where we can encounter conditions of silence, peace, and tranquillity that facilitate our looking inward.

In one way, this understanding is not completely erroneous. For example, silence and solitude can certainly play a useful role in cultivating the spirit. It is also sometimes helpful to take time out from our daily busy-ness to gain a new perspective. Yet the fragmented view that separates body and spirit is fundamentally reductionist because it fails to explore the riches present in a human being understood more holistically. Spirituality should be understood not just as a way of living certain moments of our lives but rather as a way of *being* a person.

Before going further, it is critical to emphasize that a human being, viewed concretely, is constituted as a complex whole. When we speak of a "whole" this means that there do not exist parts in juxtaposition, but rather all within is dynamically knit together as a living system, interconnected and harmonized. When we speak of "complex" this means that the human being is not simple, but rather a symphony of multiple factors and multiple dimensions that together constitute *being*. Speaking more directly, we can discern three fundamental dimensions within the coherent oneness of the human being: exteriority, interiority, and depth.

Exteriority: Embodiment

In the sense we use it here, *exteriority* refers to all the varied collection of relationships that human beings enter into with the cosmos, with nature, with society, with others, and with the reality that encompasses and sustains them: the air they breathe, the food they eat and enjoy, the water they drink, the garments that clothe them, and the energy that vitalizes their bodies.

Normally, this is understood as the bodily dimension, but the body is not a corpse. Rather, each human being is a whole, immersed in time and space, but alive. In a succinct manner, humans may be described as animals of the phylum of vertebrates, the class of mammals, the order of primates, the family of hominids, the genus homo, and the species sapiens—a being gifted with a body of some hundred trillion cells continually renewed by its genetic system, a being who was formed over the course of 3.8 billion years (or perhaps more accurately, if we consider the precursors of life, 14 billion years) of evolutionary history.

The human may be further described as a being with a complex brain consisting of roughly a hundred billion neurons (and up to a quadrillion—10^{15}—synapses) organized on three levels: the reptilian brain, which first emerged some 220 million years ago and corresponds to our instinctive actions; this is surrounded in turn by the limbic brain, which began to emerge some 125 million years ago and corresponds to emotions, affectivity, and a sense of care; and, finally, the cerebral cortex, only three million years old, which provides the ability for conceptualization and abstract thought.

The human is also gifted with feelings, intelligence, love, compassion, and ecstasy. The body as a whole lives in a complex interweaving of relationships that extend both outward and inward. If one understands the human in this way, it seems more accurate to speak of the human as an *embodied being* rather than a being *with* a body.

Interiority: The Human Psyche

Interiority is made up of the universe of the psyche, a universe just as complex as the exterior world, inhabited by impulses, desires, passions, powerful images, and ancestral archetypes. Arguably, desire constitutes the most basic structure of the human psyche. Its dynamic seems to know no limits. As beings with desires, we do not simply desire this or that. We desire all and *the* All.

The hidden and constant object of desire is *Being* in its totality. The temptation, however, is to identify Being with one of its manifestations, such as beauty, possessions, money, health, career, a loved one, children, and so on. When this happens, a fixation with the desired object is formed. This represents the illusory identification of the Absolute with something relative, of the unlimited Being with a limited entity. The effect is ultimately one of frustration because the dynamic of desire is characterized by its wanting all, not just a part—so desiring a limited entity always results in failure. From this, in turn, comes the feeling of not realizing oneself, and, consequently, of the existential void.

As human beings, we always need to take care to direct our desires in such a way that, as they pass through the various objects to which they are directed (which is unavoidable) that they do not lose the blessed memory of the One great entity that will allow them to truly rest—Being, the Infinite, the Source or Wellspring of Reality, or what we conventionally refer to as "God." The God that emerges here is not the simple God of religion, but rather the God of the personal journey, the ultimate source of value, the sacred dimension within each of us, that which is both non-negotiable and nontransferable. These qualities and descriptions point to the one whom, existentially, we most commonly call God.

Interiority may also be referred to in terms of the human mind, understood here as the totality of the human being turned within, capturing all the resonances that the external world provokes there.

Depth: The Spirit

Finally, human beings possess *depth*. We have the capacity to go beyond mere appearances—beyond what we see, hear, think, and love. We can apprehend the other side of things, their depth. Things are not just "things." Each possesses an additional dimension—they are symbols and metaphors of another reality that transcends them and which they remember, make present, and point to.

Therefore, the mountain is not just a mountain. In being a mountain, it also transmits the meaning of majesty. The sea evokes grandeur, the starry sky conjures immensity, and the deep eyes of a child speak of the mystery of life.

Human beings perceive values and meanings, not just events and actions. What really counts are not the things that happen to us but what these signify for our lives and the experiences they provide us with. All that passes, then, has a symbolic—or we might say, sacramental—character. Each event reminds us of what we have lived and nourishes our interiority.

This is why we fill our homes or rooms with photos and beloved objects from our parents, grandparents, and friends—from all those who enter our lives and who hold significance for us. It could be the last shirt worn by a father who died of a heart attack, the wooden comb of an aunt who died, or the passionate letter of a boyfriend that revealed his love. These things are not just objects—they are sacraments insofar as they speak to us of, remind us of, and make present those who are most significant and beloved to our hearts.

To apprehend, in this way, the depth of the world, of our selves, and of each thing constitutes that which we can call *spirit*. Spirit is not a part of a human being, but rather that moment of consciousness through which we experience the significance or value of things. Even more, it is that state of consciousness through which we apprehend the whole and our own selves as part and parcel of this whole.

Spirit enables us to have an experience of nonduality. "You are this world—all," say the Upanishads of India, pointing to the universe. Or, "You are all," as many of the yogis say. "The *Malkuta d'Alaha* ("Reign of God" or "Guiding Principles leading to the One") is within you," proclaims Jesus. These affirmations speak to us of a lived experience rather than a doctrine. The experience is that we are linked and relinked (the root meaning of the word "religion") to each other and all to the Originating Source. A thread of energy, life, and meaning passes through all beings, making them a cosmos instead of chaos, a symphony instead of a cacophony.

A plant, then, is not just something before me—it is a resonance, a symbol, and a value within me. There is within me mountain, vegetable, animal, human, and divine dimensions. Spirituality does not mean knowing this in an intellectual fashion, but rather living this out and making this the reality of my experience. As Blaise Pascal said so well: "It is the heart which perceives God and not reason" (*Pensées*). From this experience, all is transfigured. All becomes permeated with veneration and holiness.

The specificity of human beings lies in our ability to experience our own depth. Listening attentively to ourselves, we can perceive in our depths calls of compassion, harmony, and identification with others and with the great Other, God. We become aware of a Presence that always accompanies us, of a Center around which we organize our interior life and from which come both the great dreams and the ultimate meaning of life. We speak here of a primordial, birthing energy with the same right of belonging as the other energies—such as sexual, emotional, or intellectual—that are part of us.

An integral part of the process of individuation is to welcome this energy, to create space for this Center and attentively listen to these calls, integrating its life-project into ourselves. This is spirituality as understood in its basic anthropological sense. To have and nourish spirituality, a person does not need to profess a creed or adhere to a religious institution. Spirituality is not the monopoly of anyone; rather it is found in each person in all the different stages of life. This depth within us represents the human spiritual condition, that which we call spirituality.

Obviously, for religious persons, this Center is most commonly named God, and these calls are understood to come from God, being God's Word. The name we use to point to this reality, which is beyond all description or conceptualization, is really not so important, though. Indeed, some religions, like Buddhism and Taoism, do not speak directly of God, yet they deal in their own unique ways with the great mystery at the heart of all. (Buddhism, for example, speaks of *sunyata* or "the void.")

Religions live from this experience. They articulate it in terms of doctrines, rites, celebrations, and in spiritual and ethical paths. Their primordial function is to create and offer the conditions necessary to allow each person and each community to dive into the divine reality and attain a personal experience of God.

This experience—precisely because it is an experience, not a doctrine—results in an irradiation of serenity and deep peace accompanied by the absence of fear. We feel loved, welcomed, and embraced in the Divine Womb. What happens to us occurs in the love of this loving Reality. Even death no longer colors life with fear; rather, death is experienced as part of life, as the great alchemical moment of transformation that allows us to be fully in the All—in the heart of God.

Spirituality

Spirituality, in this sense, is a way of being, a fundamental attitude to be lived in each moment and in all circumstances. Whether doing daily chores at home, working in a factory, driving in a car, speaking with friends, living an intimate moment with one's beloved—persons who have created space for depth and for the spiritual remain centered, serene, and permeated with peace. They radiate vitality and enthusiasm, because they are full of God within. This God is love, who, in the words of the poet Dante, moves the heavens, the stars, and our own hearts.

This spiritual depth seems to have a biological manifestation. Recent research from the late twentieth century carried out by the neuropsychologists Michael Persinger and V. S. Ramachandran, the neurologist Wolf Singer, the neurolinguist Terrence Deacon, and technicians using modern brain imaging methods have detected what some call the "God Spot" (or "God Module") in the brain. It seems that those experiencing what could be considered mystical states have a detectable excitation of the frontal lobes of the brain, above what is normally found. These temporal lobes are linked to the limbic brain, the center of emotions and values. This would seem to indicate that the stimulation of the "God Spot" is linked not to an idea or thought but rather to emotional or experiential factors—or, in other words, to a living spirituality.

More recent studies seem to indicate that there may, in fact, be a multiplicity of regions in the brain stimulated by mystical experience—meaning that the "God Spot" may actually be a kind of "God Net," comprising regions normally associated with brain functions such as self-consciousness, emotions, and body representation. Other researchers like Eugene D'Aquili and Andrew Newberg have referred to this reality as the "mystical mind."

This mystical mind emerged as part of the cosmogenic-anthropogenic process to fulfill an evolutionary process: to apprehend and make conscious—in the human being—the presence of God (the One, the Creator) in the universal evolutionary dynamic and in each and every thing. It is in the human being that this consciousness of the Sacred emerges. It is in human beings that spirituality develops. For this reason, as philosopher-physicist Danah Zohar and psychiatrist Ian Marshall affirm, human beings are gifted not only with intellectual and emotional intelligence; they also possess spiritual intelligence.

Making this objective reality—spiritual intelligence—a conscious project, we must reinforce spirituality as a central dimension for a life that is open, sensitive, and attentive to all the multiple dimensions of the human experience. This spirituality moves us to care for life in all its manifestations because it enables us to see the excellence and value of each being. All that exists deserves to exist. All that lives deserves to live.

Spirituality helps us overcome the dangerous logic of self-interest dominant today, which impels us to dominate and appropriate things for our own utility and pleasure. Spirituality creates space for the logic of coexistence, cordiality, and reverence in the face of the unique reality—the otherness—of each being and in the face of our communion with all things and with God. The integration of spiritual intelligence with other forms of intelligence (cognitive, emotional, etc.) opens us to the loving communion of all things in an atmosphere of respect and reverence for other beings, the majority of whom are far older from an evolutionary perspective than we are, so that we may be welcomed again as companions in the great planetary and cosmic adventure.

Is the Universe Self-Conscious or Spiritual?

The reflections coming from modern cosmology and quantum physics examined throughout this book suggest that consciousness and spirit may be related to quantum phenomena that emerge from the infinite virtual background, the Nourishing Wellspring of All, the Pregnant Void, or—more scientifically—the quantum vacuum. Just as our physical being emerged from the cosmogenic process, so too did our spiritual being. Both are in some sense as old as the universe itself, because both were present—at least in potential form—from the first moment of the primordial flaring forth.

In cosmological terms, spirit can be understood as the capacity of the primeval energies and of matter itself to interact with each other in such a way that they self-create, self-organize, and constitute themselves into open systems (i.e., autopoiesis) that communicate with each other and which form an increasingly complex fabric of interrelationships which ultimately sustain the entire cosmos. From nearly the first moment of the primordial flaring forth, relationships and interactions emerged into being, birthing rudimentary entities (quarks and protons) that interacted and exchanged information with ever-increasing complexity. We can understand this as the dawn of what we now call spirit.

The cosmos, in this sense, is overflowing with spirit because it is interactive, pan-relational, and creative. From this perspective, there exist no inert beings— no dead matter—in contrast to other, living beings. All things, all entities—from the subatomic particle to the galaxies—participate in some degree in spirit, consciousness, and life. The difference between the spirit of a mountain and the human spirit is not one of *principle*, but rather of *degree*. The principles of interaction and of creation are present in both, but in different forms. The human spirit is this cosmic spirit which has become self-conscious and which now consciously speaks and communicates. The spirit that flows through all things reaches a new depth of crystallization in women and men. Yet the spirit is present in humans because, from the beginning, it was present in the cosmos.

If the spirit is life and relationship, then its opposite is not matter but rather death, or the absence of relationship. Matter is a field that is deeply permeated with energy, interaction, and information. Spirituality, in this context, is the maximum empowerment of life—and is therefore a commitment to the protection and expansion of life. Not only human life, but rather life in all is immeasurable diversity in all its facets of manifestation.

To live the reality of a cosmos that is itself a living being, to live the reality of the Earth as Gaia—the Great Mother, or the *Pachamama* in the language of Andean peoples—is to feel nature as the wellspring of living energy and to commune with each being we encounter as an entity with purpose, a sister or brother in the great adventure of the universe; it is to demonstrate that we are truly spiritual beings and to deeply live an ecological spirituality—something today so absolutely necessary for the survival of the biosphere.

The future of the Earth as an ancient, small, and limited planet; the future of humanity whose population ceases not to grow; the future of ecosystems exhausted by excessive stress from industrial processes; the future of confused, lost, and spiritually dulled persons who at the same time long for simpler, clearer, more authentic, and meaningful lives—this future depends on our capacity to develop a truly ecological spirituality. It is not enough to be rational and religious. More than anything, we must be sensitive to each other, cooperative in our activities, respectful toward other beings in nature—in one word, we must be authentically *spiritual*. Only then will we spread out as beings who are responsible and benevolent toward all forms of life, lovers of our Mother Earth and worshipers of the one Source from which all beings and all blessings come, God.

ECOLOGY, SPIRITUALITY, AND THE CHRISTIAN TRADITION

Throughout this book, we have drawn on a wide diversity of spiritual traditions as sources of wisdom in considering how to bring about a transformation toward a more life-affirming world. It is our strong belief that all these sources of wisdom are important and that we must learn to listen with openness and respect to many different voices.

Yet there are good reasons for examining in more detail the role that Christianity can play in a truly ecological spirituality. Why? First, many who read this text will have roots in the Christian tradition, whether or not they are currently active participants in it. Most people who live in the Americas or Europe are, to a large extent, inheritors of values and perceptions that have been formed by Christianity. Moreover, it is the culture of Europe, with roots in Christianity, that imposed itself on other peoples around the globe—originally through colonial exploits and more recently through the current dis/order promoted by global corporate capitalism.

It is only reasonable to ask, then: To what extent has Christianity played a role in the shaping of our current, dysfunctional and pathological culture of industrial pillage and consumerism? Is this the result of the teachings of Jesus himself, or is it rather a distortion of them? Could a different understanding of Jesus and the key theological ideas arising from the Gospels contribute to the healing of our planet?

At first glance, it seems apparent that Christianity has played some role in the genesis of our current world dis/order. It was Europeans professing Christianity who conquered half the world, often destroying vast forests and disrupting ecosystems as they also exploited the peoples they colonized. It was in Europe and North America that the industrial revolution began and capitalism arose. Further, as we have seen in our examination of the cosmology of domination, certain strands of Christianity—in particular, some forms of Puritanism—seem to have contributed to the ideology that viewed forests, rivers, minerals, land, creatures, and even people as resources to be exploited and commodities to be bought and sold. Indeed, these ideas have become almost synonymous with the modern "Western" civilization that developed under the influence of Christianity.

Yet, for the first fifteen centuries or so after the birth of Jesus, a much more holistic and ecological cosmology underpinned European society. Christian monastic communities, in particular, helped contribute to the ecological recovery of many areas once dominated by the destructive Roman Empire. Going back further to Christianity's roots, the life and teachings of Jesus are marked by a clear opposition to an imperial ideology based on the exploitation of the poor and of the Earth itself.

Despite this, there can be no doubt that some interpretations of both the Hebrew and Christian Scriptures have been used in ways that reinforce a worldview that separates humans from the wider community of life and that seem to counterpose body and spirit. For example, many Christians have interpreted the first chapter of Genesis to mean that humans must subdue and dominate nature. Others distorted the teachings of St. Paul, asserting that "flesh" is evil while "spirit" is good. In this view, we must forget "worldly" things and pursue "the kingdom of heaven." The body is seen as a source of temptation—and by extension, nature itself is seen as a corrupting force. The world we inhabit, in this view, is sinful and fallen, and we must focus instead on the life to come in heaven. Eventually, these distortions were combined with new ideas that arose during the Enlightenment and became a virtual license to use and destroy the Earth as we saw fit.

In actual fact, though, many of these ideas derive much more strongly from Neoplatonism and other Greek schools of philosophy than from the teachings of the Hebrew and Christian Scriptures. Indeed, traditional Middle Eastern cosmology and psychology would consider a split between spirit and body to be totally alien. Instead, spirit is understood in terms of the "breath" (*ruha* in Aramaic or *ruah* in Hebrew)[1]—that which gives life to the body.

A deeper reading of the first chapters of Genesis, for example, first reveals that all of creation belongs to God alone and that all God has made is "very good" and blessed. The words so often translated to imply that we should subdue the Earth and have dominion over its creatures can also be understood in terms of an empowerment of human consciousness—or a deepening of interiority—that carries both new potentialities and risks.

Neil Douglas-Klotz points out that the Hebrew root *khabash*, normally translated as "subdue" can also be understood as "the ability of human consciousness to move with a greater amount of free will," which "was here extended to include an ability to override its own subconscious self, instincts, and other interior abilities, which are a heritage from the interiority of older beings" (1995, 182).

Similarly, the Hebrew root *radah*, normally translated as "have dominion," "points to a singular power to radiate diversity and differentiation, a power that spreads out, unfolds, and occupies space by its nature, that moves with firmness and perseveres in its own will" (1995, 162). In both cases, the words can be understood to portray creation entering a new phase in which a capacity is given to humans to exercise free will, to act consciously and make choices, to differentiate and diversify. All of these are a far cry from giving license to exploit and

---

1. These words may also be transliterated as *rucha* and *ruach,* where the "h/ch" sound (Aramaic and Hebrew letter *het* or *heth*) is an aspirated "h" sound similar to the "j" in Spanish.

destroy. Instead, the text would seem to imply a strong sense of the responsibility that comes from participating in God's creative action.

Given this reading, we no longer have to read this Genesis text in an anthropocentric manner. Instead of being the "crown of creation," we can see ourselves in terms of a new stage dependent on all that has passed before. In fact, the progression of creation by days as presented in the first chapter of Genesis can easily be understood in this fashion. Brian Swimme often speaks of humanity as the emerging consciousness (or perhaps, one aspect of the emerging consciousness) of the Earth. Instead of being over and above the rest of creation, we can understand this text in similar terms—as saying that a new capacity has been given to our planet to act consciously and to create new possibilities through the emergence of humanity.

Jewish theologian Arthur Waskow suggests something along these lines in his commentary on the first part of chapter 2 in Genesis. He notes that the word used for "human," *adam*, is intimately connected to the word used for earth (soil), *adamah*. A good translation, therefore, for *adam* would be "Earthling" or "Earth-creature."

> Notice that "earth" here is not an "environment," because there are no "environs" for the human. It is not outside, separate, a wholly "other." Instead, the *adam* is intertwined within *adamah*, and the *adamah* is deeply entwined in the *adam*. How could you disentangle them?
>
> Intertwined, yet distinct. The last letter/syllable of the name of earth, the "ahh" of *adamah*, is the letter "Hey," the sound of breathing, the only letter that appears twice in God's Name—YHWH—which can only be pronounced (it has no vowels, whatever you have heard about "Jehovah" or "Yahweh") by simply breathing.
>
> Somehow God breathes this single letter, the "breath of life" from the living earth, into the Earthling's nostrils, so that s/he comes to live. The letter of the breathing, the "hey," vanishes from public visibility, vanishes from the Earthling's name, because it goes within: nostrils, lungs, blood, every inch of body. The breath becomes immanent, and therefore invisible, disappears.
>
> The last letter/syllable of the name of earth, the "ahh" of *adamah*, is also the female ending for many Hebrew nouns. The "forming" of *adam* is a kind of birthing from the mother's womb, where the two had been profoundly intertwined—but it is different from an ordinary birthing. For here the newborn also continues to contain the mother, as if there is a series of "Chinese wombs" in which each contains the other in a larger and larger, deeper and deeper, way. (Waskow 1997)

So, humanity is seen in Genesis as an expression of Earth. Indeed, we are in some way created in a manner that gives us a special connection to the planet, formed from its very self as though we were Earth's children. We are Earth in which breath has become immanent. We are the Earth made conscious in a new way. We are not over and above, but rather a part of the Earth.

We are therefore called to live in a deep and conscious relationship with the

Earth and its creative process. We are restored to our own humanity in our restoration to earthiness, in recognition that we are part of the great community of Earth.[2]

Looking more explicitly at Christian theology itself, we can see the incarnation of Christ as an affirmation of the goodness of the body, and indeed of the entire realm of matter. God becomes human, becomes flesh and blood. Spirit and body are not in opposition, as the weaving of breath and earth in the second chapter of Genesis already makes clear. Indeed, the Divine itself is immanent in matter. The cosmos itself is infused with the Sacred.

In the Gospels, Jesus' own personal connection to the natural world is also readily evident. Jesus almost always prays out-of-doors. He preaches beside the Sea of Galilee, surrounded by the beauty of creation. His teachings are full of references to animals (sheep, fish, birds), to growing things, and to the fruitfulness of the Earth. He speaks of God's care for all creatures: "Are not five sparrows sold for two pennies? Yet not one of them is forgotten in God's sight" (Luke 12:6). In the Beatitudes, Jesus teaches us that the humble—in Aramaic, those who have truly surrendered to God and softened all that is rigid within—shall receive the vigor and strength of the Earth itself (Matthew 5:5). Indeed, the Aramaic language that Jesus spoke is itself largely built on agricultural images related to the cultivation of living things. Jesus thought and spoke in this idiom. His entire teaching presumes a cosmology where the Earth is understood as a living subject, not an object for exploitation.

Later, the Christian tradition continued to develop many of these ideas. St. Basil (329-379), the father of monasticism in the Eastern Church, taught the following prayer:

> O God, enlarge within us a sense of fellowship with all living things, our brothers and sisters the animals, to whom you gave the Earth as their home in common with us. We remember with shame that in the past we have exercised high dominion with ruthless cruelty, so that the voice of the Earth, which should have gone up to you in song, has been a groan of travail. May we realize that they live not for us alone but for themselves and for you, and that they love the sweetness of life. (Quoted in Fitzgerald and Fitzgerald, 2005, 76)

As we will explore in more detail later in this chapter, St. Francis taught us to praise God for Brother Sun, Sister Moon, Brother Wind, and Sister Water. Indeed, many Christian saints and mystics have experienced and celebrated God's presence in the midst of creation. The great theologian St. Thomas Aquinas wrote, "The whole universe together participates in divine goodness

---

2. To further explore the relationship between Christianity and ecology, see the volume from Harvard's series on religion and ecology entitled *Christianity and Ecology: Seeking the Well-being of Earth and Humans* (Hessel and Ruether, 2000).

more perfectly, and represents it better, than any single creature whatever." The Rhineland mystic Meister Eckhart said, "Every creature is full of God, and is a book about God. If I spent enough time with the tiniest creature, even a caterpillar, I would never have to prepare a sermon. So full of God is every creature." Similarly, Martin Luther wrote, "God writes the Gospel, not in the Bible alone, but on trees, flowers, clouds, and stars."

In this section, then, we would like to reflect in more depth on how we can integrate Christian spirituality with an ecological paradigm. This is not grafting something new onto Christianity but rather returning it to its roots and drawing connections between those roots and the insights of modern cosmology and ecology. In so doing, we will consider the Christian image of God as well as our ideas about revelation, grace, salvation, and the destiny of human beings in the cosmos.

As should be clear, the new cosmology is conceived within the context of broadened evolution. This process of evolution is not linear. It is marked by halts, reverses, advances, destructions, and renewed attempts. Yet, despite all of these circumambulations, looking back over its course we can discern an undeniable direction, an arrow of time reaching onward and encompassing all.

Yet we know that many famous scientists refuse to accept the idea that the universe is evolving with directionality. For them, the universe has no intrinsic meaning. Others disagree with this view. For example, the well-known British physicist Freeman Dyson affirms: "The more I examine the universe and the details of its architecture, the more evidence I find that the universe in some sense must have known we were coming" (1979, 250).

In fact, looking back at the process of evolution that has now been unfolding for some 13.7 billion years, we cannot deny that there has been an ongoing progression: energy turns into matter, chaos organizes itself, the simple becomes more complex, from a complex entity life arises, and from life emerges consciousness. There is a purpose—a progression that suggests meaning—that cannot be denied. This is what is referred to by the Anthropic Principle (see pp. 273-74), which states that if things had not happened—often in their most minute details—as they have, we humans would not be here to speak of these things.

It is with good reason, then, that the well-known mathematician and physicist Stephen Hawking wrote in his book *A Brief History of Time*:

> The laws of science, as we know them at present, contain many fundamental numbers, like the size of the electric charge of the electron and the ratio of the masses of the proton and the electron. . . . The remarkable fact is that the values of these numbers seem to have been very finely adjusted to make possible the development of life. For example, if the electric charge of the electron had been only slightly different, stars either would have been unable to burn hydrogen and helium, or else they would not have exploded. . . . It

seems clear that there are relatively few ranges of values for the numbers that would allow the development of any form of intelligent life. Most sets of values would give rise to universes that, although they might be very beautiful, would contain no one able to wonder at that beauty. One can take this either as evidence of a divine purpose in Creation and the choice of the laws of science or as support for the strong anthropic principle. (1998, 129)

How Does God Arise within the New Cosmology?

The question of God, in our opinion, arises when we pose the question: What was there before the beginning, before the primordial flaring forth commonly called the Big Bang? Who gave the initial impulse? Who sustains the universe as a whole and each being in it so that it continues to exist and expand?

Nothing?[3] But from nothing, nothing can come. If despite this, beings appear, this is a sign that Someone or Some Reality called beings into existence and nourishes them throughout time.

What we can sensibly say without immediately formulating a theological answer is that, before the moment when time and space were born, there existed the Unknowable, there lived the Mystery. About this Mystery, about the Unknowable, by definition we can say nothing. By its nature, such a reality exists before words, energy, matter, space, time, and thought.

Now, as it happens, the Mystery and the Unknowable are precisely names that religions, including Christianity, use to refer to God. God is always both Mystery and Unknowable. Silence is worth more than words when facing this reality. Despite this, s/he can be perceived through the reverent use of reason and may be felt by the heart as a Presence that fills the cosmos and engenders in us a feeling of grandeur, majesty, respect, and veneration.

Placed between the Earth below and the heavens above, gazing at the myriad of stars, we hold our breath and we are filled with reverence. Naturally, questions arise in us: Who made all of this? Who is hidden behind the Milky Way? In our climate-controlled offices or between the four white walls of a classroom we can say anything and doubt all. But immersed in the complexity of nature and imbued with its beauty, we cannot stay silent. It is impossible to despise the breaking of the dawn, or to remain indifferent to the bloom of a flower, or to fail to be amazed when contemplating a newborn child. Almost spontaneously, we are moved to proclaim that God put all in motion and that it is God who sustains it. S/he is the originating Source and the Void that nourishes all.

Another important question arises at the same time: Why exactly does this universe exist and not another? And why are we placed here? What does God wish to express through creation? Responding to these questions is the preoccupation not just of religious consciousness but of all of science.

---

3. While at times we have drawn in this book on the image of "the pregnant void," this is more a mystical or metaphorical way of speaking of something beyond our imagination or our ability to perceive. The so-called quantum vacuum, for example, is a sea of energy beyond our comprehension. Similarly, the pregnant void is not a nothing, but rather a plenitude beyond "thingness" from which all is born.

Once again, the words of Stephen Hawking can serve as an illustration: "Why does the universe go to all the bother of existing? . . . If we find the answer to that, it will be the ultimate triumph of human reason—for then we would know the mind of God" (1998, 190-91). Even today, then, scientists and the learned are still investigating and searching for the hidden design of God.

From a religious perspective, we can succinctly say that the meaning of the universe and of our own conscious existence lies in our ability to serve as mirror in which God may see her/his self. God has created a universe as an overflowing of her/his fullness of being, kindness, and intelligence. God creates so that others may participate in her/his superabundance. Human beings are created with consciousness so that we can hear the messages that the cosmos desires to communicate—so that we can apprehend the stories of created beings, of the heavens, the seas, the forests, the animals, and of the human process itself, and re-link (Latin, *re-ligar*, as noted, the root of "religion") all with the originating Source from which it comes.

The universe, and each being within it, still does not reveal all that they are and all they contain since they find themselves still in a process of evolution and expansion. The cosmos is still being born; it is still in a process of genesis. For that reason, each being and each entity are full of potentialities not yet realized. The universe—and especially the human being—carries within it a promise and a future (Haught 1993). The tendency of all things is to be able to realize and manifest their hidden potentialities. Therefore, expansion and evolution also signify revelation. Only when all has been fully realized will the revelation of the design of the Creator be complete. Only then will we discover the formula that God used to conjure the splendid system that is the universe in its relationships and in its beings relating to each other.

God is manifest in this process—animating, attracting, and coalescing—sustaining the process from below and drawing it forward from beyond. God is the Omega Point, the great Attractor of all energy and all forms of matter, alluring them all so that they arrive at the ultimate culmination where promise becomes reality and where that which is now virtual (or that which exists only as potentiality) becomes a delightful concretization.

How to Name God in the New Cosmology?

How should we name this God-who-is-mystery, this God-beyond-knowing, from the perspective of an evolutionary cosmology?

Our first thought is to name this reality *Energy*—supreme, conscious, organizing, sustaining, and loving. Energy, as we have said, is the most primordial and mysterious of all realities, coming before the universe that we know, present in the pregnant void.

We can also understand God in anthropological terms and say that God manifests as infinite *Passion* of communication and expansion, since the cosmos is filled with movement, creating time, space, information, and—finally—beings, as it ceaselessly expands.

We can also say that God bursts forth as *Spirit* that interpenetrates all and each part so that an underlying order is continually created beginning with the initial, generative chaos and opening toward forms ever more complex, open, intelligent, and interrelated.

God, finally, appears as the absolute *Future*, the *Omega Point* where all the promises present in evolution are fully realized.

All things enter into communion with each other and, therefore, with the Originating Source. God is a *God-in-Communion*, a *God-in-Relation*. This insight opens us to understanding the Christian experience of God as Trinity, as a communion of divine Persons, as Mother/Father, Son/Child, and Holy Spirit, as we will soon examine in more detail.

Panentheism: God in All and All in God

As is apparent, the ecological cosmovision emphasizes the immanence of God in the process of cosmogenesis. God accompanies all processes from within, without losing her/himself in them because, as Mystery and Beyond Knowing, God overflows and engulfs them on all sides. Moreover, God orients the arrow of time toward the emergence of ever more complex, dynamic, and purposeful levels of order.

God is present in the cosmos and the cosmos is present in God. Classical theology expressed this mutual interpenetration with the concept of *perichoresis* (Greek), meaning literally to "rotate or dance around," or the "interpenetration of one with the other." Modern ecumenical theology coined another expression, "panentheism," from the Greek *pan* (all), *en* (in), and *theos* (God): In other words, God in all and all in God (Moltmann 1993).

Panentheism must be clearly distinguished from *pantheism*. Pantheism (from the Greek *pan* + *theos* or all-God) affirms that all is God and God is all. It maintains that God and the cosmos are identical, that the cosmos is not the creation of God but that rather the cosmos is the essential mode of God's existence. Pantheism does not accept any difference—all is identical, all is God.[4]

If all is God and God is all, it makes no difference what I occupy myself with: working on behalf of the assassinated street kids of Rio de Janeiro or having fun during carnival; playing football or advocating for the Kayapó indigenous people under threat of extinction; doing work with people with AIDS or watching movies on television; spraying my carefully manicured lawn with pesticides or starting a community gardening project based on agro-ecology. No matter what I am doing, I am experiencing the reality of God. God is all, so there are no real differences.

Yet this view seems clearly to violate common sense and to offend any sense of ethics. One thing is not another. It is one thing to say that God is present in all things, another to say that God is all. There are differences in the world. These differences are respected by panentheism but negated by pantheism.

Not all is God. But God is *in all* and all is *in God*. By the very act of creation,

---

4. It is only fair to note that many religious traditions that have been labeled in the past by the West—in particular, by Christianity—as pantheistic may actually be panentheistic. Often the perception that a religion is pantheistic has been based on a shallow or incomplete understanding of that tradition.

God leaves her/his trademark on each thing and each being, guaranteeing God's permanent presence in each creature. This is the true meaning of "providence": Each creature always depends on God and carries God within itself.

God and the world are different—one is not the other—but neither are they separated from or closed off to each other. Each is open to the other in such a way that each is inextricably linked to and interpenetrated by the other. If they are different from each other, it is so that they can communicate with each other and be united with each other through communion and mutual presence.

One of the most beautiful expressions of this idea can be found in a hymn by Hildebert of LeMans, a bishop in the late eleventh and early twelfth centuries:

Super cuncta, subter cuncta,	Over all, under all,
Extra cuncta, intra cuncta;	Outside all, inside all
Intra cuncta, nee inclusus,	Within, but not enclosed,
Extra cuncta, nee exclusus;	Without, but not excluded,
Super cuncta, nee elatus,	Above all, but not raised up,
Subter cuncta, nee substratus;	Below all, but not suppressed,
Super totus, præsidendo,	Wholly above, presiding,
Subter totus, sustinendo,	Wholly beneath, sustaining,
Extra totus, completendo,	Wholly without, embracing,
Intra totus, implendo.	Wholly within, fulfilling.

By reason of this mutual presence, both simple transcendence and pure immanence are surpassed. These categories, which originated in Greek thought, effectively established an abyss between God and the world; however, we can reconceptualize these terms so that they cease to be seen as opposites but rather are seen in a dynamic of *perichoresis* where immanence and transcendence interpenetrate each other. In this way, a diaphaneity (or transparency) emerges where transcendence is present in immanence and immanence is present in transcendence. Understood in this way, God and the cosmos become mutually transparent to each other.

Pierre Teilhard de Chardin lived, as no one else in the twentieth century, a deep spirituality of diaphaneity. As he said so well, "The great mystery of Christianity is not exactly the appearance, but the transparence, of God in the universe. *Yes, Lord, not only the ray that strikes the surface, but the ray that penetrates. Not only your epiphany, Jesus, but your* diaphany" (1964, p. 131). Or as he expressed it in this prayer: "Once again, Lord, I ask which is the more precious of these two beatitudes: that all things for me should be in contact with you? Or that you should be so 'universal' that I can undergo and grasp you in each creature?" (1964, 127).[5]

The universe in cosmogenesis invites us to live out the experience that underlies panentheism: in even the smallest manifestation of being; in each movement, and in each expression of life, intelligence, and love—we are enveloped by the Mystery of the cosmos-in-process. People sensitive to the sacred and to mystery

---

5. For more on the thought of Teilhard de Chardin, see *Teilhard in the 21st Century: The Emerging Spirit of Earth* (Fabel and St. John, 2003).

give witness, as did St. Paul, to the fact that it is in God that "we live and move and have our being" (Acts 17:28). To make this a lived experience is the origin of authentic spirituality.

The Holy Trinity as an Interplay of Inclusive Relationships

An ecological discourse makes it both possible and plausible to speak of God as a Trinity of Persons, as do Christians who believe in the coexistence, simultaneity, and co-eternity of the Mother/Father, Son/Child, and Holy Spirit.[6]

Ecology, as we have always affirmed in our reflections, can be understood as a fabric of interdependent and inclusive relationships that sustain and encompass our universe. Together with unity (only one cosmos, one planet Earth, one human species) reigns also diversity (galactic clusters; solar systems; biodiversity; a multiplicity of races, cultures, and individual persons). This coexistence between unity and diversity opens a space to situate a trinitarian and communal understanding of God. Just the act of speaking of the Trinity in place of simply speaking of God presupposes that we move beyond a simplistically monotheistic or substantialist vision of divinity. The Trinity puts us at the center of a vision of relationships, reciprocities, and intercommunion in keeping with ecological thought and perception.

So, when Christians say that God is Trinity—Mother/Father, Son/Child, and Holy Spirit—they are not merely adding up the numbers in the form 1 + 1 +1 = 3. If we were to speak of God in terms of numbers, God would be One and not Trinity. It is not our intention as Christians to multiply God by referring to the mystery of the Trinity, but rather to express our singular experience of God-as-communion, not solitude.

Pope John Paul II emphasized this point during his first visit to Latin America in 1979 in Puebla, Mexico: "It has already been said, in a beautiful and profound manner, that our God in his/her most intimate mystery is not solitary but rather a family, because God carries within her/his self parenthood, childhood, and the essence of family which is love; this love, of the divine family, is the Holy Spirit." God-Trinity is, therefore, quintessential relationality.

In the philosophical and theological traditions of the Middle Ages, the persons of the Trinity are said to be in "subsistent relations"—that is, a total relational-

---

6. The traditional terminology for the Trinity has been "Father, Son, and Holy Spirit," but this can be problematic in terms of the very masculine image of God that it implies. The word that Jesus used to refer to God in the "Lord's Prayer" was actually *Abwoon*, a word that was not clearly gendered as either male or female at the time he lived. It can be translated in many ways, including Divine Mother, Father, or Parent (parenthood in a spiritual sense). Its mystical meaning portrays a source of unity from which a birthing breath emanates into vibration, evoking the image of the cosmic creator.

The Aramaic word used for "Son" *bar*, is clearly masculine That being said, Jesus was also understood as the incarnation of Holy Wisdom (*hokhmah* or *chokhmah*), which once again is feminine in Aramaic.

The word for Spirit, *ruha*, is clearly feminine in Aramaic (as is *ruach* in Hebrew). This was translated as *pneuma* (neutered) in Greek and finally as *spiritus* (masculine) in Latin.

ity of each one with respect to the others in such a way that each is reciprocally involved in and included in the others at all times and in each moment without one ever being the other.

In this logic, we should understand that each Person of the Trinity is unique and there is no other like her/him: the Mother/Father is unique, the Son/Child is unique, the Holy Spirit is unique. Each is unique. And the One, as mathematicians know, is not a number but rather the absence of number.

So, do we have three Ones? Three gods? That would seem to be a logical argument, but the logic of trinity is otherwise. It is not substantialist and static but rather process-oriented and relational. This logic states that the Ones relate with each other so absolutely—that they are so intimately and inextricably intertwined, that they love each other so radically—that they become One. This is not a communion that results from Persons who, once constituted in and for themselves, begin to interrelate. No, this communion exists simultaneously with the Persons from the beginning. They exist, from all eternity, as Persons-in-communion, Persons-in-relationship. So there is only one, God-in-communion-relationship-of-Persons.

Each Person is irreducible. One is not the other, but they always exist connected to each other. It is not enough, then, to see each Person in itself and for itself but rather the circularity that always involves and envelops them in an intrinsic, uninterrupted interplay of relationships. The very words Mother/Father, Son/Child, and Holy Spirit suggest a relational circularity. The Mother/Father exists only because s/he is the parent of the Son/Child. The Son/Child is always the child of the Divine Parent. And the Holy Spirit is always the living breath (*ruha* or *ruach*) of the Mother/Father and Son/Child. St. Augustine, the great expositor of this vision of God-in-communion, wrote in his *De Trinitate*, each of the divine Persons "are in each, and all in each, and each in all, and all in all, and all are one" (Book VI, 10:20).

It would be difficult for a modern ecologist to express this interplay of relationships better than the way that the Christian faith formulated it, especially since this interplay constitutes the basic logic of cosmogenesis and the ecological vision.

If God is communion and relationship, then all in the cosmos lives in relationship and all is in communion with all at all points and in every moment, as we have already discussed. All emerges as a sacrament of the Holy Trinity.

In more direct language, based more on a lived-out faith than on doctrine, we could express the Trinity in this way: The God who is over us and who is our originating Source we name the Mother/Father; the God who is at our side and who shows him/herself as brother/sister, we call the Son/Child. And the God who lives within us and who reveals her/himself as exuberance we name the Holy Spirit. They are one God-in-communion-and-love.

The Holy Spirit Dwells in Creation

One of the names of God that religious and spiritual traditions have used is Spirit. That is, to speak of Spirit, of the divine breath, is to speak of life, dynamism, interaction, and purpose. For Christians, the Spirit is the third Person of the Holy Trinity, or the Holy Spirit. S/he is traditionally named *Spiritus Creator*, or Creator Spirit. S/he fills the Earth and renews all things—a quintessentially ecological affirmation.

So it is that the Spirit is present in the first creation (Genesis 1:2). The Spirit is active and profusely present in Jesus of Nazareth. The Gospels attribute the incarnation of the Son/Child to the Spirit: "Mary conceived of the Holy Spirit" (Matthew 1:20). The Gospel of Luke says that the Spirit overshadows and inhabits Mary, something which means that she was raised to a nearly divine standing; for this reason, that which is born of her is Holy and the Child of God.

It is also the Spirit that raises Jesus from the dead, inaugurating a new, complete, fullness of life, free from entropy and now with the characteristics of divinity (Romans 1:4; 1 Timothy 3:16). The Spirit also gives origin to the church, the community that carries the memory and inheritance of Jesus through history (Acts 2:32). It is the Spirit that is made present as enthusiasm, exuberance, and life in each human being.

The multiplicity of beings, the diversity of life, the immense variety of creative energies of the cosmos—all of these bear witness to the diversified action of the Spirit, who appreciates differences. We find this, too, in the human community with its diversity of talents: "There is a variety of gifts, but the same Spirit," as St. Paul expresses it.

We see the same in ecology: there is a variety of energies, particles, beings, life forms, and types of intelligence, but there exists only one mysterious Spirit which underlies and sustains all, and only one cosmos and one Earth. What is true for the Christian faith community is true also for the cosmic, planetary, and human community: "to each is given a manifestation of the Spirit for the common good" (1 Corinthians 12:7) that is never just human, but rather all-encompassing and cosmic.

The Spirit is a factor of communion and communication. Just as on Pentecost all heard in a diversity of languages the same liberating message (Acts 2:11), so too does the diversity of energies and beings return to the same creative source, to the *Dominus vivificans*, the God who is "giver of life" as is recited in the Nicene Creed.

The incarnation of the Word is one of the central doctrines of Christianity, yet few are accustomed to hear of speaking of the Spirit inhabiting her/his creation. Just as the Son/Child "is made flesh and pitches his/her tent among us" (John 1:14), the Holy Spirit "pitches her/his tent" among us through Mary (see Luke 1:35) and "placed her/his dwelling" in the universe.

To say that s/he pitched her tent and dwells in creation signifies that s/he participates in the advances and retrogressions that occur. S/he rejoices in creation, suffers with it, and groans with other creatures awaiting the fullness of redemption and liberation. Because s/he loves and pitches her tent in creation, s/he can be "suppressed" and "grieved" by its drama, as the Scriptures imply (1 Thessalonians 5:19; Ephesians 4:30).

From the Orient comes a poem that expresses this pan-spiritualism: "The

Spirit sleeps in the rock, dreams in the flower, remembers in the animal, and comes to know what it remembers in the human being."

The Spirit permeates all as an entanglement of the universe with itself; as an awakening of consciousness, desire, and enthusiasm; as a cry of liberation, and, as a force of communication and communion.

This vision provides us with a cosmic-ecological mysticism. We find ourselves immersed in a field of absolute Energy—the *Spiritus Creator*—who manifests the energies of the universe and in our own vital and spiritual energy. We form a whole with and in the Spirit. The spirituality that is born of this faith feels itself linked to natural and cosmic processes. To allow oneself to be imbued and filled by these processes is to live according to the Spirit in a natural and conscious manner.

The Cosmic Christ

The proclamation that the Son/Child of God was made flesh and dwelt among us (John 1:14) belongs essentially to Christianity. Stated in terms of an integral ecology, this means that the Son/Child is made of cosmic dust (Duve 1995) and with the same elements of which all beings and bodies are composed. Today we know that, with the exception of helium and hydrogen (which are the simplest, original, and irreducible elements), almost all the elements of the cosmos were formed in the interior of large stars through a process called "nucleosynthesis" (T. Berry and Swimme 1992).

Our solar system, the Earth, and each being and person, contain recycled material from these stars that were released into the wider cosmos through supernova explosions. The body of Jesus, therefore, possessed this same ancestral origin and was made from the cosmic dust birthed in the interior of ancient stars that long predated our planet and solar system. The iron that ran through his veins, the phosphorus and calcium that fortified his bones, the sodium and potassium that facilitated the transmission of signals through his nerves, the oxygen that made up 65 percent of his body and the carbon that made up an additional 18 percent—all of this makes the incarnation a truly cosmic event. The Son/Child dressed himself in this reality when he emerged from the process of cosmogenesis (Boff 2008b).

The christological Council of Chalcedon (450 C.E.) reaffirmed that Jesus in his humanity is co-substantial with us, in both his body and his soul. This means that, in our cosmology, Jesus too is the product of the primordial flaring forth and of the great red giant stars that died in supernova explosions (and in so doing spread the elemental seeds that would burst into life). It means that Jesus' roots are found in the Milky Way, that his cradle is the solar system, and his house our planet Earth.

Jesus participated in the unfolding of life and the emergence of consciousness, just like any other human being—child of the universe and the Earth. He is a member of the human family—and every human being is a being in which the cosmos itself has reached self-consciousness and has discovered the Sacred, a biological-anthropological locus where divinity bursts from within matter.

This reality enables us to understand why the incarnation includes not only the person of Jesus but all of humanity. The Second Vatican Council, in the Pastoral Constitution on the Church in the Modern World (*Gaudium et Spes*), notes explicitly: "By His incarnation, the Son of God has united Himself in some fashion with every human" (22). All of us, by being sisters and brothers of Jesus, are called to be assumed—in our own way—by the Word. The incarnation is a process still under way. The Word will continue to emerge from matter, from the cosmos, and from the great mass of humanity until it verbalizes the entire universe and brings it fully into the reign of the God (*malkuta d'Alaha*), the perfect expression of the purpose that guides us to the One.

The incarnation roots Jesus in the cosmos, but it also limits him within the bonds of space-time. Incarnation is an act of limitation, of accepting constraints, of moving from the universal to the particular—and because of this, it is implies a process of emptying (*kenōsis*), of letting go. Jesus was a Jew and not a Roman; he was a man and not a woman; he was born a *Homo sapiens sapiens,* and not an *Australopithecus,* in the time of Caesar Augustus; he died under Pontius Pilate.

It was within these limitations, and not despite them, that the Word was revealed and came to sanctify us.

By the resurrection, however, all the bonds of space and time were torn apart. Christ took on a truly cosmic dimension. Evolution came to know a true revolution through this process.

The cosmic Christ bursts forth, then, as a driving force of evolution that both liberates and fulfills. St. Paul says that "Christ is all and in all" (Colossians 3:11) and that in Christ "all things were created" (Colossians 1:16). Without Christ, all things would be simply a torso, lacking the most expressive part, which is the head. For this reason, the Epistle to the Ephesians affirms that it is important to "unite all things under one head in Christ" (1:10). Christ recapitulates and encompasses all.

The most expressive text of this cosmic Christology can be found in an agraphon (a saying of Jesus not found in the canonical Gospels) in logion 77 of the *Coptic Gospel of Thomas.* Here the ubiquity of the cosmic Christ assumes its full force: "I am the light that is over all things. I am all: from me all came forth, and to me all attained. Split a piece of wood; I am there. Lift up the stone, and you will find me there."

Here we truly encounter what we may call "pan-Christicism," derived from a global vision of the mystery of Christ. What we embrace in the world, what we penetrate in matter, what we feel in fields of force and energy, what we experience in our most humble and arduous labors such as splitting wood or lifting stones—all are points of access enabling us to be in contact with the cosmic, resurrected Christ.

Here a space is opened to experience the ineffable communion with the whole Christ as it is continually actualized in the mystery of the Eucharist. The bread and wine are not just a portion of matter, a piece of bread and a cup of wine on the altar. Through faith in the cosmic Christ and in the indwelling Spirit, the entire universe is transformed into bread and wine to become the body and blood of the cosmic Christ.

The Malkuta and the Tao

No idea is more central to the life and teaching of Jesus than that of the "reign of God" or "kingdom of heaven." This reality lies at the very heart of Jesus' message. He speaks in parables—of sowing seeds, of caring for flocks, of widows seeking justice—to explain this mysterious wisdom. In listening to these, we gain a sense of an organic, living principle or process unfolding in the world; yet the words that have been used to translate this concept—"kingdom," "reign," or even "realm"—seem to evoke something quite different—far more static and, in the case of "kingdom of heaven," even otherworldly.

The actual word that Jesus used in Aramaic, though—*malkuta*—is much more similar to the concept of the Tao or to the Buddhist Dharma than to any kind of "kingdom" we might imagine. Indeed, what Jesus proclaims is a reality far more dynamic, and also more subtle and powerful, than any kind of realm we can conceive.

The ancient root of *malkuta* is related to the word *malkatuh*, a name for the great Mother (Earth) in the Middle East. As Douglas-Klotz notes, "The ancients saw in the earth and all around them a divine quality that everywhere takes responsibility and says 'I can.' Later those who expressed this quality clearly were recognized as natural leaders—what we call queens and kings" (1990, 20)

The Malkuta, then, is that which gives us the sense of "I can," an empowering vision rooted not in domination but in the presence of the divine in the cosmos itself—a power that may be invoked, but which belongs to God alone. The Malkuta points to the governing principles that guide the evolutionary processes of the cosmos itself.

One way of understanding these ruling or governing principles of the Malkuta is in terms of liberation, as a process leading the cosmos toward ever greater communion, differentiation, and interiority. This is essentially a creative, cosmogenic process. As we noted in the introduction to the book, the word's roots elicit "the image of a 'fruitful arm' poised to create, or a coiled spring that is ready to unwind with all the verdant potential of the Earth" (Douglas-Klotz 1990, 20).

In speaking of the *malkutakh d'bwashmaya* ("kingdom of heaven"), Jesus was referring not to some other reality divorced from our world. In Aramaic, the word *d'bwashmaya* is based on the root *shem*, referring to the reality of all forms of vibration, be they light, sound, or even one's "atmosphere" or "name."[7] In some sense, we can think of "heaven" as the realm of that which exists in potentiality, the sphere of vision and possibilities. It is closely related to the whole idea we discussed earlier that each entity and each being is full of potentialities not yet realized—that the cosmos is a process of cosmogenesis, in which future potentialities will become manifest over time.

When we ask for the Malkuta "to come," we are seeking to put our own personal and community aspirations in harmony with those of the divine. In his prayer, Jesus used the word *teytey* to express this, a word evoking images

---

7. For more details, see our previous discussion on the *shemaya* (heaven) and *ar'ah* (earth) on p. 174 above.

of a nuptial chamber where "mutual desire is fulfilled and birthing begins" (Douglas-Klotz 1990, 20). In other words, we could think of this as harmonizing our own desires with that of the Malkuta, of acting and thinking in accordance with the great Way or Tao.

From the point of view of an evolutionary cosmology, then, we can understand the Malkuta as the principles, tendencies, and impulses that guide the cosmos toward its ultimate fulfillment, or the Omega Point. The Malkuta is present both within us and around us. (Indeed, when Jesus spoke of the Malkuta as being among us and within us, he was using the same Aramaic preposition, *men*, for both of these!) God's vision for the world is already at hand, we simply need to open ourselves to its presence—evident in the story of the cosmos itself—and allow ourselves to be guided by it. Then we will experience the creative "I can" that will enable us to be conscious participants in the unfolding creation of the cosmos. We could, indeed, understand this task as the very essence of spirituality in the Christian tradition.

Ecological Spirituality

These reflections serve as a foundation for an ecological Christian spirituality—that is, an experience of God in contact with nature and with the unfolding process of cosmogenesis and liberation.

Theology is one thing and spirituality yet another. Theology works with—and thinks in terms of—concepts. Spirituality experiences and works with deep emotions. When we move from the head to the heart, spirituality arises. Spirituality is not *thinking about* God in the cosmos, it is *experiencing* God in all things.

A good door for entering into an ecological and cosmic spiritual experience is to contemplate the image of the Earth reproduced in myriads of forms through various communications media. The iconic globe transmits an experience of sacredness and reverence—our planet Earth, framed by the black canvas of the universe, small and fragile but full of evocations (Macy and Brown 1998).

The same astronauts who transmitted these images of our planet to us also shared with us moving testimonies of their great power to inspire. For example, James Irwin, speaking of seeing the Earth as he traveled to the moon, said:

> The Earth reminded us of a Christmas tree ornament hanging in the blackness of space. As we got farther and farther away it diminished in size. Finally it shrank to the size of a marble, the most beautiful marble you can imagine. That beautiful, warm, living object looked so fragile, so delicate, that if you touched it with a finger it would crumble and fall apart. Seeing this has to change a man, has to make a man appreciate the creation of God and the love of God. (Reagan 1999, 158)

Similarly, Gene Cernan confessed:

> When I was the last man to walk on the moon in December 1972, I stood in the blue darkness and looked in awe at the Earth from the lunar surface.

What I saw was almost too beautiful to have happened by accident. It doesn't matter how you choose to worship God. . . . [God] has to exist to have created what I was privileged to see. (White 1998, 37-38)

Reverence, veneration, and thanksgiving arise spontaneously in the human heart when experiencing such beauty, majesty, and wonder. It is for this that humans exist in the cosmos.

Seeing the Earth from beyond the Earth, the human being awakens to an understanding that s/he and the Earth form a unity, and that this unity in turn is part of a greater, more encompassing unity called the solar system, which in turn is encompassed by the galaxy and a cluster of galaxies—and finally—the entire cosmos. And this, then, returns us finally to the originating Source of all—that is, to God. "I think the view from 100,000 miles could be invaluable in getting people to work together to work out joint solutions," observes astronaut Michael Collins. "The planet we share unites us in a way far more basic and far more important than differences in skin color or religion or economic systems" (White 1998, 37).

All are united in the one planet Earth. It is this whole that, ecospiritually, we understand as the temple of the Spirit; this whole belongs to the reality assumed by the Word. To feel in one's heart the all-encompassing reality of being, to live the feeling that vibrates, to perceive that which extends forever, and to allow the heart to be inundated with compassion and tenderness—all of this is to have an ecospiritual experience.

From the perspective of ecospirituality, *hope* assures us that, despite all the threats of devastation by the aggressive machine of destruction that humans have built and use against the Earth, a good and beneficial future is ultimately assured because the Earth and the cosmos are temples of the Spirit and the Word. And in that future, something of our humanity—both feminine and masculine—has already been eternalized along with the universe itself. Something has penetrated the threshold of the absolute dynamic realization—something of us is already in the heart of the Trinity itself.

Ecospiritually, *love* moves us to identify more and more with the Earth, because love is the great unifying and integrative force of the universe. For centuries, we thought *about* the Earth. We were the subject of thought and the Earth was the object and content. Now, after becoming conscious of the fact that the Earth and humanity form a single reality, it is important that we come to think *as* the Earth, to feel *as* the Earth, to love *as* the Earth.

We are not just on the Earth. We are the Earth itself that in this phase of its evolution has begun to feel, think, love, reverence, and care. For this, the word *human* comes from *humus*, meaning "fertile earth." Similarly, in Hebrew, the word *adam*, meaning "human," comes from *adamah*, meaning "soil," or "fertile earth." We are the fruit of Earth's fecund soil.

Through love, we deepen this inherent identification with the Earth. We embrace the world, the Earth, and all things—and in so doing we embrace God, entering into communion with the Spirit as it acts in natural and historical processes; we embrace as well the cosmic Christ, who is propelling evolution toward its culmination in the Malkuta.

We need this ecological, transformative spirituality for our time since it will help us to care for the Earth and all it encompasses. It will even permit us to experience God in the form that s/he wishes to be encountered, known, and served in the historical phase in which we live—a phase in which we are reaching a new level of consciousness of the Earth and humanity, a phase in which we have been gifted with knowledge that we have never before accumulated regarding the history of the cosmos and our place in it alongside other beings—but also a phase in which, for the first time, we are confronted with the very real threat of ecocide, a phase when we will need this newfound wisdom as never before to guide us toward sanity and well-being for all of the Earth community.

Francis of Assisi: Icon of Ecological Spirituality

In the West, we find a Christian with exceptional human and religious qualities who lived a deep cosmic spirituality. He is Francis of Assisi (1182-1226). Lynn White Jr., in his 1967 article entitled "The Historical Roots of Our Ecological Crisis," accused the Judeo-Christian tradition—because of its visceral anthropocentrism—of being the principal factor of the crisis which in our current time has become a clamor. On the other hand, though, he recognized that Christianity itself had an antidote to this crisis in the cosmic mysticism of St. Francis. To reinforce this idea, he suggested that St. Francis be proclaimed the "patron saint for ecologists," something that Pope John Paul II actually did on November 29, 1979.

Not surprisingly, all of St. Francis's biographers, such as Thomas of Celano and St. Bonaventure as well as the *Legend of Perugia* and other sources of the time, attest to the "friendly union that Francis established with all creatures; he was filled with ineffable joy every time he saw the sun, contemplated the moon, and directed his glance at the stars and the firmament." He gave the sweet name of sisters and brothers to each creature, to the birds of the heavens, the flowers of the fields, and to the wolf of Gubbio. Thomas of Celano even says that "he had such deep love for creatures that even those without reason could recognize his affection and sense his loving kindness" (1 Celano, 59). At the same time, he entered into community with the most discriminated against and marginalized people of his day, including lepers. Nor were his relationships bounded by religion, as can be seen by the friendship he formed with the Muslims he encountered in Egypt.

The philosopher Max Scheler in his well-known study *The Essence and Forms of Sympathy* dedicated to St. Francis many brilliant and deep pages. Scheler maintains that "never in the history of the West has a figure with such a force of sympathy and universal emotion emerged like we find in St. Francis. Never again could the unity and wholeness of all elements be conserved as St. Francis did in the field of religion, the erotic, social action, art, and thought" (1926, 110). Perhaps it is for this reason that Dante Alighieri called him the "Sun of Assisi" (*Paradise* XI, 50).

This cosmic mysticism is revealed in all its beauty in Francis's "Cantico di Frate Sole" (Canticle to Brother Sun). Here we find the complete synthesis between interior and exterior ecology. As the French philosopher and theologian Eloi Leclerc (1977) demonstrates, the exterior elements such as the sun, earth, fire, water, wind, and others are not just objective realities but also emotional ones, true archetypes that dynamize the psyche in the sense of a synthesis and experience of unity with the Whole.

These sentiments, born of sensitive reason and warm, compassionate intelligence are urgently needed today if we desire to reestablish a covenant of synergy and benevolence with the Earth and its ecosystems.

With good reason, the great English historian Arnold Toynbee observed:

> To maintain a habitable biosphere for the next two thousand years, we and our descendants will have to forget the example of Pedro Bernardone (the father of St. Francis)—a great textile businessman in the thirteenth century who pursued his own material well-being—and instead begin to follow the model of his son, St. Francis, the best of all men who have lived in the West. The example given by St. Francis is that which we of the West must imitate with all our hearts, because he is the only westerner who can save the Earth. (1972, 10-11)

Today, St. Francis has become the universal brother who transcends all confessions and cultures. Humanity can be proud to have produced a son with such love, tenderness, and care for all that exists and lives. He is the spontaneous point of reference for an ecological attitude that befriends all beings, who lives lovingly with them and protects them from threats, who cares for them as sisters and brothers. He knew how to find God in all things. He welcomed with joy the sufferings and contradictions of life. He even came to call death itself his sister. He established a covenant with the deepest of roots in the Earth and with great humility joined with all beings to sing—*together with them*, and not just *through them*—hymns of praise to the beauty and wholeness of creation.

As an archetype, Francis broke through to the collective unconscious of humanity, in the West and in the East, and from this place the beneficent energies that open us to loving relationships with all creatures, as though we were living in an earthly paradise. He shows us that we are not condemned to being the persistent aggressors of nature. Instead, we can choose to be guardian angels who protect, care for, and transform the Earth into a common home for all, the entire earthly and cosmic community.

THE ROLE OF RELIGIONS

St. Francis clearly embodies an authentic ecological spirituality, a spirituality characterized by its concern for communion (especially with both the poor and marginalized as well as with other creatures), respect for diversity (including openness to other faiths, such as Islam), and deepening interiority. His example has inspired millions of people—not only Christians but people of every faith, and even people with no explicit religious tradition whatsoever.

The power of St. Francis's example clearly illustrates the potential power of religious figures to inspire and motivate us to change our way of living. Religious traditions—which often began as movements of followers of such spiritual leaders—have a similar power. Yet this power can be used for good or for ill.

It is not hard, for instance, to find examples of religious movements that violate the principle of diversity by insisting that they alone possess the truth and that only those who follow their path may find salvation. Indeed, religious fundamentalism of this kind—essentially, a religious ideology of monoculture—has often led to discrimination, marginalization, conflicts, and violence.

Yet that does not mean that we should simply abandon religion and the wisdom it can offer the world. Fundamentalism should be understood as a distortion of religion, something that occurs when religion is manipulated to become a tool of dominating power. Fundamentalism actually represents a betrayal of God's purpose and vision for the world; it is never a way leading to true harmony, peace, and right relationship. It lacks the essential attitude of respect for the other that is a precondition for love. It is contrary to the Tao and to the liberation that the Tao embodies.

Religion is meant rather to be a way to "re-link" (*re-ligar*) us to the Source, to help us to harmonize our lives with the Tao. Religions, churches, and spiritual traditions—above all—must serve to safeguard the sacred memory of the experience of the Mystery of God. Never should they allow human beings and societies to descend into forgetfulness. For this reason, they possess an educational function. They can teach us to have reverence and respect—not just for sacred texts and places but for each creature in creation and for the vast diversity that characterizes the cosmic story. Each being came forth from the heart of God. Each one reveals something of God's majesty and grandeur. Without this sense of reverence and respect, it will be extremely difficult to impose limits on the voracity of consumerism, industry, and predatory production, which attack living beings and devastate ecosystems.

Ecology and Religion

Ecology, as was shown previously, has become the context in which we must consider all human problems. In the ecological vision, nature is no longer seen as something given, like some kind of primordial piece of data that encompasses all the immense variety of phenomena. Rather, nature is seen as an open system, an intertwined set of relationships, or as an intricate fabric of energies in constant movement which passes from chaos to ever-more complex depths of order.

More precisely, matter exists only tendentially: that which exists, according to the theory of relativity and quantum physics, is a universe of energy. A certain kind of crystallization of energies in equilibrium appears as matter. Another, extremely complex form arises as consciousness and spirit. But all of these are immersed in a dynamic, diverse, and unified whole.

In this understanding of nature, the fundamental law is that of *relationship*. Nothing exists outside of its relationship to other entities. Everything relates to everything else at all points and at every moment. From this perspective, then, we do not worry about threatened species in isolation, but rather in the context of their relationship with the regional ecosystem, with the biosphere, with the planet, and ultimately, with the entire cosmos of which we are a part.

Because of this, we should not compartmentalize knowledge into isolated disciplines. It is important to develop an understanding of the transversality (interconnected or cross-disciplinary nature) of knowledge, perceiving how one contribution relates to another—complementing it, correcting it, and forming all into a great synthesis. In this process, we must take care that we not only pay attention to contributions that come from our own cosmology, worldview, religion, or culture. All the contributions of other cultural and spiritual traditions must come into play: those from ancestral knowledge, those from popular culture, and those from the beliefs and dreams of each people. Each of these represents a window giving us access to diverse and complementary dimensions of nature.

Therefore, it is imperative that we *listen*. We must listen to our inner selves, listen to our genetic code, listen to the deepest pulses of our desire. We must listen to the messages that come to us through each and every thing, besides being things, they are also bearers of significance and doors to new insights. We must listen to the voice of each people and each person, as well as the voice of each and every spiritual tradition. And we must learn from these voices. From this process of listening and learning, a universal symphony will be born. Indeed, the very existence of dissonance and chaos calls us to create a symphony that must be nourished and safeguarded.

Awakening Humanity

As it happens, the immense, dynamic equilibrium of life on our planet is now threatened by the uncontainable aggressivity of the most complex and mysterious being on Earth: the human. In the last few centuries, humanity has so deeply wounded the planet that now, by its feverish warming, it manifests its disease. We can also perceive this same sickness in our own human relationships throughout the world: We live in a wounded global society, injured and marked with too many signs of death.

We must understand the threat of biocide, or ecocide, to be the most important religious and spiritual question of our time. How can we break this dynamic? How can we collectively limit our desire to privately possess and accumulate? How can we develop a sense of self-limitation, of fair measure, and of solidarity between present and future generations? We must safeguard the ecological conditions that will allow creation to regenerate, to continue being fruitful and creative, and to co-evolve, reaching increasingly synergetic forms until bursting into the divine.

The whole life system, and with it humanity, is under threat. There is no

Noah's Ark waiting to save some while leaving the rest to perish. Either we are all saved together or we run the risk of an ongoing degradation of life ultimately leading to death.

The basic question is no longer that of the future of any particular religious tradition. How many religions are still fixated primarily on expanding their own numbers? How many are still preoccupied primarily with their own organizational survival and not the survival of the complex web of life itself?

No, the key religious and spiritual concern of our time must be: What is the future of planet Earth and of humanity as a whole? To what extent do churches, religions, and spiritual traditions help us to safeguard the good creation of God and within this, how do we find our proper place? This is the central, radical question for all faiths in our time. Within this new perspective, we need to relativize intra-systematic and intra-ecclesial problems and subordinate our discourse to the truly important discussion that speaks of the totality of the Earth and of the interdependent beings that inhabit it—diverse, complementary, and mutually supportive because we share a common destiny.

A great part of humanity still orients itself less by ideologies and economic interests than by religious values that are the foundation of spiritual goods. Indeed, about 85 percent of humanity participates in one of the ten thousand or so different religious traditions on our planet. Two-thirds of humanity follows one of the three largest traditions: Christianity, Islam, and Hinduism (Gardner 2006). The potential power of religions to motivate humanity to a new awakening to our current crisis that will lead to effective, transformative action, then, can hardly be overestimated.

This is particularly true because religious and spiritual traditions already carry within themselves key values that are important to the development of an ecological culture. They speak to us of the sacredness of all life, they emphasize the importance of love, of cooperation, of compassion, of care, and of concern for the poor; they call us to seek justice and peace. These attitudes are benevolent and effectively lead us toward a respectful, nonaggressive relationship with nature.

These same values teach us to live in simplicity and frugality, to control our instinct to possess and dominate, and to seek to care for all beings—especially the weakest and the suffering.

At the same time, each religious and spiritual tradition carries its own unique insights and approaches. Each has its own particular way of seeking out the Source of all, its own path to harmony with the Tao. For example:

- Many indigenous spiritual traditions emphasize the importance of respecting Mother Earth and seeing ourselves in relationship to all other creatures who share our common home—not just animals and plants but even the living water, air, stones, and soil. We are taught to see ourselves in the context of "all our relations" and to consider the implications of our actions for seven generations into the future. "Aboriginal spirituality teaches that you look after what the Creator has given you and those things will look after you. It's a symbiotic relationship" (Sanderson 2004, 12).

- In the Hindu tradition, "the cosmos is the divine body of the Divine spirit. The galaxies, solar systems, planets, all life including humanity—all of these are sub-systems of the cosmos. The human being is just a cell in the divine body. And the whole is greater than the aggregate of its parts" (Sharma 2004). So, humanity, the Earth, and all its creatures form an interdependent web, as is illustrated by the image of the Net of Indra (see p. 187 above): "Each person, each object in the world, is not merely itself, but involves every other person and object and, in fact, on one level is every other person and object" (Avatamska Sutra).

- The teachings of Taoism (Daoism), particularly those of the *Tao Te Ching*, have been referred to often throughout this book. As we noted in the introduction, the Tao can be understood as a principle of order that constitutes the common ground of the cosmos; it is both the way that the universe works and the flowing cosmic structure that cannot be described, only tasted. The Tao is the wisdom that lies at the very heart of the universe, encapsulating the essence of its purpose and direction. Taoism teaches us that true wisdom lies in harmonizing ourselves with the Tao, including living simply and renouncing all forms of domination. Rather than using and exploiting nature, we must seek to observe and understand it. For Taoists, the wealth of a community is measured not by its accumulation of goods but rather by the diversity of life it supports (ARC 2009).

- We have made many references also to Buddhism in this text. Buddhism is particularly adept at explaining the human psychology of desire and suffering as well as the danger of the three poisons: aversion, addiction, and delusion (see p. 88-89 and the discussion on the dynamics of powerlessness). Buddhism also provides us with important insights about the nature of change through its understanding of complex/reciprocal causality or "dependent co-arising" (see p. 211). Further, the understanding of the Dharma, the "way things work," provides a complementary concept to the Tao or Malkuta. Finally, Buddhists greatly value compassion and seek the liberation of all sentient beings from suffering.

- From Judaism, we have seen the ecological insights inherent in the first chapters of the book of Genesis portraying humans both as a new phase in creation with the capacity to exercise free will, to act consciously and make choices, to differentiate and diversify—and as "Earth-creatures" formed by the intermingling of the divine breath and living soil. Judaism is also a religion strongly attuned to the rhythm of the seasons, with major festivals following a lunar calendar. The Jewish tradition teaches the importance of Sabbath—of taking time to refrain from work in order to enjoy creation, and of giving the Earth itself a rest every seven years. The idea of the Jubilee also makes provision for the redistribution of wealth; indeed, the ethic of justice is at the heart of the law and of the prophetic tradition in Judaism.

- Islam, which means "peace," sees peace as the fruit of submission to the One, Allah, who gives birth to compassion and mercy. To be a Muslim means to be one who submits. All of creation is understood to be Muslim, because each creature submits to the One and follows the will of Allah. In this understanding, each creature can be understood as a teacher, as one who can instruct us in the path of submission. Humans are good Muslims—they submit only to the One—insofar as they limit their use of the Earth to satisfy their authentic needs. "All creation is God's family as its sustenance is from God. Therefore the most beloved to God is one who does good to God's family" (the Prophet Muhammad, as quoted in Motiar 2004). In praying five times a day, Muslims prostrate themselves and in this gesture recall their connection to the four-legged creatures of the Earth. As well, they touch their heads to the living soil to remember that we are formed of the Earth and to it we shall return when we die.

This is but a brief sampling of some of the riches of ecological wisdom that different religious traditions offer us.[8] What seems clear is that each spiritual path offers unique insights that deepen our understanding of the Creator, of the cosmos, of our relationship to other creatures, of human psychology, and of the nature of the process of liberation itself. Each tradition is infused by the Tao; but in each, unique aspects of the Source are revealed. It is as though each reveals new facets of a reality that can never be fully understood or described. Each allows us to step closer to the truth; each enriches our understanding of the hidden purpose at the heart of the cosmos.

From an ecological perspective, we should see this vast diversity of teachings and insights not as a threat but as a strength. An ecosystem is always stronger and more resilient when it is more diverse. Similarly, the many ways to perceive and approach the great Mystery are an immense treasure of wisdom that we must draw on at this time of crisis. If we can do so, working cooperatively among different traditions with respect and openness, we can do much to awaken humanity to the reality of the crises we face and at the same time give hope and practical insights that will lead toward a more just and sustainable world.

Working for Transformation

In many ways, we are just beginning to tap the true potential of religious and spiritual traditions to mobilize humanity to seek solutions to our current crises. Much remains to be done to harness fully the immense transformative power for good that these traditions could unleash. That being said, it is helpful to point out a few concrete examples of ways that religions and religious organizations are working on themes related to ecology and justice. Most of these are drawn from Christian churches and ecumenical organizations, but we have no doubt that just as many examples exist in other traditions:

- Within the Christian tradition, the Catholic Church in various countries has promoted campaigns of conscientization to raise awareness about

---

8. See the Web site of the Alliance of Religions and Conservation at www.arcworld.org for more examples. Another excellent resource is the so-called Green Rule available through the Canadian initiative "Faith and the Common Good" at www.faith-commongood.net.

human responsibility for the future of life. For example, the Brazilian Conference of Bishops (CNBB) in their Campaigns of Fraternity during Lent has focused on themes such as water, the Amazon, and indigenous peoples. These themes are discussed in all the parishes and base ecclesial communities (CEBs), helping to awaken church participants to the key importance of ecology.

- In Canada, the ecumenical coalition Kairos: Canadian Ecumenical Justice Initiatives (www.kairoscanada.org) has worked on a number of ecological concerns over the years, integrating these with concerns for justice in a Christian faith perspective. This work has included a major campaign on water as well as another focusing on energy use and climate change.

- In the United States, Web of Creation (www.webofcreation.org) works to foster a movement for personal and social transformation from a religious perspective, focusing in particular on finding ways to green Christian congregations.

- In Sri Lanka, the Buddhist-inspired movement Sarvodaya Shramadana works in nearly two-thirds of the country's twenty-four thousand villages both to promote healthy and beautiful ecosystems and to ensure the provision of basic human needs like clean water, a balanced diet, housing, education, and healthcare. In so doing, it endeavors to integrate ecological, cultural, spiritual, and material sustenance (Gardner 2006).

- At a global level, the World Council of Churches (WCC), which is made up of nearly 350 Protestant and Orthodox churches from around the world, has for over twenty years used the theme of Justice, Peace, and the Integrity of Creation as a central focus for its work. More recently, they have also worked with other ecumenical organizations, including the World Alliance of Reformed Churches (WARC), on the topic of "Poverty, Wealth, and Ecology" to understand more clearly the interconnection between the unjust systems that create vast accumulations of "wealth" at the expense of the poor and the Earth itself.[9]

- In addition, the WCC has worked extensively with both Christian churches and other faith traditions to address questions related to climate change and has taken up the challenge of the two imperatives proposed by the Intergovernmental Panel on Climate Change (IPCC): both *mitigation* and *adaptation*. Mitigation addresses the causes that produce global warming and other manifestations of climate change—in particular, our predatory mode of production and consumption without limits and without solidarity. Adaptation, on the other hand, addresses the effects of climate change, particularly on the most vulnerable in the global South, which demand compassion and solidarity from all since failing to adapt will result in great loss of human life.

---

9. See, for example, "Alternative Globalization Addressing Peoples and Earth (AGAPE)" at www.oikouneme.org.

- Important interfaith initiatives around issues of ecology and justice are also evident. Since 2004, Faith & the Common Good (www.faith-commongood.net) has been working on the theme of "Renewing the Sacred Balance" in Canada. This includes a major initiative for green religious buildings as well as work on a Green Rule poster drawing together ecological insights from thirteen faith traditions.

- There are also a number of initiatives to collect ecological insights from different faith traditions, including ARC: The Alliance of Religions and Conservation as well as the Forum on Religion and Ecology at Yale University.

- The Forum on Religion and Ecology based at Yale University is the largest international multireligious project of its kind. Through its conferences, publications, and Web site (http://fore.research.yale.edu), the forum explores different religious worldviews, ethical traditions, and texts in dialogue with other disciplines in order to seek comprehensive solutions to both local and global ecological problems.

- The Ecumenical Patriarch of the Orthodox Church has organized an initiative called Religion, Science & the Environment (http://www.rsesymposia.org), which has sponsored a series of symposia including a diversity of faiths and religious traditions to draw on the riches of different theological traditions to address the imperative to protect the natural world.

All of these examples are positive, and no doubt myriads of others exist in every spiritual tradition and in every part of the world. Yet, by and large, we have not yet seen religious leaders and faith communities truly recognize ecocide and the threat of the dominant global dis/order as the central spiritual challenges of our time. We have not yet seen the full power of spiritual traditions focused on the pressing global problems we face. It is time, then, for each of us to do our own part in our own spiritual tradition to reorient its energies and concerns.

Now is the time to recognize that we are living—and indeed, that many peoples have now lived for centuries—without respecting the basic laws of life, including the laws of balance and of self-limitation. We have forgotten the ancient wisdom that taught us that we do not command nature, but rather are totally dependent on nature's bounty and goodwill. It is easier to send people to the moon and bring them back to Earth than to make humans respect the rhythms of nature and the limits of ecosystems. Because of this, we are now harvesting the poisoned fruits of the desacralization of life brought about by the power of techno-science at the service of the accumulation of the few.

Each of us must look again into our own spiritual tradition and seek out the insights that move us to reverence for all life, to an ethic of sharing and care, and to a vision of the sacred incarnate in the cosmos. If we can do so, we can draw on a deep and enduring wellspring of inspiration that can serve to unleash a spiritual revolution that can truly heal the Earth and, at the same time, enrich the quality of human life.

12.

The Ecology of Transformation

The supreme good is like water,
which gives life to all things without striving to.
It is content with the low places that people disdain.
Thus it is like the Tao.

In dwelling, live close to the earth.
In matters of the heart, seek depth.
In relationships, be kind and generous.
In speaking, be truthful and sincere.
In leading, be just and fair.
In work, strive to be competent.
In acting, remember that proper timing is everything.

Be content to live in accordance with your own nature.
Don't compete with others, and none will resent you.
Move in harmony with the demands of the present moment,
seizing opportunities as they arise.

(*Tao Te Ching* §8)

The Tao does not act,
yet through it all things are done.
The Tao does nothing,
yet from it springs forth all of creation.

If leaders could remain centered in the Tao,
the whole world would be spontaneously and radically transformed.
If the old habits and desires were to emerge anew,
The nameless simplicity would quickly quell them.
All would be freed from desire
and harmony and peace would emerge of their own accord.

(*Tao Te Ching* §37)

Over the course of this book, we have searched to find a Way—a "walking wisdom"—that can guide us as we work to effect the profound transformations needed to bring about the Great Turning leading to an Ecozoic era. This Way, which we call the Tao of Liberation, is a dynamic process unfolding from the very heart of the cosmos itself; it is both a creative energy and a universal attractor orienting the course of evolution toward ever-greater communion, diversity, and interiority. Like the Malkuta that Jesus proclaimed, it allows us to stand up against all odds and say "I can"; it is a life-enhancing power that—like fragile grass rising up through cracks in cement or like water wearing down a stone—displays a patient persistence that can overcome what would otherwise seem invulnerable.

This great Way has been evident since the primordial flaring forth gave birth to the universe some fourteen billion years ago. It is a hidden, organizing principle like the Dharma—"the way things work"—an "orderly process" guiding the unfolding story of the universe. The miracle of the evolution of life on Earth and the cooperative dynamics of Gaia bear witness to it. In this Tao lies our great hope, for if we learn to tap into its dynamic wisdom, if we open ourselves to be guided and nourished by it, then truly we can find a Way—despite all odds—toward a much more just and sustainable world where human beings flourish as part of the greater community of life on Earth.

Yet, while we are inspired and sustained by the Tao, we must never underestimate the immensity of the challenges we face. The pace of ecological destruction and the chasm of inequality between rich and poor have never been greater in human history. The obstacles to change are many, and these have become deeply rooted in the human psyche and in our cultural, economic, and political structures. Indeed, the pathological system that currently depletes the Earth, poisons life, and generates poverty and inequality has now been developing for thousands of years—since at least the time when the first empires began to arise around five millennia ago—and in the past century or so has reached new levels of sophistication.

Much of humanity, particularly the richest 20 percent or so of us, has adopted life-threatening habits, endangering the entire web of life in order to satisfy our greed for ever more. The cultural, political, and economic systems we have created are bent on domination and exploitation, destroying the living wealth of our planet to accumulate a dead abstraction called money. These same systems seem to have taken on a kind of life of their own, subtly warping human desires to suit their purposes. By combining the forces of cancerous growth, distorted maldevelopment, the rule of corporate pseudo-persons, parasitic finance, and monoculture of the mind with the age-old exercise of dominating power, the current global dis/order has become a veritable monster devouring life on our planet.

Even here, though, lies a seed of hope. While this system has grown to be extremely powerful, once its pathological nature becomes apparent we can clearly see that it is fundamentally irrational. No one, not even the richest and most powerful, truly wants to live in a degraded world where beauty and diversity have become but a distant memory. No one desires to live in a world where the divisions between rich and poor lead to violence and insecurity for all. No one wishes to see the possibilities of future generations undermined for centuries, or even millennia, to come.

Furthermore, we can clearly see that the current pathological dis/order is essentially based on false assumptions—for instance, that consumption can grow without limits on a finite planet; that a fictitious abstraction called money is alone the true gauge of value; and that unbridled greed, competition, and the pursuit of self-interest result in well-being for all. As our subsequent exploration of cosmology clearly reveals, there is nothing "natural" or inevitable about our current world dis/order. It violates the principles of evolution that have guided the unfolding of life on our planet, and indeed the story of the cosmos itself.

Looking back into human history, we have explored the origins of some of the beliefs, attitudes, perspectives, and practices that undergird the system of domination and exploitation currently wreaking havoc in our world. In particular, we have drawn on the insights of deep ecology to critique anthropocentrism—the belief that humans alone have intrinsic value and that all other beings and entities are only valuable insofar as they serve human interests—as being scientifically irrational, morally objectionable, and disastrous in practice. We have also looked to ecofeminism to deepen and broaden our critique, examining the relationship between patriarchy and anthropocentrism and their origins in human history as well as their manifestations in modern corporate capitalism.

In so doing, we have discovered the links between different forms of discrimination and oppression—including those based on race, class, gender, and sexual orientation—and the subjugation of nature itself in the exercise of power conceived as domination (or *power-over*). We have also examined alternative ways to reconceptionalize and reconstruct power—both in terms of *power-from-within* (the intrinsic power of *Te*, or empowerment) and *power-with* (the power of collective synergy). Together these constitute the kind of enabling power needed to effect liberating transformation.

At the same time, though, we have seen how the current pathological system of domination actually seeks to reinforce the dynamics of powerlessness to prevent authentic transformation, actively promoting the "three poisons" of aversion (denial and internalized oppression), addiction, and delusion (despair). It does so both by the use of overt repression and violence and by more subtle means, including systems of education that tend to fragment our vision and mass media promoting the pseudo-cosmology of consumerism.

Ecopsychology provides us with further insights into the roots of our disempowerment—our disconnection from the wider community of life—and in so doing provides important clues for overcoming our powerlessness through the reawakening of the ecological self. In practical terms, we may cultivate this wider sense of self and overcome our powerlessness by reawakening to awe and beauty, engaging in despair and empowerment work (or "the work that reconnects"), nurturing compassion, building community, cultivating will, and recovering vision and purpose. In this final chapter, we will take some of these themes up again and deepen them as we examine the importance of vision and the fourfold path toward liberation.

From ecopsychology, we moved on to deepen our reflections, seeking the roots of our crisis in the loss of a functional cosmology that truly situates us and enables us to feel at home in the cosmos. Few of us seriously question the largely unconscious assumptions we hold about the nature of reality and the "way things work." Yet these assumptions affect our very perception of the world and the problems we face. Perhaps even more importantly, they tend to limit our imaginations and reduce the effectiveness of our endeavors to create a more just and ecologically harmonious world.

While most traditional cosmologies valued our connection to the wider Earth community, those that have arisen over the past five thousand years or so have progressively distanced us from this vision. This is particularly true of the "cosmology of domination" that has been developing since the beginning of the "Enlightenment" in Europe. By conceiving of the cosmos as a machine as opposed to a living organism and by reducing the dynamic whole into a collection of parts, we began to see the world as a collection of dead objects rather than a community of subjects. This, in turn, removed ethical constraints on the exploitation of nature and, at the same time, promoted a deterministic vision that severely limited our ability to believe in the possibility of radical transformation. Moreover, the image of an eternal, infinite, clockwork universe gradually winding down toward thermodynamic death removed a sense of both story and purpose from the cosmos. While Darwinian evolution did at least show a spark of hope in the evolution of life, it also promoted an ideology of ruthless competition and "survival of the fittest." Overall, then, the universe in this cosmology is far from a friendly place. Humans are understood to be engaged in a ruthless struggle with the forces of nature—we are not truly "at home" in the cosmos, but rather involved in an endless effort to subdue it to our will.

Over the past century, however, a new and much more hopeful cosmology has begun to emerge from science. In many ways, this vision is difficult to understand—full as it is of both mystery and paradox. Yet it also is far more hopeful and creative than the cosmology of domination. In many respects, it resembles traditional cosmologies that situate humans within an ongoing story and the greater community of life. At the same time, it has its own unique attributes that may, in some respects, open us to an even greater sense of awe and to the immense potential for creative, life-enhancing transformation.

Instead of a fragmented, machine-like universe composed of dead, unrelated things, the new cosmology implicit in quantum physics reveals a world where the fundamental reality is that of dynamic relationships—a reality in which space, time, energy, matter, and even mind are part of a greater unity. Atoms themselves are no longer bits of things, but rather vortices of dancing waveforms. Even "empty space" is seen as dynamic, a pregnant void full of potentiality like the *sunyata* of Buddhism. Mind and consciousness themselves seem to be woven into the fabric of a cosmos that, in some ways, resembles a giant, dynamic hologram. In this vision, we must abandon both the comfort *and* the despair of a predictable universe and opt instead for a cosmos of complex relational creativity, a place (or unfolding process) where paradox and surprise create endless space for the unexpected to break through.

Systems theory further deepens this vision where the whole is more than the mere sum of its parts. Instead of a machine, the cosmos resembles an organism, a living system made up of other living systems that can self-organize, evolve, adapt, and even jump suddenly to new ways of being. Instead of hierarchy, these systems manifest holarchy—or systems nested within systems in such a way that larger systems creatively emerge from smaller ones with new properties not contained in their constituent parts. All such living systems, which include more than what we normally consider "alive," have the ability to self-organize and respond to changing conditions, and this implies a kind of mind or mental process at work in them. The cosmos as a whole can be considered a self-organizing system. In such a reality, the relationship between cause and effect is complex and reciprocal: even tiny actions can have immense effects. The nature of this "dependent co-arising" gives hope for transformative action—especially since systems can "jump" to new states of equilibrium with surprising rapidity when conditions are ripe, particularly in times of stress or crisis. Indeed, from the systems view, we can understand liberation itself as a self-organizing process, an art that calls us to discern the right action at the right place and right time through contemplation, creativity, and relational engagement.

The systems perspective is further enriched by considering the possibility that memory itself is somehow implicit in the cosmos, perhaps in the form of morphic fields. If this is so, it may well be that there are no fixed or eternal laws in the cosmos, but rather evolving habits. Some of these habits, such as those associated with what we normally call physical laws, may indeed be so stable that significant change to them is extremely improbable. Others, including the form of living species and social structures, may be difficult to change but can obviously be transformed, at times with surprising suddenness. The phenomenon of "punctuated evolution" demonstrates this kind of change. This suggests that it is possible for individuals—and even more for groups and communities—to help create new morphic fields by practicing new habits, new ways of being in the world. By embodying a new vision, they make it easier for others to do the same over time through the phenomenon of "morphic resonance."

The story of the universe reveals to us an evolutionary cosmos birthed from the unity of the primordial flaring forth. On Earth, we see life evolve largely through the cooperative process like symbiogenesis. Indeed, our planet as a whole reveals dynamics of self-regulation and self-organization—and even of cooperative altruism—that make it resemble in many ways a single living entity that many now call Gaia. The evolution of the cosmos as a whole—and of Earth in particular—reveals a sense of purpose or of the Tao, as though a universal attractor or Omega Point was drawing all toward greater diversity, communion, and interiority (or mindfulness). We, as humans, can see ourselves as part of this process: we are a part of the cosmos—a part of the living Earth—that has emerged into consciousness. As such, we are challenged to reinvent the human so that we can take a conscious part in the cosmic story—not as agents acting to reverse ecological succession and the process of evolution—but rather, as participants who facilitate the process of liberation by seeking to foster and enhance communion, diversity, and interiority.

Ultimately, this is a spiritual challenge. We need to apprehend the Sacred in all so that we may move beyond the dangerous logic of self-interest; we must widen our consciousness through empathy and compassion to embrace all of creation. Religious traditions, as a key wellspring of spiritual insight for most of humanity, can therefore play an important role in awakening humanity to a new consciousness and our connection with the cosmos. In the particular case of Christianity, for example, the theology of the Trinity provides rich insights into God-as-Communion-in-Diversity while Jesus' teachings on the Malkuta and those of St. Francis regarding care for the poor and our relationship with all of creation provide valuable insights into a genuinely ecological spirituality of liberation. To the extent that each spiritual tradition can share its wisdom and receive in openness the insights of others, religions can help humanity meet the key ethical challenge of our day: the threat of ecocide.

It is our hope that this journey has enabled us to adopt a fundamentally new perspective about the cosmos, and particularly about the vast potential for radical, life-enhancing transformation actually present in the great Way, the Tao. The multifaceted wisdom we have explored—drawn from such diverse fields as spiritual traditions, modern science, ecopsychology, ecofeminism, and deep ecology—is both inspiring and hopeful. Yet, as Joanna Macy and Molly Young Brown point out, they will not truly help to liberate us if they remain intellectual "playthings of the mind" (1998). They can only enable the Great Turning if we put them into practice, allowing them to transform our lives and our very way of being and acting in the world. To do this, we will now attempt to ground our insights, both by attempting to imagine what an Ecozoic society might look like and by endeavoring to sketch the outlines of a liberating form of transformative praxis based on our new cosmological vision.

Points of Leverage for Transformative Action

It is obviously impossible to create any kind of recipe for effective, transformative action leading to the creation of a just and ecologically sustainable society. At best, we can suggest some of the key considerations that should inform us as we endeavor to move from insights into action.

As a general point of reference, we should keep in mind that not all actions have the same transformative impact. For example, some kinds of action tend to improve the existing system, but do not challenge its fundamental assumptions or push toward an authentic change in the system itself. Donella Meadows (1999) went so far as to identify twelve "leverage points" in systems. She points out that about 95 to 99 percent of human interventions in systems take place at the level of what she calls "changing parameters"—essentially making relatively minor adjustments (like lowering income tax rates) that rarely, if ever, change behaviors in meaningful ways. In contrast, actions aimed at modifying feedback loops—enabling systems to regulate themselves more effectively—have a much larger impact. For example, reducing population and economic growth rates reduces the amplifying effects of destructive positive feedback loops while improving nutrition and preventative medicine improves the self-regulation of a negative feedback loop.

Still more effective are actions that improve the flow of information, providing meaningful and accurate data and analysis. For instance, access to information about major polluters can create pressure to force them to curb or eliminate emissions. Yet more important are changes to the fundamental rules governing a system. This would include things like constitutional change or the negotiation of international trade and investment agreements. Another key example would be to change the rules that govern corporations: in particular, removing their status as legal persons and enacting provisions making them more socially accountable and responsible.

A stronger form of intervention lies in the power actually to modify the nature of a self-organizing system. One way to do this, for example, would be to add a totally new feedback loop. Shifting taxes to reward ecologically sustainable behaviors and to penalize those that are destructive, for example, could create feedback loops that actually encourage energy efficiency and waste reduction. By making sustainable behaviors more economically viable, a real potential for systemic change is unleashed.

Changing the fundamental goal of the system is more important still. For instance, if we were to set our goal not as maximizing economic growth (or GDP) but rather as maximizing social well-being and happiness (as the Himalayan kingdom of Bhutan has done since 1972), we would need also to fundamentally reorient our system. One measure that could be a reflection of such a change in goal would be to move away from GDP as a measure of progress toward an alternative indicator like the Genuine Progress Indicator (GPI) or Bhutan's Gross National Happiness (GNH).

The final two levels of transformation are deeper still, yet also more challenging. The first is to shift to a new mind-set, paradigm, or cosmology. Yet, while this is difficult, Meadows points out:

> There's nothing necessarily physical or expensive or even slow in the process of paradigm change. In a single individual it can happen in a millisecond. All it takes is a click in the mind, a falling of scales from the eyes, a new way of seeing. Whole societies are another matter. They resist challenges to their paradigm harder than they resist anything else. Societal responses to paradigm challenge have included crucifixions, burnings at the stake, concentration camps, and nuclear arsenals.
>
> So how do you change paradigms? . . . In a nutshell, you keep pointing out the anomalies and failures of the old paradigm, you keep speaking louder and with assurance from the new one, you insert people in places of public visibility and power. You don't waste time with reactionaries; rather you work with active change agents and with the vast middle ground of people who are open-minded. (1999, 20)

Meadows goes on to say that systems theorists often seek to "change paradigms by modelling a system on a computer which takes you outside the system and forces you to see it as a whole." Perhaps in some ways this book itself can be seen as a similar exercise—particularly the opening chapters, where we tried to gain an understanding of the current system dominating our planet and to analyze its pathological nature. It would seem that the next step, though, would be to model a new system based on a new cosmology—to create a vision of change—and over time to test this vision in practice and to attempt to refine it by doing so.

The deepest level of transformative action, though, is to transcend paradigms completely. This is, perhaps, even more enigmatic, but it is a healthy caution to any attempt to embody a new worldview. No vision, no paradigm, will ever be perfect. We must always be open to new insights and new sources of wisdom. Whatever we do, whatever we embody, must always be understood as in some sense provisional. As the Zen proverb goes, "Try not to seek after what is true, only cease to cherish opinions." Clinging to any paradigm, however beautiful it may seem, may result in the kind of fanaticism characteristic of fundamentalism, and this is surely not in accord with the mystery of the Tao, which, ultimately, is beyond knowing. No human paradigm or worldview can ever fully embody it. The best we can hope is to remain open and to strive continually to seek out the right way of being in the time and place in which we find ourselves. Over time, all paradigms must adapt and evolve, as the cosmos itself does.

The idea of leverage points helps us to frame our reflections on transformative praxis. Yet another way to think of liberating action is in terms of the roles of the reformer, the prophet, and the visionary. All three are necessary, but not all are equally appropriate at a given time. Reform aims at modifying and improving structures without challenging the basic systemic pattern or its underlying paradigm. Effectively, it is part of the homeostatic process which continually fine-tunes the system to its environment. Prophetic action, in contrast, critiques and challenges the systemic pattern itself, helping to push it further toward a bifurcation point and radical transformation. Visionary action actually tries to initiate new patterns, experimenting with possible ways to concretize an emerging new paradigm. As such, it serves a function analogous to a new morphic field pulling transformation past the bifurcation point to a new pattern of stability.

At times of crisis such as these, there is an urgent need to go beyond the homeostatic function of the reformist. Prophetic action continues to serve an important function, but visionary action becomes perhaps even more important. Marilyn Ferguson (1987, 428-29) recounts a myth from the Jewish mystical tradition of the Kabala that seems pertinent: When the world is to be remade, the "children from the chamber of yearning" (prophets) will trigger a state of chaos by shaking the very roots of the old order while "the masters of construction" (visionaries) will focus the fire of revolution into new forms.

A similar perspective comes from Macy and Brown (1998, 17-24) when they speak of three kinds of action:

- *Holding actions* in defense of life seek to prevent further injustice and damage to the Earth. This includes actions to improve laws, to protest

injustice, and to boycott corporations. These actions are necessary insofar as they may slow, and even halt, that which harms life and impoverishes humanity—but they do not go so far as to actually repair the
damage already done or move us toward new ways of living in the world.
At times, we could consider such actions to be basically reformist, but
often they go beyond that to clearly denounce the injustice and destruction at a systemic level and are in this sense more prophetic in nature.

- Actions that *seek out structural causes* or *build alternatives* are more
  clearly prophetic in nature. These may include educational initiatives
  aimed at raising consciousness, collaborative living arrangements like
  ecovillages, the implementation of alternative indicators of progress, and
  the formation of community gardens or local currency systems. Many of
  these, insofar as they contain the seeds of a new paradigm, may actually
  encompass forms of visionary action.

- Actions aimed at *shifting perceptions and paradigms* actively seek to
  embody the new cosmology found in holism, systems theory, deep ecology, ecofeminism, the Gaia theory, and the emerging story of the universe. This could include, for example, despair and empowerment work
  or the remything of the cosmic story. In some ways, this is the least clearly
  defined area of action, in part because it can be the most challenging to
  conceive clearly. Yet it is arguably also the sphere with the greatest potential for radical transformation.

Once again, all three forms of action are important, but the first (holding
actions) can never move us beyond our current crisis. Ultimately, authentic liberation will be the fruit of actions based on a deep understanding of our current crisis that seek to build new alternatives that truly embody an ecological
paradigm.

CONCEIVING A NEW VISION

To undertake such actions will require a certain clarity of vision. While all
visions are ultimately provisional, they still serve as a key source of inspiration and guidance. As we have previously noted, we will need both courage and
wisdom to move beyond our current crisis and confront the structures impeding
liberation. Guilt and fear can never motivate us to confront the dangers involved
nor to make the sacrifices required—indeed, they may rather serve to paralyze
us, moving us into a state of delusion through the dynamics of aversion, addiction, and despair. Instead, we need a compelling vision (or visions) that can
inspire us, drawing us toward a new reality through beauty, hope, and wonder.
As Duane Elgin notes:

> When we can collectively envision a sustainable and satisfying pathway into the
> future, then can we begin to construct that future consciously. We need to draw

upon our collective wisdom and discover images of the future that awaken our enthusiasm for evolution and mobilize our social energies. (1993, 14)

Similarly, in discussing the whole concept of will (pp. 124-25), we noted that Roberto Assagioli described five stages needed to exercise will, which here can be understood as our power to effect change. First, we need a clear goal or motivation toward which we wish to move—a *vision* that inspires and illuminates us. Only then can we move on to the other stages: deliberation (or discernment), affirmation, planning, and directing the execution of the plan.

To be truly compelling and satisfying, this vision needs to be based on values of what really matters in life—not money and the quest for power but rather relationships, love, a sense of belonging, beauty, awe, and the enjoyment of life. This must not be a romantic return to a mythical golden age that never existed, but rather a moving forward. Morris Berman (1981) notes that this may well mean that we need to *recapture* insights and ways of being that are found in traditional societies—particularly the awareness that we are part of a greater community of life—but it must not be a *going back* to the past. Indeed, given the size of the human population and the damage we have already done, some forms of modern technology may actually be essential to whatever transformed society we create; but the way we use technology, along with its scale and purpose, will need to change in fundamental ways.

Thomas Berry speaks of how an artist often experiences "something akin to dream awareness that becomes clarified in the creative process itself." In the same way, "we must have a vision of the future sufficiently entrancing that it will sustain us in the transformation of the human project that is now in process" (1999, x). Obviously, the vision does not need to be complete before we begin, for there is a dialectical interaction between vision and action. As we experiment with new ways of being in the world, the vision will be refined and clarified. In the end, our path will become clear only once we have walked it. Yet the dream is still in some sense what inspires us and sustains us on the journey: In Berry's words, "the dream drives the action" (1999, 204).

One way to think of this is in terms of "anticipatory fidelity"—we must be faithful to the vision we hope for, even though it is not yet here. Feminist theologian Letty Russell speaks of this using the Greek term *hōs mē*, "as if not."

[We are to] live *as if not*; as if the facts of the situation are only provisional because of the horizon of freedom. The . . . anticipation of the new world is breaking in and all other aspects of life cannot be taken with utter seriousness. . . .

Living *hōs mē* is more an attitude toward life itself than a particular action. It is a calling to look critically at what is going on in the world, to see the problems and then to act in such a way that the problem itself is in some way contradicted and people begin to be transformed. (1974, 45-46)

A more positive way to restate this would be to say that we must *live as if* the reality we wish to see were already here; we must attempt to embody the vision we wish to see for the world. From the perspective of morphic resonance, we attempt to create and practice new habits, new ways of being, so that they may become easier for others to practice and so spread over time. At first, this may sound immensely challenging, but to the extent that we are also *recapturing* perceptions and habits practiced in former times by humanity (and even today by some indigenous peoples), and to the extent that we are attempting to align ourselves with the great universal attractor—the Tao—we are not creating new habits from nothing, but rather adapting perceptions and habits that have already existed to our own time and place.

The Bioregional Alternative

Throughout this book, we have begun to discern the outlines of a truly transformed human society living in harmony with the wider Earth community. In considering the current pathological global dis/order, we saw the need to move from an economy based on cancerous growth to a steady-state economy in continual evolution in qualitative terms. On a political level, we saw the need to find ways to move from dominating power-over to liberating power-from-within and power-with. On a cultural level, we saw the need to value diversity and to encourage more fluid gender roles. Our subsequent reflections on systems theory provided valuable insights into the dynamics of evolution, self-organization, holarchy, and dynamic stability while our examination of the Earth Charter rooted us in a common ethical framework.

Bolivia's current minister of foreign affairs, David Choquehuanca, drawing on indigenous Andean philosophy, speaks of moving from the goal of "living better" (the ethic of endless progress and development) to the goal of "living well" (or an ethic of sufficiency). "Living better" pushes us toward competition with others and into the endless race to accumulate more. In contrast, "living well" always means well-being for the entire community: An individual cannot live well if the community as a whole is not well. Furthermore, living well is not based on material wealth (although it presupposes the necessities of life), but rather on the well-being of persons and communities in all their dimensions. Moreover, a community cannot live well in a degraded ecosystem—indeed, we must extend our very idea of community to embrace other creatures as well as the air, water, and soil that sustain them.

What kind of society might reflect this goal of living well in harmony with the greater Earth community? How can we ground the ethics of respect, care, beauty, and right relationship in a concrete social vision? In considering these questions, we should keep in mind that a functional, sustainable human society should draw on the wisdom revealed in living, self-organizing systems such as mature ecosystems. Based on our knowledge of living systems, and enriched with other insights we have gained over the course of our reflections, we can list some key characteristics of an alternative social vision:[1]

---

1. Many of these characteristics are based on those outlined by David Korten (1995, 272-74; 2006, 292-94).

- *Sustainability.* We must embrace limits, being careful to consume no more than our ecosystem can sustainably produce and creating no waste that it cannot safely absorb and recycle. We need to shift toward creating lasting products that are functional, efficient, and beautiful. We must create economies that reuse and recycle materials wisely—mimicking ecological cycles wherever possible. We must be frugal with resources but generous in creativity and love to guarantee that future generations may live with abundance.

- *Economic justice and equity.* The authentic needs of all must be met, ensuring a modest but dignified lifestyle for all. Equity does not mean that all must have the same level of wealth, but it does mean that differences of wealth are not so great that they manifest a fundamental lack of fairness that can lead to resentment, outrage, or violence. The principle of justice also means ensuring that meeting the needs of humanity does not compromise the well-being of other species or the needs of future generations.

- *Biological and cultural diversity.* We should seek to maximize diversity in culture and to ensure the widest possible diversity of creatures and eco-systems. Diversity is a sign of a mature, well-functioning system since it makes a system both more efficient and more resilient. Indeed, one of the best ways to measure the true wealth of a community is by the diversity of life, art, cultures, and spiritualities it harmoniously sustains.

- *Rootedness in place.* Like any other biological community, we must know our local ecosystem and seek to live, as much as possible, within the limits it imposes. As we noted in discussing ecofeminism, to truly inspire and motivate us to action, our identification with the Earth must be rooted in an emotional bond to real people, places, and biotic communities. At the same time, insofar as we successfully adapt ourselves to the place in which we live, we can learn to live in ways that respect the true carrying capacity and contribute meaningfully to the wider ecological community. Furthermore, when we live within our local means, energy expended in transportation is minimized and the temptation to export pollution and other problems "out of sight and out of mind" is reduced. We are much less likely to foul our own nest—or exhaust wealth—if we live primarily within the bounds set by our local ecosystem.

- *Self-reliance and openness.* While rootedness in place emphasizes the need for self-reliance, local communities and economies—like all living systems—also need to have permeable boundaries. Trade and commerce will always be necessary, but production should be local whenever possible. People and ideas should be able to move freely, and local communities need to maintain an openness to creativity and cultural expressions arising beyond their boundaries. World-renowned economist John Maynard Keynes maintained that "economic entanglements" should be minimized, but that other areas called for wider sharing: "Ideas, knowledge, science, hospitality, travel—these are the things that by nature should be international. But let goods be homespun wherever it is reasonable and conveniently possible and, above all, let finance be primarily national" (quoted in Athanasiou 1996, 218-19).

- *Democracy, participation, and subsidiarity.* As much as possible, people should actively participate in the decisions that affect them. According to the principle of subsidiarity, matters should be dealt with at the smallest, lowest, or most local systemic entity. Larger, more inclusive levels of the systemic holarchy should deal only with matters that affect the wider system and cannot be addressed effectively at a lower level.

- *Cooperative self-organization.* Economies and cultures must be free to self-organize creatively within the boundaries of shared values and the need to ensure the well-being and sustainability of the community. This implies a fairly wide degree of freedom in economic, political, and cultural enterprises, yet such a freedom also comes with real responsibilities.

- *Sharing of knowledge and wisdom.* Knowledge should never be privatized, but should be shared as widely as possible. The flow of information and the sharing of wisdom strengthen systems and makes them more responsive and resilient.

- *Responsibility and rights.* Individuals and the community must be free to exercise their basic rights to life, health, participation, and expression. At the same time, the exercise of these rights must not compromise the responsibility of the community to provide basic necessities for all and to ensure the sustainability and health of local ecosystems.

- *Balance.* In all things, a sense of balance must reign. There are *yin* and *yang* tensions between rights and responsibilities, self-reliance and sharing, generosity and conservation. Always, we must take care that, in maximizing one value, others are not compromised; that is, we must embody the ethics of the *optima* rather than the *maxima*.

One vision that captures and synthesizes these elements is that of *bioregionalism*. Ecofeminist Judith Plant (1990) sees bioregionalism as an "integrating idea" that allows us to put our visions of a new world into practice; it is a *praxis* (theory integrated with practice, or a kind of "walking wisdom") that enables us to live what we believe. The ideas of bioregionalism are not new—indeed they draw in part on the traditional ways that humans lived for millennia before the first empires arose five thousand years ago. In its modern form, the bioregional movement is now over twenty years old; yet for many its key ideas may still need an introduction.

A bioregion is a geographic entity, normally defined by a watershed catchment area. It exhibits certain commonalities in terms of vegetation, landforms, and wildlife (Nozick 1992). It is large enough to allow for a degree of diversity and the possibility of basic economic self-sufficiency, but small enough to facilitate in-depth knowledge of the region. This latter point is important, because at the heart of bioregionalism lies the idea of "becoming native to a place" once again, of regaining a profound connection with nature at a local level. In the bioregional vision, we must fit ourselves into the ecosystem and natural economy of the particular place, rather than trying to mold the place to suit our personal tastes (albeit, presumably, some mutuality of shaping does occur). Kirkpatrick Sale refers to this in terms of the need to become true "dwellers in the land":

> To become dwellers in the land, to relearn the laws of Gaea [sic], to come to know the earth fully and honestly, the crucial and perhaps only all-encompassing task is to understand place, the immediate specific place where we live. The kinds of soil and rocks under our feet; the source of the waters we drink; the meaning of the different kinds of winds; the common insects, birds, mammals, plants, and trees; the particular cycle of the seasons; the times to plant and harvest and forage—these things that are necessary to know. The limits of its resources; the carrying capacities of its lands and waters; the places where it must not be stressed; the places where its bounties can best be developed; the treasures it holds and the treasures it withholds—these things must be understood. And the cultures of the people, of the populations native to the land, of those who have grown up with it, the human social and economic arrangements shaped by and adapted to the geomorphic ones, in both urban and rural settings—these are things that must be appreciated. (Sale 1985, 41-42)

To do this requires a radical reorientation in the way we live. As Mary Gomes and Allen Kanner note:

> Embracing the bioregional vision requires more than recycling or driving less, or even minimizing our consumption, although all these are important. It involves a change in our sense of identity, so that we allow our surroundings to grow *into* us, to let the land reclaim us like ivy growing over an old house, or wildflowers pushing up through cracks in the pavement. It means the death of the old industrial self and the birth of something new. (1995, 121)

The five goals of bioregionalism can be summarized as self-reliance, harmonizing with nature, meeting individual needs, building community culture, and achieving community control. Sale (1985) adds that the implementation of the bioregional vision requires that we gain a knowledge of the land and local ecosystem; that we learn the local lore—the history and culture of the place; that we develop the potential of the bioregion by discovering how to realize the possibilities of the place within its carrying capacity while cultivating regional self-sufficiency; and that we seek the liberation of the Self by promoting people's personal growth in the context of a supportive community. The following table contrasts the bioregional vision with the current dominant dis/order (*adapted from* Sale 1985):

	Bioregional Model	Corporate Capitalism/ Industrial Growth
Scale:	Region/Community	State/Nation/World
Economy:	Conservation/Restoration	Exploitation
	Stability/Evolution/Adaptation	Growth/Progress
	Local/Self-sufficiency	Global/Specialization and Trade
	Cooperation Primary	Competition Primary
Polity:	Decentralization	Centralization
	Complementarity/Subsidiarity	Hierarchy/Control
	Diversity/Consensus	Uniformity/Majority Rule
	Participation/Empowerment	Domination/Control
Culture:	Symbiosis	Polarization
	Evolution/Qualitative Growth	Quantitative Growth/Violence
	Plurality/Diversity	Monoculture

In considering this comparison, we must take care not to create false dichotomies. While the fundamental unit of the bioregion is the local community, that does not mean that larger, more encompassing systemic units are not important. Presumably, according to the principle of subsidiarity, larger interregional, as well as national (or similar) and international levels of organization would still be needed, including those working at the global level. The key idea, though, is that the bioregional level becomes in many ways the primary unit for making decisions and organizing the economy. That being said, we are also part of a wider planetary community and some issues—such as climate change—affect us all and require coordinated action, even if many of those actions are actually implemented locally. The idea of a "glocal" vision is helpful here: we must think and act both locally *and* globally, and indeed we must see the fundamental unity that relates the local to the global. We should know our local reality and how best to act within it, but we are also informed by the global reality and the experiences of other regions.

Similarly, while cooperation and symbiosis may be primary values, competition will also come into play. Indeed, the principle of diversity would mean that a wide variety of economic enterprises would exist and these would inevitably compete with each other to some extent. As we have seen, competition is indeed a necessary part of a healthy ecosystem, but on a wider scale cooperation and symbiosis are more important dynamics. This must also be reflected in our economic system—perhaps drawing on the example of David Korten's "community enterprise economy" consisting of "a market economy composed primarily, though not exclusively, of family enterprises, small-scale co-ops, worker-owned firms, and neighbourhood and municipal corporations" (1995, 312).

Economics: Sustainable Community Rooted in Place

In a bioregional vision, economics must be centered on values such as self-reliance, sustainability, equity, and justice. The idea of an "economy of enough" or "living well" is at the center of this vision: an economy that can equitably satisfy real human needs (vs. wants and desires) while also enabling us to truly *live* and at the same time respect the limits of our local (and global) ecosystem. Theodore Roszak (1992) calls this the principle of *plenitude*, which challenges us to assess our authentic needs. We need to ask what wealth really is and what it is really for. Instead of seeking to acquire things beyond what is truly necessary, we could seek instead other kinds of wealth, particularly in the form of time for friendship, family, reflection, meditation, creativity, nature, and play.

In many ways, the bioregional economy resembles the subsistence economies we previously discussed (see pp. 36-37). Economic activity aims not at the production of money or commodities for capital accumulation or the acquisition of luxuries, but rather at the creation and re-creation of life. Priority is given to fulfilling basic needs, both material and spiritual. This requires a shift from the trend of globalization to that of local self-sufficiency. As Marcia Nozick explains:

> First, by concentrating on local production for local needs, we minimize the distances which products must travel for distribution, thus cutting down on transportation costs, wasteful energy use and pollution. Second, local demand for goods (community and surrounding region) can be met by smaller scale industries and technologies which can be more easily managed by the community. Decentralized development—using a scaled down technology to produce smaller amounts for fewer people—disperses impacts of development more evenly throughout the biosphere, giving nature more time to absorb and reprocess the waste. Third, by decentralizing industry and creating more small scale businesses to replace megaprojects, we can increase the numbers of jobs and people's access to them, thereby creating a more equitable distribution of wealth. Fourth, at smaller scale enterprises, workers can have greater say over their work environment and therefore find work more meaningful. (1992, 14-15)

A bioregional economy is founded on both the optimization of scale and the recycling and conserving of its resources. Both of these aspects ensure sustainability—that is, the ability to satisfy society's real needs without diminishing the prospects of future generations in the biotic community (Capra and Steindl-Rast 1991). Instead of adapting the environment to the needs of people, people adapt themselves to harmonize with the natural world and maintain ecological balance. The economy aims to minimize its use of nonrenewable resources and ecological destruction while maximizing its ability to recycle and use human creativity and labor.

One example where the idea of a local economy such as that envisioned by bioregionalism is already beginning to take off is in the movement toward a "hundred mile diet"—that is, trying to eat only food grown in one's local region. Obviously, this is somewhat more challenging to achieve in some places than others due to factors of climate and agricultural productivity, but the basic principle is sound. Locally grown food requires less transportation and is fresher than food coming from afar. On another level, eating local food helps root us in place. This is particularly true when we engage in Community Supported Agriculture, where a group of persons organize to buy the production of a local farmer. Often, such groups form a living relationship between consumers and producers by visiting the farm and even lending a hand in the productive activities. Similarly, growing our own food in a garden—either by our own home or in a community plot—roots us in place *and* gives us access to fresh, organically grown food. Ultimately, of course, all agriculture in a bioregional model would aim to be truly sustainable, based on principles of organic farming and agroecology.

At the heart of the bioregional economy must lie a renewal of human work as a life-sustaining activity, along the lines discussed when considering ecofeminist alternatives. Instead of "jobs," we must seek to create authentic livelihoods that are useful, meaningful, and life-giving. On a local scale, it is possible creatively to reunite consumption and production. Work can become less specialized and more varied, and the strict division between work and recreation can be overcome.

Central to this vision must also be the eradication of the division of labor along gender lines. In particular, men must take an active role in the basic domestic chores involved in the sustenance of life, including childcare. Similarly, instead of valuing intellectual pursuits above all, activities involving direct contact with nature and those involved in the direct sustenance of life would be given higher value.

It is conceivable that computers and modern communication technologies could actually help facilitate this new model by allowing people to center more work around the home, as was once the case in preindustrial times. In general, instead of using technology to eliminate jobs or to accelerate the accumulation of wealth, we should aim to reduce the time spent working and to increase free time for relationships, recreation, art, and activities aimed at restoring ecosystems and sustaining life.

If the bioregional economic vision at first seems utopian, it must be remembered that subsistence economies have traditionally provided sustenance for millions of people while allowing for a significant degree of ecological harmony. Obviously, the conversion to such an economy will require an end to the sumptuous levels of consumption now existing in the global North, but there is no reason to believe that basic needs cannot be met. By freeing up the tremendous resources now dedicated to capital accumulation and militarism, both ecological sustainability and the satisfaction of basic needs could be met. Indeed, for the vast majority of the world's people, the bioregional model promises a significant improvement in the fulfillment of their material needs. At the same time, this improved satisfaction of basic needs combined with the empowerment of women through the restructuring of work (and power), could create the conditions necessary to stabilize human population more quickly.

Culture: Community and Diversity

The bioregional model proposes a renewal not only of economics but of human culture as well. With the ordering of human activity onto a local scale, the possibility for authentic community is renewed. Living ecologically based ethics begins to become a real possibility because the consequences of our actions become more readily apparent: for example, pollution and poverty can no longer be exported out of sight. We can more easily persuade people to do what is right because it is more immediately apparent that this is in their own personal and their own community's self-interest. A better knowledge of place and a closer connection to the land also creates a spontaneous ecological awareness from which the new ethics can flow.

A key aspect of building authentic local communities lies in the regeneration of local culture. Wendell Berry (1988) argues that a strong local culture can exert a kind of centripetal force that holds soil, memories—and the communities built around these—together. In the past (and to this day, in some autochthonous cultures), a child's destiny was to succeed his or her parents; youth were steeped in local traditions, stories, and lore. Today, children are educated, not to return home, but to leave it and to earn money in "a provisional future that has nothing to do with place or community" (W. Berry 1988, 11). Lacking a local economy, families and neighbors are no longer useful to one another. People have become dependent on outsiders who live far away, and the hegemony of professionalism has replaced local culture. Lacking an authentic local culture and local economy, places become "open to exploitation, and ultimately destruction, from the center" (W. Berry 1988, 13). Nozick elaborates:

> Culture is the *glue* that holds communities together and makes them last over generations, even more than economic or political power. *Culture is the soul and life force of a community*—the collective expression of values, perceptions, language, technology, history, spirituality, art and social organization in a community. I am referring here to culture as a way of life, distinct from culture as the "high brow" arts. (1992, 181)

The success of bioregional communities, then, depends on developing local culture in direct contraposition to the trend toward monocultures of the mind. Each community has its own particular foods, customs, values, and art. Part of the task of building a viable bioregional culture lies in recovering, re-creating, affirming, and promoting a culture truly indigenous to place. As noted earlier, this requires knowing the land and its creatures as well as the local history and stories.

In doing so, however, the aim is not to create a single, uniform culture, but to respect a multiplicity of cultural expressions. This is particularly true in today's world, where migration has led to an intermingling of cultures, languages, and religious traditions. Such an encounter is not a threat but rather an opportunity for cultural enrichment. At the core of this diversity must lie the value of *respect*, including respect for more fluid gender roles. Instead of diversity being seen as a threat, it should be seen as a strength to celebrate (and not merely "tolerate").

A bioregional culture also seeks to deepen interiority through our participation in the "cosmos-creating endeavor." Instead of pursuing fulfillment in material accumulation, a bioregional culture strives to enhance life-giving expressions of creativity, be they what have traditionally been considered artistic activities or the creative participation in the restoration of complex ecosystems.

Similarly, such a culture values what we might call the "spiritual arts" including meditative practices, spiritual dance and movement, and the cultivation of mystical identification with the Earth and the cosmos itself, all of which aim directly to deepen interiority. Ultimately, a bioregional spirituality will always be closely related to the Earth and to the land. Indeed, a tremendous spiritual potential can be unleashed when we develop a true relationship to a place, its soil, and its diverse forms of life.

An intriguing example of this is that of the community of Findhorn, located in an inhospitable climate in northern Scotland. Starting in the early 1960s, Peter Caddy began to farm in the sandy soil of Findhorn together with his family and a few friends. With no farming experience, but with a deep spiritual sense and the techniques of Rudolph Steiner's biodynamic method, he and the community that gradually gathered around him achieved startling results. Vegetables grew to astounding sizes and plants attained unheard-of rates of growth. Sir George Trevelyan, who visited Findhorn in 1969 observed:

> I make no claim to be a gardener but I am a member of the Soil Association, interested in organic methods and have seen enough to know that compost and straw mulch alone mixed with poor sandy soil is not enough to account for the garden. . . . What appears to be new at Findhorn is that here is a group of amateurs, starting gardening from scratch, using a direct mental contact with the Devic [nature-spirit] world and in fullest consciousness basing their work on this co-operation. . . . They are literally demonstrating that the desert can blossom as the rose. They also show the astonishing pace which this can be brought about. If this can be done so quickly at Findhorn, it can be done in the Sahara. (Hawken 1975, 166-67)

One does not have to have a literal belief in Divas and nature spirits to appreciate the implications of such an experience. By apprehending the Sacred present in creation, respect and care flow naturally from us. By developing a close, loving relationship to the land and its creatures, by harmonizing with their very spirit, we can greatly accelerate the process of restoring Earth's ecological health and balance. This also serves to develop a wider compassion, which in turn builds and sustains authentic community.

The development of a viable bioregional culture depends not only on cultivating a relationship to the land but also on transmitting and deepening local knowledge and history. Story plays an important role in this task. Story, too, helps root local knowledge in a larger, cosmological vision through the remything of the universe story itself. All members of the local community have a place in these endeavors; all are called to be creators and artists who recount the story through a diversity of media.

Indeed, the purpose of local culture is to celebrate the wealth of diversity both within itself and beyond itself. Just as each culture affirms its own unique characteristics within the global cultural milieu, so too it affirms the unique contribution of each individual. Growth is encouraged, but it is growth in diversity and depth rather than growth in quantity. Indeed, as Thomas Berry (1999) points out, while physical energy and material resources are diminished by use, psychic and spiritual energies actually increase as they are shared. Wealth in a bioregional culture, then, will be measured not by capital accumulation and consumption but by the rich diversity of cultural and artistic expressions it produces.

The bioregional culture, like any open system, also interacts and enriches itself with the wealth of other cultures; this sharing, however, would be based on equality and mutuality rather than the hegemony of one culture over all the others. The potential of such interaction to stimulate the evolution of knowledge and the human spirit is virtually unlimited, especially in a world where modern communications and the Internet facilitate the sharing of information as never before.

Politics: Putting New Models of Power into Action

A mutuality of participation must characterize the bioregional community in all its aspects: production, culture, and governance. At its root lies an emphasis on the affirmation of power-from-within and power-with. At the same time, community gives a context where these forms of power can, in fact, be cultivated and the dynamics of powerlessness overcome.

In order to facilitate the exercise of participatory forms of power and minimize the exercise of power-over, the structures of governance at the community level should reflect the principles of consensus, subsidiarity, and self-organization.

Consensus is based on the image of the circle and originates with the Quaker belief that every person holds a *piece* of the truth. The objective of consensus is to take all these pieces (even those that appear to be contradictory) and weave together a decision that reflects a greater wisdom (Nozick 1992). This is in accord with the systems perspective that values the role of fluctuations and diversity as a source of creativity and transformation—as opposed to majority voting, which effectively suppresses them (Jantsch 1980). An individual with a strong ethical objection may even block a decision from proceeding. To be truly effective, though, consensus requires a nonadversarial approach based on listening sincerely to the voice of the other and an openness to "step aside" and accept the wisdom of the larger group. It will work only in a relatively small group of people who are able to meet face to face or communicate interactively with one another.[2]

Subsidiarity reflects a systems understanding of power rather than a hierarchical one and minimizes the abuses of power-over. At the same time, it expresses the holarchical nature of living systems where larger, more encompassing systems emerge from smaller ones. Subsidiarity implies that any decision that can

---

2. Another interesting decision-making process that seems to reflect consensus principles is embodied in the "talking circles" found in many native North American traditions.

be made at a "lower" level (subsystem) should be made there; it is referred to the next "higher" (more encompassing) level of authority only if the lower level cannot resolve the matter—for instance, if consensus at the grassroots level fails or if the matter being dealt with requires a more inclusive, interregional approach (Capra and Steindl-Rast 1991). In accord with this, it should be noted that the bioregional model does not exclude coordination in economic and political matters at a broader, even global, level; however, respecting subsidiarity, these more-encompassing structures would not be given hegemonic power.

Self-organization is also a basic characteristic of living systems. Human societies spontaneously organize themselves as families, clans, tribes, villages, and guilds. If such structures are truly healthy, the fundamental "glue" holding them together is not authoritarian power-over but rather the ethic of care and mutual respect (Roszak 1992). Ultimately, these small social structures are effective to the degree that they facilitate cooperation and enable a creative response to changing needs and conditions. Leadership should be widely distributed and fluid, changing over time as the organization itself evolves. It is only in such a context that true power-with can flourish.

Similarly, governance in the bioregion itself would be based more on function than authority. Presumably, a wide variety of offices such as magistrates, sheriffs, treasurers, and clerks would still exist, but these would only be special functions based on service and responsibility rather than authority (power-over). The community as a whole would always maintain the priority in its exercise of its power. Competition for political power in such a model would be kept in check, and with it, the short-term perspective of most politicians trying to buy the votes of their constituents could be eliminated.

Education: From Information to Wisdom

In exploring the renewal of the psyche, we discovered the importance of recovering what Roszak calls, the "ecological ego," the "innately animistic quality" that we experience as children. In recapturing this form of consciousness and integrating it with other forms of perception and knowing, we gain "a sense of ethical responsibility with the planet" which it "seeks to weave. . . into the fabric of social relations and political decisions" (1992, 320-21). Similarly, David Korten speaks of our need to awaken "from a deep cultural trance" (1995, 325). The bioregional community provides a context for this awakening to occur, a place where we can recover our ecological ego by becoming truly rooted in place and by allowing the wider ecological community to become our teacher.

At all levels, be it with children, youth, or adults, education in the bioregional vision must help us shift from a cosmology that sees the world as a collection of objects to another in which relationships are understood as the primary reality. Gregory Bateson went so far as to argue that relationships should be the basis of all definitions—that we can only truly know a thing in the context of its relationship to others (Capra 1982). Certainly this relational, ecological vision should ground all educational endeavors in the bioregional perspective.

The original root of the word "educate" comes from the Latin *educere* which means "to draw or lead out." Education is not fundamentally concerned, then, with accumulating information—although the availability and flow of quality information *are* necessary to maintain a healthy living system; rather, education must be understood as an intrinsically transformative process that enables us, as humans, to become more attuned to both our local ecosystem and the wider cosmic story while facilitating a creative and harmonious interaction with other humans and the wider Earth community. In other words, education should draw us ever closer to the Tao, enabling us to act consciously, creatively, and harmoniously with the unfolding purpose of the cosmos.

In this perspective, we are not seeking knowledge that is simply memorized, but rather something that becomes part of our very being—something that draws out our true, ecological self, and integrates it into consciousness. Education touches not only the mind but also the heart. Instead of focusing on information, or even knowledge, it seeks to help us grow in wisdom. Matthew Fox refers to this transformation by stating that we must move from "knowledge factories" to "wisdom schools" (1994, 170).

At the base of this shift lies the transition from the idea of knowledge as power (understood as control or domination) to the idea of knowledge as love. Knowledge as love implies an empathetic sensibility, an effort to identify with that which one seeks to know. In this vision, perception takes precedence over conceptualization, and attentive contemplation becomes more important than analysis. This kind of holistic, intuitive apprehension has largely been downplayed, or even lost, in a scientific rationality based on reductionalism. This does not mean that analysis cannot play a useful role, but it must be complemented with other modes of knowing.

One way to do this is to actively engage in experiential learning. Mind and body must learn together—we must learn not only by seeing and hearing but by tasting, feeling, and smelling. Like learning to ride a bicycle, such knowledge cannot really be taught; it is rather "caught" and absorbed somehow into our very being, never again to be forgotten. As noted previously, Morris Berman (1981) speaks of *mimetic learning*, a kind cognition integrated with the whole body based on "participatory consciousness" rather than the detached mind of the "objective" observer[3] (see pp. 165-66). Traditionally, mimetic learning involved repetitive tasks in direct contact with experience—for example, learning a craft. Yet it can also take place through a great work of theatre or music that moves others to identify emotionally with the actors or performers.

How can such a participatory consciousness be evoked when we seek to learn the lessons of the land, to become truly "native to our place"? How can we expand this consciousness to embrace the wider story of the cosmos itself? Certainly, the role of ritual, myth, and even creative play may facilitate this kind of emotional identification with our local ecological community, the living Earth, and the cosmos itself. To the extent that we can awaken this kind of participatory consciousness, we can move beyond learning mere facts "about" our bioregion, our planet, and our universe (as important as those may be) to genuine

---

3. Although, in truth, as our reflections on quantum physics show, we are always in some sense participants in what we observe.

empathetic identification and love. We need to *experience* our participation in the ongoing story of cosmic evolution truly to apprehend (or "catch") what it means in our lives.

At the same time, we need to explore new ways of learning that value and incorporate experiential learning, participatory consciousness, and the development of intuition. By intuition, we are referring to a holistic form of cognition that is distinct from discursive thinking. Intuition, as we have previously noted, is not irrational, it is simply a different form of rationality which attempts to apprehend directly that which is implicit. Most of what we perceive, in fact, never becomes fully conscious. Intuition is a way of holistically accessing these diffuse perceptions and enabling the subconscious to integrate them into new insights.

To incorporate intuitive learning does not mean that we abandon discursive or analytical thought; rather, we use them both in a complementary fashion. One way we can do this is by visualizing learning as a cycle. In some ways, this cycle resembles the traditional see-judge-act method used in many varieties of popular education. We begin by gathering information on a problem or matter on which we are seeking insights, including our own experience (see); we analyze the causes and consequences to discover the roots of the matter and propose possible solutions, at times enriched in faith communities with theological reflections (judge); and finally we synthesize the insights gained and create a plan of action (act). An additional step in the cycle is to evaluate the actions undertaken as a new starting point to begin again.[4] This process of praxis is very useful, but it could be much enriched by adding an intuitive component as illustrated by the following process:

A Holistic Learning Cycle

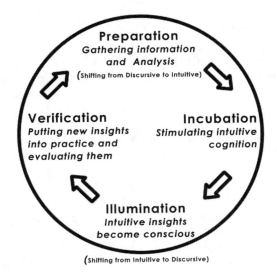

Preparation
*Gathering information
and Analysis*
(Shifting from Discursive to Intuitive)

Incubation
*Stimulating intuitive
cognition*

Illumination
*Intuitive insights
become conscious*

Verification
*Putting new insights
into practice and
evaluating them*

(Shifting from Intuitive to Discursive)

---

4. In many ways this process parallels Kolb's (1984) learning cycle starting with Concrete Experience (practice), going to Reflective Observation and Abstract Conceptualization (theory), and returning again to practice, enriched by new insights (Active Experimentation).

1. *Preparation*. We begin by gathering information on the matter we are studying. This will involve discursive processes, including the gathering and analysis of data as well as drawing on our own experience. At the same time, there is a gradual shift from a discursive to an intuitive-perceptual mode.

2. *Incubation*. Methods such as meditation, art, embodiment practices, dream-work, and visualization are used to stimulate the intuitive process, creating space for new perceptions, insights, and inspirations to emerge.

3. *Illumination*. The unconscious insights gathered through intuition are made conscious. This is normally a spontaneous process that happens in bursts; it cannot be forced or predicted. Once an insight has emerged, however, discursive thought can help articulate and clarify it.

4. *Verification*. We attempt to put our new insights into action, and these are evaluated over time for effectiveness. The cycle can then begin again.

We must understand this cycle of learning to be continual. In actual practice, the four phases overlap. While acting, a new insight may suddenly come upon us. And indeed, while acting day to day we may also be incorporating practices that stimulate our intuition, or that gather information to prepare the ground for further discoveries. The important point is to recognize the important role that intuition and creativity play in the process and to intentionally seek to stimulate and value their contributions. Data collection, reflection, and analysis are also necessary components, but alone they are not sufficient truly to break through to deeper levels of transformative learning.

Grounding the Vision

In considering the bioregional vision, our intention has been to outline a kind of "attractor" that may serve to inspire us on the journey from pathology to health. Over time, though, as we move toward such an attractor, it will continue to evolve; its outlines will surely shift and the vision will also become clearer and more detailed.

Will this vision—or one that resembles it—actually become a reality? Standing where we do at this moment, it may seem hard to believe that this could really come about; yet, if we look closely, we might be surprised to find that in countless small ways, it is already emerging in many places around the globe. Indeed, David Suzuki and Holly Dressel (2002) have collected a whole book full of case studies of projects and initiatives embodying the kind of vision of sustainable community we are speaking of here.

A particularly intriguing example is that of the Gaviotas community, located in the eastern savannahs of war-torn Colombia (Gardner 2006). Since 1971, this ecovillage has been working to become a living model of sustainable community.

What makes it particularly inspiring is that it has managed to do so in one of the most violent places on Earth and in a region with relatively poor soil and few natural resources. Despite these challenges, Gaviotas has attracted a group of students, laborers, scientists, and refugees who have managed to employ a host of sustainable technologies using little more that their own creative talents, including solar energy, biogas, organic agriculture, and an innovative deep-water pump. In addition, they have established a school and a hospital to provide needed services to the local population. At the same time, they have begun an ambitious reforestation project that already provides useful employment in the community.

Gaviotas's founder, Paolo Lugari, says that "Gaviotas is a state of mind, more than anything. It is not really so much a place. It's a way of living and thinking. It means not just thinking outside the box, but constant innovation and re-invention." The village has no mayor, no police, nor any kind of formal rules. Instead, at the heart of the community are a number of principles that facilitate the kind of creative self-organization characteristic of healthy living systems (Kaihla 2007):

- The community keeps meetings to a minimum, preferring instead to make all the community's work and activities a kind of continual, open-ended brainstorming session.

- They invent through a collective process of continual improvements and tweaking.

- In tackling a problem, the community seeks to abandon all previous assumptions and open itself to completely new insights.

- Gaviotas eschews all forms of hierarchy and status based on professional qualifications. The opinions and ideas of each community member are valued on their own merit, not on the basis of who the person is or what that person has formally studied.

- The community promotes a culture in which all are encouraged to express themselves freely and participate fully.

- Gaviotas encourages the cross-fertilization of ideas and interdisciplinary thought by rotating specialists into areas outside their traditional fields and encouraging all community members to become, at least to some extent, generalists.

- The community avoids overscheduling its members' time, encouraging them to devote their working time to whatever task most inspires them so as to make room for creativity.

One of the most intriguing aspects of the Gaviotas experience is that the community has thrived despite the relatively harsh conditions of life in Colombia. Yet, in another sense, there is a certain logic in this from a systems perspective: it is often on the margins of a system, in the places where the stresses are greatest, that creative evolution is most likely to occur. As we have seen in the case of punctuated evolution, such stresses can lead to bifurcation points where a new systemic order emerges as a kind of breakthrough.

One way of thinking about this is in terms of "creativity from the margins." Those who are struggling for survival, those who do not reap the benefits from the current systemic dis/order, are more likely to take risks to create something new. Often, necessity is indeed the mother of invention: persons living on the margins have needed to develop and hone their creative skills in order to survive, and if this creativity can be harnessed, amazing things can emerge. In this lies an immense, and only partially tapped, force for deeply transformative action.

It is also on the margins that functioning subsistence economies can still be found. The "women producing survival," of whom Vandana Shiva speaks (1989), for example, are rich sources of wisdom and inspiration in the struggle for a sustainable future. By tapping into this wisdom and building on it, much can be done to strengthen subsistence economies and local cultures under threat from globalization and monoculture. In other cases, where losses are more advanced, it may be necessary to facilitate processes through which knowledge, history, and ecological wisdom can be recovered, renewed, and reimplemented.

In all these processes, the most important role for those working toward integral liberation and the creation of sustainable communities will be to affirm the participants' dignity and to value their indigenous knowledge and culture. To do so, activists and grassroots educators must be extremely sensitive to the dynamics of power in their practice, even if they share the same cultural and class background as the participants. Often, the mystique of the outside "expert" can otherwise undermine the transformative process. By adopting a participatory work style, encouraging the sharing of leadership roles, and fostering awareness, much can be done to create a space where the dynamics of internalized powerlessness, especially internalized oppression, can be partially neutralized so that the essential process of transformative learning can truly begin.

While the margins are certainly a privileged place for transformative action, a good argument can also be made for working with those who receive significant benefits from the current structures of political and economic domination. Certainly, there is an urgent need to undermine the exploitative dynamics of the current structures as quickly as possible. While many of the real alternatives may emerge and develop on the margins, any action that serves to subvert the controlling power of the center will further the possibilities of transformation. Moreover, to the extent that the voracious appetites of the center are slowed, time is bought to allow for change.

It should be remembered, too, that the concepts of "margins" and "center" are themselves often relative. Many who benefit from the system of domination in one aspect may also find themselves oppressed by it in another—for example, middle-class women who benefit materially but still suffer the violence of patriarchy. A gay man may be an upwardly-mobile professional, but he also experiences the pain of discrimination based on sexual orientation. Others, through a sickness like cancer, become aware of the health threat posed by the chemical contamination of our food supply and begin to organize an organic community-supported agriculture initiative. In some sense, then, there are islands of marginality close to the center that provide special opportunities for change.

Two courses of action, in particular, seem to suggest themselves when seeking ways to subvert the center. The first revolves around restructuring gender roles, an issue that directly touches all human beings. According to Rosemary Radford Ruether's analysis (1992), achieving greater parity in the sexual division of labor could serve to reorient men toward more life-producing roles. Over time, this could serve to undermine the very foundations of patriarchy. In this regard, the feminist movement is serving as a powerful vehicle for raising the consciousness of women in all social strata. It should be noted, however, that the initiative for change need not be restricted to women: Many men also feel a deep dissatisfaction with the role that patriarchy assigns them. By tapping into this dissatisfaction and making it conscious, steps can be taken leading to greater gender parity.

A second suggestion for subverting the center is the use of futures oriented education. By developing a conscious connection to future generations (something accessible to most people through a reflection on the lives of their own children, grandchildren, nieces, or nephews), concern for the state of the planet and its future can be cultivated. This approach may well be effective even with those closest to the very center of power.

Yet other potential catalysts for change include spiritual practices, faith reflection, and cross-cultural encounters. All of these can help shift us out of our normal way of perceiving the world, opening us to a radical shift in our worldview.

Indeed, there are inspiring stories of corporate executives and influential politicians who have truly been converted to a new worldview and who have become important spokespersons. The example of Al Gore and his film *An Inconvenient Truth* on climate change comes to mind, as does the case of Ray Anderson, chairman of Interface flooring who made his company a leader in recycling and waste reduction after reading Paul Hawken's *The Ecology of Commerce* (1993). We should never underestimate the potential for such conversions to a new paradigm—indeed, as Donella Meadows has pointed out, it only takes the right catalyst for the blinders to fall and to make a breakthrough to a new way of seeing and being in the world.

A FOURFOLD PATH TOWARD LIBERATION

Our final step in this journey is to reflect on a new style of praxis that can lead us toward the vision of sustainable community that we seek for the world. Just *how* do we go about working for liberation? How can we put our cosmology into practice? How can we open ourselves to the Tao and allow it to guide us as we work to strengthen communion, broaden diversity, and deepen the interiority of the Earth community?

All our reflections on the holistic paradigm and the new cosmology will be in vain if we cannot translate them into practical guidelines and principles that enable us to work more fruitfully to transform a system that is devouring humanity and the planet itself. We need to take the vision we have conceived, the ethical framework we have considered, and the spiritual intuitions we have gained and put them into practice in a meaningful way.

On the one hand, we cannot create a magic recipe for transformation, but we can discern processes and principles to guide us. At the same time, we must always recall that the Tao, the Dharma, the Malkuta, is a living reality that is already present and active among us. Its guidance is already written in our hearts: cosmic grace enfolds us. To become agents for change, we need but to open ourselves to it, to invoke it, to be filled with its liberating power; yet that, in itself, requires that we learn new ways of being and acting in the world.

An image from the holographic analogy (pp. 187-91) may help to clarify our task. On the one hand, there exists an implicate order, a unifying all-pervasive substratum that is also the Tao, the great Way guiding the unfolding of the universe. On the other hand, there exists the manifest world, the explicate order, which corresponds to the Te, the way the Tao becomes embodied in a particular form.

As we have noted previously (p. 174), Middle Eastern cosmology also speaks of a different but similar distinction: There is the reality of the *shemaya* (Aramaic; *shemayim* in Hebrew) and the reality of *ar'ah* (Aramaic; *ha'aretz* in Hebrew). In essence, both realities are the reflection of a deeper, underlying unity. We normally translate these two aspects as "heaven" and "earth," but the *shemaya* can be understood to be the archetype of vibration, sound, light, and waveforms while *ar'ah* corresponds to the archetype of concretized forms, like a particle (Douglas-Klotz 1999). In terms of quantum physics, these express the wave-particle reality. Both are present, but which one we will perceive depends on how we focus our attention.

We can understand the Tao or the *shemaya* to be in some sense the realm of vision, of possibilities, of potentiality, while the *Te* or *ar'ah* is that of concrete embodiment. When, in Jesus' prayer, he speaks of "on earth as it is in heaven," it points to the need of embodying the Malkuta in reality. In practical terms, in working for liberation, we must always be conscious of uniting the two realms or archetypes. Prayer and action—spirit, energy, and matter—must not be separated. The realm of the *shemaya* and the Tao inspires and guides us, but this must be incarnated if it is to transform the world. Mysticism and action must always be united if we are to work effectively for liberation.

Christian theologian Matthew Fox (1983) has long argued the importance of this kind of unity of mysticism and prophetic action, of a truly embodied spirituality. In reflecting on these questions, he devised a useful framework that can guide our subsequent reflections which he refers to as the four "paths" of creation spirituality.

- *The Via Positiva* is the way of rooting ourselves in the goodness of creation; of celebrating the presence of the Sacred in all; of awakening to awe, beauty, and praise.

- *The Via Negativa* is the path of emptying ourselves; of clearing space for the Sacred to dwell; of lament and letting go; of experiencing the pregnant void.
- *The Via Creativa* is the way of creating and giving birth; of reuniting to the empowering vision of the Malkuta; of reconnecting ourselves to the great cosmic story and aligning ourselves with its unfolding purpose; of breaking through to new insights and perspectives.
- *The Via Transformativa* is the path of embodying the vision and giving it form; of working actively to transform the world; of building community and solidarity.

In practice, all four paths intermingle and interconnect. We do not move from one to another in a linear or even circular fashion. There is a creative dialectic particularly evident between the Via Positiva and the Via Negativa, on the one hand, and between the Via Creativa and Via Transformativa on the other, but all paths relate to each other and, in actual practice, often overlap. Together they create a way to frame our reflections on the processes and dynamics involved in liberating praxis. For this reason, we will use them to speak of a fourfold path toward liberation.

In using the fourfold path, we assume that the way toward liberation is a spiritual path, understanding spirituality here in a very ecological, embodied sense. In the Hindu tradition, this might be understood as a kind of "karma yoga"—a spiritual discipline of action, or "union through action." In practice, though, this yoga is one that united other forms, including those focused more on meditation or contemplative aspects.

We are also aware that Buddhism describes an eightfold path to enlightenment (or liberation) consisting of right view, right intention, right speech, right action, right livelihood, right effort, right mindfulness, and right concentration. In speaking of a fourfold path, we see these as complementary rather than conflicting perspectives; indeed, the components described in the eightfold path are also apparent in some form in the four paths we shall explore.

The fourfold path is readily evident in Middle Eastern spiritual traditions, particularly in the first four lines of Jesus' prayer and in the opening *surah* (or chapter) of the Qur'an, the Surah Fateha ("The Opening"). Together, these two prayers are recited on a regular basis by roughly half of humanity. We will draw on both as key sources of wisdom as we explore the fourfold path.[5]

---

5. In particular, we will draw on the "midrashic" renderings of these prayers by Neil Douglas-Klotz. Unlike traditional translations, Douglas-Klotz uses a form of "expanded" translation that seeks to encompass the multiple layers of meaning inherent in the root meanings of the Aramaic and Arabic words. In the case of Jesus' prayer (the "Our Father" or "Lord's Prayer"), we use our own renderings based on the renderings and reflections found in Douglas-Klotz's *Prayers of the Cosmos* (1990) and *Desert Wisdom* (1995, 249)—often providing two complementary versions. For more information (including sound files for the complete Aramaic version of the Lord's Prayer), visit the Abwoon Resource Center Web site at www.abwoon.com. The renderings of the Surah Fateha are drawn, with some minor some adaptations (in the first line), directly from *Desert Wisdom* (pp. 90-93).

At the same time, the fourfold path also has close analogies to the teaching of the four directions found in many indigenous traditions in North America. In one understanding, the Via Positiva corresponds to the South, the Via Negativa to the North, the Via Creativa to the East, and the Via Transformativa to the West (M. Fox 1991, 24). This provides yet another complementary perspective that can enrich our framework.

Invocation: Opening to the Tao

Abwoon d'bwashmaya.

O creative Breath, Father-Mother of the Cosmos
ebbing and flowing through all forms.

O shimmering Sound
Thy radiant Name dances in and about all-that-is.

(Renderings of the first line of the Aramaic Prayer of Jesus)

Bismillahir rahmanir rahim,
Alhamdulillahi rabbi-l'alamin,
arrahman irrahim.

In the light of the one,
who gives birth to compassion—both intrinsic and responsive,
we affirm that whatever the Cosmos does, small or large,
through any being or communion of beings that helps further its purpose,
this act celebrates the Source of our unfolding story.

Therefore, give praise and celebrate with joy,
this Being of beings who mysteriously nurtures and sustains,
grows and brings to maturity,
all worlds, universes, and pluriverses,
all aspects of consciousness and knowledge.
This Source is the Originating Womb of Love in all its aspects.

(Rendering of the first three lines of the Surah Fateha)

The first path toward liberation is the path of invocation, the path of opening ourselves to the grace of the Tao, of remembering our connection to the Source and our communion with all beings, of celebrating and praising the goodness of creation. This path is closely related to finding our place and feeling at home in the cosmos as well as with sensing the sacredness of life. At the same time, it relates to perceiving the underlying sense of story and purpose unfolding in evolution.

We can open ourselves first and foremost through the cultivation of *awareness*. We open ourselves to the Tao, to the Source, by becoming mindful of its all-pervasive presence. Further, awareness is key to creating liberating forms of power—

power-with and power-from-within—as we have seen in our previous reflections. Similarly, Joanna Macy (1991a) points out that Buddhism teaches that the mind is liberated not by setting itself apart from phenomena but rather through a radical attentiveness that enables it to perceive the dynamics of dependent co-arising.

It is perhaps easiest to do this by starting with experiences of beauty, awe, wonder, and reverence; these spontaneously lead us into greater mindfulness. Beauty, particularly the beauty of nature, is perhaps the most potent way to open ourselves through attention. At the same time, it reconnects us to power-from-within. As Rachel Carson wrote:

> Those who contemplate the beauty of the Earth find reserves of strength that will endure as long as life lasts. There is a symbolic as well as actual beauty in the migration of birds, the ebb and flow of tides, the folded bud ready for spring. There is something infinitely healing in the repeated refrains of nature—the assurance that dawn comes after the night and spring after the winter. (Quoted in Suzuki and McConnell 1997, 221)

On a collective level, work around "Earth literacy" can serve as a doorway to this kind of awareness, especially if the kind of learning involved transcends the realm of information to truly serve as an experiential awakening to the beauty and wisdom of the local ecosystem.

The Buddhist teacher Thích Nhât Hanh speaks of how we must cultivate mindfulness in all our daily activities—whether washing dishes, eating, cleaning house, or working in the garden. Any kind of activity—but perhaps especially simple tasks that can be done in silence—provides an opportunity for meditation and the development of awareness.

On a practical level, we might begin by taking time to engage in what we truly love to do. Indeed, a first step may simply be to reflect on what truly gives us energy, what makes us happy, where we find joy. If we consciously engage in these activities—taking a walk by a river, drinking a cup of tea, or spending time with a good friend—they can become "gateways to reverence" that enable us to develop a greater sense of awareness. Often, engaging in these activities on a regular basis helps as well to reorient our values and priorities, for we find that many do not involve spending money, acquiring goods, or exploiting the Earth.

Over time, we can extend our practice of mindfulness to include more "mundane" activities. Often, though, as we learn to cultivate awareness, we find that things we once considered to be chores can indeed become opportunities to develop mindfulness, and even a sense of inner peace.

Finally, we need to extend our awareness to encompass as well those places and situations where beauty has been sullied, where suffering abounds, where life has been destroyed, and where injustice reigns. The path of awareness, then, will inevitably lead us to the Via Negativa. In this way, however, we truly learn to cultivate our compassion and our capacity for empathy. In so doing, we can widen our sense of being to encompass the ecological self.

Closely related to awareness is the practice of *remembrance*. In Sufism, the practice of *zikr*, or the "remembrance of the One," is a central spiritual activity through which practitioners seek to "polish the mirror of the soul" by remembering, at the deepest level of being, that there is no reality outside of the One: *La illaha illa 'llahu.*

Similarly, the invocation in the Surah Fateha—*Bismillah*: in the light/name (*sm*) of the One (*Allah*)—presents an image of a source of unity from which the reality of light, sound, and vibration is birthed from the womb (*rhm*, found in both *rahman* and *rahim*) of compassion. The first line of Jesus' prayer presents a comparable image—a parenting oneness (*Abwoon*) from which the *shemaya* bursts forth. Both, then, can be understood on one level as recalling the moment when the cosmos was birthed in the primordial flaring forth.

In truly *remembering* the moment of cosmic birth, the unity from which all sprang, we also reconnect ourselves to the story of the universe and our fundamental kinship with all entities and all beings. Traditional prayers, especially when reframed in this fashion, can serve as a way to remember, in a very real and experiential manner, our communion with all and our connection to the Source of all. The power of these practices should never be underestimated since—through the dynamics of morphic resonance—their power to transform us has been greatly multiplied over time. Indeed, it seems especially fitting that we should consciously draw on these fields of memory as we endeavor to remember.

The very act of breathing, if we become aware of it, can become a doorway to remembrance. With each breath we take, we inhale atoms that were exhaled by every other human being, and nearly every other living creature, who has ever inhabited the Earth (save, perhaps, those newly born).[6] Those atoms, then, were once a part—at least for a time—of those other living creatures. They were also a part of the ancient supernova that birthed all elements more complex than hydrogen and helium in our solar system. In breath, then, we are all connected to one another, to all our ancestors, to the entire community of life who have gone before us—as well as to the Earth and stars themselves. In this sense:

> Every breath is a sacrament, an affirmation of our connection with all other living things, a renewal of our link with our ancestors and a contribution to generations yet to come. Our breath is a part of life's breath, the ocean of air that envelops Earth. Unique in the solar system, air is both the creator and the creation of life itself. (Suzuki and McConnell 1997, 38)

---

6. "The eminent Harvard astronomer Harlow Shapley . . . calculated that each breath contains about 30,000,000,000,000,000,000, or 3.0×10^{19}, atoms of argon plus quintillions of molecules of carbon dioxide. Suppose you exhale a single breath and follow those argon atoms. Within minutes, they have diffused through the air far beyond the spot where they were released, travelling into the neighbourhood. After a year, those argon atoms have been mixed up in the atmosphere and spread around the planet in such a way that each breath you take includes at least 15 atoms of argon released in that one breath a year earlier! All people over the age of twenty have taken at least 100 million breaths and have inhaled argon atoms that were emitted in the first breath of every child born in the world a year before!" (Suzuki and McConnell 1997, 37-38).

Yet another pathway to remembrance is the use of myth and ritual to connect us to the story of Earth and the cosmos. The use of such processes, especially those that evoke participatory consciousness, can also reawaken us to awe, wonder, and awareness. To the extent that we come to understand and live the cosmic story, it becomes our teacher. Brian Swimme, for example, speaks of the gravitational attraction in the universe as an early form of love and compassion. (Interestingly, this echoes the Sufi idea of *ishq*—the attractive force of love that serves as the glue that binds the entire cosmos together, first discussed on p. 286 above.) Ritual can help us to actually experience this kind of insight—not only with our minds but also with our bodies and souls. As we re-myth the cosmic story to incorporate these teachings and create rituals that transmit such wisdom experientially, we also create opportunities to open ourselves to the liberating power of the Tao.

Ultimately, these experiences move us to joy, praise, celebration, and thanksgiving as we taste the Source who is the "Originating Womb of Love in all its aspects." Indeed, a profound sense of gratitude and praise is, perhaps, one of the most powerful forces to inspire us to work with energy and compassion to transform our world.

Letting Go: Embracing the Void

Nethqadash shmakh.

Prepare the ground of our being
and hallow a place for the planting of thy Presence.

Penetrate the deepest recesses of our hearts
and clear a space where thy shining Name may enkindle us.

(Renderings of the second line of the Aramaic Prayer of Jesus)

Iyyaka n'abadu wa iyyaka nasta'ain.

Cutting through all distractions, addictions, diversions, and forms of delusion,
all conflicting taboos, ideologies, theologies, offenses, and misunderstandings,
we affirm that we will act only from this Universe Purpose,
we will develop abilities only in the service of the Real,
we will bow to and venerate only the deepest Source of all Life,
and we will expect help and guidance only from this direction,
The ration of what we need, freely given from the One.

(Rendering of the fifth line of the Surah Fateha)

The path of letting go and embracing the void coexists in a complementary fashion with the path of opening and invocation: we can truly open ourselves only if first we have cleared away the cobwebs of delusion and created space for the Sacred to dwell. Yet it is often only when we are filled with the sense of awe, beauty, and praise that is the fruit of the path of invocation that we find the courage to let go and sink into the fertile darkness of the void.

In reflecting on the holistic microcosm, we encountered the idea of the quantum vacuum, an apparently empty void from which subatomic particles can both emerge and disappear in an instant. This void is a vast sea of energy pregnant with possibility, like the mystery of *sunyata* in Buddhism.

Attempting to let go so that we can experience this void is, perhaps, one of the most challenging journeys we can undertake. As soon as we try to find a quiet center, most of us experience the reality that our minds are full of thoughts clamoring for attention. It can take years of practice to truly find the still point for more than fleeting moments, yet even brief experiences of the void can fill us with an energy that renews our being—a shining Name or Presence that enkindles us and serves as fertile ground for new inspiration and insights.

Many traditional forms of meditation and contemplation can lead us to this experience. Most are quite simple to learn, at least in theory. Some use a mantra (prayer word) or chant as a focus for our attention, others simply seek to follow the breath, yet others use body awareness (like Tai Chi or spiritual dance), and some seek to cultivate a new point of awareness from which we may watch our thoughts arise in a detached, objective fashion. All are ways of developing a radical sense of awareness. These practices are strengthened when we exercise them in the context of a community; it would seem that a kind of resonance builds in a group that facilitates concentration and letting go.

As we have noted, Marilyn Ferguson, reflecting on the holographic analogy, points out the importance of cultivating what she calls "coherent states of consciousness" such as those that are the fruit of practicing meditation as well as other activities because these are "more nearly attuned to the primary level of reality, a dimension of order and harmony" (1987, 23). Indeed, any activity in which we enter into "a sense of flow," be it an artistic endeavor or an athletic performance, may help to facilitate closer union with the Tao.

In a similar way, this same awareness enables us to begin to perceive the dynamics of dependent co-arising and so develop new intuitions that can guide our actions. At the same time, as we have previously noted, the insights of reciprocal causality inherent in *paticca samuppada* mean that we must transcend the dichotomy between world and self; so, cultivating a harmonious state of mind has a real effect on the world. To the extent that we purify our minds of preconceptions and predispositions, we also open ourselves to the possibility of new realities—of liberating transformation in the world.

Closely related to clearing space is the need to purify ourselves of the webs of delusion that enslave and disempower us. Meditation, in fact, also helps serve this role, facilitating healing from addiction, denial, internalized oppression, and despair, as well as helping us to let go of past habits so that we can embrace new ways of perceiving, thinking, and being:

All beings are both relationship and process. Meditation teaches us to be with darkness, to be in the present. Fully in the present, which means to let go of the past and the future, all schemes, all projections, all projects, and all patterns. Therefore, it means to be open to the future pattern, to the not yet, to the unborn. (M. Fox and Sheldrake 1996a, 117)

At the same time, by teaching us to concentrate and focus awareness, meditation practices also facilitate the cultivation of *will*, the power to direct our attention and to act freely in accord with our own deepest nature rather than external compulsion (see p. 124). This, too, plays a part in liberating us from the webs of delusion that ensnare us. In so doing, it also opens the way to the path of creative empowerment.

On a communal level, the use of Joanna Macy's methodology of "despair and empowerment" work, or the "work that reconnects," can also be a powerful tool helping us to overcome the delusion of denial, internalized oppression, addiction, and despair (see p. 120). By acknowledging our pain and fear for our world and engaging honestly and courageously in the work of lament, we can also open ourselves to our interconnectedness to each other and all living creatures. Many guidelines for engaging in this work can be found in the book *Coming Back to Life* (Macy and Brown 1998).

On a practical level, overcoming our addiction to consumerism also implies that we learn to let go of that which we do not truly need, that we cease to acquire things that have been produced by exploitation of the poor and the living systems of the Earth. In shifting to a simpler lifestyle and living more lightly on the Earth, we can move toward other sources of value and enjoyment instead, such as relationships, time spent in nature, ritual, prayer, athletic pursuits, literature, and art. In so doing, we may also find new opportunities to experience our "gateways to reverence," allowing us to further open to the Tao.

Creative Empowerment: Reconnecting to Te

Teytey malkutakh

In this nuptial chamber where desire bears fruit
conceive the creative potency that enables us to say "I can."

Let the rhythm of thy counsel reverberate through our lives
so that it may empower us with thy creative vision.

(Renderings of the third line of the Aramaic Prayer of Jesus)

Maliki yaumadin.

It says "I can" on the day when all elements part company and return home,
when the threads of interweaving destiny unravel and the invoices come due.
The Universe Being accepts the mission to resolve the unresolvable.

(Rendering of the fourth line of the Surah Fateha)

The third path seeks to reconnect us with the intrinsic power of *Te*, embodying the power of the Tao in an authentic manner from the heart in a way that combines both intuition and compassion. *Te* is the intrinsic power that enables us to see clearly and act decisively at the right place and the right time, that, like the Malkuta, enables us to stand up and say "I can" despite all odds (or to resolve what seems irresolvable). This sense of empowerment fills us with a kind of royal dignity, evoking the sense of natural leadership which embodies the sacred quality characteristic of the Great Mother, Gaia, or Pachamama. At the same time, it is a creative energy ready to spring forth with the life-giving power of the Earth.

In the first two paths, we were focused very much on opening ourselves to the Tao, with clearing a space and emptying ourselves of preconceptions and delusion so that we could harmonize ourselves with its purpose, vision, and dynamic unfolding. In this third path, we move more concretely toward action and embodiment, although in some sense this is a kind of turning point or breakthrough analogous to illumination in the holistic learning cycle. The image of the word *teytey* in the Aramaic Prayer of Jesus is that of a nuptial chamber: on one level, it means "come" but on another it "includes the images of mutual desire, definition of a goal" (or purpose), "a place where mutual desire is fulfilled and birthing takes place" (Douglas-Klotz 1990, 20).

In our reflections, we have seen how complex systems can be extremely sensitive to change: a very small alteration in initial conditions, a minor adjustment to feedback loops, or any other subtle shift can have extraordinary effects (like the image of the butterfly "causing" a hurricane on the other side of the globe). In such systems, determinism gives way to creative engagement. The key to transformation is to find the appropriate action for the place and time in which we are present. Given the subtle play of dependent co-arising, even small shifts in our perceptions, thoughts, and beliefs—and how these in turn color our words, emotions, and deeds—can have a real effect in the world.

This underlines the wisdom of the Buddhist eightfold path. Along with right action, right speech, and right livelihood (ethical conduct), we also need wisdom (right understanding and intention) as well as mental discipline (right effort, mindfulness, and concentration). Not only *what* we do, but the understanding of what we do, the intentions behind our actions, and our spiritual disciplines, affect ourselves and those around us. This clearly illustrates the link between the Via Positiva and the Via Negativa with transformative praxis.

At the same time, the sense of finding the right action for the moment at hand underlines the need for developing a deep sense of *intuition*. If our action is to be fruitful,[7] if it is to be appropriate and effective, we will need a keen insight into the situation at hand. Analysis and discussion can certainly assist in such a process, but ultimately the chaotic nature of living systems, especially as they move away from equilibrium in a time of crisis, means that a more holistic form of cognition—intuition—is also crucial. This is an essentially hopeful insight since the ability to effect change depends not on brute force but rather on

---

7. Recall our earlier discussion of intuiting the Tao and the idea of good ("ripe") and evil ("rotten" or "unripe") in Aramaic. See p. 216.

the subtle webs of relationality inherent in power-with and the self-organizing potential of power-from-within.

The letting go of the Via Negativa plays an important role in preparing the ground for intuitions to arise. As Danah Zohar and Ian Marshall, drawing on the lessons from quantum systems, observe:

> When the brain first perceives a very heterogeneous field of which it cannot make sense with its habitual perceptual categories [i.e., it is faced with the "unresolvable"], it puts itself "on hold." All the diverse data are held together in the limbic system while the brain goes through a process of deconstruction leading to resynthesis. Deconstruction is very much like letting itself get into an indeterminate state—it lets go of its old concepts and categories, it "decides" to look at the data afresh. Then, during the process of resynthesis [or illumination], new concepts and new categories are evolved that can integrate the diversity with which the brain has been challenged. (1994, 329-30)

Intuition cannot be forced, but it can be cultivated. Indeed, many of the practices described in the first two paths do much to prepare the ground. In addition, the oriental martial arts—in particular Tai Chi and Aikido—as well as practices like Qigong rely heavily on intuitive insight and their practice can lead to a honing of its faculties. In general, the kinaesthetic sense involved in moving of the body through space seems to be an especially powerful way to develop intuition. Sacred dance, for example, has a way of transporting participants into a state of deep perception of the whole. As Piero Ferrucci notes:

> Every movement in sacred dance has a meaning that not only is understood with the mind but is realized with one's whole being—body and soul. The movements used in sacred dance can have many meanings: They can include human beings in the harmony of celestial spheres; interconnect each dancer with the All; join humans with the divine world; or represent progression from multiplicity to unity. A swirling rotation can symbolize the process of becoming, around the still Center of Being, and so on. But mental understanding is incomplete. The realities represented in sacred dance cannot be fully expressed in words. Sacred dance speaks the ineffable. It has the function of reawakening intuition and of opening one's organism to a vaster world, at the moment of heightened receptivity. (1990, 177)

The practice of such sacred dances—particularly those like the Dances of Universal Peace, which are communal in nature and draw as well on the power of ancient mantras—is also a way of reawakening both power-from-within and power-with. Often, one can experience in a very real way the sense of "I can" by engaging in such dances. Communities involved in transformative action could benefit greatly by such practices—not only creating fertile ground for new insights but bonding together on a deeper level and experiencing an empowerment coming from beyond their individual selves.

Another way to cultivate intuition is to develop an awareness of *synchronicity*, what psychologist Carl Jung understood as "meaningful coincidences." Sometimes, for example, we see something in a dream that later actually becomes manifest in reality, or we run into a person we have just been thinking about but have not actually seen for years. Our reflections on the holistic microcosm and on living systems both suggest a deep, underlying unity, a world where the relationship between cause and effect is in many ways beyond our understanding. Synchronicity, for Jung, was a kind of "acausal connecting principle." As David Peat explains, Jung believed that "there are patterns in nature, and connecting patterns in consciousness . . . that are not generated by any mechanical cause. Moreover, these patterns often have a numinous meaning for us. If the universe is spanned by meaningful patterns, this suggests an activity of meaning within nature" (Peat 1990, 158). In essence, what might appear to be "bizarre coincidences" are actually doorways that can allow us to glimpse a deeper purpose at work unfolding through the complex dynamics of reciprocal causality. Indeed, Jung saw synchronicities as evidence of a "meaningful orderedness," what we might call the Tao, the Dharma, or Malkuta.

Cultivating awareness of meaningful coincidences—paying attention to synchronicities—facilitates the development of our intuition. If such an awareness were practiced in the context of a community, it could be greatly amplified and might serve as a rich source of insight for discerning creative new paths of action.

Jung also believed that ancient tools of divination such as the I Ching (The Book of Changes), a text and practice rooted in Taoism, could serve as ways to become more aware of reciprocal causality and cultivate intuitive discernment. To use the oracle, the participant(s) must first choose a clear question in which they are seeking guidance. The question must be sufficiently open to be appropriate, not an either/or dichotomy. After purifying their intentions and entering an attentive, meditative state, coins or yarrow sticks are tossed to build a pattern corresponding to one of sixty-four possible different combinations of yin and yang. Then, the I Ching is consulted to find the hexagram (actually two: one corresponding to the present situation and another to how it is transforming itself) which represents the correlation that resulted. Accompanying this, there is a short text that gives counsel in accordance with the situation. Normally, the text itself is rather enigmatic, requiring still further contemplation to become clear.

As "superstitious" as such a method may at first sound, it is in fact in harmony with the basic tenets of the systems view of causality and the relationship between mind and matter described in the holographic analogy. For instance, Jung Young Lee points out that in the I Ching "the principle of changes . . . presupposes a relationship between cause and effect. The process of changes is the process of transition from the cause to effect and from effect to cause" (1971, 87). That is, the process is based on an understanding of reciprocal causality, or dependent co-arising. Similarly, David Peat notes that, from the point of view of the holistic microcosm knit together by non-local connection:

If the human mind and body could enter into direct communion with this ocean of active information, it would have access to forms and patterns that transcend the boundaries between inner and outer, mind and matter—in other words, to synchronicities. The Chinese sages had their own account of the synchronicities of the I Ching. Our manifest world is, they said, the reflection of a much deeper reality that lies outside the domain of time. Synchronicities are embryonic moments that contain the enfolded potentialities of this transcendent reality. Through contemplations of the patterns that can be discerned within these special moments, it becomes possible to unfold the potentialities of the manifest universe. Likewise, to see the universe as a vast ocean of information suggests that we can grasp within it particular images that contain hints of the transcendent unfolding of the universe. (1991, 186)

From the perspective of the Tao, "the way that can be trodden or the way that can be spoken is not the true Tao. . . . The Tao involves a principle that is deeper . . . and more elusive. . . . Jung wished to indicate that this is the very nature of the I Ching, that its inner principle consistently moves it *beyond whatever causal condition* is established in a given moment" (Progoff 1973, 29). The key to the effectiveness of this method of tapping into our own intuitive faculties to access complex information is in our state of mind. Jung Young Lee (1971) compares the proper attitude to that of a Taoist artist who only begins to paint after achieving a contemplative unity with the object being painted; one consults the I Ching only after purifying the heart of controlling intentions and unifying oneself with the sincere search for truth.

Generally, the I Ching has been used as a tool for individual discernment. It would be interesting, though, to use it in a community or organizational context. For example, using traditional tools of analysis and reflection, a group might arrive at a question (or series of questions) it wishes to discern. Then group participants could use the I Ching to seek guidance. The group could then come back together to share the oracles they encountered and their subsequent reflections on them. The reflections of other group members could enrich this. Over time, a more inclusive image of a way to move forward would begin to emerge.

Dreams can serve a similar function, especially when reflected upon in a group context. A community considering a particular problem or challenge could ask participants to record their dreams over a period of time, and each member of the group could choose a dream that they felt was significant to share with the larger community. The work of Jeremy Taylor (1983), for example, provides excellent guidelines for this kind of process as well as concrete examples of groups that have used this kind of process to tap into the creative power of intuition.

In a more general sense, any activity that stimulates our creativity, including both art and play, can serve as a stimulus both for cultivating intuition and for reconnecting to synergetic forms of power. On the one hand, creative endeavors focus our attention while at the same time helping us suspend discursive thought and engage instead in a more holistic form of knowing. On the other, these activities can free us from the constraints and pressures that may block our perceptions.

By putting us in touch with the deepest levels of human experience and tapping our intuition, creativity can serve to restore our sense of vision and purpose. We can then move beyond the delusion of despair and the prison of preconceptualizations to new hope and new possibilities.

Incarnating the Vision: The Art of Liberation

Nehwey tzevyyanach aykanna d'bwashmaya aph b'ar'ah

So that, fully united with the vortex of thy desire,
we truly embody the light of thy purpose.

Harmonize our own goals and purposes with thine own;
As from the emanation and vision, so too in form.

(Renderings of the fourth line of the Aramaic Prayer of Jesus)

Ihdina sirat almustaquim.

We ask you to reveal the next harmonious step.
Show us the path that says, "Stand up, get going, do it!"
which resurrects us from the slumber of the drugged
and leads to the consummation of Heart's desire,
like all the stars and galaxies in tune, in time, straight on.

(Rendering of the sixth line of the Surah Fateha)

In the Via Transformativa, we seek to incarnate that which we have discerned through the Via Creativa; we seek to embody fully the power of *Te*, to "stand up" and "get going"; we move creatively between the visionary realm of *shem-aya* and the manifest realm of *ar'ah* in an interactive manner reflective of dependent co-arising. To do this faithfully and responsibly, though, we must always seek to harmonize our own desires and purposes with the great Way of the Tao. From an ecological perspective, we must attempt to act as conscious participants of the greater Earth community, working to make the world we live in a more just and harmonious place and to further its evolution toward greater diversity, interiority, and communion.

David Spangler (1996) speaks of this process of moving from vision to embodiment in terms of the art of *manifestation*—a process combining visualization, affirmation, and faith. In many ways, we could understand manifestation as related to prayer, although manifestation is often associated with specific techniques and does not necessarily involve a belief in God. The idea, though, is similar—to make something a reality, we must first come to see clearly *what* we desire and then we must *ask*, with all our being, that it come to fruition. In the case of manifestation, asking normally takes a particular form through the use of affirmation—essentially, we ask with such a sense of faith and trust that we affirm that it will, in fact, become a reality.

To be truly effective, manifestation presupposes that, through the dynamics of the Via Positiva, Via Negativa, and Via Creativa—we have truly sought to root ourselves in the Tao and to discern the right direction, the harmonious step that will "lead to the consummation of Heart's desire." We must honestly seek to ensure that our own purpose and desires are in harmony with those of the Way, the unfolding purpose of the cosmos, the Malkuta.

Unfortunately, some people have distorted the idea of manifestation by contaminating it with the cosmology of consumerism; for them, manifestation is simply a technique to acquire what they desire. Such methods—if they are rooted in a mechanistic cosmology—and our own, narrow egotistical desires can, in fact, be quite dangerous insofar as they actually reinforce the addictive delusions of consumerism; they are certainly *not* in harmony with the Tao. Such a distorted form of manifestation is not, however, what Spangler describes or advocates:

> My perspective is that manifestation has much more to with incarnation—with shaping ourselves and our world—than with acquisition. It is an act of love and sharing with the rest of creation, possessing as all acts of love do as much of giving in it as of getting. Without a sense of passion and presence, it becomes a technique of mindless acquisition, one that dulls our lives rather than enlivening these with spirit.
>
> Manifestation is an act of trust. It is the soul pouring itself out into its world, like a fisherman casting a net to gather in the fish he seeks; with each cast properly made, we will bring what we need to us, but first we must hurl ourselves into the depths without knowing just what lies beneath us. (1996, 37-38)

As an act of incarnation, manifestation presupposes that we first work to purify our own personal desires, that we practice the paths of invocation, letting go, and creative empowerment combined with intuitive discernment. Only then can manifestation become an act that opens the way toward liberating transformation.

Manifestation presupposes a cosmos whose fundamental reality is that of relationship unfolding from a state of primordial unity: "Spirit and matter, soul and personality, magic and labour, the extraordinary and the ordinary are all aspects of one reality, one flow of energy and events. It is the vision and experience of this wholeness that we wish to cultivate, for it is the source of power for our acts of manifestation" (Spangler 1996, 18).

Manifestation also assumes that the universe is, indeed, a friendly place that cares about the well-being of the entire Earth community, and of ourselves within it. At the same time, though, since manifestation is understood as a way of participating in the unfolding purpose of the cosmos, it becomes more effective as we enter more deeply into communion with the world around us.

Normally, the actual method of manifestation is quite simple. We begin by visualizing what we desire. As we have noted, though, this first assumes that we do not simply try to acquire something for personal gain or indulgence, but rather that we first seek deeply to find the vision needed for the moment at hand.

In visualizing, we attempt to see, as clearly as possible, that which we wish to manifest. At the same time, visualization requires an openness to change—what is truly needed may not be what we first imagine. Being too specific, especially at the beginning of the process, may actually stifle creativity and reduce the power of the vision. We must be open to receiving new insights, new direction, even as we begin the process of manifestation. Still, over time, we must come to see clearly what we are attempting to manifest in our mind's eye.

Visualization is essentially a form of asking, of making clear that which we desire to come about. The next step is that of affirmation: creating a statement that reinforces the vision. If I visualize a new organization working to restore my local ecosystem, the statement might be, "We are creating an effective, life-giving organization working to restore our watershed." In one way, this may seem quite different than asking, yet, it is essentially a way of attesting to the faith that what we ask for will, in fact, come about.

The third step, normally called "positive thinking," means to carry forward with that same attitude as we move toward action, expressing a basic trust and faith that our vision will, in fact, become a reality. Finally, we work to put our vision into action, a step that itself is sometimes called manifestation.

At first, this approach may seem strange to us. Can it really work? Yet the use of these methods (or ones similar to them) has been employed by athletes and performers with success for many years. Why should those of us working for liberating change not also put them into practice?

The effectiveness of manifestation can be greatly multiplied when used in a community or organizational context. Each member of the organization, for example, can begin by forming a vision of what he or she wishes to happen. These can be shared, and the group can discern together a collective vision for the whole organization. In this way, the vision can be deepened as we ask questions: What will this vision mean for future generations? What implications might it have? What will be involved in making the vision come about? Then, together, the group seeks to visualize all of this more clearly, seeing the steps involved and the possible pitfalls to avoid. Next, we can use affirmation to move forward toward the vision with an attitude of "I can." Finally, we move toward manifestation by choosing the right team, making sure we are attuned to each other and the common vision we hold. As Cherokee Chief, peacemaker, and Buddhist spiritual leader Dhyani Ywahoo points out:

> Success comes from holding the ideal very clearly in your minds and making certain that the ideal is beneficial to people [and the wider Earth community] unto seven generations. The idea is in the minds of the people rather than something imposed upon the people. To sit back and think it will happen because you visualize it is not enough. You consciously look for the right connections, consciously weed the garden of the mind, consciously gather the funds [needed]. Community building, relationship, is very active. (1989, 277-78)

David Spangler affirms that using manifestation in a community context can also be a wonderful way to gain insights about the workings and character of the group, exploring the holistic context in which the organization functions and revealing patterns and interconnections that might otherwise never be recognized. As an art of "incarnation and empowerment," manifestation is a way of "deepening into a systemic and co-creative perspective of oneself and one's world, and of touching sources of inner power that enhance both individuality [or differentiation] and group endeavour [or communion]" (1996, 231).

Manifestation is not a technique, a magical formula that we employ to get results, but rather an art requiring attunement to the reality at hand, passion, and soul. The art of manifestation is *not* based on the premise that we can make something come about by simply *thinking* about it. Rather, the key attitude is that of *presence*. Spangler uses the image of a supersaturated solution to explain this. We must first "boil away" our "normal perceptions, expectations, habits, histories, and futures," loosening their bonds on our consciousness. Then, "into this moment of supersaturated potentiality" an image drops—a particular vision that serves as a seed to precipitate a new reality. The key is to become *present* to the new image, to let the vision precipitate so that it may emerge into reality through the process of manifestation (1996, 83).

From the perspective of living systems, we can think of manifestation as an art that attempts to form new attractors which draw the system toward new forms. From the point of view of morphic fields, we could understand it as a way to create new fields that facilitate the formation of new habits through the phenomenon of morphic resonance. From the outlook of the holographic analogy, what we seek may already exist, in an enfolded form, in the holoflux. Manifestation, then, becomes a way of repatterning, of generating the appropriate conditions and energy to "reorganize our lives into the new pattern we seek." In such an understanding, "we do not *acquire* that which we desire, we *become* it" (Spangler 1996, 46-47)

To be successful, manifestation must be infused by a spirit of generosity and abundance. We must move beyond ourselves and the narrow bounds of the ego to embrace a more inclusive self, tapping into forces woven into the depths of our own beings *and* the "beingness of everything else in the world. . . . They are the deep creative energies that give all things form and existence. Therefore, on this level, manifestation is the art of incarnation" (Spangler 1996, 6).

Jesus' teachings on prayer can serve as a complementary perspective to enrich our understanding of the process of moving from vision to embodiment (or incarnation). Matthew 7:7, normally translated simply as "Ask, and it shall be given you; seek, and you shall find; knock, and it shall be opened to you," is especially instructive if we consider it in the form of an expanded translation from the Aramaic (Douglas-Klotz 2006, 51-53):

> Ask intensely –
> like a straight line engraved toward the object you want;
> pray with desire –
> as though you interrogated your own soul about
> its deepest, most hidden longings;
> and you will receive expansively –

not only what your desire asked, but where the elemental breath led you –
love's doorstep, the place where you bear fruit
and become part of the universe's power of generation and sympathy.

Search anxiously –
from the interior of your desire to its outer embodiment
let the inner gnawing and boiling lead you to
act passionately –
no matter how material or gross your goal seems at first;
then you find fulfilment
of the drive of the flesh to accomplish its purpose and see its destiny.
Like a spring unbound, you will gain the force
of profound stillness after an effort –
the earth's power to grow new each season.

Knock innocently –
as if you were driving a tent stake or striking one clear note,
never heard before.
Create enough space within to receive the force you release;
hollow yourself—
purified of hidden hopes and fears
and it shall be opened easily –
a natural response to space created,
part of the contraction-expansion of the universe;
and penetrated smoothly –
as the cosmos opens and closes around the words of satisfied desire.

In moving from vision to action, we would also do well to keep in mind a
form of action in keeping with the Tao. As we have already noted, the force of
our action is far less important than its appropriateness for the time and place
we find ourselves in. At the same time, the *way* we act makes a difference. The
image found in the *Tao Te Ching* (§78; see p. 80) of water wearing down a stone
is instructive; water can wear away a stone through the use of a persistent, flowing motion that embraces rather than strikes. It is not, therefore, sheer force
that triumphs but rather persistent energy working with the natural flow of the
Tao.

The philosophy of yielding in order to overcome is applied, often with
impressive results, in the area of oriental martial arts. In particular, Aikido and
the martial form of Tai Chi (both of which are almost exclusively defensive in
nature) utilize the force of the opponent to ward off an attack. Instead of resisting force with force (*yang* with *yang*), one yields in a controlled way and subtly redirects the force so as to throw the attacker off balance, thus causing the
aggressor to topple.

Aikido, in particular, relies on the principle of "blending" with the energies
of the aggressor. In Aikido, the defender enters into the attacker's motion, moving into its very heart. This is not with the intention to inflict harm, but rather

to begin to identify with and blend with the aggressor. Blending requires a kind of empathy with the attacker, seeing the world from his or her stance. This new perspective can actually lead to compassion, allowing the Aikidoist to redirect the aggressive energy of the attacker in such a way that a nonviolent resolution can be found. These same principles can be applied in daily life, be it to verbal or physical aggression (Saposnek, 1985, 182).

Essentially, Aikido applies a systems approach that includes the notion of mutual causality. Practitioners of Aikido see themselves in the context of a total system, including the challengers and spatial/temporal factors. They place themselves at the center of a dynamic sphere of interactions. The central axiom for response is to "turn when pushed, enter when pulled," producing spherical motions rather than linear ones. By doing this, the Aikidoist employs mutual causality: "The quick blending of forces makes indistinguishable the cause-effect relationships and makes apparent only the circularity of forces blended together for mutual problem-solving" (Saposnek 1985, 180-81). The success of this strategy depends on letting go of forceful, linear ways of thinking and acting out another quality of *yin*, intuition. Indeed, a problem with beginners learning Aikido is that they tend to try too hard, using linear thinking and force. To be successful, the practitioner needs to relax and let go of reflexive, habitual ways of doing things, trusting that a positive outcome will result if the individual uses intuition and moves with the flow.

In a complementary fashion, physicist David Peat speaks of the need to find a new style of working for change, which he calls "gentle action." Instead of seeking to isolate individual problems, analyzing a specific situation, and then proposing a solution, gentle action attempts to operate throughout the system in a gentle, nonlocal fashion based on "careful and sensitive observation and gentle instinct for balance and harmony" (1990, 163). He later elaborates:

> Gentle action is global. It arises out of the whole nature and structure of a particular issue. It addresses itself not just to practical issues, such as the price of oil or the efficiency of a given factory, but also to values, ethics, and the quality of life. Gentle action begins in a highly intelligent and coordinated fashion within a wide variety of situations. And like the ripples around the point, it moves inward to converge on a particular issue. Gentle action works not through force and raw energy but by modifying the very processes that generate and sustain an undesired or harmful effect. . . .
>
> Gentle action . . . gives a new dimension to the whole idea of social action. . . . Just as the cell and organism can be pictured as dance of meaning and communication, so, too, can society and the individual. . . . It suggests that the origins of effective action can lie in ordinary people, both as individuals and as members of a group—and with their values, ethics, goals, and desires. (1991, 220, 222-23)

This image of converging ripples in the pool underlines the need for networking at a global level. While many actions may take place locally, both our thinking *and* our action must encompass the local *and* the global. The combination of many ripples reaching out from a wide variety of places multiplies the effects of our action through resonance, particularly if we work in a way that combines a communion of purpose and a diversity of manifestations.

Yet another dimension of incarnating the vision through liberating praxis lies in the area of the work that each one of us does. Most of us spend the greatest part of our waking hours engaged in some kind of work—whether paid employment or tasks directly related to our ongoing sustenance and that of our families and communities. We need to move from the perspective of "jobs"—a mechanistic, reductionist idea that tends to separate work from life—to that of *livelihood*, seen always in some way as work related to bringing about the Great Turning.

This sense of "right livelihood" will obviously mean, in the first place, that we stop engaging in activities that harm others—we must cease to work in ways that directly exploit the planet or our fellow human beings. All our work, all our activities, must seek the ongoing sustenance of life and/or the process of transformation leading to a more just and sustainable world.

This means that each of us, in our own way, must carefully discern our *vocation*—our unique purpose situated within the unfolding purpose of the cosmos itself, the Tao. Drawing on the Surah Fateha (line 5), how can we ensure that we are truly developing our abilities in "the service of the Real," that what we do serves to venerate "the deepest Source of all Life"?

In more practical terms, each of us needs to discern how we can put our unique gifts, passions, and skills at the service of liberation. To do this, it is helpful for each one of us to reflect: What angers or upsets me the most? What most deeply concerns me? At the same time, each of us needs to draw on our passion and joy: What do I truly love to do? What talents and gifts do I have to contribute? Looking at all these, we can find insights into our deepest calling, the purpose for which we have come into being, our own unique part to play in the cosmos: What can I do that combines my concerns, interests, and passions in the concrete work for transformation?

Obviously, in considering these questions we still need to find ways to sustain ourselves and our families. This may mean that we will need to reorient our lives gradually, or seek out opportunities to volunteer outside of our regular work or "job." The important thing, though, is to take time to discern where and how we can best work to move the world toward the Great Turning and then find ways to move ourselves, progressively, in that direction.

In all our actions, we must also keep in mind that we will be most effective when we work with others, building community and the synergy of power-with. Community, of course, can take many forms. It may be an organization dedicated to focusing on a specific issue, ecosystem, or group of people; it may be a faith community; or it may simply be our neighborhood, village, or town. In thinking of community, we should also always seek to expand this vision to include the wider biotic community of which we are a part.

Working with others, of course, can be challenging. To be truly liberating, a community cannot be based on oppressive relationships or inequalities of power and respect. A new kind of community is called for, one that is founded on mutuality and a common commitment to growth and transformative action in communion with the wider Earth community of which we are a part. The perspectives on consensus and participation that we explored in the bioregional vision may serve as guidelines as we reflect on the kind of community we wish to move toward.

We should also look for ways to expand our sense of community, reaching out in solidarity to others who share our concerns or who in different ways are involved in the struggle for sustainable community. We can seek to form communities of communities, networks that encompass an entire region, or even the entire globe.

To the extent that we create community and work in solidarity with others, we also create a context for our action and the possibility for mutual support. As we have seen, working with others can enhance our capacity to enter into the pregnant void through meditation, to deepen our intuition, and to enrich our envisioning and manifestation. By networking yet more widely with others, we can tap the potential of gentle action to work in "subtle but global ways and seek to restore harmony through gentle correlations" (Peat 1990, 164).

Sustenance in a Time of Labor

Hawvlan lachma d'sunqanan yaomana.
Washboqlan khaubayn (wakhtahayn) aykana daph khnan shbwoqan
l'khayyabayn.
Wela tahlan l'nesyuna, ela patzan min bisha.
Metol dilakhie malkuta wahayla wateshbukhta l'ahlam almin. Ameyn.

With passion and soul may we generate
the sustenance and understanding we need to take the next step.
Loosen the cords of past mistakes and disentangle us from frustrated hopes,
as we, too, release others and restore to them that which has been usurped.
Let us not be enmeshed by the nets of delusion
or become lost in the forgetfulness of distractions
which divert us from our purpose,
but illuminate for us the opportunities of the present moment.
For from thy fertile ground springs forth the empowering vision,
the life energy that creates and sustains,
and the harmonious song that enkindles wonder,
From age to age, let it in truth be so.

(Rendering of the fifth through eighth lines of the Aramaic Prayer of Jesus)

Sirat alladhina an'amta 'alayhim
ghayril maghdubi 'alayhim wa laddalin.

The orbit of every being in the universe is filled with delight.
When each travels consciously,
a sigh of wonder arises at the expanse, the abundance.
This is not the path of frustration, anger, or annoyance,
which happens only when we temporarily
lose the way and become drained, roaming too far
from the Wellspring of Love.

(Rendering of the seventh line of the Surah Fateha)

In working for liberation through the fourfold path, we must always keep in mind that, despite our best efforts to discern our actions and root them in our sense of the Tao, there is no guarantee that any specific action or initiative will actually be successful. The very nature of complex systems means that we can never be absolutely certain that what we are doing is, in fact, the most appropriate action for the time and place in which we find ourselves. The best we can do is seek to root ourselves ever deeper in a sense of the Tao, to try harmonize ourselves with the unfolding purpose of the Malkuta. In terms of the holistic learning cycle, we must always keep in mind the step of verification, of trying things out to see if they actually bear fruit. Indeed, sometimes we learn more from our failures than from our successes, and these lessons can enrich and inform our subsequent praxis.

Even here, though, we must be careful. In what, truly, lies success? What might at first appear to be fruitless, in the longer term may actually prove to be richly fertile, while what appears at first to be fruitful may in fact wither over time. We therefore need to cultivate an attitude of healthy detachment from immediate results. As Vandana Shiva notes:

I've learned from the Bhagavad Gita and other teachings of my culture to detach myself from the results of what I do, because those are not in my hands. The context is not in your control, but your commitment is yours to make, and you can make the deepest commitment with a total detachment about where it will take you. You want it to lead to a better world, and you shape your actions and take full responsibility for them, but then you have detachment. And that combination of deep passion and deep detachment allows me always to take on the next challenge because I don't cripple myself, I don't tie myself in knots. I function like a free being. . . . I think that what we owe each other is a celebration of life and to replace fear and hopelessness with fearlessness and joy. (Quoted in Korten 2006, 357-58)

We must always, then, take things one step at a time, seeking only the sustenance and wisdom for the current stage of the journey. At the same time, we must let go of past mistakes and frustrated hopes, in a sense taking each day as a fresh start. The Via Negativa is key here: while we need to learn from the past, we must also let go of past disappointments as well as the nets of delusion (despair, denial, internalized oppression, and addictions) that would divert us from our purpose.

Simultaneously, we must remember that, while the struggle for integral liberation is certainly a serious matter, this does not mean that we must be solemn about it. To be truly effective, all our actions for change must be infused with the playfulness and celebration inherent in all creative endeavors, including the creativity of the cosmos itself. Play, in particular, lies at the very heart of our humanity as we saw in our discussion about neoteny (p. 285). If we do not take this into account, we will soon become de-energized and depressed by the struggle. The Via Positiva—the way of celebration, wonder, and awe, the way of remembering and relinking to the fruitful Source of all—as well as the playfulness and even humor that can be associated with the Via Creativa, have an important role is sustaining us as we struggle for a more just and sustainable Earth community.

Indeed, authentic joy, celebration, and play seem to capture a spirit that is deeply subversive to the dominant system's controlling dynamics: music, dance, and laughter lie at the very heart of our struggle for life. In Colombia, for example, in the midst of one of the most violent situations in the world, human rights activists know the value of going out for an evening of dancing to touch once again the deep source of life that inspires them to continue in the struggle— what some of them call "dancing the revolution."

As we enter still more profoundly into the struggle to renew the Earth, we may find in our communities and in our rediscovered connection to the cosmos a new source of joy, a joy that flows out of the deepening of our compassion. Joanna Macy (1983, 32) refers to this with the Buddhist term *muditha,* "the joy in the joy of others," which comes from a sharing of our gifts and powers in the struggle. As we become more deeply connected to each other and to the cosmos itself, the power of this joy becomes unstoppable. Ultimately, it is this force—this life energy that creates and sustains, this song that enkindles us with wonder—that will drive the Great Turning toward a new era for humanity and all the Earth.

Continuing the Journey

The Tao of Liberation is, by its nature, just one step on a path which will continue to unfold over time. If you are interested in continuing to explore the ideas in this book, please visit the book website at: **www.taoofliberation.com**. During the upcoming months, we hope to post follow-up resources that can help facilitate a deeper discussion of the themes and questions we have introduced in this text. For example, we plan to develop a study guide for groups wishing to reflect on the book and to examine its implication for their lives and transformative praxis.

As well, Mark Hathaway is working to form a new, participatory research center that will continue to delve deeper into the themes we have explored and share the insights gathered with the wider public. This center will endeavor to connect activists and scholars, collect case studies, and explore both visions of a sustainable future and paths toward authentic liberation. If you are interested in participating in this project or contributing to its work, please visit the website of The Centre for Transformative Ecology at: **www.centreco.org**

References

Adams, Patricia. 1991. *Odious Debts: Loose Lending, Corruption, and the Third World's Environmental Legacy.* Toronto: Probe International.

ARC. 2009. Alliance of Religions and Conservation Web site: http://www.arcworld.org/.

Arendt, Hannah. 1970. *On Violence.* New York: Harcourt Brace Jovanovich.

Assagioli, Roberto. 1965. *Psychosynthesis: A Manual of Principles and Techniques.* San Francisco: Aquarian Press.

Athanasiou, Tom. 1996. *Divided Planet: The Ecology of Rich and Poor.* Boston: Little, Brown.

Ayres, Ed. 1998. "The Fastest Mass Extinction in Earth's History." *World Watch Magazine* [Washington, D.C.: Worldwatch Institute], September/October 1998, 6-7.

———. 1999a. *God's Last Offer: Negotiating a Sustainable Future.* New York: Four Walls Eight Windows.

———, ed. 1999b. "Just a Minute." *World Watch Magazine*, July/August 1999, 39.

———, ed. 2002. "Matters of Scale." *World Watch Magazine*, January/February 2002, 23.

Bakan, Joel. 2004. *The Corporation: The Pathological Pursuit of Profit and Power.* Toronto: Viking Canada.

Barrow, John D., and Frank J. Tipler. 1986. *The Anthropic Cosmological Principle.* New York: Oxford University Press.

Barrows, Anita. 1995. "The Ecopsychology of Child Development." In *Ecopsychology: Restoring the Earth, Healing the Mind*, edited by T. Roszak, M. Gomes, and A. Kanner. San Francisco: Sierra Club Books.

Berman, Morris. 1981. *The Reenchantment of the World.* Ithaca, N.Y.: Cornell University Press.

Berman, Tzeporah. 1993. "Towards an Integrative Ecofeminist Praxis." *Canadian Woman Studies* 13:15-17.

Berry, Thomas. 1999. *The Great Work: Our Way into the Future.* New York: Bell Tower.

Berry, Thomas, and Brian Swimme. 1992. *The Universe Story: From the Primordial Flaring Forth to the Ecozoic Era—A Celebration of the Unfolding of the Cosmos.* San Francisco: HarperSanFrancisco.

Berry, Wendell. 1988. "The Work of Local Culture." The 1988 Iowa Humanities Lecture. Oakdale Campus, Iowa City: Iowa Humanities Board.

Bochte, Bruce, ed. 1990. *Canticle to the Cosmos: Study Guide.* San Francisco: Tides Foundation.

Boff, Leonardo. 2000. *Holy Trinity, Perfect Community*. Translated by Phillip Berryman. Maryknoll, N.Y.: Orbis Books.

———. 2008a. *Essential Care: An Ethics of Human Nature*. Translated by Alexandre Guilherme. Waco, Tex.: Baylor University Press.

———. 2008b. *Evangelho do Cristo cósmico: A busca da unidade do Todo na ciência e na religião*. Rio de Janeiro: Editora Record.

Bohm, David, and F. David Peat. 1987. *Science, Order, and Creativity*. Toronto: Bantam Books.

Britto García, Luis. 1990. "Guaicaipuro Cuauhtémoc cobra la deuda a Europa." *El National* [Caracas] October 18, 1990. Accessed at http://www.kaosenlared.net/noticia/sucederia-si-guaicaipuro-cuauhtemoc-cobra-deuda-europa (July 6, 2009).

Brown, Lester R., Christopher Flavin, and Sandra Postel. 1991. *Saving the Planet: How to Shape an Environmentally Sustainable Global Economy*. New York: W. W. Norton.

Brown, Lester R., et al. 1994. *State of the World: 1994*. New York: W. W. Norton.

———. 1997. *State of the World: 1997*. New York: W. W. Norton.

Bunch, Charlotte. 1987. *Passionate Politics: Essays, 1968-1986. Feminist Theory in Action*. New York: St. Martin's Press.

Bunting, Ikaweba. 1999. "The Heart of Africa." *New Internationalist Magazine*, Issue 309. Posted at http://www.newint.org/features/1999/01/01/anticolonialism.

Bunyard, Peter. 2000. "Fiddling While the Climate Burns." *Ecologist* 30:48-49.

Capra, Fritjof. 1982. *The Turning Point: Science, Society, and the Rising Culture*. New York: Simon & Schuster.

———. 1996. *The Web of Life: A New Scientific Understanding of Living Systems*. New York: Doubleday.

———. 2002. *The Hidden Connections: Integrating the Biological, Cognitive, and Social Dimensions of Life into a Science of Sustainability*. New York: Doubleday.

Capra, Fritjof, and David Steindl-Rast. 1991. *Belonging to the Universe: Explorations on the Frontiers of Science and Spirituality*. San Francisco: HarperSanFrancisico.

Chang, Larry, ed. 2006. *Wisdom for the Soul: Five Millennia of Prescriptions for Spiritual Healing*. Washington: Gnosophia Publishers.

Chatterjee, Pratap. 1997. "Conquering Peru: Newmont's Yanacocha Mine Recalls the Days of Pizarro." *Multinational Monitor*, vol. 18, no. 4 (April).

Chomsky, Noam. 1989. *Necessary Illusions: Thought Control in Democratic Societies*. Montreal: CBC Enterprises.

Commoner, Barry. 2002. "Unraveling the DNA Myth: The Spurious Foundation of Genetic Engineering." *Harper's Magazine*, February.

Conlon, Jim. 1994. *Earth Story, Sacred Story*. Mystic, Conn.: Twenty-Third Publications.

Conn, Sarah A. 1995. "When the Earth Hurts, Who Responds?" In *Ecopsychology: Restoring the Earth, Healing the Mind*, edited by T. Roszak, M. Gomes, and A. Kanner. San Francisco: Sierra Club Books.

Daly, Herman E. 1996. *Beyond Growth: The Economics of Sustainable Development*. Boston: Beacon Press.

———. 2008. "The Crisis: Groundbreaking Economist, Herman Daly, Zeroes in on the Root Cause of Our Financial Meltdown." *Adbusters* 19 (November 2008), http://www.adbusters.org/magazine/81/the_crisis.html (accessed January 16, 2009).

Daly, Herman E., and John B. Cobb, Jr. 1989. *For the Common Good: Redirecting the Economy toward Community, the Environment, and a Sustainable Future*. Boston: Beacon Press.

Daly, Ned. 1994. "Ravaging the Redwood: Charles Hurwitz, Michael Milken and the

Costs of Greed." *Multinational Monitor,* September, http://www.essential.org/monitor/hyper/issues/1994/09/mm0994_07.html.

Dankelman, Irene, and Joan Davidson. 1988. *Women and the Environment in the Third World: Alliance for the Future.* London: Earthscan Publications.

Davies, Paul. 1988. *The Cosmic Blueprint: New Discoveries in Nature's Creative Ability to Order the Universe.* New York: Simon & Schuster.

Devall, Bill, and George Sessions. 1985. *Deep Ecology: Living As If Nature Mattered.* Layton, Ut.: Peregrine Smith Books.

Dillon, John. 1997. *Turning the Tide: Confronting the Money Traders.* Ottawa: Canadian Centre for Policy Alternatives.

Douglas-Klotz, Neil. 1990. *Prayers of the Cosmos: Meditations on the Aramaic Words of Jesus.* San Francisco: Harper & Row.

———. 1995. *Desert Wisdom: Sacred Middle Eastern Writings from the Goddess through the Sufis.* San Francisco: HarperSanFrancisco.

———. 1999. *The Hidden Gospel: Decoding the Spiritual Message of the Aramaic Jesus.* Wheaton, Ill.: Quest Books, Theosophical Publishing House.

———. 2006. *Blessings of the Cosmos: Benedictions from the Aramaic Words of Jesus.* Boulder, Colo.: Sounds True.

Dreher, Diane. 1990. *The Tao of Inner Peace.* New York: HarperCollins.

Durning, Alan Thein. 1995. "Are We Happy Yet?" In *Ecopsychology: Restoring the Earth, Healing the Mind,* edited by T. Roszak, M. Gomes, and A. Kanner. San Francisco: Sierra Club Books.

Duve, Christian de. 1995. *Vital Dust: Life as a Cosmic Imperative.* New York: Basic Books.

Dychtwald, Ken. 1982. "Reflections on the Holographic Paradigm." In *The Holographic Paradigm and Other Paradoxes: Exploring the Leading Edge of Science,* edited by Ken Wilber, 105-13. Boulder, Colo.: Shambhala.

Dyson, Freeman. 1979. *Disturbing the Universe.* New York: Harper & Row.

Einstein, Albert. 1995. *Out of My Later Years.* Secaucus, N.J.: Citadel.

Elgin, Duane. 1993. *Awakening Earth: Exploring the Evolution of Human Culture and Consciousness.* New York: William Morrow.

Fabel, Arthur, and Donald St. John, eds. 2003. *Teilhard in the 21st Century: The Emerging Spirit of Earth.* Maryknoll, N.Y.: Orbis Books.

Feng, Gia-fu, and Jane English, translators. 1989. *Tao Te Ching.* New York: Vintage Books.

Ferguson, Marilyn. 1987. *The Aquarian Conspiracy: Personal and Social Transformation in Our Time.* Los Angeles: J. P. Tarcher.

Ferrucci, Piero. 1982. *What We May Be: Techniques for Psychological and Spiritual Growth.* Los Angeles: J. P. Tarcher.

———. 1990. *Inevitable Grace—Breakthroughs in the Lives of Great Men and Women: Guides to Your Self-realization.* Los Angeles: J. P. Tarcher.

Fitzgerald, Judith, and Michael Oren Fitzgerald. 2005. *The Sermon of All Creation: Christians on Nature.* Bloomington, Ind.: World Wisdom.

Flannery, Tim. 2001. *The Eternal Frontier: An Ecological History of North America and Its Peoples.* New York: Atlantic Monthly Press.

Foucault, Michel. 1980. *Power/Knowledge: Selected Interviews and Other Writings 1972-1977.* New York: Pantheon Books.

Fox, Matthew. 1983. *Original Blessing: A Primer in Creation Spirituality.* Santa Fe, N.M.: Bear.

———. 1991. *Creation Spirituality: Liberating Gifts for the Peoples of Earth.* San Francisco: HarperSanFrancisco.

———. 1994. *The Reinvention of Work: A New Vision of Livelihood for Our Time*. San Francisco: HarperSanFrancisco.

Fox, Matthew, and Rupert Sheldrake. 1996a. *Natural Grace: Dialogue on Creation, Darkness, and the Soul in Spirituality and Science*. New York: Doubleday.

———. 1996b. *The Physics of Angels: Exploring the Realm Where Science and Spirit Meet*. San Francisco: HarperSanFrancisco.

Fox, Warwick. 1990. *Towards a Transpersonal Ecology: Developing New Foundations for Environmentalism*. Boston: Shambhala.

Gardner, Gary. 2001. "The Virtue of Restraint: Is There Such a Thing as Too Much Choice?" *World Watch* 14:12-18.

———. 2006. *Inspiring Progress: Religions' Contribution to Sustainable Development*. Washington, D.C.: Worldwatch Institute.

Glendinning, Chellis. 1995. "Technology, Trauma, and the Wild." In *Ecopsychology: Restoring the Earth, Healing the Mind*, edited by T. Roszak, M. Gomes, and A. Kanner. San Francisco: Sierra Club Books.

Goldsmith, Edward. 1998. *The Way: An Ecological World-view*. Rev. ed. Athens, Ga.: University of Georgia Press.

Gomes, Mary, and Allen Kanner. 1995. "The Rape of the Well-maidens: Feminist Psychology and the Environmental Crisis." In *Ecopsychology: Restoring the Earth, Healing the Mind*, edited by T. Roszak, M. Gomes, and A. Kanner. San Francisco: Sierra Club Books.

Gorbachev, Mikhail. 1987. *Perestroika: New Thinking for Our Country and the World*. London: Collins.

———. 2001. "The World: Nature Will Not Wait." *World Watch* 14:4-5.

Gore, Albert. 2000. *Earth in the Balance: Ecology and the Human Spirit*. Boston: Houghton Mifflin.

Gould, Stephen Jay. 1977. *Ontogeny and Phylogeny*. Cambridge, Mass.: Belknap Press of Harvard University Press.

Graham, Colin. 1998. "Will the Public Expect Global Economy to Self-destruct?" *The CCPA Monitor* [Ottawa: Canadian Centre for Policy Alternatives], July/August, pp. 20-21.

Greenway, Robert. 1995. "The Wilderness Effect and Ecopsychology." In *Ecopsychology: Restoring the Earth, Healing the Mind*, edited by T. Roszak, M. Gomes, and A. Kanner. San Francisco: Sierra Club Books.

Haught, John F. 1993. *The Promise of Nature: Ecology and Cosmic Purpose*. New York: Paulist Press.

Hawken, Paul. 1975. *The Magic of Findhorn*. New York: Harper & Row.

———. 1993. *The Ecology of Commerce: A Declaration of Sustainability*. New York: HarperCollins.

Hawking, Stephen W. 1998. *A Brief History of Time: From the Big Bang to Black Holes*. New York: Bantam Books.

Heider, John. 1986. *The* Tao *of Leadership: Leadership Strategies for a New Age*. New York: Bantam Books.

Heinberg, Richard. 1999. *Cloning the Buddha: The Moral Impact of Biotechnology*. Wheaton, Ill.: Quest Books.

Henderson, Hazel. 1996. *Building a Win-win World: Life beyond Global Economic Warfare*. San Francisco: Berrett-Koehler.

Herbert, Nick. 1993. *Elemental Mind: Human Consciousness and the New Physics*. New York: Dutton.

Herman, Edward S., and Robert W. McChesney. 1997. *The Global Media: The New Missionaries of Corporate Capitalism*. Washington: Cassell.

Hessel, Dieter T., and Rosemary Radford Ruether, eds. 2000. *Christianity and Ecology: Seeking the Well-being of Earth and Humans*. Cambridge, Mass: Harvard University Press.

Heyneman, Martha. 1993. *The Breathing Cathedral: Feeling Our Way into a Living Cosmos*. San Francisco: Sierra Club Books.

Hillman, James. 1996. *The Soul's Code: In Search of Character and Calling*. New York: Random House, 1996.

Ho, Mae-Wan. 1999. "One Bird—Ten Thousand Treasures." *Ecologist* 29:339-40.

Houston, Jean. 1982. *The Possible Human: A Course in Extending Your Physical, Mental, and Creative Abilities*. Los Angeles: J. P. Tarcher.

Inayat Khan, Hazrat. 1983. *The Music of Life*. New Lebanon, N.Y.: Omega.

Jantsch, Erich. 1980. *The Self-organizing Universe: Scientific and Human Implications of the Emerging Paradigm of Evolution*. Oxford: Pergamon Press.

Joseph, Lawrence E. 1990. *Gaia: The Growth of an Idea*. New York: St. Martin's Press.

Joy, Bill. 2000. "Why the Future Doesn't Need Us." *Wired Magazine*, April, http://www.wired.com/wired/archive/8.04/joy.html.

Kaihla, Paul. 2007. "The Village That Could Save the Planet." http://money.cnn.com/2007/09/26/technology/village_saving_planet.biz2/ (accessed September 27, 2007).

Kanner, Allen, and Mary Gomes. 1995. "The All-consuming Self." In *Ecopsychology: Restoring the Earth, Healing the Mind*, edited by T. Roszak, M. Gomes, and A. Kanner. San Francisco: Sierra Club Books.

Karliner, Joshua. 1997. *The Corporate Planet: Ecology and Politics in the Age of Globalization*. San Francisco: Sierra Club Books.

Kheel, Marti. 1990. "Ecofeminism and Deep Ecology." In *Reweaving the World: The Emergence of Ecofeminism*, edited by I. Diamond and G. Feman Orenstein. San Francisco: Sierra Club Books.

Khor, Martin. 1990. *The Uruguay Round and Third World Sovereignty*. Penang, Malaysia: Third World Network.

Kolb, David A. (1984). *Experiential Learning: Experience as the Source of Learning and Development*. Englewood Cliffs, NJ: Prentice-Hall.

Korten, David. 1995. *When Corporations Rule the World*. West Hartford, Conn.: Kumarian.

———. 1999. "The Post-corporate World." *Yes Magazine* 9:12-18.

———. 2006. *The Great Turning: From Empire to Earth Community*. San Francisco: Berrett-Koehler.

Lasn, Kalle. 1999. *Culture Jam: The Uncooling of America*. New York: Eagle Brook.

Leclerc, E. 1977. *Le "Cantique des créatures" ou les Symboles de l'union, un analyse de saint François d'Assise* [The canticle of creatures or the symbols of union: An analysis of St. Francis of Assisi]. Paris: Fayard.

Lee, Jung Young. 1971. *The Principle of Changes: Understanding the I Ching*. New Hyde Park, N.Y.: University Books.

Lemkow, Anna F. 1990. *The Wholeness Principle: Dynamics of Unity within Science, Religion, and Society*. Wheaton, Ill.: Quest Books.

Lerner, Michael. 1986. *Surplus Powerlessness: The Psychodynamics of Everyday Life—and the Psychology of Individual and Social Transformation*. Oakland, Calif.: Institute for Labor and Mental Health.

Little, Bruce. 2000. "Century of Productivity, Inequality." *The Globe and Mail* [Toronto], Monday, April 17.

Lovelock, James. 1988. *The Ages of Gaia: A Biography of Our Living Earth*. New York: W. W. Norton.

———. 2006. *The Revenge of Gaia: Why the Earth Is Fighting Back—and How We Can Still Save Humanity*. London: Penguin Books.

Lovins, Amory B., and L. Hunter Lovins. 2000. "A Tale of Two Botanies." *Wired Magazine*, April, http://www.wired.com/wired/archive/8.04/botanies_pr.html.

Macy, Joanna Rogers. 1983. *Despair and Personal Power in the Nuclear Age*. Philadelphia: New Society.

———. 1991a. *Mutual Causality in Buddhism and General Systems Theory: The Dharma of Natural Systems*. Albany: State University of New York Press.

———. 1991b. *World as Lover, World as Self*. Berkeley, Calif.: Parallax.

———. 1995. "Working through Environmental Despair." In *Ecopsychology: Restoring the Earth, Healing the Mind*, edited by T. Roszak, M. Gomes, and A. Kanner. San Francisco: Sierra Club Books.

Macy, Joanna, and Molly Young Brown. 1998. *Coming Back to Life: Practices to Reconnect Our Lives, Our World*. Gabriola Island, BC: New Society.

Margulis, Lynn. 1998. *Symbiotic Planet: A New Look at Evolution*. New York: Basic Books.

May, Rollo. 2007. *Love and Will*. New York: W. W. Norton.

McKibben, Bill. 1998. *Maybe One: A Personal and Environmental Argument for Single-child Families*. New York: Simon & Schuster.

McLeod, Myles. 2006. "And Life Created Continents . . . ." *New Scientist Magazine*, issue 2544, March 24.

Meadows, Donella. 1999. *Leverage Points: Places to Intervene in a System*. Asheville, N.C.: Sustainability Institute. See http://www.sustainer.org/pubs/Leverage_Points.pdf.

Meadows, Donella, Dennis Meadows, and Jørgen Randers. 1992. *Beyond the Limits: Confronting Global Collapse, Envisioning a Sustainable Future*. Post Mills, Vt.: Chelsea Green.

———. 2004. *The Limits to Growth: The 30-year Update*. White River Junction, Vt.: Chelsea Green.

Metzner, Ralph. 1995. "The Psychopathology of the Human-Nature Relationship." In *Ecopsychology: Restoring the Earth, Healing the Mind*, edited by T. Roszak, M. Gomes, and A. Kanner. San Francisco: Sierra Club Books.

Mies, Maria. 1986. *Patriarchy and Accumulation on a World Scale: Women in the International Division of Labour*. London: Zed Books.

Mies, Maria, and Vandana Shiva. 1993. *Ecofeminism*. Halifax, NS: Fernwood.

Milanovic, Branko. 1999. *True World Income Distribution, 1988 and 1993—First Calculations, Based on Household Surveys Alone*, vol. 1. The World Bank.

Mitchell, Alanna. 2009. *Sea Sick: The Global Ocean in Crisis*. Toronto: McClelland & Stewart.

Mitchell, Stephen, translator. 1988. *Tao Te Ching: A New English Version, with Foreword and Notes by Stephen Mitchell*. New York: Harper & Row.

Moltmann, J. 1993. *Doutrina ecológica da criação* [Ecological Doctrine of Creation]. Petrópolis, Brazil: Vozes.

Motiar, Ahmed. 2004. "The Path of Submission and the Renewal of the Sacred Balance: An Islamic Perspective." *Scarboro Missions*, April, p. 11.

Muller, Charles, translator. 1997. *Tao Te Ching*. Published at http://www.mindgazer.org/tao/ (accessed July 25, 2006).

Nadeau, Robert, and Menas Kafatos. 1999. *The Non-local Universe: The New Physics and Matters of the Mind*. New York: Oxford University Press.

Naess, Arne. 1989. *Ecology, Community, and Lifestyle: Outline of an Ecosophy*. New York: Cambridge University Press.

Nhât Hanh, Thích. 1997. *The Miracle of Mindfulness: A Manual on Meditation*. Boston: Beacon Press.

Nickerson, Mike. 1993. *Planning for Seven Generations: Guideposts for a Sustainable Future*. Hull, PQ: Voyageur.

Norberg-Hodge, Helena. 1999. "The March of the Monoculture." *Ecologist* 29:194-97.

Nozick, Marcia. 1992. *No Place like Home: Building Sustainable Communities*. Ottawa: Canadian Council on Social Development.

O'Murchu, Diarmuid. 1997. *Quantum Theology: Spiritual Implications of the New Physics*. New York: Crossroad.

Orr, David. 1999. "Verbicide." *Conservation Biology* 13, no. 4 (August): 696-99.

Peat, F. David. 1987. *Synchronicity: The Bridge between Matter and Mind*. Toronto: Bantam Books.

———. 1990. *Einstein's Moon: Bell's Theorem and the Curious Quest for Quantum Reality*. Chicago: Contemporary Books.

———. 1991. *The Philosopher's Stone: Chaos, Synchronicity, and the Hidden Order of the World*. New York: Bantam Books.

———. 1994. *Lighting the Seventh Fire: The Spiritual Ways, Healing, and Science of the Native American*. New York: Birch Lane.

Perlin, John. 2005. *A Forest Journey: The Story of Wood and Civilization*. Woodstock, Vt.: Countryman.

Pitts, Gordon. 2009. "$2-trillion Loss: Being a Billionaire Is a Lot Lonelier This Year." *The Globe and Mail* [Toronto], March 11.

Plant, Judith. 1990. "Searching for Common Ground: Ecofeminism and Bioregionalism." In *Reweaving the World: The Emergence of Ecofeminism*, edited by Irene Diamond and Gloria Feman Orenstein, 155-61. San Francisco: Sierra Club Books.

Prigogine, Ilya, and Isabelle Stengers. 1984. *Order out of Chaos: Man's Dialogue with Nature*. Boulder, Colo.: Shambhala.

Progoff, Ira. 1973. *Jung, Synchronicity, and Human Destiny: Noncausal Dimensions of Human Experience*. New York: Julian Press.

Reagan, Michael, ed. 1999. *The Hand of God: A Collection of Thoughts and Images Reflecting the Spirit of the Universe*. Atlanta, Ga.: Lionheart Books.

Rensch, Bernhard. 1959. *Evolution above the Species Level*. New York, Columbia University Press.

Rockefeller, Steven C. 1996. "Principles of Environmental Conservation and Sustainable Development: Summary and Survey." Available at http://www.earthcharterinaction .org/invent/details.php?id=272 (accessed July 13, 2009).

Rockhill, Kathleen. 1992. "Dis/connecting Literacy and Sexuality: Speaking the Unspeakable in the Classroom." Unpublished manuscript.

Roszak, Theodore. 1992. *The Voice of the Earth*. New York: Simon & Schuster.

———. 1995. "Where Psyche Meets Gaia." In *Ecopsychology: Restoring the Earth, Healing the Mind*, edited by T. Roszak, M. Gomes, and A. Kanner. San Francisco: Sierra Club Books.

———. 1999. *The Gendered Atom: Reflections on the Sexual Psychology of Science*. Berkeley, Calif.: Conari.

Ruether, Rosemary Radford. 1992. *Gaia and God: An Ecofeminist Theology of Earth's Healing*. San Francisco: HarperSanFrancisco.

Russell, Letty M. 1974. *Human Liberation in a Feminist Perspective: A Theology*. Philadelphia: Westminster.

Sale, Kirkpatrick. 1985. *Dwellers in the Land: The Bioregional Vision*. San Francisco: Sierra Club Books.

———. 2001. "There's No Place like Home." *Ecologist* 31:40-43.

Sampat, Payal. 1999. "Earth's Stocks Down by One-third." *World Watch Magazine* 12, no. 4:8-9.

Sanderson, Frances. 2004. "A Mutually Caring Relationship: An Aboriginal Perspective." *Scarboro Missions*, April, p. 12.

Saposnek, David. 1985. "Aikido: A Model for Brief Strategic Therapy." In *Aikido and the New Warrior*, edited by Richard Strozzi Heckler, 178-97. Berkeley, Calif.: North Atlantic Books.

Saul, John Ralston. 1995. *The Unconscious Civilization*. Concord, ON: House of Anansi.

Scharper, Stephen Bede. 1997. *Redeeming the Time: A Political Theology of the Environment*. New York: Continuum.

Scheler, M. 1926. *Wesen und Formen der Sympathie* [Essentials and Forms of Sympathy]. Bonn: Friederich Cohen.

Seed, John, Joanna Macy, et al. 1988. *Thinking like a Mountain*. Philadelphia: New Society.

Sewall, Laura. 1995. "The Skill of Ecological Perception." In *Ecopsychology: Restoring the Earth, Healing the Mind*, edited by T. Roszak, M. Gomes, and A. Kanner. San Francisco: Sierra Club Books.

Sharma, Tulsi Ram. 2004. "Hinduism." *Scarboro Missions*, April, p. 13.

Sheldrake, Rupert. 1988. *The Presence of the Past: Morphic Resonance and the Habits of Nature*. New York: Times Books.

———. 1990. *The Rebirth of Nature: The Greening of Science and God*. London: Century.

———. 1995. "The Variability of Physical Constants," http://www.sheldrake.org/experiments/constants/ (accessed August 21, 2006).

Shiva, Vandana. 1989. *Staying Alive: Women, Ecology, and Development*. London: Zed Books.

———. 1993. *Monocultures of the Mind: Perspectives on Biodiversity and Biotechnology*. Penang, Malaysia: Third World Network; London: Zed Books.

Sliker, Gretchen. 1992. *Multiple Mind: Healing the Split in Psyche and World*. Boston: Shambhala.

Spangler, David. 1996. *Everyday Miracles: The Inner Art of Manifestation*. New York: Bantam Books.

Spretnak, Charlene. 1990. "Ecofeminism: Our Roots and Flowering." In *Reweaving the World: The Emergence of Ecofeminism*, edited by I. Diamond and G. Feman Orenstein. San Francisco: Sierra Club Books.

Star, Jonathan, translator and commentator. 2001. *Tao Te Ching: The Definitive Edition*. New York: J. P. Tarchar/Putnam.

Starhawk. 1987. *Truth or Dare: Encounters with Power, Authority, and Mystery*. San Francisco: Harper & Row.

Suzuki, David, and Holly Dressel. 2002. *Good News for a Change: Hope for a Troubled Planet*. Toronto: Stoddart.

Suzuki, David, and Peter Knudtson. 1992. *Wisdom of the Elders: Honoring Sacred Native Visions of Nature*. New York: Bantam Books.

Suzuki, David, with Amanda McConnell. 1997. *The Sacred Balance: Rediscovering Our Place in Nature*. Vancouver, BC: Greystone Books.

Swimme, Brian. 1985. *The Universe Is a Green Dragon: A Cosmic Creation Story*. Santa Fe, N.M.: Bear.

————. 1996. *The Hidden Heart of the Cosmos: Humanity and the New Story.* Maryknoll, N.Y.: Orbis Books.

————. 1997. "Human Soul and the Cosmic Heart." Lecture at the University of St. Michael's College, Toronto, June 26.

————. 2001. "Comprehensive Compassion." *Enlightenment Magazine,* no. 19 (Spring/Summer).

Talbot, Michael. 1991. *The Holographic Universe.* New York: HarperPerennial.

Taylor, Jeremy. 1983. *Dream Work: Techniques for Discovering the Creative Power in Dreams.* New York: Paulist Press.

Teilhard de Chardin, Pierre. 1964. *Le milieu divin: An essay on the interior life.* London: Collins Fontana Books.

Tolkien, J. R. R. 1999. *The Fellowship of the Ring: The Lord of the Rings,* Part I. London: HarperCollins.

Toolan, David. 2001. *At Home in the Cosmos.* Maryknoll, N.Y.: Orbis Books.

Torres, Rosa Maria. 1986. *Educación popular: Un encuentro con Paulo Freire* [Popular Education: An Encounter with Paulo Freire] (Peruvian edition - 1988). Lima: Tarea.

Toynbee, A. 1972. *Diario ABC* (Madrid), pp. 10-11.

United Church of Canada. 2007. *Living Faithfully in the Midst of Empire: Report to the 39th General Council.* Toronto: United Church of Canada.

Walsh, Roger. 1984. *Staying Alive: The Psychology of Human Survival.* Boston: Shambhala New Science Library.

Waskow, Arthur. 1997. "Sacred Earth, Sacred Earthling." *Gnosis,* no. 33:58-62.

Weber, Renée. 1982. "The Physicist and the Mystic—Is a Dialogue between Them Possible? A Conversation with David Bohm." In *The Holographic Paradigm and Other Paradoxes: Exploring the Leading Edge of Science,* edited by Ken Wilber, 187-214. Boulder, Colo.: Shambhala.

Welwood, John. 1982. "The Holographic Paradigm and the Structure of Experience." In *The Holographic Paradigm and Other Paradoxes: Exploring the Leading Edge of Science,* edited by Ken Wilber, 127-35. Boulder, Colo.: Shambhala.

White, Frank. 1998. *The Overview Effect: Space Exploration and Human Evolution.* Reston, Va.: American Institute of Aeronautics and Astronautics.

Wiener, Norbert. 1950. *The Human Use of Human Beings.* New York: Houghton Mifflin.

Wilber, Ken, ed. 1985. *Quantum Questions: Mystical Writings of the World's Great Physicists.* Boston/London: Shambhala.

————. 1996. *A Brief History of Everything.* Boston: Shambhala.

Wilson, Edward Osborne. 1971. *The Social Insects.* Cambridge, Mass.: Harvard University Press.

————. 2002. *The Future of Life.* New York: Alfred A. Knopf.

Winter, Deborah Du Nann. 1996. *Ecological Psychology: Healing the Split between Planet and Self.* New York: HarperCollins College Publishers.

Worldwatch Institute. 2007. *Vital Signs 2006-7: The Trends That Are Shaping Our Future.* New York: W. W. Norton.

Young-Sowers, Meredith L. 1993. *Spiritual Crisis: What's Really behind Loss, Disease, and Life's Major Hurts.* Walpole, N.H.: Stillpoint.

Ywahoo, Dhyani. 1989. "Renewing the Sacred Hoop." In *Reweaving the Visions: New Patterns in Feminist Spirituality,* edited by Judith Plaskow and Carol Christ. New York: HarperCollins.

Zohar, Danah, and Ian Marshall. 1994. *The Quantum Society: Mind, Physics, and a New Social Vision.* New York: William Morrow.

Additional Reading

Andruss, Van, Christopher Plant, Judith Plant, and Eleanor Wright, eds. 1990. *Home: A Bioregional Reader*. Philadelphia: New Society.

Assagioli, Roberto. 1973. *The Act of Will*. Baltimore: Penguin Books.

Berman, Morris. 1989. *Coming to Our Senses: Body and Spirit in the Hidden History of the West*. New York: Simon & Shuster.

Berry, Wendell. 1992. *Sex, Economy, Freedom, and Community*. Toronto: Random House of Canada.

Biehl, Janet. 1991. *Rethinking Ecofeminist Politics*. Boston: South End Press.

Boff, Leonardo. 1995. *Ecology and Liberation: A New Paradigm*. Maryknoll, N.Y.: Orbis Books.

———. 1997. *Cry of the Earth, Cry of the Poor*. Maryknoll, N.Y.: Orbis Books.

———. 1998. *Holy Trinity, Perfect Community*. Translated by Phillip Berryman. Maryknoll, N.Y.: Orbis Books.

———. 2006. *Francis of Assisi: A Model of Human Liberation*. Maryknoll, N.Y.: Orbis Books.

Brecher, Jeremy, John Brown Childs, and Jill Cutler, eds. 1993. *Global Visions: Beyond the New World Order*. Boston: South End Press.

Eisler, Riane. 1987. *The Chalice and the Blade: Our History, Our Future*. San Francisco: Harper & Row.

Huxley, Laura Archera. 1975. *Between Heaven and Earth: Recipes for Living and Loving*. New York: Farrar, Straus and Giroux.

Lazlo, Ervin. 1989. *The Inner Limits of Mankind: Heretical Reflection on Today's Values, Culture, and Politics*. London: Oneworld.

Lowe, David, and Riane Eisler. 1987. "Chaos and Transformation: Implications of Nonequilibrium Theory for Social Science and Society." *Behavioral Science* 32:53-65.

Nachmanovitch, Stephen. 1990. *Free Play: Improvisation in Life and Art*. Los Angeles: J. P. Tarcher.

People-Centred Development Forum. 1993. *Economy, Ecology, and Spirituality: Toward a Theory and Practice of Sustainability*. Quezon City, Philippines: Asian NGO Coalition.

Plaskow, Judith, and Carol Christ. 1989. *Weaving the Visions: New Patterns in Feminist Spirituality*. San Francisco: Harper & Row.

Rifkin, Jeremy. 1991. *Biosphere Politics: A New Consciousness for a New Century*. New York: Crown.

Suzuki, David, and Peter Knudtson. 1992. *Wisdom of the Elders: Honoring Sacred Native Visions of Nature*. Toronto: Stoddart.

Swimme, Brian. 1985. *The Universe Is a Green Dragon: A Cosmic Creation Story*. Santa Fe, N.M.: Bear.

Tart, Charles T. 1989. *Open Mind, Discriminating Mind: Reflections on Human Possibilities*. San Francisco: Harper & Row.

Tucker, Mary Evelyn. 2003. *Worldly Wonder: Religions Enter Their Ecological Phase*. Chicago: Open Court.

Watts, Alan. 1975. Tao: *The Watercourse Way*. New York: Pantheon.

Weissman, Robert. 1996. "Grotesque Inequality." *Multinational Monitor*, September 1996, p. 6.

Williams, R., and J. Stockmyer. 1987. *Unleashing the Right Side of the Brain*. Lexington, Mass.: Stephen Greene Press.

Index

Also in the Ecology and Justice Series